ARGYLL

VOLUME 2 LORN

PLATE I   BARCALDINE CASTLE (279) from W

ARGYLL

AN INVENTORY OF THE ANCIENT MONUMENTS

Volume 2
LORN

THE ROYAL COMMISSION ON THE
ANCIENT AND HISTORICAL MONUMENTS OF SCOTLAND

1975

Printed in Scotland by Her Majesty's Stationery Office at HMSO Press, Edinburgh
Dd 244595 K10 3/75 (10463)

CONTENTS

	Page
Table of Figures	vii
Table of Plates	xv
List of Commissioners	xxvi
Nineteenth Report	xxvii
List of Monuments which the Commissioners consider to be most worthy of preservation	xxxi
Register of Monuments by Civil Parishes	xxxv
Abbreviations used in the References	xli
Editorial Notes	xlv
Conversion Tables, Metric to British values	xlvii
Introduction	I

Inventory of the Ancient and Historical Monuments of Lorn

Chambered Cairns	37
Cairns and Barrow	45
Burials and Cists	57
Cup-and-ring Markings	61
Standing Stones and Stone Circle	62
Forts	64
Brochs	75
Duns	77
Crannogs	93

CONTENTS

		Page
Miscellaneous Earthworks and Enclosures	. . . .	95
Ecclesiastical Monuments	. . . .	97
Castles, Tower-houses and Fortifications	. . . . .	168
The Burgh of Oban	. . . .	242
Domestic Architecture from the 17th to the 19th century	. .	243
Farms, Townships and Shielings	. . . . . .	267
Industrial and Engineering Works, including Quarries	. .	276
Roads and Bridges	. . . .	294
Architectural Fragments, Carved Stones, etc.	. . . .	298
Indeterminate Remains	. . . .	300
Armorial	. . . .	301
Glossary	. . . .	303
Index	. . . .	311
Map showing the position of the principal Monuments in Lorn	. . . .	*in end pocket*

TABLE OF FIGURES

Fig.	Title	Page
1	Topographical map of Lorn	2
2	Distribution map of chambered cairns and cairns	8
3	Distribution map of cists, cup-and-ring markings and standing stones	11
4	Distribution map of Bronze Age pottery and metalwork	13
5	Distribution map of forts, brochs and duns	17
6	Comparative plans of medieval churches in Lorn: A, Old Parish Church, Kilchattan, Luing (No. 256); B, Chapel, Keil (No. 250); C, Church, Baile Mhaodain, Ardchattan (No. 220); D, Old Parish Church, Inishail (No. 247); E, Old Parish Church, Kilmore (No. 264); F, Old Parish Church, Eilean Munde (No. 245); G, Chapel, Innis Sèa-Ràmhach (No. 248); H, Dunstaffnage Chapel (No. 243); J, Old Parish Church, Muckairn, Taynuilt (No. 268)	24
7	Chambered cairn, Achnacree (No. 1); after Smith	38
8	Chambered cairn, Achnacreebeag (No. 2)	39
9	Chambered cairn, Ardchonnell (No. 3)	40
10	Chambered cairn, Auchachenna (No. 4)	41
11	Chambered cairn, Cladich (No. 5)	41
12	Chambered cairn, Dalineun (No. 6)	42
13	Chambered cairn, Port Sonachan (No. 8)	44
14	Chambered cairn, Shuna Cottage, Shuna, Nether Lorn (No. 9)	44
15	Cairn, Achacha (No. 10)	45
16	Cairn, Ballachulish House (No. 19)	46
17	Cairn, Barr Mór 1, Lismore (No. 27)	47
18	Cairns, Castle Farm, Barcaldine (No. 32)	48
19	Cairn, Clachadow 2 (No. 34)	49
20	Cairn, Culcharron (No. 43); after E J Peltenburg	50
21	Cairn, Druim an Uinnsinn 1, Lismore (No. 48)	51
22	Cairns, Kilmore (No. 57)	52
23	Cairn, Kilmore (No. 57, 4)	53
24	Cairn, Làrach Bàn (No. 59)	53
25	Cairn, Lerags (No. 61)	54
26	Cairn, Strontoiller (No. 78)	56
27	Stone circle, Strontoiller (No. 120)	63
28	Fort, Ardanstur 1 (No. 123)	64
29	Fort, Balvicar, Seil (No. 125)	65
30	Fort, Cnocan Dubha (No. 127)	66
31	Fort, Cnoc an Tighe Mhóir, Seil (No. 128)	66
32	Fort, Colagin (No. 129)	66
33	Fort, Dùn Creagach (No. 134)	68
34	Fort, Dùn Iadain (No. 135)	68

35 Forts and dun, Dùn Mac Sniachan (No. 136) . . . 69
36 Fort, Dùn Ormidale (No. 137) 71
37 Fort, Dùn Uabairtich (No. 138) 72
38 Fort, Kilcheran, Lismore (No. 140) 72
39 Fort, The Little Horse Shoe, Kerrera (No. 142) . . 73
40 Fort, Losgann Larnach (No. 143) 74
41 Fort, Tom an Iasgaire (No. 144) 74
42 Fort, Torr a' Chlaonaidh (No. 145) 75
43 Broch (probable), An Dùn, Loch Fiart, Lismore (No. 146) . 75
44 Broch, Tirefour Castle, Lismore (No. 147) . . . 76
45 Dun, An Dùnan, Minard Point (No. 149) . . . 77
46 Dun, An Dùn, Clenamacrie (No. 150) 77
47 Dun, An Dùn, Sloc a' Bhrighide, Lismore (No. 151) . . 78
48 Dun, Ardanstur 1 (No. 152) 78
49 Dun, Ardanstur 2 (No. 153) 79
50 Dun, Ballycastle, Luing (No. 155) 79
51 Dun, Barguillean (No. 156) 80
52 Dun, Barr a' Chaistealain (No. 157) 80
53 Dun, Barr Mór (No. 158) 80
54 Dun, Caisteal Suidhe Cheannaidh (No. 159) . . . 81
55 Dun, Camuslaich, Seil (No. 160) 81
56 Dun, Castles (No. 161) 82
57 Dun, Dunach (No. 163) 82
58 Dun, Dùnan Molach (No. 165) 83
59 Dun, Dùn Aorain, Seil (No. 166) 83
60 Dun, Dùn Bachlach (No. 168) 84
61 Dun, Dùn Bhlaran (No. 169) 84
62 Dun, Dùn Chathach (No. 170) 85
63 Dun, Dùn Chrùban, Lismore (No. 171) 85
64 Dun, Dùn Cuilein, Lismore (No. 173) 86
65 Dun, Dùn Fadaidh (No. 174) 86
66 Dun, Dùn Leigh (No. 175) 86
67 Dun, Dùn Mhic Raonuill (No. 176) 87
68 Dun, Dùn Mhuirageul (No. 177) 87
69 Dun, Dùn Mór, Balygrundle, Lismore (No. 178) . . 88
70 Dun, Dùn Mucaig, Seil (No. 179) 88
71 Dun, Eilean an Atha, Luing (No. 184) 89
72 Dun, Fiart, Lismore (No. 185) 89
73 Dun, Gallanach (No. 186) 90
74 Dun, Kilcheran, Lismore (No. 187) 90
75 Dun, Leccamore, Luing (No. 189) 91
76 Dun, Loch a' Phearsain (No. 190) 92
77 Dun and enclosure, Sean Dùn, Lismore (No. 193) . . 92
78 Dun, Tom a' Chaisteil (No. 194) 93
79 Crannogs, Loch Awe (No. 198) 94
80 Earthwork, Ard Luing, Luing (No. 201) 95

81 Enclosure, Balliveolan, Lismore (No. 202) 95
82 Earthwork, Dùn Ablaich, Luing (No. 205) 96
83 Earthwork, Dùn Mór, Bonawe (No. 206) 96
84 Enclosure, Kilmun (No. 208) 97
85 Enclosure, Làrach na h-Iobairte (No. 209) 97
86 Old Parish Church, Appin (No. 214); plan 98
87 Parish Church, Ardchattan (No. 216); plan 99
88 Ardchattan Priory (No. 217); plan 100
89 masons' marks: A, B, H, refectory pulpit; C, refectory doorway;
    D, G, east crossing arch; E, piscina drain-outlet; F, north transept
    window 101
90 profile mouldings: A, recesses in south choir wall; B, internal choir
    string-course; C, sacristy doorway; D, plinth of east choir wall; E,
    pulpitum 102
91 recesses in S choir wall 102
92 detail and profile mouldings: A, respond of south transeptal chapel;
    B, south-east angle of south transept 103
93 N transept window 104
94 profile mouldings and details: A, vaulting-rib of refectory pulpit;
    B, refectory window; C, refectory doorway; D, hood-mould of niche
    in refectory pulpit; E, vaulting-rib stops in refectory pulpit . . 105
95 refectory pulpit 106
96 pier of refectory pulpit: A, elevation looking west (base recon-
    structed); B, elevation looking north; C, section X-X¹; D, plan . 107
97 plan and elevation of niche in refectory pulpit 108
98 section and details of refectory roof 109
99 cross-decorated stone 111
100 carved fragments 111
101 fragments of window-heads 112
102 Church, Baile Mhaodain, Ardchattan (No. 220); plan . . . 116
103 Chapel and burial-ground, Ballachuan, Seil (site) (No. 221); plan . 116
104 Caibeal, Lochavich (No. 226); plan 117
105 Chapel and burial-ground, Cill-an-Suidhe, Lismore (site) (No. 229);
    plan 118
106 Burial-ground (possible), Clachan, Lismore (No. 231); plan . . 119
107 Cashel (possible), Cladh a' Bhearnaig, Kerrera (No. 232); plan . 120
108 Burial-ground, Cladh na h-Anaid, Taynuilt (No. 234); plan . . 121
109 Chapel and burial-ground, Cladh Uaine (No. 235); plan . . 121
110 Chapel (site), burial-ground and well, Cladh Churiollan, Creagan
    (No. 237); well-house 122
111 Cross-decorated stone, Clenamacrie (No. 238) 122
112 Chapel and burial-ground, Creag a' Chaibeil, Ballimeanoch (No. 239);
    plan 123
113 Parish Church, Dalavich (No. 241); plan 124
114 Dunstaffnage Chapel (No. 243); plan 125
115 masons' marks 125

116   profile mouldings: A, B, G, north and south chancel windows; C, capital of south chancel window; D, hood-mould of south nave doorway; E, label-mould of south chancel windows; F, east chancel windows; H, base of north doorway; J, angle-shaft . . . 126

117   N and S chancel windows (partially reconstructed) . . . 127

118   Parish Church, Duror (No. 244); plan 129

119   elevation 130

120   Old Parish Church and burial-ground, Eilean Munde (No. 245); plan 130

121   Parish Church, Glenorchy, Dalmally (No. 246); plan . . . 132

122   cross-decorated stone 133

123   Old Parish Church, Inishail (No. 247); plan . . . 135

124   carved fragment 135

125   altar frontal 136

126   Chapel, Innis Sèa-Ràmhach (No. 248); plan . . . 137

127   Church, Inverghiusachan (No. 249); plan 138

128   Chapel, Keil (No. 250); plan 139

129   Old Parish Church, Kilbride (No. 253); plan . . . 141

130   carved fragment 141

131   Old Parish Church, Kilchattan, Luing (No. 256); plan . . 144

132   graffiti (A) 144

133   graffiti (D) 145

134   graffiti (E) 145

135   Parish Church, Kilchrenan (No. 259); plan 146

136   S elevation (partially reconstructed) 147

137   carved fragment 148

138   fragment of cross-decorated stone 148

139   Chapel and burial-ground, Kilmaha (site) (No. 261); rock-carving . 150

140   cross-decorated stone 150

141   cross-decorated stone 151

142   Church and burial-ground (possible), Kilmaronag (site) (No. 262); plan 152

143   Old Parish Church, Kilmore (No. 264); plan . . . 153

144   tomb-recess 154

145   profile moulding of tomb-recess 154

146   cross-decorated stone 155

147   Chapel and burial-ground, Kilmun (site) (No. 265); plan . . 155

148   Cathedral of St Moluag and Parish Church, Lismore (No. 267); plan 156

149   profile mouldings: A, F, sedilia shafts; B, sedilia capital; C, choir plinth; D, nave plinth; E, sedilia base; G, north choir doorway; H, window-jamb 157

150   piscina, sedilia and doorway in S choir wall . . . 158

151   masons' marks: A, C, E, south choir doorway; B, north choir doorway; D, sedilia; F, piscina 159

152   N choir doorway 160

153   Old Parish Church, Muckairn, Taynuilt (No. 268); plan . . 163

154   Parish Church, Muckairn, Taynuilt (No. 269); plan . . 164

155   S elevation 164
156   fragment of grave-slab 165
157 Episcopal Church, Portnacroish (No. 272); plan 166
158   S elevation (partially reconstructed) 167
159 Achadun Castle, Lismore (No. 276); ground-floor plan . . . 169
160   first-floor plan 170
161   masons' marks: A, B, south-east range; C, detached fragment . 170
162 Achallader Castle (No. 277); floor-plans 172
163   pistol-holes (A, B) 173
164   pistol-holes (C, D) 174
165 Ardfad Castle, Seil (No. 278); plan 175
166 Barcaldine Castle (No. 279); floor-plans 176
167   corbelling of SW angle-turret 177
168 Caisteal nan Con, Torsa (No. 280); plan 181
169 Caisteal na Nighinn Ruaidhe, Loch Avich (No. 281); plan . . 183
170 Castle Coeffin, Lismore (No. 282); floor-plans and section . . 185
171   carved fragment 186
172 Castle Shuna, Appin (No. 284); floor-plans 187
173 Castle Stalker (No. 285); general plan 188
174   floor-plans 190
175   sections 192
176   profile mouldings: A, B, D, second-floor fireplace; C, ground-floor
        entrance; E, third-floor fireplace 193
177 Dunollie Castle (No. 286); general plan 196
178   first- and second-floor plans of tower-house 197
179   carved fragment 197
180 Dunstaffnage Castle (No. 287); ground-floor plan . . . 200
181   first- and second-floor plans 201
182   plan at parapet-level 203
183   profile mouldings: A, fireplace in east range; B, entrance-doorway 204
184   S window-embrasure in E curtain 206
185   N window-embrasure in E curtain 207
186   arrow-slit in W tower (partially reconstructed) 209
187 Fortified dwelling, Eilean Tighe Bhàin, Loch Tromlee (No. 289);
        plan 212
188 Castle, Fraoch Eilean (No. 290); general plan 214
189   upper floor-plans and section 215
190   carved fragment 216
191 Gylen Castle, Kerrera (No. 291); general plan 218
192   floor-plans of tower-house 218
193   NE elevation 219
194   profile mouldings and details: A, E, north angle-turret; B, entrance-
        doorway; C, oriel-window; D, eaves-cornice; F, corbelling of
        chamber above stair-tower 220
195   gun-loops 221
196   oriel-window 222

197   Innis Chonnell Castle (No. 292); general plan . . . facing 223
198   inner bailey; first- and second-floor plans 224
199   inner bailey; plan at parapet-level 226
200   inner bailey; section 227
201   inner bailey; masons' marks: A, arrow-slit in south-east angle-tower; B, C, D, south-east tower 228
202   inner bailey; profile mouldings: A, entrance-gateway; B, lobby fireplace in west range 228
203   inner bailey; window and gun-loop in SE tower. . . . 229
204   inner bailey; arrow-slit in SE angle-tower 230
205   Kilchurn Castle (No. 293); general plan and lower ground-floor plan of NW and NE ranges . . . . . . facing 231
206   first-floor plan and upper floor-plans of tower-house . . 233
207   masons' marks: A–H, tower-house (c. 1440–60); J, K, tower-house door-lintel (1693) 235
208   tower-house; profile mouldings: A, first-floor corbel; B, angle-turret corbels; C, third-floor corbel 236
209   gun-loops and pistol-holes: A, south angle-turret of tower-house; B, south angle-tower; C, D, north angle-tower . . . 237
210   Fortified dwelling, Loch a' Phearsain, Kilmelford (No. 294); plan . 240
211   Castle, Rarey (site) (No. 297); plan 241
212   Airds House (No. 304); principal elevation and floor-plans . facing 244
213   Appin House (No. 305); first-floor plan 245
214   profile mouldings: A, entrance-doorway; B, fireplace . . . 246
215   Ardmaddy Castle (No. 310); ground- and first-floor plans of early Georgian house 248
216   principal elevation of early Georgian house (partially reconstructed) 250
217   Glenure (No. 322); ground- and first-floor plans . . . 257
218   Kilmore House (No. 326); ground-floor plan . . . 260
219   Kulmani, Duror (No. 328); ground-floor plan . . . 261
220   Lochnell House (No. 330); ground-floor plan . . . 262
221   principal elevation of early Georgian house (partially reconstructed) 264
222   barn 265
223   Lady Margaret's Tower 266
224   Shielings, Airidh nan Sileag (No. 337); plan . . . 268
225   Cruck-framed byre, Bonawe (No. 338); plan . . . 269
226   Cruck-framed building, Cadderlie (No. 339); plan . . 269
227   Cruck-framed building, Clachadow (No. 340); section . . 270
228   Cottages, Glencoe village (No. 342); plan . . . 270
229   section 271
230   Shielings, Glen Risdale (No. 343); plan 272–3
231   Tigh-cuil township (No. 345); plan 274–5
232   Cruck-framed byre, Torr-an-tuirc (No. 346); plan. . . 276
233   Limestone-quarries and workers' dwellings, An Sàilean, Lismore (No. 348); plan of dwelling-house 276

234 Slate-quarries and workers' dwellings, Easdale, Seil (No. 356); plan of
cottage 279
235 Glen Kinglass Ironworks (No. 358); plan of furnace . . . 280
236 Lorn Furnace, Bonawe (No. 362); site-plan 282
237 general plan of furnace 283
238 upper plan of furnace 284
239 elevation and section of furnace 285
240 elevation of E charcoal-shed 286
241 plan and section of furnace, ore-shed and charcoal-sheds . facing 286
242 roof-details and section of E charcoal-shed 287
243 roof-details and section of W charcoal-sheds 288
244 ground- and first-floor plans of NE workers' dwellings . . 289
245 ground- and first-floor plans of SE workers' dwellings . . 290
246 elevation of SE workers' dwellings 291
247 ground- and first-floor plans of Bonawe House 292
248 Graffito, Creagan (No. 373) 298

TABLE OF PLATES

Plate

I   (*Frontispiece*) Barcaldine Castle (No. 279) from W

2   Mesolithic implements, Oban (p. 5) (*Photo: National Museum of Antiquities of Scotland*)

3 A   Pottery vessel, Achnacree (No. 1) (*Photo: National Museum of Antiquities of Scotland*)

3 B   Beaker, Slaterich, Kerrera (No. 100, 1) (*Photo: National Museum of Antiquities of Scotland*)

3 C   Food Vessel, Ledaig (p. 12) (*Photo: National Museum of Antiquities of Scotland*)

3 D   Food Vessel, Corran Park, Oban (No. 98, 8) (*Photo: National Museum of Antiquities of Scotland*)

4 A   Cinerary Urn, McKelvie Hospital, Oban (No. 98, 7) (*Photo: National Museum of Antiquities of Scotland*)

4 B   Bronze dagger, Kilmore (No. 57, 4) (*Photo: National Museum of Antiquities of Scotland*)

4 C   Bronze armlet, Melfort House (No. 97) (*Photo: National Museum of Antiquities of Scotland*)

5 A   Bronze axe, Achanrear (p. 13) (*Photo: National Museum of Antiquities of Scotland*)

5 B   Bronze swords, Shuna, Nether Lorn (p. 13) (*Photo: National Museum of Antiquities of Scotland*)

5 C   Bronze axe, Barr Mór, Lismore (p. 13) (*Photo: National Museum of Antiquities of Scotland*)

5 D   Bone pin, Kerrera (p. 22) (*Photo: Mr Robert Turner; by courtesy of Mrs T Lethbridge*)

6 A   Chambered cairn, Achnacreebeag (No. 2); SE chamber from E

6 B   SE chamber from N

6 C   NW chamber from N

7 A   Chambered cairn, Dalineun (No. 6); chamber from N

7 B   secondary cist from SE

8 A   Cairn, Lochan nan Ràth (No. 64), from S

8 B   Cairn, Clachadow 2 (No. 34), from NW

9 A   Cairn and standing stone, Strontoiller (No. 78), from E

9 B   Standing stones, Duachy (No. 116), from W

9 C   Standing stone, Acharra (No. 110), from N

10 A   Broch, Tirefour Castle, Lismore (No. 147); view from S

10 B   view from SW

10 C   detail of walling from NE

10 D   mural gallery from S

11 A   Dun, Dùn Chrùban, Lismore (No. 171), from SW

xv

11 B	Dun, Leccamore, Luing (No. 189); SW entrance, from outside
11 C	SW entrance, detail of jamb and bar-hole
11 D	staircase
11 E	Field-bank, Black Crofts, North Connel (No. 203)
12 A	Old Parish Church, Appin (No. 214); view from SE
12 B	S doorway
12 C	detail of S doorway
12 D	Parish Church, Ardchattan (No. 216); view from N
12 E	communion-table
12 F	interior
13 A	Ardchattan Priory (No. 217); mansion from SE
13 B	choir and Ardchattan burial-aisle from SE
14 A	choir and Lochnell burial-aisle from N
14 B	interior of choir from SE
15 A	detail of recesses in S choir wall
15 B	recesses in S choir wall
15 C	detail of recess in N choir wall
15 D	interior of S transept from SE
15 E	NE angle-shaft and plinth of choir
15 F	archways of crossing from W
16 A	N transept window
16 B, C	details of N transept window
16 D	doorway of Ardchattan burial-aisle
16 E	W doorway of Lochnell burial-aisle
16 F	N doorway of Lochnell burial-aisle
16 G	window in N nave-aisle
17 A	refectory pulpit
17 B	heads of refectory windows
18 A–E	details of refectory pulpit
18 F	detail of refectory doorway
18 G	Prior's Room
19 A, B	carved stones
19 C	grave-slab
20 A, B	recumbent slabs
20 C	table-tomb
20 D	armorial panel
21 A	Parish Church, Dalavich (No. 241); view from SW
21 B	recumbent slab
21 C	Church, Baile Mhaodain, Ardchattan (No. 220); interior of E wall
22 A	Dunstaffnage Chapel (No. 243); view from SW
22 B	exterior of S wall
22 C	S chancel windows
22 D	interior of N wall
23 A	detail of E window
23 B	base of N doorway
23 C	Dunstaffnage burial-aisle

23 D   pediment
23 E   detail of recumbent slab
24 A   Parish Church, Duror (No. 244); view from N
24 B   interior
24 C   Old Parish Church, Eilean Munde (No. 245); view from S
24 D   recumbent slab
24 E   detail of recumbent slab
25 A   table-tomb
25 B, C   recumbent slabs
25 D   pediment
26 A   Parish Church, Glenorchy, Dalmally (No. 246); view from SW
26 B   grave-slab
26 C   view from SE
26 D   grave-slab of a child
27 A   interior of roof
27 B   mortsafe
27 C   interior
28 A   Old Parish Church, Inishail (No. 247); cross-decorated slab
28 B, C   Chapel, Keil (No. 250); recumbent slabs
28 D   view from SW
28 E   S window
28 F   Church, Inverghiusachan (No. 249), from S
29 A   Old Parish Church, Kilbride (No. 253); view from SW
29 B   detail of Campbell of Lerags Cross
29 C   Campbell of Lerags Cross, front
29 D   Old Parish Church, Kilbrandon, Seil (No. 252); recumbent slab
30 A   Kilcheran, Lismore (No. 257), from SE
30 B   Old Parish Church, Kilchattan, Luing (No. 256); view from SW
30 C   graffiti
30 D   table-tomb
30 E   detail of headstone
31 A   Old Parish Church, Kilmore (No. 264); tomb-recess
31 B   view from SW
31 C   Parish Church, Kilchrenan (No. 259); grave-slab
31 D   view from SW
31 E   McIntyre monument
31 F   McIntyre tablet
32 A   Cathedral of St Moluag and Parish Church, Lismore (No. 267); view from NW
32 B   view from SW by Erskine Beveridge, 1882
33 A   exterior of S choir doorway
33 B   interior of choir
33 C   interior of S choir doorway
33 D   sedilia
33 E   piscina
33 F   archway of pulpitum

34 A	corbel-stop of N choir doorway
34 B	interior of N choir doorway
34 C	corbel-stop of N choir doorway
34 D, E	grave-slabs
34 F	MacGregor monument
35 A	Parish Church, Muckairn, Taynuilt (No. 269); table-tomb
35 B	view from SW
35 C	interior
35 D, E	carved stones
35 F	bell
36 A	Free High Church, Oban (No. 270); view from SW
36 B	pulpit
36 C	interior
36 D	Burial-enclosure, Sonachan (No. 274); armorial panel
36 E	Episcopal Church, Portnacroish (No. 272), from SE
37 A	Achadun Castle, Lismore (No. 276); general view from NE
37 B	mural stair
37 C	general view from S
37 D	exterior of NE curtain-wall
38 A	interior of courtyard from SW
38 B	interior of NW curtain-wall
38 C	Achallader Castle (No. 277); view from N
38 D	view from E
38 E	detail of entrance-doorway
38 F	window in N wall
39 A, B	pistol-holes in N wall
39 C	interior of E wall
39 D	Ardfad Castle, Seil (No. 278), from W
40	Barcaldine Castle (No. 279); view from S
41 A, B	armorial panels
41 C	SW angle-turret
41 D	view from NW
42 A	entrance-door and yett
42 B	detail of yett
42 C, D	door-furniture
43 A	hall
43 B	kitchen-fireplace
43 C	sundial
44 A	Caisteal nan Con, Torsa (No. 280); view from N
44 B	view from E
44 C	detail of masonry
45 A	Castle Coeffin, Lismore (No. 282); general view from E
45 B	view from NE
46 A	interior from E
46 B	mural staircase
46 C	fish-trap

46 D	Castle Shuna, Appin (No. 284); view from S
46 E	view from N
47	Castle Stalker (No. 285); view from E
48 A	view from NW
48 B	view from SW
48 C	Board of Ordnance drawing, *c.* 1748 (*By courtesy of the Trustees of the British Museum*)
49 A	view from E by Richard Pococke, 1760 (*By courtesy of the Trustees of the British Museum*)
49 B	view from E by John Clerk of Eldin, *c.* 1750–70
50 A	principal entrance
50 B	window in NE wall
50 C	ground-floor entrance
50 D	detail of postern-doorway
50 E	gun-loop
50 F	vault of pit-prison
50 G	carved stone
51 A	garderobe vent-shaft
51 B	detail of window in S angle-round
51 C	S angle-round
51 D	pistol-hole
51 E	detail of stair-newel
51 F	fireplace-jamb
51 G	stair-doorways and prison hatch
52 A	Dunollie Castle (No. 286); view from SE
52 B	tower-house and courtyard from SE
53 A	view from W
53 B	tower-house from SW
53 C	tower-house and courtyard from NW
54 A	interior of tower-house
54 B	imprint of wicker-centering
54 C	exterior of W curtain-wall
54 D	interior of W curtain-wall
54 E	slab-corbelled ceiling
54 F	carved fragment
55 A	Dunstaffnage Castle (No. 287); view from NE
55 B	view from E
56 A	view from SE
56 B	view from SW
57 A	view from NW
57 B	gatehouse from E
58 A	interior of dwelling-house
58 B	interior of courtyard from S
58 C	first-floor apartment of gatehouse
58 D	window-embrasure in gatehouse
58 E	dormer-windows of gatehouse

58 F   window in dwelling-house
59 A   interior of courtyard from W
59 B   interior of courtyard from N
59 C   detail of SW parapet-walk
59 D   SE parapet-walk
60 A   Castle, Fraoch Eilean (No. 290); aerial view from NE (*Photo: Planair, Edinburgh*)
60 B   view from SE
61 A   aerial view from E (*Photo: Planair, Edinburgh*)
61 B   view from E
62 A   view from S
62 B   pilaster-buttress
62 C   dwelling-house from NW
62 D   mural staircase
62 E   interior of dwelling-house from NE
62 F   carved fragment
63 A   Gylen Castle, Kerrera (No. 291); general view from NW
63 B   general view from SE
63 C   view from SW
64 A   view from NE
64 B   view from N
64 C   detail of NE façade
64 D   N angle-turret
65 A   detail of window
65 B   fireplace
65 C   interior from E
65 D, E   carved fragments
65 F   archway of pend
65 G   carved fragment
66 A   Innis Chonnell Castle (No. 292); inner bailey, view from S
66 B   inner bailey, SE angle-tower
66 C   view from W
66 D   exterior of entrance-gateway
66 E   view from NE
66 F   interior of entrance-gateway
67 A   S courtyard-range
67 B   interior of SE tower
67 C   hall and kitchen
67 D   hall forestair
67 E   window and gun-loop
67 F   cellar doorway
68 A   hall lobby
68 B   canopied fireplace
68 C   forestair of N curtain-wall
68 D   S parapet-walk
68 E   W parapet-walk

69 A	Kilchurn Castle (No. 293); view from S
69 B	view from NE
70 A	view from NW
70 B	view from W
71 A	view from E, 1808 (*By courtesy of the Curators of the Bodleian Library*)
71 B	view from SW by P Sandby, *c.* 1779 (*By courtesy of the Trustees of the National Library of Scotland*)
72 A	tower-house, view from W
72 B	N angle-turret
72 C	E angle-turret
72 D	interior from N
72 E	interior from SE
72 F	lintel of entrance-doorway
72 G	interior of pistol-hole
73 A	S angle-tower from NE
73 B	courtyard from E
73 C	SE curtain-wall
74 A	courtyard from SE
74 B	interior of NE range
74 C	NE range from E
75 A	interior of NE range from S
75 B	interior of NW range
75 C	dormer-window pediment
75 D	water-inlet in NE range
76	The Burgh of Oban (Nos. 298–301); detail of plan by R Stevenson, 1846
77 A	view from S by A Stanley, *c.* 1857
77 B	Piermaster's House, South Pier, Oban (No. 301), from E
78 A	Achlian (No. 302); view from N
78 B	entrance-doorway
78 C	drawing-room
78 D	staircase
78 E	Achnaba (No. 303); cast-iron fireback
79 A	Airds House (No. 304); view from SW
79 B	view from NE
80	principal façade
81 A	detail of principal façade
81 B	pavilions
81 C	entrance-doorway
81 D	doorway in quadrant-wall
82 A	principal staircase
82 B	entrance-hall
82 C	drawing-room chimney-piece
82 D	second-floor room
82 E	home farm
82 F	timber door-lock

82 G   gatelodge

83 A   Appin House (No. 305); view from S

83 B   cupboard

83 C   staircase

84 A, B, C   fireplaces

84 D   Appin Post-office, Tynribbie (No. 306), from W

85 A   Ardanaiseig (No. 307); ground-floor plan by William Burn, 1833

85 B   view from E

86 A   entrance-doorway

86 B   main block from SW

86 C   Ardencaple House, Seil (No. 308); view from N

86 D   chimney-piece

86 E   Ardlarach, Luing (No. 309), from S

87 A   Ardmaddy Castle (No. 310); view from N

87 B   window

87 C   SW range from S

88 A   view from N, c. 1772 (*By courtesy of the Trustees of the National Gallery of Scotland*)

88 B   forestair and portico

88 C   detail of pediment

88 D   carved panel

89 A   boat-house

89 B   bridge

89 C   dining-room fireplace

89 D   first-floor room

89 E   brass rim-lock

89 F   court of offices from SW

90 A   Ballachulish House (No. 311); view from NW

90 B   staircase

90 C   Barcaldine House (No. 313); view from NW

90 D   dining-room chimney-piece

90 E   library chimney-piece

91 A   Balliveolan (Druimavuic) (No. 312), from W

91 B   Dalmally Manse (No. 315), from SE

91 C   The Manor House, Dungallon (No. 317), from SE

91 D   Old Schoolhouse, Ferlochan (No. 319), from NE

91 E   Dunollie House (No. 318), from S

91 F   Degnish (No. 316), from SE

92 A   Gallanach (No. 320); early view from N (*By courtesy of Major J William-son of Gallanach*)

92 B   detail of view, 1800 (*By courtesy of Major J Williamson of Gallanach*)

92 C   view from NE

93 A   ground-floor plan by William Burn, 1814 (*By courtesy of Major J Williamson of Gallanach*)

93 B   drawing-room

93 C   staircase

94 A	ground-floor plan, probably by Gillespie Graham, 1812 (*By courtesy of Major J Williamson of Gallanach*)
94 B	principal elevation, probably by Gillespie Graham, 1812 (*By courtesy of Major J Williamson of Gallanach*)
95 A	Glenure (No. 322); view from NW
95 B	kitchen-fireplace
95 C	staircase
95 D	first-floor room
96 A	Kilbrandon House, Seil (No. 325), from S
96 B	Glenstockdale (No. 321), from N
96 C	Kilmore House (No. 326); view from E
96 D	view from W
96 E	Hayfield (No. 323); steading from SE
97 A	Kinlochlaich (No. 327); view from NW
97 B	view from W
97 C	door-case
97 D	detail of plaster vault
97 E	detail of drawing-room ceiling
97 F	Lerags House (No. 329), from W
97 G	Kulmani, Duror (No. 328), from SE
98 A	Lochnell House (No. 330); view fron NE
98 B	view from NW
98 C	barn
99 A	view from S
99 B	oriel-window
99 C	sundial
99 D	mock arrow-loop
99 E	drawing-room chimney-piece
100 A	Rarey (No. 333), from N
100 B	Upper Sonachan House (No. 336); view from N
100 C	carved panel
100 D	Old Schoolhouse, North Ledaig (No. 332), from W
100 E	Muckairn Manse, Taynuilt (No. 331), from SE
101 A	Cottages, Glencoe village (No. 342); view from SE
101 B	interior
101 C, D	details of crucks
101 E	Cruck-framed building, Clachadow (No. 340); cruck-truss
101 F	Dunstaffnage Mains Farm (No. 341), from NE
102 A	Tigh-cuil Township (No. 345); general view from N
102 B	byre-dwelling A
102 C	general view from SW
103 A	detail of estate-plan by Alexander Langlands, 1809 (*By courtesy of the Scottish Record Office*)
103 B	Thatched houses, Kilchrenan (p. 32); view by the Rev. J B MacKenzie, *c.* 1870–80 (*By courtesy of the Natural History and Antiquarian Society of Mid Argyll*)

104 A Limestone-quarries and workers' dwellings, An Sàilean, Lismore (No. 348); general view from SE

104 B lime-kilns

104 C Old quarries, Ardentallan (No. 349); working-face

104 D Old quarry, Barrnacarry (No. 351); millstone-quarry

105 A Slate-quarries and workers' dwellings, Ballachulish (No. 350); general view of East Laroch quarry from SE

105 B view of East Laroch quarry from NW

105 C cottages, West Laroch

106 A Slate-quarries and workers' dwellings, Easdale, Seil (No. 356); general view from NE

106 B cottages, Ellanbeich

106 C, D harbour, Easdale Island

107 A Lighthouse, Eilean Musdile, Lismore (No. 357); view from SW

107 B view from NE

108 A ground-floor plan, 1829 (*By courtesy of the Northern Lighthouse Board*)

108 B section, 1829 (*By courtesy of the Northern Lighthouse Board*)

109 elevations, 1829 (*By courtesy of the Northern Lighthouse Board*)

110 A lantern

110 B, C, D details of superstructure

110 E keeper's house

110 F bridge

110 G courtyard entrance

111 A Lorn Furnace, Bonawe (No. 362); general view from S

111 B general view from E

112 A early view of furnace from N (*Photo: Valentine, Dundee*)

112 B furnace from NW

113 A loading-mouth

113 B cast-iron lintel

113 C furnace-hearth

114 A ore-shed and E charcoal-shed from NE

114 B E charcoal-shed from N

114 C W charcoal-sheds from SE

115 A E charcoal-shed roof

115 B, C, D details of W charcoal-shed roofs

116 A NE workers' dwellings from N

116 B SE workers' dwellings from NE

116 C staircase in SE workers' dwellings

116 D Bonawe House from N

116 E entrance-doorway of Bonawe House

117 A Gunpowder-works, Melfort (No. 363); storage-shed roof

117 B court of offices

117 C Old Ferryhouse, South Shian (No. 367), from NE

117 D Old Ferryhouse, Port Appin (No. 364), from N

118 A Lime-kilns, Port Kilcheran, Lismore (No. 365), from W

118 B   Limestone-quarries and workers' dwellings, Port Ramsay, Lismore (No. 366); general view from W

118 C   lime-kilns

118 D   cottages from E

119 A   Bridge of Awe (No. 368), from NW

119 B   Clachan Bridge, Seil (No. 369), from SW

119 C   Bridge and embankment, Dalmally (No. 370); bridge from E

119 D   Military Road, Tyndrum–Kinlochleven (No. 372); Bridge of Orchy from SW

120 A   Architectural fragments, Druimneil House (No. 374); staircase

120 B   Graffito, Creagan (No. 373)

120 C   Armorial panel, Dunstaffnage House (No. 375)

120 D   Armorial panel, Old Smithy, Port Appin (No. 376)

120 E   Architectural fragments, St Conan's Church, Lochawe (No. 377); window from St Mary's Parish Church, South Leith

120 F   window-tracery from Iona Abbey

120 G   bell from Skerryvore Lighthouse

ROYAL COMMISSION ON THE ANCIENT AND
HISTORICAL MONUMENTS OF SCOTLAND

LIST OF COMMISSIONERS

The Right Honourable The Earl of Wemyss and March, K.T., LL.D., J.P. (*Chairman*)

Professor G. Donaldson, M.A., Ph.D., D.Litt.

Professor A. A. M. Duncan, M.A.

J. D. Dunbar-Nasmith, Esq., B.A., R.I.B.A., P.P.R.I.A.S.

A. Graham, Esq., M.A., F.S.A.

Professor K. H. Jackson, M.A., Litt.D., D.Litt., D.Litt.Celt., D.Univ., M.R.I.A., F.B.A.

P. J. Nuttgens, Esq., M.A., Ph.D., R.I.B.A.

Professor Stuart Piggott, C.B.E., B.Litt., D.Litt., F.B.A., F.S.A., F.R.S.E.

Secretary
K. A. Steer, Esq., M.A., Ph.D., F.S.A., F.R.S.E

NINETEENTH REPORT

of the Royal Commission on the Ancient and Historical Monuments of Scotland

TO THE QUEEN'S MOST EXCELLENT MAJESTY

MAY IT PLEASE YOUR MAJESTY,—

We, Your Majesty's Commissioners, appointed to make an Inventory of the Ancient and Historical Monuments and Constructions connected with or illustrative of the contemporary culture, civilisation and conditions of life of the people in Scotland from the earliest times to the year 1707, and such further Monuments and Constructions of a date subsequent to that year as may seem in our discretion worthy of mention therein, and to specify those which seem most worthy of preservation, humbly present to Your Majesty the Report on the Ancient Monuments of Lorn, being the Nineteenth Report on the work of the Commission since its first appointment.

2. We record with grateful respect the receipt of the gracious message that accompanied Your Majesty's acceptance of the volume embodying our Eighteenth Report with Inventory of the Ancient Monuments of Kintyre.

3. It is with great regret that we have to record the resignation through ill-health, and subsequent death, of Mrs Annie Isabella Dunlop, O.B.E., Ph.D., D.Litt., LL.D., who gave valued service to the Commission for many years.

4. We have to thank Your Majesty for the appointment of Mr James Duncan Dunbar-Nasmith, R.I.B.A., P.R.I.A.S., under Your Majesty's Royal Sign Warrant of 9th December 1971.

5. Following our usual practice we have prepared a detailed, illustrated Inventory of the Ancient Monuments of Lorn, being the second volume of the Inventory of the County of Argyll, which will be issued as a non-Parliamentary publication.

6. In the archaeological field, the survey has disclosed unrecorded examples of almost every class of monument included in the Inventory. From the wide range of prehistoric remains represented in Lorn, special mention may be made of the small but important group of Neolithic chambered burial-cairns of the 3rd millennium BC; we have been able to undertake some productive excavations on two of them, which have added significantly to our understanding of their structural history and affinities. Excavation, too, has resulted in the identification of a hitherto unrecognised category of Bronze Age burial-cairn of the 2nd millennium BC.

Together with the examples already published in the Kintyre volume, more than one hundred and sixty Iron Age forts and duns have now been recorded in Argyll.

7. Lorn is particularly rich in castles, and as well as including detailed re-appraisals of several well-known medieval strongholds, such as Dunstaffnage and Dunollie, the present volume describes a number of hitherto unrecorded structures of this class. Domestic architecture, too, is well represented by an interesting group of Georgian mansions and by a corresponding series of small lairds' and tacksmen's houses, while selected examples of the numerous peasant townships and shielings of the same period have also been included. The most notable ecclesiastical monuments in the region are the Valliscaulian monastery of Ardchattan and the cathedral church of the diocese of Argyll on Lismore Island, both of which retain important remains of medieval date, while among post-Reformation buildings mention may be made of a small but unusually diverse group of Gothic Revival churches. Lorn also contains one of the outstanding monuments of the early Industrial Revolution, namely the charcoal blast-furnace and iron-works at Bonawe, whose extensive remains are fully described for the first time, while other examples of industrial and engineering enterprise now recorded include slate-quarries, lime-works, illicit stills, and a Stevenson lighthouse.

8. We wish to acknowledge the assistance accorded to us, during the preparation of this Inventory, by the owners and occupiers of ancient buildings and sites, and by parish ministers, throughout the region. Our thanks are due especially to the late Duke of Argyll, Mr I. M. Campbell, W.S., Mr C. T. Reid, W.S., Major J. Williamson, M.C. and the General Manager of the Northern Lighthouse Board, for access to, and information about, buildings, records, or relics in their possession; to Mr F. Celoria, Ph.D., F.R.G.S., and Mr D. J. Turner, B.Sc., F.S.A., for information in advance of publication concerning excavations which they have conducted in Lorn; to the members of the Lorn Archaeological Society for help with the field surveys and with excavation; to the Cambridge University Committee for Aerial Photography for permission to reproduce air-photographs; to the Institute of Geological Sciences, and particularly to Mr G. H. Collins, B.Sc., F.G.S., one of its officers, for advice on geological questions; to the Scottish Development Department for facilities for the study of air-photographs; and to the staffs of the Department of the Environment, the Forestry Commission, the National Library of Scotland, the National Museum of Antiquities of Scotland, the Glasgow Art Gallery and Museum, the Hunterian Museum, University of Glasgow, the Archaeology Division of the Ordnance Survey, the Scottish Record Office and Your Majesty's Stationery Office for continual and valued co-operation.

9. We wish to record our appreciation of the high standard of work maintained by our executive staff, including those who are not employed in the preparation of the Inventories but on surveys or archival duties for the National Monuments Record of Scotland. In the present volume, the articles and the sections of the Introduction dealing with prehistoric monuments have been written by Messrs A. MacLaren, M.A., F.S.A., G. S. Maxwell, M.A., F.S.A. and J. N. G. Ritchie, M.A., Ph.D., F.S.A., and those dealing with medieval and later buildings by Messrs J. G. Dunbar, M.A., F.S.A. and I. Fisher, M.A. The descriptions of the Early Christian and late medieval carved stones have been contributed by the Secretary. The architectural

drawings have been produced by Messrs S. Scott, D. R. Boyd, G. Fraser and A. Leith under the guidance of Mr G. D. Hay, A.R.I.B.A., F.S.A., while Mr I. G. Scott, D.A. has been responsible for the drawings of the prehistoric monuments and other illustrative work. The photographs have been taken by Messrs G. B. Quick, A.I.I.P., A.R.P.S. and J. D. Keggie, and general assistance has been given by Miss A. E. H. Muir, Miss M. Isbister and Mrs M. Jenkins. The volume has been edited by the Secretary, with the help of Messrs Dunbar and MacLaren, and the index has been compiled by Miss Muir and Dr Ritchie.

WEMYSS, *Chairman* ANGUS GRAHAM
GORDON DONALDSON K. H. JACKSON
JAMES DUNBAR-NASMITH PATRICK NUTTGENS
A. A. M. DUNCAN STUART PIGGOTT
KENNETH A. STEER, *Secretary*

LIST OF MONUMENTS IN LORN
WHICH THE COMMISSIONERS CONSIDER TO BE
MOST WORTHY OF PRESERVATION

The selection of monuments for this list is based on an objective appraisal of various factors such as architectural merit, historical associations, and known or potential value for archaeological research. Inclusion in the list does not confer any statutory protection on the monuments in question, and no account is taken of external circumstances which might make preservation difficult or impracticable.

The list itself is divided into two parts. Part I consists of monuments whose importance can be readily assessed from the surviving remains. Part II comprises monuments which are, in general, less well preserved than those in Part I, but which may nevertheless be valuable subjects for further research by excavation or other means.

PART I

Chambered cairn, Achnacree (No. 1)
Chambered cairn, Achnacreebeag (No. 2)
Chambered cairn, Ardchonnell (No. 3)
Chambered cairn, Auchachenna (No. 4)
Chambered cairn, Dalineun (No. 6)
Cairn and standing stone, Achacha (No. 10)
Cairn, Achanamoine (No. 12)
Cairns, Aon Garbh, Lismore (No. 16)
Cairns, Balure (No. 21)
Cairns, Balygrundle (South), Lismore (No. 23)
Cairn, Barochreal (No. 25)
Cairns and standing stone, Castle Farm, Barcaldine (No. 32)
Cairn, Clachadow 2 (No. 34)
Cairn, Cnoc Aingil, Lismore (No. 38)
Cairn, Dalnacabeg (No. 44)
Cairn, Dalvuie 1 (No. 46)
Cairn, Glen Etive (No. 54)
Cairns, Kilmore (No. 57)
Cairn, Lochan nan Ràth (No. 64)
Barrow, Lochnell Arms Hotel (No. 65)
Cairn, Musdale (No. 67)
Cairn, Salachail (No. 70)
Cairn, Shuna Point, Shuna, Nether Lorn (No. 75)

Cairn, Slatrach Bay, Kerrera (No. 76)
Cairn and standing stone, Strontoiller (No. 78)
Cup-and-ring markings, Kilchrenan (No. 105)
Standing stone, Acharra (No. 110)
Standing stone, Benderloch 1 (No. 112)
Standing stone, Benderloch 2 (No. 113)
Standing stones, Duachy (No. 116)
Stone circle, Strontoiller (No. 120)
Fort, Balvicar, Seil (No. 125)
Forts and dun, Dùn Mac Sniachan (No. 136)
Broch (probable), An Dùn, Loch Fiart, Lismore (No. 146)
Broch, Tirefour Castle, Lismore (No. 147)
Dun, Ballycastle, Luing (No. 155)
Dun, Caisteal Suidhe Cheannaidh (No. 159)
Dun, Dùn Aorain, Seil (No. 166)
Dun, Dùn Chrùban, Lismore (No. 171)
Dun, Dùn Mucaig, Seil (No. 179)
Dun, Gallanach (No. 186)
Dun, Leccamore, Luing (No. 189)
Dun, Tom a' Chaisteil (No. 194)
Appin-murder cairn, Ballachulish (No. 213)
Old Parish Church, Appin, with associated funerary monuments and carved stones (No. 214)

Parish Church, Ardchattan (No. 216)

Ardchattan Priory, with associated funerary monuments and carved stones (No. 217)

Church, Baile Mhaodain, Ardchattan (No. 220)

Carn Chailein (No. 227)

Cross-decorated stone, Clenamacrie (No. 238)

Parish Church, Dalavich, with associated funerary monument (No. 241)

Dunstaffnage Chapel, with associated funerary monuments and carved stones (No. 243)

Parish Church, Duror (No. 244)

Old Parish Church and burial-ground, Eilean Munde, with associated funerary monuments and carved stones (No. 245)

Parish Church, Glenorchy, Dalmally, with associated funerary monuments (No. 246)

Old Parish Church, Inishail, with associated funerary monuments and carved stones (No. 247)

Chapel, Innis Sèa-Ràmhach (No. 248)

Chapel, Keil, with associated funerary monuments (No. 250)

Old Parish Church, Kilbrandon, Seil, with associated funerary monuments (No. 252)

Old Parish Church, Kilbride, with funerary monuments and other associated remains (No. 253)

Old Parish Church, Kilchattan, Luing, with associated funerary monuments (No. 256)

Kilcheran, Lismore (No. 257)

Parish Church, Kilchrenan, with associated funerary monuments (No. 259)

Chapel and burial-ground, Kilmaha (site), with carved stones and other associated remains (No. 261)

Old Parish Church, Kilmore, with associated funerary monuments (No. 264)

Cathedral of St Moluag and Parish Church, Lismore, with funerary monuments and other associated remains (No. 267)

Old Parish Church, Muckairn, Taynuilt (No. 268)

Parish Church, Muckairn, Taynuilt, with associated funerary monuments and carved stones (No. 269)

Free High Church, Oban (No. 270)

Episcopal Church, Portnacroish (No. 272)

Cross, Taynuilt (No. 275)

Achadun Castle, Lismore (No. 276)

Achallader Castle (No. 277)

Barcaldine Castle (No. 279)

Caisteal na Nighinn Ruaidhe, Loch Avich (No. 281)

Castle Coeffin, Lismore (No. 282)

Castle Shuna, Appin (No. 284)

Castle Stalker (No. 285)

Dunollie Castle (No. 286)

Dunstaffnage Castle (No. 287)

Fortified dwelling, Eilean Tighe Bhàin, Loch Tromlee (No. 289)

Castle, Fraoch Eilean (No. 290)

Gylen Castle, Kerrera (No. 291)

Innis Chonnell Castle (No. 292)

Kilchurn Castle (No. 293)

Piermaster's House, South Pier, Oban (No. 301)

Achlian (No. 302)

Airds House (No. 304)

Ardanaiseig (No. 307)

Ardmaddy Castle (No. 310)

Ballachulish House (No. 311)

Dalmally Manse (No. 315)

Gallanach (No. 320)

Glenure (No. 322)

Kilmore House (No. 326)

Kinlochlaich (No. 327)

Lochnell House (No. 330)

Muckairn Manse, Taynuilt (No. 331)

Cottages, Glencoe village (No. 342)

Limestone-quarries and workers' dwellings, An Sàilean, Lismore (No. 348)

Slate-quarries and workers' dwellings, Easdale, Seil (No. 356)

Lighthouse, Eilean Musdile, Lismore (No. 357)

Lorn Furnace, Bonawe (No. 362)

Bridge of Awe (No. 368)

Clachan Bridge, Seil (No. 369)

Bridge of Orchy and selected sections of military road, Tyndrum-Kinlochleven (No. 372)

Architectural fragments, Druimneil House (No. 374)

Armorial panel, Dunstaffnage House (No. 375)

Architectural fragments, St Conan's Church, Lochawe (No. 377)

PART II

Chambered cairn, Cladich (No. 5)

Chambered cairn, Port Sonachan (No. 8)

Chambered cairn, Shuna Cottage, Shuna, Nether Lorn (No. 9)

Cairn, Achaleven (No. 11)

Cairn, Achanancarn (No. 13)

Cairns, Achnaba (No. 14)

Cairn, Allt an Dùnain (No. 15)

Cairn (probable), Ariogan 1 (No. 17)
Cairn (probable), Ariogan 2 (No. 18)
Cairn, Ballachulish House (No. 19)
Cairn, Balygrundle (North), Lismore (No. 22)
Cairn, Barbreck (No. 24)
Cairn, Barr Beag (No. 26)
Cairn, Barr Mór 1, Lismore (No. 27)
Cairn, Barr Mór 2, Lismore (No. 28)
Cairn, Càrn Bàn, Achnacarron (No. 29)
Cairn, Càrn Breugach, Kerrera (No. 30)
Cairn, Càrn Mór, Lismore (No. 31)
Cairn, Clachadow 1 (No. 33)
Cairn, Clachan Bridge, Seil (No. 35)
Cairns, Clenamacrie (East) (No. 36)
Cairns, Clenamacrie (West) (No. 37)
Cairn, Creag an Fhithich, Lismore (No. 41)
Cairn, Cruach Achadh na Craoibhe (No. 42)
Cairn, Culcharron (No. 43)
Cairn (probable), Dalranach (No. 45)
Cairn, Druim an Uinnsinn 1, Lismore (No. 48)
Cairn, Dùnan Buiaig (No. 50)
Cairn (probable), Dunstaffnage House (site) (No. 51)
Cairn, Duntanachan (No. 52)
Cairn, Gualachulain (No. 55)
Cairn, Kilmelford (No. 56)
Cairn, Lagganbeg (No. 58)
Cairn, Làrach Bàn (No. 59)
Cairn, Ledaig, (No. 60)
Cairn, Lerags (No. 61)
Cairn, Lochan a' Chuirn (No. 62)
Cairns, Lochan na Beithe (No. 63)
Cairn, Pennyfuir (No. 68)
Cairn, Rockhill (No. 69)
Cairn, Shuna Cottage 1, Shuna, Nether Lorn (No. 73)
Cairn, Shuna Cottage 2, Shuna, Nether Lorn (No. 74)
Cist, Aon Garbh, Lismore (No. 82)
Cist, Barr Mór, Lismore (No. 85)
Cists, Slaterich, Kerrera (No. 100)
Cup-markings, Ardteatle (No. 101)
Cup-markings, Clachadow (No. 102)
Cup-markings, Clenamacrie (No. 103)
Cup-markings, Keppochan (No. 104)
Cup-markings, Killiechonich (No. 106)
Cup-markings, Kilmaronag (No. 107)
Cup-markings, Loch Gleann a' Bhearraidh (No. 108)
Cup-markings, Oban Esplanade (No. 109)
Standing stones, Barcaldine (No. 111)
Standing stone, Clenamacrie (No. 114)
Standing stone, Inverfolla (No. 118)
Standing stone, Taynuilt 1 (site) (No. 121)
Standing stone, Taynuilt 2 (No. 122)
Fort, Ardanstur 1 (No. 123)
Fort (probable), Castle Coeffin, Lismore (No. 126)
Fort, Cnocan Dubha (No. 127)
Fort, Cnoc an Tighe Mhóir, Seil (No. 128)
Fort, Colagin (No. 129)
Fort, Dùnan Corr (No. 131)
Fort, Dùnans, Glen Cruitten (No. 132)
Fort, Dùn Creagach (No. 134)
Fort, Dùn Iadain (No. 135)
Fort, Dùn Ormidale (No. 137)
Fort, Dùn Uabairtich (No. 138)
Fort, Eilean Mór (No. 139)
Fort, Kilcheran, Lismore (No. 140)
Fort (probable), Kilmore (No. 141)
Fort, The Little Horse Shoe, Kerrera (No. 142)
Fort, Losgann Larnach (No. 143)
Fort, Tom an Iasgaire (No. 144)
Fort, Torr a' Chlaonaidh (No. 145)
Dun (probable), An Dùnan, Dalintart (No. 148)
Dun, An Dùnan, Minard Point (No. 149)
Dun, An Dùn, Clenamacrie (No. 150)
Dun, An Dùn, Sloc a' Bhrighide, Lismore (No. 151)
Dun, Ardanstur 1 (No. 152)
Dun, Ardanstur 2 (No. 153)
Dun, Arduaine (No. 154)
Dun, Barguillean (No. 156)
Dun, Barr a' Chaistealain (No. 157)
Dun, Barr Mór (No. 158)
Dun, Camuslaich, Seil (No. 160)
Dun, Castles (No. 161)
Dun, Clachadow (No. 162)
Dun, Dunach (No. 163)
Dun, Dùn an Fheurain (No. 164)
Dun, Dùnan Molach (No. 165)
Dun, Dùn Bachlach (No. 168)
Dun, Dùn Bhlaran (No. 169)
Dun, Dùn Chathach (No. 170)
Dun, Dùn Creagach (No. 172)
Dun, Dùn Cuilein, Lismore (No. 173)
Dun, Dùn Fadaidh (No. 174)
Dun, Dùn Leigh (No. 175)
Dun, Dùn Mhic Raonuill (No. 176)
Dun, Dùn Mhuirageul (No. 177)
Dun, Dùn Mór, Balygrundle, Lismore (No. 178)
Dun, Duntanachan (No. 183)
Dun, Eilean an Atha, Luing (No. 184)
Dun, Fiart, Lismore (No. 185)
Dun, Kilcheran, Lismore (No. 187)
Dun, Loch a' Phearsain (No. 190)

Dun (possible), Park, Lismore (No. 191)
Dun, Rubh' an Tighe Loisgte (No. 192)
Dun and enclosure, Sean Dùn, Lismore (No. 193)
Crannog, An Doirlinn, Eriska (No. 195)
Crannogs, Loch Awe (No. 198)
Crannog (possible), Loch Seil (No. 199)
Crannog, Moss of Achnacree (site) (No. 200)
Earthwork, Ard Luing, Luing (No. 201)
Enclosure, Balliveolan, Lismore (No. 202)
Field-bank, Black Crofts, North Connel (No. 203)
Earthwork, Cleigh (No. 204)
Earthwork, Dùn Ablaich, Luing (No. 205)
Earthwork, Dùn Mór, Bonawe (No. 206)
Enclosure, Kilmun (No. 208)
Enclosure, Làrach na h-Iobairte (No. 209)
Earthwork, Lochan nan Ràth (No. 210)
Earthwork, South Ledaig (No. 211)
Burial-ground, Achallader (No. 212)
Chapel and burial-ground, Ballachuan, Seil (site) (No. 221)
Chapel and burial-ground, Bernera (site) (No. 224)
Caibeal, Lochavich (No. 226)
Chapel and burial-ground, Cill-an-Suidhe, Lismore (site) (No. 229)
Cill Choluim-chille, Benderloch (site) (No. 230)
Burial-ground (possible), Clachan, Lismore (No. 231)
Cashel (possible), Cladh a' Bhearnaig, Kerrera (No. 232)
Burial-ground, Cladh na h-Anaid, Auchnacloich (No. 233)
Burial-ground, Cladh na h-Anaid, Taynuilt (No. 234)
Chapel and burial-ground, Cladh Uaine (No. 235)
Chapel (site), burial-ground and well, Cladh Churiollan, Creagan (No. 237)
Chapel and burial-ground, Creag a' Chaibeil, Ballimeanoch (No. 239)
Burial-ground and well, Creag Mhór (No. 240)
Church and burial-ground (possible), Kilmaronag (site) (No. 262)
Parish Church, Kilmelford, with associated funerary monuments and carved stones (No. 263)
Chapel and burial-ground, Kilmun (site) (No. 265)
Parish Church and burial-ground, Kilninver (No. 266)
Ardfad Castle, Seil (No. 278)
Caisteal nan Con, Torsa (No. 280)
Fortified dwelling, Eilean Stalcair, Loch Tulla (site) (No. 288)
Fortified dwelling, Loch a' Phearsain, Kilmelford (No. 294)
Fortified dwelling, Loch Nell (site) (No. 296)
Shielings, Airidh nan Sileag (No. 337)
Tigh-cuil township (No. 345)
Glen Kinglass Ironworks (No. 358)
Indeterminate remains, Saulmore (No. 378)

REGISTER OF MONUMENTS IN LORN
BY CIVIL PARISHES

ARDCHATTAN AND MUCKAIRN PARISH

Chambered cairn, Achnacree (No. 1)
Chambered cairn, Achnacreebeag (No. 2)
Cairn and standing stone, Achacha (No. 10)
Cairn, Achaleven (No. 11)
Cairn, Achanamoine (No. 12)
Cairn, Achanancarn (No. 13)
Cairns, Achnaba (No. 14)
Cairns, Balure (No. 21)
Cairns and standing stone, Castle Farm, Barcaldine (No. 32)
Cairn, Clachadow 1 (No. 33)
Cairn, Clachadow 2 (No. 34)
Cairns, Clenamacrie (East) (No. 36)
Cairns, Clenamacrie (West) (No. 37)
Cairn, Culcharron (No. 43)
Cairn (probable), Dalranach (No. 45)
Cairn, Dalvuie 1 (No. 46)
Cairn (possible), Dalvuie 2 (No. 47)
Cairn, Duntanachan (No. 52)
Cairn, Glen Etive (No. 54)
Cairn, Gualachulain (No. 55)
Cairn, Ledaig (No. 60)
Cairn, Lochan a' Chuirn (No. 62)
Cairns, Lochan na Beithe (No. 63)
Cairn, Lochan nan Ràth (No. 64)
Barrow, Lochnell Arms Hotel (No. 65)
Cairn (possible), Moss of Achnacree (No. 66)
Cist, Achnaba (site) (No. 81)
Burial, Ardachy (site) (No. 83)
Cists, Balure (sites) (No. 84)
Cist, Keil (site) (No. 93)
Cist, Kintaline (No. 95)
Cist, Ledaig (site) (No. 96)
Cup-markings, Clachadow (No. 102)
Cup-markings, Clenamacrie (No. 103)
Cup-markings, Kilmaronag (No. 107)
Standing stones, Barcaldine (No. 111)

Standing stone, Benderloch 1 (No. 112)
Standing stone, Benderloch 2 (No. 113)
Standing stone, Clenamacrie (No. 114)
Standing stone, Connel (site) (No. 115)
Standing stone, Taynuilt 1 (site) (No. 121)
Forts and dun, Dùn Mac Sniachan (No. 136)
Dun, An Dùn, Clenamacrie (No. 150)
Dun, Barguillean (No. 156)
Dun, Clachadow (No. 162)
Dun, Dùn Bachlach (No. 168)
Dun, Dùn Chathach (No. 170)
Dun, Dùn Creagach (No. 172)
Dun, Dùn Leigh (No. 175)
Dun, Duntanachan (No. 183)
Crannog, An Doirlinn, Eriska (No. 195)
Crannog, Moss of Achnacree (site) (No. 200)
Field-bank, Black Crofts, North Connel (No. 203)
Earthwork, Dùn Mór, Bonawe (No. 206)
Earthwork, Lochan nan Ràth (No. 210)
Earthwork, South Ledaig (No. 211)
Old Parish Church, Ardchattan (No. 215)
Parish Church, Ardchattan (No. 216)
Ardchattan Priory (No. 217)
Church, Baile Mhaodain, Ardchattan (No. 220)
Burial-ground, Balliveolan (No. 222)
Cill Choluim-chille, Benderloch (site) (No. 230)
Burial-ground, Cladh na h-Anaid, Auchnacloich (No. 233)
Burial-ground, Cladh na h-Anaid, Taynuilt (No. 234)
Cross-decorated stone, Clenamacrie (site) (No. 238)
Burial-ground and well, Creag Mhór (No. 240)
Church, Inverghiusachan (No. 249)
Church and burial-ground (possible), Kilmaronag (site) (No. 262)
Old Parish Church, Muckairn, Taynuilt (No. 268)
Parish Church, Muckairn, Taynuilt (No. 269)
Cross, Taynuilt (site) (No. 275)
Barcaldine Castle (No. 279)
Achnaba (No. 303)
Balliveolan (Druimavuic) (No. 312)

Barcaldine House (No. 313)
Old schoolhouse, Ferlochan (No. 319)
Glenure (No. 322)
Inverawe House (No. 324)
Lochnell House (No. 330)
Muckairn Manse, Taynuilt (No. 331)
Old schoolhouse, North Ledaig (No. 332)
Taynuilt Hotel (No. 334)
Cruck-framed building, Cadderlie (No. 339)
Cruck-framed building, Clachadow (No. 340)
Cruck-framed building, Narrachan (No. 344)
Charcoal-burning stances, Achanlochan (No. 347)
Old quarry (possible), Bridge of Awe (No. 354)
Glen Kinglass Ironworks (No. 358)
Charcoal-burning stances, Loch Creran (No. 360)
Charcoal-burning stances, Loch Etive (No. 361)
Lorn Furnace, Bonawe (No. 362)
Old ferryhouse, South Shian (No. 367)
Bridge of Awe (No. 368)

GLENORCHY AND INISHAIL PARISH

Chambered cairn, Cladich (No. 5)
Cairn, Allt an Dùnain (No. 15)
Cairn, Barbreck (No. 24)
Cairn, Càrn Bàn, Achnacarron (No. 29)
Cairn, Làrach Bàn (No. 59)
Cairn, Rockhill (No. 69)
Cairn, Stronmilchan (site) (No. 77)
Cup-markings, Ardteatle (No. 101)
Cup-markings, Keppochan (No. 104)
Cup-and-ring markings, Kilchrenan (No. 105)
Standing stone, Taynuilt 2 (No. 122)
Fort, Tom an Iasgaire (No. 144)
Dun, Barr a' Chaistealain (No. 157)
Dun, Castles (No. 161)
Dun (probable), Dùn Athaich (site) (No. 167)
Dun, Dùn Mhuirageul (No. 177)
Dun (possible), Dùn na Cuaiche (No. 180)
Dun, Tom a' Chaisteil (No. 194)
Crannog (possible), Lochan na Gealaich (No. 197)
Crannogs, Loch Awe (No. 198)
Burial-ground, Achallader (No. 212)
Chapel and burial-ground (possible), Auch Gleann (site) (No. 219)
Caibeal Chiarain (site) (No. 225)
Parish Church, Cladich (No. 236)
St Conan's Well, Dalmally (No. 242)

Parish Church, Glenorchy, Dalmally (No. 246)
Old Parish Church, Inishail (No. 247)
Burial-enclosure, Sonachan (No. 274)
Achallader Castle (No. 277)
Castle, Castles Farm (site) (No. 283)
Fortified dwelling, Eilean Stalcair, Loch Tulla (site) (No. 288)
Fortified dwelling, Eilean Tighe Bhàin, Loch Tromlee (No. 289)
Castle, Fraoch Eilean (No. 290)
Kilchurn Castle (No. 293)
Achlian (No. 302)
Ardanaiseig (No. 307)
Bothan na Dige, Stronmilchan (site) (No. 314)
Dalmally Manse (No. 315)
Hayfield (No. 323)
Tigh Mór, Stronmilchan (site) (No. 335)
Upper Sonachan House (No. 336)
Shielings, Airidh nan Sileag (No. 337)
Cruck-framed byre, Bonawe (No. 338)
Millstone-quarry, Barran (No. 352)
Whisky-still, Brackley (site) (No. 353)
Old quarry (possible), Bridge of Awe (No. 354)
Bridge of Awe (No. 368)
Bridge and embankment, Dalmally (No. 370)
Military road, Inveraray-Tyndrum (No. 371)
Military road, Tyndrum-Kinlochleven (No. 372)
Architectural fragments, St Conan's Church, Lochawe (No. 377)

KILBRANDON AND KILCHATTAN PARISH

Chambered cairn, Shuna Cottage, Shuna, Nether Lorn (No. 9)
Cairn, Clachan Bridge, Seil (No. 35)
Cairn (possible), Sgeir Carnaich (No. 71)
Cairn, Shuna Cottage 1, Shuna, Nether Lorn (No. 73)
Cairn, Shuna Cottage 2, Shuna, Nether Lorn (No. 74)
Cairn, Shuna Point, Shuna, Nether Lorn (No. 75)
Cist, Degnish (site) (No. 88)
Fort, Balvicar, Seil (No. 125)
Fort, Cnoc an Tighe Mhóir, Seil (No. 128)
Dun, Ballycastle, Luing (No. 155)
Dun, Camuslaich, Seil (No. 160)
Dun, Dùn Aorain, Seil (No. 166)
Dun, Dùn Fadaidh (No. 174)
Dun, Dùn Mucaig, Seil (No. 179)
Dun, Eilean an Atha, Luing (No. 184)

Dun (possible), Kilchoan Loch (No. 188)
Dun, Leccamore, Luing (No. 189)
Earthwork, Ard Luing, Luing (No. 201)
Earthwork, Dùn Ablaich, Luing (No. 205)
Chapel and burial-ground, Ballachuan, Seil (site) (No. 221)
Old Parish Church, Kilbrandon and Kilchattan, Seil (No. 251)
Old Parish Church, Kilbrandon, Seil (No. 252)
Chapel, Kilbride, Seil (site) (No. 255)
Old Parish Church, Kilchattan, Luing (No. 256)
Chapel and burial-ground, Kilchoan House (site) (No. 258)
Burial-enclosure, Shuna, Nether Lorn (No. 273)
Ardfad Castle, Seil (No. 278)
Caisteal nan Con, Torsa (No. 280)
Ardencaple House, Seil (No. 308)
Ardlarach, Luing (No. 309)
Ardmaddy Castle (No. 310)
Degnish (No. 316)
Kilbrandon House, Seil (No. 325)
Marble-quarry, Caddleton (No. 355)
Slate-quarries and workers' dwellings, Easdale, Seil (No. 356)
Clachan Bridge, Seil (No. 369)

KILCHRENAN AND DALAVICH PARISH

Chambered cairn, Ardchonnell (No. 3)
Chambered cairn, Auchachenna (No. 4)
Chambered cairn, Port Sonachan (No. 8)
'Cairns', Ballimeanoch (No. 20)
Cairn, Cruach Achadh na Craoibhe (No. 42)
Burial, Kames (site) (No. 92)
Dun, Barr Mór (No. 158)
Dun, Caisteal Suidhe Cheannaidh (No. 159)
Crannogs, Loch Awe (No. 198)
Enclosure, Kilmun (No. 208)
Enclosure, Làrach na h-Iobairte (No. 209)
Caibeal, Lochavich (No. 226)
Chapel and burial-ground, Creag a' Chaibeil, Ballimeanoch (No. 239)
Parish Church, Dalavich (No. 241)
Chapel, Innis Sèa-Ràmhach (No. 248)
Parish Church, Kilchrenan (No. 259)
Chapel and burial-ground, Kilmaha (site) (No. 261)
Chapel and burial-ground, Kilmun (site) (No. 265)
Caisteal na Nighinn Ruaidhe, Loch Avich (No. 281)
Innis Chonnell Castle (No. 292)

KILMORE AND KILBRIDE PARISH

Chambered cairn, Dalineun (No. 6)
Cairn (probable), Ariogan 1 (No. 17)
Cairn (probable), Ariogan 2 (No. 18)
Cairn, Barr Beag (No. 26)
Cairn, Càrn Breugach, Kerrera (No. 30)
Cairn, Connel (site) (No. 39)
Cairn, Dalnacabeg (No. 44)
Cairn (probable), Dunstaffnage House (site) (No. 51)
Cairns, Kilmore (No. 57)
Cairn, Lerags (No. 61)
Cairn, Musdale (No. 67)
Cairn, Pennyfuir (No. 68)
Cairn, Slatrach Bay, Kerrera (No. 76)
Cairn and standing stone, Strontoiller (No. 78)
Cairn (possible), Strontoiller 2 (No. 79)
Cist, Cleigh (site) (No. 86)
Burials, Dùn an Fheurain (sites) (No. 89)
Burials and cist, Dunollie (sites) (No. 90)
Cist, Gallanachbeg (site) (No. 91)
Burials and cists, Oban (sites) (No. 98)
Cist, Saulmore (site) (No. 99)
Cists, Slaterich, Kerrera (No. 100)
Cup-markings, Killiechonich (No. 106)
Cup-markings, Loch Gleann a' Bhearraidh (No. 108)
Cup-markings, Oban Esplanade (No. 109)
Stone circle, Strontoiller (No. 120)
Fort, Colagin (No. 129)
Fort, Dùnan Corr (No. 131)
Fort, Dùnans, Glen Cruitten (No. 132)
'Fort', Dunbeg (site) (No. 133)
Fort, Dùn Creagach (No. 134)
Fort, Dùn Iadain (No. 135)
Fort, Dùn Ormidale (No. 137)
Fort, Dùn Uabairtich (No. 138)
Fort, Eilean Mór (No. 139)
Fort (probable), Kilmore (No. 141)
Fort, The Little Horse Shoe, Kerrera (No. 142)
Dun (probable), An Dùnan, Dalintart (No. 148)
Dun, An Dùnan, Minard Point (No. 149)
Dun, Dunach (No. 163)
Dun, Dùn an Fheurain (No. 164)
Dun, Dùnan Molach (No. 165)
Dun, Dùn Bhlaran (No. 169)
Dun (possible), Dùn Neil (No. 181)
Dun (possible), Dunstaffnage (site) (No. 182)
Dun, Gallanach (No. 186)
Crannog, Loch a' Mhuillin (site) (No. 196)
Earthwork, Cleigh (No. 204)

Chapel and burial-ground, Bar-a-goan, Kilvarie (site) (No. 223)
Cashel (possible), Cladh a' Bhearnaig, Kerrera (No. 232)
Chapel and burial-ground, Cladh Uaine (No. 235)
Dunstaffnage Chapel (No. 243)
Old Parish Church, Kilbride (No. 253)
Burial-ground, Kilbride, Glen Feochan (site) (No. 254)
Old Parish Church, Kilmore (No. 264)
Free High Church, Oban (No. 270)
Dunollie Castle (No. 286)
Dunstaffnage Castle (No. 287)
Gylen Castle, Kerrera (No. 291)
Fortified dwelling, Loch Nell (site) (No. 296)
Back Combie Street, Oban (No. 299)
Cawdor Place, Oban (No. 300)
Piermaster's House, South Pier, Oban (No. 301)
The Manor House, Dungallon (No. 317)
Dunollie House (No. 318)
Gallanach (No. 320)
Kilmore House (No. 326)
Lerags House (No. 329)
Dunstaffnage Mains Farm (No. 341)
Cruck-framed byre, Torr-an-tuirc (No. 346)
Old quarries, Ardentallan (No. 349)
Armorial panel, Dunstaffnage House (No. 375)
Indeterminate remains, Saulmore (No. 378)

KILNINVER AND KILMELFORD PARISH

Cairn, Barochreal (No. 25)
Cairn (possible), Corrielorne (No. 40)
Cairn, Dùnan Buiaig (No. 50)
Cairn, Kilmelford (No. 56)
Cairn, Laggenbeg (No. 58)
Cairns (possible), Shelachan (No. 72)
Cists, Melfort House (sites) (No. 97)
Standing stones, Duachy (No. 116)
Standing stone, Kilninver (site) (No. 119)
Fort, Ardanstur 1 (No. 123)
Fort (possible), Ardanstur 2 (No. 124)
Fort (possible), Creag Aoil (No. 130)
Fort, Losgann Larnach (No. 143)
Dun, Ardanstur 1 (No. 152)
Dun, Ardanstur 2 (No. 153)
Dun, Arduaine (No. 154)
Dun, Dùn Mhic Raonuill (No. 176)
Dun, Loch a' Phearsain (No. 190)
Dun, Rubh' an Tighe Loisgte (No. 192)

Crannog (possible), Loch Seil (No. 199)
Burial-ground, Ath Dearg (site) (No. 218)
Carn Chailein (No. 227)
Burial-ground, Cill an Inbhire (site) (No. 228)
Parish Church, Kilmelford (No. 263)
Parish Church and burial-ground, Kilninver (No. 266)
Fortified dwelling, Loch a' Phearsain, Kilmelford (No. 294)
Castle, Loch na Sreinge (site) (No. 295)
Castle, Rarey (site) (No. 297)
Rarey (No. 333)
Shielings, Glen Risdale (No. 343)
Tigh-cuil township (No. 345)
Old quarry, Barrnacarry (No. 351)
Gunpowder-works, Melfort (No. 363)

LISMORE AND APPIN PARISH

Chambered cairn (probable), Portnacroish (site) (No. 7)
Cairns, Aon Garbh, Lismore (No. 16)
Cairn, Ballachulish House (No. 19)
Cairn, Balygrundle (North), Lismore (No. 22)
Cairns, Balygrundle (South), Lismore (No. 23)
Cairn, Barr Mór 1, Lismore (No. 27)
Cairn, Barr Mór 2, Lismore (No. 28)
Cairn, Càrn Mór, Lismore (No. 31)
Cairn, Cnoc Aingil, Lismore (No. 38)
Cairn, Creag an Fhithich, Lismore (No. 41)
Cairn, Druim an Uinnsinn 1, Lismore (No. 48)
Cairn (possible), Druim an Uinnsinn 2, Lismore (No. 49)
Cairn (possible), Fasnacloich (No. 53)
Cairn, Salachail (No. 70)
Cairns, West Laroch (sites) (No. 80)
Cist, Aon Garbh, Lismore (No. 82)
Cist, Barr Mór, Lismore (No. 85)
Burial, Cnoc Aingil, Lismore (site) (No. 87)
Burial, Kilcheran, Lismore (site) (No. 94)
Standing stone, Acharra (No. 110)
Standing stone, Eilean Musdile, Lismore (site) (No. 117)
Standing stone, Inverfolla (No. 118)
Fort (probable), Castle Coeffin, Lismore (No. 126)
Fort, Cnocan Dubha (No. 127)
Fort, Kilcheran, Lismore (No. 140)
Fort, Torr a' Chlaonaidh (No. 145)
Broch (probable), An Dùn, Loch Fiart, Lismore (No. 146)
Broch, Tirefour Castle, Lismore (No. 147)
Dun, An Dùn, Sloc a' Bhrighide, Lismore (No. 151)

Dun, Dùn Chrùban, Lismore (No. 171)

Dun, Dùn Cuilein, Lismore (No. 173)

Dun, Dùn Mór, Balygrundle, Lismore (No. 178)

Dun, Fiart, Lismore (No. 185)

Dun, Kilcheran, Lismore (No. 187)

Dun (possible), Park, Lismore (No. 191)

Dun and enclosure, Sean Dùn, Lismore (No. 193)

Enclosure, Balliveolan, Lismore (No. 202)

Enclosure, Eilean Balnagowan (No. 207)

Appin-murder cairn, Ballachulish (No. 213)

Old Parish Church, Appin (No. 214)

Chapel and burial-ground, Bernera (site) (No. 224)

Chapel and burial-ground, Cill-an-Suidhe, Lismore (site) (No. 229)

Burial-ground (possible), Clachan, Lismore (No. 231)

Chapel (site), burial-ground and well, Cladh Churiollan, Creagan (No. 237)

Parish Church, Duror (No. 244)

Old Parish Church and burial-ground, Eilean Munde (No. 245)

Chapel, Keil (No. 250)

Kilcheran, Lismore (No. 257)

Chapel, Killandrist, Lismore (site) (No. 260)

Cathedral of St Moluag and Parish Church, Lismore (No. 267)

Chapel, Port Maluag, Lismore (site) (No. 271)

Episcopal Church, Portnacroish (No. 272)

Achadun Castle, Lismore (No. 276)

Castle Coeffin, Lismore (No. 282)

Castle Shuna, Appin (No. 284)

Castle Stalker (No. 285)

Airds House (No. 304)

Appin House (No. 305)

Appin Post-office, Tynribbie (No. 306)

Ballachulish House (No. 311)

Glenstockdale (No. 321)

Kinlochlaich (No. 327)

Kulmani, Duror (No. 328)

Cottages, Glencoe village (No. 342)

Limestone-quarries and workers' dwellings, An Sàilean, Lismore (No. 348)

Slate-quarries and workers' dwellings, Ballachulish (No. 350)

Lighthouse, Eilean Musdile, Lismore (No. 357)

Whisky-stills (sites), Lismore (No. 359)

Old ferryhouse, Port Appin (No. 364)

Lime-kilns, Port Kilcheran, Lismore (No. 365)

Limestone-quarries and workers' dwellings, Port Ramsay, Lismore (No. 366)

Military road, Tyndrum-Kinlochleven (No. 372)

Graffito, Creagan (No. 373)

Architectural fragments, Druimneil House (No. 374)

Armorial panel, Old Smithy, Port Appin (No. 376)

ABBREVIATIONS USED IN
THE REFERENCES

Adomnan, *Columba* (Anderson)	Anderson, A O and M O (edd.), *Adomnan's Life of Columba*, Edinburgh, 1961.
Anderson, *Early Sources*	Anderson, A O (ed.), *Early Sources of Scottish History 500 to 1286*, Edinburgh, 1922.
APS	*The Acts of the Parliaments of Scotland*, Edinburgh, 1814–75.
Arch. J.	*The Archaeological Journal.*
Argyll Synod Minutes	Mactavish, D C (ed.), *Minutes of the Synod of Argyll*, vol. i (1639–51), SHS, 1943; vol. ii (1652–61), SHS, 1944.
Blaeu's *Atlas* (Lorn)	Pont-Gordon Map of second quarter of 17th century, first published in Scottish volume of Blaeu's *Atlas* in 1654.
B.M.	British Museum.
Burrell, 'Tour'.	Burrell, Sir W, 'Tour' (n.d., dated 1758 from internal evidence), Nat. Lib. of Scot. MS 2911.
Cal. Docs. Scot.	*Calendar of Documents relating to Scotland*, Edinburgh, 1881–8.
Cal. Scot. Supp., ii	Dunlop, A I (ed.), *Calendar of Scottish Supplications to Rome 1423–1428*, SHS, 1956.
Campbell, *Argyll Sasines*	Campbell, H (ed.), *Abstracts of the Particular and General Registers of Sasines for Argyll, Bute and Dunbarton, otherwise known as the Argyll Sasines*, Edinburgh, 1933–4.
Campbell, *Highland Dress*	Campbell, Lord A, *Highland Dress, Arms and Ornament*, London, 1899 (reprinted 1969).
Carmichael, *Lismore*	Carmichael, I, *Lismore in Alba*, (Perth, 1948).
Cast. and Dom. Arch.	MacGibbon, D and Ross, T, *The Castellated and Domestic Architecture of Scotland*, Edinburgh, 1887–92.
Clan Campbell	Campbell, Sir D, *The Clan Campbell*, Edinburgh, 1913–22.
Cowan, *Parishes*	Cowan, I B, *The Parishes of Medieval Scotland*, SRS, 1967.
DES (date)	*Discovery and Excavation, Scotland*, Annual publication of Scottish Regional Group, Council for British Archaeology.
Douglas, *Baronage*	Douglas, Sir R, *The Baronage of Scotland*, Edinburgh, 1798.
Drummond, *Monuments*	Drummond, J, *Sculptured Monuments in Iona and the West Highlands*, Edinburgh, 1881.
Dunstaffnage Case	*Joint Print of Documents in causa His Grace the Duke of Argyll against Angus John Campbell of Dunstaffnage and Another*, Edinburgh, 1911.
Easson, *Religious Houses*	Easson, D E, *Medieval Religious Houses, Scotland*, London, 1957.
Eccles. Arch.	MacGibbon, D and Ross, T, *The Ecclesiastical Architecture of Scotland*, Edinburgh, 1896–7.
ECMS	Allen, J Romilly and Anderson, J, *The Early Christian Monuments of Scotland*, Edinburgh, 1903.
ECMW	Nash-Williams, V E, *The Early Christian Monuments of Wales*, Cardiff, 1950.
Exch. Rolls	*The Exchequer Rolls of Scotland*, Edinburgh, 1878–1908.
Faichney, *Oban*	Faichney, A M, *Oban and the District Around*, Oban, 1902.
Fell, *Iron Industry*	Fell, A, *The Early Iron Industry of Furness and District*, Ulverston, 1908 (reprinted 1968).

Fergusson, *Argyll* . . . Fergusson, Sir J, *Argyll in the Forty-Five*, London, 1951.

Forbes, *Journals* . . . Craven, J B (ed.), *Journals of the Episcopal Visitations of the Right Rev. Robert Forbes, M.A. 1762 & 1770*, second edition, London, 1923.

GAJ . . . . *Glasgow Archaeological Journal.*

Garnett, *Tour* . . . Garnett, T, *Observations on a Tour through the Highlands and part of the Western Isles of Scotland*, London, 1800.

Geog. Coll. . . . Macfarlane, W, *Geographical Collections relating to Scotland*, SHS, 1906–8.

Gillies, *Netherlorn* . . . Gillies, P H, *Netherlorn, Argyllshire, and its Neighbourhood*, London, 1909.

Groome, *Ordnance Gazetteer* . Groome, F H (ed.), *Ordnance Gazetteer of Scotland*, new edition, Edinburgh, 1901.

Hay, *Post-Reformation Churches* . Hay, G, *The Architecture of Scottish Post-Reformation Churches 1560–1843*, Oxford, 1957.

Henshall, *Chambered Tombs* . Henshall, A S, *The Chambered Tombs of Scotland*, Edinburgh, 1963–72.

Highland Papers . . . Macphail, J R N (ed.), *Highland Papers*, SHS, 1914–34.

Hist. MSS. Comm. . . . *Reports of the Royal Commission on Historical Manuscripts*, London, 1870–   .

Howson, *Antiquities* . . . Howson, J S, 'On the Ecclesiastical Antiquities of Argyllshire', in *Transactions of the Cambridge Camden Society*, 1842 and 1845.

Inchaffray Chrs. . . . Lindsay, W A, Dowden, J and Thomson, J M (edd.), *Charters, Bulls and other documents relating to the Abbey of Inchaffray*, SHS, 1908.

Inventory of [*County*] . . Royal Commission on the Ancient and Historical Monuments of Scotland: *Inventory of the Ancient and Historical Monuments and Constructions in* [the county stated].

Johnston, *Campbell Heraldry* . Johnston, G H, *The Heraldry of the Campbells*, Edinburgh, 1920–1.

JRSAI . . . . *The Journal of the Royal Society of Antiquaries of Ireland.*

Leyden, *Tour* . . . . Leyden, J, *Journal of a Tour in the Highlands and Western Islands of Scotland in 1800*, Edinburgh and London, 1903.

Lorn Presbytery Minutes . . MS minute-books of Presbytery of Lorn in custody of clerk of Presbytery.

MacDonald, *Argyll* . . . MacDonald, C M, *The History of Argyll up to the beginning of the sixteenth century*, Glasgow, (1950).

Mackinlay, *Non-Scriptural Dedications* . . . . Mackinlay, J M, *Ancient Church Dedications in Scotland: Non-Scriptural Dedications*, Edinburgh, 1914.

Mackinlay, *Scriptural Dedications* Mackinlay, J M, *Ancient Church Dedications in Scotland: Scriptural Dedications*, Edinburgh, 1910.

Monro, *Western Isles* . . . Munro, R W (ed.), *Monro's Western Isles of Scotland and Genealogies of the Clans 1549*, Edinburgh, 1961.

Muir, *Eccles. Notes* . . . Muir, T S, *Ecclesiological Notes on some of the Islands of Scotland*, Edinburgh, 1885.

Name Book . . . . Original Name-books of the Ordnance Survey, County of Argyll.

Nat. Lib. of Scot. . . . National Library of Scotland.

Newte, *Tour* . . . . Newte, T, *Prospects and Observations; on a Tour in England and Scotland: Natural, Oeconomical and Literary*, (new edition), London, 1791.

N.M.R.S. . . . . National Monuments Record of Scotland.

NSA . . . . *The New Statistical Account of Scotland*, Edinburgh, 1845.

Origines Parochiales . . *Origines Parochiales Scotiae*, Bannatyne Club, 1851–5.

O.S. . . . . . Ordnance Survey.

Pennant, *Tour* (*1769*) . . (Pennant, T), *A Tour in Scotland; MDCCLXIX*, fifth edition, London, 1790.

Pennant, *Tour* (*1772*) . . (Pennant, T), *A Tour in Scotland; and Voyage to the Hebrides; MDCCLXXII*, (new edition), London, 1790.

Pitcairn, *Trials* . . . Pitcairn, R (ed.), *Criminal Trials in Scotland from 1488 to 1624*, Edinburgh, 1833.

Pococke, *Tours* . . .	Kemp, D W (ed.), *Tours in Scotland, 1747, 1750, 1760, by Richard Pococke, Bishop of Meath*, SHS, 1887.
PPS	*Proceedings of the Prehistoric Society.*
P.R.O.	Public Record Office.
PSAS	*Proceedings of the Society of Antiquaries of Scotland.*
RMS	*Registrum Magni Sigilli Regum Scotorum*, Edinburgh, 1882–1914.
Roy's Map . . .	Military Survey of Scotland, 1747–55 (original in B.M.; photostat copies at Edinburgh University Library and elsewhere).
RPC	*The Register of the Privy Council of Scotland*, Edinburgh, 1887– .
St Fond, *Journey* . .	St Fond, B Faujas de, *A Journey Through England and Scotland to the Hebrides in 1784*, revised edition, Glasgow, 1907.
Scots Peerage . . .	Balfour Paul, Sir J (ed.), *The Scots Peerage*, Edinburgh, 1904–14.
Scott, *Fasti* . . .	Scott, H, *Fasti Ecclesiae Scoticanae*, revised edition, Edinburgh, 1915– .
Scottish National Memorials .	Paton, J (ed.), *Scottish National Memorials*, Glasgow, 1890.
Shedden, *Lorn* . .	Shedden, H, *The Story of Lorn, its Isles and Oban*, Oban, 1938.
SHR	*The Scottish Historical Review.*
SHS	Scottish History Society.
SHS Misc. . . .	*The Miscellany of the Scottish History Society*, SHS, 1893– .
Simpson, *Dunstaffnage* .	Simpson, W Douglas, *Dunstaffnage Castle and the Stone of Destiny*, Edinburgh, 1958.
Skene, *Celtic Scotland* .	Skene, W F, *Celtic Scotland: A History of Ancient Alban*, Edinburgh, 1886–90.
Smith, *General View* . .	Smith, J, *General View of the Agriculture of the County of Argyll*, Edinburgh, 1798.
Smith, *Loch Etive* . .	Smith, R A, *Loch Etive and the Sons of Uisnach*, new edition, London and Paisley, 1885.
S.R.O.	Scottish Record Office, H.M. General Register House, Edinburgh.
SRS	Scottish Record Society.
Stat. Acct. . . .	*The Statistical Account of Scotland*, Edinburgh, 1791–9.
Steer and Bannerman, *Monumental Sculpture* . . .	Steer, K A and Bannerman, J W M, *Late Medieval Monumental Sculpture in the West Highlands*, forthcoming.
Stoddart, *Local Scenery* .	Stoddart, J, *Remarks on Local Scenery and Manners in Scotland during the years 1799 and 1800*, London, 1801.
Taymouth Bk. . . .	*The Black Book of Taymouth*, Bannatyne Club, 1855.
TDGAS . . .	*Transactions of the Dumfriesshire and Galloway Natural History and Antiquarian Society.*
Telford, *Atlas* . . .	*Atlas to the Life of Thomas Telford, Civil Engineer*, London, 1838.
Telford, *Life* . . .	Rickman, J (ed.), *Life of Thomas Telford, Civil Engineer, written by himself*, London, 1838.
TGAS	*Transactions of the Glasgow Archaeological Society.*
TGSI	*Transactions of the Gaelic Society of Inverness.*
Third Stat. Acct. (Argyll) .	*The Third Statistical Account of Scotland, The County of Argyll*, Glasgow, 1961.
TISS	*Transactions of the Inverness Scientific Society and Field Club.*
TSES	*Transactions of the Scottish Ecclesiological Society.*
Watson, *Celtic Place-names* .	Watson, W J, *The History of the Celtic Place-names of Scotland*, Edinburgh and London, 1926.
Watt, *Fasti* . . .	Watt, D E R, *Fasti Ecclesiae Scoticanae Medii Aevi ad annum 1638*, second draft, St Andrews, 1969.
White, *Knapdale* . .	White, T P, *Archaeological Sketches in Scotland, Knapdale and Gigha*, Edinburgh, 1875.
Wordsworth, *Tour* . .	Wordsworth, D, *Recollections of a Tour made in Scotland, A.D. 1803*, Edinburgh, 1874.

EDITORIAL NOTES

Maps, Grid References and Dates of Visit

At the end of each article will be found the National Grid Reference of the monument in question, the number of the O.S. 6-inch sheet on which it occurs, and the last date on which it was examined.

When this volume went to press, the O.S. 6-inch National Grid sheets were in preparation, and therefore they are quoted in preference to the second edition of 1900 (County Series). Since the first two letters of the 6-inch sheet number indicate the relevant 100-kilometre square, the letters have been omitted from the six-figure references.

Metrication

The plans in this volume are provided with scales in both British and metric units. The text was originally prepared using British units of measurement, but in anticipation of the adoption of the Metric System, and in order to maintain a uniformity of presentation throughout the several volumes that will eventually constitute the *Inventory of Argyll*, all measurements have been converted into metric units, the primary unit of length being the metre. For area measurements the equivalent British units are given alongside the metric units where these occur in the text, and, as a rough guide to assist the reader to find the approximate British values for all other measurements, simplified conversion-tables are printed on pp. xlvii–iii. A copy of these conversion tables is also enclosed in the end-pocket. Unless otherwise stated, the ranging-poles that have been included in some of the photographs for scale purposes are of metric type, each division measuring 0·5 metre.

Scales

To facilitate comparison, the plans of similar earthworks and buildings have been reproduced wherever possible at uniform scales. The representative fractions principally employed are: (*a*) for the majority of prehistoric monuments, 1 : 1000; (*b*) for smaller prehistoric monuments and for plans of buildings, 1 : 250; and (*c*) for elevations and sections of buildings, 1 : 150.

Inscriptions

Square brackets occurring in the text of an inscription indicate that the words or letters within them are illegible but have been restored, a question-mark being added when the restoration is uncertain. Words or letters in round brackets have never existed in the inscription but have been inserted for the sake of clarity.

Place Names

The spelling of place names normally follows the spelling currently adopted by the Ordnance Survey.

xlv

Personal Names

The spelling of personal names is usually modernized, except where these occur in inscriptions, or in direct quotations from early records.

Reproductions

Unless otherwise stated, the contents of the volume are all Crown Copyright, but copies of the photographs, and prints of the plans and other line drawings, can be obtained from the Secretary, The Royal Commission on the Ancient and Historical Monuments of Scotland, 54 Melville Street, Edinburgh EH3 7HF. The records of the Commission, which include a number of unpublished photographs of monuments, buildings and relics referred to in this volume, may also be consulted at that address.

CONVERSION TABLES, METRIC TO BRITISH VALUES

1. *Metres to Feet and Inches*[1]

METRES	FEET	INCHES	METRES	FEET	INCHES	METRES	FEET	INCHES	METRES	FEET
0·006	0	0¼	1·14	3	9	2·34	7	8	8·84	29
0·013	0	0½	1·17	3	10	2·36	7	9	9·14	30
0·019	0	0¾	1·19	3	11	2·39	7	10	9·45	31
0·03	0	1	1·22	4	0	2·41	7	11	9·75	32
0·05	0	2	1·25	4	1	2·44	8	0	10·06	33
0·08	0	3	1·27	4	2	2·46	8	1	10·36	34
0·10	0	4	1·30	4	3	2·49	8	2	10·67	35
0·13	0	5	1·32	4	4	2·52	8	3	10·97	36
0·15	0	6	1·35	4	5	2·54	8	4	11·28	37
0·18	0	7	1·37	4	6	2·57	8	5	11·58	38
0·20	0	8	1·40	4	7	2·59	8	6	11·89	39
0·23	0	9	1·42	4	8	2·62	8	7	12·19	40
0·25	0	10	1·45	4	9	2·64	8	8	12·50	41
0·28	0	11	1·47	4	10	2·67	8	9	12·80	42
0·31	1	0	1·50	4	11	2·69	8	10	13·11	43
0·33	1	1	1·52	5	0	2·72	8	11	13·41	44
0·36	1	2	1·55	5	1	2·74	9	0	13·72	45
0·38	1	3	1·58	5	2	2·77	9	1	14·02	46
0·41	1	4	1·60	5	3	2·79	9	2	14·33	47
0·43	1	5	1·63	5	4	2·82	9	3	14·63	48
0·46	1	6	1·65	5	5	2·85	9	4	14·94	49
0·48	1	7	1·68	5	6	2·87	9	5	15·24	50
0·51	1	8	1·70	5	7	2·90	9	6	15·55	51
0·53	1	9	1·73	5	8	2·92	9	7	15·85	52
0·56	1	10	1·75	5	9	2·95	9	8	16·15	53
0·58	1	11	1·78	5	10	2·97	9	9	16·46	54
0·61	2	0	1·80	5	11	3·00	9	10	16·76	55
0·64	2	1	1·83	6	0	3·02	9	11	17·07	56
0·66	2	2	1·85	6	1	3·05	10	0	17·37	57
0·69	2	3	1·88	6	2	3·35	11	0	17·68	58
0·71	2	4	1·91	6	3	3·66	12	0	17·98	59
0·74	2	5	1·93	6	4	3·96	13	0	18·29	60
0·76	2	6	1·96	6	5	4·27	14	0	18·59	61
0·79	2	7	1·98	6	6	4·57	15	0	18·90	62
0·81	2	8	2·01	6	7	4·88	16	0	19·20	63
0·84	2	9	2·03	6	8	5·18	17	0	19·51	64
0·86	2	10	2·06	6	9	5·49	18	0	19·81	65
0·89	2	11	2·08	6	10	5·79	19	0	20·12	66
0·91	3	0	2·11	6	11	6·10	20	0	20·42	67
0·94	3	1	2·13	7	0	6·40	21	0	20·73	68
0·97	3	2	2·16	7	1	6·71	22	0	21·03	69
0·99	3	3	2·18	7	2	7·01	23	0	21·34	70
1·02	3	4	2·21	7	3	7·32	24	0	21·64	71
1·04	3	5	2·24	7	4	7·62	25	0	21·95	72
1·07	3	6	2·26	7	5	7·93	26	0	22·25	73
1·09	3	7	2·29	7	6	8·23	27	0	22·56	74
1·12	3	8	2·31	7	7	8·53	28	0	22·86	75

[1] The form of this conversion table has been dictated by the fact that the text was originally prepared using British units of measurement. The table shows the metric equivalents, correct to two decimal places, of feet and inches by intervals of one inch up to 10 feet, then by intervals of one foot up to 100 feet, and thereafter by intervals of 10 feet up to 1000 feet.

METRES	FEET	METRES	FEET	METRES	FEET	METRES	FEET	METRES	FEET
23·17	76	30·18	99	97·54	320	167·64	550	237·74	780
23·47	77	30·48	100	100·58	330	170·69	560	240·79	790
23·77	78	33·53	110	103·63	340	173·74	570	243·84	800
24·08	79	36·58	120	106·68	350	176·78	580	246·89	810
24·38	80	39·62	130	109·73	360	179·83	590	249·94	820
24·69	81	42·67	140	112·78	370	182·88	600	252·98	830
24·99	82	45·72	150	115·82	380	185·93	610	256·03	840
25·30	83	48·77	160	118·87	390	188·98	620	259·08	850
25·60	84	51·82	170	121·92	400	192·02	630	262·13	860
25·91	85	54·86	180	124·97	410	195·07	640	265·18	870
26·21	86	57·91	190	128·02	420	198·12	650	268·22	880
26·52	87	60·96	200	131·06	430	201·17	660	271·27	890
26·82	88	64·01	210	134·11	440	204·22	670	274·32	900
27·13	89	67·06	220	137·16	450	207·26	680	277·37	910
27·43	90	70·10	230	140·21	460	210·31	690	280·42	920
27·74	91	73·15	240	143·26	470	213·36	700	283·46	930
28·04	92	76·20	250	146·30	480	216·41	710	286·51	940
28·35	93	79·25	260	149·35	490	219·46	720	289·56	950
28·65	94	82·30	270	152·40	500	222·50	730	292·61	960
28·96	95	85·34	280	155·45	510	225·55	740	295·66	970
29·26	96	88·39	290	158·50	520	228·60	750	298·70	980
29·57	97	91·44	300	161·54	530	231·65	760	301·75	990
29·87	98	94·49	310	164·59	540	234·70	770	304·80	1000

2. *Kilometres to Miles*

KM	MILES
1	0·62
2	1·24
3	1·86
4	2·49
5	3·11
6	3·73
7	4·35
8	4·97
9	5·59
10	6·21

3. *Area measurements*

The metric unit of area is the square metre; ten thousand square metres=one hectare (1 ha). One hectare is approximately two and a half acres (1 ha=2·47 acres).

INTRODUCTION
to the Inventory of the Ancient and Historical Monuments of Lorn

PART I. GENERAL

THE LAND AND ITS RESOURCES

The district of Lorn[1] takes its name from the Dalriadic chief Loarn Mór, son of Erc, whose tribe occupied it in the Dalriadic settlement of Argyll, traditionally dated to the middle of the 5th century. Adomnan, in the late 7th century, mentions the '*genus Loerni*',[2] and the tribal name likewise appears in some later Irish annals.[3] The district occupies the north-east corner of the county, being bounded to the north and north-east by Inverness-shire and Perthshire and abutting to the south on Mid Argyll (Fig. 1). Its west side lies on the Firth of Lorn and Loch Linnhe, and it here incorporates the islands of Shuna (Appin), Lismore, Kerrera, Seil, Luing, Shuna (Nether Lorn) and some smaller islets. It measures 54 km from its northeast extremity on the Moor of Rannoch to the south point of Luing, and 26 km transversely, from Duror to near Tyndrum.

At its north-east corner, Lorn impinges on the end of the Grampian chain, with Bidean nam Bian (1146 m) as its highest summit. An outlier on the Perthshire border is Ben Lui (1131 m), and Ben Cruachan (1125 m) stands conspicuous on the southern margin of the group. The more southerly and lower-lying regions are, however, still mountainous in character, as many of the summits exceed 750 m in height. The other main feature of the landscape is the series of long narrow valleys, some of which form sea-lochs where they reach the coast; thus Loch Leven (14 km) and Loch Etive (31 km) represent the seaward ends of long glens running down from the Grampians, while Loch Creran (15 km) stands in a similar relation to the high ground of Appin. Loch Awe (37 km)[4] is structurally another valley of the same kind, again taking drainage from the Grampian mass, but it fails to reach the sea as its south-west end has been blocked by glacial deposits, and it now discharges by the River Awe into Loch Etive. The Sounds of Seil and Shuna, in combination, bear every appearance of a similar ancient valley, now drowned by the sea. Other large indentations of the coast are Loch Feochan (8 km) and Loch Melfort (6 km), and the whole shore-line is much broken up by small bays and inlets.

---

[1] Although this name is almost invariably spelled 'Lorne' in the Argyll family title, the forms with and without the final 'e' have both been in common use since the Middle Ages. It therefore seems undesirable to depart from the current official spelling in favour of the alternative 'Lorne', which the Ordnance Survey used in 1875 'to agree with the spelling adopted by the Marquis of Lorne' (Name Book, No. 53, p. 27) but dropped in 1946.

[2] Adomnan, *Columba* (Anderson), 456.
[3] Ibid., 37, 55–9; Anderson, *Early Sources*, ii, index, s.v. 'Lorn'.
[4] Eight kilometres of this length are in Mid Argyll.

In addition to Loch Awe, there are several large inland lochs, such as Loch Avich, Loch Bà, Loch Nell, Loch Scamadale and Loch Tulla.

The oldest rocks of Lorn are sandstones, limestones and shales of the Moine and Dalradian assemblages, which have been strongly deformed and metamorphosed by mountain-building movements of the Caledonian period. After this folding and metamorphism, rocks of Lower Old Red Sandstone age were deposited on the eroded remnants of the Caledonian mountain-chain. Plateau lavas cover a wide area, and conglomerates and sandstones were laid down

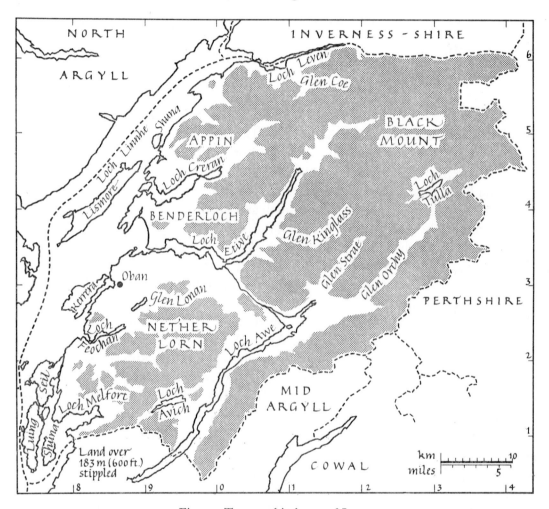

Fig. 1. Topographical map of Lorn

during periods of quiescence. Contemporary igneous intrusions include the large masses of granite and diorite that form the mountains around Glen Coe and Loch Etive. Much later intrusions, belonging to the Tertiary sequence of igneous rocks, are in the form of regional dykes emanating chiefly from the volcanic island of Mull. The whole area has been heavily glaciated. The Moor of Rannoch was a great gathering-ground from which ice flowed radially outwards, over-deepening such main valleys as Glen Orchy, Loch Awe, and Glen Etive with its sea-loch extension, and leaving typical deposits of glacial drift.

The greater part of Lorn is shown on the maps of the Land Utilisation Survey as heath, moorland and rough pasture, with arable and permanent grass mainly at the heads of sea-lochs and the mouths of the larger streams.[1] Lismore, however, is specially favoured, as its soil is derived from limestone. Narrow belts of cultivation are also found along the coast and on the shores of the lochs, where the slopes are not too steep, and in these zones there is likewise a good deal of scrub. Holdings tend to be small, and the Survey's report[2] distinguishes (i) the Loch Awe scrub and crofting area, with cultivable land of limited extent on alluvial areas and lower drift-covered slopes, and much plantation and scrub; (ii) the Lorn pastoral and crofting area, where the best land is on alluvial flats and raised beaches, the improved areas being interspersed with woods, and at the higher elevations with rough grazings; (iii) the Loch Etive scrub and moorland, with hill grazing and much scrub and plantation. Large areas have been planted by the Forestry Commission, mainly along the west shore of Loch Awe and in Muckairn, Benderloch and Duror. Woodland and mineral resources were once of considerable importance, as it was the former that supplied the fuel required for iron-smelting, initially in Glen Kinglass (Loch Etive) and later at Bonawe Furnace, while slate was worked at Ballachulish, Seil and Easdale and limestone on the island of Lismore. There were granite quarries at Bonawe and Kentallen, but only the former is still in production.

The climate is damp,[3] and is notable for a high rainfall, which, however, varies greatly with the elevation of the land. Thus at several points in the Grampian region the average annual maximum for 1916–50 exceeded 3205 mm (125 inches), and a small high-lying area west of Loch Awe received as much as 2564 mm (100 inches); while even Oban, in the drier coastal zone, showed a figure of 1451 mm (56·59 inches), the wettest month being October (172 mm or 6·71 inches) and the driest March (82 mm or 3·18 inches). Roy's map of Scotland (1747–55) marks 'Much Water' in the area north-east of Ben Cruachan.

Records of temperature and sunshine are available only for Oban, and consequently have little significance outside the coastal zone, but for what they are worth the average figures for 1931–60 show that the warmest month was August, with a daily maximum of 12·3°C (54°F) and minimum of 10·9°C (52°F), and the coldest January with corresponding figures of 5·9°C (43°F) and 1·3°C (34°F). The sunshine duration was 1241 hours, with the maximum in May (197 hours) and the minimum in December (27 hours).

Lorn evidently remained in a fairly primitive condition until at least the second half of the 18th century, and Roy's map shows all the centres of population, including Oban, as simple hamlets. Oban had, in fact, taken a first step forward about 1714, when a Renfrew trading-company built a storehouse there as a local outlet for its merchandise, much as earlier adventurers had opened 'factories' in the Far East; but no Custom-house was found necessary until about 1760, and a proposal that the British Fisheries Society should establish a station there for the herring-fishery came to nothing.

Internal communications were correspondingly poor. The earliest map, one of the Argyll dukedom as in 1734, shows a track coming in from the east on the line of A85, giving access to Loch Etive at Bonawe, and branching at Tyndrum to Glen Coe and Ballachulish as A82 does

---

[1] For a comprehensive survey of contemporary vegetational cover in the West Highlands generally, see McVean, D N and Ratcliffe, D A, *Plant Communities of the Scottish Highlands* (1962).

[2] *The Report of the Land Utilisation Survey of Great Britain: The Highlands of Scotland* (1944), 542–5.

[3] For the following data the Commissioners are indebted to the Superintendent of the Meteorological Office, Edinburgh.

today. From Bonawe further roads, eked out by ferries, gave access to Appin by Benderloch; to Dunstaffnage Bay, again with a branch to Benderloch; and south-eastwards to Loch Awe and Inveraray. Roy's map, rather later in date and much better made, shows several additions— for example in Appin and Benderloch; from Connel to Oban and thence by the coast south- wards; across the central moorlands between the coast and Loch Awe; and along the western shore of Loch Awe. The scarcity of bridges is illustrated by the fact that the predecessor of A85 is shown as keeping to the right bank of the Awe all the way down to its mouth—the bridge at Bridge of Awe was not, in fact, built until 1779. External trade, apart from the droving of cattle, must have been entirely by sea, while the number of small 'ports' and landings helped to make up for the deficiencies of the roads by facilitating movement by water. Ferries, too, were numerous, crossing, for example, Loch Leven at Ballachulish and Glencoe; the narrows between Appin and Lismore; Loch Creran from Appin at Rubha Garbh; Loch Awe near Kil- chrenan and at Dalavich; Loch Etive at Connel and Bonawe; and the Sounds of Seil and Kerrera at several points. Some or most of these ferries were used for droving in the 18th and 19th centuries, and not least the open-water link between Kerrera and Grass Point in Mull. Much frequented, likewise, by drovers were the tracks across the central moorlands, and before the days of regular road-improvement little distinction is likely to have been made between the kinds of track used by men and by cattle. The existence of local traditions of pilgrim traffic to Iona following tracks which were later known as drove-roads[1] consequently possesses some interest.

[1] Haldane, A R B, *The Drove Roads of Scotland* (1952), 89.

PART II. THE MONUMENTS

1. THE MESOLITHIC PERIOD (c. 4500–3000 BC)

From the middle of the fifth millennium BC, small groups of hunters and fishermen were moving about the southern part of the Atlantic seaboard of Scotland making use of the natural resources of the sea, the lochs and the forests. The subsistence economy practised by these mesolithic people necessitated seasonal movement from camp to camp in order to take full advantage of the game, fish, shell-fish and the harvests of nuts and berries that were their sources of food. Two types of camp site have been found in Lorn, coastal caves and rock-shelters in Oban Bay and inland caves above Melfort, perhaps indicating settlements at different periods of the year. The excavations of a number of mesolithic sites in Oban were undertaken in the late 19th century during the expansion of the town, and two in particular, the MacArthur Cave (NM 859304)[1] and the Druimvargie Rock-shelter (NM 857296),[2] situated at heights of 10·4 m and 14·6 m OD respectively, provide much information about the way of life of their occupants. Their diet is indicated by mollusc shells, fish bones and animal bones, including those of red deer, roe deer and boar. Stone tools include long rolled pebbles, known as 'limpet-hammers', round hammer-stones (Pl. 2), and a few small flake tools of flint. The bone-work comprises scrapers, punches and borers, but the most distinctive objects are barbed antler-points which were probably used as fish-spears (Pl. 2). Objects from the Distillery Cave (NM 859301) include a spatulate piece of deer-horn (Pl. 2), a bone borer and five unworked flints; human bones were also discovered in this cave as well as in the MacKay Cave (NM 859305), where they were associated with shells, bone and flint.[3] An occupied shelter containing similar deposits with limpet shells, 'limpet-hammers' and stone scrapers was excavated on the island of Shuna, Appin, in 1958 (NM 915497).[4]

A rock-shelter locally called the Cave of the Crags (NM 822175), 3·5 km north-north-west of Melfort and at a height of 228 m OD, yielded a small group of finished flint tools,[5] but on typological grounds the prolific occupation-deposit in a cave near the top of An Sithean (NM 840147), is likely to represent the earliest settlement known in the Melfort area.[6] The flint industry here contained large projectile points, burins, scrapers and knives, and probably dates to the fourth or fifth millennium BC.

Evidence for the date of the coastal deposits is provided by two sources, geological observation and radiocarbon dating. The stratigraphy in the MacArthur Cave showed that the earliest occupation had taken place at a time when the Early Post-Glacial sea had not receded any great distance, for shingle could still be washed into the cave to cover the lower of the two mesolithic levels. The beginning of the regression is thought to have occurred about the middle of the Atlantic period and this hypothesis is confirmed by radiocarbon dates from a comparable site at Cnoc Sligeach, Oronsay.[7] Samples of bones and shells yielded dates of 3805 bc ± 180

[1] *PSAS*, xxix (1894–5), 423–38.
[2] Ibid., xxxii (1897–8), 298–306.
[3] Ibid., xxix (1894–5), 410–23, 431–8.
[4] *DES* (1958), 2–3.
[5] *DES* (1963), 9.
[6] *DES* (1959), 4.
[7] In accordance with current practice 'bc' is used for uncorrected radiocarbon dates to distinguish them from calendar years.

and 3065 bc ± 210;[1] when the appropriate adjustments have been made, these dates show that the mesolithic occupation of the region had certainly taken place by the middle of the fifth millennium BC.[2] There is even earlier material, dating to before the maximum extent of the Early Post-Glacial sea, at Lussa Bay, Jura. Also from Jura come the most recent radiocarbon dates for the mesolithic period (2670 bc ± 140 and 2250 bc ± 100) which, when corrected, show that this way of life lasted in the region until at least the end of the fourth millennium BC.[3]

In the past the distinctive material from the Oban caves, and from the shell-middens on Oronsay and Risga, has been seen in isolation and has been regarded as typical of an 'Obanian culture'.[4] Recent excavations on Jura, however, have greatly added to our knowledge of this period and it may be suggested that the Obanian material is merely one facet of the mesolithic period in the west of Scotland, and that it should no longer enjoy cultural status in its own right.[5] Variations in the types of object found on these camp sites may be the result not of population or 'cultural' changes, but of responses to different environments and to different seasonal activities.[6] Whether or not this is so, it can be assumed that Lorn continued to be inhabited by itinerant bands of hunters and fishermen, no doubt in very small numbers, until at least the end of the fourth millennium BC and probably longer.[7]

2. THE NEOLITHIC PERIOD (*c.* 3500 BC–2000 BC)

The knowledge of agriculture and stock-rearing was introduced into Lorn before the end of the fourth millennium BC with the arrival of a new group of people. No settlement sites of these incomers have so far been recognised in the region, presumably because they were constructed of perishable materials, and only their stone-built burial-monuments remain. These tombs were intended to receive communal burials over a number of generations and were accordingly designed to allow periodic access to the burial-chamber. Detailed study of the ground-plans and building-styles has shown that the Scottish tombs comprise a number of different types, distinct in both architecture and distribution. The northern part of Argyll (Ardnamurchan, Morvern and Lorn) is of some interest in this study as in that region the distributions of two types of tomb overlap, thus providing evidence of colonisation from two directions. Of the eight surviving chambered cairns in Lorn (Fig. 2), six belong to the type described as *Clyde Cairns* and two belong to that known as *Passage-Graves*.[8] Four of the Clyde Cairns have been found round the northern part of Loch Awe, and one each at the south end of Loch Nell and on the island of Shuna, Nether Lorn. The cairn at Portnacroish (No. 7), which has been completely destroyed, may also have belonged to the Clyde group.[9] This distribution seems to indicate that the builders of these monuments came from the north end of Loch Fyne, from the Kilmartin area, or up the western seaboard. On the other hand, the

[1] *PPS*, xxxviii (1972), 412–13 (GX–1904 and 1903).
[2] *Scottish Archaeological Forum*, iii (1971), 79.
[3] *Quaternaria*, xiii (1970), 177–9 (BM–556 and 555).
[4] For a full discussion of the Obanian culture see Lacaille, A D, *The Stone Age in Scotland* (1954), 196–245; *PSAS*, lxxxix (1955–6), 91–106; *Archaeologia Aeliana*, 4th series, xlviii (1970), 337–46. For recent excavations on Oronsay, *Nature*, 231 (1971), 397–8.

[5] *Quaternaria*, xiii (1970), 177–83 summarises the work on Jura.
[6] See also *TDGAS*, xlv (1968), 67–71; *PPS*, xxxvii (1971), 319.
[7] The Commissioners are indebted to Dr J M Coles and Mr J Mercer for their assistance in the preparation of this section.
[8] Henshall, *Chambered Tombs*, ii, 15–157.
[9] Ibid., 361–2.

two passage-graves situated on the northern edge of the Moss of Achnacree, near the mouth of Loch Etive, are outliers from the main concentration of this class in the Hebrides.

Cairns of Clyde type contain burial-chambers of rectangular ground-plan, constructed of massive side-slabs and roofed either by a large slab, as at No. 6, or by a series of smaller slabs, as at No. 3. The chambers are divided by transverse slabs into a number of compartments, usually between two and five, and are normally situated towards one end of the cairn. A typological scheme for such chambers has recently been put forward, in which closed- or single-compartment chambers with relatively high transverse slabs are placed early in the sequence; it is suggested that chambers with two compartments then developed from this simple type, and that finally more complex chambers with several compartments were built. Many chambers have a complicated structural history which can only be fully understood by excavation. In broad terms the simpler Lorn tombs such as Cladich (No. 5), Dalineun (No. 6), Port Sonachan (No. 8) and Shuna Cottage (No. 9) may be considered to belong to the second stage of this sequence, dating to the early third millennium BC, while Ardchonnell (No. 3) and Auchachenna (No. 4) appear to be more complex and thus later in date. The two well-preserved cairns of the first group (Dalineun and Port Sonachan) are oval, whereas those at Ardchonnell and Auchachenna are trapezoidal on plan, measuring about 30 m in length and up to 14 m in breadth, with their chambers at the broader end. It is possible, however, that Ardchonnell was originally a simple two-compartment chamber with a small cairn, and that subsequently an additional pair of portals was added, and the present trapezoidal cairn constructed with its long axis on a slightly different alignment from that of the chamber. Only one Clyde Cairn in Lorn (Dalineun) has been scientifically excavated, and severe robbing made it impossible to establish its structural history precisely; but a two-compartment chamber evidently formed the focus for a series of later burials, and the cairn continued in use until the middle of the second millennium BC, with resulting alteration of its original shape.

The Passage-Grave contrasts in plan and building-technique with the Clyde type of tomb. It comprises a round or oval chamber built of upright stones, often with some dry-stone walling between them, and entered through a distinct passage; in order to lessen the span of the roof, corbelling was frequently employed. At Achnacreebeag (No. 2) excavations revealed that a passage-grave had been added to one side of a cairn which already covered a simple closed chamber, but unfortunately there was no indication of the date of the earlier structure. Elements of both Clyde cairn and passage-grave traditions can be seen in the chamber of Càrn Bàn, Achnacree (No. 1). Although the chamber is not accessible at the present time, excavations conducted in 1871 showed that it might incorporate two structural periods. The earlier of the two hypothetical periods would be represented by the inner two compartments, which in building technique and plan are comparable to a two-compartment Clyde chamber and which may have been covered by a small cairn; subsequently, it is suggested, a corbelled chamber and a long passage were added to the front of this structure and the cairn was increased to its present size.[1] The sequence demonstrated by excavation at Achnacreebeag and postulated for Achnacree, is significant as it shows that a megalithic tradition, represented by the simple chamber at the former and by the inner two compartments at the latter, was already established before the local introduction of the passage-grave.

[1] Ibid., 142.

Altogether four of the Lorn chambered tombs have been excavated (Nos. 1, 2, 6 and 8); there were apparently no finds from the last, but the relics that were recovered from two of them (Nos. 2 and 6) not only throw light on the early burials in these tombs but also provide information about the date of the final burials. Three pottery bowls discovered at Achnacree (No. 1) are in a distinctive style which has been named after the site;[1] the vessels are round-based and carinated, and have vertical necks. Two sherds of a vessel with a rounded rim,

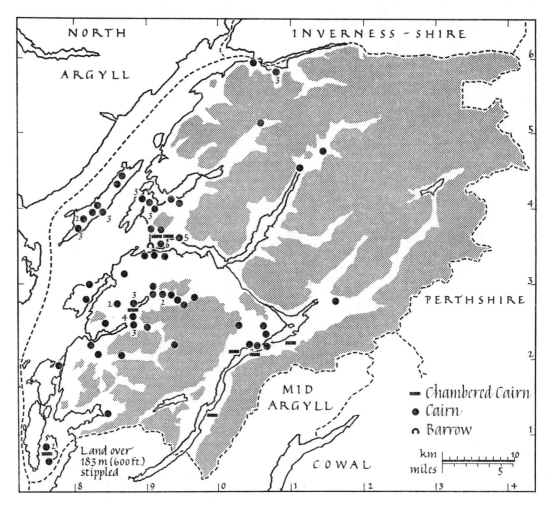

Fig. 2. Distribution map of chambered cairns and cairns.

probably a finely-made carinated bowl, were found at Dalineun (No. 6), and in the earlier level of the passage-grave at Achnacreebeag (No. 2) were sherds of a plain round-based bowl, a carinated bowl of Beacharra ware and sherds of two indeterminate vessels. The dating of such pottery is still a matter of discussion. The only other finds that can be firmly associated with this phase of the tomb's history are quartz pebbles from No. 1, a plano-convex flint knife from No. 2 and a number of other flints. No skeletal material has survived.

The terminal burials at Achnacreebeag appear to have been part of a single ritual act, as

[1] Henshall, *Chambered Tombs*, ii, 100–1.

8

sherds of Beaker pottery, flint objects, jet disc-beads and some tiny fragments of cremated bone were found scattered throughout a filling of stones and earth in the chamber and passage. Finally the entrance to the tomb was sealed by a blocking of stones which made further access to the chamber impossible. At Dalineun, too, the makers of Beaker pottery were responsible for the final deposits in the chamber, here associated with inhumation burials, but there was no dating evidence for the insertion of a small cist in front of the tomb, or for the blocking of the entrance to the chamber. At this site a cist of more massive proportions, situated behind the main chamber, appears to be a secondary insertion, originally, perhaps, containing a Food Vessel and a cremation burial (see *infra* p. 43); if so, it would point to the continuing sanctity of the site a millennium after the building of the cairn. The Beaker pottery found within the chambers at Achnacreebeag and Dalineun is evidence of the arrival of an intrusive group of people. Although their predominant burial rite in Scotland is that of individual interment in a short cist, as at No. 91, their use of chambered cairns as well as of cists may indicate that the change in ritual and the assimilation of this new element in the population were effected only gradually.

Although the distribution of chambered cairns may be thought to indicate in general terms the areas of settlement of their builders and users, some further information of the extent of neolithic activity is provided by a small number of unassociated finds of polished stone axe-heads; these have been discovered at Kilmore, Oban and Taynuilt. Two other artifacts, presumably late neolithic in date, are the carved stone ball said to be from the neighbourhood of Inverawe[1] and the jadeite axe-head from Appin.[2]

3. THE BRONZE AGE (*c.* 2000–500 BC)

In the absence of any known habitation-sites, our information comes exclusively from funerary monuments and stray finds; there can be little doubt, however, that the distribution of the round burial-cairns of this period represents, at least to some extent, the settlement pattern of their builders.

One barrow, eighty-five cairns and twelve possible cairns are recorded in this volume, of which twenty are situated on off-shore islands and the rest on the mainland. Their distribution (Fig. 2) is predominantly maritime, with three-quarters of the total occurring within 2·5 km of the coast and at heights of less than 90 m OD, and indicates a preference for the sheltered vicinity of sea lochs where advantage could be taken of the light gravel soils that offered suitable areas for settlement, as they had done previously to the builders of the chambered tombs. In this respect two regions of the mainland appear to have been particularly attractive. The first is centred on Benderloch, with easy access from Loch Creran, Loch Etive and the shores of Ardmucknish Bay. There are twenty-eight cairns and one barrow forming a fairly compact group in this area, and it is reasonable to regard the thirteen examples on the adjacent island of Lismore as comprising part of this concentration; if counted together, the Lismore-Benderloch complex as a whole contains more than two-fifths of the total number recorded in Lorn. The second region is centred on the flood-plain of the River Nell, extending south-west from the

[1] *PSAS*, xv (1880–1), 7; xvi (1881–2), 12. [2] Ibid., c (1967–8), 185–6.

southern end of Loch Nell and easily approached from the head of Loch Feochan. This area contains ten cairns, all situated within 2 km of one another, which form the nucleus of a group, and in it can be included other examples associated with the river-valleys that drain into Loch Nell and Loch Feochan. Though more widely dispersed than the Lismore-Benderloch concentration, this group nevertheless comprises some thirty cairns, all mutually associated through their relationship to Loch Feochan. The remaining twenty-five cairns occur in loose groupings at the north-east end of Loch Awe, in the Loch Melfort and Oban areas, in Glen Etive and Glen Creran, and on the south shore of Loch Leven in the vicinity of Ballachulish.

The cairns range in size from 4 m to 42·7 m in diameter, more than half the total lying within the bracket 10 m to 19 m. Few of them are more than 2 m high and all have suffered in varying degrees from stone-robbing. With the exception of the one barrow (No. 65), they are all built predominantly of stone, and about a dozen of them either contain, or are known to have contained, burial-cists. Otherwise the only visible structural feature is a peripheral kerb of boulders, recorded in fifteen instances. In six of the kerbed examples the size of the kerb-stones is strikingly large in proportion to the relatively small diameter of the cairn, and as a result of the excavation of one of them (No. 78) by the Commission's officers it has been possible to distinguish for the first time a separate category of round cairn, for which the term *kerb-cairn* has been adopted. Cairns of this type occur not only in Lorn, Morvern, Mull and Mid Argyll, but also in Perthshire, Aberdeenshire and Inverness-shire. Although several examples have been excavated, there is no firm indication of their date, but in general terms the affinities of this group are with the *ring-cairns* of north-east Scotland.[1] It is thus possible to link this type of cairn to the single example of a ring-cairn in Lorn, at Castle Farm, Barcaldine (No. 32, 3). The abundance of quartz chips was a feature of two of the Lorn kerb-cairns (Nos. 43 and 78) and two have settings of stones which may be interpreted as 'false portals' (Nos. 34 and 43), reminiscent perhaps of the portal stones flanking the entrance at Castle Farm, Barcaldine (No. 32, 3). Both these features are present in the cairn at Kintraw (Mid Argyll).[2] In size the kerb-cairns fall into two main groups, namely those between 4 m and 6 m (Nos. 10, 34, 61 and 78) and those between 8 m and 12 m (Nos. 32(3), 43 and 59). Outlying standing stones are a feature of two sites (Nos. 10 and 78), but the closest association was at Castle Farm, Barcaldine where originally the stone was only 3·1 m from the cairn.

In general only scanty reports, if any, survive of the contents of the cists discovered under cairns. At Ballachulish (No. 19), however, and at Kilmore (No. 57, 4) recent re-excavation by one of the Commission's officers has resulted in the recovery of a Food Vessel of Irish Bowl type from the former, and at the latter has yielded evidence that the cist contained two successive burials, both cremations—the later accompanied by a bronze riveted dagger, and the earlier by three flint flakes.

The disposition of certain cairns within the two major concentrations already mentioned suggests that they were in some instances grouped together in local cemeteries. The most striking example of such a grouping is provided by an alignment of cairns at Kilmore, which may be regarded as forming a linear cemetery comparable to that at Kilmartin in Mid Argyll.[3] At Kilmore there are four round cairns (Fig. 22, 1, 4, 6 and 10) which, together with the

[1] *Scottish Archaeological Forum*, iv (1972), 1–17.
[2] *PSAS*, xcix (1966–7), 54–9.
[3] Ibid., xciv (1960–1), 50.

chambered cairn No. 6, extend from north-north-west to south-south-east in an almost straight line over a distance of 1·8 km. The primary or 'Founder's' cairn would be the chambered cairn at Dalineun (No. 6), with its burial-chamber of Clyde type; about 180 m to the north-north-west is the round cairn No. 57, 1, and to the south-south-east lie the three cairns (p. 53, nos. 4, 6 and 10). Another such alignment may be seen in Benderloch, formed by the largest of the cairns at Balure (No. 21, 1), the cairn at Achanamoine (No. 12) and the westernmost of the cairns at Castle Farm, Barcaldine (No. 32, 3); these three cairns are spaced at almost equal

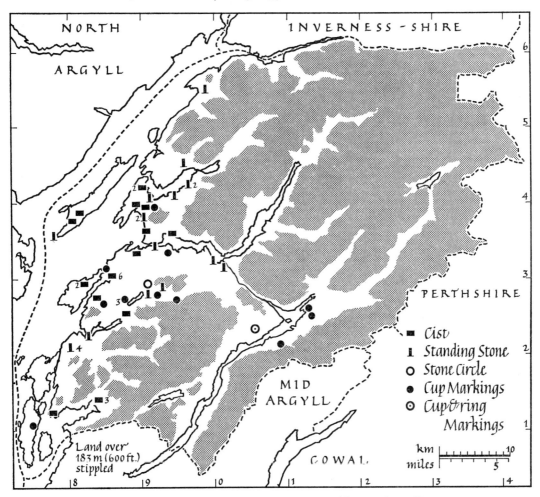

Fig. 3. Distribution map of cists, cup-and-ring markings and standing stones.

intervals over a distance of nearly 2 km on a line running from north-west to south-east. In addition to their linear arrangement it is interesting to note that all seven round cairns in these two alignments measure more than 19·5 m in diameter, and are thus among the largest known in Lorn. Other cairn cemeteries are indicated by a cluster of five cairns at Achnaba (No. 14), and by the seven cairns and one barrow situated on and around the Moss of Achnacree (Nos. 13, 46–7 and 62–6).

In addition to the cists already mentioned, at least twenty-five others have been found, normally occurring just below ground-surface without any covering mound or cairn. Their distribution, as known at present (Fig. 3), is complementary to that of the cairns and serves to emphasise their coastal disposition. In several instances (Nos. 84, 97 and 98) two or more cists have been discovered close together, but otherwise they usually occur singly. Two contained Beakers (Nos. 91 and 100), three yielded Food Vessels (Nos. 98 (3 and 8) and 100), and an 'urn' of unspecified type is reported in one other (No. 93). The most important assemblage of grave-goods, however, came from one of three cists found near Melfort House (No. 97); this cist, which was of considerably larger than average size, contained an extended inhumation accompanied by the remains of a crescentic jet necklace and a pair of identical bronze armlets of which only one survives (Pl. 4c). The dimensions of the Melfort cist place it within the comparatively small group of long cists designed to accommodate a body lying extended at full length and not in the crouched attitude that is typical of the inhumation burials in short cists of this period. The bronze armlets belong to Coles's 'rib' type, whose ancestry may lie ultimately in Únetician armlets of central Europe.[1] The precise date of such objects is still undecided, but in his re-assessment of Scottish Early Bronze Age metalwork[2] Coles sees the lenticular decoration on the Melfort armlet as being most closely comparable with the similar ornamental style used on a strip of sheet bronze in the Migdale hoard,[3] and hence a central date of about 1500 BC would be appropriate. The date of the jet necklace, a type of personal ornament often, if not exclusively, found in association with Food Vessels, would also fall within the period 1650–1400 BC.[4]

Several burials not in cists have been recorded, most of them cremations contained within, or accompanied by, Cinerary Urns, and other vessels of this type can doubtless be included among the unspecified 'urns' that are now lost. Mention may here be made of three instances in which pottery of this period has been discovered in caves. At Ledaig a Food Vessel (Pl. 3c) was recovered from a cave at the foot of Creag an Èig (NM 904375) but there is no record of any burial-remains; in a cave (NM 860300) behind Oban Gasworks (No. 98, 4) two sherds of what was probably a Cinerary Urn were found together with human remains and other relics; and a cave deposit at Ardantrive,[5] on Kerrera (NM 841300) yielded sherds of Bronze Age pottery and stone implements, including a broken leaf-shaped flint arrowhead, a flint knife, a flint scraper, fragments of Arran pitchstone[6] and several stone 'limpet-hammers'.

Only one example of cup-and-ring markings and thirteen instances of plain cup-markings are here recorded (Fig. 3), and their comparative scarcity in Lorn is in marked contrast to the profusion of this type of rock art in the more southerly parts of the county, notably in Mid Argyll[7] and Kintyre.[8] With two exceptions—a schist slab found under the cairn at Culcharron (No. 43), and a slate slab now serving as a jamb of the south-west entrance to the dun at Leccamore, Luing (No. 189)—the markings all occur on detached boulders.

Although the status of the nineteen standing stones (Fig. 3) is uncertain, it has already been noted above that in three instances a standing stone is situated near a cairn; it has yet to be proved, however, that in any of these cases the cairn and standing stone are contemporary. Most of the stones are singletons, but at Duachy (No. 116) there are four disposed as a line of

[1] *PSAS*, ci (1968–9), 51.
[2] Ibid., 72.
[3] *Inventaria Archaeologica*, GB. 26, no. 54.
[4] Coles, J M and Simpson, D D A (edd.), *Studies in Ancient Europe* (1968), 209.
[5] Lethbridge, T C, *Herdsmen and Hermits* (1950), 7–9.
[6] Information from Mr G H Collins, Institute of Geological Sciences.
[7] *PSAS*, xcv (1961–2), 29–35.
[8] *Inventory of Argyll*, i, Nos. 89–129.

three with a single outlier nearby, and Nos. 115 and 121 may originally have belonged to settings of several stones. The date and affinities of the stone circle No. 120 are unknown. A radiocarbon date recently obtained for the field-bank at Black Crofts (No. 203) suggests that some sort of farming activity was taking place about the middle of the 2nd millennium BC.

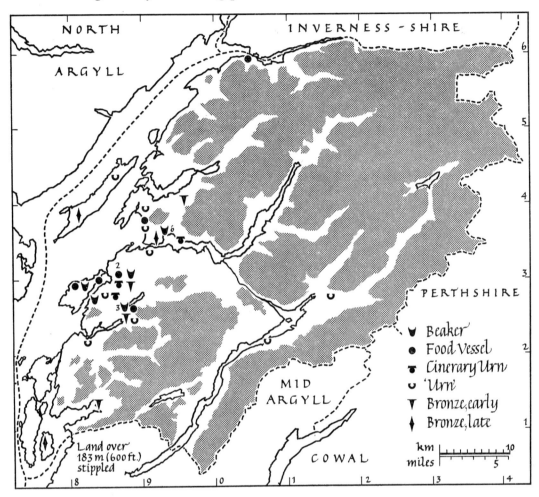

Fig. 4. Distribution map of Bronze Age pottery and metalwork.

The earliest bronze objects from Lorn are the two armlets from the Melfort House cist already mentioned (p. 12), and the riveted dagger from Kilmore (also sometimes described under the names Cleigh, Moleigh and Loch Nell). This dagger (No. 57, 4, Pl. 4B), of flat type with omega hilt-mark, dates to about the period 1500–1400 BC.[1] Of broadly similar date are the two flanged axes, found near Oban and at Achanrear, Barcaldine (Pl. 5A) respectively. A remarkable hoard of three bronze swords of Ewart Park type (Pl. 5B), which were found together on the island of Shuna, Nether Lorn, sticking vertically in the peat with the points downward, may have been a votive deposit. These swords and three socketed axes, from the Moss of Achnacree, Dunollie and Barr Mór (Pl. 5C), are not likely to be earlier than the 8th century BC.[2]

[1] *PSAS*, ci (1968–9), 43, 89.　　　　　[2] Ibid., xciii (1959–60), 67, 104.

LIST OF BRONZE AGE POTTERY AND METALWORK
FOUND IN LORN (FIG. 4)

The following abbreviations are used: CMAE—University Museum of Archaeology and Ethnology, Cambridge; GAGM—Glasgow Art Gallery and Museum; NMA—National Museum of Antiquities of Scotland, Edinburgh. In Fig. 4 the classification of Bronze Age metalwork follows that adopted by Coles in *PSAS*, xciii (1959–60), 16–134; xcvii (1963–4), 82–156; ci (1968–9), 1–110.

OBJECT	PROVENANCE, PARTICULARS AND ARTICLE NUMBER	REFERENCES	MUSEUM AND ACCESSION NUMBER
Beakers (6)	Achnacreebeag, Chambered Cairn (No. 2) *In chamber-blocking and cairn material*	*PSAS*, cii (1969–70), 31–55	NMA: EO 1018–22, 1022a
Beakers (3)	Dalineun, Chambered Cairn (No. 6) *Chamber deposits and blocking*	Ibid., 50–1	NMA: EO 1054–6
Beaker	Gallanachbeg, Cist (No. 91)	*The Scotsman*, 21 April 1897; Faichney, *Oban*, 18–19; *PSAS*, xxxi (1896–7), 238	Private possession, Gallanach
Beaker	Oban, Breadalbane Street (No. 98, 2)	*The Scotsman*, 21 April 1897; Faichney, *Oban*, 19	Lost
Beaker	Slaterich, Kerrera, Cist (No. 100, Pl. 3B)	*PSAS*, lxvi (1931–2), 406–7	NMA: L 1931.1
Food Vessel (possible)	Ardantrive, Kerrera *Found in a cave*	Lethbridge, T C, *Herdsmen and Hermits* (1950), 7–9	CMAE: 51.1055
Food Vessel	Ballachulish House, Cairn (No. 19) *Cist*	*DES* (1972), 59	NMA: EE 163
Food Vessel	Dalineun, Chambered Cairn (No. 6) *?Secondary deposit*	*DES* (1971), 58	NMA: EO 1057
Food Vessel	Ledaig (Pl. 3C) *Found in a cave*	*PSAS*, ix (1870–2), 87; Smith, *Loch Etive*, 171	NMA: L. 1955. 76
Food Vessel	Oban, Corran Park, Cist (No. 98, 8, Pl. 3D)	*PSAS*, lvi (1921–2), 364–5	Oban Museum
Food Vessel	Oban, 'Road to Dunollie', Cist (No. 98, 3) *Inhumation*	Ibid., xi (1874–6), 468–9	Lost
Food Vessel	Slaterich, Kerrera, Cist (No. 100) *Quartz pebbles*	Ibid., lxvi (1931–2), 406	NMA: L 1931.2
Cinerary Urn	Ardachy, Burial (No. 83) *Cremation*	Ibid., lxxix (1944–5), 176	NMA: EA 231
Cinerary Urn (possible)	Oban, Gasworks Cave, Burial (No. 98, 4)	Ibid., xxix (1894–5), 417–18	NMA: HL 378–9

OBJECT	PROVENANCE, PARTICULARS AND ARTICLE NUMBER	REFERENCES	MUSEUM AND ACCESSION NUMBER
Cinerary Urn	Oban, McKelvie Hospital, Burial (No. 98, 7, Pl. 4A) *Cremation*	Ibid., xxxii (1897–8), 58–9	NMA: EQ 251
'Urn'	Near Cnoc Aingil, Lismore, Burial (No. 87) *Containing 'ashes'*	*Stat. Acct.*, i (1791), 493	Lost
'Urns'	Connel, Cairn (No. 39)	Name Book, No. 19, p. 19	Lost
'Urn'	Dùnan Buiaig, Cairn (No. 50) *Cist, containing 'ashes'*	*NSA*, vii (Argyll), 68	Lost
'Urn'	Keil, Cist (No. 93) *Bones 'wonderfully entire'*	Ibid., 500	Lost
'Urn'	Kilmore, Cairn (No. 57, 6) *With cremation in a cist*	Name Book, No. 19, p. 78; Smith, *Loch Etive*, 247	Lost
'Urn'	Ledaig, Cairn (No. 60) *Cremation, flint arrowhead*	*NSA*, vii (Argyll), 500; Name Book, No. 1, p. 64	Lost
'Urns'	Oban, McKelvie Hospital, Burial (No. 98, 7)	*PSAS*, xxxii (1897–8), 58–9	Lost
'Urn'	Rockhill, Cairn (No. 69) *?Cist with bones*	Pococke, *Tours*, 68	Lost
'Urn'	Stronmilchan, Cairn (No. 77) *Cist*	*NSA*, vii (Argyll), 98; Name Book, No. 6, p. 17	Lost
Riveted Dagger	Kilmore, Cairn (No. 57, 4, Pl. 4B) *Cist, cremation*	*PSAS*, x (1872–4), 84, 458	NMA: DI 1
Armlets (2)	Melfort House, Cist (No. 97, Pl. 4C) *Extended inhumation, crescentic jet necklace*	Ibid., xix (1884–5), 134–6	NMA: DO 51; one now lost
Swords (3)	Shuna, Nether Lorn (Pl. 5B) *Found within a short distance of each other, points downwards*	Ibid., xi (1874–6), 121; xciii (1959–60), 38–9, 104	GAGM: 774–28; NMA: DL 21; St Andrews University Museum: N 159
Flanged Axe	Achanrear, Barcaldine (Pl. 5A)	Ibid., ci (1968–9), 80	NMA: DC 39
Flanged Axe	'near Oban'	Ibid., 81, 93	Lost
Socketed Axe	Barr Mór, Lismore (Pl. 5C)	Ibid., xciii (1959–60), 67	NMA: DE 123
Socketed Axe	*'near Dunollie'		NMA: L 1963.51
Socketed Axe	Moss of Achnacree	Ibid.	NMA: DE 11
'Gold ornaments'	*Loch an Leoid	Ibid., xxv (1890–1), 127	Lost

*Not included in the distribution map (Fig. 4) as the type of object or its provenance is not known with sufficient accuracy.

4. THE IRON AGE (*c.* 600 BC–*c.* AD 400)

INTRODUCTORY

In the almost total absence of distinctive cultural material, our knowledge of the native Iron Age peoples of Lorn, as of those in Kintyre, necessarily derives, to a great extent, from a study of their habitations, which are predominantly of a defensive character.

It is not yet possible to decide which tribal group or groups occupied the district at this period. We know that by the later 1st century AD the Kintyre peninsula was inhabited by a tribe known to Ptolemy as the *Epidii*,[1] and it is possible that their territory extended as far north as Loch Leven. On the other hand, as Watson suggested,[2] it is equally likely that Lorn formed part of the lands of the *Cerones*, or possibly *Creones*, whom Ptolemy described as living immediately to the north of the *Epidii*. The hypothesis that the northernmost part of Lorn belonged to the *Caledonii* at this time,[3] cannot, however, be supported as it depends upon the erroneous equation of Loch Linnhe with *Lemannonius Sinus*.[4]

The same system of classification that was used for the Iron Age monuments in the first volume of this *Inventory*[5] has again been adopted. Most of the sites are forts or duns, although two brochs have also been recorded, one of them Tirefour Castle (No. 147), being the most impressive prehistoric monument in the district; the distribution of these monuments is shown in Fig. 5. It is also probable that some at least of the crannogs (Nos. 195–200) and the miscellaneous earthworks and enclosures (Nos. 201–11) belong to the same period.

FORTS

Compared with those of Kintyre, the forts of Lorn form a remarkably homogeneous group, comprising, in the main, structures of no great size, all but one of which have been defended by a single dry-stone wall. It is thus often difficult to draw a dividing line between the smaller examples of this class and duns, and the distinction made in this volume, in accordance with the practice adopted in Kintyre, depends almost entirely on internal area—forts being large enough to have served the needs of a small community and duns only those of a family group.

Dùn Ormidale (No. 137), with an internal area of 3 ha (7·5 acres), is by far the largest fort in Lorn, and on account of its exceptional size it may claim to be recognized as yet another member of the class of hill-forts to which the term 'minor *oppidum*' has been applied. Although such forts are normally thought to be the tribal centres of their regions, the absence of any trace of dwellings at Dùn Ormidale, coupled with the slightness of the artificial defences and the exposed nature of the site, inevitably gives rise to doubts about its purpose. The next largest, the earlier vitrified fort at Dùn Mac Sniachan (No. 136), has an internal area of 0·6 ha (1·5 acres), and it is noteworthy that both it and the three forts immediately following it in order of size, Kilcheran (No. 140), Balvicar (No. 125) and Castle Coeffin (No. 126), occupy

[1] *Inventory of Argyll*, i, pp. 1, 15.
[2] Watson, *Celtic Place-names*, 23.
[3] Ordnance Survey, *Map of Roman Britain* (3rd ed., 1956); see also Richmond, I A (ed.), *Roman and Native in North Britain* (1958), 135–6.
[4] Cf. Watson, *Celtic Place-names*, 19. Ptolemy (*Geographia*, II 3, 1) clearly indicates that *Lemannonius Sinus* lies to the east of the Kintyre peninsula, opening on to the Firth of Clyde.
[5] *Inventory of Argyll*, i, pp. 15–20.

fairly level rocky ridges close to the sea-shore. The remaining forts are much smaller, their average internal dimensions being 44 m by 23 m, or 0·07 ha (one-sixth of an acre).

As noted above, all the forts but one are univallate; the exception is Dùn Iadain (No. 135), which has been defended by two dry-stone walls. Almost half the remainder were, however, provided with additional protection in the form of outworks, whose general purpose was to impede access to the fort where the lie of the ground offered an easy avenue of approach.

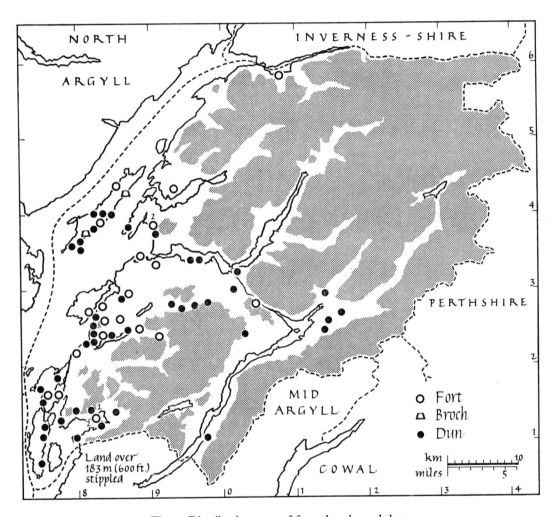

Fig. 5. Distribution map of forts, brochs and duns

In the majority of cases the enclosing wall was built of solid stone, but in two forts (Nos. 128 and 134) the core material included an admixture of earth. At Dùn Mac Sniachan (No. 136) on the other hand, where a large univallate fort is overlain by a smaller univallate fort and a dun, the walls of both forts are heavily vitrified, indicating that each structure incorporated a timber framework. The presence of a mass of vitrification in the core of the fort wall at Balvicar (No. 125) suggests that at least part of its perimeter was similarly constructed. There is a marked concentration of vitrified forts and duns in North Argyll and in the southern parts of

Inverness-shire,[1] and it would not be unreasonable to assume that Balvicar and Dùn Mac Sniachan are broadly contemporary with them. Unfortunately the partial excavation of the latter site undertaken in 1873–4[2] failed to establish a firm date for either the earlier or the later fort. However, radiocarbon assay of primary material from timber-laced forts elsewhere in Scotland[3] indicates that such western examples may have been constructed as early as the middle of the sixth century BC. It may be added that Dùn Mac Sniachan is the only fort in Lorn where more than one structural period can be observed, but, although it bears a general resemblance to the complex site at Dùn Skeig in Kintyre,[4] where a univallate fort was overlain by a vitrified dun and subsequently by a solid-walled dun, it is impossible to determine in this case the exact relationship of the two secondary structures.

The largely wasted condition of the Iron Age forts in Lorn precludes any comment on such minor constructional details as they may have possessed, but it is probable that, as in Kintyre, forts and duns had several architectural characteristics in common.

Traces of round timber-houses have been found at only two sites (Nos. 125 and 143), and it is possible that the curving stony bank observed at a third (No. 138) may represent the remains of a stone-walled dwelling. In a number of cases (e.g. Nos. 135 and 144) the interiors of the forts slope so steeply that houses of either type could scarcely have been erected except on platforms excavated into the hillside, and the absence of any signs of these suggests that the forts in question were not intended for permanent occupation.

DUNS

The most numerous class of Iron Age monument in Lorn is that of the dun, which comprises no fewer than forty-eight examples. For the purposes of this Inventory, as explained above, the dun has been defined as a comparatively small defensive structure with a dispro-portionately thick dry-stone wall, usually but not always sub-circular or oval on plan, and enclosing an area seldom exceeding about 375 sq. m (4000 sq. feet); it would thus normally accommodate only a single family group. The enclosing wall consists of a solid rubble core with inner and outer facings, frequently of massive proportions (e.g. Nos. 155, 157, 169, 170, 175 and 177); the external face occasionally exhibits a marked batter (e.g. No. 189). In a number of cases, such as Dùn Skeig (Kintyre),[5] Rahoy (Morvern),[6] or the recently discovered site at Dùn Daraich (Cowal),[7] vitrification of the core indicates that the walls in question were originally timber-laced. Although most duns are sub-circular or oval on plan, there are a few, situated on the summits of isolated rocky stacks, which are markedly irregular on plan—the course of the wall being dictated by the outline of the summit area. These structures have been referred to previously as 'stack forts',[8] but the recent excavation of one example in Kintyre,[9] and the examination of occupation material found in the midden of another, in Lorn (No. 164), have shown that no useful purpose is served by classifying them separately from duns.

Although no site is quite as diminutive as Sunadale in Kintyre,[10] the duns of Lorn vary

[1] *Arch. J.*, cxi (1954), 74–8.
[2] *PSAS*, xii (1876–8), 13–19.
[3] *Antiquity*, xliii (1969), 17.
[4] *Inventory of Argyll*, i, No. 165.
[5] Ibid.

[6] *PSAS*, lxxii (1937–8), 23–43.
[7] *DES* (1968), 4.
[8] Ordnance Survey, *Field Archaeology* (1963), 77.
[9] *Inventory of Argyll*, i, No. 203.
[10] Ibid., No. 236.

quite widely in size, the smallest recorded being Dùn Mhuirageul (No. 177), the internal area of which is about 49 sq. m (530 sq. feet). The average dimensions are, however, about 15·4 m in internal diameter or 18 m by 13 m axially. Apart from Castles (No. 161) and the island-site at Eilean an Atha (No. 184), the duns of Lorn appear to favour, to a greater degree than those of Kintyre, positions of considerable natural strength; indeed in some cases, e.g. Caisteal Suidhe Cheannaidh (No. 159) and Dùn Fadaidh (No. 174), a remote and inaccessible situation seems to have been selected in preference to positions of comparable strength at a lower altitude.

Owing to the wasted condition of the majority of duns, architectural details are rarely visible, but a very few well-preserved sites (e.g. Nos. 159, 171 and 189), as well as those where excavations of varying date and extent have taken place, furnish instances of the practical skill and technical expertise of their builders. At Gallanach (No. 186), and probably also at An Dùn, Sloc a' Bhrighide (No. 151), an internal revetment has been used to give added stability to the rubble core of the enclosing walls. Similar features have been observed in the walls of Iron Age defensive structures in Kintyre and other widely separated parts of Britain.[1] Intramural chambers occur only at Dùn Aorain (No. 166) and Leccamore (No. 189). In the latter case, where there are two chambers, one on either side of an entrance passage, they should perhaps be interpreted as guard-cells; indeed it has been argued[2] that the presence of double guard-cells here betokens the presence of southern innovators amongst the native fort-builders. Access to the wall-head of the dun, a necessary provision if the site was to be adequately defended, was gained up an intramural staircase issuing from the rear of one of these cells; this is the only instance in Lorn where such a feature can still be seen. Another unusual feature, this time at Dùn Aorain (No. 166), is the local thickening of the wall on either side of the entrance in a manner which recalls the so-called 'gate-house' forts elsewhere in the Atlantic Province.[3] The purpose of the expansion at Dùn Aorain is unknown, but it may have been to allow the wall to be carried to a greater height at the most vulnerable part of its perimeter.

Of the six examples where the entrances are comparatively well-preserved, only three have been checked or rebated for a wooden door, the width of the passage varying between 1·5 m and 1·75 m externally and between 1·7 m and 2·1 m internally; of the remainder, which do not appear to have been rebated, two are of uniform width throughout, i.e. 1·3 m and 1·5 m respectively, while the other measures 1·5 m in external width, but increases gradually to a width of 1·8 m on the line of the inner wall-face. In one case (No. 189) the entrance passage, as well as being rebated, also exhibits slots for the housing and securing of a heavy wooden door-bar. The same dun is also remarkable in having two entrances, a peculiarity it shares with duns in other parts of Argyll.[4] In the absence of adequate excavation practically nothing is known about the internal features of duns in Lorn, but almost one-third of them have outworks, which consist in general of comparatively slight stone walls designed to give added protection on particularly vulnerable sides. At Leccamore (No. 189), and possibly at Dùn Neil (No. 181), these defences have been supplemented by rock-cut ditches, while in at least one other case (No. 166) the outwork also served to enclose an annexe.

---

[1] Ibid., pp. 16–17.
[2] GAJ, ii (1971), 62–4.
[3] Hamilton, J R C, Excavations at Clickhimin, Shetland (1968), 54–61.

[4] E.g. Kildalloig (Inventory of Argyll, i, No. 219) and Druim an Duin, Mid Argyll (PSAS, xxxix (1904–5), 285–7).

The earliest securely datable material to be associated with any dun in Lorn is the rim-fragment of a samian bowl of the late 1st century AD found in a midden-deposit at Dùn an Fheurain (No. 164),[1] but it is clear from evidence available elsewhere in the Atlantic Province that some examples of the dun class, as defined in this volume, could date to a much earlier period, possibly the fifth or sixth century BC,[2] while others, like No. 164, were still being used, if not constructed, in the Early Christian period. It would appear, nevertheless, that many, if not the majority, were built in the 1st or 2nd century AD.[3]

BROCHS

The typical features of the brochs are so well known and the problems of their date and origin have been so fully discussed,[4] that it is unnecessary to do more in this context than provide a brief description of their appearance and distribution, and emphasise their affinity to other examples of galleried-wall construction.

The broch is a dry-stone walled defensive structure, usually circular on plan, measuring from about 7·6 m to 12·2 m in internal diameter and up to 15 m in height. Its distribution is densest in the Northern Isles, Caithness and Sutherland, Skye and the Outer Hebrides, but a few instances are known in the islands of northern Argyll, while scattered outliers have been recorded in central, eastern and southern parts of the mainland. Recent excavation has given added weight to the hypothesis that brochs evolved from small stone forts of the Atlantic Province in the 1st century BC.

Only one certain and one probable broch have been recorded in Lorn, both on the island of Lismore. About Tirefour Castle (No. 147), the better-preserved of the two, there can be no doubt, in view of its circular plan, its thick dry-stone wall with massive base and upper mural gallery, and the scarcement and characteristic aperture in its inner wall-face. An Dùn, Loch Fiart (No. 146), closely resembles Tirefour Castle in plan, wall-thickness and the possession of a mural gallery, but owing to its ruined condition its tentative identification as a broch needs to be confirmed by excavation.

CRANNOGS

Of the twenty-one crannogs recorded in this volume only two (Nos. 195 and 200) have been excavated. The former produced artifacts which, without being closely datable, suggested that the site was occupied in the medieval period; no artifacts of any kind were found in the latter, but its style of construction was comparable in a general way with that of the crannog at Lochan Dughaill,[5] which may have been constructed in the 2nd century AD. Of peculiar interest is the recent discovery of no fewer than sixteen crannogs (No. 198) in that part of Loch Awe which falls within the district of Lorn. While none of these has yet been excavated, the occurrence in several examples of harbours or jetties similar to that discovered in the excavation of Milton Loch crannog, Kirkcudbrightshire,[6] suggests that some, at least, may also be of Iron Age origin.

[1] For a recent re-examination of this material cf. *PSAS*, ciii (1970–1), 100–12.
[2] I.e. timber-laced duns; see *supra*, p. 18.
[3] For recent dating evidence from duns in Kintyre and in Ross and Cromarty, cf. *Inventory of Argyll*, i, p. 19; also *DES* (1969), 44–5.

[4] *PSAS*, lxxxi (1946–7), 48–99; *PPS*, xxxi (1965), 93–146; Hamilton, J R C, *Excavations at Clickhimin, Shetland* (1968); *GAJ*, ii (1971), 39–71.
[5] *Inventory of Argyll*, i, No. 241.
[6] *PSAS*, lxxxvii (1952–3), 134–52.

MISCELLANEOUS EARTHWORKS AND ENCLOSURES

Apart from the field-bank at Black Crofts (No. 203), which is dated to the second millennium BC, none of the eleven earthworks and enclosures included in this section has been excavated, and little can therefore be said about their date or purpose, although it is possible that some were constructed and used in the Iron Age. Dùn Ablaich (No. 205) and Ard Luing (No. 201) occupy positions of considerable natural strength, such as dun-builders might have favoured, but both are enclosed by banks composed mainly of earth. The enclosure at Sean Dùn, Lismore (No. 193), appears to have been constructed when the adjacent dun and its outwork were no longer in use.

5. THE EARLY CHRISTIAN PERIOD

Under this head are considered monuments of the period that begins with the first Scottish appearance of Christian memorials (in Galloway in the 5th century), and ends with the introduction of the Romanesque style of architecture into Western Scotland in the 12th century.

The recorded history of Christianity in Lorn begins in the second half of the 6th century, when a small monastic outpost was established from Iona at a site as yet unidentified near Loch Awe[1] and a major community was founded by St Moluag on the island of Lismore. The physical remains of this important monastery have proved less permanent than at least one relic of the saint, whose crozier, the *bachull mór*, has recently been restored to the custody of its hereditary keepers, the Livingstone family of Bachuil, Lismore.[2] The outline of the monastic enclosure may, however, have been perpetuated in the boundary of the medieval churchyard (cf. p. 156). Two other sites that may be monastic in origin are the possible cashel at Cladh a' Bhearnaig, Kerrera (No. 232), where the enclosed area is sub-divided, as in many Irish sites of this character, and the promontory site at Kilmaha on the north-west shore of Loch Awe (No. 261), where the remains of several buildings have been recorded, together with a rock-carving and two carved stones of Early Christian date.

The diffusion of Christian worship throughout the inhabited parts of the region in this period is attested by the frequent occurrence of *Kil*-names. In many cases the sites associated with place-names of this type remained in use throughout the medieval period and any earlier features have been obliterated. The medieval chapel that existed at Cill-an-Suidhe, Lismore (No. 229), however, has itself disappeared leaving only the remains of a circular ditched enclosure some 38 m in diameter. A similar enclosure has been recorded near Clachan, on the same island (No. 231), and both sites may be tentatively identified as cemeteries of Early Christian date, the former developed by the addition of a chapel and the latter 'undeveloped'.[3] Smaller enclosed burial-grounds of irregular shape survive at two of the six places in the region that

[1] Adomnan, *Columba* (Anderson), 268–9.
[2] *Origines Parochiales*, ii, part i, 163; Carmichael, *Lismore*, 63–5, 171–80. It has been suggested by Joseph Anderson (*PSAS*, xliv (1909–10), 274–5), that the early iron bell enclosed within the 12th-century Kilmichael Glassary bell-shrine was the bell of St Moluag, which was still venerated at Lismore in 1509.

[3] Cf. Thomas, C, *The Early Christian Archaeology of North Britain* (1971), 50–68, 81–9.

bear forms of the name *Anaid* (Nos. 233 and 234), a name which in Scotland usually seems to be associated with an ancient chapel or cemetery.[1]

Except possibly at Dunollie (p. 197), no secular monuments of this period have been identified. For lack of specific information a supposed Viking burial behind Mount Pleasant House, Kerrera (NM 842302),[2] and a 'ship-burial' said to have been found in the vicinity of Oban railway-station (NM *c.* 857298),[3] have not been included in the *Inventory*. Also omitted is a structure described as an 'earth house' which was situated at the northern end of Kerrera (NM *c.* 844311), and which produced an animal-headed bone pin (Pl. 5D) showing an amalgam of Norse and native traditions.[4] It has not been possible to identify the site, and its precise nature is uncertain: it is, however, clear from correspondence with the finder that it was not a typical Iron Age earth-house, and it is not known whether the relics recovered, which included several other pins and a single-sided iron knife, were in the primary occupation layer. The hipped shank of the animal-headed pin, and the position of the zoomorphic head at right-angles to the shank, seem to be native features of 7th–9th century date, while the proportions of the pin and the vigour of the carving indicate 9th–century Norse influence.[5]

Of the few Early Christian carvings in Lorn, the oldest is probably the rock-carving at Kilmaha (p. 150) which could be as early as the 7th or 8th century. Although poorly executed, the incised ring-cross appears to be of 'Maltese' type, and with its handle may have been inspired by the *flabellum*. In Wales incised crosses of this form, in some cases associated with figures, are thought to be of 7th–9th century date,[6] while most of the Irish examples are tentatively ascribed to the 8th century. The wheel-cross slab on Inishail (p. 135, no. 1), and the cross-decorated stone from Clenamacrie (No. 238), are both unlikely to be earlier than the 9th century and could be appreciably later, while the two carved stones at Kilmaha (p. 150, nos. 1 and 2) are probably 11th or 12th century. Lastly, although an earlier date has been proposed, Mr R B K Stevenson has argued persuasively for a 10th-century date for the most remarkable monument in this group, the elaborately ornamented cross-slab at Ardchattan Priory (p. 110, no. 1).[7]

6. THE MIDDLE AGES AND LATER

ECCLESIASTICAL MONUMENTS

The principal ecclesiastical building of Lorn, the cathedral church of the diocese of Argyll, was situated on the island of Lismore, probably from the foundation of the see before 1189, but no part of the existing remains appears to be earlier in date than the 14th century (No. 267). In plan-form it was the least elaborate of the medieval cathedrals of Scotland, having neither transepts nor aisles, except for a small chapel or sacristy on the north side of the presbytery. The doorways and sedilia of the latter are executed in an idiosyncratic style bearing little

[1] Cf. Nos. 214 and 219; a small township near Kilchrenan is named Annat (NN 035223). Smith, *Loch Etive*, 262, describes a site near Strontoiller named 'Cleidh-na-h-Annait' which was not recorded by the Ordnance Survey. The name *Annaid* is discussed by Watson, *Celtic Place-names*, 250–3.
[2] *DES* (*1965*), 9.
[3] Shetelig, H (ed.), *Viking Antiquities in Great Britain and Ireland*, part vi (1954), 75.

[4] Lethbridge, T C, *Herdsmen and Hermits* (1950), 95.
[5] Hamilton, J R C, *Excavations at Jarlshof, Shetland* (1956), 115, 124, fig. 58.
[6] *ECMW*, 20, fig. 5.
[7] *JRSAI*, lxxxvi (1956), 93–4.

relationship to other surviving medieval work in the West Highlands, and appear to belong to the early 14th century.[1] In the late medieval period the choir was separated from the nave by a massive stone pulpitum, which became the west wall of the church when the nave and its added west tower fell into ruin after the Reformation. The choir, with its wall-head lowered in the 18th century, was preserved as the parish church of Lismore, and the full extent of the original building was revealed only by excavation in the 1950s.

Ardchattan Priory (No. 217), founded by Duncan MacDougall of Lorn in 1230, was one of three houses of the Valliscaulian order to be established in Scotland at about the same date, the others being Pluscarden, Moray, and Beauly, Inverness-shire. It preserves considerable remains of the earliest buildings, and the general plan of the original cruciform church has been identified during the present survey, although the precise extent of the choir remains uncertain. The nave had a narrow north aisle, and each transept opened into twin eastern chapels of unusually shallow projection. The latter feature is more closely paralleled in earlier work in the north transept of Iona Abbey than in the contemporary architecture of the Cistercians, on whose usages the Valliscaulian rule was modelled. The use of round angle-shafts (cf. p. 105) is another feature that is probably due to local influence. The ritual choir was entirely contained within the eastern limb, being separated from the crossing by a solid wall penetrated by an arched opening some 2·5 m in width. The total number in each Valliscaulian community, including lay-brothers, was limited to twenty,[2] and the conventual buildings at Ardchattan were of modest extent, having no west range. The refectory was rebuilt in the 15th century; although now sub-divided it preserves two notable features of that date, its original open timber roof and the two-bay pulpit which has recently been restored. The choir of the church was rebuilt on a larger scale at the same period, with interesting sculptural decoration, additional fragments of which have recently come to light in re-use within the later mansion.

The third major ecclesiastical building of Lorn is another MacDougall foundation, the 13th-century chapel at Dunstaffnage (No. 243) which, although only a little larger than some of the medieval parish-churches of the area (cf. Fig. 6), far surpasses them in architectural elaboration. Its richly-decorated chancel bears a close resemblance, in the design of its paired windows and in the detail of some mouldings, to the chancel of Killean Church, Kintyre.[3] Dunstaffnage, however, lacks the Romanesque features that are prominent at Killean, being distinguished by a profusion of dog-tooth ornament similar to that found in the original cloister-arcades of Iona Abbey, and the use of filleted and deeply undercut mouldings suggests a date late in the first half of the 13th century.

The parochial churches and chapels of the area form a striking contrast with those of Kintyre, many of which appear to be of 12th-century date. Only the parish church of Kilchattan (No. 256) can be ascribed to that period; Keil Chapel (No. 250), although similar to Kilchattan in plan-form, has masonry and lintelled windows of characteristic late-medieval type, and may represent a remodelling of a Romanesque building. Work of the 13th century

[1] The mouldings of the sedilia are similar, although cruder in execution, to those of the piscina in the 14th-century south aisle of Fortrose Cathedral, Ross and Cromarty.
[2] Bull of Innocent III (1205), in Birch, W de G (ed.), *Ordinale Conventus Vallis Caulium* (1900), 139–41. The history and observances of the order are summarized in Anson, P F, *A Monastery in Moray* (1959), 8–33.

[3] *Inventory of Argyll*, i, No. 287.

23

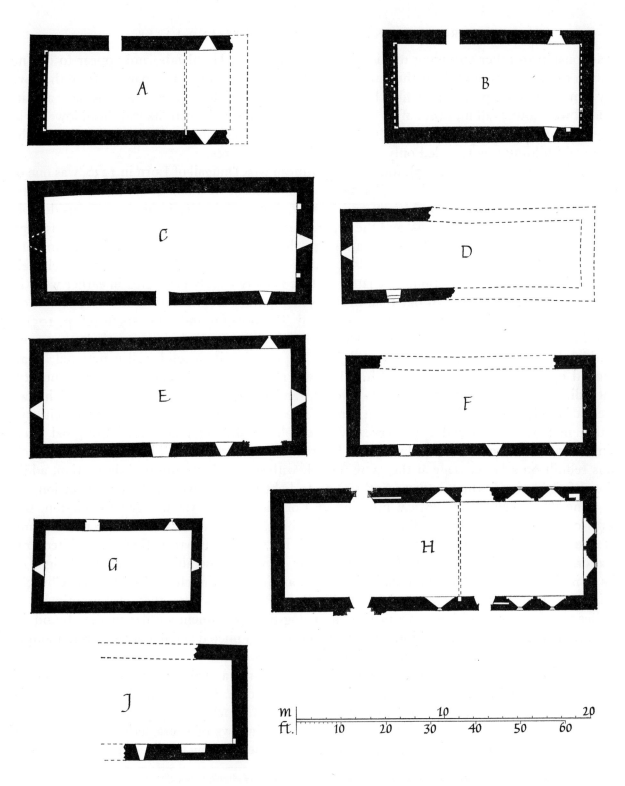

Fig. 6. Comparative plans of medieval churches in Lorn: A, Old Parish Church, Kilchattan, Luing (No. 256);
B, Chapel, Keil (No. 250); C, Church, Baile Mhaodain, Ardchattan (No. 220); D, Old Parish Church, Inishail
(No. 247); E, Old Parish Church, Kilmore (No. 264); F, Old Parish Church, Eilean Munde (No. 245); G, Chapel,
Innis Sèa-Ràmhach (No. 248); H, Dunstaffnage Chapel (No. 243); J, Old Parish Church, Muckairn,
Taynuilt (No. 268)

has been identified only in the form of carved masonry-fragments re-used in several later buildings (Nos. 220, 247, 253 and 259). With the exception of Kilchattan, all the churches and chapels are of late medieval date and have undergone no structural alteration during that period; in layout they conform to the oblong unicameral type characteristic of the 13th-century churches of Kintyre. Analysis of their comparative plans (Fig. 6) shows that two pairs of closely similar buildings survive. The churches of Baile Mhaodain, Ardchattan (No. 220) and Kilmore (No. 264) measure about 17 m by 6 m internally, and in each case the entrance doorway was probably situated near the centre of the south wall. The island churches of Eilean Munde (No. 245) and Inishail (No. 247), although only a little shorter, are much narrower; their attenuated plans, each having a doorway towards the west end of the south wall, correspond closely with that of the parish church of Kilchousland, Kintyre,[1] as remodelled in or about the 16th century, and they may be ascribed to the same period. The chapel on Innis Seà-Ràmhach (No. 248), probably associated with the nearby castle of Innis Chonnell (No. 292), is intermediate in scale between the parochial churches and the other dependent chapels of which only fragmentary remains survive (Nos. 221, 235, 239 and 265).

Many of the graveyards associated with these churches and chapels remained in use long after the buildings had become ruinous, and the wells found near several of them were likewise held in popular veneration. Most of these now appear simply as natural springs, but the well at Cladh Churiollan, Creagan (No. 237), renowned in the 17th century for its therapeutic qualities, is enclosed within a well-house resembling others in Ireland and Wales.[2]

There was little post-Reformation church-building in Lorn until the 18th century, and the structures erected then were modest in scale and mediocre in execution. Several required subsequent enlargement by the construction of a wing, producing a T-plan, a process which in Lowland Scotland had occurred a century earlier.[3] Most of them are now ruinous or have been completely remodelled. An exception is Kilchrenan (1771, No. 259) where the S elevation is of considerable merit as an example of Classical design. A number of interesting churches were built to the designs of eminent metropolitan architects during the first half of the 19th century. James Elliot's Glenorchy Church (1809–11, No. 246), an octagonal structure with an imposing tower, and David Cousin's Free High Church, Oban (1846, No. 270), a Puginesque design adapted to the traditional Presbyterian T-plan, were erected under the direct patronage of, respectively, the 4th Earl and the 2nd Marquess of Breadalbane. This volume also includes two Parliamentary Churches, at Duror (No. 244) and Muckairn (No. 269), which were constructed under the personal supervision of Joseph Mitchell to a high degree of precise craftsmanship.[4] Ardchattan Parish Church (1836, No. 216), an incompetent essay in the Gothic style by a local architect, is of interest as the only church to retain its original long communion-table. The Episcopal Church at Portnacroish (1815, No. 272), was one of the earliest churches of that denomination to be built in the Highlands, and its internal layout, in common with Presbyterian buildings of that period, was centred on the pulpit.

About one hundred late medieval crosses and funerary monuments have been recorded in

---

[1] *Inventory of Argyll*, i, No. 281.
[2] Cf. the inner chamber at St Gwenfaen's Well, Rhoscolyn, Anglesey.
[3] Cf. Hay, *Post-Reformation Churches*, 22–3, 52–63, 86–92, 120–2.

[4] Although Thomas Telford is usually considered as architect of these churches (and their associated manses), the standard designs were produced by one of his assistants, James Smith (cf. p. 129).

this volume, the principal groups being at Ardchattan Priory (No. 217), Dalmally (No. 246), Kilbride (No. 253), Kilchrenan (No. 259), the former cathedral of Lismore (No. 267), and on the island of Inishail (No. 247). The earliest are two late 13th- or early 14th-century grave-slabs at Kilchrenan (p. 148, no. 1) and Kilmore (p. 154, no. 1), which bear cross-heads of a geometric design employed in many parts of Britain. This design was, however, rapidly superseded in the West Highlands by others evolved in the schools of carving that were established there in the 14th and 15th centuries, and in Lorn the majority of the carvings made before 1500 are the work of a school centred in the Loch Awe region. Unlike the contemporary craftsmen of the other West Highland schools, the Loch Awe carvers seem to have been peripatetic, journeying from place to place as their services were required, and using whatever suitable stone lay readily to hand.[1] Their grave-slabs, and occasional effigies and crosses, are usually uninscribed, and in the quality of the decoration they compare unfavourably with the monuments of the Iona school, an outstanding example of which is the memorial to Somerled MacDougall and his family at Ardchattan (p. 112, no. 11(i)). Two other pre-1500 slabs, both on Lismore (p. 161, nos. 3–4), are of particular interest since they bear representations of tau-headed staves. From about 1500 until the Reformation, when production ceased, the local trade in minor monumental sculpture passed into the hands of independent craftsmen who were responsible for a series of idiosyncratic carvings such as the Campbell of Lerags Cross at Kilbride (p. 143), the lid of a tomb-chest on Lismore (p. 162, no. 8), and a stone panel, probably an altar frontal, containing a Crucifixion scene, on Inishail (p. 136. no. 13).

The earliest of the post-Reformation memorials is a grave-slab at Ardchattan (p. 113, no. 18), probably of late 16th-century date. Otherwise the later funerary monuments are notable for the rarity of those headstones bearing trade insignia which are so numerous in Kintyre. Individual recumbent slabs of the 17th century at Eilean Munde (p. 131, no. 4) and Dunstaffnage Chapel (p. 128, no. 4) deserve mention for, respectively, a lengthy eulogistic inscription in Scots, and a detailed representation of a couple in fashionable costume. The most interesting series of monuments, spanning the 17th and 18th centuries, is at Ardchattan Priory (No. 217), where the elaborate table-tombs of the Campbells of Lochnell bear armorial achievements of outstanding quality. Monumental sculpture in the slate-quarrying areas of Lorn displays little of the calligraphic virtuosity of its English counterparts, but at Eilean Munde (No. 245) and Keil Chapel (No. 250) there are some charmingly naive carvings of early 19th-century date.

CASTLES, TOWER-HOUSES AND FORTIFICATIONS

Lorn contained more medieval castles than any other region of Argyll, and a high proportion of these survive today, including several well-preserved structures of considerable architectural interest. Two of the earliest are Innis Chonnell and Achadun, which belong to a well-defined group of early Scottish stone castles sometimes termed 'simple rectangular castles of enclosure', whose dominating feature was a stout curtain-wall, pierced with few openings, enclosing a square or oblong courtyard.[2] Castles of this type survive mainly in the

---

[1] Cf. 'The Loch Awe School' in Steer and Bannerman, *Monumental Sculpture*.

[2] Cf. Dunbar, J G and Duncan, A A M, 'Tarbert Castle', *SHR*, 1 (1971), 7–9.

Highlands, and examples occur elsewhere in the county at Castle Sween and Duart, as also, on a rather larger scale, at Tarbert.[1] In its original form Innis Chonnell (No. 292) comprised a curtain-wall surrounding a courtyard some 19 m square, around which there were ranged a number of domestic buildings. The curtain-wall was strengthened by one or more square angle-towers of slight projection, and on one side there was also a substantial mid-buttress. The castle thus bore a considerable resemblance, both in plan and in overall dimensions, to the late 12th-century castle of Sween; but in view of the presence of arrow-slits of a fairly sophistic-ated type in the primary work, Innis Chonnell may more probably be ascribed to a date within the first half of the following century. Much of this early work was swept away when the castle came to be remodelled during the first half of the 15th century. New courtyard-buildings were erected at this period, including a spacious first-floor hall with an associated series of private apartments housed partly within an adjacent tower, while the wall-head defences were entirely recast. Although the buildings are now roofless, the castle is unusually well preserved and ranks as one of the most outstanding monuments of the county.

The episcopal castle of Achadun (No. 276), probably built shortly before 1300, is less well preserved, but has undergone fewer alterations. The courtyard measured about 22 m square and the whole of one side was occupied by a substantial stone-built range of buildings which probably incorporated a first-floor hall. Recent excavations have shown that one of the two entrances was equipped with a forework incorporating a miniature drawbridge-pit. An interesting series of small finds of late medieval date includes personal ornaments and English and Scottish silver coins.

The developed castle of enclosure, with fortified curtain-wall and round angle-towers, is well represented by Dunstaffnage (No. 287), which was probably erected in about the second quarter of the 13th century. In its original form the castle appears to have comprised a quad-rangular enclosure with three cylindrical angle-towers, one of which flanked a simple entrance-gateway. Another of the towers, considerably larger than the other two, probably formed a keep, on each side of which ranges of domestic buildings, including a first-floor hall, stood against the inner face of the curtain-wall. The remaining sections of the curtain-wall contained a series of defensive embrasures incorporating tall fish-tailed arrow-slits, while at parapet-level there was a continuous wall-walk which communicated with the upper floors of the towers. The general arrangement resembled those of Dirleton, East Lothian, Coull,[2] Aberdeenshire, and Inverlochy, Inverness-shire, although in all these cases the angle-towers were of much bolder projection. The castle was extensively remodelled about the turn of the 15th and 16th centuries, when a gatehouse was built and the courtyard buildings partially reconstructed, while further alterations continued to be made up to the time that the castle was abandoned as a private residence in 1810.

In addition to these three 13th-century castles of enclosure, Lorn also contains the remains of at least two hall-houses of the same period. The most interesting of these is Fraoch Eilean (No. 290), which was probably erected by, or on behalf of, Alexander III during the third quarter of the 13th century. Like Innis Chonnell, the castle is situated on a small island in Loch Awe, and the original building comprised an unvaulted cellarage beneath a large first-floor

---

[1] *Inventory of Argyll*, i, No. 316.

[2] Simpson, W Douglas, 'The Excavation of Coull Castle, Aberdeenshire', *PSAS*, lviii (1923–4), 45–99.

hall probably covered by an open timber roof set within a wall-walk. The hall was unusually wide, the floor-joists being supported by a stout axial beam resting upon timber posts or masonry piers constructed within the undercroft.[1] There is no evidence of mural fireplaces, and the hall was probably heated by means of a central hearth ventilated by a louver. The castle has affinities with other Scottish examples of its class such as Lochranza, Island of Arran, and Knock, Skye, but the closest parallel in terms of overall size and plan-form appears to be the English royal castle of Greencastle, County Down, built in about the middle of the 13th century.[2] Fraoch Eilean was partially remodelled in the 17th century to form a small dwelling-house, and when this was abandoned the whole structure fell into ruin. The poor condition of the building, coupled with its remoteness of situation, led earlier writers to underestimate its importance, but recent investigations have shown that the shell of the original hall-house survives, and steps have now been taken to arrest further decay. Castle Coeffin (No. 282), although very ruinous, can be recognized as a building of similar character. In this case, however, the width of the structure was considerably restricted by the nature of the site, and there is no evidence of the existence of an axial supporting-beam beneath the hall floor. The hall itself was equipped at its upper end with a mural fireplace whose flue discharged beneath the parapeted wall-walk.

Excluding the doubtful examples of Caisteal na Nighinn Ruaidhe (No. 281) and Caisteal nan Con (No. 280), there are nine surviving castles of tower-house type within the area under review, and of these the earliest is probably Kilchurn (No. 293), founded by Sir Colin Campbell, 1st of Glenorchy, shortly before the middle of the 15th century. The original castle, comprising an oblong tower-house with an associated barmkin, was subsequently remodelled by successive members of the Glenorchy family, the final and most extensive series of alterations being undertaken by the 1st Earl of Breadalbane between about 1690 and 1698. This scheme of reconstruction, which ranks as one of the last major essays in private fortification in Britain, involved the addition of cylindrical angle-towers equipped for firearm defence and the erection of barrack-blocks capable of accommodating a garrison of more than two hundred men. Although the defensive arrangements of these buildings are distinctly old-fashioned, their plan-form anticipates some of the features of the typical Board of Ordnance barrack of the following century. Following the breakdown of a proposal to sell the castle to the government for use as a permanent Highland garrison in 1747, Kilchurn was abandoned and the fabric rapidly began to disintegrate, but the existing remains are extensive. Another oblong tower-house of the 15th century, similar in size to the one at Kilchurn, but of more massive construction, formerly stood at Ardmaddy. The upper portion of the tower was subsequently demolished, however, and only the lowest storey now survives, forming the basement of an early Georgian house (No. 310).

A third major tower-house of 15th-century date stands at Dunollie, near Oban, on a site formerly occupied by a fortress of the rulers of North Dalriada. The layout of the castle (No. 286) is somewhat unusual in that the tower-house projects forward obliquely from one corner of the barmkin, thus partially flanking the two adjacent sections of the barmkin-wall. The

[1] The arrangement is an uncommon one but appears to have been employed occasionally elsewhere, e.g. in the 13th-century Irish hall-house of Castle Carra, Co. Mayo, and perhaps also at Duffus Castle, Morayshire.

[2] *An Archaeological Survey of County Down* (1966), 211–19.

square four-storeyed tower is strongly constructed, and some of the techniques employed, such as the use of slab-corbelling and wicker-centering,[1] probably reflect local building-practice.

The best-preserved and most noteworthy of the later tower-houses are Castle Stalker, Gylen and Barcaldine. Stalker (No. 285) was probably erected by Alan Stewart of Appin some time during the second quarter of the 16th century, but the upper storey was remodelled a hundred years later, following the acquisition of the castle by Sir Donald Campbell of Ardnamurchan. The tower, which is exceptionally solidly built, shows considerable refinement both of planning and execution, and two of the principal apartments are provided with remarkable sculptured fireplaces. The early 17th-century upperworks incorporate covered parapet-walks equipped for firearm defence, together with a small living-room contained within a cap-house. Gylen (No. 291), a late 16th-century residence of the MacDougalls of Dunollie, is much smaller in scale than Castle Stalker, but no less carefully planned and detailed. The tower-house is of L-plan, comprising a square main block with a staircase-tower of unexpectedly generous dimensions at the rear. The main entrance-doorway occupies its usual position at the foot of the staircase but, because the building straddles the neck of a promontory, access is obtained by means of a vaulted passage passing through the ground-floor area of the main block. Although the tower is equipped for defence, there is also much embellishment, and the upperworks display a rich assemblage of homespun Renaissance detail, much of it probably carved by a sculptor whose work can also be recognized at Dundarave Castle, Mid Argyll.

The master-mason responsible for the design of Dundarave (1596) may also have had a hand in the erection of Barcaldine Castle (No. 279), for the layout of the two buildings is much the same. The L-plan arrangement, with extruded staircase, allows both main block and wing to be given over to living-accommodation, thus enabling a private room to be formed *en suite* with the hall on the principal floor. The castle gains additional interest by virtue of the survival of an early inventory of fittings, which provides a room-by-room description of the building as it stood not many years after its completion in 1609. Sir Duncan Campbell of Glenorchy, the founder of Barcaldine, was a notable castle-builder (cf. p. 238), and among his other activities in Lorn was the construction of a small tower-house at Achallader (No. 277) shortly before 1600. The building was attacked and burnt by Jacobites in 1689, but the surviving fragment contains an interesting series of gun-loops comparable with those at Gylen and Kilchurn.

Just as it was customary in the Highlands and Islands to site major stone castles upon conveniently placed inshore islands (cf. Nos. 281, 285, 290 and 292), so was the practice widespread of erecting lesser defensive buildings of timber and other materials upon artificially-constructed islets,[2] and a number of these sites can be identified in Lorn. An islet of this nature in Loch Nell (No. 296) appears to have been occupied in the late 14th century, while another in Loch Tulla (No. 288), mentioned in a mid-15th-century charter, still retains part of a heavy timber substructure. The islands in Loch Tromlee (No. 289), Loch na Sreinge (No. 295) and Loch a' Phearsain (No. 294), on the other hand, seem to be mainly natural in origin. All con-

---

[1] Another example of the use of wicker-centering in the West Highlands occurs in late medieval work at Castle Tioram, Inverness-shire; the practice was also widespread in Ireland.

[2] *PSAS*, vi (1864-6), 132; *Geog. Coll.*, ii, 159, 161-3.

tain the remains of simple stone buildings, and at Loch a' Phearsain, which is known to have been occupied as late as the 17th century, the entire island appears to have been enclosed by a dry-stone wall.

THE BURGH OF OBAN

In contrast to Campbeltown and Inveraray, which were established as planned towns by the Argyll family,[1] Oban developed during the second half of the 18th century in a piecemeal and irregular fashion, in response to increasing use of its fine natural harbour (cf. No. 298). It was described in 1800 as 'a small straggling village',[2] and the expansion of the northern part of the town in the following decade, although planned on a grid-pattern, was also haphazard in execution. The earliest harbour-buildings, the South Pier and its adjacent Piermaster's House (No. 301), were built about 1814 at the south extremity of the burgh, close to the best anchorage but inconveniently placed in relation to the development of the town.

The late 18th- and early 19th-century street-architecture of the burgh was unpretentious (Nos. 299 and 300), and much of it was swept away during the rapid commercial expansion of the second half of the 19th century. The most notable monument of that period, the Great Western Hotel on Corran Esplanade, was built to the designs of Charles Wilson of Glasgow in 1862,[3] and falls outside the scope of this *Inventory*. The Free High Church within the burgh is dealt with elsewhere in this Introduction (cf. p. 25).

DOMESTIC ARCHITECTURE FROM THE 17TH TO THE 19TH CENTURY

The unsettled state of society in Lorn throughout the 17th century was not favourable for the development of unfortified residences, and the only substantial domestic structure to survive from that period is a late 17th-century range at Lochnell House (No. 330). More stable conditions in the early 18th century encouraged a number of the resident landowners to build mansions, the earliest of these being the now-demolished principal block of Appin House (No. 305). An outstanding group of buildings of this type was erected in the years 1737-9 by the Campbell lairds of Airds and Lochnell, and by the 2nd Earl of Breadalbane's factor at Ardmaddy. Airds House (No. 304) and the early Georgian block at Lochnell House (No. 330) are remarkably similar in scale, each being based on a double cube of 30 feet (9·1 m) and having a ground-floor entrance set within a three-bay pedimented frontispiece. The former preserves its flanking pavilions, linked by quadrant corridors to a main building whose elevational treatment may be derived from that of the south front of Marble Hill House, Twickenham (1724-9),[4] although lacking the horizontal articulation of that design. The princi-

[1] *Inventory of Argyll*, i, No. 318; Lindsay, I G and Cosh, M, *Inveraray and the Dukes of Argyll* (1973), *passim*.
[2] Leyden, *Tour*, 31.
[3] Gomme, A and Walker, D, *Architecture of Glasgow* (1968), 283.

[4] Illustrated in Campbell, C, *Vitruvius Britannicus*, iii (1725), pl. 93. Donald Campbell of Airds was factor of Morvern for the 2nd Duke of Argyll, who was a patron of the architect Roger Morris and, as a trustee for Mrs Howard, had been concerned with the building of Marble Hill House (cf. Draper, M P G and Eden, W A, *Marble Hill House and its Owners* (1970), 10, 12, 19).

pal façade of Lochnell House displays a certain gaucherie in the handling of similar elements, such as the lack of relationship between the cornices of the side-bays and that of the frontis-piece. One of the masons employed at Lochnell was John Johnstone, an associate of the mason-architect John Baxter and of Sir John Clerk of Penicuik, and certain distinctive features of the design appear in other buildings where Johnstone and Baxter collaborated.[1] Ardmaddy Castle (No. 310), although a much smaller house than Airds and Lochnell, was equally advanced in its use of fashionable architectural motifs, and its unknown architect made skilful use of the *piano nobile*, imposed upon him by the retention within the new building of the vaulted lowest storey of a medieval tower-house. The now-ruined mansion of Hayfield (No. 323), built about 1780 by a successful lawyer of local descent, was of a conventional late 18th-century pattern.

The mansions of the early 19th century, as befitted their picturesque settings and the historic traditions of the families for whom they were built, were in the Gothic Revival style. The most distinguished example was the large castellated wing added in 1820 to Lochnell House (No. 330); this was probably designed by Archibald Elliot, and its bold asymmetry, as contrasted with his earlier houses, may be attributed to his experience of designing prisons at Edinburgh (Calton Jail, 1815), and at Jedburgh (1820). William Burn and James Gillespie Graham each received several commissions for country-house designs in Lorn, and their alternative schemes for Gallanach (No. 320), of which that by Burn was executed on a reduced scale in 1814–17, illustrate the simple ornament and classical planning of the early phases of the Castellated Gothic style. Its later Jacobethan phase is seen in Burn's mansion at Ardanaiseig (No. 307) and Graham's extension of Ardmaddy Castle. Kinlochlaich (No. 327) is a charming small Gothic Revival house, and a wing in the same style was added about 1831 to Appin House.

The residences of the lesser lairds and tacksmen in the 18th century, like their grander counterparts, were constructed principally by masons from the Lowlands, and their planning followed the models previously developed in that area. Glenure (No. 322), which is of the symmetrical two-storeyed central-staircase plan common in Stirlingshire from about 1700, retains two rooms fitted with original pine-panelling, and its development and furnishing is well documented. Ballachulish House (No. 311) is another well-preserved building of the same type, and among the smaller houses mention may be made of Upper Sonachan (No. 336), and of Ardlarach (1787, No. 309) and Degnish (1786, No. 316), both of which bear date-panels. Achlian (No. 302) and Ardencaple (No. 308), both ascribed to the last quarter of the 18th century, are distinguished by the addition of semicircular stair-towers. The early tacksmen's houses at Achnaba (No. 303) and Rarey (No. 333) appear to have been single-storeyed.

During the first half of the 19th century a number of manses were erected, some of them by local builders, the earliest being that at Dalmally (1805, No. 315). Kilbrandon House (1827, No. 325) and Kilmore House (1828, No. 326), both originally built as manses, are similar in scale to the contemporary proprietor's residence at Lerags (No. 329). This volume also includes examples of the alternative designs for Parliamentary Manses, the single-storeyed type being found at Duror (1827, No. 328), and the less common two-storeyed version at Muckairn (1828, No. 331).

[1] Cf. the use of panelled pilasters, flanking the upper portion of the centrepiece, at Galloway House, Wigtownshire, built by Baxter and Johnstone to designs by the architect John Douglas.

Farms, Townships and Shielings

Scanty documentary references to the destruction of buildings during the Highland warfare of the 17th century provide the earliest source of information about the dwellings of the tenant-farmers in Lorn. The tenants on the Dunstaffnage estate, whose homes were burnt by Montrose's army in 1644, possessed chambers, byres, barns, a kiln, and a mill with attached dwelling, all identified by the number of cruck-couples that they incorporated.[1] The houses of this class erected during the 18th century resembled those of Kintyre,[2] and the south-west Highlands generally, in being rectangular byre-dwellings with cruck-framed roofs and straight gables. The ruined shells of many buildings of this type survive throughout the region; a typical example at Cadderlie (No. 339) has been recorded, and others are found at Tigh-Cuil Township (No. 345). These buildings have, without exception, lost their internal furnishings such as canopied chimneys, which are known only from early travellers' descriptions,[3] and the only intact cruck-framed roof-structure recorded in the present survey was in a cottage of later type at Glencoe (No. 342). This house incorporated scarf-jointed cruck-couples with yokes, within solidly-built walls of lime-mortared masonry, bearing witness to the strong tradition of cruck-framed building in the area.[4]

Although structures of the form described were predominant, two other types of peasant dwelling have been recorded. One of these, now represented only by small outhouses in the Glencoe area (cf. p. 271) but observed also in dwellings in Appin in the 19th century,[5] was influenced by the hip-roofed round-angled houses of the neighbouring area of North Argyll. A more widely-distributed variation from the normal type is found in the occurrence within a wholly rectangular structure of end-crucks for a hipped roof. This feature, recorded in several buildings in Lorn (Nos. 338, 344 and 346) and also at Auchindrain, Mid Argyll,[6] suggests that the gable-ended method of building may have replaced an earlier hipped-roof tradition, distinct from that of the 'Skye House'.[7]

The peasant houses of Lorn were, until the 19th century, invariably thatched. As early as 1804 a factor of the Breadalbane estate in Argyll complained that the excessive cultivation of corn 'for the sake of the straw for thatch' made it difficult to introduce a correct crop-rotation system,[8] but until the early years of the 20th century thatch was common even in those areas, such as Ballachulish, where supplies of roofing slate were readily available. Although no thatched roof survives in the region, early photographs show that several techniques were employed in the late 19th century. Whereas the roped thatch characteristic of the Western Isles was common,[9] there were several examples of 'scollop thatching', cruder in execution but similar in method to those found at the present day in Northern Ireland.[10] Two varieties of

[1] *Dunstaffnage Case*, 165–7. For a similar reckoning in cruck-couples in 1645, cf. *Taymouth Bk.*, 101.
[2] *Inventory of Argyll*, i, p. 27.
[3] St Fond, *Journey*, i, 292; Lettice, I, *Letters on a Tour through Various Parts of Scotland in the Year 1792* (1794), 281–2; for extant examples at Camserney, Perthshire, cf. *PSAS*, xc (1956–7), 87–9.
[4] The remains of scarf-jointed cruck-couples secured with iron bolts were noted at Upper Gylen Farm, Kerrera (NM 812270).
[5] Photographs of houses at Duror, taken by E Beveridge in 1882, in N.M.R.S.

[6] *Folk-Life*, iii (1965), 62–4.
[7] Illustrations of buildings at Inveraray and Kilchrenan (Pl. 103B), noted by R A Gailey (*Gwerin*, iii (1960–2), 13–14), and photographs of a house at Duror (in N.M.R.S.), show structures with square angles and steeply-pitched hipped roofs.
[8] S.R.O., Breadalbane Collection, GD 112/47/1, letter from John Campbell dated 30 July 1804.
[9] Lettice, op. cit., 281.
[10] Cf. Buchanan, R H, 'Thatch and Thatching in North-East Ireland', *Gwerin*, i (1956–7), 123–42.

scollop thatching were in use, namely that which employed rods bent into the form of staples to secure the bundles of straw,[1] and another type in which horizontal fixing-rods were themselves held in place by pegs or 'hairpin-rods'.[2] Just outside the boundary of Lorn, at Onich, Inverness-shire, there were several buildings where both forms of scollop were used on the same roof. A rarer thatching-type, hitherto identified only in a limited area of Co. Antrim,[3] was that known as pegged thatch, in which horizontal ropes were fixed by wooden pegs; these performed the function of the vertical ropes of conventional roped thatch.[4]

Until the last quarter of the 18th century, the normal unit of settlement was the joint-farm, cultivated in run-rig by a group of tenants. Even within the limits of a single estate, agricultural improvement was introduced intermittently and with varying degrees of efficiency. Thus, while the 4th Earl of Breadalbane had the township of Stronmilchan divided into crofts by a professional surveyor, John MacArthur, as early as 1784,[5] his factor in Nether Lorn re-organised farms in that region, some years later, only in a half-hearted way, making no provision for the introduction of new techniques of building and agriculture. The tenants of the joint-farm of Ardnahua who, as part of this re-organisation, were moved in 1790 to a new settlement at Tigh-Cuil (No. 345), built houses which were thoroughly traditional both in construction and layout. From about 1800, however, improvement was pursued vigorously, through subsidies or direct building, by landlords in most parts of Lorn, and large barns or complete steadings were constructed on the home farms of many estates (cf. pp. 258–9, 265). Those members of the tenant-farmer class who rose to become farmers of amalgamated holdings were accommodated in well-built two-storeyed houses, such as Dunstaffnage Mains Farm (No. 341), which are similar to the tacksmen's houses of the previous generation (cf. Nos. 309 and 316). Single-storeyed cottages with gable-fireplaces became the standard form of housing for agricultural as well as industrial workers (cf. No. 356), and many earlier dwellings, such as Cadderlie (No. 339), were adapted to this type.

Lorn was noted as a centre for the rearing of black cattle, and deserted shieling-sites for summer grazing are numerous. The two examples included in this volume (Nos. 337 and 343) are similar in character to those recorded in Kintyre,[6] but are of interest because of the documentary evidence for their continued use until the 1790s.

Industrial and Engineering Works, including Quarries

The outstanding item in this category is the foundry at Bonawe (No. 362), whose extensive and well-preserved remains constitute one of the most notable monuments of the early Industrial Revolution in Britain. Iron-smelting by means of primitive bloomery furnaces had been practised in many parts of Scotland from a very early date, but large-scale manufacture was seldom attempted before the first half of the 18th century. At this period the industry was still charcoal-based, and it was almost inevitable that English and Irish ironmasters, compelled

---

[1] Photographs of buildings at Glencoe in N.M.R.S.
[2] Photographs of buildings at Duror, Glencoe and Kilchrenan, in N.M.R.S.
[3] Buchanan, op. cit., 134 and fig. 1 on p. 129 (incorrectly captioned).
[4] Photographs of buildings at Oban and Stronmilchan, in N.M.R.S.
[5] S.R.O., Breadalbane Collection, GD 112/9/51, Argyll Rental, 1783–4; cf. Wordsworth, *Tour*, 141.
[6] *Inventory of Argyll*, i, Nos. 341, 345.

to look ever further afield for supplies of fuel, should decide to exploit the vast timber resources of the West Highlands. The earliest of the Scottish charcoal blast-furnaces appears to have been the one at Glen Kinglass (No. 358), on upper Loch Etive, established by an Irish company in or before 1725, and this was soon followed by ironworks at Glengarry (1727) and Abernethy (c. 1730), both in Inverness-shire, Bonawe (1753), and Goatfield (1754), Mid Argyll, all of which were undertaken by English operators. In most cases iron-ore was imported by sea from the Furness district of Lancashire, but local sources of bog-iron were also utilized where available. Timber rights were negotiated with neighbouring proprietors, making provision for the periodic felling of suitable woodland and the construction of charcoal-burning stances (Nos. 360 and 361), whence charcoal was transported directly to the furnaces. This last operation was usually undertaken by water, the deeply penetrating network of sea-lochs along the western seaboard affording easy communication with large areas of otherwise inaccessible forest.

The enterprises of the 1720s and 1730s were short-lived and have left few traces, although part of the furnace itself may still be seen at Glen Kinglass. At Goatfield and Bonawe, however, production continued well into the 19th century and considerable remains survive. All these ironworks were, of necessity, established in comparatively remote districts, and tended to form small self-contained industrial communities, peopled mainly by incomers whose way of life was quite alien to Highland traditions. The architectural effects of this isolation are clearly evident at Bonawe, where the Newland Company made itself responsible, not only for the erection of a furnace with its associated charcoal- and ore-sheds, but also for the provision of workers' dwellings, a manager's house, and numerous ancillary buildings. Moreover, several of these buildings display distinctive techniques of construction indicating that they were erected under the direction of English Lake-District craftsmen employing materials imported from that area. The most interesting of the structures now remaining at Bonawe are being consolidated and repaired by the Department of the Environment.

Another local enterprise undertaken by the proprietors of the Bonawe ironworks was the establishment of a gunpowder-works at Melfort (No. 363) in 1838. Here, too, it was necessary to import some of the principal ingredients in the manufacturing-process, such as sulphur and saltpetre, but there was an abundant supply of charcoal, and water-power was readily available to operate the grinding-mills. Production ceased following an explosion in 1867, but some of the buildings subsequently continued in use as a saw-mill. The most interesting structures to survive are the mill-lade and the storage-sheds, one of which is very similar in character to those at Bonawe.

The most important centres of quarrying in Lorn were at Easdale (No. 356) and Ballachulish (No. 350), which produced high-quality slate suitable for most building purposes, especially roofing. It is evident that the slate-beds of the Easdale district were worked sporadically during the medieval period, since grave-slabs of slate dating from the 15th century, if not earlier, are common in that area,[1] whereas the Ballachulish quarries were not opened until the end of the 17th century. Both quarries were considerably developed during the following century, although production at Easdale was hampered by the fact that the best beds lay near

---

[1] Slate employed in the construction of several West Highland castles, including Moy, Mull, and Breachacha, Coll, was probably derived from the Easdale area.

sea-level and were susceptible to flooding. This difficulty was, however, overcome by the introduction of improved methods of pumping, and with the rapid expansion of the building-industry in the 19th century both quarries entered upon a period of great prosperity, serving markets throughout the British Isles and as far afield as America. But after reaching a peak of production during the last quarter of the 19th century the industry swiftly declined, manufacture at Easdale ceasing in about 1914 and at Ballachulish in 1955. The principal remains comprise disused quarries and spoil-heaps, harbours and several groups of workers' dwellings dating from about the first quarter of the 19th century.

In contrast to slate, freestone suitable for building-purposes was in short supply in Lorn, and recourse was generally had to neighbouring areas of the county such as Carsaig, on the Isle of Mull, and the Lochaline district of Morvern. When available, however, local deposits were worked, as for example at Bridge of Awe (No. 354) from which sandstone for the construction of Fraoch Eilean Castle (No. 290) appears to have been obtained during the second half of the 13th century. By the later Middle Ages the sandstone outcrops at the mouth of Loch Feochan (Nos. 349 and 351) and on the south shore of the island of Kerrera (p. 217) were also being exploited, and at Ardentallan (No. 349) production continued into the 19th century, at which period there was also some development of sandstone quarrying in Oban itself in consequence of the rapid expansion of the burgh (p. 242). The Barrnacarry outcrops, Loch Feochan (No. 351), again, were utilized for the production of millstones, although these were also quarried individually in the localities within which they were required (No. 352). About the middle of the 18th century the company that operated the Easdale slate-quarries attempted to develop a marble-quarry at Ardmaddy (No. 355), but this venture soon failed owing to a shortage of skilled workmen and increasing difficulties of extraction.

Another important branch of the quarrying-industry in Lorn was associated with the manufacture of lime for agriculture and building. The main centre of activity was the island of Lismore, where limestone is present in great quantity. Lime-burning on a commercial scale was begun on Lismore towards the end of the 18th century, but the main development of the industry took place during the following century, after which there was a rapid decline. The three principal centres of production were Port Kilcheran (No. 365), Port Ramsay (No. 366) and An Sàilean (No. 348), the last of which retains an interesting group of kilns with associated workers' dwellings and a small harbour.

Fewer traces survive of another once-flourishing Lismore industry, namely illicit whisky-distilling. Barley was plentiful on the island, and the rugged limestone terrain lent itself to the concealment of the stills (No. 359) and to secrecy in the shipping of the finished product to neighbouring districts. The industry reached its peak during the early years of the 19th century, but subsequently declined following changes in the law.

Finally in this section mention may be made of the lighthouse on Eilean Musdile (No. 357), off the south-west point of Lismore, which was erected in 1833 from a design by Robert Stevenson, engineer to the Commissioners of Northern Lights. This is a particularly well-preserved example of its period, and although the reflector-mechanism has been renewed, the original superstructure, which incorporates a wealth of meticulously-detailed cast-ironwork, remains almost intact.

ROADS AND BRIDGES

The two military roads that pass through Lorn were constructed soon after the Forty-Five under the direction of Major Edward Caulfield, with the object of establishing additional links between the military bases in the Lowlands and the rudimentary network of roads and garrisons developed in the Central and Northern Highlands during the two previous decades. Between them these two routes brought Fort William into direct communication with Stirling, Dumbarton and Inveraray, thus creating the basis of the present West Highland road-system. Both routes presented formidable difficulties of terrain, and nowhere were these more marked than in the combined section of road that traverses Black Mount and the Devil's Staircase (p. 297). Few bridges were erected at first, but the fine single-arch structure at Bridge of Orchy (p. 297) dates from *c.* 1751, while other early examples survive in the neighbourhood of Dalmally (p. 296).

Other notable bridges in Lorn are those at Dalmally itself (No. 370) and at Bridge of Awe (No. 368), both erected by the Commissioners of Supply *c.* 1780, and the well-known 'Atlantic Bridge' at Clachan, Isle of Seil (No. 369), whose design appears to have been amended by the architect Robert Mylne.

ARCHITECTURAL FRAGMENTS, CARVED STONES ETC.

The most notable items in this category are the group of miscellaneous architectural fragments and fittings now incorporated into, or preserved within, St Conan's Church, Loch Awe (No. 377). These include a late medieval window formerly at St Mary's, Leith, portions of window-tracery from the abbey of Iona and a bell from Skerryvore Lighthouse. At Creagan (No. 373) there is an interesting graffito of a West Highland galley which may be compared with the carvings at the Old Parish Church at Kilchattan, Luing, described under No. 256.

INVENTORY
of the Ancient and Historical Monuments
of Lorn

CHAMBERED CAIRNS

The code number in round brackets immediately following the title of each article in this section conforms to the system outlined by Henshall, *Chambered Tombs*, ii, 312–13.

1. Chambered Cairn, Achnacree (ARG 36). This impressive cairn stands in trees on the N edge of the Moss of Achnacree at a distance of 0·6 km SW of the farmhouse of Achnacreemore. The peat does not appear to have grown over the perimeter of the cairn, but leaves a natural hollow round it which may be compared with the hollow surrounding cairn No. 64. The cairn was excavated by Smith in 1871 and, as the passage and chamber are no longer accessible, the following description and plan (Fig. 7) are partly based on the published report.[1]

The cairn is about 24·4 m in diameter and now stands to a height of some 3·4 m on the S and 4·1 m on the NE, although it is said to have been about 4·6 m high before excavation; it consists of small and medium-sized stones, interspersed with a few large boulders. A low platform of cairn material, now grass-covered and about 1 m high, extends round the base of the cairn and increases the overall diameter to about 40 m. The entrance to the passage is on the SE side of the cairn and is marked by four upright stones, one of which is now leaning out of position. The central pair, set about 1·2 m apart and protruding 1·3 m and 0·4 m above the cairn material, are the portal stones on either side of the passage, while the flanking pair may be the remains of a shallow forecourt.[2] The passage, which measured 6·4 m in length and 0·6 m in width, was constructed of upright slate slabs about 1 m in height, and the roof was composed of similar slabs. The excavator recorded that the passage was filled with stones, and these seem to indicate a deliberate blocking after the final burial-deposit. The chamber comprised three compartments. The outer, measuring 1·8 m by 1·2 m and about 2·1 m in height, was constructed of upright slabs and dry-stone walling supplemented by corbelling, and was covered by a single capstone. The central compartment, measuring 2·0 m by 0·7 m and 1·6 m in height, was entered across a large transverse slab, and the entrance itself appeared to have been deliberately sealed with stones 'built firmly in after the chamber had been completed'.[3] The sides of this chamber were formed of blocks of stone supplemented by dry-stone walling, and it was roofed by a single capstone. The inner compartment was entered across a sill-stone, and measured 1·4 m by 0·9 m and 1·7 m in height. A combination of slabs and dry-stone walling had been employed in its construction, and it was roofed by a single massive capstone some 0·4 m thick. Each side-wall was constructed of two slabs set lengthwise one above the other, in such a way that a narrow ledge was formed at their junction. On these two ledges a number of white quartz pebbles had been deliberately deposited. One end of the capstone of the inner compartment can still be seen in the disturbed central crater of the cairn, through which Smith gained access to the chamber. Three Neolithic pottery bowls were discovered in the course of the excavation—a fragmentary vessel from the outer compartment, and one complete (Pl. 3A) and one fragmentary bowl from the inner compartment. These finds are in the National Museum of Antiquities of Scotland.

About 9 m to the NW of the edge of the cairn the tops of three upright slabs can be seen, and it is possible that these are what Smith described as the remains of a cist;[4] their present arrangement, however, is not consistent with this interpretation, and it seems unlikely that they belong to a prehistoric structure.

922363   NM 93 NW   May 1971

2. Chambered Cairn, Achnacreebeag (ARG 37). This cairn (Fig. 8) stands in pasture 275 m W of the farmhouse of Achnacreebeag and 700 m E of the chambered cairn of Achnacree (No. 1). Two burial-chambers are visible in amongst the surviving cairn material, and between 1968 and 1970 officers of the Commission undertook the excavation of the site in order to examine the relationship between the chambers and to explore the possibility that they represented different phases in the cairn's history. The excavation confirmed that there were two periods of construction, the first comprising a simple chamber covered by a round cairn. Subsequently a small passage-grave was added to the SE edge of the cairn, and the cairn itself was enlarged to assume its present oval shape. The following account is a summary of the published excavation report.[5]

The original, or NW, chamber (Pl. 6c) is composed of

---

[1] *PSAS*, ix (1870–2), 409–15.
[2] Henshall, *Chambered Tombs*, ii, 355.
[3] *PSAS*, ix (1870–2), 413.
[4] Ibid., 99.
[5] Ibid., cii (1969–70), 31–55.

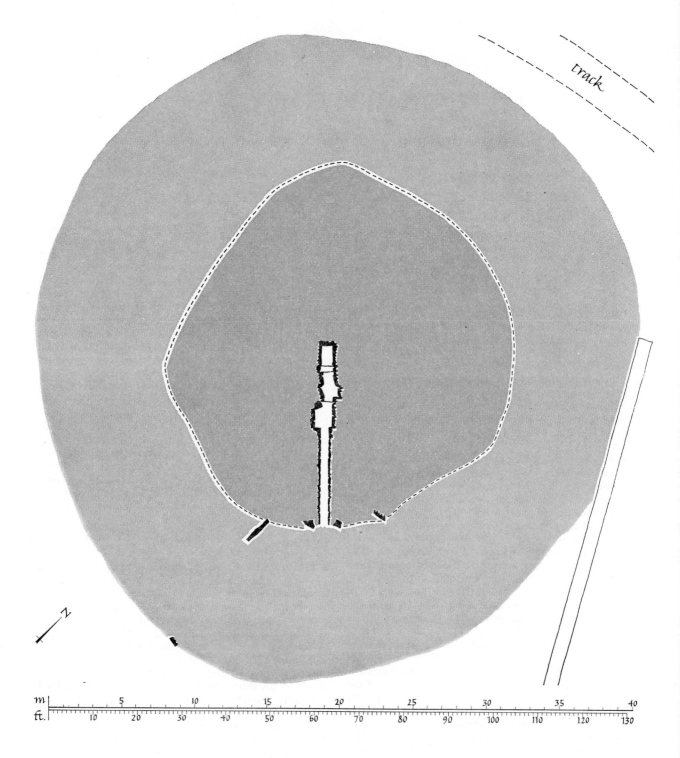

track

m
5　10　15　20　25　30　35　40
ft.
10　20　30　40　50　60　70　80　90　100　110　120　130

Fig. 7. Chambered cairn, Achnacree (No. 1); after Smith

38

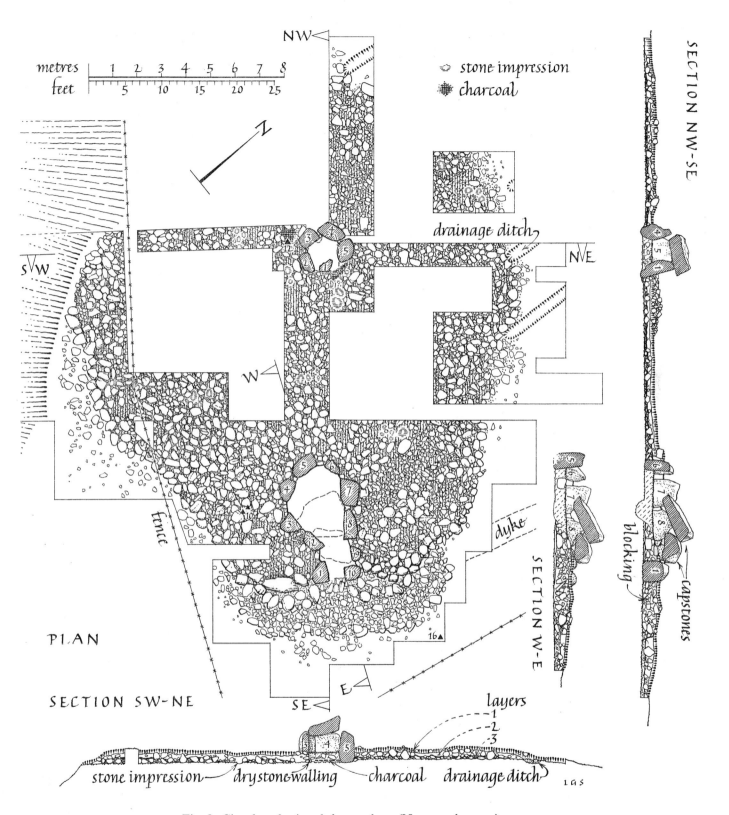

metres 1 2 3 4 5 6 7 8
feet 5 10 15 20 25

N

NW

⌐ stone impression
▥ charcoal

drainage ditch

SW

NE

W

SECTION NW-SE

fence

dyke

SECTION W-E

blocking

capstones

PLAN

SECTION SW-NE

SE

E

layers
—1
—2
—3

stone impression — drystone walling — charcoal — drainage ditch

I G S

Fig. 8. Chambered cairn, Achnacreebeag (No. 2; scale 1:150)

39

five upright boulders with a flat granite capstone; the enclosed area measures 0·9 m by 1·25 m and between 0·9 m and 1·2 m in height. Entry to this simple chamber could have been made only between stones Nos. 1 and 5, and once the surrounding cairn had been built no further access would have been possible, as there was no indication of a passage through the cairn material. The cairn had been severely robbed and only the basal layer of stones remained; the kerb-stones, however, which survived in two places on the S and NE, showed that the cairn had been roughly circular on plan, and had measured about 18 m in diameter. Three small fragments of unworked flint were the only objects that could be associated with this phase of activity on the site.

The passage-grave, constructed on the SE perimeter of the cairn, was entered through a passage, 1·4 m in length, 1·1 m in breadth and about 0·9 m in height; the chamber consists of seven large granite blocks with dry-stone walling between them (Pl. 6A, B). Two of the capstones survive, but only one, which covers the rear half of the passage, remains in its original position. In order to cover the passage-grave the original cairn was increased in length to 20·7 m, maintaining its original breadth of 18 m at the NW end. After the deposition of the final burials, the chamber and passage were sealed with a blocking of earth and stones which extended in a semicircle outside the entrance to give the cairn its final oval shape.

Although the interior of the chamber had been considerably disturbed, evidence of two distinct burial-phases was discovered in the SW half, which remained comparatively intact. The earlier phase was represented by sherds of several Neolithic vessels and a plano-convex flint knife, and the final deposit, which may be linked to the blocking of the tomb, was associated with sherds of Beaker pottery, a number of flints, jet disc-beads and small fragments of cremated bone. The finds are now in the National Museum of Antiquities of Scotland.

929363   NM 93 NW   September 1970

3. Chambered Cairn, Ardchonnell (ARG 50). This impressive cairn (Fig. 9) occupies a clearing in a large forestry plantation on the E side of Loch Awe, 1·2 km ENE of Ardchonnell. It appears at the present time as a bare stony mound, trapezoidal on plan and rising to a maximum height of 4·3 m, with the long axis aligned NE and SW. Its length is about 33 m, and the breadth decreases from 19 m at the NE end to about 12 m at the SW end, where the cairn has been considerably disturbed and is traversed by a modern stone wall. At the broader end of the cairn are the substantial remains of a burial-chamber. It measures 3·7 m in overall length and 0·8 m in maximum breadth, and is entered between a pair of portal stones, 0·5 m apart, and through a short ante-chamber with two flanking slabs at an angle to the passage. The chamber is irregular on plan and is composed of seven upright slabs and one surviving capstone. The S side of the chamber consists of two overlapping slabs, but the four slabs on the N side appear to be less carefully placed; this, however, may be due to the dis-

turbance of the chamber. Only the inner half of the chamber is still roofed, and the capstone, measuring 1·4 m by 1·4 m and up to 0·2 m in thickness, has been placed on the top of the upright slabs at a height of about 1 m above the present floor-level. The angle at which the portal stones are set in relation to the longer axis of the

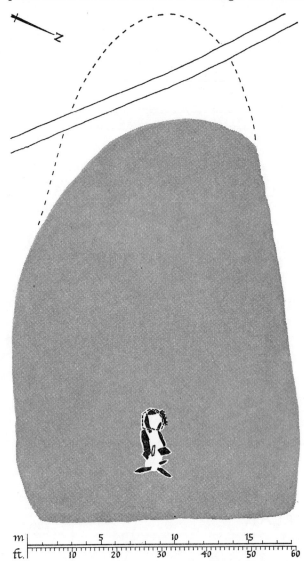

Fig. 9. Chambered cairn, Ardchonnell (No. 3)

chamber suggests that they may originally have formed part of a concave façade to the cairn, in front of which there appears to be a considerable deposit of material blocking access to the tomb.

992127   NM 91 SE   May 1971

4. Chambered Cairn, Auchachenna (ARG 49). This cairn (Fig. 10) is situated 220 m SE of Auchachenna and within 500 m of the NW shore of Loch Awe. It has been built along a slight rocky spine and measures about 30 m in length with its long axis aligned NW and SE. Although it has been heavily robbed to provide stones for a wall which runs across its NW end, the surviving material, measuring 14 m in maximum breadth at the SE end and narrowing to about 11 m at the other, suggests that it was originally trapezoidal on plan. At the SE end of the cairn, where it stands to a height of 1·7 m above the surrounding ground, there are the remains of the chamber. It

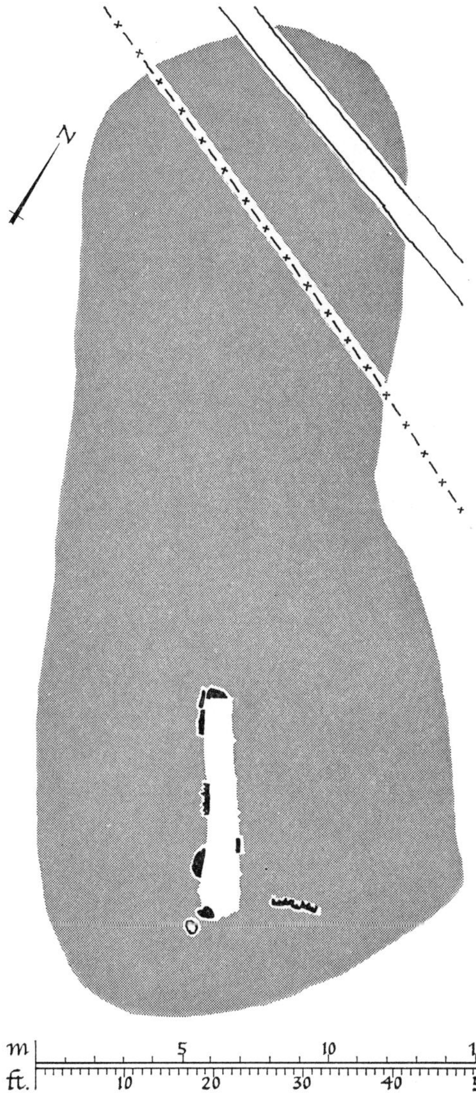

Fig. 10. Chambered cairn, Auchachenna (No. 4)

measures 6·9 m in length by 1·1 m in breadth and, although only one stone of the NE side survives, four slabs of the SW side and the rear-slab remain. The most impressive feature of the site, however, is the SW portal-stone which rises to a height of 1·45 m above the cairn. Three other stones of the façade, protruding up to 0·45 m

through the turf, are visible in the debris that blocks the forecourt area.

023210   NN 02 SW   June 1969

5. Chambered Cairn, Cladich (ARG 4). This cairn stands at a height of 90 m OD on a slight natural knoll in a cultivated field 550 m NE of Cladich village and 100 m SE of the public road. It has been so severely reduced by stone-robbing and ploughing that without excavation it is impossible to determine the original outline precisely, but as indicated on the plan (Fig. 11) it was probably oval in shape, measuring at least 25 m by 21 m, with the longer axis aligned NE and SW. Towards the NE end can be seen the remains of a burial-chamber,

Fig. 11. Chambered cairn, Cladich (No. 5)

now roofless, measuring about 4 m in length and 1·1 m in width internally, and having its longer axis aligned with that of the cairn. The stones now visible comprise the terminal slab, two adjacent side-slabs and a short transverse slab, forming the rear compartment of the chamber, together with another side-slab, one of the portal stones and what appears to be the stump of the other. Apart from the terminal slab, which protrudes 0·5 m above ground, and the NW portal-stone, which stands 1·1 m in height and is now leaning towards the SE,

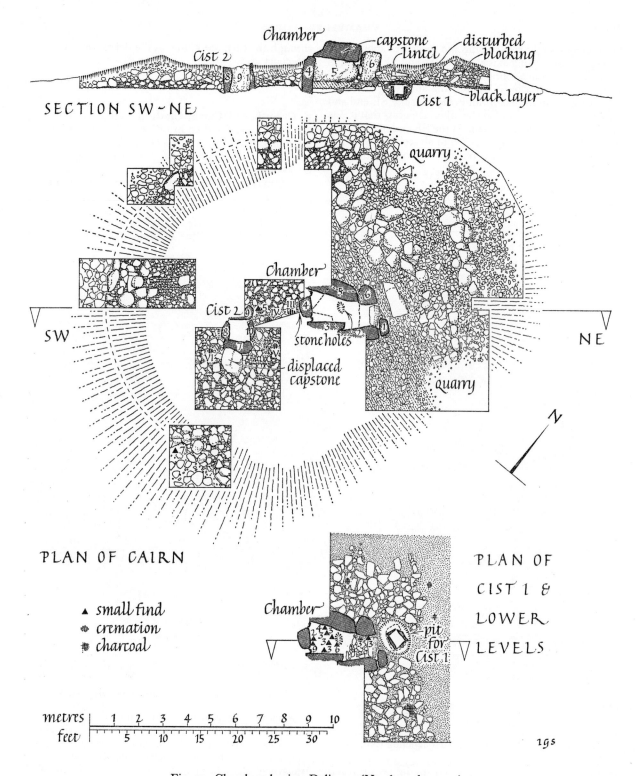

SECTION SW~NE

Chamber
capstone
lintel
disturbed blocking
Cist 2
black layer
Cist 1

quarry

Chamber

Cist 2

stone holes

displaced capstone

quarry

SW

NE

N

PLAN OF CAIRN

▲ small find
⊕ cremation
⊞ charcoal

Chamber

pit for Cist 1

PLAN OF CIST 1 & LOWER LEVELS

metres 1 2 3 4 5 6 7 8 9 10
feet   5   10   15   20   25   30

ig s

Fig. 12. Chambered cairn, Dalineun (No. 6; scale 1:150)

42

only the upper edges of the stones are visible. Each of the two triangular stones situated to the SSE of the NW portal-stone appears to be a broken stump, and while both of them may represent the shattered remains of the SE portal-stone, the SW one may possibly belong to the outermost side-slab of the SE side of the chamber. A large slab, measuring 1 m square and 0·4 m in greatest thickness, which is lying prone immediately SE of the chamber, is probably one of the original capstones.

100222   NN 12 SW   May 1970

6. Chambered Cairn, Dalineun (ARG 3). This cairn (Fig. 12) is situated 275 m S of the farmhouse of Dalineun at the S end of Loch Nell, and 180 m S of the round cairn (p. 52, no. 1). At the present time it is oval on plan, measuring 18 m by 15 m, with the longer axis aligned NE and SW; although it has been severely robbed of its stone, the grass-covered remains still stand to a height of 1·25 m. In the centre a chamber of Clyde type is exposed amongst the surviving cairn-material, and behind it the tops of the slabs of a large stone cist protrude above the turf. The excavation of the site was undertaken by the Commission's officers in 1970 and 1971 in an attempt to establish the chronological relationship between the two structures, and the following account is a summary of the excavation report.[1]

Because of the disturbance caused by the previous stone-robbing, the evidence provided by the excavation was not entirely conclusive, but four distinct phases of construction could be distinguished. The first phase saw the construction of the main burial-chamber within a heel-shaped cairn measuring about 12·5 m by 11 m. The chamber, which measures internally 2·5 m by 1·2 m and up to 1·4 m in height, is aligned NE and SW, and is composed of six large upright slabs roofed by a massive granite capstone. Two of the stones (Nos. 1 and 6 on Fig. 12) are the entrance-portals, and were originally spanned by a lintel-stone discovered in the course of the excavation lying dislodged outside the tomb (Pl. 7A). Entered across a low sill-stone, the chamber had been divided into two compartments by a transverse slab, but only the shallow socket in which this had been set was found, the stone itself having been removed. Although the deposits within the chamber had been previously rifled, two periods of burial were indicated by the finds. Two sherds of Neolithic pottery and a flint point probably represent the primary phase, and sherds of three Beaker vessels and a flint flake belong to the secondary period of burial in the tomb. In the second phase a small cist, measuring 0·6 m by 0·4 m and about 0·3 m in depth, was inserted into a pit in front of the entrance; cremated bones were discovered throughout the gravel fillings of both the cist and the pit. After the final burials in the chamber a semicircular blocking of stones (phase three) was piled in front of the tomb and the cairn assumed its present oval shape.

At a distance of 2 m behind the main chamber there is a massive cist measuring 0·85 m by 0·85 m and 1 m in depth (Pl. 7B). The cist itself, and the cairn material in the immediate vicinity, had suffered considerable disturbance, but it seems most likely that the cist was inserted into a hollow dug into the existing cairn (phase four). A Food Vessel associated with a number of cremated bones, which were found close to the N side of the cist, probably formed the original burial-deposit. All the finds from the site are now in the National Museum of Antiquities of Scotland.

879267   NM 82 NE   August 1971

7. Chambered Cairn (probable), Portnacroish (Site) (ARG 42). In the mid-18th century two travellers recorded their visits to a large cairn situated on the N side of Loch Laich opposite Castle Stalker (No. 285). Writing in 1758,[2] Burrell referred to 'a very large circular Heap of Stones, called Cairnbane, in which are said to be several Subterraneous Apartments, the Passages leading to them, supported by large Beams of Timber in some Places, in others by large Stones, the Entrance is now closed with a Stone . . .'. Two years later, however, Pococke[3] was able to enter the cairn, and recorded that 'on the west side of it a little way up is a very difficult entrance which leads to a cell about two yards long and one and a half broad, and this by a sort of door place to another about the same dimensions. I observed in some parts the stones on the sides are laid flat, in others edge way, and a little sloping, and large stones are laid across on the top; To the north of it is a low heap of stones, in which three mouths of entrances are very visible, and there seemed to be two more; these were probably for different Branches of the family; the large one is twelve yards long at the top and about a yard broad: It is not improbable that these Cells were built all round and several stories of them one over another. They are something in the style of the Picts houses but the entrance in the Cells of those were at the Bottom'. This cairn, which was probably a prehistoric chambered cairn,[4] is no longer visible.

c. 9247   NM 94 NW   May 1970

8. Chambered Cairn, Port Sonachan (ARG 5). The denuded remains of this cairn (Fig. 13) stand on a terrace about 70 m above the SE side of Loch Awe and 235 m SE of the Port Sonachan Hotel. The cairn, which is aligned E and W, was originally trapezoidal on plan, measuring 29·5 m by 13 m, but it has been heavily robbed of its stone, and a rectangular secondary enclosure has been built on its E end. The chamber, at the broader (W) end, measures at least 3·5 m by 1 m internally, but only its inner end is undisturbed. The innermost side-slabs measure 2·2 m and 1·2 m in length respectively, and the end-slab at the rear is 0·9 m in length; the S side-slab protrudes 0·8 m above the

---

[1] *PSAS*, civ (1971–2), forthcoming.
[2] Burrell, 'Tour', fol. 25.
[3] Pococke, *Tours*, 95.
[4] Henshall, *Chambered Tombs*, ii, 361–2.

present floor-level. The only other slab on the S side, which stands at the entrance to the chamber, may be a portal stone, but its partner on the N lies dislodged nearby, and without excavation it is impossible to interpret this part of the chamber fully. Lying to the NW of the chamber, beyond the perimeter of the cairn, there are two large slabs which may originally have been

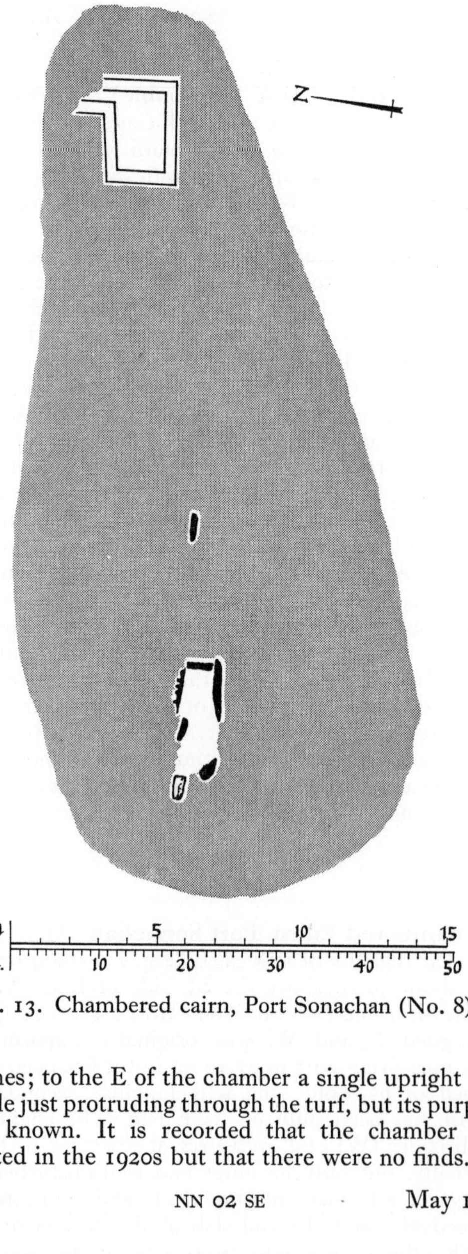

robbed, probably to provide material for the modern track and stone wall that pass it on the E side. The cairn appears as an irregular grass-covered mound of earth and stones measuring 15 m by 10·5 m and standing to a height of about 2 m. One possible kerb-stone remains in position on the SW side. At the broader end of the cairn four stones protrude through the turf, comprising the transverse slab and three side-slabs of a roofless chamber measuring at least 3·7 m by 1·4 m internally. The chamber has consisted of two compart-

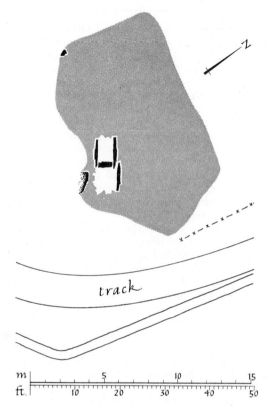

Fig. 14. Chambered cairn, Shuna Cottage, Shuna, Nether Lorn (No. 9)

Fig. 13. Chambered cairn, Port Sonachan (No. 8)

capstones; to the E of the chamber a single upright slab is visible just protruding through the turf, but its purpose is not known. It is recorded that the chamber was excavated in the 1920s but that there were no finds.[1]

050206   NN 02 SE   May 1971

9. Chambered Cairn, Shuna Cottage, Shuna, Nether Lorn (ARG 51). This cairn (Fig. 14) is situated on the SW side of the island of Shuna, 213 m ENE of Shuna Cottage. The cairn and its chamber have been extensively

ments with a transverse slab between them. Only the N side-slab of the front compartment survives *in situ*, overlapping the side-slab of the inner compartment and protruding 1 m above the turf; the S side-slab has been dislodged and now lies at the side of the mound. The N side-slab of the rear compartment, which has measured 1·5 m by 1·0 m internally, protrudes 0·5 m through the turf but the S side-slab is only just visible. Because of the damage done to the site it is no longer possible to determine either the original shape of the cairn or the position of any forecourt or façade.

760075   NM 70 NE   May 1970

[1] *DES (1955)*, 8.

CAIRNS AND BARROW

10. Cairn and Standing Stone, Achacha. A cairn and a standing stone are situated in an area of upland pasture between Cnoc Reamhar and the Allt Garraich burn at a height of about 50 m OD. The cairn (Fig. 15) is oval on plan and measures 4·6 m from N to S by 4·0 m transversely. It is kerbed by a series of large boulders, mainly granite erratics measuring up to 0·7 m in height, fifteen of which remain *in situ*; others are lying dislodged nearby. The cairn material is rather lower than the kerb,

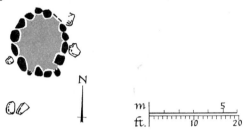

Fig. 15. Cairn, Achacha (No. 10)

standing to a height of only 0·3 m above the surrounding ground, and it seems unlikely that it was ever appreciably higher. This cairn belongs to a distinct class of monument, which is further discussed on p. 10.

The standing stone is situated 89 m to the E of the cairn and is 2·5 m high; it is aligned approximately E and W and measures 0·65 m by 0·33 m at the base, rising with a taper to a slightly rounded top.

943407 (Cairn)   NM 94 SW   May 1970
944407 (Standing Stone)

11. Cairn, Achaleven. This cairn stands at a height of about 15 m OD in level pasture S of the railway and some 40 m NW of the house called Cairnhill at Achaleven. It appears as a grass-covered stony mound measuring 16 m by 14 m and 1·25 m in height. An electricity-pole has been erected on its E perimeter.

921341   NM 93 SW   May 1971

12. Cairn, Achanamoine. A large cairn is situated at 15 m OD on a low ridge in an arable field about 275 m NW of Achanamoine farmhouse and 75 m SW of the public road. Heavily overgrown with scrub, it measures at least 23 m in diameter and stands to a maximum height of 1·8 m. A considerable quantity of stones has been removed from the top, but the amount of cairn material that survives suggests that the lower levels remain relatively undisturbed.

901408   NM 94 SW   May 1966

13. Cairn, Achanancarn. Situated in a small patch of scrub 65 m SW of Achanancarn farmhouse, and at a height of about 25 m OD, there are the wasted remains of a cairn measuring 23 m by 20 m and 0·9 m in maximum height. It is so heavily overgrown that very few stones are visible.

926356   NM 93 NW   April 1967

14. Cairns, Achnaba. The following five cairns are all situated within 500 m of Achnaba farmhouse (No. 303) at heights between about 20 m and 30 m OD.

(1) Situated 90 m SE of the farmhouse, this cairn stands by the E side of the approach road at 946364. It has been severely robbed and subsequently used as a dump for field clearance, and now measures 15 m in diameter and 0·9 m in height. A number of large boulders are lying scattered over the surface of the cairn but none of them are in their original positions.

(2) A second cairn is situated 135 m SSW of (1) in an arable field S of the approach road at 945362. Largely grass-grown, it has been trimmed by the plough to a squarish shape and now measures 22·5 by 21 m and 1·8 m in height. An electricity-pole has been erected on it.

(3) A third cairn, 170 m SSW of (2), stands in trees at 944361 on the edge of the bluff overlooking Loch Etive. It has been so severely damaged by robbing and later dumping that without excavation it is no longer possible to determine its size; it seems likely, however, that it originally measured at least 23 m in diameter and 2 m in height.

(4) A fourth cairn, 230 m NW of (3), is situated at 942363, beside the N edge of the approach road and 135 m ENE of the spot where the cist No. 81 was discovered. A prominent grass-grown stony mound with a lone tree growing on it, it measures 15·3 m in diameter and 1·7 m in height. Fifteen original kerb-stones are still visible *in situ*, nine of them forming an almost unbroken arc on the W perimeter of the cairn.

(5) A fifth cairn (940363) stands 185 m W of (4) on a low natural rise at the W edge of an arable field. Now largely grass-grown, it measures 18·6 m in diameter and 2·4 m in greatest height. A quarry has been driven into the centre from the E.

NM 93 NW   April 1967

15. Cairn, Allt an Dùnain. This cairn, 1·5 km NW of Hayfield, is situated at a height of about 120 m OD in broken ground above the E bank of the Allt an Dùnain. It is 10 m in diameter and still stands to a height of 1 m, although it has been robbed to provide material for a small rectangular enclosure which adjoins it on the E side.

062245   NN 02 SE   May 1970

16. Cairns, Aon Garbh, Lismore. Three cairns are situated approximately in line from NE to SW on the crest of the ridge known as Aon Garbh.

(1) The first, situated at the SW end of the group, measures about 12·2 m in diameter and 1·4 m in height. It is composed of large angular blocks and several kerb-stones are visible intermittently round the perimeter.

(2) The second is situated in a saddle of the ridge about 18 m NE of (1). It is partly grass-grown, measures from 9·1 m to 7·6 m in diameter, and stands to a height of about 1 m.

(3) The third, situated about 105 m NE of (2), measures 7·6 m in diameter and 1 m in height.

(1) and (2) 802375,   NM 83 NW   June 1968
(3) 803376

17. Cairn (probable), Ariogan 1. On the summit of a low hill about 280 m NNW of Ariogan farmhouse there are the much-denuded remains of what has probably been a prehistoric cairn. Roughly circular on plan, it appears as a largely grass-grown stony mound measuring approximately 4·9 m in diameter and not more than 0·3 m in height. Where the mound has been disturbed by recent stone-robbing, it can be seen to consist mainly of rounded boulders of no great size.

863275   NM 82 NE   May 1967

18. Cairn (probable), Ariogan 2. The irregularly-shaped stony mound situated on a gently sloping shoulder of moorland some 840 m W of Ariogan farmhouse appears to represent the wasted remains of a burial-cairn of prehistoric date. It measures about 6 m across, stands to a height of 0·6 m, and has been severely disturbed by stone-robbing.

857273   NM 82 NE   May 1967

19. Cairn, Ballachulish House. The remains of this cairn (Fig. 16) are situated 300 m N of Ballachulish House (No. 311), on the N end of a low gravel ridge.

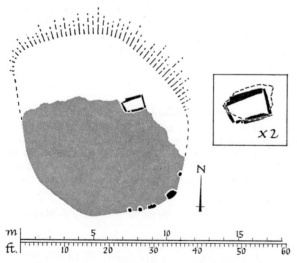

Fig. 16. Cairn, Ballachulish House (No. 19)

The N half has been destroyed, and the irregular shape of the S half, which measures 11·4 m by 8 m, is due largely to recent damage by ploughing and to the

dumping of stones cleared from the adjacent field. Five of the original kerb-stones, however, remain in position on the SE perimeter, and at the present time the cairn stands to a maximum height of 0·75 m. At the N edge there is a cist which has been partly dug into the natural gravel; it measures 1·3 m by 0·7 m and 0·6 m in depth, and is covered by a massive capstone (1·6 m by 1·0 m and 0·35 m in maximum thickness). Excavation by the Commission's officers revealed that the contents had been previously disturbed, but, although no skeletal remains were recovered, several fragments of a Food Vessel were found on the floor of the cist.[1] The Food Vessel is now in the National Museum of Antiquities of Scotland.

The 'cairn' recorded by Christison 120 m to the W appears to be an isolated natural gravel mound.[2]

048595   NN 05 NW   August 1972

20. 'Cairns', Ballimeanoch. It has been stated that two long mounds situated about 640 m NNW of the farm of Ballimeanoch on the E side of Loch Awe may be the remains of prehistoric long cairns.[3] Examination of the mounds suggests, however, that they are of natural origin.

008172   NN 01 NW   May 1971

21. Cairns, Balure. About 750 m SW of Balure farmhouse there is a group of three cairns, situated on a bleak heather-covered moss at a height of about 12 m OD.

(1) The most westerly of the group, which has the name Càrn Bàn, measures about 23 m in diameter and 3 m in height. A shallow pit has been sunk in the top, but otherwise the cairn appears to be undisturbed.

(2) Situated 220 m ENE of (1), the centre cairn[4] measures 13·7 m in diameter and 1·2 m in greatest height. A considerable quantity of stones has been removed from it, and the capstone of a large cist is now partly exposed. It is a massive slab measuring at least 3 m by 2·1 m and 0·4 m in thickness; a portion of one of the side-slabs supporting the capstone is also visible. The interior of the cist is choked with debris.

(3) The easternmost cairn, 135 m ESE of (2), measures 12 m in diameter and 0·5 m high above present ground-level. A trial excavation, however, carried out in 1963 by members of the Lorn Archaeological Society,[5] revealed that the visible cairn material represents only a comparatively small proportion of the whole, the remainder

[1] The Commissioners are indebted to Commander I T Clark, OBE, Mr H J Haldane, WS, and the Ballachulish Estate Company Limited for assistance during this work.
[2] *PSAS*, xxv (1890–1), 130.
[3] *DES (1960)*, 4; Henshall, *Chambered Tombs*, ii, 364 (ARG 47).
[4] Listed by Henshall as an unclassified chambered cairn (ARG 43), *Chambered Tombs*, ii, 362.
[5] *DES (1963)*, 8. A further report has been deposited in the N.M.R.S.

being hidden by a layer of peat estimated to be at least 1·5 m thick. The cairn material, consisting of water-worn stones of smallish size, shells, quartz pebbles and soil, was removed to a depth of about 0·8 m below turf-level, but further investigation became impossible because of the waterlogged condition of the site. Probing, however, suggested that the cairn may originally have measured as much as 3 m in height and 18 m in diameter. At the end of the investigation the cairn was restored, as far as possible, to its previous state.

(1) 893414, (2) 895414,   NM 84 SE   April 1967
(3) 897414

22. Cairn, Balygrundle (North), Lismore. This grass-covered cairn stands 60 m SW of the dun No. 178. It is 17 m in diameter and has been heavily robbed of its stone to provide material for nearby dry-stone walls and possibly also for the dun itself, but it still stands in places up to 1·5 m in height and is now surmounted by a modern cairn.

836399   NM 83 NW   May 1968

23. Cairns, Balygrundle (South), Lismore. There are two cairns situated in broken ground S of Balygrundle farmhouse and within 200 m of the shore.

(1) One cairn, named Dùn Uamha Chradh, stands on a rocky ridge 500 m SSE of Balygrundle at a height of about 35 m OD. Largely grass-grown, it measures 16 m in diameter and 1·8 m in height; the top has been levelled and is surmounted by a small modern cairn. Five kerb-stones are visible on the S arc of the perimeter.

(2) The other cairn, 365 m SW of (1), is situated near the N end of a rock ridge at a height of about 30 m OD. Measuring 14·6 m in diameter and 1·4 m in height, it is almost completely turf-covered. No kerb-stones are visible, but in the SW quadrant a long thin slab, measuring 1·0 m in length, 0·4 m in breadth and 0·15 m in thickness, can be seen protruding above the cairn material. Although clearly dislodged, its size and shape suggest that it may originally have formed part of a cist.

(1) 840395, (2) 836394   NM 83 NW   May 1968

24. Cairn, Barbreck. This cairn is situated at a height of 90 m OD in broken ground 640 m ESE of Barbreck farmhouse and 135 m NNW of the dun No. 180. It appears as a grass-grown stony mound measuring 8·7 m by 9·0 m and 1·0 m in height. Near the E perimeter a large block can be seen protruding 0·5 m above the surface.

049218   NN 02 SW   May 1971

25. Cairn, Barochreal. Situated in the middle of a level field, about 185 m W of Barochreal farmhouse, there is a roughly circular grass-grown cairn measuring 9·8 m in average diameter and 1·7 m in height. It appears to have been kerbed by a series of massive

boulders, several of which survive *in situ* on the perimeter of the S half, the largest measuring 1·1 m by 0·5 m and protruding as much as 0·8 m above ground-level.

833206   NM 82 SW   May 1966

26. Cairn, Barr Beag. The summit of a natural knoll on the lower slopes of Barr Beag, about 320 m NNW of Strontoiller farmhouse, is occupied by the remains of an oval cairn. It appears as a grass-covered stony mound measuring 11·0 m by 13·3 m and standing to a height of 1·2 m; its centre has been severely disturbed by stone-robbing.

907297   NM 92 NW   May 1972

27. Cairn, Barr Mór 1, Lismore. The cairn (Fig. 17) situated on the summit of Barr Mór (126 m OD) is surmounted by an Ordnance Survey triangulation station. It measures 6·9 m in diameter by 1·2 m in height,

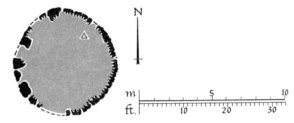

Fig. 17. Cairn, Barr Mór 1, Lismore (No. 27)

and the kerb, which is formed of large boulders up to 0·55 m in height, is almost complete. In some places two courses of kerb-stones are visible, but this may be due to the fact that the cairn was rebuilt in 1933.[1]

814388   NM 83 NW   May 1968

28. Cairn, Barr Mór 2, Lismore. This cairn stands at a height of 100 m OD on the SW slopes of Barr Mór and about 400 m SW of the summit. Situated on top of a small rocky hillock, it measures 17 m by 15·5 m and 2·3 m in height. A considerable quantity of stones has been removed from the top and flanks of the cairn to build a near-by wall.

812385   NM 83 NW   July 1970

29. Cairn, Càrn Bàn, Achnacarron. This cairn occupies the summit of a natural knoll which overlooks the NW side of Loch Awe 700 m SW of Achnacarron. It is a flat-topped grassy mound measuring about 23 m in diameter and standing to a height of 1·5 m. Four massive kerb-stones survive on the SW side, measuring 0·7 m by 0·5 m and up to 1·0 m in height.

053218   NN 02 SE   May 1970

---

[1] *TGAS*, new series, ix (1937–40), 110.

30. Cairn, Càrn Breugach, Kerrera. On the summit of Càrn Breugach (188 m OD), the highest point on the island, there is a roughly circular grass-grown cairn measuring 15·5 m in diameter and 1·75 m in maximum height. It appears to have been composed for the most part of fairly small stones, but several massive boulders which protrude through the turf on the S and SSW perimeter may belong to an original kerb. The centre of the cairn has been disturbed by treasure-seekers, and more recently a wooden bench, a small marker cairn and an Ordnance Survey triangulation station have been erected on it.

815278   NM 82 NW   April 1970

31. Cairn, Càrn Mór, Lismore. This cairn stands on a spine of rock 182 m W of the cathedral (No. 267), at a height of about 60 m OD. Measuring 11 m by 8 m and 1·7 m in height, it is composed of smallish stones and has recently been used as a dump for stones cleared from the surrounding fields.

859435   NM 84 SE   May 1969

32. Cairns and Standing Stone, Castle Farm, Barcaldine. Situated 170 m SE of Castle Farm, Barcaldine, there are three cairns disposed in an irregular line running approximately NE and SW.

(1) The NE cairn (Fig. 18, 1) stands to a height of 0·8 m, and a number of kerb-stones show that it originally measured about 9 m in diameter. It is now grass-covered and the centre is slightly hollowed.

(2) The central cairn (Fig. 18, 2), 33 m SW of (1), is also about 9 m in diameter and stands to a height of 1 m; stone-robbing has disturbed the outline on the N and S. It consists for the most part of small stones, although some of the surviving kerb-stones are massive boulders, the largest measuring 1·0 m by 0·6 m and 0·5 m in height.

(3) The SW cairn (Fig. 18, 3), 18 m W of (2), is one of the most unusual in Lorn; it is encircled by a low stone-revetted bank, and both cairn and bank have been built on an artificial platform about 22 m in diameter. The cairn is 9·8 m in diameter and stands to a height of 0·6 m; it consists of small stones within a kerb of large boulders, measuring up to 0·8 m by 0·4 m and protruding 0·8 m above the present level of the platform. The surrounding bank, which is about 3·7 m from the cairn, measures 3 m in width and 0·6 m in height above the ground outside. In the SE quadrant there is an entrance flanked by two upright slabs; the W slab measures 0·8 m by 0·3 m at its base and 1 m in height, while the other is 1·1 m by 0·4 m and 0·8 m in height.

This group of cairns was originally accompanied by a standing stone, which, according to Pennant, was situated about 10 feet (3·1 m) from the SW cairn and stood to a height of 7 feet (2·1 m).[1] Subsequently the stone fell and was re-erected on the N tip of an esker 120 m

---

[1] Pennant, *Tour* (1772), i, 413.

Fig. 18. Cairns, Castle Farm, Barcaldine
(No. 32; scale 1:500)

E of the cairns.[1] As it stands at present, it measures 0·45 m by 0·15 m at its base and 2·1 m in height.

(1) and (2) 910403, (3) 910402; Standing Stone 911402
NM 94 SW   May 1967

33. Cairn, Clachadow 1. This cairn, is situated beside the River Lonan a little less than 1 km NW of the ruined steading of Clachadow. It appears at present as a grass-grown mound 18·3 m in diameter and 1·9 m in height; in the centre there is a shallow depression, which contains, embedded in the turf, a flat slab measuring 1·22 m by 0·76 m and at least 0·15 m in thickness. Smith records[2] that, when the slab was raised during the 1870s, it was found to have served as the capstone of a cist, which measured internally 0·91 m in length, 0·50 m in breadth and 0·63 m in depth. The cist itself was nearly filled with earth, which contained a few small fragments of human bone but no grave-goods of any kind.

939280   NM 92 NW   May 1969

34. Cairn, Clachadow 2. This cairn (Fig. 19, Pl. 8B) is situated 320 m N of the ruined farmhouse of Clachadow on a slight rise above the valley floor of the River Lonan. Oval on plan, it measures 5·3 m by 4·3 m and has a kerb of large boulders, nine of which form a continuous arc round the W perimeter; the E side has been severely disturbed, however, and only three kerb-stones remain *in situ*. Outside the kerb, on the S, two stones protruding through the turf may have formed

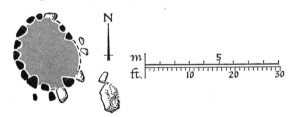

Fig. 19. Cairn, Clachadow 2 (No. 34)

part of a 'false portal' comparable to that found at No. 43. If this interpretation is correct, this setting would have been flanked by two of the tallest stones of the kerb, 0·8 m and 0·9 m in height, but the E stone has now fallen outwards from its original position. The cairn material rises to a height of only 0·4 m and it is unlikely that it was ever appreciably greater. There are several small cairns in the vicinity, but without excavation it is not possible to determine whether they are of prehistoric origin or are merely clearance cairns associated with the near-by rig-and-furrow cultivation.

947276   NM 92 NW   May 1969

35. Cairn, Clachan Bridge, Seil. This cairn is situated on a rocky spine separating two strips of cultivated ground some 700 m SW of Clachan Bridge (No. 369). Roughly circular on plan, it appears as a grass-covered

stony mound measuring about 22 m in diameter and 2 m in height. Several large kerb-stones are still visible on the S and W arcs of the perimeter, but elsewhere the remains have been greatly disturbed by stone-robbing.

779192   NM 71 NE   May 1966

36. Cairns, Clenamacrie (East). There is a small cairn situated on the N side of the public road through Glen Lonan, 830 m ESE of Clenamacrie farmhouse. The W side of the cairn has been severely damaged during the extraction of timber, but excavation of the E half by the Commission's officers showed that it was composed of a mixture of stones and earth and had originally measured about 6 m in diameter and 0·6 m in height.[3] Several stones of a rough kerb survived on the SE and N sides, but although the central area had not previously been disturbed there was no sign of a cist or a burial-deposit. Two further mounds to the NE, which measure respectively 4 m by 2·5 m and 0·2 m in height and 4·4 m by 4 m and 0·8 m in height, may be similar cairns, but without excavation it is not possible to be certain of this, since there are also several mounds of apparently field-gathered stones in the vicinity.

932283   NM 92 NW   July 1972

37. Cairns, Clenamacrie (West). Two cairns are situated in rough ground between the public road and the River Lonan in the vicinity of Clenamacrie farmhouse.

(1) The larger, which lies 35 m W of the standing stone No. 114, appears as an oval stony mound measuring 19·1 m by 17·2 m and as much as 2·6 m in height.

(2) The second cairn, similar in general appearance to the first, is situated about 300 m WNW of Clenamacrie farmhouse; it measures 18·6 m by 17·4 m and stands to a height of 1·9 m.

(1) 924285, (2) 921287 NM 92 NW   May 1972

38. Cairn, Cnoc Aingil, Lismore. The largest cairn in Lorn is situated 550 m NE of the cathedral (No. 267) at a height of about 60 m OD. Measuring 42·7 m in diameter and standing to a height of about 7·3 m, it is now grass-covered and is crossed by a modern dry-stone wall. It is possible that the size of the cairn has been emphasised by an underlying rock outcrop.

863439   NM 84 SE   May 1968

39. Cairn, Connel (Site). Nothing can now be seen of the cairn that once stood 90 m SE of the Dunstaffnage Arms Hotel and close to the road leading to the Connel Bridge. It is recorded[4] that several 'urns' were found in it in the 19th century, but nothing further is known of them.

910342   NM 93 SW   April 1967

[1] Smith, *Loch Etive*, 176.
[2] *PSAS*, x (1872–4), 87.
[3] The Commissioners are indebted to Mrs K McCorquodale, Dunach, for permission to undertake this work.
[4] Name Book, No. 19, p. 19.

40. Cairn (possible), Corrielorne. On a ridge of open moorland some 400 m SW of Corrielorne farmhouse there is a circular stony mound, largely covered with grass and heather, which may represent the remains of a prehistoric cairn. It measures about 7·6 m in diameter and stands to a height of nearly 0·6 m. A shallow central depression may indicate that the mound has already been disturbed by treasure-seekers.

866173   NM 81 NE   May 1967

41. Cairn, Creag an Fhithich, Lismore. On the SW end of a low rocky ridge about 390 m SSW of Creag an Fhithich farmhouse there is a much-denuded cairn of roughly circular shape measuring 13·7 m in diameter and 1·7 m in greatest height; it is almost totally turf-covered and is crossed by a modern dry-stone boundary-wall.

832400   NM 84 SW   May 1968

42. Cairn, Cruach Achadh na Craoibhe. There is a robbed cairn situated at a height of about 200 m OD on the highest part of the E end of Cruach Achadh na Craoibhe. It measures 18 m from NE to SW by 16 m transversely and stands to a height of 1·7 m. It is composed of medium-sized stones with some larger boulders on the NE side and is surmounted by a small modern cairn.

027246   NN 02 SW   June 1969

43. Cairn, Culcharron. The remains of this cairn are situated 400 m NNW of Culcharron farmhouse to the W of the public road between Connel and Ballachulish. Half of the cairn was completely destroyed during the construction of the branch-railway to Ballachulish, but

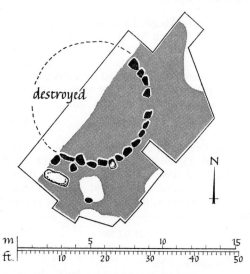

Fig. 20. Cairn, Culcharron (No. 43); after E J Peltenburg

excavation revealed that the rest remained undisturbed (Fig. 20).[1] The most impressive feature was a substantial kerb of granite boulders which would have formed a circle about 8 m in diameter. Within this kerb there was a filling of large boulders covered by smaller stones which stood to a height of about 1 m; outside it an irregular band of stones increased the overall diameter of the cairn to about 15 m. White quartz chips were wedged around the kerb-stones and there was a distinct apron of quartz outside this line measuring 0·5 m in width and 0·15 m in depth; the whole cairn had also been strewn with quartz chips. On the S quadrant an arrangement of stones consisting of two granite erratics set at right angles to the kerb and flanking a schist slab formed a 'false portal' to the cairn; lying in front of this setting was a further schist slab decorated with thirteen cup-marks on one face, five of which are very small, and a single cup on the other face. About 2 m S of the kerb there was a small upright stone associated with a pit dug into the natural gravel. The 'false portal' may be compared to that suggested at Clachadow (No. 34).

913397   NM 93 NW   May 1972

44. Cairn, Dalnacabeg. This cairn, some 260 m W of Dalnacabeg farmhouse, is situated on the edge of a level shelf above the flood-plain of the Feochan Bheag. A conspicuous oval mound, it measures 19·5 m by 17·4 m and stands to a maximum height of 2·3 m. Although almost completely grass-grown at present, the cairn can be seen to have been bordered by a carefully built kerb of massive boulders, particularly well preserved on the SE arc, where the largest stone is 1·3 m long and 0·8 m high. On the SW, however, the kerb has been largely removed by stone-robbing for adjacent field-walls.

900243   NM 92 SW   June 1969

45. Cairn (probable), Dalranach. A large mound of stones, which probably represents the remains of a burial-cairn, stands on a small tidal island off the S shore of Loch Creran, 255 m WNW of Dalranach. The mound is oval in shape, and measures 17 m by 10 m and 0·9 m in height.

935411   NM 94 SW   April 1967

46. Cairn, Dalvuie 1. This cairn is situated on the Moss of Achnacree, 300 m S of Dalvuie and 230 m SW of the chambered cairn No. 1. It stands on the crest of a scarp overlooking the S edge of a cultivated field from a height of about 15 m OD, and measures 19 m by 16·5 m and 2 m in height. Much of the E half of the cairn has been removed by stone-robbing, but the W portion appears to be largely intact and the primary burial may still remain undisturbed.

920362   NM 93 NW   May 1970

---

[1] This account, and the accompanying plan, are based upon information kindly supplied to the Commissioners by the excavator, Dr E J Peltenburg, in advance of publication.

47. Cairn (possible), Dalvuie 2. A low grass-grown mound situated at a height of 15 m OD on level ground 75 m S of Dalvuie may be the remains of a burial-cairn. Ragged in shape, it measures about 15 m in diameter and 1·25 m in height. Round the S half of the perimeter, where it has been dug into, it can be seen that the mound consists of a mixture of earth and stones.

920365   NM 93 NW   May 1970

48. Cairn, Druim an Uinnsinn 1, Lismore. This cairn (Fig. 21), standing in pasture 720 m SSW of Frackersaig farmhouse at a height of 45 m OD, measures 13·5 m in diameter and 1·4 m in height. It has been severely robbed, presumably to provide material for the near-by wall, but the remains of three cists are still visible. The central cist is represented by a single side-slab (1·4 m long, 0·25 m thick and at least 0·6 m in depth), and by the capstone (1·5 m by 1·4 m and 0·2 m thick), which now stands upright in the centre of the

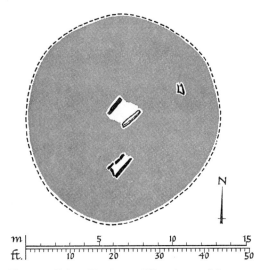

Fig. 21. Cairn, Druim an Uinnsinn 1, Lismore (No. 48)

cairn. The central area has been considerably disturbed, possibly when the cist was emptied some years before the date of visit. The remains of two inhumation burials are said to have been found, as well as a number of animal claws and nutshells, all probably modern.[1]

To the E there is a small cist, the side-slabs of which survive almost in their original positions, but the end-slabs have slipped out of place. It has measured 0·4 m by 0·2 m and up to 0·5 m in depth; the capstone (0·8 m by 0·7 m and 0·1 m thick) now lies broken near by. The cist contained the cremation of a young adult intermixed with a deposit of black earth and stones.[2] The third cist is to the S of the centre of the cairn; two side-slabs and one end-slab still surive, but the N side-slab is broken into three fragments and the S side-slab into two. The cist has measured internally about 1·4 m by 0·5 m and

about 0·6 m in depth; not only has it been robbed but it has apparently been excavated to below the original floor-level.

824396   NM 83 NW   May 1969

49. Cairn (possible), Druim an Uinnsinn 2, Lismore. Situated in an isolated patch of level arable ground, 320 m SW of the cairn No. 48, there is a grass-grown mound of earth and stones measuring 13·7 m by 9·1 m and 1·0 m in height. It has been trimmed to its present shape by cultivation along the NW and SE sides, and stones gathered from the surrounding field have been dumped on it. Abutting on the NE end there are the collapsed remains of a small kiln.

822393   NM 83 NW   May 1968

50. Cairn, Dùnan Buiaig. The severely wasted remains of this cairn[3] are situated near the edge of a level field at the mouth of the River Euchar about 175 m N of Kilninver Post Office. Although it appears at present as an irregularly shaped stony mound measuring 25 m by 20 m and 1 m in height, it is probable that its original dimensions were considerably greater, as the cairn was 'barbarously demolished' c. 1810 by local masons in quest of building materials.[4] On that occasion it is recorded that workmen came upon a stone cist containing a cremation in an 'urn', but the vessel has since been lost and the cist itself is no longer visible.

822219   NM 82 SW   May 1969

51. Cairn (probable), Dunstaffnage House (Site). No visible traces now remain of what was probably a cairn, situated in a small plantation 120 m W of the junction of the main Connel–Oban road and the approach road to Dunstaffnage House. It was destroyed during the second half of the 18th century, when the main road was constructed. Although previously described as a stone circle, consisting of eleven upright stones,[5] it is much more likely that the structure was originally a cairn, having a massive stone kerb like those recorded at Strontoiller (No. 78) and Culcharron (No. 43).

897338   NM 83 SE   April 1967

52. Cairn, Duntanachan. This cairn is situated on the summit of a low knoll immediately to the SW of Duntanachan farmhouse. A flat-topped stony mound, measuring 18·3 m in diameter and 2·25 m in maximum height, it is almost entirely grass-grown; it exhibits a

---

[1] Information from Mr and Mrs J Cooper.
[2] The Commissioners are indebted to Mr T F Spence, BSc, Department of Anatomy, University of Birmingham, for undertaking the examination of the bones.
[3] Wrongly located on the 1st (1875) and 2nd (1900) editions of the O.S. 6-inch map, sheet cx.
[4] NSA, vii (Argyll), 68.
[5] Name Book, No. 19, p. 24.

fairly regular profile on all sides except the NE, where extensive stone-robbing has taken place, presumably to provide material for the adjacent farm building.

966282   NM 92 NE   May 1969

53. Cairn (possible), Fasnacloich. There is a pile of stones, possibly representing the remains of a cairn, on the W side of Loch Baile Mhic Chailein, 350 m S of Fasnacloich. It measures 9·4 m in diameter and about 1·5 m in height. The site has also been described as a crannog,[1] but in the absence of excavation this cannot be substantiated.

020473   NN 04 NW   May 1971

54. Cairn, Glen Etive. One of the best-preserved cairns in Lorn is situated in pasture on the W bank of the River Etive, some 700 m S of Invercharnan. Bowl-shaped in profile, it measures 8·25 m in diameter by 1·6 m in height, and has been constructed with a kerb of boulders on which a second retaining course of stones has been carefully set.

143476   NN 14 NW   May 1971

55. Cairn, Gualachulain. This cairn occupies a small clearing in forestry about 60 m SW of Gualachulain at the head of Loch Etive. It measures 7·7 m in diameter by 1·6 m in height, and its irregular outline, particularly on the E side, may have been caused by stone-robbing to provide material for the near-by wall.

112454   NN 14 NW   May 1971

56. Cairn, Kilmelford. This cairn is situated at a height of about 10 m OD at the N edge of a low-lying field 600 m SW of Kilmelford village. Heavily robbed, and encroached upon by ploughing, it now appears as a ragged grass-grown mound of stones and earth measuring about 18 m in diameter and 1·2 m in greatest height; its present height, however, has been exaggerated by the dumping of stones cleared from the field. According to local information several large upright slabs, presumably the remains of a cist, could still be seen in the centre of the cairn until comparatively recent times, but they are no longer visible.

844127   NM 81 SW   May 1966

57. Cairns, Kilmore. There is a remarkable concentration of cairns in the valley between the SW end of Loch Nell and the head of Loch Feochan, all lying within 1·5 km of Kilmore village (Fig. 22). The cairns are situated on the farms of Dalineun (1–3), Moleigh (4–5) and Cleigh (6–7), and E of the former manse, now Kilmore House (No. 326) (8–10).

(1) This cairn is situated at the W end of the esker locally known as the 'Serpent Mound' and 120 m

SW of Dalineun (NM 880268).[2] Circular on plan, it measures about 19·7 m in diameter and 1·3 m in height, but it has been considerably disturbed by stone-robbing and also by excavation undertaken in 1871. In the centre the excavation revealed a massively-built cist, triangular on plan, containing a cremation deposit, a flint knife and hazelnut shells, the last probably modern. One stone

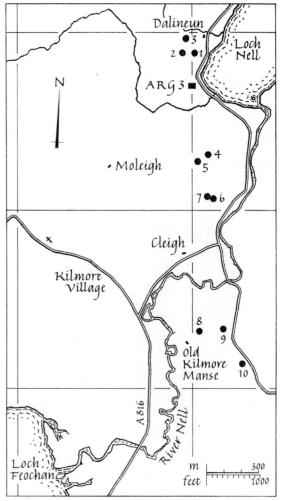

Fig. 22. Cairns, Kilmore (No. 57)

of this cist can still be seen; it measures 0·8 m in length by 0·3 m in thickness and protrudes about 0·8 m above the debris.

(2) Situated 70 m W of (1), this cairn is grass-covered and measures 12·5 m by 11 m across and 0·9 m in height (NM 879268).

(3) At a distance of 91 m NW of (1), the cairn measures 12·8 m by 9·3 m and 1 m in height (NM 879269).

---

[1] *PSAS*, vi (1864–6), 175.
[2] Listed by Henshall as an unclassified chambered cairn (ARG 46), *Chambered Tombs*, ii, 363–4.

(4) One of the best-preserved cairns of this group is situated 550 m E of Moleigh farmhouse (Fig. 23); it measures about 21·3 m in diameter and, although it has been reduced by stone-robbing, stands to a height of 1·4 m above the surrounding field (NM 880263). Several of the granite kerb-stones survive round the perimeter of the cairn, the largest standing to a height of 0·7 m, and in the centre a cist has been exposed.

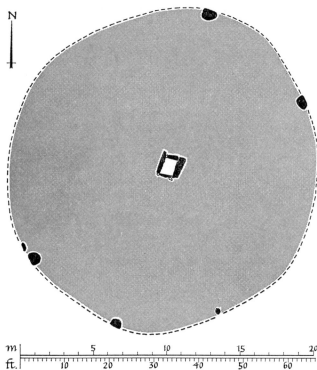

Fig. 23. Cairn, Kilmore (No. 57, 4)

Measuring 1·1 m by 0·8 m internally, and about 1·2 m in depth, it is constructed of four slabs measuring between 0·5 m and 0·2 m in thickness. The cist has been excavated on two occasions, first in the 1870s when it was cleared out to a depth of about 0·6 m and a cremation deposit and a bronze riveted dagger (Pl. 4ʙ) were discovered.[1] When it was re-examined by the Commission's officers in 1967 a second cremation burial was found, sealed from the upper one by a thin layer of clay and a layer of sand and gravel.[2] The lower deposit, probably the remains of a woman, was associated with three flakes of calcined flint. The dagger and the flints are now in the National Museum of Antiquities of Scotland.

(5) Situated 91 m to the SW of (4), this cairn measures 9·1 m in diameter and 0·5 m in height (NM 880262).

(6) Some 365 m NNE of Cleigh, this cairn stands to a height of 1·8 m above the surrounding field, but it has been enlarged to its present diameter of 31·4 m by the dumping of cairn material round the perimeter when the central area was pillaged in the 19th century (NM 881260). Two slabs, which may have been the sides of a cist measuring about 1·0 m in length, 0·6 m in width and 0·8 m in depth, lie in the centre of the cairn. The cairn had already been excavated by the 1870s and it is recorded that the cist contained a cremation in an 'urn',[3] but the vessel no longer exists.

(7) There is a small cairn immediately on the NW side of (6) measuring about 7·3 m in diameter and 0·6 m in height (NM 880260).

(8) In a small conifer plantation 85 m NE of Kilmore House there is a cairn known as Cnoc Buidhe; it measures 18·3 m in diameter and 2·4 m in height (NM 880253).

(9) A severely-robbed cairn, measuring 13·7 m in diameter and 1·3 m in height, is situated 200 m ENE of Kilmore House (NM 881253).

(10) On a slight rise about 220 m SE of (9), and crossed by a field-dyke, there is a cairn measuring 26·8 m in diameter and 3·4 m in greatest height (NM 882251).

NM 82 NE   June 1967

58. Cairn, Lagganbeg. This cairn is situated in a cultivated field some 750 m E of Lagganbeg farmhouse. Roughly circular on plan, it appears as a grass-covered stony mound measuring about 14 m in diameter and 2·1 m in height. Much of the perimeter of the cairn has been disfigured by stone-robbing and the subsequent deposition of stones gathered from the surrounding field.

864204   NM 82 SE   May 1966

59. Cairn, Làrach Bàn. This unusual cairn (Fig. 24) stands on a rise in a former plantation 400 m NW of Làrach Bàn and at a height of about 100 m OD. The

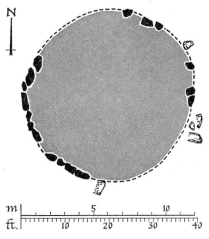

Fig. 24. Cairn, Làrach Bàn (No. 59)

site has been considerably disturbed, not only by excavation but also during the felling and subsequent extraction of the trees, and a covering of fallen trunks

---

[1] *PSAS*, ix (1870–2), 105; x (1872–4), 84, 458.
[2] Ibid., c (1967–8), 190–2.
[3] Name Book, No. 19, p. 78; Smith, *Loch Etive*, 247.

has made it difficult to interpret. The cairn is 11·8 m in diameter and has a kerb of large boulders, long stretches of which remain on the W side and intermittent boulders on the E. The stones are up to 0·85 m in height and stand above the low inner filling of earth and stones. Outside the kerb on the W side there appears to be a build-up of earth and stones which extends for a distance of 3·8 m. In the absence of excavation, however, it is not possible to determine whether this represents an outer band of cairn material, as at Culcharron (No. 43), or whether it is the result of later disturbance of the site.

067234   NN 02 SE   May 1970

60. Cairn, Ledaig. The grass-grown foundations of a cairn can be seen by the E side of the public road immediately S of the Old Schoolhouse, Ledaig (No. 332), and at a height of about 12 m OD. Parts of the N and W sectors have been completely destroyed, and what survives now measures 18·3 m by 14·6 m and 1·2 m in greatest height. It is recorded[1] that about 1835, when the approach road to the schoolhouse was being made, an 'urn' containing cremated bones and a flint arrowhead was discovered in the cairn.

905373   NM 93 NW   April 1967

61. Cairn, Lerags. This cairn (Fig. 25) is situated at a height of 50 m OD in hill pasture 380 m NW of Lerags House (No. 329). Now largely grass-covered, it measures 5·8 m in diameter and stands to a maximum height of

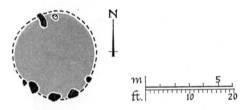

Fig. 25. Cairn, Lerags (No. 61)

0·4 m; it has, however, been considerably disturbed, especially in the centre and in the N half. On the S edge three granite kerb-stones protrude up to 0·8 m above the surrounding turf, and the disposition of these suggests that the site is a ruined kerb-cairn (see Introduction, p. 10).

841248   NM 82 SW   May 1967

62. Cairn, Lochan a' Chuirn. Situated in a small clump of trees 37 m SE of Lochan a' Chuirn, and at a height of about 25 m OD, this cairn has been seriously disturbed by stone-robbing and by the construction of a wall which traverses the remains. Its outline has been further distorted by the dumping of stones cleared from adjacent

fields, but its original diameter was probably about 24 m. At the present time the cairn stands to a maximum height of 2·1 m.

927354   NM 93 NW   April 1967

63. Cairns, Lochan na Beithe. The following three cairns are all situated within 300 m of Lochan na Beithe farmhouse, overlooking the N shore of Loch Etive from a height of about 15 m OD.

(1) On the N side of the public road immediately E of the farm there are the severely denuded remains of a cairn, appearing as a light spread of smallish stones largely overgrown by grass and whins. The stones now extend over an area measuring about 29 m across, but the original structure was probably somewhat smaller in diameter. Smith,[2] however, records that it was a large cairn, and that nothing was found in it when it was demolished to provide material for the construction of the farm buildings.

(2) The last vestiges of a second cairn can be seen a short distance S of the road and 180 m ESE of (1). Heavily overgrown by whins, it is now represented by a spread of stones measuring about 16 m in diameter and not more than 0·5 m in height.

(3) A third cairn stands 100 m ESE of (2) and 20 m S of the road. It, too, is largely concealed by a dense covering of whins, but it is in a better state of preservation than the other two, measuring 18·5 m by 17·0 m and 2·0 m in height. Considerable quantities of stones have been removed from the top and the sides, but the core of the cairn appears to be relatively undisturbed.

(1) 915349, (2) 917348, NM 93 SW   May 1971
(3) 918347

64. Cairn, Lochan nan Ràth. This cairn (Pl. 8A), known as 'The Baron's Cairn', is situated at a height of about 15 m OD on the Moss of Achnacree, 135 m E of the S end of Lochan nan Ràth. Measuring 19·2 m from N to S by 18·3 m transversely and 2·3 m in height, it stands in a hollow in the moss and is itself completely free of peat. Several shallow depressions visible in the top and flanks may represent the exploratory trenching done by Smith about 1870,[3] when he established that the cairn was not chambered. He makes no mention of internal structures, and it is probable that any primary burial remains undisturbed.

921353   NM 93 NW   April 1967

65. Barrow, Lochnell Arms Hotel. This barrow stands in trees 120 m ESE of the Lochnell Arms Hotel, overlooking the N shore of Loch Etive from a height of about 10 m OD. It measures 12·2 m in diameter by 2 m in height, and appears to be composed of earth and gravel.

909347   NM 93 SW   May 1970

[1] Name Book, No. 1, p. 64; NSA, vii (Argyll), 500.
[2] Smith, Loch Etive, 169.
[3] PSAS, ix (1870–2), 101–2.

66. Cairn (possible), Moss of Achnacree. Situated in open moorland on the N shore of an unnamed loch in the Moss of Achnacree, about 380 m WNW of Achanancarn farmhouse, there is a grass-covered mound of stones which may represent the remains of a prehistoric burial-cairn. Roughly circular in shape, it measures approximately 11 m in diameter and 0·6 m in maximum height.

923358   NM 93 NW   May 1970

67. Cairn, Musdale. This cairn, some 310 m E of Musdale farmhouse, is situated on steeply sloping ground at a height of 205 m OD. It appears as a grass-covered stony mound of roughly conical shape, measuring 11·0 m in diameter and standing to a height of 1·8 m; the top and sides have suffered slight disturbance by stone-robbing.

938220   NM 92 SW   May 1967

68. Cairn, Pennyfuir. On the summit of a ridge 280 m SE of Pennyfuir Cemetery there are the remains of a cairn which has been robbed to provide material for a later enclosure on its NE side. At the present time the cairn is turf-covered and measures 12·2 m by 8·2 m and about 1·4 m in height.

868313   NM 83 SE   May 1972

69. Cairn, Rockhill. The summit of a steep-sided conical hillock immediately overlooking the SE shore of Loch Awe, about 320 m W of Rockhill farmhouse, is crowned by a roughly circular cairn. A flat-topped grassy mound, whose sides merge almost imperceptibly into the natural slope, the cairn now measures about 7·5 m in diameter and 1 m in height, but before the afforestation of the hillock in modern times its dimensions may have been somewhat greater.

It is possible that Pococke may have been referring to this site when he mentioned[1] the discovery near Rockhill shortly before 1760 of a 'vault with an urn and bones in it'. The relatively small size of the cairn, however, suggests that the 'vault' should be interpreted as a stone cist, rather than a burial-chamber, although the nature of the burial rite and the identity of the accompanying vessel must remain uncertain.

No traces survive at the foot of the hillock of the low revetting wall and small 'rectangular' cairns described by Christison,[2] but it seems likely from his account that these were of comparatively recent origin.

068218   NN 02 SE   May 1970

70. Cairn, Salachail. This cairn is situated at a height of about 90 m OD on the N side of a forestry road 400 m NE of the old farm of Salachail. It is 12·5 m in diameter and stands to a maximum height of 1·15 m. Sixteen kerb-stones survive round the perimeter, the largest measuring about 1·1 m by 0·5 m. Now largely grass-covered, the cairn has been damaged on the N side by recent deep ploughing for afforestation.

059513   NN 05 SE   October 1967

71. Cairn (possible), Sgeir Carnaich. The summit of Sgeir Carnaich, a rocky islet on the NE coast of Luing about 1 km NNW of Ardinamar farmhouse, is surmounted by a ragged mound of stones measuring 15·2 m by 10·7 m and standing to a height of 1·2 m. Although formerly identified as a crannog[3] because of the alleged presence of a framework of wooden beams, recent inspection of the site suggests that what earlier observers recorded may have been no more than a chance assemblage of driftwood; a massive piece of undressed timber was noticed by officers of the Commission at the time of visit. Accordingly it would seem more likely that the mound represents the remains of a burial-cairn of prehistoric date, similar to that at Dalranach (No. 45).

751129   NM 71 SE   May 1966

72. Cairns (possible), Shelachan. On the level pasture-land bordering the right bank of the River Euchar opposite Shelachan farmhouse there are two circular stony mounds, which, though somewhat obscured by piles of stone gathered from the surrounding fields, may possibly represent the remains of prehistoric cairns.

(1) The larger, which is situated 300 m NNE of Shelachan farmhouse, is mainly grass-covered, measuring about 18 m in diameter and 1·1 m in greatest height; a depression in the centre may be the result of stone-robbing.

(2) The second mound, lying 500 m W of (1), measures only 9·8 m in diameter and stands to a height of 0·9 m; it is more or less flat-topped and almost completely covered with turf.

(1) 872206, (2) 868205   NM 82 SE   May 1966

73. Cairn, Shuna Cottage 1, Shuna, Nether Lorn. This cairn stands 250 m NW of Shuna Cottage, and at a height of about 10 m OD, at the W edge of a piece of level ground which was formerly under cultivation. The cairn measures 13·5 m in diameter by 2·0 m in height and is now largely grass-grown. A ragged depression in the top indicates that it has been disturbed, and a large flat slab, which is now standing upright with its base loosely embedded in the cairn material, may originally have formed part of a cist. Several large kerbstones are still in position round the perimeter of the cairn.

757077   NM 70 NE   May 1970

[1] Pococke, *Tours*, 68.
[2] *PSAS*, xxv (1890–1), 128–9.
[3] Ibid., xxx (1895–6), 25.

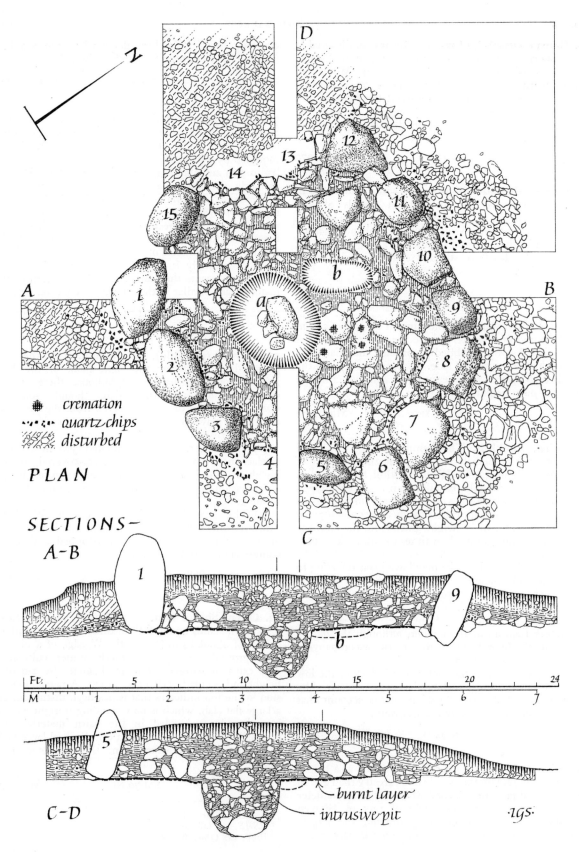

N

cremation
quartz chips
disturbed

PLAN

SECTIONS—
A-B

A   B

C-D

Ft.
M   1   2   3   4   5   6   7
5   10   15   20   24

burnt layer
intrusive pit

·IGS·

Fig. 26. Cairn, Strontoiller (No. 78; scale 1:50)

74. Cairn, Shuna Cottage 2, Shuna, Nether Lorn. This cairn is situated in pasture about 195 m ENE of Shuna Cottage and 20 m W of the chambered cairn No. 9. It measures 13 m by 11 m and 1 m in height and has been disturbed both on the S side and in the centre.

760075   NM 70 NE   May 1970

75. Cairn, Shuna Point, Shuna, Nether Lorn. Situated 350 m NE of the most southerly point of Shuna, and at a height of about 8 m OD, this cairn stands on the S end of a small isolated ridge of outcrop. Now overgrown by a light covering of peat and heather, it measures 12·5 m by 9·5 m at the base and rises to a height of 4 m. On the top, and especially down the NE side where some disturbance has been caused by stone-robbing, it can be seen that the cairn material consists only of stones with no earth intermixed; some small areas of living rock are visible intermittently round the flanks.

763064   NM 70 NE   May 1970

76. Cairn, Slatrach Bay, Kerrera. There is a small cairn close to the shore about 365 m NE of the E end of Slatrach Bay and opposite the island of Eilean nan Gamhna. The cairn, which stands on a slight rise, at about 7·6 m OD, is a grass-covered mound of stones and earth some 9 m in diameter and 0·6 m in height.

820300   NM 83 SW   April 1970

77. Cairn, Stronmilchan (Site). Nothing can now be seen of a cairn (c. 45 m OD) which formerly stood 120 m S of the public road opposite Laganbuidhe; the site is at present in an arable field. At some time during the first half of the 19th century[1] a cist containing an 'urn' was found in the cairn, but the urn is now lost.

161278   NN 12 NE   May 1970

78. Cairn and Standing Stone, Strontoiller. Situated in pasture 450 m S of Strontoiller farmhouse on the flood-plain at the N end of Loch Nell, this cairn and its associated standing stone (Pl. 9A) are 185 m SSE of the stone circle No. 120. The cairn was excavated in 1967 and the following account is a summary of the published report.[2]

Approximately circular on plan (Fig. 26), and measuring some 4·5 m in overall diameter, it has been kerbed by fifteen large boulders, twelve of which survive. All but one of the kerb-stones are granite erratics, measuring up to 1·3 m in height on the S side and apparently decreasing in size on the N. Excavation revealed that white quartz chips had been deliberately placed round the bases of the kerb-stones. The cairn material, composed of earth, gravel and stones, was lower than the surrounding kerb, standing to a height of only 0·75 m above the natural ground-level, and it is unlikely that it was originally of greater height. On the old land-surface there was a layer of burning and an unexplained hollow ('b' on Fig. 26), while in the basal layer of cairn material a very small

quantity of cremated bone was discovered. An intrusive pit ('a' on Fig. 26) was the result of an earlier excavation.[3] For further discussion of this class of cairn see p. 10.

The standing stone, situated 11·6 m NW of the cairn, is a large block of granite standing to a height of about 4 m; it measures 1·2 m by 0·9 m at the base and rises with a slight taper to a flat top.

907289   NM 92 NW   June 1967

79. Cairn (possible), Strontoiller 2. The summit of a low rocky spur projecting into arable ground about 75 m SE of the stone circle No. 120 is crowned by a roughly circular stony mound, which may represent the remains of a prehistoric burial-cairn. Measuring about 18·3 m in diameter and 1·7 m in height, the mound has been subject to extensive stone-robbing, presumably to provide material for adjacent field-walls.

907290   NM 92 NW   May 1969

80. Cairns, West Laroch (Sites). The three small cairns that stood at a height of about 9 m OD in a field extending between the W bank of the River Laroch and the houses of West Laroch village have been destroyed. In 1834 an empty cist was discovered in the easternmost cairn.[4]

079581   NN 05 NE   May 1970

BURIALS AND CISTS

81. Cist, Achnaba (Site). Nothing can now be seen of a cist discovered over a hundred years ago[5] about 400 m SW of Achnaba farmhouse (No. 303), in what is at the present time a level arable field.

941362   NM 93 NW   April 1967

82. Cist, Aon Garbh, Lismore. In a slight hollow on the NE flank of Aon Garbh, and about 25 m NE of the O.S. triangulation station, there are the remains of a stone cist which has measured 0·9 m by 0·5 m internally. Now roofless, the cist is aligned ENE and WSW and is represented by the W side-slab and by the S half of the E side-slab. At the present time the two stones project 0·5 m at most above the turf. What has probably been the S end-slab lies dislodged near by.

804377   NM 83 NW   May 1968

83. Burial, Ardachy (Site). An inverted Cinerary Urn containing the cremated remains of an adult was discovered near the NW corner of a field about 121 m W of Ardachy farmhouse.[6] The vessel, which is of undecorated

---

[1] *NSA*, vii (Argyll), 98.
[2] *GAJ*, ii (1971), 1–7.
[3] *PSAS*, x (1872–4), 84–5.
[4] Name Book, No. 22, p. 25; *NSA*, vii (Argyll), 244.
[5] Name Book, No. 1, p. 76.
[6] *PSAS*, lxxix (1944–5), 176.

Cordoned Urn type, is preserved in the National Museum of Antiquities of Scotland.

954354   NM 93 NE

84. Cists, Balure (Sites). In March 1954 a cist was discovered during ploughing operations in an arable field NE of Balure farmhouse and within 150 m of the S shore of Loch Creran.[1] A second cist, situated a short distance away in the same field, which had been discovered many years before, was also examined at the same time.

(1) The first cist, situated about 150 m NNE of the farmhouse, was encountered at a depth of 0·3 m when the uppermost of its two massive cover-slabs was struck by the plough. When this slab (1·9 m by 1·2 m and 0·3 m in greatest thickness) was removed it was found to be resting on a second cover-slab (2·0 m by 1·5 m and 0·4 m in thickness). The cist, which was aligned roughly NE and SW, measured 1·52 m by 0·9 m and 0·75 m in depth internally and was formed of four large slabs, the side-slabs being about 0·13 m thick and the end-slabs 0·07 m. It had contained an inhumation burial of which only a fragment of one femur remained, lying partly embedded in a thin layer of silt which had accumulated over the gravel floor of the cist. There were no grave-goods. After examination the cist was filled with soil and is no longer visible.

(2) The second cist, situated about 55 m NNE of (1), had been severely damaged at the time of its discovery and had lain open ever since. Measuring internally 1·2 m by 0·6 m and 0·5 m in depth, with the longer axis aligned N and S, it lay about 0·4 m below ground-level. There is no record of any skeletal remains or grave-goods.

(1) 900420, (2) 901421 NM 94 SW   April 1967

85. Cist, Barr Mór, Lismore. The remains of a cist measuring about 0·6 m by 1·0 m are visible 35 m SW of the summit of Barr Mór at a height of 125 m OD.[2] The cist, which was constructed above ground and must originally have been protected by a small cairn, is aligned E and W. The N side-slab measures 1·02 m by 0·61 m in length and depth and the S side-slab is 0·76 m by 0·51 m. There are several loose slabs near by which may have formed the sides or cover of the cist.[3]

814388   NM 83 NW   May 1968

86. Cist, Cleigh (Site). The Ordnance Survey Name Book[4] records the discovery of a cist on the N side of the minor road between Cleigh and Connel and just opposite Cleigh farmhouse. There are now no visible remains.

879256   NM 82 NE   May 1969

87. Burial, Cnoc Aingil, Lismore (Site). About 1790 an urn containing skeletal remains and ashes was found on a farm near Cnoc Aingil (No. 38).[5] As there is no mention of a cist it is likely to have been a cremation deposit in a Cinerary Urn.

c. 8643   NM 84 SE

88. Cist, Degnish (Site). In 1960 the two side-slabs of a cist were revealed by the plough in a low-lying field 550 m SW of Degnish (No. 316). The site is within 100 m of the N shore of Loch Melfort, and a short distance N of a track leading from the shore to the farmhouse. The sandstone slabs, each measuring 2·3 m by 0·6 m and 0·2 m in thickness, were set on edge about 0·5 m apart with their long axes aligned roughly N and S; the filling between them consisted simply of plough-soil. The capstone and end-slabs were missing, having presumably been removed when the cist was disturbed on a previous occasion. The two side-slabs are now lying 6 m S of their original position on a rocky patch of uncultivated ground. Close beside them the top edge of another large slab is exposed. When, on the date of visit, the soil and loose stones in which it is embedded were cleared back, it was found to measure 1·3 m by at least 0·5 m and 0·2 m in thickness. It seems likely that it was the original capstone, since one face bears a number of plough-scars while the other face is unmarked. There is no record of anything having been found in the cist.

777123   NM 71 SE   May 1971

89. Burials, Dùn an Fheurain (Sites). It is recorded that during the building of the road to Gallanach two human skeletons were found not far from Dùn an Fheurain (No. 164). There is, however, no evidence of the date of the burials which were 'redeposited in a crevice of the rock by the roadside'.[6]

c. 823265   NM 82 NW

90. Burials and Cist, Dunollie (Sites). A number of burials of unknown date are reported to have been found near Dunollie Castle (No. 286).

(1) A quantity of human bones were found in a cave about 800 m N of Dunollie when it was emptied to form an ice-house.[7]

(2) Three skeletons were uncovered in a cave below the castle, and a stone cist, containing a skeleton and a sword, was found near by; coins, a gold brooch and a finger ring are said to have been found close to the cist.[8]

(3) In 1906 the bones of an infant were discovered in the course of excavations in a rock shelter about 1·1 km

---

[1] *The Scotsman*, 26 March 1954.
[2] Name Book, No. 22, p. 153.
[3] *TGAS*, new series, ix (1937–40), 110–11.
[4] Name Book, No. 19, p. 114.
[5] *Stat. Acct.*, i (1791), 493.
[6] Faichney, *Oban*, 15.
[7] Name Book, No. 19, p. 32.
[8] Ibid., p. 34.

NE of Dunollie Castle. There is nothing to suggest that the burial was of prehistoric origin, although it is possible that the layers of ash and quantities of shells found in deposits beneath it represent earlier occupation.[1]

(1) 855322, (2) *c.* 852314, (3) *c.* 858323

          NM 83 SE

91. Cist, Gallanachbeg (Site). In 1897, in the course of building operations at the farm of Gallanachbeg, a cist was uncovered at a depth of about 1·83 m below ground-level.[2] The sides of the cist sloped inwards, and although it measured 0·91 m in length by 0·84 m in breadth at the top, it narrowed to 0·69 m by 0·38 m at the bottom. The cist, which was about 0·51 m in depth, was covered by a number of flat slabs and contained a Beaker, sherds of which are at present preserved at Gallanach.

836276   NM 82 NW   July 1968

92. Burial, Kames (Site). The Ordnance Survey records the discovery of human remains near a group of boulders, formerly thought to be a stone circle,[3] about 120 m E of Ardchonnell school. The arrangement of the boulders is, however, natural, and the date of the human remains is uncertain.

978105   NM 91 SE   May 1971

93. Cist, Keil (Site). The discovery of a cist on the farm of Keil, near Lochnell House (No. 330), is recorded in the *New Statistical Account*.[4] The cist was found in natural gravel under a layer of peat some 1·2 m in thickness; it contained an 'urn', now lost, in which there were well-preserved human bones.

c. 9039   NM 93 NW

94. Burial, Kilcheran, Lismore (Site). About 1850 some human bones were discovered during the building of a small house 150 m E of Kilcheran.[5] No further details are known.

826387   NM 83 NW   May 1968

95. Cist, Kintaline. The remains of a cist can be seen 27 m S of the entrance-gate to Kintaline, immediately W of the wall bordering the W side of the public road. At the time of its discovery, about 1870,[6] it was covered by a small cairn, measuring not more than 1·2 m across. Nothing was found inside and all traces of the cairn have since disappeared. When the cist was re-examined in 1963[7] a large number of white quartz pebbles, many small fragments of bone, and a tooth were recovered from it. At the present time three flat slabs survive, but only one of these appears to be still *in situ*; it measures 0·8 m by 0·6 m and about 0·1 m in thickness and is aligned approximately NE and SW with its bottom edge

buried and its top edge protruding about 0·5 m above ground-level. Its position suggests that it may originally have been one of the side-slabs of the cist. A second slab, of similar size, which may have formed the opposite side of the cist, is leaning over at an angle some 0·5 m to the NW, while a third slab is lying flat near by.

897397   NM 83 NE   April 1967

96. Cist, Ledaig (Site). Smith records the discovery of a cist in a gravel mound situated S of Ledaig village on the W side of the road to Connel.[8] Constructed of boulders, and measuring about 0·6 m in length internally, it appears to have been oval on plan and to have been covered by two slate slabs. No human remains were found.

c. 9036   NM 93 NW   June 1969

97. Cists, Melfort House (Sites). About 1878 three cists were discovered some 180 m from Melfort House, during the construction of a new road on the E bank of the River Oude.[9] Two of the cists were of normal dimensions, measuring about 1·2 m in length, but the third was over 1·5 m in length and was covered by a capstone 2·13 m long. One of the smaller cists contained a partly cremated skeleton and a flint scraper. The massive cist contained an extended inhumation, a crescentic jet necklace and a pair of bronze armlets (Pl. 4c), of which only one now survives. The finds are further discussed on p. 12. The flint and necklace are in the British Museum, and the armlet is in the National Museum of Antiquities of Scotland.

839141   NM 81 SW   May 1968

98. Burials and Cists, Oban (Sites). On a number of occasions, particularly in the latter part of the 19th century, prehistoric burials, some of them in cists, have been discovered in Oban. The majority have been found in the northern part of the town, broadly between Breadalbane Street and Corran Park.

(1) Two cists, each containing bones, were discovered during the digging of the foundations of the E side of Breadalbane Place, a building on the E side of Breadalbane Street (NM 859304). A third cist was found on the N side during these operations, but there were no burial-remains.[10]

[1] *PSAS*, xli (1906–7), 181–2; Lacaille, A D, *The Stone Age in Scotland* (1954), 210–11.
[2] *The Scotsman*, 21 April 1897; Faichney, *Oban*, 18–19.
[3] Name Book, No. 53, p. 233; *PSAS*, xxiii (1888–9), 415.
[4] *NSA*, vii (Argyll), 500.
[5] Name Book, No. 22, p. 157.
[6] Smith, *Loch Etive*, 186.
[7] *DES* (1963), 9.
[8] *PSAS*, ix (1870–2), 90; Smith, *Loch Etive*, 162–3.
[9] *PSAS*, xix (1884–5), 134–6; *Inventaria Archaeologica*, GB. 25.
[10] Name Book, No. 79, p. 10; shown on O.S. 25-inch map, 1st ed. (1868), sheet xcviii, 7.

(2) At the time of the discovery of the cist burial at Gallanachbeg (No. 91), attention was drawn to a vessel found some years previously during the digging of the foundations of the Argyllshire Gathering Halls, Breadalbane Street (NM 858305). Although the vessel is now lost, the description of the decoration suggests that it was a Beaker, and it had no doubt originally accompanied a burial.[1]

(3) A cist containing an inhumation and a Food Vessel was discovered in 1875 in a gravel mound at the side of the road from Oban to Dunollie (c. NM 8530). The Food Vessel, now lost, was of Irish Bowl type. The cist, which measured 0·74 m in length, 0·41 m in breadth and 0·53 m in depth, was only 0·46 m from the surface of the mound.[2]

A second cist of similar dimensions was found in the mound and is said to have contained 'broken pieces of bone'. An unusual cremation deposit was discovered at the same time; it was contained within a 'small tomb', which had its 'sides and ends made of a thin layer of clay instead of stones'. A third cist was found in another mound near by.[3]

(4) A cave, which formerly existed behind the gas-works in Oban (NM 860300), has now been completely destroyed by quarrying. It is said to have contained several human skeletons, and in 1877 two fragments of pottery, a flint chip and quantities of shells were recovered, in addition to human and animal remains.[4] The pottery, which appears to be of Cinerary Urn style, and the flint flake are preserved in the National Museum of Antiquities of Scotland.

(5) In 1878 an unusual discovery was made during peat-cutting in Dalrigh, which at that time was situated outside the burgh boundary (c. NM 860307). A wooden coffin (originally described as a canoe) had been buried 0·6 m below the surface of the peat, and had been covered by a mound of broken stones and peat, measuring about 12 m in diameter and 1·2 m in height.[5] The coffin had been hollowed out of a trunk of oak and its ends were composed of pieces of wood inserted into prepared grooves at either side. It measured 1·8 m in length, 0·6 m in breadth internally, and 0·5 m in depth, and had been covered by a series of birch and hazel branches. Several logs had been carefully placed to keep the end-boards in position and to protect the corners of the coffin. The coffin, which was filled with greasy soil mixed with charcoal, yielded no skeletal-remains, but contained several pieces of birch bark. One piece, a fragment of which is preserved in the National Museum of Antiquities of Scotland, measured about 0·15 m square and was pierced by a series of holes along one edge.

Although there is no direct evidence for the date of this coffin, it might possibly represent a wooden prototype for the well-known group of grooved stone cists of the mid-second millennium BC recorded in other parts of the county.[6]

(6) During the excavation of the MacArthur Cave (NM 859304) in 1894, parts of the skeletons of at least four individuals were discovered.[7] The burials cannot,

however, be associated with the mesolithic material from the cave (p. 5), as they were found on top of and within the thick layer of debris that sealed these deposits; their date is not known.[8]

(7) In August 1897, during the construction of the road to the McKelvie Hospital, in Gleann Sheileach (Glenshellach), a short distance to the S of Oban, three urns containing cremated bones were discovered (c. NM 8528).[9] One of the vessels, a large Cordoned Urn (Pl. 4A), was found at a depth of about 0·53 m below the surface 'in very black soil, as if largely mixed with charcoal and ashes'. The two other urns are said to have been about 0·23 m in height; one of these was restored and placed in the Reading Room of the Oban Scientific and Literary Association, but it can no longer be traced.[10] A stone battle-axe of Roe's Calais Wold group,[11] was found close beside the Cordoned Urn. This urn and a cast of the battle-axe are preserved in the National Museum of Antiquities of Scotland; the original battle-axe has been lost.

(8) In January 1922 a cist containing a Food Vessel (Pl. 3D) was discovered on the SE side of the road through Corran Park, and approximately on the site of the present car-park (NM 857305).[12] It had been inserted into the raised-beach gravel, at a height of some 9 m OD, and lay with its long axis approximately E and W. The cist measured 1·4 m in length, 0·6 m in breadth, and 1·1 m in depth, and had been covered by a single large slab. The Food Vessel is at present in Oban Museum.

(9) The Cave of the Skulls (Uamh nan Claigionn), which is situated just S of Oban on the Gallanach road (NM 848293), is mentioned in the *Statistical Account* in 1794 as containing a collection of human bones, traditionally associated with 17th-century raiders, and a gold-headed cane and a silver brooch are said to have been found in it.[13] In 1870 the Ordnance Survey Name Book recorded that 'a great quantity of human bones were taken from it a few years ago'.[14] There is clearly nothing to suggest that these remains were of prehistoric origin.

(1–6) and (8) NM 83 SE,
(7) NM 82 NE, (9) NM 82 NW

99. Cist, Saulmore (Site). About 1874 a cist was discovered in the course of digging for sand in a partly natural mound situated inland from Saulmore farmhouse.[15] The cist was immediately destroyed and the

---

[1] *The Scotsman*, 21 April 1897; Faichney, *Oban*, 19.
[2] *PSAS*, xi (1874–6), 468–9.
[3] Ibid.
[4] Ibid., xxix (1894–5), 417–18.
[5] Ibid., xiii (1878–9), 336–8; xxxix (1904–5), 181–2.
[6] Ibid., xciv (1960–1), 46–61; ci (1968–9), 111–14.
[7] Ibid., xxix (1894–5), 211–30, 423–38.
[8] Lacaille, A D, *The Stone Age in Scotland* (1954), 204.
[9] *PSAS*, xxxii (1897–8), 58–9.
[10] Faichney, *Oban*, 20.
[11] *PPS*, xxxii (1966), 225.
[12] *PSAS*, lvi (1921–2), 364–5.
[13] *Stat. Acct.*, xi (1794), 126–7.
[14] Name Book, No. 19, pp. 60–1.
[15] Smith, *Loch Etive*, 170.

stones were built into a wall bordering the public road nearby. No further details are known.

892335   NM 83 SE   April 1967

100. Cists, Slaterich, Kerrera. On the S side of a natural pinnacle of conglomerate near Sithean Riabhach, and about 470 m NNE of Slaterich, there are the remains of two cists situated practically alongside one another, only about 1 m apart.[1]

(1) The tops of one side-slab and one end-slab of the W cist can still be seen protruding above the turf. The cist was formed of four upright slabs and measured about 1 m in length and 0·61 m both in breadth and in depth. A slab lying close to the cist, and measuring 0·9 m by 0·66 m, may possibly be the dislodged capstone. The cist contained a Beaker (Pl. 3B).

(2) The E cist originally measured 1·35 m in length, 0·38 m in breadth and 0·66 m in depth; one side-slab and one end-slab are still visible above the present ground-level. A large slab measuring 1·72 m in length, part of which may be seen to one side of the cist, may have been the original capstone. The cist contained a Food Vessel and a number of quartzite pebbles. The finds from both cists are in the National Museum of Antiquities of Scotland.

820295   NM 82 NW   April 1970

CUP-AND-RING MARKINGS[2]

101. Cup-markings, Ardteatle. There are two cup-marked stones situated within 500 m of Ardteatle and at heights of between 60 m and 90 m OD.

(1) A boulder (2·3 m by 1·3 m and 0·5 m high), situated 365 m SW of Ardteatle and 70 m SE of the public road. It bears on its level upper surface at least seven plain cups, ranging from 35 mm to 75 mm in diameter and from 10 mm to 25 mm in depth.

(2) A boulder (2·0 m by 1·6 m and 1·25 m high), situated on the top of a low hillock in broken ground 460 m NW of Ardteatle and 75 m SSW of a stone wall. Its gently sloping upper surface bears one genuine cup-mark (60 mm by 70 mm and 20 mm deep) and some other depressions which may be of natural origin.

(1) 132254, (2) 130259   NN 12 NW   May 1970

102. Cup-markings, Clachadow. These markings occur on a large rounded granite boulder (1·3 m by 0·75 m and 0·75 m high) which is incorporated in the wall running SW from Clachadow farmhouse to a stone sheepfold. Near the SW end of the NW face of the stone there is one large cup (85 mm in diameter and 30 mm deep), and there are two others near the NE end (40 mm and 30 mm in diameter and 20 mm and 10 mm in depth respectively). The upper surface bears two hollows, one circular and the other oval, which are probably of natural origin.

946273   NM 92 NW   May 1970

103. Cup-markings, Clenamacrie. On a broad natural shelf in the hillside that rises from the S side of Glen Lonan, and 365 m SSW of Clenamacrie farmhouse, there is a squarish boulder measuring 1·5 m by 1·0 m and 0·8 m in height. On its upper surface there are two plain cups, 70 mm and 50 mm in diameter and 20 mm and 12 mm in depth respectively.

921282   NM 92 NW   May 1970

104. Cup-markings, Keppochan. These markings occur on a large boulder which lies on the summit of a ridge situated in rising ground 600 m ESE of Keppochan farmhouse. Measuring 2·4 m by 1·9 m and 0·9 m in height, it bears on its upper surface at least twenty-four plain cups, ranging from 30 mm to 100 mm in diameter and from 5 mm to 40 mm in depth. Nine of the cups, including the largest, are disposed in a straight line running down the centre of the boulder.

089214   NN 02 SE   May 1972

105. Cup-and-ring Markings, Kilchrenan. About 1·6 km ENE of Kilchrenan there is a large boulder (2·6 m by 1·8 m and 1 m high) situated by the N side of the road to Ardanaiseig (No. 307). Known locally as the 'Holy Stone' or the 'Slaughter Stone', it bears on its level upper surface at least sixty plain cups, ranging from 20 mm to 60 mm in diameter and from 5 mm to 15 mm in depth. Near the edge of the upper surface a group of four small cups is accompanied by a short arc of what appears to have been an enclosing ring. It is 20 mm wide and very shallow; if complete, it would have measured about 180 mm in diameter.

053235   NN 02 SE   May 1970

106. Cup-markings, Killiechonich. There are three cup-marked stones situated between the track that leads from Killiechonich to Glencruitten and the unnamed stream that flows from the SW end of Lochan a' Bhuilg Bhith to Loch Nell.

(1) A large rectangular granite boulder (1·5 m by 1 m and 1·1 m high), situated 70 m SSW of the track and 6 m W of a ruined turf wall. Its upper surface bears at least eight shallow cups, 50 mm and 15 mm in maximum diameter and depth respectively.

(2) A rounded granite boulder (1 m by 1 m and 0·5 m high), situated 265 m ESE of (1) in what has at some time been a cultivated field; it lies 85 m SW of the track and close to the junction of two electricity transmission lines. It has in its upper surface one plain cup, 50 mm in diameter and 10 mm deep.

(3) A squarish granite boulder (0·8 m by 0·7 m and 0·6 m high), situated 10 m NE of the burn and 80 m downstream from a waterfall. There is one possible cup on its upper surface.

(1) 878274, (2) 880273, NM 82 NE   May 1970
(3) 876274

---

[1] *PSAS*, lxvi (1931–2), 406–7.
[2] See also Nos. 43 and 189.

107. Cup-markings, Kilmaronag. An isolated granite boulder is situated in rough grazing 800 m S of Kilmaronag and 18 m SE of the track leading to Black Lochs. Measuring 1·4 m by 1·1 m and 0·5 m high, it bears on its sloping upper surface seven small cups, 25 mm to 40 mm in diameter and up to 10 mm in depth. Five of them are evenly disposed in a straight line running lengthwise down the centre of the stone. The other two are parallel to, and almost opposite the topmost pair of, the line of five.

936337   NM 93 SW   May 1970

108. Cup-markings, Loch Gleann a' Bhearraidh. About half-way along the NW side of Loch Gleann a' Bhearraidh (Oban reservoir) there is a granite boulder (2·1 m by 1·8 m and 0·6 m high); lying in the water just off shore, it is normally visible, but on occasions is submerged. On its level upper surface there are twelve plain cups, measuring up to 80 mm in diameter and 20 mm in depth.

846270   NM 82 NW   May 1970

109. Cup-markings, Oban Esplanade. By the W side of the road, close to the lighthouse at the N end of the Esplanade, there is a massive granite boulder measuring 1·8 m by 1·5 m and 2·9 m in height. It is recorded[1] that it was originally situated about 7 m E of its present position, but was moved when the road was being constructed at the end of the 19th century. On what was previously the upper surface of the boulder (now the S and E faces) there were thirty-four shallow cups and 'three arcs of circles'. These markings are no longer visible, but local residents have confirmed the accuracy of the diagram accompanying the newspaper article cited above, which shows twelve cups on the S face and twenty-two cups on the E face.

852309   NM 83 SE   May 1970

STANDING STONES[2]
AND STONE CIRCLE

110. Standing Stone, Acharra. One of the most impressive standing stones in Lorn (Pl. 9C) is situated in a level field 180 m NW of Acharra. It measures 3·7 m in height and 1·1 m by 0·6 m at the base, and tapers to a pointed top about 0·4 m in thickness; the long axis lies NE and SW.

986545   NM 95 SE   May 1967

111. Standing Stones, Barcaldine. There are two standing stones in a field 46 m SW of Barcaldine School. Only one of them, however, is now *in situ*, the other, which is propped against the first, having been moved from its original position to facilitate cultivation.

The undisturbed stone is rectangular in profile and has a pointed top; it is aligned NNW and SSE and measures 1·7 m in height, 0·85 m in breadth and 0·2 m in thickness. The second stone measures 1·6 m in height, 0·6 m in breadth, 0·3 m in thickness and tapers to a point on its N side.

963421   NM 94 SE   May 1970

112. Standing Stone, Benderloch 1. This stone stands in an arable field to the W of the public road at the S end of Benderloch village. It measures 2·1 m high and 1·2 m by 0·5 m at the base; the longer axis is aligned NW and SE.

903380   NM 93 NW   April 1967

113. Standing Stone, Benderloch 2. This standing stone is situated in a level field at the N end of Benderloch village, immediately N of Lochnell Primary School. It measures 1·5 m in height and 1·1 m by 0·2 m at the base; the longer axis is aligned N and S.

906386   NM 93 NW   April 1967

114. Standing Stone, Clenamacrie. About 100 m E of Clenamacrie farmhouse there is a four-sided monolith situated on level ground immediately S of the public road. It measures 0·7 m by 0·6 m at the base and stands to a height of 1·45 m. Close beside it to the W there are two large boulders, but without excavation it is impossible to tell whether or not they are associated with the standing stone.

924285   NM 92 NW   June 1969

115. Standing Stone, Connel (Site). The stone that formerly stood within the area now occupied by Connel Station was presumably removed shortly before 1880, when the railway was being constructed. It is described[3] as 'a large standing stone' having 'around it marks where others, well remembered, lately stood'. Nothing, however, is known of the size or disposition of these other stones.

917340   NM 93 SW   April 1967

116. Standing Stones, Duachy. A little over 300 m W of Duachy farmhouse, and about 45 m SE of Dubh Loch, there is a group of four standing stones (Pl. 9B) situated in a pasture field at a height of 40 m OD. Three of the stones are disposed in a straight line running NNW and SSE, while the fourth, now reduced to a mere stump, stands apart, 38 m to the E of the alignment.

The most northerly of the line of three measures 0·7 m by 0·5 m at the base and 2·8 m in height, and rises with a

---

[1] *The Oban Times*, 10 September 1921.
[2] See also Nos. 10, 32 and 78.
[3] *PSAS*, x (1872–4), 83–4.

slight taper to an almost level top. The centre stone, which is situated at distances of 2·7 m and 2·1 m from the N and S stones respectively, is now leaning towards the E at an angle of about 30° from the horizontal; it measures 0·6 m by 0·5 m in girth and 1·9 m in length, but a portion appears to have been broken off the tip. The S stone measures 0·7 m by 0·6 m at ground-level and stands 2·2 m in height. Like the N stone its sides are smooth and its top level.

Until recently the isolated stone to the E was still erect, though tilted at a considerable angle to the W. A large natural split in the stone had developed to such an extent that in 1963 it was knocked down to prevent it from becoming a danger to livestock. The stump, measuring 0·8 m by 0·5 m and 0·3 m in height, has been left in position and a fragment lies close beside it. The main body of the stone, still in one piece, now lies 45 m to the SSW at the edge of a small marshy hollow; this piece measures 2·4 m in length and 0·7 m by 0·5 m in maximum girth. When in its original state the stone would have stood to a height of about 2·5 m.

801205   NM 82 SW   May 1966

117. Standing Stone, Eilean Musdile, Lismore (Site). The stone recorded by Faujas de Saint Fond in 1784[1] as standing on the highest point of Eilean Musdile has since disappeared. Described as an unworked pillar of grey granite measuring 0·9 m in breadth, 0·6 m in average thickness and 2·75 m in height, it stood with its base embedded to a depth of 0·6 m below ground-level and was held firmly in position by two other stones.

On a survey map of the island,[2] dated 1829, which was made in preparation for the construction of the lighthouse (No. 357), the stone is located 174 m NE of the lighthouse-tower, and it was probably removed during the subsequent building-operations.

779351   NM 73 NE   July 1971

118. Standing Stone, Inverfolla. This stone, now fallen, is situated close to its original position on the S side of the public road through the Strath of Appin, 150 m NNE of Inverfolla. It measures 3·8 m in length, 0·7 m in breadth at the base, and about 0·13 m in average thickness.

958450   NM 94 NE   May 1970

119. Standing Stone, Kilninver (Site). The standing stone marked on the 1st edition of the O.S. 6-inch map[3] on the E bank of the River Euchar, some 330 m N of Kilninver, has since been destroyed. It is recorded that it measured 1·2 m in height.[4]

825220   NM 82 SW   May 1970

120. Stone Circle, Strontoiller. The only known stone circle in Lorn (Fig. 27) is situated on the flood plain at the N end of Loch Nell, 280 m SSW of the farm of Strontoiller and 185 m NNW of the cairn and standing

stone No. 78. The NE half is now in an area of marshy ground but the SW half lies at the edge of an arable field. The circle measures about 20 m in diameter, and is composed of thirty-one rounded boulders of varying sizes, the largest measuring not more than 1 m in height. Four other stones, which have probably been displaced, are situated

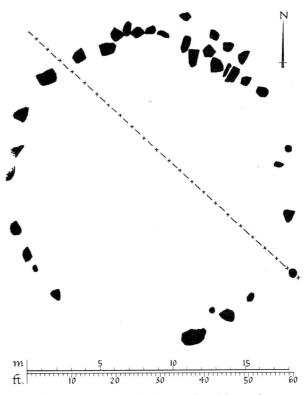

Fig. 27. Stone circle, Strontoiller (No. 120)

a short distance outside the circle on the NNE. Many of the boulders forming the circle are now partly grass-covered, and without excavation it is impossible to tell whether or not they are precisely in their original positions. The interior of the circle is featureless.

906291   NM 92 NW   May 1967

121. Standing Stone, Taynuilt 1 (Site). The granite monolith that now stands on a prominent knoll immediately E of Taynuilt village (NN 005310) was originally situated about 1·6 km to the NW on a low ridge, named Barra na Cabar, SW of Airdsbay House.[5] It was removed to its present position in 1805 by the workmen of the Lorn Furnace (No. 362) and erected as a memorial to Lord Nelson. Thomson states[6] that the stone was lying

[1] St Fond, *Journey*, ii, 7–8.
[2] Contract-drawing in the possession of the Northern Lighthouse Board.
[3] Sheet cx (1875).
[4] Name Book, No. 53, p. 35.
[5] *PSAS*, lxi (1926–7), 230–1.
[6] Ibid.

prone at the time of its removal and that, according to local tradition, there had been other 'pillar stones' lying in the same field in the past. This would suggest that it was originally a standing stone, possibly forming part of a setting of such stones and thus comparable with the standing stone No. 115.

As it stands at the present time, it measures 1·17 m by 0·91 m by 0·66 m at the base and rises to a height of 3·43 m; its N face bears a dedicatory inscription.

c. 995320   NM 93 SE   June 1969

122. Standing Stone, Taynuilt 2. About 800 m E of Taynuilt village there is a small standing stone situated near the corner of an arable field 230 m NW of the Oban–Dalmally road. It is a granite boulder, roughly triangular in shape at the base, and measuring 0·75 m by 0·60 m by 0·55 m at ground-level. It now stands to a height of 1·2 m, but pieces have been split off in comparatively recent times and it may originally have been taller.

012311   NN 03 SW   June 1969

FORTS

123. Fort, Ardanstur 1. On the W side of the point known as Rubh' Ard an Stùrra, which juts into the N side of Loch Melfort, there are the remains of a fort (Fig. 28). There is a sheer drop on the W side to the

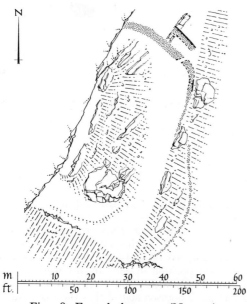

Fig. 28. Fort, Ardanstur 1 (No. 123)

loch some 35 m below, and at the S end the ground falls steeply in a series of vertical scarps; on the N and E sides, however, there is easy access from the level top of the promontory. The fort is situated on an elongated ridge and measures 53 m by 36 m internally, but a large

part of the interior is occupied by an extensive rock outcrop. The main defence has comprised a stone wall which can now be seen only on the N and E sides. On the N, where it measures about 2·4 m in thickness, the wall can be clearly traced and the entrance-passage is still indicated; on the E, however, it is reduced to a thin band of debris lying on the flank of the ridge. The approach from the N has been protected by a short outwork, which runs from a spine of outcrop almost to the crest of the ridge. This wall is 1·8 m thick, and the lowest course of outer facing-stones, consisting of massive boulders up to 1 m high, survives for a length of 8·2 m.

822131   NM 81 SW   May 1971

124. Fort (possible), Ardanstur 2. An isolated rocky ridge beside the N shore of Loch Melfort, about 350 m S of Ardanstur farmhouse, is occupied by the wasted remains of an oblong enclosure which may have been a small fort. The site affords moderately strong natural protection, its steep rock-studded flanks rising to a height of 3 m above the surrounding ground on the N and as much as 7·6 m on the S.

The enclosure has measured about 33 m from N to S by 17 m transversely within a single stone wall built round the edge of the level summit; but at present the wall is represented by only an intermittent band of stony debris, nowhere more than 1·8 m thick. Although the actual entrance can no longer be recognised, it was probably located on the WNW, where a natural grassy ramp gives easier access to the summit. Virtually the whole of the interior has at some time been under cultivation.

824132   NM 81 SW   May 1967

125. Fort, Balvicar, Seil. On the summit of an elongated rocky ridge, aligned NE and SW, about 280 m SE of Balvicar village, there are the denuded remains of a vitrified fort (Fig. 29), which measures internally 93 m by 44 m. Precipitous rock-faces have rendered artificial defence unnecessary on the NW flank of the ridge, while steep rock-studded slopes, now overgrown with impenetrable scrub, present a scarcely less formidable obstacle on the SE. Easy access is thus to be gained only along the spine of the ridge on the NE or SW.

The defences comprise a wall (A), drawn round the margin of the summit area on all sides except the NW, with outworks (B, C, D) at either end of the ridge. Wall A is best preserved on the NE and SW, where it is represented for the most part by a grass-grown stony scarp 1 m high, in which several stretches of outer facing-stones have survived in position as shown on the plan; no stones of the inner face can now be seen. On the SE, however, most of the wall has been destroyed and only a thin band of debris, 18·6 m in length, survives on the very crest of the steep slope to show that the work was originally continuous. A large mass of vitrified core-material which lies embedded in the scarp at the SW end of the fort indicates that the wall was originally timber-laced; several smaller lumps of vitrifaction have been incorporated in the boundary-walls of adjacent fields. A gap in the wall-debris on the SSW, measuring 2 m in width, probably marks the position of

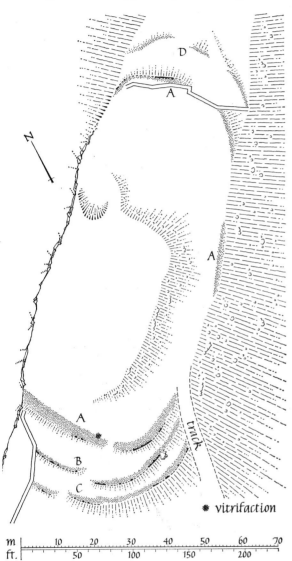

m | 10   20   30   40   50   60   70
ft. | 50   100   150   200

Fig. 29. Fort, Balvicar, Seil (No. 125)

the entrance at this end, and it is possible that a second entrance was located somewhere in the broad gap at the NE end, where the line of wall A is crossed by a turf-and-stone dyke of recent date.

The outworks on the SW originally consisted of two dry-stone walls (B, C) drawn round in a protective arc from the edge of the cliffs on the NW flank of the ridge and probably butting against the outer face of wall A on the SE. Unfortunately the actual point of junction is obscured by a broad modern track which has broken

through the outworks and the main wall on this side. On the NW the outworks have been truncated by the construction of a modern turf dyke. Both walls have been reduced throughout to mere scarps of stony debris in which a number of outer facing-stones can still be seen. The entrances in B and C, both about 2·4 m wide, appear to have been staggered in such a way as to give only oblique access to the entrance in wall A.

Outwork D, which lies at an average distance of 7·6 m outside wall A on the NE, is in an extremely denuded condition, being represented at best by a thin scatter of core material. It is not certain which of the two wide gaps is the site of the original entrance.

The interior is divided into two levels by a sinuous rocky outcrop, 4·6 m in greatest height, at the N end of which there is a crescentic scarp, presumably defining the rear edge of a stance for a round timber house some 6 m in diameter. It is probable that cultivation of the interior in recent times has obscured the remains of other house-sites.

771164   NM 71 NE   May 1967

126. Fort (probable), Castle Coeffin, Lismore. On the level summit of a rocky ridge 90 m NE of Castle Coeffin (No. 282) there are the last vestiges of what has probably been a stone-walled fort. Easy access to the summit can be gained across gentle grassy slopes on the NE, but on all other sides steep or vertical rock-faces 7·6 m in height afford strong natural protection.

A sub-rectangular area measuring about 80 m from NE to SW by 36 m transversely has been defended by a single stone wall, the mutilated remains of which can still be seen on the NE, where it was drawn in a shallow arc across the spine of the ridge, barring the line of easiest access. Here it survives for a distance of 33 m as a ragged stony bank 3·7 m in average width and 0·5 m high, a gap 2·4 m wide near its mid-point presumably indicating the position of the entrance. No traces of a wall have been preserved along the flanks or at the SW end of the ridge, but whether this is because the defences have been completely destroyed on those sides, or because the strong natural protection was deemed sufficient, cannot be determined without excavation. The whole of the interior appears to have been subject to intensive cultivation in comparatively recent times.

854438   NM 84 SE   May 1968

127. Fort, Cnocan Dubha. On the summit of the more northerly of the two rocky bosses known as Cnocan Dubha, immediately N of the village of East Laroch, there are the tenuous remains of a stone-walled fort (Fig. 30). The boss, which rises to a height of about 18 m above the surrounding coastal plain, is protected on the NE and SE by sheer rock-faces, but elsewhere, apart from a low crescentic scarp on the S, the immediate approach is over a grassy incline of only moderate steepness.

Although no trace of any defences can now be seen on

the E half of the perimeter, it is probable that the fort, which measures internally about 36 m from E to W by 27 m transversely, was originally defended by a continuous wall drawn round the irregular outline of the summit area, with an outwork restricting access on the more vulnerable W flank. The surviving portion of the

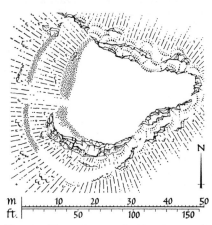

Fig. 30. Fort, Cnocan Dubha (No. 127)

main wall appears as a low grass-grown spread of core material, 0·6 m to 2·4 m wide, in which no inner or outer facing-stones are now visible. A similar band of debris, although only 1·5 m in greatest width, indicates the course of the outer wall.

The entrance lay on the W, its position being marked by gaps in the inner wall and the outwork measuring 1·8 m and 5·1 m in width respectively. The interior is largely occupied by bare rock.

079585   NN 05 NE   May 1971

128. Fort, Cnoc an Tighe Mhóir, Seil. The denuded remains of a fort occupy the summit of a small isolated ridge 275 m S of Kilbride farmhouse at a height of 30 m OD. Sub-rectangular on plan (Fig. 31), the principal defence has consisted of a wall, which follows the margin of the summit to enclose an area measuring 43 m by 25 m. Many of the stones have been removed to build field-dykes, two of which now traverse the fort. No facing-stones are visible but the remnants of the core material, composed of a mixture of earth and stones, can still be traced for most of the circuit as a grass-grown bank. On the SE, where it is best preserved, the bank is spread to a maximum thickness of 7·3 m and rises to a height of 2 m externally and 1 m internally. For a distance of about 26 m on the NW side the wall has been completely destroyed, but its approximate course is still indicated by the collapsed remains of a comparatively modern turf-dyke. The position of the entrance is represented by a gap 4·3 m wide on the NE.

Two isolated stretches of terrace, situated some 9 m outside the line of the wall on the SE and SW respec-

tively, are probably the seatings for an outer wall or rampart of which no traces remain.

756163   NM 71 NE   May 1966

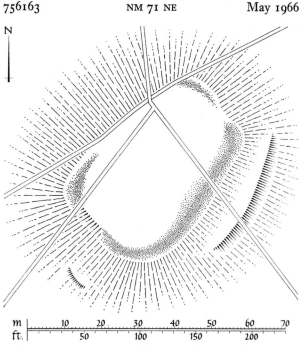

Fig. 31. Fort, Cnoc an Tighe Mhóir, Seil (No. 128)

129. Fort, Colagin. This fort (Fig. 32) is situated on the nose of a conspicuous promontory overlooking the valley of the Allt Criche about 530 m NE of Colagin farmhouse. On all sides except the N, where relatively easy access may be gained across a level neck of land, precipitous or vertical rock-faces up to 15 m in height provide strong natural protection.

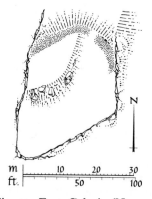

Fig. 32. Fort, Colagin (No. 129)

Approximately kite-shaped on plan, and measuring internally 37 m by 27 m, the fort has been defended on the N by an arc of walling now reduced to a grass-covered stony bank 1·5 m to 3 m thick and 0·2 m high, in which only two stones of the outer face are now visible. In view of the great natural strength of the site it is unlikely that any defences were constructed on the remaining sides.

The entrance is situated on the NNE, and the interior, which falls as much as 4·9 m from NE to SW, is divided by a low rock-studded scarp into two shelves of unequal size.

858264   NM 82 NE   May 1967

130. Fort (possible), Creag Aoil. On the northern tip of Creag Aoil, a rocky headland on the S shore of Loch Melfort situated a little over 1 km WNW of Kames farmhouse, there are the wasted remains of what may have been a promontory fort. The position is one of great natural strength, being protected on the N, E and W by cliffs which fall almost without interruption to the shore 15 m below, while the approach on the landward side is over rough ground interspersed with rock out-crops.

A line of walling, now represented by a grass-grown band of rubble 2·1 m to 3 m wide and of negligible height, has been drawn across the headland from E to W on the crest of a low rocky scarp, thus cutting off a D-shaped area which measures about 32 m along the chord by 16·5 m transversely. The position of the entrance is probably indicated by a gap 1·5 m wide near the mid-point of the wall. Apart from traces of recent cultivation, the interior is featureless.

810114   NM 81 SW   May 1967

131. Fort, Dùnan Corr. The summit of Dùnan Corr, a rocky knoll situated 360 m WSW of Lerags farmhouse, is occupied by the severely denuded remains of a stone-walled fort, whose overall dimensions are about 37 m from E to W by 18 m transversely. On the S and W, where a nameless tributary of the Allt Mór Lerags winds round the base of the knoll in a ravine up to 12 m deep, the site is strongly defended by nature; on the E, how-ever, its flanks are grass-covered and less steeply inclined, while on the N easy access is available across a saddle which links the knoll to the rising ground on that side.

At present the fort is obscured by a dense growth of trees, and the only visible trace of its defences is a low grass-grown bank on the N margin of the summit area, representing the spread core-material of a dry-stone wall which doubtless once enclosed the whole of the summit. The bank, which measures 2·4 m in average thickness and only 0·3 m in height, appears to be interrupted for an entrance opposite the point of easiest access, but the recent extraction of timber makes it impossible to be certain that this is not merely the result of modern disturbance.

834242   NM 82 SW   May 1967

132. Fort, Dùnans, Glen Cruitten. Little now remains of the stone-walled fort that once occupied the W summit of Dùnans, a steep-sided eminence in Glen Cruitten,

380 m ESE of the West Highland Cottage Hospital, Oban. The summit, of elongated oval shape and aligned NE and SW, is protected on the NW by a sheer precipice 15 m high, and by steep rocky slopes on the SW and SE, but the immediate approach at the NE end is over a grassy incline offering comparatively easy access.

The fort, measuring internally about 55 m from NE to SW by 18 m transversely, has been defended, probably on all sides except the NW, by a stone wall constructed on the margin of the summit area. At present the wall is reduced to an intermittent grass-grown band of stony debris, which is up to 3·7 m wide on the NE, but on the SE appears as a thin scatter of core material; elsewhere it has completely vanished. Separated from the main wall at the NE end by an interval of about 8 m, there has been an outwork, drawn in an arc across the line of easiest access; although it is now so severely mutilated that its precise course can no longer be determined, it seems unlikely that it ever continued round the whole of the SE flank as Christison suggested.[1]

The entrance was probably situated at the NE end of the fort, but its exact position is not apparent. An oval depression on the brink of the cliff near the middle of the NW side is said to be the site of a well.[2]

869296   NM 82 NE   May 1967

133. 'Fort', Dunbeg (Site). No traces are visible of the 'fort' reported by Christison[3] on nearly level ground at the head of Dunstaffnage Bay and about 73 m from the shore. According to Christison's brief description and plan the structure had none of the characteristics of a fort or dun, and there is no evidence to support the suggestion, perpetuated by subsequent writers,[4] that it was vitrified. On the contrary it seems to have consisted simply of a low grassy bank, largely composed of earth, which formed an irregularly-shaped enclosure with a maximum internal measurement of about 15 m; there was an entrance in the centre of the S side. The date and purpose of the structure are unknown.

c. 8733   NM 83 SE   May 1970

134. Fort, Dùn Creagach. The slight remains of a fort (Fig. 33) can be seen at the S end of Dùn Creagach, a rocky ridge which is a prominent feature of the broken ground SW of Connel between the railway and the minor public road to Kilmore. Though some 15 m lower than the N end of the ridge, the S tip (60 m OD) provides a position of great natural strength, being defended on the E, S and W by sheer rock-faces up to 12 m high, and separated from the remainder of the ridge by a small transverse gully about 3 m in depth.

The visible remains consist of a grass-grown bank of earth and rubble, representing the core material of a

[1] *PSAS*, xxiii (1888–9), 387.
[2] Name Book, No. 19, p. 54.
[3] *PSAS*, xxiii (1888–9), 383–4.
[4] E.g. Childe, V G, *Scotland Before the Scots* (1946), 135, no. 39.

wall, which extends in a gentle arc along the S lip of the gully, thereby cutting off an area measuring about 38 m by 30 m. The entrance probably lay somewhere within the gap at the SE end where the bank has been completely destroyed. The bank is now between 3·6 m and 4·6 m in thickness at the base and stands up to 0·6 m above the level of the interior. Its surface is very uneven

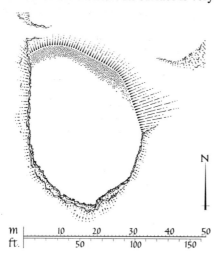

Fig. 33. Fort, Dùn Creagach (No. 134)

and pitted with numerous depressions where the facing-stones have been torn away. A considerable proportion of the material for the wall was obtained from the gully, the sides of which show evidence of quarrying, particularly at either end. No trace is now visible of any walling elsewhere, and owing to the natural protection afforded by the rock faces it is likely that any defences on the other three sides would have been of a less substantial nature. The interior is featureless.

907334   NM 93 SW   June 1969

135. Fort, Dùn Iadain. This fort (Fig. 34), 490 m SW of Kilbride farmhouse, occupies the summit of Dùn Iadain, an isolated round-topped hill, overlooking the E end of Glen Feochan from a height of about 110 m OD. The site, which commands extensive views to the E and W, is protected on all sides by steep grass-covered slopes.

Measuring internally about 57·6 m by 19·2 m, the fort has been defended by two boulder-faced rubble-cored walls, one of which is drawn round the somewhat irregular margin of the summit area, taking advantage wherever possible of low rocky scarps, as shown on the plan, while the other follows, in the greater part of its course, the outer edge of a level terrace lying 1 m to 2 m below the summit; the walls apparently converged at the S end of the fort, where a rock fall has removed all trace of the defences. The inner wall appears as a grass-grown stony scarp of varying height, in which no facing-stones are now visible; it has been interrupted for an entrance on the SSE. The outer wall has been much more

severely mutilated; for most of the E side, and for a short distance on the SW, it survives as a turf-covered band of core material 1·2 m in greatest width, but elsewhere it is reduced for the most part to a mere crest-line. On the NNW and NNE the terrace has been quarried to a depth of about 1 m to provide material for both walls.

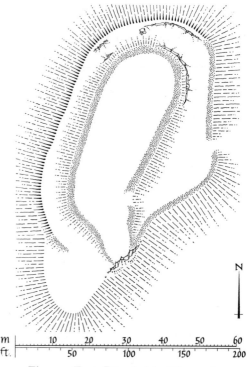

Fig. 34. Fort, Dùn Iadain (No. 135)

No trace of the outer defence can now be seen on the SSW, where it crossed the neck of a spur. The position of the entrance through the outer wall is indicated by a gap in the wall debris on the E.

The ground enclosed is steeply inclined, and it is noteworthy that it shows no signs of house-platforms (cf. Introduction, p. 18).

911240   NM 92 SW   May 1967

136. Forts and Dun, Dùn Mac Sniachan. An important group of remains[1], comprising two successive forts and a dun (Fig. 35), is situated on the summit of Dùn Mac Sniachan, a steep-sided isolated ridge which stands close to the NE shore of Ardmucknish Bay, overlooking Benderloch Village from a height of 40 m OD. The higher (SW) part of the summit area joins the lower (NE) part at the head of a gully named Bealach na Banrigh, which cuts into the SE flank of the ridge. The gully affords a steep but practicable means of access to the

---

[1] To which the spurious name *Beregonium*, a misreading of Ptolemy's *Rerigonium*, was mistakenly applied by Hector Boece in his *Scotorum Historiae*.

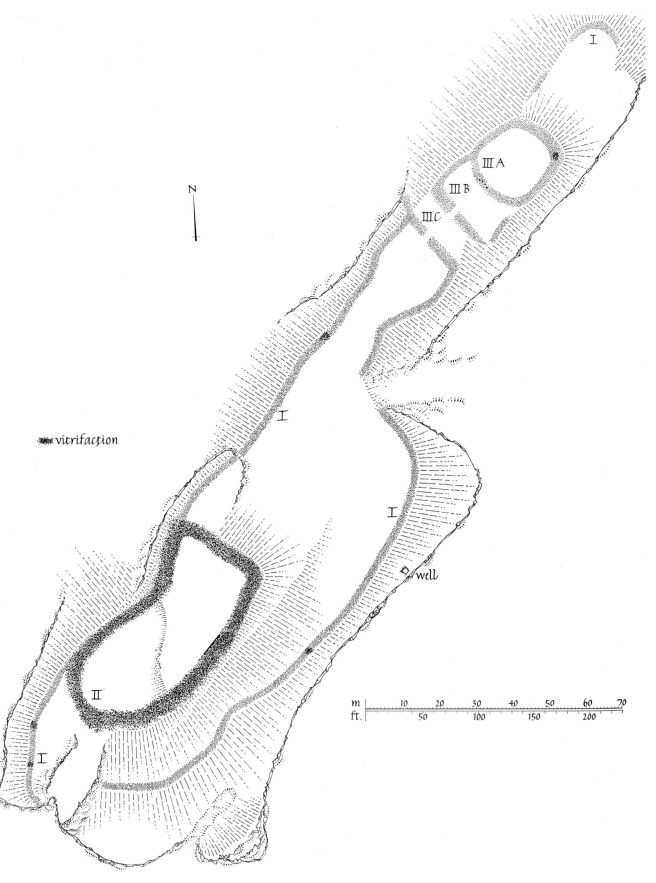

N

III A

III B

III C

I

vitrifaction

I

I

well

II

I

| m | | 10 | | 20 | | 30 | | 40 | | 50 | | 60 | | 70 |
ft. | | | 50 | | 100 | | 150 | | 200 | |

Fig. 35. Forts and dun, Dùn Mac Sniachan (No. 136)

summit, but the easiest approach is up a gentle slope from the NE.

The earlier of the two forts measures about 245 m in length by a maximum of 50 m in breadth internally. Traces of its wall (I) can still be detected almost all the way round the margin of the summit area of the ridge in the form of a grass-grown band of stony debris, in which five separate masses of vitrified material, apparently fused with the underlying rock, are visible as shown on the plan. The entrance was probably at the head of the gully on the SE. The interior is largely covered by scrub and there are no indications of buildings.

The later fort, situated near the SW end of the ridge, measures 52 m by 21 m within a vitrified wall (II) which, on the NW side, overlies the wall of the earlier fort. The remains of wall II appear as a grass-covered stony bank spread to a maximum thickness of 6 m, in which a stretch of inner facing-stones is exposed for a length of 7 m on the SE side. The position of the entrance is not apparent. Excavations carried out by Smith in 1873–4,[1] although inconclusive, established that the wall was preserved to a height of nearly 2 m and that its core material was heavily vitrified. Smith also found that at the NE end the wall had been rebuilt, vitrified material from the older structure being incorporated in the new. Some evidence of this reconstruction may be provided by the remains visible at the present time, which show an unexpected salient at the N corner, whereas Smith's plan shows in addition the line of a vitrified wall continuing straight across the base of the salient. Further excavation, however, would be required to establish the nature and extent of the rebuilding. Within the interior Smith found traces of rectangular stone buildings, now no longer visible, and the finds included part of a tanged iron sword, an iron dagger, an iron ring, an enamelled bronze circular mount, and a bronze ring, together with several querns and a considerable quantity of animal bones (sheep, pig and cattle). The metal objects are now in the National Museum of Antiquities of Scotland.

The dun, situated at the lower (NE) end of the ridge, measures about 18·3 m by 15·2 m within a wall (IIIA), which now appears as a grass-grown band of stony debris about 3 m in thickness. The removal of some of the debris on the E arc of this wall has revealed a mass of the vitrified core-material of wall I underneath. The dun is protected on the SW by two outer walls (IIIB and IIIC), running transversely across the ridge at distances of about 9 m and 18 m respectively from wall IIIA. The nearer wall (IIIB) appears to have been connected to wall IIIA on the S and W, but there is no trace of a similar junction between walls IIIB and IIIC. Each of the outer walls has an entrance centrally placed; there is no corresponding gap visible in wall IIIA, and the position it would occupy, if it were situated in line with the other two, is now blocked by four large earthfast boulders.

While it is clear that the larger fort preceded both the smaller fort and the dun, there is at the present time nothing to show whether or not these latter structures were contemporary. The possibility, however, that the dun succeeded the smaller fort is suggested by a comparable group of remains at Dùn Skeig (Kintyre),[2] where a threefold sequence has been demonstrated. For further discussion, see pp. 17–18.

WELL. On the steep SE flank of the hill, 6 m outside wall I, there is a cavity in the rock measuring about 1·3 m square and normally filled with water. When cleared out in 1871,[3] it was found to be 1·7 m in greatest depth. The cavity was originally a natural feature, subsequently enlarged and deepened to provide a well fed by water percolating through a crack in the rock above.

903382   NM 93 NW   May 1969

137. Fort, Dùn Ormidale. By far the largest fort (Fig. 36) in Lorn is situated on Dùn Ormidale (175 m OD), a conspicuous hill which forms the S end of a long ridge of high ground overlooking Gallanach to the S and the Sound of Kerrera to the W. Occupying the whole of the summit plateau, it contains an area of 3 ha (7·5 acres). On the N a grassy incline about 20 m in height provides relatively easy access to the plateau from the crest of the ridge, but on the other sides the site is bounded by steep, and in places precipitous, slopes.

No traces of any defences can now be seen on the S and W sides, where the sheer rock-faces may have been thought to afford adequate protection, but on the N and E the remains of what has been a substantial wall are visible intermittently. The wall is, however, reduced to a mere band of stony debris, measuring 3·7 m in greatest thickness and standing not more than 1 m in height; a few outer facing-stones survive in position at the NE angle together with a single example on the E. A gap in the N side, about 3 m wide, is approached from the outside by a winding track and probably represents the original entrance.

Apart from a knoll in the NE quarter, the interior is more or less level; no surface indications of buildings can be seen. For further discussion, see p. 16.

829263   NM 82 NW   May 1970

138. Fort, Dùn Uabairtich. The wasted remains of a fort occupy the summit of a small but prominent knoll which forms part of the SW extension of the ridge of high ground that rises abruptly from the E side of the Sound of Kerrera, N of Port nan Cuile. Situated at a height of 60 m OD, it is bounded on the NW by crags and by steep grassy slopes in all other directions.

D-shaped on plan (Fig. 37), the fort has measured about 23 m by 21 m within a single stone wall. No traces of the wall are now visible along the cliff edge on the NW, and on the NE it has been reduced to a low grassy scarp, but a few stretches of outer face can still be

---

[1] *PSAS*, x (1872–4), 78–80; xi (1874–6), 299–300; xii (1876–8), 14–15, pl. i (plan).
[2] *Inventory of Argyll*, i, No. 165.
[3] *PSAS*, ix (1870–2), 85, 396.

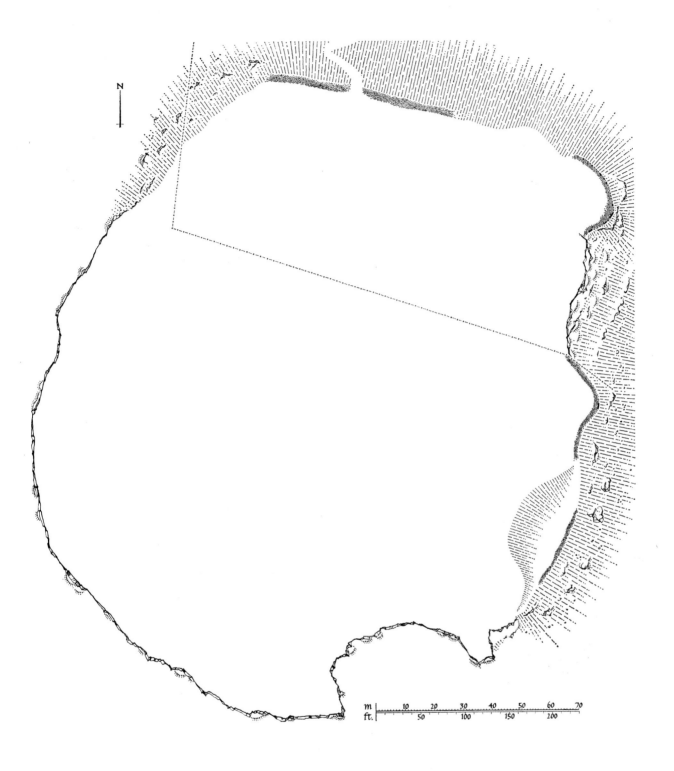

N

m
ft.

Fig. 36. Fort, Dùn Ormidale (No. 137; scale 1:1250)

71

seen round the S half of the perimeter, standing at best to a height of 1 m in five courses. The entrance probably lay within the gap on the ENE, where a modern track passes obliquely into the fort from the N. Within the

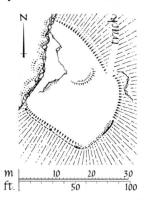

Fig. 37. Fort, Dùn Uabairtich (No. 138)

interior, a little to the W of the entrance, there is a low stony grass-grown bank, about 1·2 m thick, which forms a shallow arc. In the absence of excavation, its purpose is not clear.

832280   NM 82 NW   April 1970

139. Fort, Eilean Mór. On the moderately level summit of an isolated rocky knoll in the middle of Eilean Mór, the larger of two islands situated at the mouth of Loch Etive, there are the last vestiges of a fort. On all sides but the E, where grass-covered slopes provide relatively easy access, the way to the summit is barred by steep cliffs up to 9 m in height.

An irregular oval on plan, the fort has measured internally about 44 m from NE to SW by 25 m transversely. It has been defended round the E half of the perimeter by a stone wall built on the edge of the summit area, and also by two outworks, shown on a sketch-plan by Christison,[1] at the foot of the knoll on the E and S sides. All that survives of the inner wall is an intermittent grass-grown band of stony debris, nowhere more than 2 m in thickness, while the outer walls have been completely removed. The entrance appears to have been situated near the head of a steeply inclined path on the S, where the inner wall approached the cliff edge.

887347   NM 83 SE   May 1970

140. Fort, Kilcheran, Lismore. Some slight remains of a fort (Fig. 38) occupy the SW end of a rocky ridge 175 m E of Kilcheran, overlooking Port Kilcheran from a height of 25 m OD. The extreme SW tip of the ridge has been quarried and now presents a sheer rock-face, and the SE flank is also steep and rocky. The NW flank, however, falls less abruptly as a grassy slope to the public road, while from the NE there is easy access over almost level ground.

The fort has been defended by a single wall which encloses an area measuring at least 120 m in length by 40 m in greatest breadth. Quarrying has removed a stretch of the wall at the SW end, and no remains are

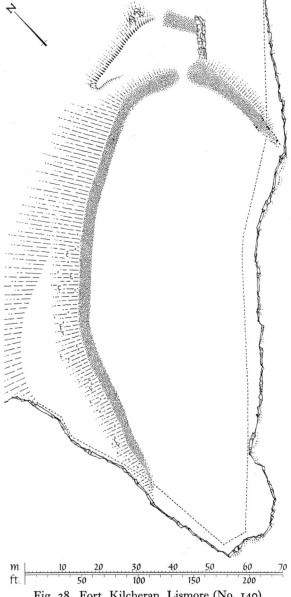

Fig. 38. Fort, Kilcheran, Lismore (No. 140)

now visible along the SE side, but its course can be traced along the NW side and round the NE end by a band of stony debris. The entrance is situated on the NE, and on either side of it the wall debris is standing to a height of 1 m; at one point on the ENE a few stones of both the inner and the outer faces survive *in situ*, indicating that the wall had a thickness of about 3 m.

---

[1] *PSAS*, xxiii (1888–9), 383.

About 10 m to 12 m outside the fort on the NE there are slight vestiges of an outer wall which has been drawn across the ridge to provide a protective screen for the entrance. Only a short stretch of this outwork can now be seen, appearing as a band of rubble, some 4·5 m thick, which extends NW for a distance of 9 m from the NE end of a natural rock outcrop across the line of the entrance-passage to give a staggered approach. After a gap measuring 2 m in width, the outer wall probably continued westwards for a further 25 m along the forward edge of a natural terrace before the steepness of the slope on the N made it no longer necessary; no trace of it, however, is now visible in this sector.

The interior of the fort is uneven, the SW half rising some 4·5 m higher than the NE portion. The only features that can be distinguished are what appear to be the ruined foundations of sub-rectangular buildings, now too indefinite to plan. As at least two of them overlie the fort wall, they are clearly secondary and probably of no great age.

826387   NM 83 NW   May 1968

141. Fort (probable), Kilmore. On the summit of an elongated knoll which projects from the W face of Sròn Mhór, about 320 m NNW of Kilmore farmhouse, there are the denuded remains of what has probably been a stone-walled fort; its overall dimensions are 37 m from NW to SE by 14 m transversely. The knoll can be approached with relative ease from either end, but on the NE and SW flanks steep rocky slopes, up to 5·5 m in height, make access extremely difficult. The summit area has been enclosed by a wall, at present visible for a short distance on both the NW and SE, where it appears as a low grass-covered band of rubble 2 m in average thickness. No facing-stones can now be seen, but on the SE a series of shallow quarry-scoops, lying as much as 1·6 m below the level of the summit, indicates the approximate line of the outer face.

The position of the entrance is marked by a gap in the debris, 1·5 m wide, at the NW end; the interior of the fort is featureless.

884252   NM 82 NE   May 1969

142. Fort, The Little Horse Shoe, Kerrera. This fort occupies the level summit of an isolated rocky hillock overlooking the S side of the bay called 'The Little Horse Shoe', and within 100 m of the shore. Although it stands at a height of only 15 m OD, the fort is difficult of access since the flanks of the hillock consist of sheer rock cliffs, broken at two points, on the NW and NE, by steep grass-covered slopes.

Oval on plan (Fig. 39), the fort measures 36 m by 27 m within a single wall drawn round the extreme edge of the summit of the knoll. Though reduced for the most part to a slight band of stony debris, the line of the wall can be traced for the whole circuit apart from a short gap on the NE; it appears to have measured from 2·5 m to 3 m in average thickness. On the SW, however, where the

rubble core survives as a grass-grown bank to a height of about 1 m, with a considerable number of stones belonging to the lowest course of both the inner and outer faces still in position, the thickness of the wall increases to a maximum of 3·6 m on either side of the entrance. The entrance itself is approached from the outside up a slight cleft in the rock, which has been widened and accentuated by the fort-builders. At its outer end the entrance-

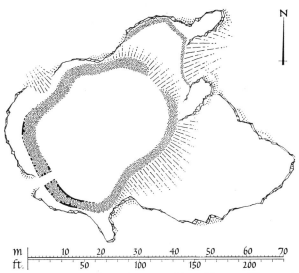

Fig. 39. Fort, The Little Horse Shoe, Kerrera (No. 142)

passage is 2·4 m wide, narrowing slightly to 2·1 m at its inner end, the side-walls giving no indication of having been checked for a door. Within the level interior of the fort there are several irregular spreads of stones, now overgrown by grass; as they do not appear to form any significant pattern, they probably represent debris discarded by the stone-robbers.

Outside the fort wall on the NE a thin band of stony debris, measuring up to 1·2 m in thickness, evidently represents the remains of a wall built round the margin of a fairly level shelf some 3 m below the summit, and across the neck of a steep grassy gully leading up to the shelf through the cliff. Clearly this outwork was of a much less substantial nature than the fort wall, but it seems likely that it was built at the same time since the gap in the fort wall on the NE may well mark the position of a postern giving access from the interior of the fort to the outwork.

817271   NM 82 NW   April 1970

143. Fort, Losgann Larnach. This fort (Fig. 40) occupies the NE summit of Beinn Mhór (182·3 m OD), which is known locally as 'Losgann Larnach' (The Toad of Lorn) because of its resemblance to a crouching toad. Unrivalled within the region for its great natural strength and the wide view that it commands over the Firth of Lorn to the NW, the summit is rendered impregnable to assault on that side and on the NE by almost vertical cliffs 6 m to 12 m in height, from the foot of which the ground falls steeply away, the seaward slopes being also encumbered by very large fallen boulders. On the S precipitous rock-faces afford moderately strong natural protection along most of the perimeter, but access to the summit is available on the SE, where the line of low cliffs is interrupted by a gully 9 m wide.

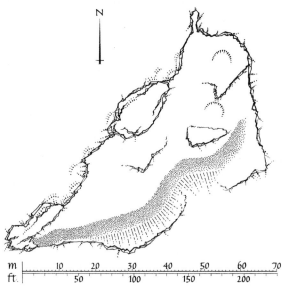

Fig. 40. Fort, Losgann Larnach (No. 143)

Roughly triangular on plan, the fort has measured internally about 76 m in length by a maximum of 21 m in width, and has been defended by a single stone wall drawn across the more vulnerable S and SE sides. The wall, which butted against the base of a rocky boss at the SW angle and probably terminated on the brink of the precipice on the E, is now in a heavily-robbed condition, being represented merely by a stony scarp in which no facing-stones are visible. The core material is spread in places to a width of 10 m, but the original wall-thickness was probably about 4 m. The entrance was presumably located on the SE, at the head of the debris-choked gully, but its exact position can no longer be identified.

The interior of the fort consists of steeply-inclined grassy shelves interspersed with rock outcrops. Two crescentic scarps at the NE end, each 5·2 m across, indicate the sites of round timber houses, and it is possible that a number of irregularly-shaped platforms elsewhere in the fort represent the remains of others.

799217   NM 72 SE   May 1966

144. Fort, Tom an Iasgaire. On the summit of Tom an Iasgaire (186·5 m OD), a conspicuous isolated hill dominating the NW end of the Pass of Brander, there is a fort (Fig. 41). Precipitous rocky slopes present an almost insuperable obstacle on the N, E and S, but access to the summit may be gained either directly over grass-covered slopes on the NW, or by means of a gentle

incline from the level shelf situated immediately below the fort on the SW.

An irregular oval on plan, the fort has measured 40·5 m by 24·4 m within a stone wall originally drawn round the margin of the summit, but now surviving on the W half of the perimeter only, where it appears as a grass-grown band of stony debris 3·0 m wide and of negligible height. Several short stretches and a few isolated stones of the outer face have been preserved in position, as shown on the plan, but no inner facing-stones can now be seen. A gap on the WSW, 2·4 m wide, may indicate the position of the entrance. Access to the summit has been further restricted by an outer wall, which sprang from the edge of the precipitous drop on the N and may

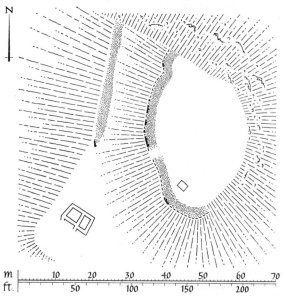

Fig. 41. Fort, Tom an Iasgaire (No. 144)

originally have continued along the flank of the hill immediately above the shelf on the SW. It has been reduced to a mere scatter of rubble 1·5 m to 2·7 m wide, in which one short stretch of outer facing-stones is visible. To the SW of the fort it has been completely removed, possibly to construct the rectangular structure of recent date whose foundations can still be seen on the adjacent shelf.

A radio repeater station has been erected in the S part of the interior, which is otherwise featureless.

044283   NN 02 NW   June 1969

145. Fort, Torr a' Chlaonaidh. This fort (Fig. 42) is situated at a height of about 75 m OD on the wooded NE end of a prominent isolated ridge 1·2 km W of Ardnaclach. The ridge is of a type commonly found in the locality, having precipitous flanks and steep rocky ends some 30 m in height. The ground occupied by the fort is separated from the rest of the summit area by a broad natural gully, which lies athwart the ridge and would help to protect the site against assault from the SW.

The defences consist of a single wall which may originally have enclosed the whole of the top of this end of the ridge, but which is now visible only on the SW side, where it runs along the crest of the gully. In this sector it is reduced to a band of rubble from 1 m to 2 m in thickness. No inner facing-stones can be seen, but

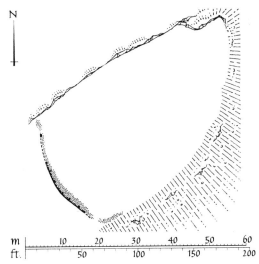

Fig. 42. Fort, Torr a' Chlaonaidh (No. 145)

the outer face still stands to a maximum height of 0·7 m in three courses; it is composed of large blocks of stone measuring up to 1·4 m long, 0·7 m high and 0·4 m thick. At either end of the wall there is a gap, the southernmost of which probably marks the position of the original entrance, while the other appears to be a relatively recent breach.

933434   NM 94 SW   May 1971

BROCHS

146. Broch (probable), An Dùn, Loch Fiart, Lismore. The remains of what is probably a broch with outworks (Fig. 43) stand on the NE end of a ridge overlooking Loch Fiart from a height of about 35 m OD. The steep sides of the ridge afford strong natural protection in all directions except the NE and SW, but additional defences have been drawn across the ridge only on the N. As a result of stone-robbing the remains now consist largely of a heavy band of grass-grown rubble representing the core material of a substantial wall; standing to a height of 1·2 m above the interior, it encloses a roughly circular area measuring about 13 m in diameter. Round the NW half of the perimeter some stretches of the outer face of the wall are exposed, standing at best to a height of 0·8 m in three courses. The only visible

inner facing-stones, however, are on the W, where the wall has a thickness of about 4·9 m. The entrance is on the NE; only one of the side-slabs of the passage can be seen but originally it was at least 3·6 m in length and 1·5 m in width. Within the thickness of the wall on the W side a narrow lintelled gallery, measuring 0·4 m in width, can be traced for a distance of 6 m. Its depth cannot be determined without excavation as it is choked with debris to within 0·7 m of the underside of the lintels. The narrowness of this gallery indicates that, as at the broch No. 147, its function must have been structural.

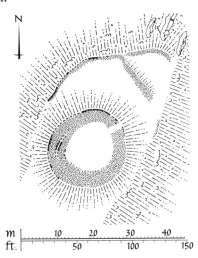

Fig. 43. Broch (probable), An Dùn, Loch Fiart, Lismore (No. 146)

Additional defences, designed to protect the entrance, have been drawn across the ridge on the N, thus cutting off a flat shelf some 4·6 m below the broch. The remains of a wall run round the perimeter of this shelf, and stretches of outer facing-stones may be seen on the NW with a thin spread of debris behind them; on the NE it survives as a low stony bank interrupted by a wide gap in line with the entrance to the broch. About 2 m below the level of this shelf, a further platform has been bordered by a wall now reduced to a band of stony debris, and likewise interrupted by a gap at its E end.

811376   NM 83 NW   May 1968

147. Broch, Tirefour Castle, Lismore. Standing in a prominent position on the highest point of an elongated limestone ridge 550 m SW of Port Maluag, this broch provides a conspicuous landmark on the E side of Lismore Island (Pl. 10A, B) and is one of the best-preserved prehistoric monuments in the county. From a height of 47·9 m OD the site commands an extensive prospect in all directions, especially towards the E across the Lynn of Lorn to the mainland beyond. The NW and SE flanks of the ridge fall steeply, the latter to a gently-sloping terrace about 20 m broad, whose outer limit is bounded by a precipitous cliff which rises from the shore;

access to the broch is, however, comparatively easy from the NE and SW along the crest of the ridge.

Almost circular on plan (Fig. 44), the broch is constructed, at ground-level, of a solid dry-stone wall measuring 4·5 m in average thickness, which encloses a central court about 12·2 m in diameter. Though considerably reduced by stone-robbing and collapse, the outer face of the wall (Pl. 10C) is still standing, for the most part, to a height of at least 3 m, and on the SE it

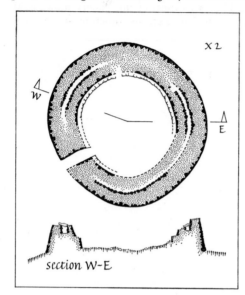

section W-E

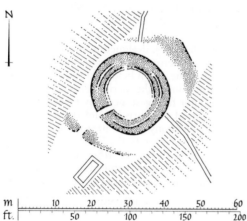

Fig. 44. Broch, Tirefour Castle, Lismore (No. 147)

rises to its maximum surviving height of 4·9 m with a uniform batter of about one in four. The footings and the first five or six courses of masonry, up to a height of about 1·5 m above ground, incorporate a considerable number of massive boulders; above this level, however, the coursing is less regular, the material used including a high proportion of thin slabs with pinnings of smaller stones.

By comparison, the inner face of the wall has suffered more severely, and the floor of the central court is

buried under a mass of debris to a depth of at least 1 m. The best surviving portion is in the NW quadrant, where the face is exposed to a height of 3·5 m. After rising almost vertically for about 1·5 m above the present surface (i.e. about 2·5 m above the floor-level), the inner face is stepped back to form a level ledge or scarcement 0·6 m wide. At the present time the scarcement can be traced for only three-quarters of the circuit, the SE quadrant being buried under a spread of fallen stones. Above the scarcement the face continues upwards for a further 1·5 m with a batter of about one in three, the quality of the masonry being much inferior to that of the lower portion. Below the scarcement on the N, the face of the wall is interrupted by a doorway 1·0 m wide; now choked with debris, this opening probably gives access either to a mural cell or to a staircase leading upwards within the thickness of the wall.

The entrance to the broch faces WSW and is 1·4 m wide at either end. The SE side-wall of the passage is straight, but the NW side is slightly concave, thus increasing the width to a maximum of 1·5 m at a point 2·7 m from its outer end. The walling at the entrance is so ruinous that no traces can be seen of door-checks, bar-holes or an entrance to a mural guard-chamber, and the floor of the passage is hidden by debris.

At a height of about 2·7 m above ground-level traces of an intramural gallery can be seen in the broch wall; it was probably continuous, but the collapse of the wall has completely destroyed it on either side of the main entrance, and elsewhere it is now more or less in a fragmentary condition. A well-preserved stretch is, however, visible for a distance of 7 m in the NW quadrant, measuring 1 m in height and 0·6 m in average breadth internally, and roofed by a series of large transverse lintels. At the open (S) end (Pl. 10D) it can be seen that the side-walls of the gallery are very unevenly finished internally and that the floor appears to be formed by the unpaved core-material of the solid broch wall below, indicating that the function of the gallery was merely structural. Another short section of the gallery, still lintelled but in a rather unstable condition, survives on the E, but elsewhere little remains visible except the outer casement, which stands to a maximum height of 0·8 m above the gallery floor. The sockets where the outer ends of lintel-stones have rested can be seen intermittently, and some of the dislodged lintels are lying embedded in the debris that now partly fills the gallery. On the NE, about 0·7 m above the level of the scarcement, the inner face of the broch wall is pierced by an opening 0·9 m wide, which appears to have served as a relieving-slit and not as a doorway.

The floor of the central court is buried under debris, and on the E, where there has been a particularly heavy collapse, a crude attempt has been made to rebuild the inner face of the wall both above and below the level of the scarcement.

On both the NE and SW sides the broch is protected by outworks consisting, in each case, of a boulder-faced rubble wall running transversely across the ridge. There is no evidence to show whether or not these walls were originally linked to form a continuous defence encircling the broch, but this seems unlikely. The NE outwork now appears as a grass-grown stony bank spread to a thickness of as much as 5·5 m and standing up to 1·5 m in height externally and 0·7 m internally. The surviving stretch of the outer face is at best 0·7 m high in three courses. At its W end the wall has been reduced to a mere scarp and there is no indication of an entrance. The SW outwork is of similar construction and appearance, measuring 3·0 m in thickness at the base and up to 1·1 m in height externally. No inner facing-stones are visible, but the outer face survives to a height of 0·7 m in two courses. There is a well-marked entrance, 1·5 m wide, situated almost in line with that of the broch.

Immediately outside the SW outwork there are the stone foundations of a rectangular building of comparatively recent date, which may be contemporary with the turf-and-stone boundary dykes indicated on the plan.

867429   NM 84 SE   May 1968

DUNS[1]

148. Dun (probable), An Dùnan, Dalintart.
The summit of an elongated rocky ridge about 330 m W of Dalintart farmhouse is occupied by the wasted remains of an oval enclosure which has probably been a dun. A precipitous rock-face, some 11 m in height, affords strong natural protection on all sides except the ENE, where there is relatively easy access up a gentle grassy slope.

The dun has measured about 18·3 m from NE to SW by 12·2 m transversely within a single stone wall drawn round the margin of the summit area. Almost completely obliterated by stone-robbing, the wall is now represented by a low grass-covered band of debris, which attains a maximum width of 4·5 m on the NE, where the entrance was most probably located, but elsewhere rarely exceeds 1·8 m; although no facing-stones have survived *in situ*, in places the approximate line of the outer face is indicated by robber trenches.

862292   NM 82 NE   May 1966

149. Dun, An Dùnan, Minard Point.
This dun (Fig. 45) occupies the summit of a rocky knoll overlooking the narrows at the mouth of Loch Feochan some 190 m E of Minard Point. The flanks of the knoll are everywhere steep, but on the NW and SW present almost vertical rock-faces up to 9 m in height.

Oval on plan, the dun has measured 11·9 m by 9·1 m within a massively-built stone wall about 4·3 m in maximum thickness. Considerable stretches of the outer face survive *in situ*, the best-preserved sector being on the E, where the wall stands to a height of 1·2 m in seven courses; the lowest course lies as much as 1·8 m below the level of the summit area. Only a few inner facing-stones are, however, visible.

The entrance was probably situated on the W, where a rock-fall has removed nearly all traces of the wall and a grassy path gives access to the summit. Immediately to the S of this area an earthfast stone, which protrudes

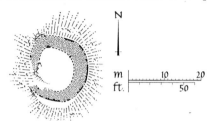

Fig. 45. Dun, An Dùnan, Minard Point (No. 149)

from the band of rubble only 1·7 m inside the line of the outer face, may indicate the presence of some intramural feature.

818235   NM 82 SW   May 1967

150. Dun, An Dùn, Clenamacrie.
This dun is situated 500 m ESE of Clenamacrie farmhouse, on the top of an isolated knoll on the S side of the public road through Glen Lonan. The following account and the plan (Fig. 46) incorporate evidence revealed by excavation carried out in 1967 by the Lorn Archaeological Society.[2]

The dun is oval on plan, measuring about 29 m by 21 m within a wall which has consisted of a compact rubble core faced on either side with large boulders. Little now remains, however, except core material, appearing as a low grass-covered stony bank through which a few outer

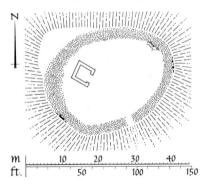

Fig. 46. Dun, An Dùn, Clenamacrie (No. 150)

facing-stones protrude on the E and SW. On the SSE the wall was 2·5 m thick on either side of the entrance, but it increased to as much as 4·6 m thick on the W. The entrance was 1·8 m wide, and the side-walls of the passage showed no indication of having been checked for a door.

Within the W half of the interior there are the founda-

---

[1] See also No. 136.
[2] *DES* (1969), 9, and additional information from Mrs U V G Betts, who directed the excavation.

tions of a small rectangular building, which is clearly secondary. The only relics recovered during the excavation were fragments of two flat rotary-querns, which had been incorporated in the dun wall.

928283   NM 92 NW   May 1968

151. Dun, An Dùn, Sloc a' Bhrighide, Lismore.
This dun (Fig. 47) is situated 800 m SW of Fiart farmhouse on the tip of a rocky promontory overlooking the shore from a height of about 30 m OD. Except on the NW, where there is comparatively easy access, the sides of the promontory are precipitous, and on the NE and SE they take the form of sheer cliffs up to 10·7 m high. Only intermittent traces of the dun wall now remain, appearing for the most part as bands of stony debris enclosing an area measuring 23 m by 20 m. No inner facing-stones are visible, but several portions of the outer face survive, the best-preserved section, on the SSE, standing to a height of 1·4 m with the lowest course set 3 m below the level of the interior. At one point on the W side two separate overlapping stretches of facing-stones can be seen, the inner stretch being set back about 1 m and some 1·2 m above the other. This feature may imply that the wall was rebuilt, but a more likely explanation is that, because of the steepness of the slope at this point, extra stability was needed and an internal revetment was introduced. A similar structural feature is recorded in the dun No. 186.

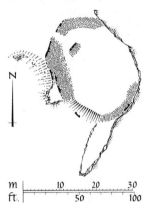

Fig. 47. Dun, An Dùn, Sloc a' Bhrighide, Lismore (No. 151)

The entrance is on the NW. A short distance to the SE, within the interior of the dun, there is an isolated spread of stony debris, which is accompanied by three earthfast boulders ranged in a straight line along its NW edge. If contemporary with the dun, this would be a very unusual, if not unique, structure, presumably intended to provide protection for the entrance. It may, however, be a secondary feature, since much of the interior of the dun has been under cultivation at some time, and the remains of a comparatively recent stone

wall can be seen overlying the dun wall between the entrance and the cliff edge on the N.

799365   NM 73 NE   May 1968

152. Dun, Ardanstur 1.
This dun (Fig. 48) is situated 150 m WNW of Ardanstur on an isolated knoll, partly tree-covered, which rises about 12 m above the surrounding ground to a height of 45 m OD. The flanks of the knoll are everywhere steep, and on the N and W present bare rock-faces up to 4·6 m in height. The dun wall encloses the whole of the top of the knoll, an area measuring 36·5 m by 16·8 m; it has been heavily robbed,

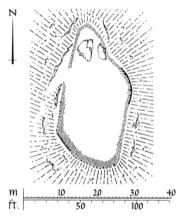

Fig. 48. Dun, Ardanstur 1 (No. 152)

but the spread of core material suggests that it had a thickness of at least 2 m. No inner facing-stones can be seen, but stretches of the outer face are exposed, especially on the NE and SW. Rock outcrops have been incorporated in the wall in several places, and, where necessary, underlying crevices have been filled with dry walling to provide a firm base. On the NE, where it is best preserved, the outer face is still standing to a height of 1·4 m. The surviving facing-stones are for the most part large blocks, measuring up to 1·1 m by 0·4 m by 0·4 m, and the lowest course is sometimes as much as 1·8 m below the ground-level inside the dun. The entrance was probably situated on the NW, where the rock face is interrupted by a natural shelf which leads obliquely from the SW to the top of the knoll.

In the higher, or N, part of the interior there are the remains of what has been a substantial walled structure, too indefinite to plan; it is, however, clearly of later date than the dun. The S part of the interior contains several quarry-scoops and a small rectangular plot which has at some time been under cultivation.

822136   NM 81 SW   May 1967

153. Dun, Ardanstur 2.
This dun is situated at a height of 75 m OD on rising ground 350 m WNW of Ardanstur and 185 m WNW of the dun No. 152. The site is a rocky promontory, sloping steeply in all direc-

tions except to the E where the immediate approach is comparatively easy; the promontory is divided by a shallow gully into two pronounced rock ridges aligned NE and SW, and the dun stands on the higher (SE) ridge.

Oval on plan (Fig. 49), the dun measures 16·7 m by 11·6 m within a wall which, at the one place where it can still be measured, has a thickness of 2·4 m. Only one inner facing-stone is now visible, but considerable stretches of the outer face survive round the S half of the perimeter, standing at best to a height of 0·8 m in two courses. Rock outcrop has been incorporated into the base of the wall in many places, especially on the S and W where the wall mounts the SW end of the bare

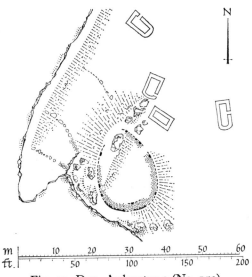

Fig. 49. Dun, Ardanstur 2 (No. 153)

rock spine and rides along its crest towards the NE. The position of the entrance is uncertain, but is most probably represented by the gap in the wall on the NE.

Beyond the dun to the N and NE there are the ruined stone foundations of at least four small rectangular buildings, clearly of later date than the dun and presumably associated with the cultivation that has at some time covered practically all the arable space both inside the dun and in the immediate vicinity. In the gully to the NW there are three small plots, formerly cultivated, which are revetted on their lower sides with boulders.

820137　　　　　　　　NM 81 SW　　　　　　　　May 1967

154. Dun, Arduaine. On the summit of an isolated steep-sided hill (60 m OD), situated some 70 m NW of the old farmstead of Arduaine, there is an oval dun measuring internally 18·3 m from NE to SW by 12·5 m transversely. It has been defended by a single wall, now reduced for most of its circuit to a ragged turf-covered band of stony debris about 4·1 m in average width and of negligible height. Several earthfast boulders which

protrude through the turf on the N and NW may possibly indicate the line of the outer face, but no inner facing-stones are visible. The entrance was probably situated on the SW, where the wall debris is interrupted for a distance of 1 m.

A flag-pole has at some time been erected on the summit of the hill, but otherwise the interior of the dun is featureless.

797105　　　　　　　　NM 71 SE　　　　　　　　May 1969

155. Dun, Ballycastle, Luing. This dun, also known locally as the 'North Fort', stands on a rocky knoll which forms the highest part of a small ridge (55 m OD) immediately E of Ballycastle farmhouse. The flanks and S end of the ridge are moderately steep, but from the N there is easy access over gently sloping ground.

Oval on plan (Fig. 50), the dun measures 32·0 m by 18·3 m within a wall which varies in thickness from about 4·0 m to 4·7 m on each side of the entrance. Considerable stretches of both the inner and outer faces are visible, but the lowest courses are everywhere hidden by a mass of fallen debris which covers most of the interior and extends down the flanks of the knoll in a scree-like spread. On the SE where it is best preserved, the inner face is exposed for a height of 2 m in ten courses, and the amount of debris suggests that it probably reached a height of at least 3 m originally. The best visible portion of the outer face is on the S, where the fallen stones have been cleared back over a distance of about 8 m to reveal it standing 1·1 m in height in four courses.

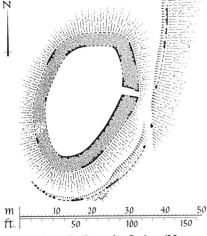

Fig. 50. Dun, Ballycastle, Luing (No. 155)

The entrance, on the E, is clearly defined. Measuring 1·45 m in width at its outer end, the passage is checked for a door at a point 1·22 m from the outside. Only the N door-check can now be seen as there has been a considerable collapse of the masonry on the S side and the passage itself is now largely filled with debris. Beyond the check the passage increases to a maximum width of 2·13 m at its inner end. Another gap in the wall on the

SW appears to be merely a modern breach caused by stone-robbing.

The wasted remains of an outer defensive wall can be seen intermittently on the edge of a narrow terrace on the E and S; all that now survives is a number of massive blocks, some of them still in position and others now lying dislodged nearby, which represent the lowest course of the outer face. Wherever possible natural outcrop has been incorporated in the line of this wall. No trace of the wall can be seen on the N and W, and its function has evidently been to afford a protective screen to the main entrance to the dun.

752120   NM 71 SE   May 1966

156. Dun, Barguillean. On an isolated knoll overlooking the E end of Glen Lonan, 250 m SSW of Barguillean farmhouse, there are the last vestiges of a dun which has been enclosed on three sides by an outer wall or bank; on the N side the slope of the knoll is so steep that any additional defence was evidently considered unnecessary.

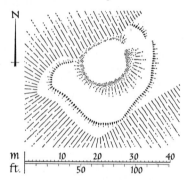

Fig. 51. Dun, Barguillean (No. 156)

Oval on plan (Fig. 51), the dun has measured about 12·8 m by 10 m internally, but all that remains of the wall is a thin band of rubble core, interrupted by an entrance at the E end. The outer work, 1·5 m below the dun, is now reduced to a mere scarp; its entrance is also on the E, roughly in line with that of the dun.

979285   NM 92 NE   May 1967

157. Dun, Barr a' Chaistealain. The remains of a dun (Fig. 52) are situated at a height of 95 m OD among a cluster of ruined cottages on a flat-topped ridge 230 m SE of Dalmally Station. Although it has been extensively damaged, the dun wall can still be traced for three-quarters of its circuit; circular on plan, it originally enclosed an area measuring about 15·5 m in diameter. Outer facing-stones survive over a continuous stretch of 20 m round the S half of the perimeter and for a much shorter distance on the N, standing at best to a height of 1·3 m in two courses; some very large blocks have been used, the largest measuring 1·3 m by 0·8 m by 0·75 m. On the N advantage has been taken of a rock outcrop, which

must originally have been incorporated into the structure of the wall. Only a few inner facing-stones are visible, situated on the SW and standing to a maximum height of 0·6 m. They indicate, however, that in this sector the wall was between 1·7 m and 2 m thick at the base. The

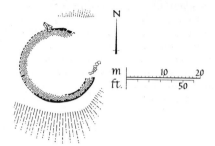

Fig. 52. Dun, Barr a' Chaistealain (No. 157)

exact position of the entrance is not known, but it was evidently situated at some point on the NE where, apart from seven dislodged boulders, there are now no surface indications of the wall.

162270   NN 12 NE   May 1970

158. Dun, Barr Mór. The dun on the summit of Barr Mór, a steep-sided tree-clad hill rising some 20 m above the SE shore of Loch Awe, is oval on plan (Fig. 53) and measures approximately 29 m by 19 m within the ruins of a dry-stone wall 3·7 m to 5 m thick. The wall is best preserved on the SW, where considerable stretches of the inner and outer faces survive *in situ*, the latter rising at

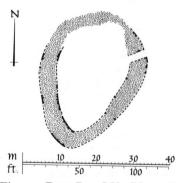

Fig. 53. Dun, Barr Mór (No. 158)

one point to a height of 0·5 m in three courses. Elsewhere, however, and particularly on the N, it has been severely denuded by stone-robbing and appears as a low band of scattered core-material in which only a few isolated stones of either face can still be seen. The entrance, measuring 2 m in width, is situated on the ENE, where the immediate approach to the dun is over less steeply sloping ground.

The interior falls 1·75 m from S to N and contains no traces of structures.

977105   NM 91 SE   May 1971

159. Dun, Caisteal Suidhe Cheannaidh. One of the best-preserved duns in Lorn occupies a commanding position overlooking the valley that runs between Taynuilt and Kilchrenan. It stands on the highest part of the E end of a rock ridge (210 m OD) situated 1·55 km NW of Kilchrenan, and is protected by steep slopes on all sides except on the W where there is a gentle approach along the crest of the ridge. Almost circular on plan (Fig. 54), the dun measures 11·9 m by 13·1 m within a wall up to 4·9 m thick. The outer face, which consists of large stones measuring 1·65 m by 0·6 m and 0·45 m in thickness, rises with a slight batter to a maximum height of over 2 m on the W. The inner face of the wall still stands to an average height of 2 m in about nine courses, but the base of the wall on both sides is now largely

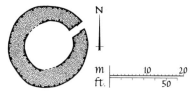

Fig. 54. Dun, Caisteal Suidhe Cheannaidh (No. 159)

obscured by fallen debris. It is recorded[1] that it stood to a height of about 6 m before it was used as a quarry for field walls. The entrance is on the NE side and measures 1·75 m externally, with large blocks forming the outer corners. The passage is checked for a door at a point 1·7 m from the outside, where it widens to 2·1 m. The inner portion of the passage, 2·4 m in length, has slightly curved sides which seem to be corbelled inwards at the top, but this may have been due to the settlement of the stones. Some excavation was undertaken in the interior in 1890,[2] in the course of which several hearths were discovered, as well as the bones of horse and deer.

029242   NN 02 SW   June 1969

160. Dun, Camuslaich, Seil. The end of a narrow rocky ridge 430 m SSW of the derelict steading of Camuslaich is occupied by a dun and its outworks (Fig. 55), once locally known as 'Caisteal Ach-a-luachrach'. On all sides except the NE, where easier access is available along the spine of the ridge, the site is protected by steep grassy slopes, interspersed with sheer-faced rock outcrops; at the present time almost impenetrable whitethorn scrub presents an additional barrier on the NW.

An irregular oval on plan, the dun has measured about 17 m by 14 m within a wall, now represented by a heather-covered stony bank 4·3 m in average thickness and as much as 1·5 m in height above the level of the featureless interior; several inner facing-stones have survived *in situ* on the NW, and a single stretch of the outer face can be seen on the SW. The entrance was probably situated on the ENE, immediately to the S of a large quarry-scoop, where a modern path leads diagonally up the flank of the ridge; a large earthfast boulder on the

NW margin of the path as it passes through the wall may indicate the position of one side of the entrance-passage.

Additional protection has been provided by two outer walls, one built round the nose of the ridge on the SW, and the other drawn across its spine to the NE. The former is represented by a low debris-strewn scarp and a single outer facing-stone. The latter, however, appears as a prominent stony bank in which short stretches of both the inner and outer faces survive, indicating an original wall-thickness of about 2·7 m; a gap on the S, where the wall is interrupted by a modern path, may mark the site of an original gateway.

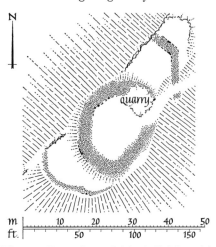

Fig. 55. Dun, Camuslaich, Seil (No. 160)

Macadam states[3] that *c.* 1845, doubtless during the extensive stone-robbing then taking place, 'a bar of gold . . . a sword and other articles' were found in the ruins of the dun. All the objects were subsequently lost, and no further details have been recorded.

771185   NM 71 NE   April 1966

161. Dun, Castles. This dun is situated 60 m NNW of Castles farmhouse on a low spur which projects towards the SE from the foot of the S slopes of Stob Maol. Its position is somewhat unusual in having little or no natural defensive strength, although there are several other sites available near by which would have been preferable in this respect. Moreover, a crescentic scarp on the N side, up to 0·6 m high, shows that the site was deliberately prepared by digging into the slope in order to provide a level platform for the dun; the modification of a natural feature in this way is a technique rarely used by dun-builders and hitherto unrecorded in the county.

Circular on plan (Fig. 56), the dun measures about 18 m in diameter within a wall now badly reduced by stone-robbing. Eleven large outer facing-stones, measuring up to 1·2 m by 0·7 m and 0·7 m in height, remain in

[1] *PSAS*, xxv (1890–1), 118–27.
[2] Ibid.
[3] Ibid., xxx (1895–6), 24.

position, and the holes from which at least twenty others have been removed are still clearly visible. On the N side several of the facing stones have their outer sides completely embedded in the scarp already mentioned. No inner facing-stones are visible and the core material appears as a low grass-grown spread of rubble, indicating that the wall was probably at least 3 m

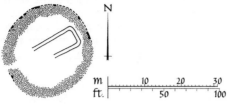

Fig. 56. Dun, Castles (No. 161)

thick. A gap on the WSW represents the original entrance. The interior has been severely disturbed, and the only recognisable feature is the foundation of a sub-rectangular building which is clearly secondary to the dun, but which may be contemporary with the medieval castle mentioned under No. 283.

138296   NN 12 NW   May 1971

162. Dun, Clachadow. The fragmentary remains of an oval dun occupy the summit of a knoll which projects from the lower S slopes of Deagh Choimhead some 500 m NW of the ruined farmhouse of Clachadow. The dun measures 11·6 m from E to W by 8·5 m transversely within a heavily-robbed stone wall, which now appears as a ragged stony bank only 3 m in average thickness and not more than 0·3 m in height. A number of massive blocks, scattered across the steep slope beneath the dun on the W and doubtless deriving from the outer face of the wall on that side, testify to its former strength.

Although the position of the entrance is not apparent, access would have been easiest across a fairly broad col on the N.

943277   NM 92 NW   May 1969

163. Dun, Dunach. This dun (Fig. 57), 570 m ENE of Dunach House, occupies the highest point of a tree-covered ridge situated close to the shore at the E end of Loch Feochan. Sheer rock-faces up to 18 m in height render the site almost impregnable on the E and W, but on the S the immediate approach is over more gently sloping ground, and to the N the line of cliffs is broken by a natural grassy ramp.

The dun wall has been severely reduced by stone-robbing and tree-planting, and now appears as a low band of rubble from 1·5 m to 2·7 m wide, enclosing a roughly oval area measuring 11·6 m by 14·3 m; no facing-stones are visible. Of the two gaps in the wall debris, that on the NNW almost certainly represents an original entrance, while the one on the E was probably caused by recent disturbance. There is no trace of the

internal 'traverse' recorded by Christison,[1] and it seems unlikely that such a feature ever existed. Inspection of his published site-plan strongly suggests that Christison mistook the natural scarp situated to the NNE of the entrance for an artificial defence-work and was therefore led to interpret the arc of dun wall lying immediately to the S of it as some form of internal blocking.

On the S, where a broad shelf slopes gently down from the dun to the shore, additional defence has been provided by an arc of walling drawn across the ridge from E to W. It too has been subjected to severe stone-robbing, all that remains being a moss-grown spread of stony debris 3 m in maximum width and 0·3 m in height. The

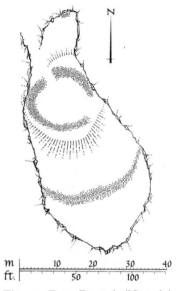

Fig. 57. Dun, Dunach (No. 163)

quarries from which the core material was probably obtained can be seen as shallow scoops lying immediately within the line of the wall. A short stretch of stony bank situated on the edge of the cliff, about 13 m N of the dun, supports Christison's claim[2] that this side also was defended by an outwork.

868249   NM 82 SE   May 1967

164. Dun, Dùn an Fheurain. This dun occupies the top of an isolated stack, about 15 m in height, which is situated close to the shore 700 m NW of Gallanach. The dun wall follows the margin of the summit area, but apart from a short stretch of outer facing-stones on the E side it is now reduced to a grass-covered stony bank. Internally the dun measures about 23 m by 12 m. The entrance was presumably on the NE, no approach being practicable from any other direction owing to the steepness of the sides of the stack.

Excavations have been undertaken on several occa-

---

[1] *PSAS*, xxiii (1888–9), 392.
[2] Ibid., 391.

sions, not within the dun itself but in the midden deposit at the base of the stack on the W side. A recent re-assessment of the finds[1] demonstrates that they fall into two distinct groups. The earlier group, which includes a sherd of samian ware, a bronze pin with a projecting ring-head, a bronze finger-ring and a bronze strap-loop, possibly of Roman origin, indicates a date about the 2nd century AD for the building of the dun. An antler pottery-stamp, a number of bone pins with globular heads and a fragment of a composite bone comb suggest a second occupation of the site in the 6th century AD or rather later.

824266   NM 82 NW   June 1968

165. Dun, Dùnan Molach. On the summit of a whale-backed ridge, 115 m SE of Lower Ardoran farmhouse, there are the remains of a sub-circular dun (Fig. 58) measuring internally about 11·6 m by 9·1 m. The wall has been reduced by stone-robbing to a grass-grown

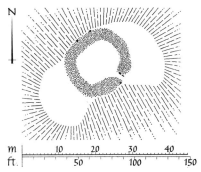

Fig. 58. Dun, Dùnan Molach (No. 165)

stony bank 3·5 m in average thickness and not more than 0·3 m in height, in which only three isolated outer facing-stones are visible. The entrance, which probably measured about 1·5 m in width, faces SE, and at least one of the stones defining the NE side of the passage is still in position. The interior is featureless.

845241   NM 82 SW   May 1967

166. Dun, Dùn Aorain, Seil. On a rocky promontory which rises to a height of 9 m above the shore, some 460 m W of Dunmore House, there are the conspicuous remains of a sub-oval dun and its outwork (Fig. 59). The site is protected on nearly every side by precipitous rocky faces, relatively easy access being available only on the NE, where the line of cliffs crossing the neck of the promontory is interrupted for a distance of about 6 m. Immediately to the NW, however, lies one of the safest landing-places on the W coast of the island.

The dun, which occupies the summit of the promontory, measures internally about 17 m in length by 12 m in greatest width. Its wall, being composed mainly of the local slate, an extremely friable material with low resistance to weathering, is in places in an advanced state of dilapidation. It is best preserved on the E,

where it has been built upon the crest of a rocky spine and appears as a grass-grown stony bank rising to a height of as much as 3·3 m above the level of the interior, but for much of the W half of the perimeter it has been reduced to a mere scarp. Several short stretches and isolated stones of the outer face can be seen protruding through the turf in places, as shown on the plan, while at one point on the S it survives to a height of 0·76 m in six courses.

A brief trial excavation conducted by one of the Commission's officers in 1970[2] revealed that the 'small recess' noticed by Christison[3] in the inner half of the wall on the SE was in fact a mural cell measuring 1·4 m

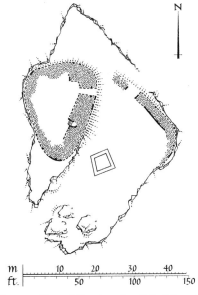

Fig. 59. Dun, Dùn Aorain, Seil (No. 166)

in length and 0·9 m in average width, which was approached from the interior by means of a staircase, handsomely built in slabs of slate; the cell was later used as a midden, the refuse with which it was gradually filled containing numerous shells such as limpet and peri-winkle.[4] Limited investigation of the interior beside the staircase suggested that there had been only one major period of occupation, but none of the objects recovered during excavation could be closely dated; they included a few crumbs of hand-made pottery, a crude slate disc and an anvil-stone.

It was further discovered that, whereas to the S of the cell the thickness of the dun wall was approximately 4·3 m, on the N it had been as much as 5·3 m, the increase being achieved by building the inner face at the foot of

[1] Ibid., ciii (1970–1), 100–12.
[2] The Commissioners are indebted to Mr I MacFarlane for permission to carry out this work.
[3] *PSAS*, xxiii (1888–9), 400.
[4] For the identification of these items the Commissioners are indebted to the Oceanographical Laboratory of the Scottish Marine Biological Association, Edinburgh.

the rocky spine along which the wall ran instead of on its crest. The greater thickness appears to have been maintained round the whole of the NE quadrant, extending for a distance of about 8 m on either side of the entrance and probably terminating on the NNE, where a line of earthfast slabs probably indicates the position of a second cell or staircase. Without excavation it is impossible to determine the purpose of such a thickening, but it may have been to facilitate the construction in this sector of intramural features, such as a gallery or guard-cell. The resulting plan is reminiscent of the so-called 'blockhouses' of promontory forts in Orkney, Shetland and Caithness.[1]

The entrance faces E, the width of the passage, at least in its outer half, being 1·5 m; the interior of the dun is for the most part level and featureless.

The outwork, consisting of a wall 2·4 m thick, has been drawn across the neck of the promontory, skirting the line of cliffs on the SE and, although the point of junction no longer survives, abutting against the dun wall a little to the N of the entrance. It thus not only provided additional protection on the landward side, where access was relatively easy, but also served to define the NE end of a roughly trapezoidal annexe measuring about 30 m by 15 m and lying as much as 3·7 m below the level of the dun. The wall of the annexe is also composed largely of slate and is severely reduced, surviving for the most part as a grass-covered stony bank, in which a single long stretch of inner facing-stones and several stones of the outer face are still visible. The gateway, which is situated opposite the break in the cliffs and in line with the dun entrance, is no less than 3·2 m in width, the side-walls of the inner part of the passageway being particularly well preserved.

Immediately below the dun on the SE there are the ruined stone foundations of a small rectangular building of no great age.

747171   NM 71 NW   May 1966

167. Dun (probable), Dùn Athaich (Site). The structure that once stood on the summit of Dùn Athaich (166 m OD), a conspicuous steep-sided hill about 1·8 km SW of Dalmally, was probably a sub-circular dun. The site is now occupied by a monument erected to the memory of the Gaelic poet Duncan Ban MacIntyre, and all that remains to be seen of the earlier structure is an arc of grass-grown stony debris bordering the E margin of the summit area. Christison estimated[2] that the overall diameter had been about 14·3 m.

144258   NN 12 NW   May 1970

168. Dun, Dùn Bachlach. This dun (Fig. 60), 800 m W of Balure farmhouse, occupies the top of an isolated rocky stack 15 m in height, which is situated within 50 m of the shore. Except on the NE and W, where there are steep grassy slopes, the stack presents almost sheer rock-faces in all directions. The dun wall is built round the margin of the summit area, the lowest course of the

outer face being bedded in the sides of the stack at a distance of as much as 2·6 m below the crest. Now largely reduced to a band of stony rubble in which only a few facing-stones are visible, the wall appears to have varied in thickness from 1·8 m on the S to about 3·6 m

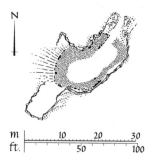

Fig. 60. Dun, Dùn Bachlach (No. 168)

on the W. The entrance, about 1·5 m wide, is on the NE, where a spine of rock affords a convenient approach. Internally the dun measures 15 m from NE to SW by a maximum of 6 m transversely.

869386   NM 83 NE   May 1969

169. Dun, Dùn Bhlaran. This dun (Fig. 61) stands at a height of 60 m OD on a small rocky knoll at the S end of a ridge 350 m NE of Minard farm. It is circular on plan, measuring about 11 m in diameter within a wall

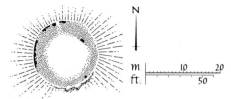

Fig. 61. Dun, Dùn Bhlaran (No. 169)

which has probably been about 3 m in thickness. Much of the wall has been robbed to provide material for two adjacent buildings of no great age, but several stretches of outer facing-stones remain in position on the NW. Massive blocks of stone have been used, two of which, on the N, may have flanked the original entrance.

826241   NM 82 SW   May 1967

170. Dun, Dùn Chathach. This dun (Fig. 62) is situated on the summit of a prominent hill which overlooks the S shore of Loch Etive 630 m E of Auchnacloich railway station. Although the immediate approach from the SE is over gently undulating terrain, on the NW the ground falls steeply down to the shore 50 m below.

Circular on plan, the dun measures 18·3 m in diameter externally. The wall, which has been about 3·4 m in

---

[1] Hamilton, J R C, *Excavations at Clickhimin, Shetland* (1968), 54–61.
[2] *PSAS*, xxiii (1888–9), 412.

average thickness, is now reduced to a low grass-grown stony bank, but considerable stretches of the outer face are still visible *in situ*. Many of the facing stones, which lie as much as 1·6 m below the level of the summit, are of massive proportions, the largest measuring 1·4 m by 1·3 m and 1·0 m in height. It is uncertain which of the three gaps now visible in the wall indicates the site of the original entrance.

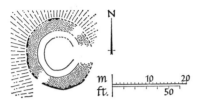

Fig. 62. Dun, Dùn Chathach (No. 170)

The interior is occupied by the foundations of a penannular enclosure of recent date, which has encroached upon the inner face of the dun wall.

967340   NM 93 SE   June 1969

171. Dun, Dùn Chrùban, Lismore. Situated 100 m S of Dalnarrow farmhouse, this dun and its outworks (Pl. 11A) stand in a conspicuous position on the NE end of a rock ridge, overlooking the shore from a height of 15 m OD. The ridge ends abruptly in a sheer cliff, up to 7·6 m high, which renders the site virtually inaccessible from the N and E, and the only unimpeded and relatively easy approach is from the SW along the crest of the ridge.

Oval on plan (Fig. 63), the dun measures about 15 m by 11 m internally. The W sector of the main wall (A), 3·6 m in maximum thickness at the base, is still in a good state of preservation. The well-built outer face,

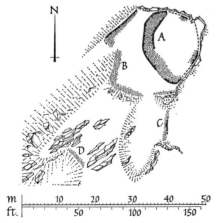

Fig. 63. Dun, Dùn Chrùban, Lismore (No. 171)

incorporating some very large blocks in the lower courses, is up to 3·4 m in height, and the core material continues even higher. A small modern cairn has been

built on the highest point. The inner face is constructed of smaller stones and, where visible, stands to a height of only 1·2 m in five courses; elsewhere, however, it is buried under a heavy spread of fallen rubble. The entrance was situated somewhere within the gap on the SSW, where the outer face is interrupted for a distance of 3 m. Its precise position is uncertain, since the wall has been rebuilt at this point in comparatively recent times.

In marked contrast to the sector just described, only very slight traces survive of any walling round the E half of the perimeter; they comprise two short lengths of outer facing-stones accompanied by a light spread of stony debris, the rest having presumably fallen over the edge of the cliff. It can be seen that the massive W part of the wall tapers off sharply at either end as it reaches the cliff edge, and on the NNW it ends in an exposed face only 1·2 m thick; this suggests that the W portion was constructed first, as a separate element, and that the E part was then abutted against it and not bonded into it. At any rate, there is little doubt that the wall in this latter sector was a much less substantial structure, the presence of the cliff rendering a continuation of the massive wall unnecessary.

The approach to the dun has been defended by an outer wall (B), which starts on the cliff face on the NW side, some 3 m below the dun. After running straight along the ridge for a distance of 12 m, it turns inwards to follow a winding course over the spine of the ridge before ending on the edge of the cliff on the S. On the NW the outer face is still standing to a maximum height of 1·5 m in five courses, but elsewhere the wall is now reduced to a stony bank up to 2 m thick and 0·5 m high. There are two gaps in this wall, on the W and SSW respectively, each of which appears to mark the site of an original entrance. Further to the S and SW there are additional outworks in the form of two short isolated stretches of walling (C and D), which have been drawn across the necks of small natural gullies.

792359   NM 73 NE   May 1968

172. Dun, Dùn Creagach. The fragmentary remains of a dun occupy the summit of a small rock stack which rises about 13·7 m above the shore of Loch Etive, opposite Abbot's Isle and 145 m NW of Auchnacloich. The stack drops precipitously to the shore on the W side, but on other sides the approach is across less steeply sloping ground. The dun has measured 26·5 m by 18·5 m externally, but to the N and E the wall has been almost completely robbed to provide material for near-by dykes. There is a short stretch of outer facing-stones on the S, and three further stretches on the W, where the line of the wall survives as a grass-covered band of debris. The facing stones are in some cases below the present summit area of the dun and measure up to 0·9 m high in four courses. The interior is tree-covered.

954340   NM 93 SE   June 1969

173. Dun, Dùn Cuilein, Lismore. Some slight remains of a dun (Fig. 64), which has measured about 25 m by 14 m internally, are situated on the highest part of a ridge of rock outcrop 180 m SW of Frackersaig farmhouse. The wall is reduced to a spread of rubble 2 m to 3 m in width on the N, and less than 1 m in width on the S side. A single stretch of outer facing-stones survives on the W.

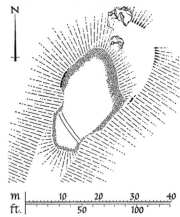

Fig. 64. Dun, Dùn Cuilein, Lismore (No. 173)

Two detached outer facing-stones, visible below the dun on the E side, are probably all that remains of an outer wall which enclosed the natural shelf on this side. The only feature in the interior of the dun is a secondary earthen bank which runs across the S end.

824401   NM 84 SW   May 1968

174. Dun, Dùn Fadaidh. Situated 750 m WNW of Degnish farmhouse, this dun (Fig. 65) stands in a position of great natural defensive strength on the top of a conspicuous hill which rises to a height of 75 m OD, commanding a wide prospect in all directions. The NE

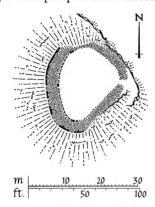

Fig. 65. Dun, Dùn Fadaidh (No. 174)

end of the hill consists of precipitous rocky crags about 30 m in height, and the other sides fall steeply as grassy slopes studded intermittently with patches of bare rock. The dun measures 19·8 m from N to S by 16·8 m

transversely within a wall which has been built round the edge of the summit area. The outer face of the wall can be traced round most of the W half of the perimeter, standing at best to a height of two courses, but only a few inner facing-stones are visible; these, however, show that the wall had an average thickness of about 3·4 m at the base. Round the E half of the circuit the course of the wall is now indicated merely by a light spread of stony debris. On the W, however, the core material is more substantial, standing up to 0·9 m above the interior. A gap in the core at the E end, 1·2 m wide, represents the original entrance. Cultivation, of which there are traces down the SW end of the hill, has encroached upon the interior of the dun.

774129   NM 71 SE   May 1967

175. Dun, Dùn Leigh. This dun (Fig. 66) is situated on a rocky ridge (45 m OD) overlooking the S shore of Loch Etive and the mouth of the River Awe. It occupies a knoll, about 10 m above the surrounding ground, which has been quarried close to the dun on the S side. The dun measures 9·8 m in diameter within a massively-

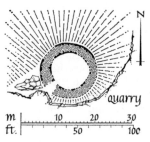

Fig. 66. Dun, Dùn Leigh (No. 175)

built wall between 2·4 m and 3·4 m in thickness, and a considerable number of both outer and inner facing-stones still survive. On the NE, where it is best preserved, the outer face rises with a distinct batter to a height of 1·2 m in three courses. The entrance is on the SW, and the inner corner-stone of the N side of the passage is still in place.

018324   NN 03 SW   June 1969

176. Dun, Dùn Mhic Raonuill. On an isolated stack of rock which rises abruptly to a height of 9 m above the shore about 830 m NNE of Barrnacarry farmhouse, there are the wasted remains of an oblong dun (Fig. 67). The sides of the stack are precipitous, but the summit can be reached, with some difficulty, by means of a narrow cleft on the SSW.

Reduced by stone-robbing to a low band of rubble 3 m in average width, in which five short stretches of outer facing-stones have survived *in situ*, the dun wall (A) encloses an area measuring 19·8 m by 10·7 m. The entrance is no longer visible, but it was presumably situated at the head of the cleft on the SSW.

The boulder-strewn foreshore to the S of the dun is

traversed by two arcs of ruined walling (B, C) of widely differing character. Wall B, drawn round the base of the stack on the SW, terminates on the E against a large rocky boss, and at its NW end is overlain by a boundary wall of comparatively recent date. It is best preserved immediately to the S of the dun, where it appears as a low grass-grown bank 3·7 m thick and up to 1 m in height; to the NW, however, it has been reduced to a stony scarp, while all that remains on the E is an irregular scatter of angular boulders. In all these sectors outer facing-stones can be seen protruding through the debris as shown on the plan. Without excavation it is impossible to determine whether the

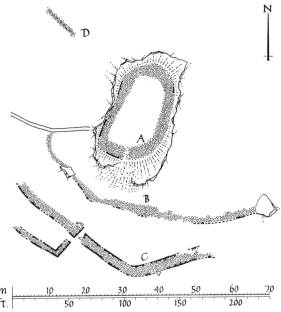

Fig. 67. Dun, Dùn Mhic Raonuill (No. 176)

gap recorded by Christison[1] immediately below the presumed dun entrance, but now obscured, marks the position of an original gateway or is simply the result of later disturbance.

The outer work (C) consists of an exceptionally well-preserved dry-stone wall, more than 3 m thick in places, which extends for a distance of 60 m from an area of broken ground on the SE to a morass on the NW, where all traces of the wall are finally lost. Both the inner and outer faces, considerable stretches of which can still be seen, are mainly composed of massive blocks of stone, the largest measuring as much as 1·5 m in length, 0·3 m in thickness and 0·8 m in height. The entrance, which faces SW, measures 1·1 m in width internally and about 1·5 m externally; at present the passage is partially blocked by a displaced facing-stone of the SE side-wall.

A comparison of walls B and C suggests that the latter, being so much better preserved and occupying ground of lower tactical value, is of later date. Both, however, constitute formidable defensive barriers and have obviously been designed to give added protection to the dun, although in different phases of its occupation.

Adjoining wall C to the W of the entrance, and probably secondary to it, there are the fragmentary remains of a rectangular enclosure measuring at least 12·2 m in length and about 6·3 m in average width. The NW end of the enclosure has been completely destroyed, but on the SW and SE sides the enclosing wall is comparatively well preserved and measures about 1·5 m in average thickness. An entrance 1·4 m wide gives access to the enclosure at its SE end.

An isolated stretch of walling (D), situated at the foot of the stack on the NW and now represented by a low band of stony debris not more than 1·2 m in width, does not appear to serve any defensive purpose and may possibly be contemporary with the enclosure.

814230   NM 82 SW   May 1966

177. Dun, Dùn Mhuirageul. This small dun occupies the summit of a slight rocky knoll (60 m OD) situated on rising ground on the E side of Glen Nant; it is about 500 m NW of Ichrachan House and 275 m E of the Taynuilt–Kilchrenan road. The knoll itself is some 5 m high and the immediate approach to it is relatively easy from all directions except the N, where there is a long steep slope.

Oval on plan (Fig. 68), the dun measures 8·2 m by 6·7 m within a wall 2·4 m thick. On the S and W a few facing-stones are visible as shown on the plan, but otherwise the wall is reduced to a stony bank not more than 1 m in height and heavily overgrown. The stones used for the faces of the wall are unusually massive blocks, measuring up to 1 m by 0·8 m by 0·6 m. Of the two gaps in the wall, the one on the W almost certainly represents the original entrance, while the one on the E has been caused by stone-robbing in comparatively recent times.

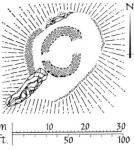

Fig. 68. Dun, Dùn Mhuirageul (No. 177)

Except perhaps on the N, the dun has been enclosed by an outer wall now represented by only a thin scatter of core material. The entrance in this wall does not seem to have been directly opposite the entrance to the dun, and was probably situated within the wide gap on the E side of the long spine of rock that runs south-westwards across the space between the dun and its outwork.

013300   NN 03 SW   June 1969

---

[1] *PSAS*, xxiii (1888–9), 395, fig. 21.

178. Dun, Dùn Mór, Balygrundle, Lismore. This dun (Fig. 69) occupies the highest point on the NE end of a rock ridge 180 m SW of Balygrundle, but it is separated from the main mass of the ridge by a cleft which runs transversely across it. The approach from the W is over level ground but the flanks of the ridge fall steeply on the other three sides. The wall of the dun

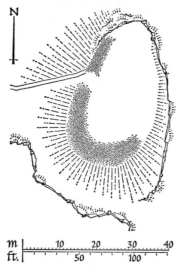

Fig. 69. Dun, Dùn Mór, Balygrundle, Lismore (No. 178)

has been drawn round the margin of the summit, and originally enclosed an oval area measuring about 30 m by 15 m. On the N and E sides the wall has now been completely robbed away, but on the S and W it is represented by a band of stones which is spread to a breadth of up to 6 m, and stands to a height of 1·4 m externally and 1·0 m internally. A gap in the debris in the centre of the W side presumably indicates the original entrance to the dun, the interior of which is featureless. A ruined wall of no great age runs up the W flank of the knoll.

837400   NM 84 SW   May 1969

179. Dun, Dùn Mucaig, Seil. This dun (Fig. 70), situated on the SW coast of the island, 110 m NE of the inlet known as Port nam Faoileann, occupies the summit of a conspicuous stack of rock which is separated from overhanging cliffs on the NE by an irregular cleft not more than 12 m wide. On all sides except the SE, where a steep grassy path gives access to a narrow shelf and thence to the summit, the stack is protected by sheer rock-faces varying from 7·6 m to 22·9 m in height.

The wall of the dun, following fairly closely the irregular outline of the summit, has enclosed an area measuring 14·6 m in length and 7 m in greatest width, although at one point, where the SW side is built across a transverse ridge, the internal width is barely 4·9 m. Like the defences of dun No. 166, the wall is composed of the local slate; for the most part it is

reduced to a low bank of stony debris, covered with a thick growth of heather and grass, in which several stretches of inner and outer facing-stones can still be seen, indicating an average thickness of about 2·8 m. On the NE, however, where the summit is overlooked by the adjacent cliffs, the remains of the wall rise to a height of 2·4 m above the interior, and on the SE, immediately to the S of the entrance, the outer face stands 1·5 m high. The entrance passage, which measures 1·83 m in width at its inner end, but only 1·52 m externally, does not appear to have been checked for a door.

On the N and E margins of the narrow shelf that lies

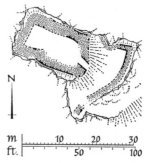

Fig. 70. Dun, Dùn Mucaig, Seil (No. 179)

below the dun on the SE there has been an outer wall, originally about 1·2 m thick; apart from a short stretch on either side of the NE angle, it is now reduced to a low stony bank. The position of an entrance is indicated by a gap 3 m wide near the S end of the wall.

751154   NM 71 NE   May 1966

180. Dun (possible), Dùn na Cuaiche. The summit of Dùn na Cuaiche (122 m OD), a steep-sided hill some 350 m NE of North Port Sonachan, is occupied by the wasted remains of what has possibly been a dun. A grass-covered bank of stony debris 3·3 m thick and not more than 0·3 m high, apparently representing the robbed foundations of a boulder-faced dry-stone wall, encloses a roughly circular area measuring 12·2 m by 11·4 m; no facing-stones are, however, visible. The position of the entrance is uncertain, but it probably lay on the NE, where the immediate approach is over relatively gentle slopes.

The highest point of the interior is occupied by a modern marker-cairn, and a turf-and-stone boundary-wall passes within 4 m of the NE side.

049217   NN 02 SW   May 1971

181. Dun (possible), Dùn Neil. About 100 m NE of Duneil farmhouse there is a prominent rocky ridge, aligned NE and SW, which rises to a height of about 35 m OD. The flanks and SW end of the ridge are steep, but a more gentle ascent from the NE leads to a fairly level summit measuring about 26 m by 12 m. Round the margin of the summit area, particularly at the NE end, a number of small ragged depressions may represent the sockets from which the facing stones of a wall have been torn. Some 15 m down the NE slope of the ridge, and about 4·5 m below the level of the summit, there is a natural crescentic shelf whose outer edge is also pitted with shallow quarry-scoops interrupted by a gap as if for an entrance. Further down the slope, and below the shelf, a very ragged rock-cut ditch runs transversely across the ridge and is intersected by a centrally-placed causeway situated roughly in line with the gap in the terrace above. At the SW end of the ridge there are two more transverse rock-cut ditches, set 2·75 m apart and each measuring about 3 m in width and 1 m in depth.

It seems possible that these features are the last vestiges of a dun with outworks, but on the other hand they may be merely the result of extensive surface quarrying which has encroached over the ridge, especially at the NE end.

903293   NM 92 NW   May 1967

182. Dun (possible), Dunstaffnage (Site). Macphail has suggested[1] that the summit of Chapel Hill, a steep-sided rocky ridge situated 160 m SW of Dunstaffnage Castle (No. 287), was fortified in early times, as it is referred to in a charter of 1572 under the name 'sendown', a transliteration of the Gaelic 'sean dùn', or 'old dun'.

The site, which enjoys strong natural protection on all sides, is largely covered with trees and dense vegetation, and no remains of defences can now be seen. If any fortification existed, however, it is likely that it was a dun, occupying the highest point of the ridge, rather than a fort with a more extensive perimeter drawn round the margin of the summit area.

880343   NM 83 SE   May 1970

183. Dun, Duntanachan. On the SW end of an isolated rocky ridge 515 m W of Duntanachan farmhouse there are the last vestiges of a roughly circular dun measuring about 15 m over all. The wall, almost completely obliterated by stone-robbing, now appears as a low band of spread core-material, 2·4 m wide, in which only one outer facing-stone (on the SW) is still visible.

The dun has been entered from the NE, where there is a narrow gap in the wall debris and relatively easy access is to be gained along the spine of the ridge.

961282   NM 92 NE   May 1967

184. Dun, Eilean an Atha, Luing. This dun (Fig. 71) occupies an islet in the bay that is bounded on the N by the promontory of Eilean an Atha; it is easily accessible at low tide by means of a natural ridge of beach pebbles which links the NW side of the islet to the shore. Roughly oval on plan, the dun measures 18 m by 11·6 m within a wall originally about 2·4 m thick. On the NE a short stretch of the wall has been destroyed by erosion,

and elsewhere it is reduced to a band of rubble in which only a few facing-stones are visible. The entrance was probably on the S, the gap in the wall on the NW being of recent origin.

748072   NM 70 NW   May 1966

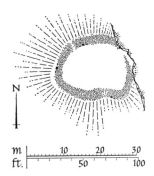

Fig. 71. Dun, Eilean an Atha, Luing (No. 184)

185. Dun, Fiart, Lismore. The remains of a small sub-rectangular dun (Fig. 72), measuring 22·9 m by 16·8 m within a wall about 4·9 m in maximum thickness, are situated on a coastal headland 190 m SSE of Fiart farmhouse. On the SW and SE, steep rocky cliffs, ranging from 4·5 m to 13·5 m in height, afford strong natural protection, and access from the landward side, albeit over fairly level ground, is impeded by transverse limestone outcrops. The dun wall is best preserved on the NE, where it appears as a bank of stony debris measuring up to 5·2 m in thickness and rising to a height of as much as 2·3 m above the level of the interior; only one short stretch of inner facing-stones and a somewhat

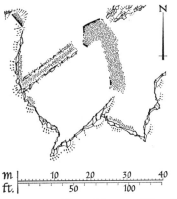

Fig. 72. Dun, Fiart, Lismore (No. 185)

longer stretch of the outer face have survived *in situ*. On the NW, however, the wall has been reduced to a light scatter of core material, about 1·2 m wide, on top of a low rocky spine, while the only evidence to suggest that the remaining sides were ever provided with artificial defence is an isolated band of rubble bordering

---

[1] *SHR*, xvii (1919–20), 271.

the cliffs on the WSW. The entrance is situated on the N, and the remains of the NE passage-wall show that it was irregular on plan, possibly because the wall at this point is awkwardly sited on the crest of the rocky spine referred to above. Owing to a dense growth of bracken, no structural remains were visible in the interior of the dun on the date of visit.

Additional protection has been provided by a dry-stone wall extending along the edge of the cliffs on either side of the dun and across the neck of a gully on the NW. The wall is now severely denuded and is represented by three disconnected bands of stony debris, in one of which a short stretch of outer facing-stones can still be seen.

806368　　　　　　　NM 83 NW　　　　　　　July 1970

186. Dun, Gallanach. This dun stands on a low rocky promontory which juts into the sea 455 m W of Gallanach (No. 320). Roughly D-shaped on plan (Fig. 73), it measures 24·4 m from N to S by 19·8 m transversely within a massive wall which varies in thickness from 2·1 m on the SSE to 4·0 m on either side of the entrance on the ENE. To provide a firm foundation for the wall the builders packed a number of underlying crevices

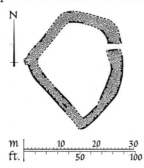

Fig. 73. Dun, Gallanach (No. 186)

with stones. The lower part of the wall incorporates large angular blocks of stone, but at a higher level smaller regularly-coursed stones are employed. Long stretches of both faces are visible, the best-preserved sector being on the E where the debris has been cleared back to reveal the outer face rising without any batter to a height of 1·5 m. By contrast the inner face is not more than 0·75 m high, but the lowest courses are at present hidden under the spread of fallen material that covers much of the interior. In places the rubble core of the wall stands as much as 1·8 m above the level of the interior.

An unusual feature of the wall, but one which has been recorded in three instances in Kintyre,[1] is the presence of an internal revetment, forming, as it were, a second outer face within the thickness of the wall. This feature is visible for a distance of only 2 m on the SSW, but may have been continuous.

The entrance, on the ENE, is 1·5 m wide. The passage itself is largely choked with debris, but the side-walls do not appear to have been checked for a door.

823259　　　　　　　NM 82 NW　　　　　　　May 1966

187. Dun, Kilcheran, Lismore. This dun (Fig. 74), 450 m SSW of Kilcheran farmhouse, is situated on the highest point of a coastal ridge whose SE flank falls at first steeply, and then precipitously, to the shore below. The site is further protected on the SW by a sheer-sided rocky chasm 6 m in depth, while to the NW and NE the immediate approach is over gently undulating ground, studded with limestone outcrops.

An irregular oval on plan, the dun measures approximately 9·5 m by 7·6 m within the robbed remains of a

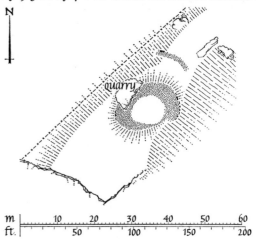

Fig. 74. Dun, Kilcheran, Lismore (No. 187)

dry-stone wall, which now appears as a grass-grown stony bank 4·3 m in maximum thickness and not more than 1·2 m in height; a few isolated outer facing-stones survive *in situ* on the E and W, but no stones of the inner face are visible. Modern quarrying has destroyed a large portion of the NW arc, while on the S the outer half of the wall appears to have collapsed down the steep seaward slope. The position of the entrance cannot be determined without excavation.

Drawn across the crest of the ridge, about 7 m to the NE of the dun, there is an outer wall now represented by a low band of spread core-material, 1·5 m wide, in which only one short stretch of the outer face can still be seen. The gap between the SE end of the outwork and the steep flank of the ridge is probably the result of comparatively recent stone-robbing.

822383　　　　　　　NM 83 NW　　　　　　　May 1968

188. Dun (possible), Kilchoan Loch. Situated on the highest part of a ridge to the W of Kilchoan Loch, and at a height of about 150 m OD, there are the last remains of a stone-walled enclosure which may possibly have been a dun. It has measured originally about 25·7 m from N to S by 17·5 m transversely within a wall which is now represented on the N and S sides by a band of debris about 3·3 m in width. Only a few stones of the wall survive on the W side, and on the E, where it overlooked the loch, it has been completely destroyed.

796142　　　　　　　NM 71 SE　　　　　　　May 1969

[1] *Inventory of Argyll*, i, p. 16.

189. Dun, Leccamore, Luing. The impressive dun of Leccamore (Fig. 75) stands within outworks on the highest part of the easternmost of the dorsal ridges of Luing at a height of 85 m OD. Known also as 'An Caisteal' and the 'South Fort', it was partially excavated

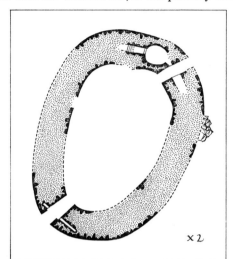

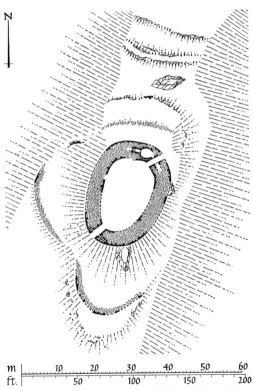

Fig. 75. Dun, Leccamore, Luing (No. 189)

in 1890 and 1892 and the following account is based on the published reports.[1]

The dun measures 19·8 m by 12·8 m within a wall from 4·0 m to 4·9 m in thickness, and has an entrance at either end. Long stretches of both faces of the wall are visible throughout the circuit, and at the S end, where it is best preserved, the outer face stands to a height of 3 m in eight well-laid courses with a batter of one in four. Many of the facing stones are massive blocks measuring up to 1·35 m by 0·46 m and about 0·38 m in thickness. The SW entrance (Pl. 11B) measures 1·7 m in width externally, and, in order to provide checking for a door, two jamb-stones have been built about 1·2 m inside the outer corners of the passage. The S jamb (Pl. 11C) is a slate slab measuring 1·32 m in height, 0·43 m in width and about 0·23 m in thickness; the inner face of this stone has at least fifteen cup-marks pecked into it, ranging between 38 mm and 76 mm in diameter and between 13 mm and 25 mm in depth. The N jamb is of similar size to the one on the S. There is a bar-hole 0·9 m in depth on the N side of the passage, and on the S side a complementary slot (Pl. 11C) for storing the bar extends for 2·7 m into the thickness of the wall. The dimensions of these features indicate that the bar probably measured about 0·23 m by 0·18 m in section. The entrance-passage, which was originally paved, is 4·3 m in total length and the walls now stand to a height of 1·8 m; after a slight expansion at the jambs, the passage narrows again to its original width. The lintel over the door, and some of the slabs forming the roof of the passage, had been removed only a short time before the excavation of 1890.

The second entrance, at the NE end of the dun, has a uniform width of 1·5 m at the present time. There is no trace of door-checks, but they may have been removed when the outer corners of the passage were destroyed. In the thickness of the wall on the S side of the passage there are the remains of a straight-sided chamber at a rather higher level than that of the present passage-floor. It extends into the wall for a distance of at least 1·2 m, but its original length is uncertain owing to the collapse of the inner end. On the N side there is an oval guard-chamber which is entered up a step (0·53 m high) and along a narrow passage. The chamber measures 2·7 m by 2·4 m; its walls, which are built of slate slabs, stand to a height of 1·4 m above the debris covering the floor of the chamber, and are corbelled inwards as they rise. A flight of steps (Pl. 11D) leads from the chamber to the wall-head, and slabs have also been used on one side of this stairway. On the NW there is a break in the inner face of the dun wall, but as it is choked with rubble and fallen stone it is uncertain whether or not this is a structural feature. The foundations of walled enclosures in the interior of the dun are clearly secondary.

The steep grassy flanks of the ridge, falling some 25 m to marshy ground on either side, afford natural protection for the dun on the E, but additional defences have been provided on the other three sides. On the N two rock-cut ditches which, to judge by their width, may also have served the purpose of furnishing building-material for the dun, have been drawn across the spine of the ridge. The outer ditch measures about 1·8 m in

[1] *PSAS*, xxv (1890–1), 476–83; xxvii (1892–3), 371, 375–80.

depth and the inner one about 3 m, while traces of walling can be seen on the scarp of the latter. On the N, W and S there is an outer wall which largely follows the natural crest-line; considerable stretches of the outer face survive on the S and there are shorter stretches of outer and inner facing-stones on the W and NW respectively, but elsewhere the wall is reduced to a band of rubble. On the SW a gap in line with the dun entrance presumably indicates the site of a gateway.

Most of the finds from the excavations are in the National Museum of Antiquities of Scotland, and a catalogue of the extant objects has recently been published;[1] they include a number of stone implements, such as pounders, discs, querns and a quartzite strike-a-light. A thin bronze stem, a fragment of an iron blade, two bone points and a piece of worked antler were also found in the domestic refuse, as well as a quantity of animal bones and shells.

750107   NM 71 SE   May 1966

190. Dun, Loch a' Phearsain. This dun is situated a little under 1 km NNE of Kilmelford village, on the highest point (120 m OD) of a rocky ridge which borders the W side of Loch a' Phearsain. Almost circular on plan (Fig. 76), it measures 16·2 m in diameter within a wall which has a maximum thickness of only 1·8 m. Although the wall is thus considerably thinner than is

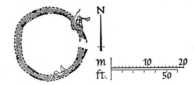

Fig. 76. Dun, Loch a' Phearsain (No. 190)

usual for this type of monument, it can be paralleled in other duns in the county.[2] Designed to incorporate patches of outcropping rock, it has been severely robbed and all that now remains are a number of inner and outer facing-stones of the lowest course, together with a light spread of core material. The entrance faces E, and probably measured about 0·9 m in width originally. Subsequently, however, the gap has been enlarged by the destruction of the N side of the passage.

851139   NM 81 SE   May 1966

191. Dun (possible), Park, Lismore. The summit of a low rounded knoll about 350 m N of Park farmhouse is occupied by the denuded remains of a stone-walled enclosure which may originally have been a dun. Oval on plan, it has measured 8·2 m by 6·4 m transversely within a wall now represented by a grass-covered stony bank 3 m in average thickness and nowhere more than 0·4 m in height. The position of the entrance is presumably indicated by a gap in the bank on the NE arc measuring about 2·4 m in width.

887459   NM 84 NE   May 1968

192. Dun, Rubh' an Tighe Loisgte. On the summit of a steep grassy knoll (30 m OD), situated 600 m W of Tullich farmhouse between the public road and the S shore of Loch Melfort, there are the last vestiges of a dun. Stone-robbing and tree-planting have virtually obliterated the wall, leaving only a slight stony bank not more than 0·3 m high, which encloses a roughly circular area measuring about 10·7 m in diameter. No facing-stones are visible, but the approximate line of the outer face of the wall is indicated by robber trenches. Three large slabs (the largest measuring 1·2 m by 0·3 m by 0·2 m), which are lying dislodged on the E flank of the knoll, suggest that the entrance may have been on that side.

829122   NM 81 SW   May 1966

193. Dun and Enclosure, Sean Dùn, Lismore. A rocky headland overlooking the Lynn of Lorn some 590 m E of Balygrundle farmhouse is occupied by the wasted remains of a dun and a later enclosure (Fig. 77). Except on the W, where gentle slopes offer relatively

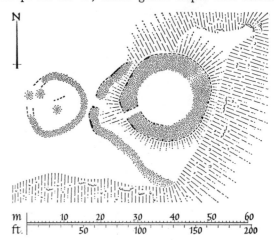

Fig. 77. Dun and enclosure, Sean Dùn, Lismore (No. 193)

easy access, the site affords great natural strength, being defended on the S and E by precipitous cliffs, and by a steep-sided gully on the N.

The dun, which has been built on the summit of a low knoll crowning the headland, is roughly circular on plan and measures 14·8 m in average internal diameter. Severely reduced by stone-robbing, the wall now appears as an overgrown bank of stony debris 1·2 m high and 5·5 m in maximum width, although the survival *in situ* of a single inner facing-stone on the SSW, as well as several short stretches of the outer face elsewhere, indicate that the original wall-thickness was about 4·1 m. The entrance, which faces WSW, was approximately 1·5 m wide, part of the passage-wall and the inner corner-stone on the N side still being visible. A gap in

---

[1] Ibid., ciii (1970–1), 110.
[2] E.g. *Inventory of Argyll*, i, Nos. 203 and 229.

the core material on the NE is probably the result of modern disturbance.

Round the base of the knoll on the S and W there has been an outer wall, now represented for the most part by a grass-grown stony scarp, at the foot of which several outer facing-stones remain in position. At the N end of the outwork, where it is best preserved, the outer face stands to a height of 1·2 m in five courses. The wall is interrupted for a gateway diagonally opposite the dun entrance; a large earthfast boulder, which lies immediately SW of the gap in the debris, probably indicates the position of one of its passage-walls.

An irregular oval on plan, the enclosure is situated on a level shelf immediately below the dun on the W; it has measured about 14 m by 12·2 m within a wall now reduced to a grass-grown stony bank 1·5 m wide and 0·3 m high, which incorporates several large boulders. There is, however, no longer any trace of the series of inner and outer facing-stones that led Christison in 1889[1] to describe the monument as a 'double stone circle'. The entrance was presumably on the W, where a considerable length of the wall has been completely destroyed by cultivation. A line of four earthfast blocks of stone near the centre of the interior may represent part of the foundations of some recent structure, possibly associated with three adjacent clearance-cairns, two of which overlie the site of the enclosure wall.

Whereas the precise date and purpose of the enclosure cannot be determined without excavation, the fact that it virtually blocks the entrance in the outwork suggests that it is secondary to the dun and its defences.

844399   NM 83 NW   May 1968

194. Dun, Tom a' Chaisteil. This comparatively well-preserved dun (Fig. 78) occupies the summit of a rocky knoll on the left bank of the Teatle Water about 930 m W of Blarchaorain farmhouse. Although surrounded by rock-strewn slopes of moderate steepness, the site is not one of great natural strength, and it would appear rather

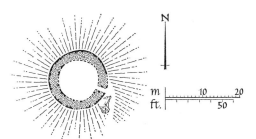

Fig. 78. Dun, Tom a' Chaisteil (No. 194)

to have been chosen for the extensive view that it commands in all directions.

Almost circular on plan, the dun measures 11 m in diameter within a wall 2·3 m to 2·9 m in thickness. The wall has suffered from stone-robbing, but the lowest courses of nearly the whole circuit of the outer face are

visible, as well as several stretches of inner facing-stones. The entrance, situated on the ESE, is 1·3 m wide.

139247   NN 12 SW   May 1970

CRANNOGS

195. Crannog, An Doirlinn, Eriska. This crannog is situated below high-water mark on the S shore of Eriska, about 275 m E of the bridge that links the island to the mainland. It is represented at present by a seaweed-covered stony mound some 20 m in diameter and not more than 1 m in height, the centre of which is disfigured by spoil-heaps and a partly-filled trench associated with the unfinished excavation of 1884.[2]

The investigation then undertaken revealed that the crannog had rested on a circular timber substructure, about 18·3 m in diameter, the bulk of which consisted of roughly-dressed horizontal beams, radially disposed, with a certain amount of brushwood towards the centre, while the perimeter had been defined by at least one row of beams laid circumferentially. Superimposed on this was a layer of stones and clay 0·9 m in depth, from the surface of which charcoal, ashes and some burned animal bones were recovered, but no artifacts of any kind.

There is no evidence to suggest that the crannog was ever linked to the island by means of a causeway.

900423   NM 94 SW   May 1970

196. Crannog, Loch a' Mhuillin (Site). A crannog was discovered in 1888 during draining operations at Loch a' Mhuillin, then an area of marshland just S of Oban and close to the Railway Engine Shed.[3] A stone structure measuring about 26 m by 16·2 m was found to be resting on a platform of horizontal timbers consolidated by a number of upright piles. During the examination of the site a number of human and animal bones were recovered. There are now no surface indications of the crannog and its precise position is not known.

c. 857293   NM 82 NE   June 1967

197. Crannog (possible), Lochan na Gealaich. About 9 m off the E shore of Lochan na Gealaich, a small hill-loch situated 1·2 km NE of Kilchrenan, an accumulation of stones, measuring between 6·0 m and 7·6 m in diameter and linked to the shore by what appears to be a causeway, has been recorded as a crannog.[4] At the date of visit only a few stones were visible above the surface of the loch.

049233   NN 02 SW   May 1970

[1] *PSAS*, xxiii (1888–9), 377.
[2] Ibid., xix (1884–5), 192–5.
[3] *The Oban Times*, 5 May 1888 and 15 June 1889; *PSAS*, xlvii (1912–13), 288. See also Pl. 76 ('Mill Loch').
[4] *DES* (1969), 10.

198. Crannogs, Loch Awe. As a result of an underwater survey of Loch Awe undertaken in 1972 by Naval Air Command Sub-Aqua Club under the direction of Dr and Mrs T D McArdle, no fewer than twenty crannogs have been positively identified.[1] The tops of many of them are visible as small stony islands, but others are permanently submerged. In at least nine instances their structure can be seen to include timber baulks, which in one example are radially disposed.

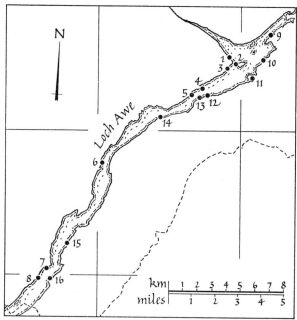

Fig. 79. Crannogs, Loch Awe (No. 198)

Causeways linking the crannog to the shore have been detected at five examples and the remains of jetties or of harbours, comparable to that discovered at Milton Loch I (Kirkcudbrightshire),[2] have been noted in six cases. The sixteen crannogs of this group that fall within the boundaries of Lorn are shown on Fig. 79 and are listed below in the order in which they occur from NE to SW, those off the NW shore of the loch being numbered 1–8 and those off the SE shore 9–16.

(1) 280 m E of Ardanaiseig (No. 307) and 20 m from the shore (NN 091248).

(2) 50 m from the W side of Inishail (NN 095244).

(3) 700 m SSE of Ardanaiseig (No. 307) and 20 m from the shore (NN 090241).

(4) 455 m SE of Làrach Bàn and 75 m from the S side of Ceann Mara (NN 073227).

(5) The island known as Càrn an Ròin, 520 m E of Achnacarron and 74 m offshore (NN 065223).

(6) The stony island known as Càrn Dubh, 490 m ENE of Inverinan and 10 m from the shore (NN 001177).

(7) 115 m SW of Barr Phort and 975 m E of Cruachan (NM 963104).

(8) Càrn Mhic Chealair, a small stony island 825 m SSE of Cruachan (NM 958098).

(9) On the S side of the loch opposite St Conan's Church and 55 m from the shore (NN 121264).

(10) 760 m NW of Achlian (No. 302) and less than 100 m from the shore (NN 115247).

(11) At the NE end of the small bay sheltered by the Inistrynich peninsula and 280 m ESE of Inistrynich (NN 108235).

(12) 1 km NW of Keppochan and 45 m from the shore (NN 077223).

(13) 170 m N of Rockhill and 10 m from the shore (NN 071220).

(14) In a bay 550 m WSW of the Port Sonachan Hotel and 15 m from the shore (NN 042207).

(15) 425 m WSW of Ardchonnell, 290 m NNE of Innis Chonnell Castle (No. 292) and 170 m from the shore (NM 978121).

(16) Close to the shore some 290 m N of Eredine (NM 968097).

(1–5, 12–13) NN 02 SE; (6) NN 01 NW; (7, 15) NN 91 SE; (8, 16) NM 90 NE; (9) NN 12 NW; (10–11) NN 12 SW; (14) NN 02 SW

199. Crannog, Loch Seil. There is an artificial island in the S half of Loch Seil, situated 85 m from the W shore and 365 m S of Duachy farmhouse. Almost totally submerged at the present time, it is said[3] to measure about 7·3 m by 5·5 m and to be built of stones, with a boat-slip on the W side and a 'square place' on the E as if for a landing-stage. No trace is visible of a causeway linking the crannog with the shore.

803202   NM 82 SW   May 1971

200. Crannog, Moss of Achnacree (Site). The site of this crannog can still be detected near the NW corner of the Moss of Achnacree, 210 m SW of Moss Cottage; it appears as an area of firmer ground rising a little above the general level of a slight boggy depression which, until it was drained during the 18th century, was a small loch comparable with others that still exist in the moss at the present time. Investigations carried out between 1869 and 1872[4] revealed that the crannog was based on a foundation constructed of at least four or five successive layers of timber and brushwood laid transversely to one another and extending over an area measuring about 18·3 m across. Although the foundation was examined in several places, no evidence was found to indicate that it had been consolidated by upright wooden piles. On this foundation-platform there were the remains of a low turf bank, consisting of a double row of turves, which enclosed an oval area measuring about 15·2 m by 8·5 m, and which probably represented the remains of a turf or wattle wall. The entrance was

[1] The Commissioners are indebted to Dr and Mrs T D McArdle for permission to include this information.
[2] *PSAS*, lxxxvii (1952–3), 136.
[3] Ibid., xxx (1895–6), 23.
[4] Ibid., ix (1870–2), 93–8, 416–17; x (1872–4), 82–3; Smith, *Loch Etive*, 228–36.

on the E and within the interior there was a well-laid floor of clay, 0·15 m thick. Three hearths were discovered, one near the entrance, a second roughly in the centre of the house, and the third and largest near the W end of the interior. There was no indication of the roofing-arrangement. The timbers were thought to consist of birch wood, but a sample recovered in 1969 shows that ash was also employed.[1]

The finds included two wooden double-sided combs, several wooden pegs, a rim fragment of a turned wooden bowl, an unfinished wooden 'ladle' and what is described as a piece of wood with a 'Greek cross with crosslets' burnt on to it; a knife, a hook, fragments of skin soles and a skin slipper were also recovered. The combs, 'ladle' and several fragments of antler are in the National Museum of Antiquities of Scotland, but the other objects are no longer extant. Neither the small finds nor an analysis of the pollen horizon of the crannog can provide a firm date for the site,[2] but a date within the medieval period is the most likely.

910366   NM 93 NW   May 1969

MISCELLANEOUS EARTHWORKS AND ENCLOSURES[3]

201. Earthwork, Ard Luing, Luing. A rocky promontory which projects from the sea-cliffs bordering the SW coast of Luing about 1·8 km SSE of Rubha Cùil, and in the area known as Ard Luing, is occupied by an earthwork of trapezoidal plan (Fig. 80). The site is well suited for defence, being protected on the S and W by precipitous rock-faces as much as 12 m in height, and by a

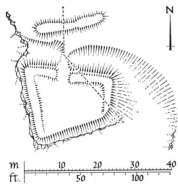

Fig. 80. Earthwork, Ard Luing, Luing (No. 201)

broad natural gully on the E, access thus being available only over a narrow col on the N. The earthwork, which measures internally 16·1 m in length by about 10·5 m in average width, has been defended by a single rampart and, on the N, by a broad external ditch, drawn across the col from the head of the gully to the cliff edge. Comparatively well preserved on all sides except the S,

the rampart is now represented for the most part by a turf-covered bank of earth and stones 3·6 m in thickness and 0·6 m in greatest height; near the middle of the N side it is pierced by an entrance measuring 2·7 m in width. The ditch measures 6·7 m in average width by about 2 m in depth and is interrupted opposite the entrance by a causeway, direct access to the outer end of which has been barred by a traverse, now appearing as a low grass-grown bank some 20 m long, 4·6 m wide and not more than 0·6 m high. A modern boundary-fence bisects this bank and crosses the NE quarter of the interior of the earthwork, which is otherwise completely featureless.

737066   NM 70 NW   May 1966

202. Enclosure, Balliveolan, Lismore. On the SW end of a ridge, 470 m N of Lismore School, a turf-covered stony bank forms a circular enclosure measuring 13·4 m internally (Fig. 81). The bank is about 3·4 m in

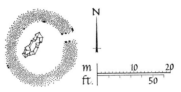

Fig. 81. Enclosure, Balliveolan, Lismore (No. 202)

thickness and 1 m in height. Several upright stones on the E indicate the position of the entrance, which is 1·8 m in width. About a quarter of the interior is occupied by a rock outcrop, but the remainder is featureless.

838412   NM 84 SW   May 1969

203. Field-bank, Black Crofts, North Connel. The Black Crofts are situated on the SE perimeter of the Moss of Achnacree, overlooking the narrows at the mouth of Loch Etive. Behind two of the crofts there are the remains of a field-bank which is built on the old land surface beneath the peat, and thus antedates the formation of the moss. Three trenches were dug by the Commission's officers in order to examine this feature, which is visible behind Croft number 3 as a low bank (about 1·8 m in width and 0·3 m in height), and which may be traced from the edge of the moss for a length of 62 m; beyond this point it has been destroyed by recent building. A short stretch of a similar bank, running obliquely to the first, is visible 88 m to the WNW, behind Croft number 1. The main bank was 1·5 m in width,

---

[1] The Commissioners are indebted to Miss K Starkey and Sir William Starkey for permission to carry out this work, and to Miss H Prentice, Royal Botanic Garden, Edinburgh, for identifying the wood.
[2] The Commissioners are indebted to Dr S E Durno, the Macaulay Institute for Soil Research, for undertaking the pollen analysis.
[3] See also Nos. 133 and 193.

covered by peat to a depth of 1·1 m, and consisted of a core of earth and stones revetted on either side with granite boulders (Pl. 11E).[1] The core material had been scooped out of quarry-ditches on either side and a deposit of grey silt in the ditches suggested that they later served as drainage channels. Two radiocarbon dates, the first for a sample taken from the original soil surface sealed beneath the bank, and the second taken from the base of the peat elsewhere on the moss,[2] suggest that the field-bank was constructed in the middle of the 2nd millennium BC.

923349　　　　NM 93 SW　　　　August 1971

204. Earthwork, Cleigh. The earthwork that is situated in pasture a little to the S of the cairns at Cleigh (p. 53, nos. 6 and 7) has been almost completely ploughed away. It consists of a bank, with slight traces of a ditch on the inside, which encloses an almost circular area 21·3 m in diameter. The bank is spread to a width of up to 5·5 m and is now not more than 0·15 m in height. A broad gap in the S side no doubt marks the position of the original entrance.

881260　　　　NM 82 NE　　　　August 1971

205. Earthwork, Dùn Ablaich, Luing. This earthwork (Fig. 82), 850 m NNE of Ardlarach farmhouse (No. 309), is situated on the top of an isolated rocky knoll which rises to a height of about 14 m OD above an expanse of low-lying marshland. The W side of the knoll presents a sheer rock-face 6 m in greatest height,

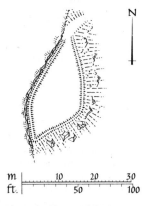

Fig. 82. Earthwork, Dùn Ablaich, Luing (No. 205)

while the E and SE flanks consist of steep grassy slopes studded with patches of rock outcrop. Around the margin of the summit area there is an earthen bank up to 2·2 m in thickness and 0·6 m in height internally. The enclosure thus formed measures 27 m by 12 m, and has an entrance 1·5 m wide at the N end, approached obliquely by a track. The interior is featureless.

738097　　　　NM 70 NW　　　　May 1966

206. Earthwork, Dùn Mór, Bonawe. Immediately to the E of the mouth of the River Awe, and about 730 m N of Bonawe House, there is an earthwork (Fig. 83), which comprises a single broad rampart and external ditch cutting off the end of a steep-sided alluvial spur; the roughly triangular area thus isolated measures about 14·6 m from NW to SE by 10·7 m transversely. The rampart is now reduced to a grassy bank about 8 m in width, which stands to a height of as much as 4·5 m above the ditch-bottom, but only 0·5 m above the level of the interior; it is surmounted at one point by a modern memorial-stone. The ditch itself is flat-bottomed and about 12 m in width, its upcast having been apparently

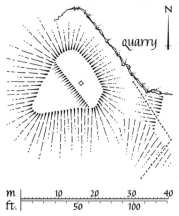

Fig. 83. Earthwork, Dùn Mór, Bonawe (No. 206)

used, as Christison observed,[3] to raise the level of the interior by as much as 3 m above the former ground-surface. At the date of visit a sherd of green-glazed pottery of medieval date was observed at a point where the filling of the ditch was exposed by weathering.

Although the earthwork bears a close resemblance, both in plan and style of construction, to certain late medieval monuments (cf. No. 297), in the absence of any documentary evidence to support this identification, its date and purpose are uncertain.

012325　　　　NN 03 SW　　　　April 1972

207. Enclosure, Eilean Balnagowan. The island known as Eilean Balnagowan comprises two rocky ridges joined by a strip of lower ground on which there are the wasted remains of a circular stone-walled enclosure measuring about 4 m in diameter within a wall 1·3 m in thickness. The wall is best preserved on the S half of its circuit, where some outer facing-stones remain in position. There is no sign of an entrance.

953539　　　　NM 95 SE　　　　May 1970

[1] *GAJ*, forthcoming.
[2] Base of peat deposit, 980 bc ± 80 (N—1468); original soil surface, 1359 bc ± 50 (SRR—219). The Commissioners are indebted to Dr G Whittington, Department of Geography, University of St Andrews, for permission to quote these dates.
[3] *PSAS*, xxiii (1888–9), 385.

208. Enclosure, Kilmun. On a fairly level shelf which projects from the face of the hill above Kames Bay, Loch Awe, some 280 m NE of Kilmun farmhouse, there are the wasted remains of a roughly circular enclosure (Fig. 84) measuring approximately 15 m in diameter within a greatly reduced stone wall. The wall

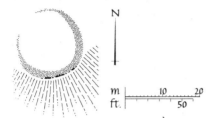

Fig. 84. Enclosure, Kilmun (No. 208)

is now represented on the S by a grass-grown stony scarp, 0·9 m in height, at the foot of which several outer facing-stones have survived *in situ*, but elsewhere only a low band of spread core-material is visible, not more than 2 m in thickness. The entrance was probably on the NW arc, where almost all the stones of the wall have been removed, presumably to provide metalling for the adjacent road from Kilchrenan to Dalavich.

973145   NM 91 SE   June 1969

209. Enclosure, Làrach na h-Iobairte. About 600 m WSW of Kilmun, and a short distance NE of the public road from Kilchrenan to Loch Avich, there are the wasted remains of an enclosure (Fig. 85), situated on a narrow shelf in rising ground in the Inverinan Forest. The site suffered considerable damage about 1850,[1] when stones were removed to build a near-by wall, and

Fig. 85. Enclosure, Làrach na h-Iobairte (No. 209)

what survives, while clear of trees, is now covered by a heavy growth of bracken. The visible remains consist of a spread of stones, through which a number of large boulders protrude, forming a roughly circular enclosure measuring about 18·3 m externally from NW to SE by 16·8 m transversely. Some of the boulders are disposed round the outer edge of the spread of stones while others are in the middle of it, and in the absence of excavation it is impossible to determine whether the two broad gaps on the NW and SW are original features or merely the result of robbing.

965142   NM 91 SE   June 1969

210. Earthwork, Lochan nan Ràth. Situated close to the SW end of Lochan nan Ràth, on the low-lying Moss of Achnacree, there are the wasted remains of an earthwork, consisting of a bank of earth and stones which has enclosed an irregularly-shaped area measuring about 42 m by 27 m. Considerable stretches of the bank on the W and ESE have been completely levelled, and the surviving portions, which measure up to 6 m in thickness at the base and 1 m in height, are covered by a heavy growth of whins. The material for the bank seems to have been obtained in part by surface-scraping on the inside and also from an external quarry-ditch, now largely filled up except on the E and SE, where it has been partly re-cut for drainage in comparatively recent times. The ditch appears to be interrupted by a causeway on the SSE as if for an entrance.

919353   NM 93 NW   May 1970

211. Earthwork, South Ledaig. About 100 m N of South Ledaig farmhouse, and 30 m E of the public road, there are the fragmentary remains of an earthen bank and external ditch which, if complete, would surround a roughly circular area measuring about 23 m in diameter. The bank has been virtually levelled except on the S side, where it stands not more than 0·5 m in height internally and 1·8 m externally. The ditch, which is largely filled up, is visible only on the N and W, measuring up to 2·4 m in width and 0·5 m in depth.

909357   NM 93 NW   April 1967

ECCLESIASTICAL MONUMENTS

212. Burial-ground, Achallader. A small burial-ground of the Fletcher family is situated about 15 m S of Achallader Castle (No. 277). It is bounded by a stone wall, probably of early 19th-century date, into which there is built a slab of schist containing a pistol-hole, evidently removed from the ruined castle. Another architectural fragment, probably from the same source, lies within the enclosure (cf. p. 173).

The earliest dated monument is a slate headstone commemorating John Fletcher at Inveroran, who died in 1805 aged 78. This is carved in relief with a shield bearing: a Greek cross, a ?flagon in the centre, between four pellets, each charged with a pheon, for Fletcher. For crest there is a horse's head couped.

322442   NN 34 SW   August 1970

213. Appin-murder Cairn, Ballachulish. This cairn stands in a Forestry Commission plantation some 135 m SE of Craigallan Cottage. It measures about 2·1 m in height and has a diameter of about 6 m at the base. Although evidently repaired and repointed in lime

---

[1] Name Book, No. 53, p. 149.

mortar fairly recently, the cairn appears to have been in existence at least as early as 1770.[1] It bears a modern metal plaque containing the inscription: THIS CAIRN IS ERECTED / ON THE SPOT WHERE / COLIN CAMPBELL / OF GLENURE / WAS MURDERED ON / 14TH MAY 1752.[2]

032593   NN 05 NW   July 1968

214. Old Parish Church, Appin. The roofless and ivy-grown shell of this church (Pl. 12A) stands within its burial-ground on the E side of the Oban–Fort William road about 1·5 km SE of Portnacroish. The building is of two main periods, and comprises an oblong main block of mid-18th-century date to which a central N aisle was added in the late 18th century, bringing the structure to its present T-plan form (Fig. 86). The original building measures 14·9 m from E to W by 5·9 m transversely within walls some 0·71 m in thickness. The masonry is of random rubble with quoins and dressings composed partly of schist and partly of buff-coloured sandstone, and the building was formerly harled. The margins of

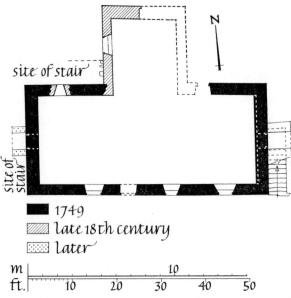

site of stair

site of stair

■ 1749
▨ late 18th century
▧ later

m | 10
ft. | 10   20   30   40   50

Fig. 86. Old Parish Church, Appin (No. 214); plan

the doors and windows are chamfer-arrised, the latter being rebated for external shutters.

The original arrangement of the interior is uncertain, but the pulpit may have occupied a central position against the S wall, as it certainly did during the later period of occupation, when the N aisle was in use.[3] If so, the existing entrance-doorway in the S wall, situated a little to the W of centre, may have been designed primarily to provide access for the minister to the pulpit. The doorway (Pl. 12B) is segmental-headed, and the keystone (Pl. 12C) bears in relief the date 1749. Two large segmental-headed windows pierce the S wall to the E of the doorway, and there is another similar window on the opposite side of the doorway. The N wall also contained at least one entrance-doorway, situated

immediately to the E of the N aisle, and one jamb of this survives. There were, in addition, high-level doorways, placed centrally in each gable-wall, giving access to galleries at both ends of the building. These doorways were approached by stone forestairs of which the E one alone remains.

The N aisle is now incomplete, but evidently measured 5·0 m from N to S by 4·4 m transversely within the walls. There appears to have been a centrally placed entrance-doorway in the N wall, and the only surviving window is situated in the W wall. To the S of this window the external wall-face shows traces of tusking which probably marks the site of a former forestair leading to a doorway serving a gallery in the aisle. The small window in the adjacent N wall of the original church was probably introduced when the forestair was built, and may replace a larger window in a similar position.

This church was erected in 1749 to serve the adjacent portion of the united parish of Lismore and Appin. It evidently superseded a building of about 1641 which itself probably stood on or near the site of an older chapel, known as Annaid (Annat),[4] whose name is preserved in a number of early maps.[5] Some evidence of continuity of occupation on the present site is afforded by the presence in the burial-ground of a tombstone of 16th- or early 17th-century date (infra). By 1776 the church was found to be too small, and it was decided to lengthen the building,[6] but this scheme was evidently abandoned in favour of one involving the erection of the N aisle. The building appears to have remained in use until 1889, when a new church was built on a fresh site.[7]

FUNERARY MONUMENTS AND OTHER CARVED STONES

(1) Immediately outside the E end of the church there is a recumbent slab with slightly tapered sides which measures 1·98 m in length by 0·66 m in width at the head. The upper corners contain (left) a small cross with one barred and three trifid terminals, and (right) a plaited knot of simple design. Beneath these motifs there is the crude outline of a claymore, with another plaited knot in the space between the hilt and the left quillon, while at the foot of the slab is a circular arrangement of plaitwork. All the decoration is incised, and badly executed. The handiwork of a local mason, the carving cannot be earlier than 1500, and may be as late as the 17th century. (White, *Knapdale*, pl. xlv, 1).

[1] Forbes, *Journals*, 312.
[2] For the circumstances of the Appin Murder, see MacArthur, W, *The Appin Murder* (1960), and Mackay, D N, *Trial of James Stewart*, (1907).
[3] Plan of 1882 (S.R.O., RHP 8178).
[4] *NSA*, vii (Argyll), 242; *Origines Parochiales*, ii, part i, 164; Watson, *Celtic Place-names*, 253; *Argyll Synod Minutes*, i, 26; Carmichael, *Lismore*, 124–6.
[5] Langlands, G, *County Map of Argyll* (1801); Johnston, W, *Argyllshire*, in Thomson's *Atlas* (1824). Part of the hillside to the N of Achnacone House is designated Coire na h'Anaid on the 2nd ed. (1900) of the 6-inch O.S. map (sheet lvii SE). Cf. *Origines Parochiales*, ii, part i, 167–8.
[6] Lorn Presbytery Minutes, v (1772–1820), pp. 33–7; *Stat. Acct.*, i (1791), 491.
[7] Scott, *Fasti*, iv, 80.

(2) Within an arched recess of no great age which has been built against the centre of the W gable-wall of the church there is preserved a headstone. This formerly stood over the Stewart of Appin grave at Culloden Moor, commemorating those who fell in the battle of 1746. The stone bears the inscription: CLAN / STEWART / OF APPIN.

939464   NM 94 NW   June 1971

215. Old Parish Church, Ardchattan. About 45 m to the E of Ardchattan Manse there stand the fragmentary remains of a rectangular building measuring about 18·4 m from E to W by 7·5 m transversely over all. The N and E walls have been almost entirely destroyed, but the S wall, which survives to a maximum height of about 1·5 m, appears to have incorporated a number of doorway- and window-openings.

This is evidently the church that was erected to serve the parishioners of Ardchattan in 1731–2. Prior to this date parish services were held in Ardchattan Priory (No. 217), which itself appears to have superseded the medieval church of Baile Mhaodain (No. 220) as the principal place of parish worship sometime during the 17th century.[1] A building-contract and other documents preserved in the Ardchattan Papers show that the church was built by James Duff, mason in Dunblane, and that work had been completed by November 1732; some of the stone used in the construction was evidently quarried from Ardchattan Priory.[2] A seating-plan of the church, preserved in the Scottish Record Office,[3] indicates that the communion table was centrally placed on the long axis of the church and that the pulpit stood against the centre of the S wall. The church is indicated on Roy's Map of about 1750 (cf. also No. 216).

976347   NM 93 SE   May 1969

216. Parish Church, Ardchattan. This church (Pl. 12D) was built in 1836, to replace an earlier building (No. 215) situated to the E of Ardchattan House and close to the site of the present manse.[4] The main block is oblong on plan and measures about 18·6 m from NE to SW by 12·3 m transversely over all. The principal entrance-doorway is situated in the SW gable-wall, which is surmounted by a belfry and flanked by short two-storeyed wings containing a vestry and retiring-rooms. The masonry is of local granite with sandstone dressings, all the detail being executed in the Gothic Revival style. The windows are mullioned and transomed and have latticed glass, while the gables are crow-stepped.

The interior (Pl. 12F), which retains much of its original character, follows the arrangement generally adopted in galleried hall-churches (Fig. 87). A horseshoe gallery, supported on moulded cast-iron columns, runs round three sides of the building, while the pulpit stands against the centre of the NE wall. The pulpit is approached by a double flight of steps and is surmounted by a sounding-board, while a lower but similar staircase gives access to the precentor's desk. The pulpit,

precentor's desk and gallery-front are panelled with blind Gothic tracery. A long communion-table (Pl. 12E) with flanking pews traverses almost the full length of the church along its central axis, the remainder of the ground-floor area being occupied by two main series of bench-pews.

A plan and specification for a new church at Achnaba (Ardchattan) was provided by John Thom, an Oban

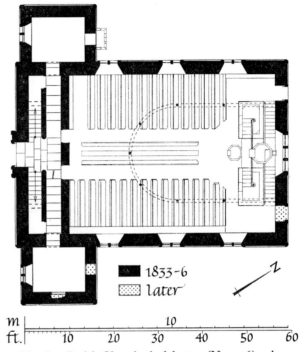

Fig. 87. Parish Church, Ardchattan (No. 216); plan

1833–6
later

architect, in September 1832, the estimated cost of the building being £972 4s 1d. It was presumably Thom's plan that was approved by the Presbytery in the following month, but in January 1833 a somewhat higher estimate by J and W Dalziel, wrights near Hamilton, was accepted. There was some delay in construction, and the church was not opened for worship until the autumn of 1836.[5]

945359   NM 93 NW   June 1967

217. Ardchattan Priory. The priory (Fig. 88, Pls. 13, 14) occupies a sheltered situation on the N shore of Loch Etive about 6 km E of North Connel. The site

---

[1] *Origines Parochiales*, ii, part i, 148; 'Memoriall & Queries for the heritors of the paroch of Ardchattan' (*c.* 1730) in Campbell of Ardchattan Papers, Ardchattan Priory, Top Drawer.
[2] Campbell of Ardchattan Papers, loc. cit.
[3] S.R.O., RHP 12329.
[4] *NSA*, vii (Argyll), 506.
[5] S.R.O., Campbell of Barcaldine Collection, GD 170/519; Lorn Presbytery Minutes, vi (1829–39), pp. 36–8, 73, 84–6, 248.

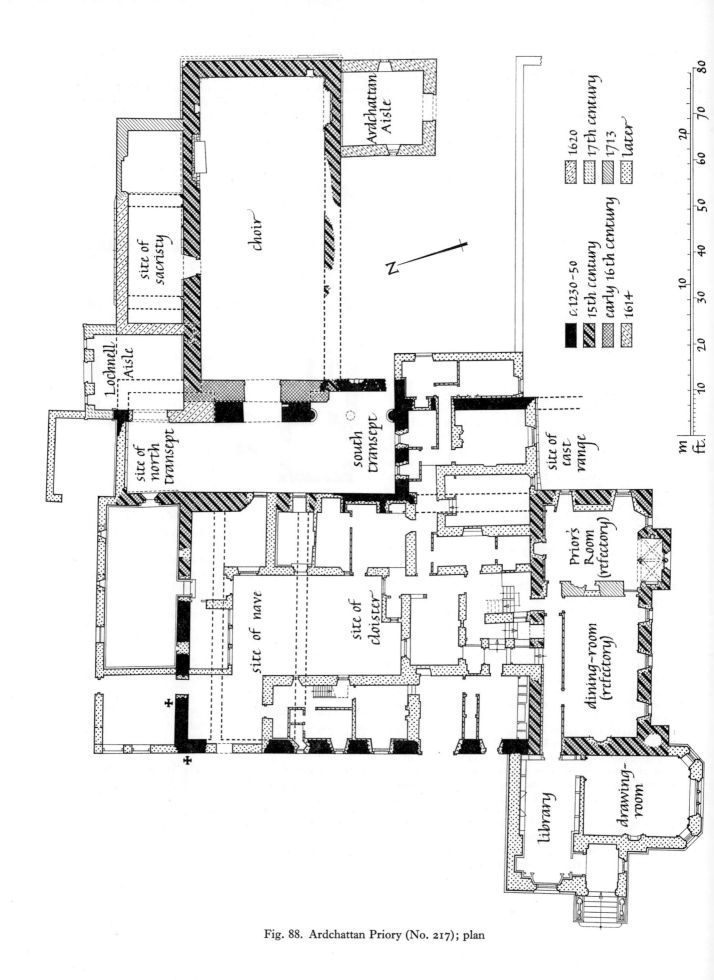

Fig. 88. Ardchattan Priory (No. 217); plan

The following labels appear within the plan:

- Ardchattan Aisle
- choir
- site of sacristy
- Lochnell Aisle
- site of north transept
- south transept
- site of east range
- site of nave
- site of cloister
- Prior's Room (refectory)
- dining-room (refectory)
- library
- drawing-room
- N

Key:
- c.1230-50
- 15th century
- early 16th century
- 1614
- 1620
- 17th century
- 1713
- later

Scale: m 0 10 20 ft. 0 10 20 30 40 50 60 70 80

forms part of a narrow strip of cultivable ground lying at the foot of the Benderloch Hills, overlooking the outer reaches of the loch, which until recent years comprised one of the main channels of communication between the interior of Lorn and the western seaboard.

The architectural development of the structure is not altogether clear, but the principal stages in the evolution of the fabric appear to have been as follows. A church with associated conventual buildings was erected soon after the foundation of the Valliscaulian priory in 1230 or 1231. This church comprised a small choir and crossing, N and S transepts with double transeptal chapels, and a nave having a narrow N aisle. The conventual buildings were disposed round a cloister on the S side of the church in the usual way, the W range, however, being represented only by a cloister-walk and an outer retaining-wall. Of the buildings of this period there remain today the S transept with its two chapels, and some fragments of the nave and crossing. Certain portions of the monastic buildings incorporated within the present mansion may also belong to this period, notably the W wall of the cloister.

A major scheme of reconstruction was begun and partially completed during the 15th and early 16th centuries, when a new and much larger choir with an adjacent N sacristy was erected and parts of the crossing, N transept and nave were rebuilt. The S range of the conventual buildings was also remodelled, a new refectory being constructed upon the site of the original one. All these buildings survive today either in whole or

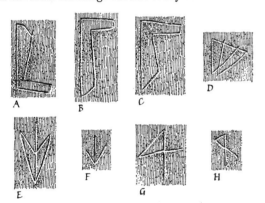

Fig. 89. Ardchattan Priory (No. 217); masons' marks: A, B, H, refectory pulpit; C, refectory doorway; D, G, east crossing arch; E, piscina drain-outlet; F, north transept window (scale 1:5)

in part. Following the cessation of religious life towards the end of the 16th century the priory was secularized, passing into the hands of Alexander Campbell, who had formerly been its commendatory prior. The Campbell family converted the S range of the conventual buildings into a private dwelling-house, while the choir and transepts of the church were used for parochial worship during the 17th and early 18th centuries, a number of private burial-aisles being added to the church during this period. Following the erection of a new parish-

church in 1731–2 the monastic church fell into disuse, except for the purposes of burial, and the fabric was subsequently quarried for building-materials. The house was enlarged and remodelled in about the middle of the 19th century, and numerous minor alterations have been carried out since, but the monastic refectory still survives as the nucleus of the present mansion, whose offices and outbuildings now extend over the site of the former nave and cloister. The remaining portions of the choir and transepts of the monastic church passed into the guardianship of the Department of the Environment in 1954.

ARCHITECTURAL DESCRIPTION

All the buildings are constructed of local granite rubble with freestone dressings. The medieval masonry is characterised by large rubble blocks set on edge and bonded with numerous slate pinnings. The 13th-century dressings appear to be composed mainly of a fine-grained greyish-green sandstone of Jurassic age, probably deriving from the Carsaig quarries on Mull. For the late medieval work, however, as seen in the choir and refectory, a medium-grained buff-coloured sandstone was generally employed, and this probably emanates from the Carboniferous beds at Inninmore Bay, Morvern.[1] Some of the stones bear incised masons' marks (Fig. 89).

THE CHOIR. The choir (Pls. 13B, 14) measures 20·1 m by 8·6 m internally, the walls having a thickness of 1·1 m. The S and E walls are in general reduced to a height of less than 2·0 m, although the SE angle rises to a height of 3·3 m; the N wall is a little better preserved, particularly at its W end, where it rises to a maximum height of 8·2 m. There is a splayed plinth, comprising a single member, on the N and S walls and a double member on the E wall (Fig. 90D, Pl. 15E), and above it a splayed string-course, which has returned round the choir at a height of about 2·1 m above ground-level. The NE and SE angles are defined by octagonal shafts (Pl. 15E) which probably rose to the wall-head. No windows now remain, but there is evidence to suggest that there were formerly three windows in the N wall, one to the W of the sacristy and two to the E of it. Nothing now remains to indicate the arrangement of windows in the S wall, except at a point 1·2 m from the SE angle, where a stone with a splayed arris may represent the ingo of a window. The arrangement of windows in the E wall is uncertain.

Internally, a moulded string-course (Fig. 90B), which may have formed a sill-course for the windows, returned round the choir at a height of about 2·0 m above floor-level. At the E end of the S wall there are three moulded arch-pointed recesses whose bases are carved with foliaceous ornament (Fig. 91, Pl. 15B). The recesses are set within a semicircular-headed arch comprising two main bands of roll-and-hollow moulding framed by a hood-mould (Fig. 90A) terminating in carved stops, of which only the westernmost, representing a lion (Pl.

[1] Information from Mr G H Collins, Institute of Geological Sciences.

15A), now survives. The upper portion of the central recess contains a piscina, decorated with arcading, while the flanking recesses incorporate what appear to be credences. It seems probable that the piscina and credences have been removed from their original positions,[1] and the situation of the external drain-outlet

Fig. 90. Ardchattan Priory (No. 217); profile mouldings: A, recesses in south choir wall; B, internal choir string-course; C, sacristy doorway; D, plinth of east choir wall; E, pulpitum

in the base-plinth suggests that the piscina, at least, formerly occupied the easternmost recess. One or both of the neighbouring recesses may have incorporated sedilia. There is an aumbry at the S end of the E wall, and another at the E end of the N wall. A little to the W of this latter aumbry there has evidently been a mural recess, but its upper part has been almost completely destroyed; the lower part contains a tomb-chest of the MacDougalls (*infra*, p. 112; no. 11). The E stop of the hood-mould of the arch that formerly framed the recess terminates in an intertwined spray of foliage (Pl. 15C), carved in relief.[2]

The sacristy was reached by means of a moulded doorway in the N wall of the choir. The head of this doorway has fallen and the dressings of the E jamb have disappeared, but the greater part of the W jamb remains *in situ* (Fig. 90C). Almost nothing now remains of the sacristy itself, although the rough stone corbels that supported its lean-to roof may still be seen in the N wall of the choir, as can the tusks of masonry into which its E and W walls were bonded. A fragment of the N wall of the sacristy remains, however, and bears a splayed plinth

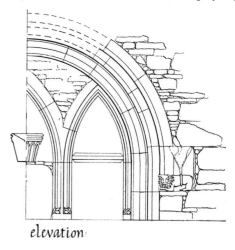

elevation

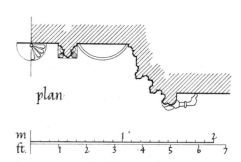

plan

Fig. 91. Ardchattan Priory (No. 217); recesses in S choir wall

which has evidently returned round the building. The plinth of the choir appears to continue within the sacristy, suggesting that the decision to incorporate a sacristy was taken only after the base-course of the choir had been laid. The sacristy was enlarged to form a burial-aisle in

[1] MacGibbon and Ross describe them as 'modern insertions' (*Eccles. Arch.*, iii, 389). In a drawing of 1820, however, the piscina and credences are shown occupying their present positions. A slightly earlier, but perhaps less reliable, drawing shows the piscina alone (Nat. Lib. of Scot. MS Adv. 30.5.22, nos. 19c, 20b).

[2] This is probably the mural recess illustrated in a drawing of 1798 (Nat. Lib. of Scot. MS Adv. 30.5.22, no. 19a), which shows part of the arch-head still *in situ*, the voussoirs being enriched with a cable-moulding and paterae. The treatment of the carved stop recalls Irish work of the 15th century, as seen e.g. at Movilla Abbey, Co. Down.

post-Reformation times, possibly to accommodate members of the family of Campbell of Inverawe (*infra*, pp. 113–14). Towards the E end of the N wall of the aisle there are the remains of a mural recess, which contains an unidentifiable tomb-slab.

THE CROSSING AND TRANSEPTS. In the original scheme both the N and S transepts appear to have incorporated double transeptal chapels, but those in the N transept were almost completely removed in the early 17th century. In the S transept (Pl. 15D) the N and S responds of the arcade through which the chapels were entered can still be seen, however, together with the base and

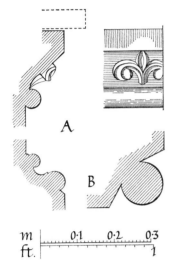

m   0·1   0·2   0·3
ft.   1

Fig. 92. Ardchattan Priory (No. 217); detail and profile mouldings: A, respond of south transeptal chapel; B, south-east angle of south transept

lower courses of the central pier. The bases are water-holding and the capital of the N respond retains traces of carved fleurs-de-lis (Fig. 92A). Each chapel probably had a single-light window in the E wall, but only the window of the northernmost chapel now remains, having been blocked with masonry when the S wall of the enlarged choir was built over it in the 15th century. The remaining fragment of the N jamb is rebated externally. In the southernmost chapel the base of an altar has recently been exposed against the E wall.

The building-sequence within the crossing is not altogether clear, but it seems likely that in the original arrangement the transepts opened directly into the crossing, as they do today, the entire area being covered with a continuous roof pitched from E to W. The nave is now separated from the crossing by a pulpitum, the central opening of which survives, although now greatly mutilated and partially blocked by masonry. The semicircular-headed arch of four orders springs from multiple shafts (Fig. 90E) and moulded capitals apparently of 15th-century character. Above the arch on the E side of the pulpitum there may be seen parts of two

sandstone corbels which may originally have carried a beam supporting a timber superstructure. In the W wall of the S transept there is another blocked-up opening, evidently a semicircular-headed doorway formerly opening on to the cloister-walk. Beyond this doorway a staircase may have risen against the W wall to give access to the monks' dormitory in the E range of conventual buildings. There appears to have been no direct communication between the N nave-aisle and the crossing.

Access from the crossing to the choir is now obtained through a massive double wall containing two separate but adjacent semicircular-headed arch-ways (Pl. 15F). The W arch, which has lost nearly all its dressed rybats and voussoirs, is probably as old as the 13th century, being the original entrance to the choir. The beam-sockets visible on each side of the arch-way, at heights of about 2·1 m and 4·2 m above ground-level respectively, may be associated with the insertion of timber galleries during the post-Reformation use of the building for parochial worship. There is, however, no trace of corresponding sockets in the opposite wall.

The E arch and its surrounding masonry, forming the present W wall of the choir (Pl. 14B), may be ascribed to the early 16th century. This wall was probably erected as the first stage of a projected reconstruction of the crossing, during the course of which it was intended to demolish the earlier W archway and the adjacent transeptal chapels. This scheme, however, was never completed and the W archway and transeptal chapels remained intact until the early 17th century, when the two N chapels were removed to make way for the Lochnell burial-aisle. The E archway is wrought on its E side with a continuous quirked roll-and-hollow moulding and is rebated for double doors opening into the crossing. Above the arch there are the remains of one, or possibly of two, carved stone heads. The W side of the arch is wrought with a continuous roll-moulding. Above the arch the W face of the wall can be seen rising behind and above the broken corework that overlies the adjacent western arch. This face has a splayed intake at a height of 3·9 m above ground-level, while part of a splayed weather-course can be seen at a higher level, together with what appears to be raggles for a roof pitched from N to S. This suggests that it was intended to carry the nave roof through the crossing, but there is nothing to suggest that this arrangement was ever put into effect. The masonry composing the wall incorporates a number of carved fragments, including some pieces of 13th-century dog-tooth ornament, evidently quarried from older portions of the fabric.

The N wall of the N transept was rebuilt in the 18th or 19th century, but the lower portion of the wall is old, as evidenced by its greater thickness and by the splayed plinth that is visible externally. The E wall incorporates an early 17th-century archway (Pl. 16E) opening into the Lochnell burial-aisle, but about 1·5 m N of the arch-way some traces still remain of the original 13th-century buttress that supported the N respond of the arcade of the transeptal chapels. The W wall of the transept

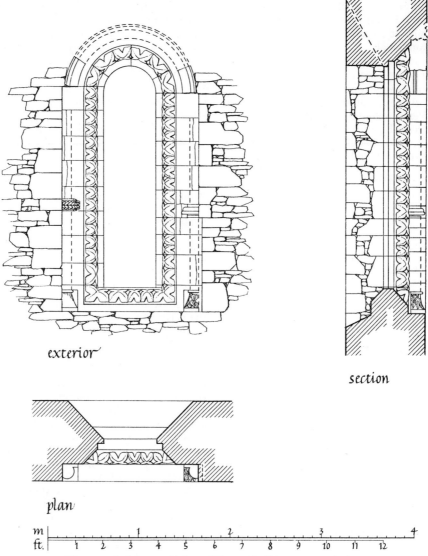

exterior

section

plan

m
ft.

Fig. 93. Ardchattan Priory (No. 217); N transept window

contains a tall deeply-splayed window having a semi-circular-headed daylight-opening set within nook-shafts (Fig. 93, Pl. 16A). The shafts, which are now missing, rose from tall bell-shaped bases to support a roll-moulded arch-head. The N annulet (Pl. 16C) is decorated with nail-head and cable ornament, and the S base (Pl. 16B) is elaborately carved with foliage similar in character to that seen in the arch-pointed recesses in the S wall of the choir. The surround of the window is carved with a continuous band of massive dog-tooth ornament. On either side of the window the internal wall-face shows traces of a moulded string-course. Although this window incorporates features of 13th-century character, it may be ascribed to the 15th century. The carving displays a clumsiness of execution not found elsewhere in the building in work of this period.

THE BURIAL-AISLES. The burial-aisle of the Campbells of Ardchattan (Pl. 13B) stands at the SE angle of the choir. It is entered from the S by a semicircular-headed doorway (Pl. 16D) wrought with rounded arrises, and incorporates a square-headed window, having chamfered arrises, in each of the side-walls. The windows, which were formerly barred, incorporate glazing-grooves. The keystone of the doorway has an ornamental pendant and bears in relief the date 1614, together with a monogram apparently comprising the initials A C K M for Alexander Campbell, 1st of Ardchattan, and his wife Katherine MacDonald. On each side of the arch-head there are carved the emblems of mortality, those on the E side incorporating the incised inscription [ME]MENTO MORI ('Remember death').

The Campbell of Lochnell aisle (Pls 14A, 16F) stands

in the angle formed by the choir and the N transept, and in part occupies the site of the former N transeptal chapels. It is entered from the W by an early 17th-century archway of two orders (Pl. 16E), and also from the N by a square-headed doorway (Pl. 16F) having an ovolo-moulded surround. On each side of this doorway there is a window above which there are carved the emblems of mortality, while over the doorway itself there is a panel bearing an incised inscription: THIS BURIELL PLACE WAS BUILT / BY ALEX^R CAMPBELL THIRD LAIRD / OF LOCHINELL ANNO 1620 AND NOU / [RE]BUILT AND ENLARGED BY ALEXR / CA[MPB]ELL SIXTH LAIRD [OF] / LOCHINELL ANNO 1713 / MANET POST FUNERA VIRTUS ('Virtue lives beyond the grave'). Above this panel there is a recess with a moulded surround, evidently intended to contain a coat of arms, but now empty.

THE NAVE. Very little now remains of the nave, the S wall and the N arcade having completely disappeared. The N aisle-wall, however, survives for its full length and is now incorporated within a hall and offices pertaining to the present mansion. Within the hall a semicircular-headed aisle-window (Pl. 16G) can be seen at a point 3·3 m W of the W wall of the N transept. This window is blocked up, its jambs and arch-head have been mutilated, and its mouldings in large part cut away; part of a foliaceous pattern remains upon the arch-head, however, its character suggesting a late medieval date. About 3·0 m to the W of this window there is a change in the nature of the masonry and, although a complete examination of the wall is not possible at present, it seems likely that the original aisle-wall may survive to the W of this point, the E portion of the wall having been rebuilt with the N transept in the 15th century. About 3·3 m W of the point at which the character of the masonry changes there may be seen a square-headed opening, now blocked, the lintel and jambs of which are rebated externally; this appears to have been a window. Further W there is a crudely-incised consecration-cross, while a second consecration-cross can be seen at the NW angle of the nave. The nave appears to have measured 15·2 m by 7·3 m internally, including the N aisle, which can have had a width of only about 1·5 m.

THE CONVENTUAL BUILDINGS. Apart from the refectory, little now remains of the monastic buildings, and the surviving fragments have been so thoroughly incorporated in the present mansion that their significance can be appreciated only by a study of the plan, Fig. 88. This indicates that the conventual buildings were grouped in the customary manner around a cloister situated on the S side of the nave. The cloister probably comprised a central garth some 9 m square, having on each side of it a covered walk or alley measuring about 3 m in width. Of the E or dorter-range very little now remains, although the wall-thicknesses and wall-alignments in this portion of the house suggest that part of the N end of the range, including the site of the chapter-house, is incorporated in the present mansion. Behind the wall-linings of a room in the E wing of the

house there may be seen the lower part of the SE angle of the S transept; the quoins are wrought with a heavy edge-roll (Fig. 92B), similar to those at Dunstaffnage Chapel (No. 243). The E range must have extended southwards beyond the limits of the present mansion, but its original extent is not known.

The best-preserved portion of the conventual buildings, the S range, was occupied by the refectory. In the S wall of this range, which forms the S front of the existing mansion, there may be seen traces of three original refectory-windows. The lower portions of the windows have been destroyed, but their pointed heads,

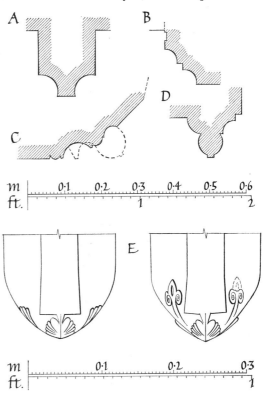

Fig. 94. Ardchattan Priory (No. 217); profile mouldings and details: A, vaulting-rib of refectory pulpit; B, refectory window; C, refectory doorway; D, hood-mould of niche in refectory pulpit; E, vaulting-rib stops in refectory pulpit

wrought with double hollow-chamfer mouldings, remain, although now blocked up (Fig. 94B, Pl. 17B). A fourth window formerly existed at the E end of the building, beyond the projecting bay that houses the refectory-pulpit, but no trace of this now remains externally. The two-light window contained within this bay is evidently original, but the stonework has been cement-rendered and the hood-mould renewed in artificial stone. At the W end of the refectory, immediately to the E of the return of a 19th-century bay-window, there is a projection, now inaccessible, which may have contained a small spiral stair leading from the refectory to an undercroft. The undercroft was evidently

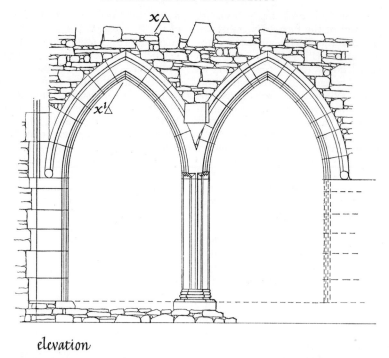

elevation

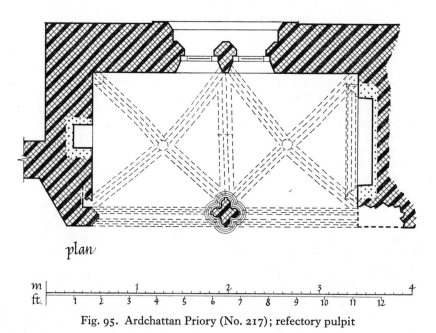

plan

Fig. 95. Ardchattan Priory (No. 217); refectory pulpit

lit by means of windows in the S wall, one of which has recently been re-discovered and opened up. The square-headed opening is wrought externally with a rebated 0·13 m chamfer, and still retains part of its original wrought-iron stanchion.

When the S range was converted to domestic use in post-Reformation times, the interior was sub-divided and additional floors were inserted. In the original arrangement there appears to have been a low unvaulted undercroft, and above it the refectory itself, whose floor lay at the same level as the cloister, that is to say at approximately the present floor-level of the 'Prior's Room' and dining-room. The refectory measured 15·2 m by 6·7 m internally and rose to an open timber roof; it

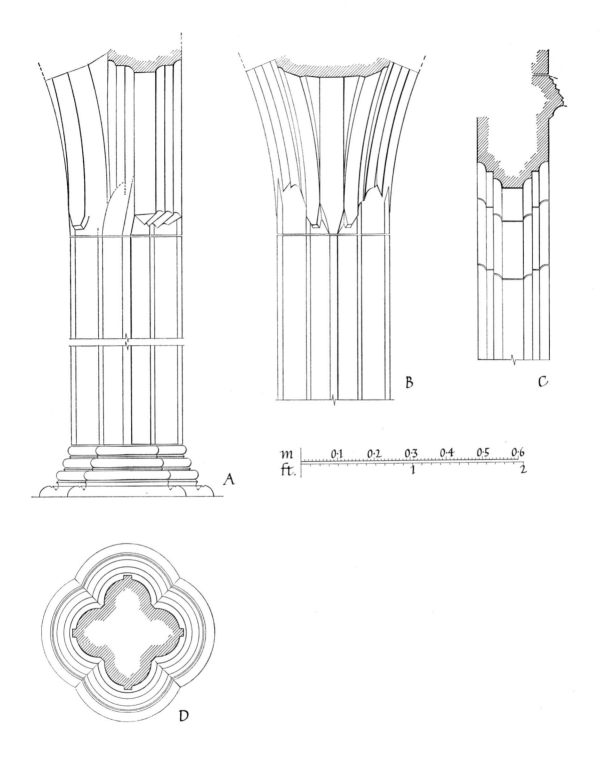

Fig. 96. Ardchattan Priory (No. 217); pier of refectory pulpit: A, elevation looking west (base reconstructed); B, elevation looking north; C, section X-X¹; D, plan

was entered from the cloister through a doorway in the N wall. A fragment of this doorway came to light during alterations carried out in 1960, and is now preserved behind the linings of the main E–W corridor on the principal floor of the house at the point indicated on Fig. 88. Only the inner part of the W jamb of the doorway survives, but it is clear that both jambs and arch-head were moulded (Fig. 94C, Pl. 18F), the latter incorporating a somewhat curiously superimposed hood-moulding which terminated in carved stops.

The most interesting feature of the refectory is the pulpit, which has recently been re-exposed to view and successfully restored (Pl. 17A). The pulpit, which is of two bays, appears to have been floored at the same level as the refectory, into which it opened through an arcade comprising two pointed arches divided by a central pier (Fig. 95, Pl. 18A–C). Presumably one of the bays served for access while the other accommodated the lectern. The responds and voussoirs of the arcade are wrought with a quirk-and-hollow moulding, and there are some remains of a hood-mould. The central pier, comprising a cluster of four filleted columns, rises from a damaged multiple-roll base, the lowest member of which appears to have been of water-holding profile (Fig. 96). There is no capital, and the transition between the mouldings of the pier and those of the arch-voussoirs is somewhat awkwardly contrived. Each bay of the pulpit is vaulted with a quadripartite vault having stout simply-moulded ribs and leaf-carved bosses and stops (Fig. 94A, E, Pl. 18D, E). The setting-out of the vaulting compartments is irregular and the masonry composing

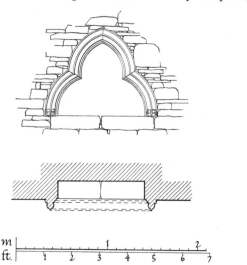

Fig. 97. Ardchattan Priory (No. 217); plan and elevation of niche in refectory pulpit

the cells varies a good deal in character from one bay to the other. The E wall of the E bay appears originally to have been intended to stand about 0·12 m further eastwards than it does at present, suggesting that the bays were at first designed to be correspondingly larger. The existing arrangement of the bays, however, leaves

more room for the broadly-splayed window-embrasure that adjoins the pulpit to the E and is evidently contemporary with it. In the W wall of the pulpit there is a trefoil-shaped niche (Figs. 94D, 97) framed by a hood-mould terminating in carved stops, but it is uncertain whether or not this feature is *in situ*. The corbel that projects above the central column of the arcade was evidently inserted in post-Reformation times to accommodate the timber runner of an upper floor.

The refectory originally rose to an open scissor-braced, collar-beam roof, but with the adaptation of the building for domestic use in post-Reformation times additional accommodation was contrived within the roof-space, while the roof itself was altered or partially reconstructed on more than one occasion. Nevertheless, the five eastern bays of the roof, at least, now partially exposed within the attic of the mansion, appear to have survived without alteration and are probably of 15th-century date. The details of construction are shown in Fig. 98; the timbers are of oak. The western section of the roof has been partially reconstructed, perhaps as a result of damage caused by the burning of Ardchattan in 1654 (*infra* p. 110). The timbers used in the reconstruction are in general of slighter dimensions than the original members, and some are of pine, but original timbers have been re-used in places. Wall-posts were introduced at this period and the heads of the cross-braces were half-lapped into the rafters instead of being tenoned. Subsequent alterations to the western portion of the roof included the replacement of the exposed wall-posts by posts embedded in the masonry of the wall and half-lapped to the sole-pieces; this modification was presumably intended to prevent the encroachment of the timbers within the first-floor bedrooms of the mansion. These details were observed when the greater part of the roof was exposed during the alterations of 1960, and although access may still be obtained to the upper part of the roof, the lower part is now for the most part again concealed behind wall-linings.

The alterations of 1960 also revealed the existence of a rough stone corbel at the E end of the S wall of the refectory and at a height of about 3·0 m above the original floor-level. This corbel, which may still be seen behind the wall-linings of a first-floor bedroom, may have been associated with an arrangement of floor-levels earlier in date than the existing arrangement, but falling within the post-Reformation period.

Any W range that might once have existed would have projected beyond the line of the W front of the church, but the plan of the conventual buildings (Fig. 88) suggests that there was, in fact, no W range, the cloister-walk being bounded on this side simply by a wall. Part of this wall remains and is incorporated in the buildings that occupy the W side of the courtyard to the N of the present mansion.

Water for the drainage-system of the conventual buildings was probably obtained from the small burn that flows past the NW and W sides of the site. Until comparatively recent times a culvert ran from this burn to pass beneath, or close by, the present mansion, before

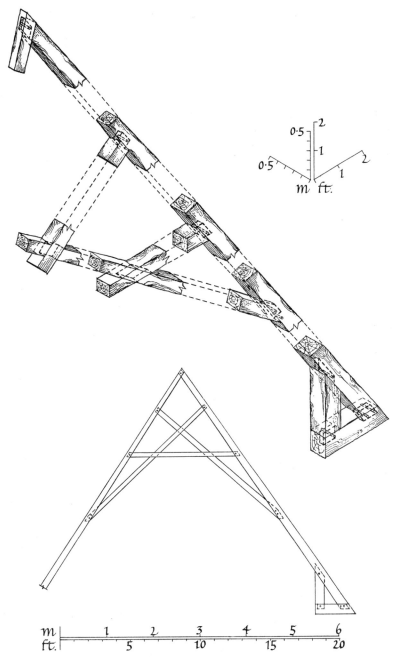

Fig. 98. Ardchattan Priory (No. 217); section and details of refectory roof

discharging into Loch Etive; stone drains are said to have been found on the site of the E range and elsewhere in and near the house. About 50 m NW of the mansion there is an artificial rectangular depression said to have been used as a fish-pond in monastic times; no doubt the pond was filled by means of a culvert linked to the burn already mentioned.

Apart from the surviving medieval fragments described above, the mansion contains no particular features of architectural interest. In the 'Prior's Room' (Pl. 18G) there is some 18th-century panelling, while an attractive mid-18th-century pine mantelpiece of English origin has recently been inserted in the dining-room; this incorporates a grate having a cast-iron fireback, apparently of 17th-century date. The drawing-room in the Victorian wing contains a recently installed chimney-piece of late 18th-century date, which incorporates a cast-iron grate formerly at Valleyfield House, Fife.

Some of the bedrooms retain stone bead-moulded fireplace-surrounds of 18th-century date, but the marble mantelpiece of late 18th- or early 19th-century date at the E end of the main block is a recent insertion.

HISTORICAL NOTE

The priory of Ardchattan was founded by Duncan MacDougall, lord of Lorn, in 1230 or 1231, being one of three houses of the Valliscaulian Order established in Scotland at that time. The endowments included lands and rights in Benderloch, Appin and Nether Lorn, as well as the teinds, or portions of the teinds, of the churches of Baile Mhaodain, Kilninver and Kilbrandon, in Lorn; Soroby, in Tiree; and Kilmarow, in Kintyre. The dedication was to St Mary and St John the Baptist.[1]

Little is known of the history of the monastery before the 16th century, although the names of some of the priors are recorded in documentary sources, and on stone memorials at Ardchattan. In a letter addressed to the pope by James V in 1538 on behalf of Prior Duncan MacArthur of Ardchattan, it is stated that Duncan had been promoted to this office by James IV thirty years previously, and that he had revived religious life there by choosing the six religious that the priory could support, and restoring the church and other buildings, which had been falling into ruin.[2] It seems likely that the existing W wall of the choir (*supra*, p. 103) represents one of the fruits of this building-activity. About the middle of the 16th century John Campbell, a younger son of Sir John Campbell of Cawdor and afterwards bishop of the Isles, was appointed commendator and prior of Ardchattan, and in 1602 Alexander Campbell, who had succeeded his father as commendatory prior in 1580, received a grant of the monastery as a secular tenantry.[3] The property has since remained in the possession of Alexander Campbell's descendants, who continue to occupy the former conventual buildings as a private residence.

John Campbell, 2nd of Ardchattan, supported the Royalist cause during the Civil War. In 1644 he is said to have helped Colkitto's army to cross Connel ferry on condition that his lands were not burnt.[4] In 1653–4 Campbell garrisoned Ardchattan on behalf of Charles II during Glencairn's rising, whereupon Captain Mutloe, the Cromwellian governor of Dunstaffnage, 'fell upon the house, and after some dispute having kill'd 3 of the Enemy, entred the house, and tooke a Lieutenant with some other prisoners, and store of armes and amunition'.[5] The laird subsequently claimed that the house had been 'brunt, plundered & destroyed',[6] but this report was probably exaggerated.

Although the conventual buildings were appropriated for domestic use, part of the monastic church was utilized for parochial worship, for it was reported to the presbytery in 1678 that 'the brethren having visited the fabrick of the old parish church of Ballevoadan (No. 220), as also the fabrick of the kirk and Quire of Ardchattan, being the ordinar place of publick worship past memory of any at present liveing, do find both ruined, and nothing but old walles'.[7] No doubt the

timber galleries, of which some traces remain within the crossing (*supra*, p. 103), were introduced during this period of post-Reformation occupation, which evidently continued until the erection of a new church on a fresh site in 1731–2 (cf. No. 215).

It is probable that some of the stone used in the construction of this church was obtained by dismantling the choir.[8] The monastery also provided a convenient quarry for use in building-operations at the adjacent mansion, and in 1798 it was reported that 'the place has been destroyed by the possessor for the sake of the stones, much to the regret of the inhabitants'.[9] A number of minor accounts relating to miscellaneous building-activity at Ardchattan during the late 17th and 18th centuries survive among the family papers, and it is known that the house was repaired by John Drummond, the Oban builder, in 1815.[10] The mansion was extended to its present size and remodelled under the direction of Charles Wilson, the Glasgow architect, between about 1847 and 1855.[11]

FUNERARY MONUMENTS AND OTHER CARVED STONES

Early Christian

(1) Leaning against the N wall of the Campbell of Lochnell aisle there is a cross-decorated stone designed to stand upright in the ground.[12] It was presumably brought to Ardchattan from some nearby Early Christian burial-ground, and all four edges of the stone have been trimmed down, possibly to adapt it for re-use as a coffin lid. At present it measures 2·0 m high, 0·68 m wide at the top, 0·55 m wide at the bottom, and from 0·10 m to 0·13 m thick.

On the front (Fig. 99) there is a wheel-cross with rounded and sunken arm-pits, the arcs of the wheel being embellished with Z-fret pattern. On the upper arm is the (? winged) figure of a man holding a book, with the head of a monster on either side; his hair is elaborately curled and his legs merge into triple-ribbon interlacing which also fills the surviving portions of the

[1] Easson, *Religious Houses*, 70; *Origines Parochiales*, ii, part i, 21–2, 149–53; Batten, E C, *The Charters of the Priory of Beauly with notices of the priories of Pluscardine and Ardchattan . . .* (1877), 140–56; Cowan, *Parishes*, 185.
[2] Hannay, R K and Hay, D (edd.), *The Letters of James V* (1954), 345–6.
[3] *Origines Parochiales*, ii, part i, 149–51.
[4] Leith, W Forbes, *Memoirs of Scottish Catholics during the XVIIth and XVIIIth Centuries* (1909), i, 312–13.
[5] Firth, C H, *Scotland and the Protectorate*, SHS (1899), 43–4.
[6] *APS*, vii (1661–9), 284.
[7] Lorn Presbytery Minutes, i (1651–84), p. 306.
[8] Campbell of Ardchattan Papers, Ardchattan Priory, Top Drawer, 'Agreement for the erection of a new church, 6 March 1731'; *NSA*, vii (Argyll), 496.
[9] Batten, op. cit., 283, quoting B.M., Add. MS 8142.
[10] Campbell of Ardchattan Papers, Ardchattan Priory, Miscellaneous Building-Papers.
[11] Thomson, David, 'The Works of the Late Charles Wilson . . .', p. 4 (paper read to the Glasgow Philosophical Society, 13 March 1882, typescript in N.M.R.S.); Campbell of Ardchattan Papers, Ardchattan Priory, Masons' wage-books.
[12] *ECMS*, part iii, 377–9 and fig. 393; *PSAS*, xxxiii (1898–9), 46–9; *JRSAI*, lxxxvi (1956), 93–6.

side-arms and the upper part of the shaft. The inter-lacing bifurcates in places, in Norse style, and occasionally incorporates rows of pellets. The rest of the cross is decorated with spiral patterns, a plaited knot, and a diagonal key-pattern. The carving to the left of the cross has been largely destroyed, but traces of an animal can be seen beside the upper arm. The spaces to the right of the cross are occupied by several strange beasts, and by a vertical row of three ecclesiastics, one of whom plays a

Fig. 99. Ardchattan Priory (No. 217);
cross-decorated stone (scale 1:15)

harp and another a pipe, while the third is holding what appears to be a crown. At the foot there is the figure of a warrior holding a spear and a rectangular notched shield.

On the back of the slab are traces of the incised outline of a cross of similar size and shape to the one on the front.

Medieval

Numbers 2–7 and parts of 10 are in the conservatory attached to the S wall of the mansion, numbers 8 and 15

in the N transept, numbers 9, part of 10, 11–13 and 16–17 in the choir, and number 14 in the Ardchattan aisle.

(2) Fragment of multiple roll-and-hollow moulding, the hollows infilled with dog-tooth ornament (Fig. 100A, *13th century*).

(3) Fragment of quirked roll-and-hollow moulding (Fig. 100B, *15th century*).

(4) Relief-carving of a dragon, possibly originally employed as a gable-skewput (Pl. 19A, *15th century*).

(5) Fragment from an arch, carved in relief with plaitwork (Pl. 19B, *15th century*).

(6) Fragments of two cusped ogee-headed windows, the spandrels decorated with interlace-ornament (Fig. 101, *15th—early 16th century*).[1]

(7) Tapered slab in two pieces, 1·80 m long by 0·60 m wide at the head, bearing the full-length effigy of a priest in low relief; the head of the figure has been broken off. He wears a chasuble and alb, and the apparel of the

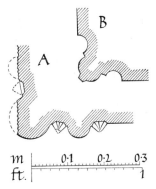

Fig. 100. Ardchattan Priory (No. 217); carved fragments

amice stands up stiffly close to the neck. The hands are joined in prayer on the breast, and on top of the maniple, which is worn on the left wrist and hangs down the centre of the body, there is a crude representation of a chalice. The feet are shown out-turned and in profile. At the foot of the slab is a running chevron-pattern. *Loch Awe school, 14th—15th century*.

(8) Tapered slab with bevelled edges, measuring over all 1·96 m in length by 0·50 m in width at the head; it is broken into three pieces. Within a border consisting of a row of elongated nail-head ornament between two plain mouldings there is an overall pattern of intertwined plant-scrolls. *Loch Awe school, 14th—15th century*.

(9) Tapered slab with bevelled edges, measuring over all 1·80 m long by 0·45 m wide at the head; it is broken across and very worn. Down the centre, within broad plain margins, there is a single plant-scroll. The name MCKICHAN has subsequently been cut in the top margin. *Iona school, 14th—15th century*.

(10) Three fragments of a free-standing disc-headed

[1] The closest parallels for the treatment of these windows are to be found in contemporary Irish work, e.g. at Carlingford Mint, Co. Louth.

cross, probably about 3·5 m in height. One fragment, the lower part of the shaft, has been re-erected inside the choir of the priory church; 0·73 m in height, it measures at the base 0·47 m in width by 0·11 m in thickness. On one face there is a galley without a sail, and a pair of animals, while the other face bears a foliated cross and the following inscription in black letter: *d(omi)n(u)s e[ugen]ius so/vorle m[a]kdwel p(r)i/or con(ven)tu[a]l(is) de ard/chata(n) fec[i]t ha(n)c cr/uce(m) [aedif]icar(i) pe/r ioh[a](n)n[em] o b(r)olcha(n) / apud ardchata(n) / a(n)no d(omi)ni mccccc* ('Sir Eugenius, son of Somerled MacDougall, conventual prior of Ardchattan, caused this cross to be erected by John O Brolchan at Ardchattan in the year of Our Lord 1500').[1]

The other two pieces, which are housed in the conservatory, are both from the head of the cross. On the

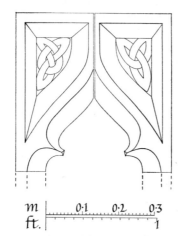

Fig. 101. Ardchattan Priory (No. 217);
fragments of window-heads

front of the disc, beneath the sacred cypher *i h s*, there has been a figure of the Crucified Saviour embowered in foliage. The back of the disc bears a representation of the Virgin, crowned and enthroned, and the inscription *maria g/racia ple(na)* ('Mary full of grace'). Eugenius probably succeeded in the priorate of Ardchattan the Dugall MacDougall mentioned in (11) below. *Iona school.*

(11) Tomb-chest built against the N wall of the choir of the priory church. The monument is a composite one, the lid being the wrong shape for the coffin and earlier in date. The two parts are therefore described separately.

(i) The lid (Pl. 19C) is a tapered slab of the Iona school measuring 2·11 m long by 0·85 m wide at the top. The foot of the stone has been chipped off, and the other edges have also sustained some damage. The decoration is in false relief and comprises six canopied figures arranged in two groups of three. Surrounding the entire composition there is an inscribed border with a debased dog-tooth moulding outside it, and the inscription, which begins in the top left-hand corner and runs clockwise round the stone, is continued on the left edge, and

terminates on a central label which separates the two groups of figures. At each of the four corners, and midway along the two longer sides, there have been roundels, the surviving three of which contain symbols of the Evangelists. The incised inscription, in Lombardic capitals, is now legible only in part, but with the help of earlier transcripts it can be restored to read: HIC IACENT [NATI / SVMERLEDI M(EIC)]DVGAILL DVNCANVS [ET DVGALLVS HVIVS MONASTERII SVCCESSIVE PRIORES VNA CVM EORVNDEM PATRI ET MATRE ET] / FR(ATR)E ALLANO QVORV(M) DVGALLVS ISTIVS MONIMENTI FABRICA[TOR] OBIIT / ANNO D(OMI)NI MCCCCCII ('Here lie the sons of Somerled MacDougall, Duncan and Dugall, successive priors of this monastery, together with their father, mother, and brother Alan. The said Dugall, creator of this monument, died in the year of Our Lord 1502').

In the upper range a cadaver, symbolising Mortality, is flanked by the priors Duncan and Dugall, clad in the habits of their order, while the three figures in the lower range represent (from left to right) Somerled MacDougall, his wife, and their son Alan. The family named in the inscription were no doubt MacDougalls of Dunollie, who seem to have been the local lay patrons of Ardchattan, and who probably had the right to nominate its prior.[2]

(ii) The coffin is undecorated but bears a black-letter inscription which, so far as it can be deciphered, reads: + [hic] iacent alla[nus] . . . [cum] suis filiis [.. / ..] (et) allano hic . . . sepult/us est ('Here lies Alan . . . with his sons . . . and Alan. Here . . . is buried'). In this context, the black letter implies that the coffin dates to the period *c.* 1500–1560, and the re-occurrence of the forename Alan, together with the adoption of a MacDougall tombstone as a lid, suggests that it was made for members of the same MacDougall family.[3]

(12) Parallel-sided slab, 1·85 m long by 0·50 m wide, with bevelled corners at the foot; it has been broken across and the top right-hand corner is missing. In a niche in the centre of the slab there is a small figure of a priest clad in Mass vestments and accompanied by a chalice, while round the margin is a black-letter inscription bordered by a row of debased dog-tooth ornament. The inscription reads: *hic iacet ven/erabilis et egregi[us] vir rodericus alexandri rector quo/ndam fyn/ani insule qui obiit anno d(omi)ni — —* ('Here lies a venerable and eminent man, Roderick, son of Alexander, formerly parson of Eilean Fhianain, who died in the year of Our Lord — —').

The stone was evidently made during Roderick's lifetime, for although space was left for it the year of death was never added. The slab was presumably carved between 1515, when he was collated to the parsonage of Eilean Fhianain (St Finan's Isle) in Loch Shiel, and 1545 when he was already dean of Morvern. An important figure in his day, Roderick was for a time bishop elect of the Isles, and he was one of two persons

---

[1] Cf. Steer and Bannerman, *Monumental Sculpture*, inscription no. 58, and fig. 17.
[2] Cf. ibid., inscription no. 57.
[3] Cf. ibid., inscription no. 59.

appointed by the Council of the Isles in 1545 to treat on their behalf with Henry VIII of England.[1]

(13) Parallel-sided slab, 1·96 m long by 0·55 m wide; it is broken across and heavily worn in places. Within a border consisting of a row of debased dog-tooth ornament between two plain mouldings, there is a foliaceous cross at the top of the stone, and centrally beneath this a claymore with animals both above and below the quillons. The spaces on either side of the sword-blade are occupied by a black-letter inscription, which reads: *hic iace[t] dugalus fili(us) | alexandri filii ioha(n)nis | . . . [qu]i obiit —— — die | mens(is) — — [a(n)no] d(omi)ni mcccccxli* ('Here lies Dugall, son of Alexander, son of John . . . , who died on the — day of the month of — in the year of Our Lord 1541'). The figures giving the precise day and month of death were never inserted. This stone may commemorate a younger son of Alexander MacDougall of Dunollie.[2]

(14) Tapered slab, 1·85 m long by 0·60 m wide at the head. Much of the surface has scaled off, but there are traces of a foliaceous pattern in the upper half, while down the right-hand margin there is a black-letter inscription, which reads: + *hic iacet tavus et alanus filii alexandri . . .* ('Here lie Thomas and Alan, sons of Alexander . . .'). *c. 1500—1560*. The persons commemorated were probably members of one of the local MacDougall families.[3]

(15) The upper two-thirds of a parallel-sided slab with bevelled corners; it is 1·55 m long by 0·51 m wide. The work of the same carver who was responsible for (7) above, it bears a similar figure of a priest set in a niche, and a border of dog-tooth ornament. In this case, however, there is no sign of an inscription. *c. 1500—1560*.

(16) Tapered slab, broken across and lacking the foot; it is 1·79 m long by 0·76 m wide. The only surviving decoration is a figure of a woman in a deeply recessed round-headed niche. She wears a long robe reaching to the ankles and a head-dress which rises to a slight peak in the centre; her hands are joined in prayer. *Probably c. 1500—1560*.

(17) The upper part of a tapered slab, 1·32 m long by 0·52 m wide at the head. Within a border of nail-head ornament there is a centrally-placed sword flanked by plant-scrolls. *14th—early 16th century*.

Post-Reformation

Number 18 is in the burial-ground, number 19 in the choir, numbers 20-3 in the sacristy, numbers 24-5 in the S transept and numbers 26-30 in the Lochnell aisle.

(18) Tapered slab of slate, 1·78 m long by 0·53 m at the wider end; it is broken across in two places and heavily damaged round the edges. Within a border decorated with intersecting arcs there is an inscription which reads: *iohne mak do[ue]ll m(a)c callen*. The most likely of several possible translations of this epitaph is: 'John MacDougall, son of Allan'. The slab probably dates to the second half of the 16th century, and the letters of the inscription show the influence of contemporary Gaelic script.[4]

(19) Recumbent slab of schist (Pl. 20A), now protected by a wooden cover. The main inscription, which occupies the lower centre of the slab, reads: THIS MONUMENT / WAS MADE BY / DUNCAN MCINTYRE / OF GLENO AND IS / DESIGNED FOR A TOMB / FOR HIM AND HIS / SPOVS MARY / CAMPBELL AND / HER SUCEESORS. A marginal inscription reads: BLESSED ARE THE DEAD WHICH DY IN THE LORD THEY MAY REST FROM THEIR LABOVRS AND THEIR WORKS DOE FOLLOVE THEM (Revelation, 14, verse 13). A third inscription carved partly at the centre, inversely, and partly on the margin reads:

WE LIVE TO LIFE
WE LIVE TO DY
WE DY TO LIVE
ETERNALLY

At the head of the stone there is a shield carved in relief and bearing the following armorial charges arranged without apparent regard for the rules of heraldry: a stag tripping, having its chest pierced by an arrow; a galley, sail furled, pennon flying; a mullet; a salmon naiant. Above the shield there is a label with pendulous terminations, carved with the monogram-initials D C M and the motto PER ARDUA ('Through adversity'). The shield is flanked by the initials of the deceased, while beneath there are carved in relief a hemispherical disc, possibly representing the globe, and a heart, together with the conventional emblems of mortality, the injunction MEMENTO MORI ('Remember death') and the date 1695.

(20) Recumbent slab of sandstone with the marginal inscription:

DUGALL CAMPBELL WAS [?TH]VS PERSONS NAM
RENOVND FOR HOHOUR (sic) AND VNDVBTED FAIM
OBIIT ANNO 1665

At the top of the stone there are carved the emblems of mortality, while in the centre there is an armorial shield set within a sunk frame and charged: quarterly, in each quarter, gyronny of eight. This stone may commemorate Colonel Dugald Campbell of Inverawe (cf. (23)).[5]

(21) Recumbent slab similar in style to (20) and evidently of about the same date. The inscription is illegible, but the shield appears to be charged for ? Campbell: quarterly, 1st and 4th, gyronny of eight; 2nd and 3rd, a galley, sail furled.

(22) Built into the W wall of the sacristy there is a stone panel (Pl. 20D) containing an armorial achievement flanked by what are probably intended to be fluted classical columns. The shield is charged: quarterly, 1st, 2nd and 4th, gyronny of eight; 3rd, gyronny of eight, in base a ?salmon naiant. Above is the motto SPERANS

[1] Cf. ibid., inscription no. 61.
[2] Cf. ibid., inscription no. 60.
[3] Cf. ibid., inscription no. 62.
[4] The Commissioners are indebted to Dr J W M Bannerman for help with this inscription.
[5] Johnston, *Campbell Heraldry*, ii, 49, gives the date of death as 1666.

('Hopeful'), and beneath the date 1682 divided by a monogram comprising the letters M N C, all in relief, except the motto, which is incised. This panel may commemorate a member of the family of Campbell of Inverawe.

(23) Recumbent slab of schist bearing the marginal inscription: HEIR LYES ALLANE CAMPBELL WHO DIED 1671. At the head of the slab the emblems of mortality are carved within a three-sided frame above which is the incised date 1689, while at the foot there is an armorial shield flanked by the initials A C and charged: quarterly, 1st and 4th, gyronny of eight; 2nd, a galley, sail furled; 3rd, a ?salmon naiant. The central area of the slab evidently contained a lengthy inscription, but this is now illegible apart from the words: CAPTANE / DOUGALL CAMPBELL. The slab was probably carved by the same sculptor as (24) and (25). In view of the rarity of the forename Alan within the Campbell family at this period it is tempting to identify the subject of this memorial with the 'Allan (also called Colin) Campbell, brother-german of Dougall Campbell of Inverawe', who is on record in 1664.[1] The coat of arms appears to represent the early form of emblazonment adopted by the Campbells of Inverawe; subsequently, however, the family coat of arms came to incorporate salmon within a bordure.[2]

(24) Recumbent slab of schist (Pl. 20B) carved in relief at head and foot with armorial shields having associated marginal inscriptions, and at the centre with a panel containing the emblems of mortality. The upper inscription reads: + HEIR LYES ANNABEL CAMPBEL FIRST SPOVSE TO PATRICK CAMPBE[L] OF INNERYELDIES WHO DIED THE 1[?1] OF IVNE 1634 OF HIR AGE [   ]. The shield is charged: quarterly, 1st and 4th, gyronny of eight; 2nd and 3rd, a galley, sail furled, oars in action. The shield is flanked by the raised initials A C, and beneath is the incised date 1689. Annabella Campbell was a daughter of Alexander Campbell of Arrivean, a cadet of Dunstaffnage; the marriage took place in 1620.[3] The lower inscription reads: HEIR LYES MARGARET CAMPBEL FIRST SPOUUASS TO IO[HN CAMPBELL] OF INNERYELDES WHO DIED THE 7 OF FEBR 1657 & OF [?HIR AGE   ]. The shield is charged: gyronny of eight, within a bordure ?vair, and is flanked by the initials [M] C. Margaret Campbell was a daughter of John Campbell of Clathic, and daughter-in-law to Annabella Campbell; the marriage took place in 1647.[4]

(25) Recumbent slab of schist probably executed by the same sculptor as (23) and (24). The upper part of the slab contains a panel carved with the emblems of mortality, and having a marginal inscription. The latter, which probably dates only from the 19th century, attempts to reproduce an original inscription, some traces of which can be seen on the sinister margin of the stone. This probably read: [HIC JACET PATRICIUS CAMPBE]LL DE INNERZALDIES QUI OBIIT [?25] MART AN DOM 1678 AETA[T] SUAE 8[6] ('Here lies Patrick Campbell of Innerzaldies who died 25 March 1678, aged 86'). Beneath the panel there is a Latin epitaph, again probably re-cut during the 19th century:

VIR PROBUS HIC SITUS EST CAUTUS / PROVIDUS PERHONESTUS / JUDICIO CLARO PROMPTUS ET INGENIO / IN APOTHYMATIBUS COMMUNIS / SERMO FLUEBAT / FACTA SUIS DICTIS CONSONA SEMPER / ERANT / PROLE PARENTE TORO REBUS VIRTUTE / SENECTA / JUSTITIA ET MERITIS LAUDE BEATUS OBIIT

('Here lies an honest man, one who was circumspect and canny, of unassailable honour, whose great powers of intellect and discernment were manifest to all. His conversation abounded with terse statements of opinion, and what he professed he never failed to practise. He died a man who had been fortunate alike in the children he reared and the parents who reared him, in the woman he married, in his material possessions, his moral worth, his length of years, his righteousness, and in his well-deserved renown'). At the foot of the slab there is carved in relief a shield, flanked by the initials P C and charged: quarterly, 1st and 4th, gyronny of eight; 2nd, a galley, sail furled, oars in action; 3rd, a fess checky between three ?crescents. Beneath the shield there is a label containing an illegible motto. Patrick Campbell, a natural son of Sir Duncan Campbell, 1st Bart. of Glenorchy, was the founder of the family of Campbell of Barcaldine (cf. No. 279).

(26) Table-tomb with inscription: HERE LAYS THE BON/NS AND ASES OF AL/EXANDER CAMPBE/LL THIRD LAIRD OF / LOCHNEALL WHO / DEPARTED THIS LIFE / THE YEARE 1645 / AND HIS LADY ISOB/ELL MCDUGALL DAUG/HTER TO THE LAIRD OF RAIGHRAY (Rarey). Alexander Campbell's armorial achievement is carved in relief at the head of the stone, the shield being charged: quarterly, 1st and 4th, gyronny of eight; 2nd, a boar's head erased; 3rd, a galley, sail furled. The motto is AUDAC[E]S IUVO ('I help the bold'). At the foot of the stone there are carved the monogram initials A C and M D, together with the emblems of mortality. This stone was probably carved by the same sculptor as (28), and evidently belongs to the first half of the 18th century.

(27) A large table-tomb (Pl. 20C) with the inscription: HERE LAYES THE BONNS AND ASHES / OF ALEXANDER CAMPBELL SIXTH / LAIRD OF LOCHINEALL WHO DEPARTED / THIS LIFE JANEUERY THE 4 THE YEARE / [?1714[5] AN]D OF AGE 63 YEARS AND HIS / [SPOUSE] MARGARET STUART DAUGH/[TER TO] THE LAIRD OF APEIN (Appin) WHO DEP/[ARTED] THIS LIFE THE 23 OF JANEUERY / 1712 AND OF AGE 56 YEARS. The armorial achievements of the deceased are carved at the head of the stone. The dexter shield is charged: quarterly, 1st and 4th, gyronny of eight; 2nd, a boar's head erased; 3rd, a galley, sail furled. The crest is a dexter hand holding a lance. The sinister shield is charged: quarterly, 1st and 4th, a fess checky; 2nd and 3rd, a galley, sail furled. The crest is a unicorn's head. Above the shields there is a label bearing the motto

[1] Campbell, *Argyll Sasines*, ii, 421.
[2] Wimberley, D, *Memorials of the Family of Campbell of Kilmartin and some notes on the Family of Campbell of Inverawe* (1894), 2–3.
[3] *Burke's Landed Gentry* (1952 ed.), 359.
[4] *Burke's Peerage* (1963 ed.), 425.
[5] Johnston, *Campbell Heraldry*, i, 28.

AUDAC[ES] IUV[O] ('I help the bold'), and beneath a second label with the motto WHITHER W[ILL YE]. The foot of the stone is carved in bold relief with two angels blowing trumpets, while between them there is an oval panel bearing the reversed monogram-initials A M C.

(28) Table-tomb of the first half of the 18th century, probably by the same sculptor as (26). The inscription is illegible. The upper part of the stone is carved in relief with an elaborate heraldic achievement comprising a central armorial panel set within a strapworked cartouche which incorporates an ancillary armorial panel at each corner. The central panel is charged, for Campbell of Lochnell: quarterly, 1st and 4th, gyronny of eight; 2nd, a boar's head erased; 3rd, a galley, sail furled. The ancillary panels at the 1st, 2nd and 4th corners of the cartouche correspond with those of the main achievement, but the one at the 3rd corner appears to incorporate a bordure, together with a saltire-shaped figure from the centre of which there hangs a hunting-horn. Between the two lower panels there are carved the reversed monogram-initials A C. The identity of the person commemorated is unknown.

(29) Table-tomb with the incised inscription: HIC IACET COLINUS CAMPBEL / DE BALIGOUN QUI OBIIT / MORTEM VICESIMO / QUARTO DIE FEBRUARII 1729 / ANNO AETATIS SUAE 49 ('Here lies Colin Campbell of Balligown, who died 24 February 1792, aged 49'). The upper part of the stone is carved in relief with an armorial achievement, the shield being charged: quarterly, 1st and 4th, gyronny of eight; 2nd, a boar's head erased; 3rd, a galley, sail furled. The crest is a dexter hand holding a lance, and the motto, now almost illegible, appears to be AUDACES IUVO ('I help the bold'). Between the inscription and the armorial achievement there are carved the emblems of mortality. Colin Campbell of Balligown, in the parish of Kilmartin, appears to have been a younger son of Alexander Campbell, 6th of Lochnell.

(30) Table-tomb inscribed: HERE LYES THE CORPS [OF DON]ALD CAMPBELL OF ARDIN[TALLAN] SON TO IOHN CAMPBELL LAIRD / OF LOCHNELL WHO DIED THE / YEAR ONE MDCCII AND OF / AGE LXXV THIS DONE BY / IOHN CAMPBELL HIS SON. Donald Campbell of Ardentallan was the third son of John Campbell, 4th of Lochnell.[1] The upper part of the stone is carved in relief with an armorial achievement, the shield being charged, for Campbell of Lochnell, as in (28). Between the inscription and the armorial there are carved the emblems of mortality. This stone may have been carved by the same sculptor as (27).

971349   NM 93 SE   August 1971

218. Burial-ground, Ath Dearg (Site). There are no identifiable traces of this burial-ground, and the site is occupied by what appear to be the remains of one or more shieling-huts.

This is said to be the burial-place of those killed at the battle fought hereabouts between the MacDougalls and the Campbells in about 1294[2] (cf. No. 227).

925183   NM 91 NW   May 1968

219. Chapel and Burial-ground (possible), Auch Gleann (Site). Close to the left bank of Allt na h-Annait, a little above its confluence with Allt Chonoghlais, there may be seen the remains of a sub-rectangular building and of an associated enclosure of roughly circular plan. The building measures about 18·3 m from SW to NE by about 5·5 m transversely over walls some 0·9 m in thickness. The walls are now reduced to their lowest courses and no details of construction are visible, except for what appear to be the remains of two separate entrance-doorways in the SE wall. The masonry was probably of dry-stone construction, but the upper courses of the walls may have been of turf.

The enclosure lies about 70 m NE of the building described above. It measures about 27 m in diameter, and the enclosing dry-stone dyke has an average width of about 1·1 m and a maximum height of about 0·6 m. Within the enclosure there may be seen about half-a-dozen roughly circular heaps of stones between 1·8 m and 3·7 m in diameter which may be either field clearance-heaps or stack-bases; other examples occur outside the enclosure.

Although the neighbouring place-names of Coire na h-Annait and Allt na h-Annait suggest that this site has some ecclesiastical significance, the existing remains are probably those of a small farmhouse with an associated cultivation-patch. There appears to be no early record of any ecclesiastical foundation in this vicinity, but the site was pointed out as that of a former 'R.C.Chapel', burial-ground and well, in 1870.[3]

346380   NN 33 NW   August 1967

220. Church, Baile Mhaodain, Ardchattan. The remains of this church stand within a burial-ground about 400 m NW of Ardchattan Priory (No. 217). The building is ruinous and much overgrown with trees and ivy, but the E gable-wall remains almost intact, whilst the N and W walls stand to a height of about 3·0 m above the present floor-level. The church is of unicameral plan and measures 17·2 m from W to E by 6·4 m transversely within walls about 1·0 m in thickness (Fig. 102). The masonry is of roughly-coursed local rubble laid in coarse lime mortar and well bonded with pinnings. The dressings, most of which have been robbed, were of yellow sandstone, probably quarried at Ardtornish. Numerous blocks of coarse-grained variegated sandstone also occur in the rubble facework of the walls and this material was probably quarried locally, perhaps at Bridge of Awe (No. 354). Some of these blocks are evidently in secondary use and probably derive from an earlier church on the same site. One such fragment, situated in the N wall about 1·7 m from the inner NW corner of the building and at a height of 1·5 m above floor-level, is wrought with a quirked edge-roll of 13th-century character. The E gable of the church is founded upon a substantial splayed plinth of rubble some 1·2 m in

---

[1] Ibid., i, 32.
[2] NSA, vii (Argyll), 68; Macdonald, *Argyll*, 120.
[3] Name Book, No. 51, p. 47.

height, while the upper portion of the wall is intaken internally at a height of 4·0 m above floor-level.

The building seems to have been served by a single entrance-doorway placed near the centre of the S wall, but this is now blocked by a dry-stone wall. In the centre of the E gable-wall there is a narrow single-light window having a lintelled ingo (Pl. 21C), and there are the remains of a similar opening towards the E end of the S wall. There may have been another window at the W end of the same wall,[1] while part of a splayed high-level window survives in the centre of the W gable-wall. The external face of the E gable-wall contains two small aumbries, flanking the site of the altar.

In the absence of architectural mouldings or details it is difficult to ascribe a precise date to the church, but it probably belongs to the 15th or early 16th century. The plan and overall dimensions correspond closely with those of the old parish-church of Kilmore (No. 264).

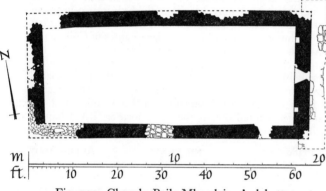

Fig. 102. Church, Baile Mhaodain, Ardchattan (No. 220); plan

This church served the former parish of Ardchattan,[2] a district which comprised Benderloch, together with an extensive tract of country lying on the E side of Loch Etive to the N of the River Awe. The dedication was either to St Modan or to St Baedan.[3] Little is known of the history of the church, and the date at which it was abandoned for worship is not recorded. The building may still have been in use in about 1630 when it was specifically designated as the parish church,[4] but in 1678 it was reported to the presbytery that 'the brethren having visited the fabrick of the old parish church of Ballevoadan, as also the fabrick of the kirk and Quire of Ardchattan, as being the ordinar place of publick worship past memory of any at present living, do find both ruined, and nothing but old walles'.[5] Directions were given for the repair of Baile Mhaodain, but an undated memorandum of about 1730 states that 'preaching & other parts of divine worship hes now for a long tyme bein administrat in the Monastrie Church of Ardchattan & the Kirk of Ballevoadan become ruinous'.[6] Both churches were superseded by a new building (No. 215) erected on a different site in 1731–2.

BURIAL-GROUND. The burial-ground was evidently enclosed by a dry-stone wall, of which some remains

can be seen on the S side of the church. The interior is very much overgrown with grass and bracken, but none of the visible tombstones appear to be of a date earlier than about the end of the 18th century.

TOBAR MHAODAIN. This is the name given to a spring situated on the right bank of the Eas Mhaodain about 50 m NE of the church. The mouth of the spring is enclosed by dry-stone masonry and is lintelled over to form a culvert from which the water discharges into a slab-built trough. This arrangement, however, probably dates from a fairly recent period.

970353 (Church)   NM 93 NE   July 1970
971353 (Well)

221. Chapel and Burial-ground, Ballachuan, Seil (Site).
These remains are situated about 400 m W of Kilbrandon House (No. 325), on a small knoll which rises 2·0 m above an area of marshy ground at the N end of Ballachuan Loch. The SW part of the site is occupied by the turf-covered foundations of an oblong building measuring 5·7 m from NE to SW by 2·7 m transversely at the NE end and 3·2 m at the SW end, within walls

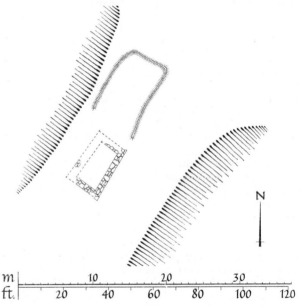

Fig. 103. Chapel and burial-ground, Ballachuan, Seil (site) (No. 221); plan

[1] Howson, writing in 1842, however, states that the church contained only three windows, all 'flat-topped' (Howson, *Antiquities*, 93).
[2] The parishes of Ardchattan and Muckairn were united in 1637.
[3] Mackinlay, *Non-Scriptural Dedications*, 148–9.
[4] *Geog. Coll.*, ii, 153.
[5] Lorn Presbytery Minutes, i (1651–84), pp. 306–7.
[6] Campbell of Ardchattan Papers, Ardchattan Priory, Top Drawer, 'Memoriall & Queries for the heritors of the paroch of Ardchattan'.

which vary in thickness from 0·8 m to 1·0 m, and stand to a maximum height of 0·7 m (Fig. 103). The masonry, where it is exposed in the inner faces of the SE and SW walls, is of rubble and slate bonded with clay mortar. To the NE there is a sub-rectangular enclosure measuring about 10·7 m from NE to SW by 5·5 m transversely.

When the officers of the Ordnance Survey visited this site in 1871, they reported that some of the graves could be traced, but the date of the last interment was unknown to the local inhabitants. One informant was able to remember the walls being 'five feet' (1·5 m) high.[1]

762153   NM 71 NE   June 1970

222. Burial-ground, Balliveolan. This burial-enclosure measures about 4·6 m square over walls 0·6 m in thickness and about 1·8 m in height. No tombstones are visible within the interior, which is grass-grown, but a stone incorporated in the W wall bears the incised inscription: [ER]ECTED / BY / ?[I C] / 1767; other initials have been inscribed at a later date.

This burial-ground belonged to the Campbells of Balliveolan,[2] and the initials are probably those of John Campbell of Balliveolan, who is on record in 1768 (cf. No. 312).

007453   NN 04 NW   April 1967

223. Chapel and Burial-ground, Bar-a-goan, Kilvarie (Site). There are no identifiable remains, and the site appears formerly to have been under rig-cultivation. This is presumably the 'burial ground or church of Marie, or the Virgin Mary' mentioned by the author of the *New Statistical Account* of the parish of Muckairn.[3]

905328   NM 93 SW   July 1968

224. Chapel and Burial-ground, Bernera (Site). The only visible remains are those of an enclosure about 11 m square surrounded by a dry-stone dyke. No tombstones are to be seen, but near the centre of the enclosure there are the remains of a stone-and-turf hut measuring about 3·7 m in diameter. The age of this hut is uncertain, but it may be contemporary with the house and kail-yard of comparatively recent origin, whose ruins stand a few metres to the SW of the enclosure.

Pont's map of about the beginning of the 17th century indicates the existence of a church or chapel in this locality,[4] while the burial-ground is recorded by the writer of the *Statistical Account*.[5] When the officers of the Ordnance Survey visited the place in about 1871-3 they reported that nothing remained of the chapel apart from a few loose stones scattered over the site.[6] The dedication is unknown.

794392   NM 73 NE   May 1968

225. Caibeal Chiarain (Site). This place was pointed out by the local inhabitants as the site of a chapel in about 1870.[7] There are no visible remains.

141260   NN 12 NW   April 1968

226. Caibeal, Lochavich. These remains are situated at a height of 250 m OD, in a Forestry Commission plantation 550 m N of Loch Avich. They comprise a circular enclosure-wall having an overall diameter of 17·5 m, within which stands a rectangular structure of lime-mortared rubble masonry measuring 5·4 m from NW to SE by 4·3 m transversely within walls having an average thickness of 0·7 m and a maximum height of 0·9 m (Fig. 104). There is no visible entrance to the latter

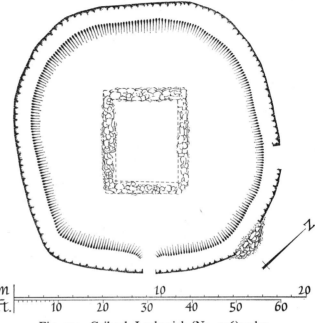

Fig. 104. Caibeal, Lochavich (No. 226); plan

structure, but the central portion of its SE wall is reduced to ground-level and may have incorporated an opening. The outer face of the enclosure-wall is of dry-stone masonry, now reduced to a height of about 0·3 m above ground-level; the inner face of the wall was obscured by a thick growth of vegetation at the date of visit, and no masonry was visible. The wall has an overall thickness of about 1·5 m, and the principal entrance is in the SE sector. No funerary monuments were identified at the date of visit.

Although these remains may occupy the site of an Early Christian burial-ground, whose existence is indicated by the place-name Kilmun, first recorded in 1414[8] and subsequently attached to the farm that once stood 650 m SW of the site, they were described by the officers of the Ordnance Survey in 1871 as a private burial-ground of the family of MacDougall of

[1] Name Book, No. 53, pp. 70-1.
[2] Ibid., No. 48, p. 71.
[3] *NSA*, vii (Argyll), 517.
[4] Blaeu's *Atlas* (Lorn).
[5] *Stat. Acct.*, i (1791), 491.
[6] Name Book, No. 22, p. 141.
[7] Ibid., No. 49, p. 163.
[8] *Origines Parochiales*, ii, part i, 125.

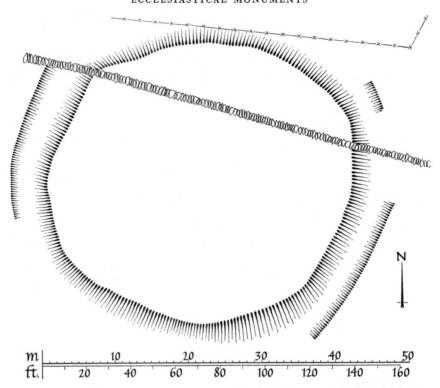

Fig. 105. Chapel and burial-ground, Cill-an-Suidhe, Lismore (site) (No. 229); plan

Kilmun, a branch of the MacDougalls of Rarey.[1] Neither the proportions nor the orientation of the inner structure supports its identification as a chapel, and it was probably never roofed. While the outer wall may perpetuate the outline of an earlier enclosure, the existing remains may be ascribed to the 18th century.

929153   NM 91 NW   June 1971

227. Carn Chailein. This name ('Colin's cairn') applies to a small cairn of stones situated about 400 m N of Loch na Sreinge, and on the left-hand side of the track that leads from Loch Avich to Loch Scammadale via the String of Lorn. The cairn measures about 3·6 m in diameter at base and stands to a height of 1·5 m. It is reputed to commemorate the death of Sir Colin Campbell of Lochawe during a battle fought in this locality between the MacDougalls and the Campbells about the year 1294.[2] The age of the cairn is not known, but it was evidently in existence before the end of the 17th century.[3]

927176   NM 91 NW   July 1971

228. Burial-ground, Cill an Inbhire (Site). There are no visible remains. It was reported in about 1870 that large blocks or slabs of stone were frequently encountered hereabouts when ploughing.[4]

825220   NM 82 SW   April 1970

229. Chapel and burial-ground, Cill-an-Suidhe, Lismore (Site). This burial-ground comprises an approximately circular enclosure having an internal diameter of about 38 m (Fig. 105). The site appears formerly to have been surrounded by a ditch, but this now remains only on the NW and SE sides, where it measures about 2·5 m in width and 1·5 m in depth. The interior is completely rush-grown, and there are no traces of burials. The burial-ground is traversed by a dry-stone wall of comparatively recent origin.

This is probably the site of the former chapel of Killean, which is reputed to have stood hereabouts;[5] the dedication was presumably to St John. The burial-ground appears to belong to a class of circular ditched enclosures for which an Early Christian origin has been postulated[6] (cf. Nos. 231 and 234).

848405   NM 84 SW   July 1970

230. Cill Choluim-chille, Benderloch (Site). There are no identifiable remains of this church, and none of the tombstones now visible in the burial-ground is of a date earlier than 1707.

[1] Name Book, No. 53, p. 137; *Burke's Landed Gentry* (1952 ed.), 1620.
[2] Macdonald, *Argyll*, 120.
[3] *Highland Papers*, ii, 85.
[4] Name Book, No. 53, p. 43.
[5] Blaeu's *Atlas* (Lorn); *Origines Parochiales*, ii, part i, 163; Carmichael, *Lismore*, 81.
[6] *Medieval Archaeology*, xi (1967), 166–7.

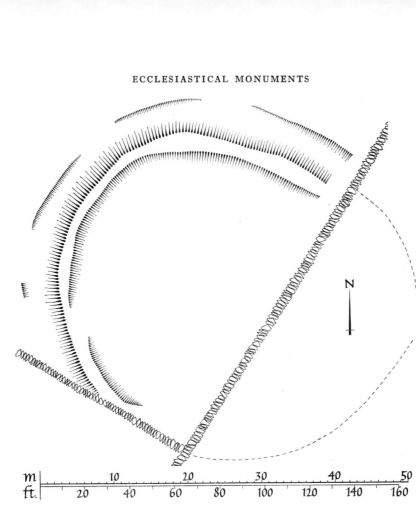

Fig. 106. Burial-ground (possible), Clachan, Lismore (No. 231); plan

A 'chappell called Killchallumchill in Beandirlogh' is mentioned in a topographical account of the Highlands written about the year 1630,[1] but in 1844 the writer of the *New Statistical Account* reported that 'the vestiges of this building are all that now remain, though the small plot of burial-ground around it continues to be used by a few families as a place of interment'.[2] The compilers of the Ordnance Survey Map, who visited the site in about 1870 and were able to identify two walls of the building, were informed that the burial-ground formerly extended over the adjacent cottage-garden and roadway.[3] This was confirmed in April 1952, when burials were discovered in the vicinity of the roadway during the laying of a new water-supply.[4]

The dedication was evidently to St Columba.

904377   NM 93 NW   May 1969

231. Burial-ground (possible), Clachan, Lismore.
The visible remains comprise an enclosure of roughly circular plan, measuring about 41 m internally, together with traces of a surrounding bank and ditch (Fig. 106). The site is traversed by a dry-stone wall of comparatively recent origin, to the SE of which nearly all traces of the bank and ditch have been obliterated by cultivation. To the NW of the wall, however, the bank attains a width of some 1·8 m and shows traces of a dry-stone core, while

the ditch, which is flat-bottomed, has a width of about 1·5 m and lies some 1·2 m beneath the top of the bank. There are no visible traces of burials.

Nothing is known of the history of this site, but it appears to belong to a class of circular ditched enclosures for which an early ecclesiastical origin has been postulated[5] (cf. Nos. 229 and 234). The only reputed ecclesiastical site in the immediate vicinity is that of the chapel at Killandrist (No. 260), some 360 m to the SE.

856430   NM 84 SE   July 1970

232. Cashel (possible), Cladh a' Bhearnaig, Kerrera.
These remains are situated on a raised beach near the extreme N point of Kerrera; the site is bounded on the NW by an outcrop of rock, from which the ground slopes gently to the S. It comprises a roughly circular enclosure, measuring some 60 m in diameter, which is divided by a curving wall into two unequal portions. Within the enclosure there are the fragmentary foundations of several structures. The enclosure-wall is best preserved in the NE sector, where it is constructed of

[1] *Geog. Coll.*, ii, 153.
[2] *NSA*, vii (Argyll), 498–9.
[3] Name Book, No. 1, p. 62.
[4] *The Glasgow Herald*, 21 April 1952.
[5] *Medieval Archaeology*, xi (1967), 166–7.

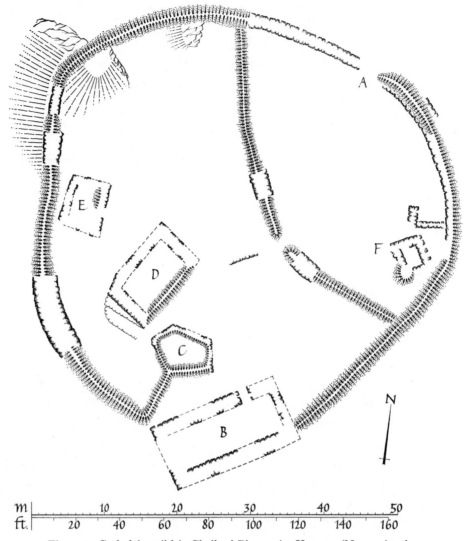

Fig. 107. Cashel (possible), Cladh a' Bhearnaig, Kerrera (No. 232); plan

dry-stone masonry with substantial facing-blocks and has a width of 1·9 m; elsewhere it appears as a low bank of turf in which occasional facing-stones remain *in situ*. The entrance is on the N (A on Fig. 107), and in the S sector the enclosure-wall is interrupted by a rectangular building (B) measuring 18·0 m from SW to NE by 9·1 m transversely over walls varying in thickness from 1·4 m to 2·2 m. Some 14 m to the NW there is a second rectangular building (D) measuring 12·2 m by 7·6 m over all, and associated with these structures there are traces of two smaller sub-rectangular or oval buildings (C, E). There are no visible remains of the structure that was observed in 1872 on the rock-outcrop at the NW limit of the site.[1] The lesser, or NE division of the enclosure, which is demarcated by a stony bank some 1·4 m in thickness, contains within the SE angle a stone-lined pit (F) measuring 2·6 m by 1·9 m internally.

This site is identified on James Dorret's map of

Scotland, published in 1750, as 'Clyvernock, an old monastery', and the stone-walled enclosure indeed resembles other cashels identified in Western Scotland,[2] although these are of smaller dimensions. It is, however, improbable that the internal structures are as early as the enclosure-wall, and they doubtless represent a domestic re-occupation of the site, although the large thick-walled building (B) may be ascribed with some probability to the medieval period.

842312   NM 83 SW   June 1971

233. Burial-ground, Cladh na h-Anaid, Auchnacloich.
The only visible remains are those of an enclosure measuring about 15 m square within a dry-

[1] *PSAS*, x (1872–4), 89.
[2] E.g. Sgor nam Ban-naomha, Canna (*Inventory of the Outer Hebrides*, No. 679); Strathcashel Point (*Inventory of Stirlingshire*, i, No. 164).

stone or turf wall some 0·9 m in thickness. The NE portion of the enclosure has been almost obliterated, and the remainder considerably mutilated, by the construction of the former Taynuilt–Oban road. There are no identifiable remains of buildings within the interior.

Nothing is known of the history of this site, which was identified as a burial-ground in about 1870.[1]

001291   NM 93 SE   July 1968

234. Burial-ground, Cladh na h-Anaid, Taynuilt.
The only visible remains are those of an enclosure of irregular pentagonal plan measuring from 14 m to 17 m within a stony bank which has an average width of

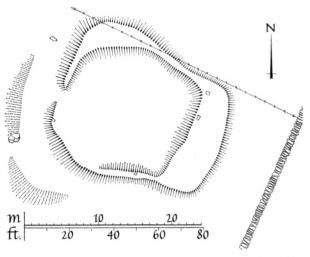

Fig. 108. Burial-ground, Cladh na h-Anaid, Taynuilt
(No. 234); plan

about 3·0 m and a maximum height of about 0·5 m (Fig. 108). There are some traces of what appears to be a narrow entrance on the NW side. There are no visible burials, but it was reported in about 1870 that the place had been used for interment 'many years ago'.[2] The site is probably of early ecclesiastical origin[3] (cf. Nos. 229 and 231).

001291   NN 02 NW   July 1970

235. Chapel and Burial-ground, Cladh Uaine. The remains of the chapel comprise the grass-grown wall-footings of a small rectangular building measuring about 8·2 m from E to W and 4·1 m transversely within walls about 1·0 m in thickness (Fig. 109). There are some traces of an entrance-doorway towards the centre of the S wall. There are no identifiable remains of the oval enclosure within which the chapel is delineated upon the 6-inch O.S. map, but in the immediate vicinity of the building there are rigs and field clearance-heaps, together with what appear to be the remains of a shieling-hut. This later cultivation seems to have obliterated all traces of the burial-ground.

Nothing is known of the history of this chapel, but gravestones were still visible in 1868–9, when officers of the Ordnance Survey were informed that interments had taken place within recent years.[4] It has been suggested that this is the site of a chapel dedicated to St

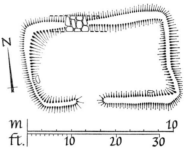

Fig. 109. Chapel and burial-ground, Cladh Uaine
(No. 235); plan

Maelrubha of which the name appears to be preserved in a late 16th-century document. In this document the Pennyland of 'Kilmorrie alius (alias) Clazemorrie (Cladhmorrie)' is included in a list of properties lying in the vicinity of Dunstaffnage Castle (No. 287), but the precise location of the land in question has not been established.[5]

881326   NM 83 SE   July 1970

236. Parish Church, Cladich. In 1736 the medieval parish-church of Inishail (No. 247) was abandoned and a new building was erected 1·8 km NE of Cladich, near the SE shore of Loch Awe, to serve the S portion of the united parish of Glenorchy and Inishail. Writing in 1843, the author of the *New Statistical Account* of the parish states that the church was 'a paltry building, erected about seventy years ago'.[6] The author of the earlier *Statistical Account*, however, makes no mention of this rebuilding, which, if the statement quoted is correct, would have been executed during his own incumbency.[7] Whereas the existing church may incorporate the 18th-century structure, it owes its present form to a remodelling which took place in 1896.[8] It is a plain rectangular building of harled rubble measuring 16·0 m from ENE to WSW by 7·1 m transversely over all, lit by four windows in each of the side-walls. The E gable is surmounted by a bell-cot containing an inscribed bell which dates from a re-casting in 1865.

108233   NN 12 SW   August 1970

[1] Name Book, No. 23, p. 20.
[2] Ibid., No. 52, p. 53.
[3] *PSAS*, c (1967–8), 132.
[4] Name Book, No. 19, p. 15.
[5] Simpson, *Dunstaffnage*, 16–17; *Dunstaffnage Case*, 85.
[6] *NSA*, vii (Argyll), 101.
[7] *Stat. Acct.*, viii (1793), 336.
[8] S.R.O., HR 738/1, Glenorchy and Inishail Heritors' Minute-book, 1894–1928.

237. Chapel (Site), Burial-ground and Well, Cladh Churiollan, Creagan. The burial-ground is situated on the lower S slopes of Beinn Churalain at an altitude of about 150 m. It is approximately rectangular on plan and measures about 30·5 m from E to W by 18·3 m transversely within a dry-stone wall some 0·6 m in thickness. The earliest identifiable memorial is a recumbent slab commemorating Duncan MacColl, who died in 1772, while a number of later stones commemorate other members of the same family. One of these, erected in memory of Hugh McColl at Caolisnacon, who died in 1794, bears an incised representation of a musket, while an undated headstone of about the same period commemorates Angus McInnes, piper to James Stewart of Fasnacloich. The burial-ground continued in use into the present century. There are no identifiable remains of the chapel.

WELL. A well lies about 300 m SW of the burial-ground, in close proximity to a rough track leading to Creagan. The well-house is a carefully constructed dry-stone building of rubble slabs and quartz boulders

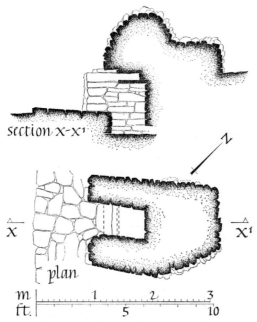

Fig. 110. Chapel (site), burial-ground and well, Cladh Churiollan, Creagan (No. 237); well-house

enclosing the mouth of a small spring. The building is U-shaped on plan and measures about 2·4 m in length, 1·8 m in maximum width and 1·5 m in height (Fig. 110). The well-chamber, which is lintelled with stone slabs, measures about 0·61 m by 0·46 m and has a height of about 1·1 m; the upper portion is shelved. The age of this building is difficult to determine, but it is probably of considerable antiquity; some restoration is known to have been carried out within the past few years.[1]

The author of an account of the Highlands written in about 1630 says of this site: 'In Loch Greverin (Creran)

ther is a hie mountayne upon the northsyd therof, in the midpart therof betwix the sea and the mountayn, ther is a Chappell called Craikwherreellan, ther ar springs of fresche water and the opinion of the wholsomnes of the water, draweth many people thither upon St. Patricks day yearlie in hopes of health from deseases be drinking therof, the toun or village of Ardnacloich is hard by, renouned for a well also, where they alledge if a deseased person go, if he be to dye he shall find a dead worm therin or a quick one if health be to follow.'[2] The chapel is named on Roy's Map of about 1750, and is mentioned as a 'religious house' by the author of the *New Statistical Account*;[3] the dedication was apparently either to St Cyril of Alexandria or to the Irish saint, St Cairrell.[4]

983452 (Chapel and Burial-ground)
980450 (Well)   NM 94 NE   July 1968

238. Cross-decorated Stone, Clenamacrie (Site). The cross-decorated stone that formerly stood on the crest of the mound known as Tom na Croise ('The knoll of the cross') on the N side of the public road through Glen Lonan, opposite the farm of Clenamacrie, is now in the National Museum of Antiquities of Scotland.[5] It is said that before it was placed on the mound it stood in an ancient burial-ground on the site

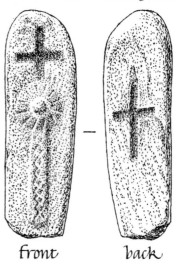

front   back

Fig. 111. Cross-decorated stone, Clenamacrie (No. 238; scale 1:15)

of the present farmyard, but no other record of this burial-ground has been found.

The stone (Fig. 111) is a roughly hewn four-sided pillar, rounded at the top; it measures 0·94 m in height,

---

[1] Information from Mr R Caig, Creagan.
[2] *Geog. Coll.*, ii, 516; *Argyll Synod Minutes*, i, 8.
[3] *NSA*, vii (Argyll), 242.
[4] Mackinlay, *Non-Scriptural Dedications*, 410.
[5] *PSAS*, lix (1924–5), 79–81; ibid., lxi (1926–7), 106–7.

Fig. 112. Chapel and burial-ground, Creag a' Chaibeil, Ballimeanoch (No. 239); plan

0·30 m in greatest width, and 0·14 m in thickness. On the front there is a deeply incised equal-arm cross, and below this a boss, 0·19 m in diameter and 0·04 m in height, which is ornamented with twelve grooves radiating from a circular groove in the centre; from the rim of the boss a shaft, cut in relief and bearing traces of an incised two-strand plait, descends almost to the foot of the stone. Contrary to what has been stated,[1] there is no indication of any decoration on the edges of the shaft or in the spaces between the shaft and the margin of the stone. On the back of the stone is a Latin cross, incised in similar fashion to the cross on the front.

923287   NM 92 NW   February 1972

239. Chapel and Burial-ground, Creag a' Chaibeil, Ballimeanoch. The only visible remains are those of a small oblong building standing within an irregularly-shaped enclosure (Fig. 112). This building, presumably

a chapel, measures about 5·5 m from E to W by 2·5 m transversely within walls some 0·8 m in thickness; there appears to be a doorway towards the W end of the N wall. To the E of the chapel there is a small open-ended building of sub-circular plan measuring about 1·8 m by 1·2 m within dry-stone walls some 0·7 m in thickness. The enclosure, which measures about 25 m by 29 m over all, contains no identifiable tombstones, apart from a small standing stone which may be a headstone.

This site was pointed out to the officers of the Ordnance Survey in about 1870 as a place in which interments had been made 'before the Reformation', but no tradition respecting the former existence of a chapel appears to have been current at that date.[2]

014167   NN 01 NW   May 1968

[1] Ibid., lix (1924–5), 80–1.
[2] Name Book, No. 54, p. 134.

240. Burial-ground and Well, Creag Mhór. This burial-ground, which lies about 250 m NW of Dalvuie Farm, is oval on plan and measures about 13·7 m from E to W by 9·1 m transversely. The enclosing dry-stone wall is now ruinous and the interior is overgrown with turf; no tombstones are visible.

TOBAR BIAL NA BUAIDH. This is the name given to a spring situated a few metres to the NE of the burial-ground. The mouth of the well is overgrown, and it presents no visible features of interest.

The burial-ground is said to have been used for the interment of unbaptized children and the last burials appear to have taken place in about 1830. The well was formerly much frequented on account of its supposed therapeutic properties.[1]

918370   NM 93 NW   June 1967

241. Parish Church, Dalavich. A separate parish of Dalavich appears to have been formed about the middle of the 17th century, but was soon afterwards united, or re-united, with the adjacent parish of Kilchrenan.[2] The present church (Pl. 21A) was erected about the year 1770, but replaces an earlier one in a similar position; the building was remodelled in about 1898.[3]

The church is a plain oblong building measuring 12·3 m from E to W by 7·6 m transversely over walls some 0·8 m in thickness (Fig. 113). The masonry is of

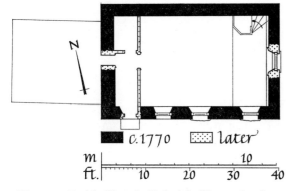

$\blacksquare$ *c.1770*   ⬚ *later*

Fig. 113. Parish Church, Dalavich (No. 241); plan

random rubble with roughly dressed quoins, and the external wall-surfaces are harl-pointed and lime-washed; the roof is gabled and slated. The S wall contains three single-light windows, all of which incorporate semi-circular-arched voussoired heads with prominent keystones; the window-sills are formed of large schist slabs which project somewhat from the wall-face. Prior to 1898 the church was entered through the vestry by means of a doorway in the W wall, the present entrance-doorway at the W end of the S wall having been formed out of an original window-opening when the church was remodelled. The round-headed window in the E wall is an insertion of the same period. The vestry on the W side of the church, which appears to be of 19th-

century date, was formerly used as a schoolroom.[4] The interior of the building presents no features of interest.

FUNERARY MONUMENTS. There are no identifiable medieval tombstones, and the only post-Reformation stone of interest is a recumbent slab placed by John McLerran in 1757 to commemorate his parents, Dugald McLerran and Sara Downie. Beneath the inscription there is a crude relief-carving apparently depicting the resurrected souls of the deceased being supported heavenwards by a winged cherub (Pl. 21B). This stone was probably carved by the sculptor responsible for the execution of one of the Campbell table-tombs at Muckairn (cf. p. 165).

968124   NM 91 SE   August 1970

242. St Conan's Well, Dalmally. This spring, which is traditionally associated with St Conan,[5] lies immediately to the N of the main Tyndrum–Oban road (A85) a little to the W of Dalmally School. The mouth of the well is enclosed by stone slabs.

171273   NN 12 NE   April 1968

243. Dunstaffnage Chapel. This ruined building (Pl. 22), whose dedication is unknown, stands about 150 m WSW of Dunstaffnage Castle (No. 287), on a small knoll which is overlooked from the S by Chapel Hill. The architectural detail of the chapel indicates that it dates from the second quarter of the 13th century. A roofless burial-aisle, designed for the use of the Campbell of Dunstaffnage family, was added to the E end in 1740, when the chapel was already ruinous.[6] The remains came into the guardianship of the Department of the Environment in 1962 and have since been consolidated.

The chapel is a single-chambered unvaulted rectangular structure measuring 20·3 m from E to W by 6·3 m transversely within walls 0·9 m in thickness (Fig. 114). Nave and chancel were separated by a wooden screen, and the chancel is also distinguished by elaborately-decorated paired windows in the N, S and E walls. The masonry is of flat stones and split boulders, laid in neat horizontal courses with many small pinnings. Pink and buff sandstone, which in places has weathered to yellow and grey, is used for window- and door-dressings and for the ashlar internal facing of the E wall. Three different masons' marks have been recorded (Fig. 115).

The external angles have bold edge-roll mouldings (Fig. 116J), whose original masonry survives only in the upper courses; they are similar to those at Iona Nunnery, and Killean Church, Kintyre,[7] and in the S

[1] Name Book, No. 1, pp. 69–70.
[2] Scott, *Fasti*, iv, 91; *Argyll Synod Minutes*, ii, 147, 190.
[3] *NSA*, vii (Argyll), 375; Roy's Map; S.R.O., HR 478/2/17.
[4] Name Book, No. 53, p. 204.
[5] *Stat. Acct.*, viii (1793), 351.
[6] Pennant, *Tour* (1772), i, 411.
[7] *Inventory of Argyll*, i, No. 287.

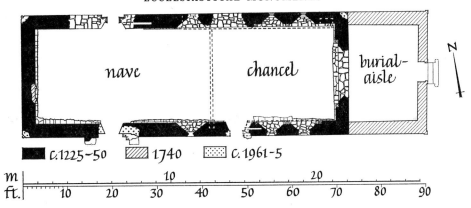

Fig. 114. Dunstaffnage Chapel (No. 243); plan

transept of Ardchattan Priory (No. 217). The principal entrance to the nave is near the W end of the S wall; it has been an elaborate arched doorway of three orders, with nook-shafts separated by keeled engaged shafts. All that survives is the lower part of the E jamb, and five voussoirs of the hood-mould (Fig. 116D), which has a deeply-undercut roll-and-fillet moulding flanked by smaller rolls. The doorway has had a pitched coping, of which the raggle survives on the W side. The chancel-entrance in the S wall has lost all of its external dressings. In the N wall, opposite the S door of the nave, there is another doorway of which only the bases remain *in situ*. This has been of two main orders with several shafts, the largest of which has had a fillet which runs continuously over the water-holding base (Fig. 116H, Pl. 23B).[1]

Both parts of the chapel are lit by windows placed opposite each other in the N and S walls (Pl. 22B–D), the nave by single windows near the dividing screen and the chancel by pairs of windows. All the surviving windows are chamfered and rebated externally; internally they have broad shallow-splayed jambs and arch-heads, and sloping sills. Two of the four surviving heads are semicircular and monolithic; the other two are pointed and the heads, which were originally monolithic, have split. There are holes in the heads and sills for central iron bars. The E window in the S wall of the chancel, whose W jamb survives, is decorated externally with bold dog-tooth ornament. Nothing remains of the external dressings of the E windows of the chancel.

The interior of the chapel was divided into nave and chancel by a timber screen situated 1·0 m W of the chancel-doorway. A beam-socket for the upper part of this screen survives in the S wall at a height of 3·2 m above present floor-level, and beneath there is a slot for a side-post, which is cut into the moulded string-course. This string-course is much weathered and incomplete, but originally it ran round the entire building at window-sill level except in the area to the W of the nave-doorways. The S doorway of the nave is completely ruinous; a moulded stone which appears to be the base of the W jamb is in fact a misplaced jamb-stone from one of the nave windows. The other doorways have plain semi-circular rear-arches with splayed ingoes, and there are draw-bar sockets in their E jambs.

The outer jambs of the chancel-windows are enriched with dog-tooth ornament having prominent central ribs. Each pair of windows has been flanked and separated by cylindrical nook-shafts with moulded mid-annulets and water-holding bases decorated with nail-head ornament. The E windows are fragmentary and only the lower part of the outer jambs survives (Pl. 23A), but the position of the remaining mid-annulet indicates the great height of the windows, which was not less than 4·7 m from sill to arch-head. The inner order displays a keeled shaft

Fig. 115. Dunstaffnage Chapel (No. 243); masons' marks (scale 1:5)

flanked on either side by a row of dog-tooth and a smaller roll-moulding (Fig. 116F); two voussoirs with similar mouldings, which probably belonged to the arch-heads of these windows, are now built into the garden-wall about 15 m NE of the castle.

The pairs of windows in the N and S walls (Figs. 116 A–C, E, G, 117; Pl. 22B–D), whose composition closely resembles that of the early 13th-century E windows at Killean Church, Kintyre,[2] are ingeniously arranged so that, while each pair forms a unified group, the windows nearer the E end are more elaborate. This is achieved by making the mouldings and ornament of the arch-heads correspond within each pair, but varying the mouldings of the inner order so that each window is paired with that directly opposite to it. The inner order rests upon the moulded string-course and runs continuously round the jambs and head of each window. In the E window of each pair it consists of a small keeled shaft clasped by two roll-mouldings, flanked by hollows; in the W windows there is a keeled shaft

---

[1] This unusual feature also occurs in the S chancel-doorway in Inchcailleach Parish Church, Stirlingshire, discovered in recent excavations (report in N.M.R.S.).
[2] *Inventory of Argyll*, i, No. 287.

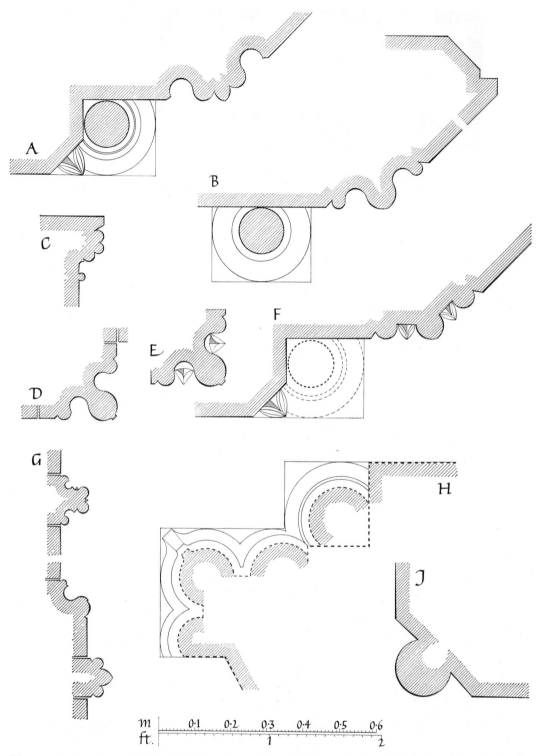

m | 0·1   0·2   0·3   0·4   0·5   0·6
ft. | 1   2

Fig. 116. Dunstaffnage Chapel (No. 243); profile mouldings: A, B, G, north and south chancel windows; C, capital of south chancel window; D, hood-mould of south nave doorway; E, label-mould of south chancel windows; F, east chancel windows; H, base of north doorway; J, angle-shaft

Fig. 117. Dunstaffnage Chapel (No. 243); N and S chancel windows (partially reconstructed)

flanked by hollows and quirked roll-mouldings. The semicircular arch-heads rise from the square abaci of the nook-shaft capitals. In each window the arch-head has a roll-and-fillet moulding between deep hollows and quirked rolls, but in addition the S windows have dog-tooth ornament in the hollows. The capitals of the outer nook-shafts of the S windows are much weathered but preserve traces of long-stalked stiff-leaf ornament; the central shaft has a moulded capital having a double roll below the abacus. The central capital of the N windows is a plain bell-capital, while that of the W nook-shaft has a band of plaited foliaceous ornament resting upon a cylindrical lower part.[1] At the E end of the N wall is an aumbry, set immediately above the string-course, which is rebated externally for a timber door.

The window in the S wall of the nave is almost intact; a keeled roll set between hollows and smaller rolls runs

continuously round the jambs and semicircular rear-arch. Small sockets, to support the centering used in the construction of the arch-head, occur at springing-level in the ingoes of this window, and also in the S windows of the chancel. The N window of the nave is very ruinous, but enough remains of the W jamb to indicate that it was identical with that in the S wall. Beneath the sill of this window is a greatly-damaged aumbry similar to that described above.

The 18th-century burial-aisle (Pl. 23C) that has been added to the E end of the chapel continues the line of its N and S walls. It measures 5·4 m from E to W by 8·2 m transversely over walls which vary from 0·7 m to 0·9 m

[1] The base of the E nook-shaft of the NE window, the only one not *in situ*, was identified at Dunstaffnage Castle at the date of visit. It has been re-used in the inserted fireplace at the N end of the E range (cf. p. 205).

in thickness. The rubble walls incorporate many moulded fragments; some of these can be identified as belonging to the medieval chapel, while others appear to be of 16th- or 17th-century date and probably came from the castle. Red and orange sandstone is employed in the quoins and a fine-grained grey sandstone for the door-surround and the moulded cornice that runs round three sides of the building. The door-surround and the quoins at either end of the E wall are set forward to receive harling of which considerable traces remain.

Pennant's view of the chapel[1] shows that the burial-aisle has never been roofed. The entrance-doorway, in the centre of the E wall, stands upon an ashlar band which runs along the whole wall at threshold-level. Flanking pilasters with Ionic capitals support an entablature above which there is a triangular pediment; this originally carried a large urn which now lies inside the aisle.[2] Above the door is an inscribed panel dated 1930 which may replace an earlier panel. On either side of the door-way there is carved a skull and thigh-bone, in very high relief. The interior of the aisle is featureless except for the monuments and carved stones described below.

FUNERARY MONUMENTS AND OTHER CARVED STONES

Medieval

In this section the stones described under (1) are built into the garden-wall some 15 m NE of Dunstaffnage Castle. Group (2) was recovered by the Department of the Environment during clearance-operations in the chapel, and on the date of visit the stones were in temporary storage at Lorn Furnace, Bonawe. Group (3) is in the Campbell of Dunstaffnage burial-aisle. Numerous re-used fragments of dressed masonry have been identified in the fabric of the latter structure (*supra*), and in the E curtain-wall of Dunstaffnage Castle (cf. p. 205).

(1) Several fragments of sandstone, of which at least eight are wrought with keel- or roll-mouldings. Two of these, which display a keeled roll flanked by dog-tooth ornament and smaller roll-mouldings, may be identified as voussoirs from the arch-heads of the E windows of the chancel.

(2) Numerous moulded fragments, some too worn to be identified. They include three voussoirs from the inner order of the arch-head of the NE chancel-window, and three arch-voussoirs of the S nave-window. Three other voussoirs wrought with a filleted roll between dog-tooth ornament are probably from the label-mould of the S windows of the chancel. The only fragment that cannot be associated with any of the extant features of the chapel is a slab of grey sandstone 0·10 m in thickness, wrought on one edge with a half-roll bearing a 0·02 m fillet. A hollow-moulding is cut into one side of the roll, and the same side of the slab bears a groove some 0·03 m in width. This fragment resembles a string-course moulding, but the survival *in situ* of the entire string-course of the chapel renders such an identification unlikely.

(3) Two fragments of yellowish sandstone having together an overall height of 0·61 m and a maximum width of 0·50 m. These fragments have evidently formed part of a small circular or octagonal structure with a hollow centre, perhaps a font; the exterior of the bowl has been decorated with blank tracery incorporating fleur-de-lis finials. These stones are probably of late medieval date.

Post-Reformation

All the stones described in this section are in the Campbell of Dunstaffnage burial-aisle. The monuments that remain in the chapel are of 18th- and 19th-century date.

(4) A recumbent slab measuring 2·03 m by 0·76 m, but now broken into two pieces. There is an incised marginal inscription: HERE LYES I[O]HN CAMPBEL OF DVNST[AFFNAGE] IN WHOSE MEMORY [T]HIS MONVMENT IS ERECTED BY ALEX[ANDER C]AMP[B]ELL HIS ELDE[S]T SONE 168[?3].[3] In the centre of the slab there is a shield: quarterly, 1st and 4th, gyronny of eight; 2nd and 3rd, a galley, sail furled. Above the shield there are carved the emblems of mortality, while beneath it the figures of a man and woman, dressed in the costume of the period, lie beneath a canopy. The figures (Pl. 23E) hold hands, and the man wears breeches or stockings, and a knee-length coat taken in at the waist and having broad cuffs. He has a wig, and what appears to be a three-cornered hat; the feet are missing because of the fracture of the stone. The woman wears a long dress gathered at the elbows, with a square-cut bosom and long, full sleeves. She is bare-headed, the hair falling to the shoulders. Below the figures there are some lines of verse now scarcely legible:

EX[?PECTES]T THO[V ?CHRIST] / THY [?FRIEN]D TO BE / PREP[ARE] TO VELCOME HIM /
EXP[EC]T[E]ST THOV DEATH / THY [F]O[E] TO BE / PREPARE TO OVERCOME / HIM

This stone evidently commemorates John Campbell, 9th of Dunstaffnage, who died in 1677.[4]

(5) A recumbent slab measuring 1·83 m by 0·81 m and bearing the incised inscription: HERE WITH HER PREDESESSORS MIN (=IN) / SCAMDL & CRACKEIG LAYS THE CORPS / OF BEATRIX CAMPBELL SPOUS TO / ARCHD CAMPBELL TACKMAN OF / CLACHANSEIL & DAUGHTER TO / DON CAMP(BELL) OF SCAMIDEL WHO DY/ED AT CLACHAN THE 24 OCTB / 1741 AGED 34 THIS MONUMENT / WAS LAID OVER HER GRA[V]E BY / THE ABOVE ARCHD CAMP HER HUS/BAND. Below there are some lines of pious verse beginning:

SNATCHED FROM ME IS MY MODEST LOVE BY DEATH.[5]
An heraldic achievement is carved in the upper part of the slab. The shield bears: quarterly, 1st, a castle of three towers; 2nd, gyronny of eight; 3rd, a fess checky; 4th, a ? boar's head cabossed. There is an anchor for crest and the motto is VIGILANDO ('Watchful'). The

---

[1] Pennant, *Tour* (*1772*), i, pl. xliii.
[2] Ibid.
[3] Alternatively the last numeral may have been a 5.
[4] *Burke's Landed Gentry* (1952 ed.), 359.
[5] These are given in full in Otter, W, *The Life and Remains of the Rev. Edward Daniel Clarke* (1824), 304–5.

Campbells of Scammadale were cadets of the house of Dunstaffnage.[1]

(6) Built into the W wall of the aisle there is an ogival-headed pediment (Pl. 23D), evidently part of some large funerary monument of which it appears to be the only surviving portion. The pediment is carved in relief with an angel who holds in each hand a trumpet from which there issues a scroll inscribed: ARISE YE DEAD & COME TO JUDGEMENT. The pediment also bears the conventional emblems of mortality; it appears to be of 18th-century date.

Unclassified

(7) A plain bell-shaped capital of uncertain date which has been designed to receive a shaft 0·19 m in diameter and a circular abacus 0·43 m in diameter. Another smaller capital of similar form was observed in May 1961, but could not be located on the date of visit.

881344   NM 83 SE   August 1969

244. Parish Church, Duror. This church (Pl. 24A) was built in 1827 to serve the adjacent portion of the combined parish of Lismore and Appin, being one of a series of 'Parliamentary kirks' erected in the Highlands

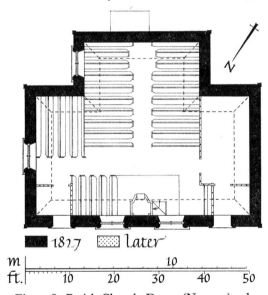

Fig. 118. Parish Church, Duror (No. 244); plan

at that time according to plans and specifications furnished by the Inverness architect James Smith and approved by Thomas Telford. Building-operations were supervised by Joseph Mitchell, the total cost of the church and adjacent manse (No. 328) being £1470.[2]

The building is of T-plan form (Fig. 118) and conforms closely to Telford's published design for a Highland church.[3] The main block measures 16·1 m from NE to SW by 9·4 m transversely over all, while the wing measures 3·7 m in depth and 9·3 m in width

over all; the walls have a thickness of 0·76 m. The masonry is of coursed rubble with offset quoins and dressings of pink sandstone. The roof is gable-ended, the SW gable being surmounted by a bird-cage belfry capped with a pyramidal finial. The principal, or NW, elevation (Fig. 119) incorporates a pair of large four-centred arch-headed windows flanked by corresponding doorways. The windows have cast-iron mullions and transoms containing small lozenge-shaped panes set within cast-iron frames. The other windows of the church are similar in form, but now lack their original mullions and transoms. The interior (Pl. 24B) has been remodelled and now presents no features of interest, but the pulpit still occupies its original position against the centre of the NW wall; there may formerly have been a gallery.

993552   NM 95 NE   July 1971

245. Old Parish Church and Burial-ground, Eilean Munde. The church stands at the W end of the island and measures 15·2 m from E to W by 4·9 m transversely within walls some 0·9 m in thickness (Fig. 120, Pl. 24C). The building is ruinous and much overgrown with ivy, but the E gable and S wall are fairly entire, while the remaining two walls stand to an average height of about 1·0 m above the present floor-level. The floor has been considerably raised by burials, however, and must now lie up to 1·0 m above the original level, while the ground-level outside the church has risen to a similar extent. The building is constructed of local rubble roughly brought to courses, and well bonded with pinnings and coarse lime mortar. Many of the rubble blocks are of large size, and some are set on edge. The quoins and dressings are of buff-coloured sandstone, but some of these have been robbed. The NW and NE quoins have evidently been made good following the removal of the original dressings. These, and some other minor alterations apart, the building appears to be homogeneous, but in the absence of any closely dateable features its age is uncertain. In all probability, however, it is of late medieval date, and it corresponds very closely in plan and dimensions with the former parish-church of Inishail (No. 247), which can be ascribed to the same period.

The entrance-doorway (Pl. 24C) is situated towards the W end of the S wall and comprises a plain lintelled opening wrought on the jambs with an 0·05 m chamfer. This doorway was probably raised in height by about 0·48 m during the 17th century, following the raising of the internal floor-level by burials. Towards the E end of the S wall there are the remains of two splayed single-

[1] Johnston, *Campbell Heraldry*, ii, 37.
[2] Telford, *Life*, 187, 490–1; Mitchell, J, *Reminiscences of my Life in the Highlands* (1883), i, 179; '6th Report of Commissioners for Building Churches in the Highlands of Scotland', 24, in *Parliamentary Papers, 1831*, ix; Maclean, A M, 'Parliamentary Churches in the Highlands and Islands', pp. 29–38, 89 (unpublished Edinburgh University thesis, 1972, copy in N.M.R.S.).
[3] Telford, *Atlas*, pl. 59.

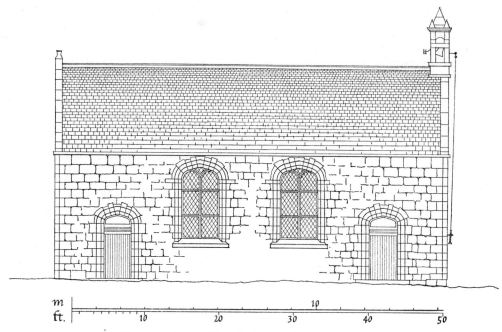

Fig. 119. Parish Church, Duror (No. 244); elevation

light windows now lacking their heads and all external dressings. The E gable-wall incorporates two put-log holes, which seem to penetrate almost the full thickness of the wall, together with a small aumbry, now at floor-level. The N wall has no recognizable openings, but a breach in the masonry towards the W end may represent the position of a former window. Two carved stones in secondary use are built into the N wall towards its E end. One of these is a window-sill having a daylight-opening of about 0·20 m and a steeply-weathered sill. The other shows traces of a roll-and-hollow moulding. Both fragments are of buff-coloured sandstone, similar to that used for the other dressings, and probably derive from an earlier church standing on the same site.

This church served the former parish of Elanmunde, which comprised, on the N side of Loch Leven, the

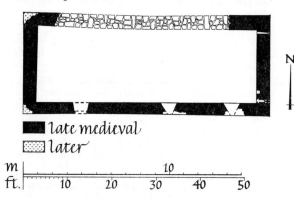

■ late medieval
▨ later

Fig. 120. Old Parish Church and burial-ground, Eilean Munde (No. 245); plan

districts of Mamore and Onich, lying in Inverness-shire, and, on the S side of Loch Leven, Glencoe and part of Appin, lying in Argyll. The parish seems to have continued in existence until about the middle of the 17th century, when the Inverness-shire districts were annexed to the parish of Kilmalie. At the same time it was proposed to unite those portions of Elanmunde lying within Argyll with the remainder of Appin (then forming part of the parish of Lismore), to form a separate parish, to be served by a newly erected church at Duror. This scheme was not realized, and the whole area was absorbed within the parish of Lismore, but the church of Elanmunde was abandoned, the last service there being held in July 1653.[1] When Bishop Forbes visited the place in 1770 he reported that all four walls of the church were still entire.[2] The island has continued to be used as a burial-place by the local inhabitants on both sides of Loch Leven. The dedication was evidently to St Munn.

FUNERARY MONUMENTS

Medieval

Numbers 1 and 2 are inside the church; number 3 is about 5 m NE of the burial-enclosure of MacDonald of Glencoe.

(1) Tapered slab with bevelled edges, 1·90 m long by 0·50 m wide at the head; the bevel is decorated with a single row of nail-head ornament. At the top of the

[1] *Origines Parochiales*, ii, part i, 170–1; *Argyll Synod Minutes*, i, 57, 150, 237, 249; Scott, *Fasti*, iv, 84–5; *NSA*, vii (Argyll), 223–4; Carmichael, *Lismore*, 85–6.
[2] Forbes, *Journals*, 310.

stone, within a border composed of two plain mouldings, there is a mounted warrior armed with a spear, while below are two pairs of animals and a single-hand sword flanked by double plant-scrolls. (Drummond, *Monuments*, pl. xciii, 1). *Iona school, 14th—15th century.*

(2) Tapered slab, 1·75 m long by 0·44 m wide at the head, broken into two pieces. Within triple plain mouldings there is a sheathed sword with lobated pommel and canted quillons expanded at the ends. To the left of the sword is a double plant-scroll surmounted by a pair of animals, and to the right a sword-belt. In the lower part of the stone are a comb, a pair of shears, and a casket. (Drummond, *Monuments*, pl. xciii, 2). *14th—15th century.*

(3) Tapered slab with pointed foot, 1·90 m long by 0·45 m wide at the head; it is very worn. At the top there may have been an inscribed panel, but no letters are now visible. The rest of the stone, which is bordered by a channel containing paterae, displays a claymore flanked by plant-scrolls. *c. 1500—1560.*

Post-Reformation

Of the following, numbers 4 and 5 lie within the church and the remainder in the burial-ground.

(4) A worn recumbent slab of schist partly covering a stone-lined burial-recess some 1·2 m in depth, within which there may be seen a human skull and other bones. A marginal inscription reads: HEIER LAYS IOHN CAM[E]RO[N] [?WHO DEPAR]TED [?THIS LIFE T]HE [?DAY OF M]ARCH ANO 1662 / IN THE 51 YE[A]R OF HIS AEGE AND / THIS DONE BY ORDER OF EWO[N] CAMERON HIS SON & MARGRET CAMPBELL HIS SPOUS[E].[1] Within the marginal inscription there are the following lines of verse:

THIS MAN WHILE HE LIVED HERE BELOW
WAS ASTEMED BY ALL WHO DID HIM KNOW
HIS VARTH MEAD HIS DEALLINGS CLEAR
WHICH GEANED HIM FRENDS BOTH FAR AND [NEAR]
HE LEAD AN UPRIGHT AND IUST LIFE
HE SHOUNED AND SLIGHTED FRIVOLOUS STRIFE
TO SUPERIOURS HE GAVE THER DUE
HIS EQUALS FOUND HIM IUST AND TRUE
HE WAS AVERC TO WRONG OR HURT
OR TO DISPISE THE MINNOR SORT
ALL HONEST MEN HE DID BEFREND
TO CONIVE AT VICE HE CULD NOT YEILD
TO WORLDLY RICHES HE WAS NO SLAVE
YET GOD SUFFICENCE [T]O HIM GAVE
HIS NIGH[T]BOURS O[FFTE]N HE COULD [?SEE]
[I]N TIME OF THERE NEEDSESETY
TO C[R]AUE HIS HELP AND HIS ADVIC
TO GIVE THEM BOTH HE WAS NOT NICE
A MAN OF [H]IS [N]ATION SELDOM HATH
BEEN MOR L[AME]NTED AT HIS DEA(T)H.

(5) A recumbent slab of slate (Pl. 24D) commemorating Duncan McKenzie, tenant at North Ballachelish, and his wife Ann Stewart, and commissioned by their grandson, Duncan McKenzie, smith at Laroch. At the foot of the stone there is a relief-carving (Pl. 24E)

showing McKenzie, arrayed in full Highland costume, in the act of killing a dragoon at the battle of Prestonpans in 1745. Beneath is the inscription: THE FATE OF AN ENGLISH DRAGOON WHO / ATTACKED D. MC. K. AT THE BATTLE OF / PREST. P. WHERE HE FOUGHT UNDER / PRINCE CHARLES STEWART. This stone is evidently of early 19th-century date.

(6) A table-tomb erected in memory of Allan Cameron of Corrychiracha, who died in 1726, by his son Donald Cameron. It bears a shield charged with three bars, for Cameron.

(7) A table-tomb (Pl. 25A) commemorating Anne Cameron, spouse to John Cameron, son to Culchennan, who died in 1756. Beneath the inscription there is an armorial achievement incorporating a shield charged with three bars, within an architectural surround. For crest there is a dexter arm, armoured, holding a sword. A label above bears the motto PRO REGE ET PATRIA ('For King and Country'). At the base of the slab there is a reversed monogram of the letters J C and A C.

(8) A recumbent slab of slate (Pl. 25B) commemorating William Rankin, successively tenant in Inshree and in Carnach, who died in 1800, and his spouse Mary MacInnes. At the base of the slab there are carved the emblems of mortality, and the conventional epitaph: AS RUNS THE GLASS / MAN'S LIFE DOTH PASS / LIFE HOW SHORT / ETERNETY HOW LONG.

(9) A large recumbent slab of slate (Pl. 25C) erected in memory of John Stewart, who died in 1817 aged 18, by his parents, John Stewart and Jean McDougall at Slate Quarry (Ballachulish). In the centre there is a remarkable pseudo-armorial achievement. The shield is charged: on a field or, a fess checky surmounted by a bend, a cinquefoil in chief. The supporters are: dexter, a wild man bearing a club; sinister, a lion. For crest, upon a (baron's) coronet of four points, there is a dove bearing in its beak an olive branch. The motto is SOLA JUVAT VIRTUS ('Virtue is the only reward').

CARVED STONE. Built into the wall of the MacDonald of Glencoe burial-enclosure, which stands above the SE shore of the island, there is a triangular pediment (Pl. 25D) carved with the monogram initials J MC D and the date 1706. An inscription records that this stone was removed from the gable of John MacDonald's house at Invercoe, which fell in 1893. John MacDonald, 13th of Glencoe, was the eldest son of the chief who was murdered in 1692, and his house is said to have stood upon the site of the one associated with the massacre.[2]

083591   NN 05 NE   August 1970

---

[1] The person commemorated was perhaps John, elder son of Alan Cameron, 16th of Lochiel, and father of the famous Sir Ewen Cameron. He married Margaret, daughter of Sir Robert Campbell, 9th of Glenorchy, and pre-deceased his father c. 1632 (*Burke's Landed Gentry* (18th ed., 1965–72), i, 116; *Memoirs of Sir Ewen Cameron of Lochiell, chief of Clan Cameron*, Abbotsford and Maitland Clubs (1842), 63). If this identification is correct, the third numeral in the date in the inscription may have been altered by recutting.
[2] Name Book, No. 49, p. 15.

246. Parish Church, Glenorchy, Dalmally. The present church at Dalmally, anciently called Clachan Dysart, is the third to occupy the island site between the River Orchy and the Orchy Bheag. A medieval church, which was 'altogidder rowinus and decayit' was rebuilt by Sir Duncan Campbell of Glenorchy in 1615, at a cost of £1000 Scots.[1] This building also had become unsafe by 1807, when the 4th Earl of Breadalbane agreed to pay for a new church. Designs for this were obtained by the Earl's factor from John Stevenson of Oban, but Lord Breadalbane preferred to entrust the work to James Elliot, the Edinburgh architect who was at that time undertaking the rebuilding of Taymouth Castle. Elliot produced a plan in 1808, and Allan Johnstone, principal mason-contractor at Taymouth, was employed in the same capacity at Glenorchy, his estimate of £1552 being accepted in 1809. The church (Pl. 26A, C) was built during the following year, and opened for worship in March 1811.[2] Extensive repairs were undertaken in 1898, at a total cost of £1255, and most of the existing furnishings date from that period.[3]

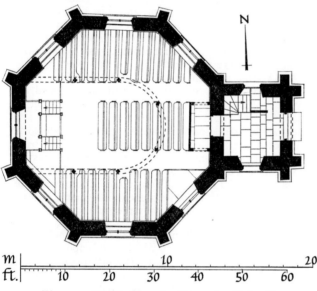

m |_____10_____|20
ft. |____10____20____30____40____50____60____|

Fig. 121. Parish Church, Glenorchy, Dalmally
(No. 246); plan

The parish of Glenorchy was extensive, comprising the areas of Black Mount, Glen Orchy, Glen Lochy and Glen Strae. It was united with that of Inishail during the 17th century. The church first comes on record in the late 14th century, as a burial-place of the Clan Gregor.[4]

The plan of the church (Fig. 121) comprises a buttressed octagon, having a span of 12·7 m within walls 0·9 m in thickness, with a tower measuring 5·7 m square over all on the E side. The walls are of rubble masonry, harled and whitewashed, with door- and window-dressings of sandstone. Polished schist is employed for the simple plinth that runs round the entire building at ground-level, and for the buttress-finials. The conical timber roof, of elaborate construction (Pl. 27A), is said to

incorporate 'the last remains of the pine-forest of Glenstrae';[5] it supports a covering of Easdale slate, with lead strips at the angles.

Each bay of the octagon contains one large arch-pointed window having chamfered jambs and a moulded head. The existing metal tracery of these windows, comprising a central mullion which branches to form twin lancets having a round light in the arch-head, was inserted in 1898. The W window, however, has wooden tracery of the same design, which is probably original; this was doubtless preserved because it contained a stained-glass memorial-window of 1889. At each angle there is a buttress having two sloping off-sets and rising above the wall-head to terminate in a pyramidal finial.

The tower, which in the opinion of Robert Southey 'would not mis-become a good English Church', was a notable symbol of Lord Breadalbane's munificence; the previous building had evidently possessed no belfry, for in 1798 the bell, recast five years earlier to a weight of 191 pounds, was hanging from a plane-tree in the churchyard.[6] It rises in four stages, divided by string-courses, to a height at parapet-level of 19·2 m. Pairs of angle-buttresses, intaken at the third stage, support pinnacles rising for a further 3·1 m, and the crenellated parapet incorporates central pinnacles of similar height. The entrance-doorway of the church, situated in the E wall of the tower, is set within a large four-centred arch wrought with a continuous broad chamfer and having a rectangular hood-mould. In the N and S walls of the lowest stage of the tower there are windows with arches and hood-moulds of similar type and incorporating simple wooden Y-tracery. In its original form the tower had large windows of perpendicular design in each wall at the second and fourth (belfry) stages. These openings are now blocked, except for the E and N openings at the second stage, which are of four lights with transoms. In the E wall at the third stage there is a square window-recess, also blocked.

The lowest stage of the tower forms a vestibule, paved with schist slabs, from which a doorway with four-centred arch-head leads into the body of the church (Pl. 27C). This was completely re-modelled in 1898, except for the fine horseshoe-shaped gallery, supported on clustered shafts of pine and having a panelled front of the same material. The present pulpit occupies the position of its predecessor, against the W wall. In the original arrangement a long communion-table was placed in the central aisle, running E to W.[7] The timber roof of the octagon (Pl. 27A), accessible only by a hatch in the ceiling above the gallery, is of impressive dimen-

[1] *Taymouth Bk.*, 47.
[2] S.R.O., Breadalbane Collection, GD 112/51/8, Church Papers; New Register House, OPR 512/2, Glenorchy Parish Register, fol. 114.
[3] S.R.O., HR 738/1, Glenorchy and Inishail Heritors' Minute-book, 1894–1928.
[4] *Origines Parochiales*, ii, part i, 134–5, 147.
[5] *NSA*, vii (Argyll), 92.
[6] Southey, R, *Journal of a Tour in Scotland in 1819* (1929), 238; New Register House, OPR 512/2, Glenorchy Parish Register, fols. 11v, 60v.
[7] Hay, *Post-Reformation Churches*, fig. 43 on p. 124.

sions; in particular, the principal tie-beam, which spans the building from SSW to NNE and carries a king-post with radiating struts, has a length of some 15 m. Shorter beams span the distance from the other angles of the octagon to the centre of the main tie, and the rafters are braced by a series of collar-beams interlocking round the king-post.

A wooden stair rises from the lobby in the lowest stage of the tower to a landing above, from which a doorway gives access to the gallery. The upper stages of the tower contain no original features, although the brick infilling of the belfry-openings is visible. A large bell bearing the date 1888 is mounted on the lead-covered roof of the tower.

FUNERARY MONUMENTS

The following monuments are all in the churchyard.

Medieval

(1) Narrow slab with pointed top, 1·91 m long (Fig. 122). It bears a long-shafted cross with triple bars, the lower pair of which have barred terminals. The shaft

Fig. 122. Parish Church, Glenorchy, Dalmally (No. 246); cross-decorated stone (scale 1:15)

has a stepped base and is flanked by plain mouldings. No close parallel is known for this type of cross-slab, but it is presumably of medieval date.

(2) Tapered slab, 2·08 m long by 0·54 m wide at the head (Pl. 26B). Like the majority of the slabs of the Loch Awe school, it has a wide border consisting of two plain mouldings which enclose a row of elongated nail-head ornament. Within this, at the top, there is a small effigy of an armed man standing in an archway formed of irregular plant-scrolls; he wears a bascinet and an aketon, and carries a sword and spear. Beneath the effigy is a griffin, with a rosette above its head, which is in combat with a ?lion. From the legs of these animals issues a diaper pattern of plant-scrolls which, apart from a plain oblong panel at the foot, fills the rest of the surface of the stone. (*PSAS*, xvii (1882–3), 341, fig. 2; ibid., xxxi (1896–7), 82, fig. 1). *Loch Awe school, 14th—15th century.*

(3) Tapered slab, 1·95 m long by 0·61 m wide at the head. The decoration is generally similar to that on (2) above, the main difference being that the armed man occupies a recessed triangular-headed niche, the animals are both leonine creatures, and there is no plain panel at the foot. (*PSAS*, xxxi (1896–7), 82, fig. 3). *Loch Awe school, 14th—15th century.*

(4) Tapered slab, 1·93 m long by 0·54 m wide at the head. A fracture has destroyed about one quarter of the surface at the foot of the stone. In the upper half there is an effigy of an armed man, larger than on (1) above and in low relief. He stands in a niche which is crowned by a pair of dragons' heads, and bears a shield as well as a sword and spear. The decoration in the lower half of the slab has consisted of two pairs of animals and interlocking plant-scrolls. (*PSAS*, xxxi (1896–7), 82, fig. 2). *Loch Awe school, 14th—15th century.*

(5) Tapered slab with pointed head, 2·0 m in length. It is broken across and the surface has scaled off in places. The decoration in the upper half is similar to that on (4) above, with the addition of a leaf-spray in the triangular space at the top. Most of the rest of the surface has been covered with plain interlacing. The border is the same as on (2) above, but the work of shaping the individual nail-heads from a continuous moulding has not been completed. *Loch Awe school, 14th—15th century.*

(6) Tapered slab, 1·80 m long by 0·48 m wide at the head. It is very worn, the decoration in the lower part of the stone being almost entirely obliterated. On three sides the border consists simply of two plain mouldings, but at the top the inner moulding is replaced by a Z-fret pattern and a running chevron has been added on the outside. The ornament has again consisted of an armed man standing in a niche crowned by dragons' heads, beneath which there is a pair of long-eared creatures and then an interlace pattern. In this case the man is not bearing a shield, and, where they cross one another, the necks of the dragons are enclosed within a circle. *Loch Awe school, 14th—15th century.*

(7) Tapered slab, 1·90 m long by 0·56 m wide at the head. The surface is divided by strips of two-strand plait into three panels, each of which is bordered by a

plain moulding and an external row of elongated nail-head ornament. The panels contain: (*top*) a cross with diagonal arms which are linked together by a circle and terminate in leaf sprays; (*centre*) a figure of an armed man similar to the one on (2) above; and (*bottom*) a pair of long-eared creatures and interlaced plant-scrolls. (A poor drawing of this slab is given in *PSAS*, xxxi (1896–7), 83, fig. 5). *Loch Awe school, 14th—15th century.*

(8) Miniature tapered slab with bevelled edges, presumably the tombstone of a child (Pl. 26D). Over all it measures 1·0 m in length by 0·41 m in width at the head. There is one row of elongated nail-head ornament on the bevel, and another, between two plain mouldings, round the margin of the upper surface. The field is divided by strips of two-strand plait into three panels which contain: (*top*) a plaited knot; (*centre*) an armed man similar to the one on (2) above; (*bottom*) a pair of animals. (*PSAS*, xvii (1882–3), 340, fig. 1; ibid., xxxi (1896–7), 85, fig. 7). *Loch Awe school, 14th—15th century.*

(9) Three fragments of a tapered slab with a pointed foot, 0·56 m wide at the head. The border is the same as on (2) above, and in the upper portion there is a small effigy of an armed man similar to those already described. Below is an irregular pattern of foliage, and at the foot is a plain panel. The statement[1] that there has been a second effigy on this stone is inaccurate. (Two of the fragments are illustrated in *PSAS*, xxxi (1896–7), 83, fig. 4). *Loch Awe school, 14th—15th century.*

(10) Tapered slab, 1·98 m long by 0·58 m wide at the head. It is very worn and all that is visible is a small figure of an armed man dressed like the one on (2) above. A secondary inscription incorporating the date 1798 has been carved on the lower part of the stone. *Loch Awe school, 14th—15th century.*

(11) Tapered slab, 1·85 m long by 0·59 m wide at the head. Within a wide border, consisting of a row of debased dog-tooth ornament between two plain mouldings, there are four panels. In the upper panel is a rudimentary foliated cross, a motif rarely used by the carvers of the Loch Awe school, while the next panel contains the effigy of a man in civil dress with head uncovered. His hair is bobbed and he wears a knee-length tunic; on his right hip he carries some object, probably a hunting-horn. In the third panel a stag is being pursued by a hound, but the decoration in the fourth panel has been obliterated by a secondary inscription dated 1819. *c. 1500—1560.*

(12) Side-slab of a tomb-chest, 1·98 m long by 0·57 m high. There is a wide plain border along the lower edge, and above this two undulating branches of foliaceous ornament which extend outwards from the centre of the stone. (There is an inverted drawing in *PSAS*, xxxi (1896–7), 83, fig. 6). *c. 1500—1560.*

Post-Reformation

(13) A recumbent slab of schist bearing the emblems of mortality, including a coffin and crossed spades, with a blank shield and the date 1684. Along one edge is the inscription: REV(EREN)D MR DOUGALL LINDSAY. The person commemorated was aged only 28 in 1684, and the

stone evidently marked the site allocated as his 'lair' when he became minister of the parish, where he remained, although not conforming to Presbyterianism, until his death in 1728.[2]

(14) A recumbent slab of schist bearing the incised initials G MᶜPH / D MᶜP, and the date 1691, with later inscriptions commemorating Alexander MacPherson, tacksman, Lochfinehead, who died in 1791, and other members of the MacPherson family.

(15–19) The following monuments of a date later than 1707 also deserve mention:

A recumbent slab (15) commemorating Duncan Campbell of Blarochorin, 3rd son of Patrick Campbell of Barcaldine, who died in 1716, and Alexander Campbell in Blarochorin and Mary Campbell his spouse. The stone is carved in relief with the emblems of mortality, and a greatly-worn armorial with the motto FOLLOU ME.

Two large slabs of schist, each carved in relief with a skull above incised cross-bones. One (16) bears an inscription of which the only part legible is the name COLIN CAMBEL. The other (17) bears an inscription with the date 1726 and the initials C C.

A neatly-executed headstone (18) bearing, within pilasters, an inscription commemorating the Rev John McVean, minister of Clachan Dysart, who died in 1764. A cherub's head and wings are carved in high relief within the broken pediment.

A headstone (19) erected by John Macnab in memory of his father, Alexander Macnab of Barran, who died in 1814. The back of the stone bears an armorial achievement framed within classical pilasters, the shield bearing, for Macnab: on a chevron three crescents; in dexter chief a dexter arm couped holding a sword; in sinister chief a sinister arm couped holding a sword; in base a galley, oars in action. The crest is a human head couped, and above and below there are carved respectively the motto DREAD NOUGHT and its Latin equivalent TIMOR OMNIS ABESTO ('Let all fear depart').

Southey, who visited the church in 1819,[3] describes a smith's tombstone which was carved with pincers, a hammer and bellows. This cannot now be identified.

Close to the entrance-doorway there stands a well-preserved cast-iron mortsafe of early 19th-century date (Pl. 27B).

167275   NN 12 NE   July 1971

247. Old Parish Church, Inishail. The remains of this church stand within a burial-ground near the W end of Inishail, a wooded island situated in the northern part of Loch Awe about 650 m SW of Fraoch Eilean (No. 290). It served a parish which included the adjoining islands and parts of the W and SE shores of the loch. The existence of a cross-decorated slab of Early Christian date establishes the ecclesiastical use of the site at that period. The parish first comes on record, however, in 1257, in which year Ath, son of Malcolm

---

[1] *PSAS*, xxxi (1896–7), 84.
[2] Scott, *Fasti*, iv, 86.
[3] Op. cit., 239.

MacNachtan, granted the teinds of 'the church of St Findoca of Inchealt' to the Augustinian canons of Inchaffray Abbey. The parish was united with that of Glenorchy in 1618, a union which was temporarily rescinded from 1650 to 1662. Services were conducted regularly on the island until 1736, when a new church was built near Cladich (No. 236). The medieval church was described as ruinous in the late 18th century.[1]

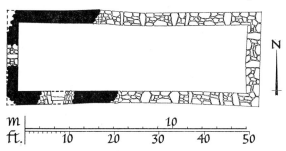

Fig. 123. Old Parish Church, Inishail (No. 247); plan

The building is extremely decayed, the walls being reduced almost to ground-level except near the W end where they stand in places to a height of about 2·1 m. The church is rectangular on plan (Fig. 123), measuring some 15·6 m from E to W by 4·6 m transversely within walls 0·84 m in thickness. The masonry is of massive rubble blocks, well coursed with small pinnings. Schist is employed in the masonry and for the quoins, which have for the most part been removed. A break at the centre of the W wall probably marks the position of a window. The entrance-doorway was situated near the W end of the S wall; part of the threshold, and the lowest course of the W side, remain *in situ*. The outer jamb-stone is of schist, wrought externally with a plain 0·08 m chamfer, checked for a door and retaining

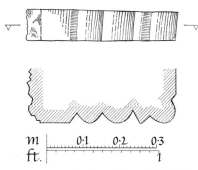

Fig. 124. Old Parish Church, Inishail (No. 247);
carved fragment

traces of a metal hinge-crook. The inner jamb-stone is of a fine-grained pinkish sandstone similar in appearance to that used at Fraoch Eilean Castle (No. 290). At the date of visit, several fragments of white sandstone, one of them being part of a filleted roll-moulding of 13th-century character, were found in the vicinity of this doorway. These afford strong evidence for the existence

of a stone-built church during the 13th century, but it is improbable that the existing remains are of that date. The doorway, which appears to be integral with the walls, may be ascribed to the late medieval period.

At the date of visit a slab of schist measuring 0·08 m in thickness was found near the E end of the church. It is dressed on two adjacent edges, the angle being wrought with an 0·08 m roll-moulding, and one edge being carved with a quirked pair of shallow rolls (Fig. 124). The purpose of this fragment is uncertain; it may possibly have formed part of an arched tomb-recess of late medieval date.[2]

The burial-ground is enclosed within a modern boundary-fence, beyond which the scanty remains of an earlier drystone enclosure-wall can be traced on the S and SW.

FUNERARY MONUMENTS AND OTHER CARVED STONES

Numbers 1, 5, 7–12 and 14 are inside the ruined church, and numbers 2–4, 13 and 15–19 in the surrounding graveyard. Number 6 could not be found on the date of visit.

Early Christian

(1) A cross-decorated slab (Pl. 28A), which formerly stood in the graveyard, has been re-erected inside the church on a pedestal which seems to have been designed for another monument. The slab measures 1·64 m high, 0·51 m in greatest breadth, and from 0·09 m to 0·41 m in thickness. Each face bears a wheel-cross slightly raised above the background and bordered by a plain moulding. The side-arms of both crosses project a short distance beyond the edges of the slab, and the circular hollows at the intersections contain bosses. The present E face is probably the front, since the bosses are more prominent than on the W face. (*ECMS*, part iii, 404–5, fig. 423; *PSAS*, xxxiii (1898–9), 49, fig. 1).

Medieval

(2) Tapered slab, 1·85 m long; the top left corner has been broken off. The border consists of two plain mouldings enclosing a row of elongated nail-head ornament. In the upper half of the stone there is a niche crowned by dragons' heads and containing a small figure of a man in armour; he wears a conical bascinet and an aketon, and carries a spear and sword. In the lower half of the stone there is a foliaceous pattern which terminates at the top in a pair of beasts. (*PSAS*, xxxiii (1898–9), 51, fig. 4; ibid., xlvi (1911–12), 430, fig. 3). *Loch Awe school, 14th—15th century.*

(3) Tapered slab with plain chamfered edges, 1·80 m long by 0·49 m wide at the head. The principal elements in the decoration are a sword with lobated pommel and canted quillons expanded at the ends, a thick-stalked plant-scroll to the right of the sword, and a casket at the

[1] *Origines Parochiales*, ii, part i, 129–31; *Inchaffray Chrs.*, 75–6; *Stat. Acct.*, viii (1793), 336.
[2] Cf. the use of thin voussoirs separating the carved panels in the arch of the MacLeod tomb at Rodel, Harris (*Inventory of the Outer Hebrides*, Fig. 89).

foot of the slab. At the top and bottom the border consists of a simple two-strand plait, while down each side there are double plain mouldings enclosing a row of elongated nail-head ornament. *Loch Awe school, 14th—15th century.*

(4) Tapered slab, 1·98 m long by 0·59 m wide at the head. In the upper half there is an overall pattern of linked plant-scrolls, which changes into plain interlacing in the lower half. At the foot is a casket. The border ornament is similar to that on (2) above. *Loch Awe school, 14th—15th century.*

(5) Tapered slab, 1·95 m long by 0·58 m wide at the head. It is very worn, all that is now visible being a man in armour in the upper half of the stone, similar to the figure on (2) above. *Loch Awe school, 14th—15th century.*

(6) Brydall illustrates a tapered slab, then in the graveyard, which could not be found on the date of visit. It measures 1·83 m long by 0·41 m wide at the head, and the bevelled edges are embellished with nail-head ornament. On the main axis of the stone there is a sword of similar type to that on (3) above, while on either side of the blade there are some slight traces of interlacing. (*PSAS*, xxxiii (1898–9), 49, fig. 3). *14th—15th century.*

(7) Tapered slab, 1·74 m long by 0·50 m wide at the head; very worn. The only decoration is the incised outline of a sword of the same type as that on (3) above. *14th—15th century.*

(8) Tapered slab, very worn and lacking the bottom left corner. It measures 1·96 m in length by 0·60 m in width at the head, and has a border composed of a row of dog-tooth ornament between plain mouldings. Within this, at the top, there is a 7-line black-letter inscription which reads: *hic iacet d(omi)n(u)s | [d]u[nc]anus mac|auis vicarius | [de] inisalt qui | obiit a[nno . . .* ('Here lies sir Duncan MacCauis, vicar of Inishail, who died in the year . . .'). The initials *d m a* for 'Duncanus MacCauis' appear in the top right-hand corner of the stone. Below the inscription there is a niche crowned by dragons' heads and containing a chalice and paten, while the lower half of the slab is decorated with a strip of three-strand plait flanked by plant-scrolls with large leaves. The date of the stone is between 1543 and 1558.[1] (*Scottish National Memorials*, 21, fig. 26).

(9) Tapered slab, probably by the sculptor who carved (8) above. It is pointed at the foot, and measures 1·70 m

in maximum length by 0·52 m in width at the head. Within a border embellished with dog-tooth ornament there is a 4-line black-letter inscription, of which only the word *ioh/a(nn)is* ('of John') at the end of the second line and beginning of the third is legible. Centrally-placed beneath the inscription there is a claymore, the hilt of which is flanked by animals and the blade by plant-scrolls. *c. 1500—1560.*

(10) Tapered slab with chamfered bottom corners, 1·71 m long; it is broken across and the right edge is missing at the top. Within a border of debased dog-tooth ornament there is the incised outline of a claymore. *c. 1500—1560.*

(11) A decorated slab which has formed the W end of a tomb-chest built against the inner face of the S wall of the church is still *in situ*. Standing about 3 m from the SE corner of the church, it is 1·10 m high by 0·61 m broad. The main element in the decoration is a cross with barred ends and a slightly splayed foot which occupies the centre of the slab and has been partly destroyed by flaking. Below the left arm of the cross is a man in armour who holds a dog by the collar, while the greater part of the area on the right of the cross is infilled with blind tracery surmounted by a tall mullioned window of two main lights, having a small lozenge-shaped light framed within the pointed arch-head. *c. 1500—1560.*

(12) Side-slab of a tomb-chest, 1·92 m long by 0·45 m to 0·52 m high. Apart from a wide plain border along the lower edge, the exterior surface is covered with crudely executed foliage, the main stems of which form overlapping arcs. This may be part of the same tomb as (11) above. *c. 1500—1560.*

(13) Parallel-sided slab, probably an altar frontal (Fig. 125). Measuring 1·95 m long by 0·57 m high, it is broken across and heavily worn. In the centre there is a Crucifix flanked by two figures, one of whom holds a chalice and the other a cup to catch the blood dripping from the wounds. To the left are two men-at-arms, and to the right an heraldic group comprising two more armed men supporting a crown which is held over a shield charged with a galley with furled sail. There is no basal margin, as would almost certainly have been the case if the slab had been the side of a tomb-chest. The fact that the warriors are wearing plate armour suggests that the carving dates to the 16th century. *c. 1500—1560.*

---

[1] Steer and Bannerman, *Monumental Sculpture*, inscription no. 63.

Fig. 125. Old Parish Church, Inishail (No. 247); altar frontal (scale 1:15)

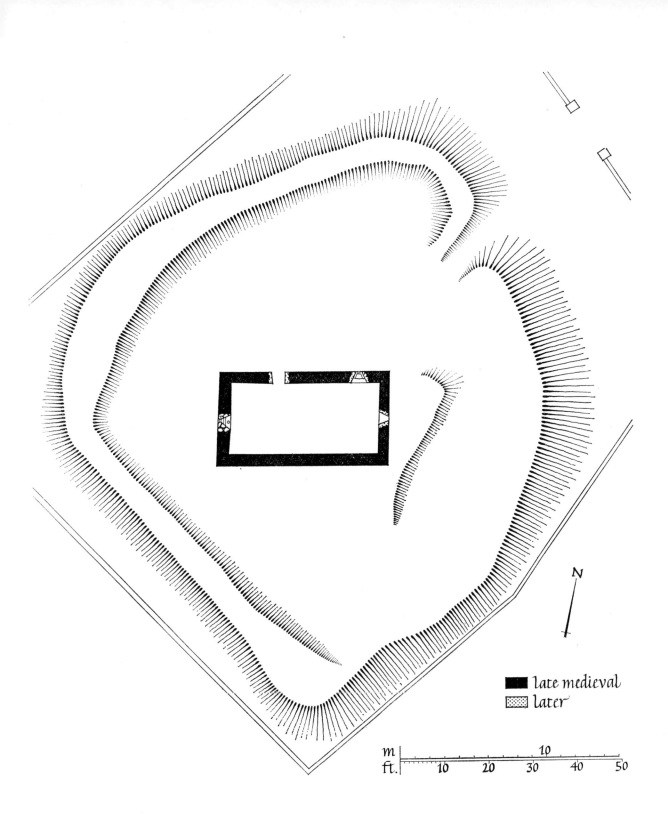

Fig. 126. Chapel, Innis Sèa-Ràmhach (No. 248); plan

(14) Tapered slab with chamfered edges, 1·80 m long by 0·50 m wide at the head; badly worn. Framed within double plain mouldings, there are two plant-scrolls in the upper half of the stone; these unite in the lower half to form large heart-shaped loops enclosing quasi-palmette ornament. *14th—early 16th century.*

(15) Tapered slab, 1·82 m long by 0·55 m wide at the head; it is fractured across the lower end and very worn. Centrally placed there is a long-shafted cross, the head of which is composed of interlocking rings and foliage, while the shaft is decorated with two intertwined stems enclosing ornament of palmette type. At the foot of the slab there are traces of a tightly-knit interlacing pattern based on circles. (*PSAS*, xxxiii (1898–9), 51, fig. 5). *14th—early 16th century.*

(16) Tapered slab with bevelled edges, probably by the same sculptor as (15). It measures 1·78 m long by 0·62 m wide, and is badly worn. Down the right-hand side there is a narrow fillet of foliage decoration, and inside this the incised outline of a sword of uncertain type. The rest of the surviving decoration, which occupies the broad space between the sword and the left margin of the stone, consists of a series of large circles filled with palmette, trefoil and fleur-de-lis ornament. (Part of the decoration is illustrated in *PSAS*, xxxiii (1898–9), 52, fig. 6). *14th—early 16th century.*

(17) Parallel-sided slab, 1·64 m long by 0·61 m wide, bearing the effigy of a priest carved in low relief. His head is bare and rests on a pillow, while his hands are joined in prayer. Below the hands is a chalice. Crude local workmanship. *14th—early 16th century.*

(18) Tapered slab, 1·45 m long by 0·44 m wide, with rebated margin. Incised on the upper surface there is a sword with a tri-lobed pommel and canted quillons, and above this an object of uncertain purpose, blunt at one end and pointed at the other. Local workmanship. *14th—early 16th century.*

(19) Tapered slab, 1·81 m long by 0·50 m wide. The decoration, including the border, is merely incised. On the main axis there is an outline Latin cross with a splayed base, and to the right of this a sword of uncertain type.

Post-Reformation

The earliest of the post-Reformation tombstones are of mid-18th-century date.

098244   NN 02 SE   August 1970

248. Chapel, Innis Sèa-Ràmhach. The remains of
this building are situated on a small island in Loch Awe, about 40 m from the E shore of the loch and about one kilometre SSW of Innis Chonnell Castle (No. 292). The island is accessible by a causeway when the water-level of the loch is low; normal access is by boat, and a path leads to the chapel from a landing-place on the NE side of the island. The chapel stands within an enclosure measuring about 28 m square, defined by an earthen bank on the NW and SW, and by ground which falls steeply to the SE and NE; the entrance is at the NE,

where the bank curves inwards. The entire site is contained within a stone enclosure-wall of recent date.

The chapel is roofless, but the lower parts of the walls are well preserved, rising in places to a height of 2·0 m. The masonry is of local rubble and schist laid in lime mortar; a certain amount of consolidation has taken place at a recent date, probably when similar work was in progress at Innis Chonnell Castle (cf. p. 223). The building, which is rectangular on plan (Fig. 126) and measures 10·1 m from E to W by 4·7 m transversely within walls 0·69 m in thickness, is entered by a doorway situated towards the W end of the N wall. This retains no features of interest and may have been rebuilt. There are single windows in the E and W walls and towards the E end of the N wall. Although the existing jambs of these openings are of recent construction, those in the W and N walls retain schist sills which have been shaped to receive windows having daylight openings of 0·15 m, wrought externally with 0·13 m chamfers and splayed internally. In the sill of the W window there is carved a small basin measuring 0·16 m in diameter and 0·08 m in depth.

The earliest dated monument in the burial-ground is a table-tomb commemorating William McAllum who died in 1732. This is carved in relief with the emblems of mortality and an axe or cleaver. The burial-ground is still in use as a place of interment.

The chapel may be ascribed to the 15th or 16th century. It has no recorded history, and the dedication is unknown.[1]

973110   NM 91 SE   August 1970

249. Church, Inverghiusachan. This is a plain rect-
angular building, now roofless, measuring 12·2 m from NE to SW by 6·1 m transversely over walls some 0·67 m in thickness (Fig. 127, Pl. 28F). It is constructed of local rubble bonded with lime mortar, and the roof was

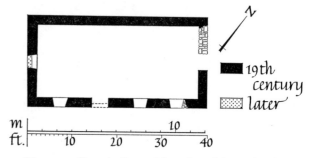

Fig. 127. Church, Inverghiusachan (No. 249); plan

evidently of slate. There is a doorway in the centre of the NE gable-wall and another in the SE wall, which also contains three plain lintelled windows; a fourth window, now blocked, can be seen in the SW gable-wall. No

[1] Cf., however, 8th Duke of Argyll in *TSES*, v (1915–18), 57, suggesting a dedication to St Conuall, and the criticism of this in Simpson, *Dunstaffnage*, 17–18.

details of the internal arrangement survive, but the pulpit probably stood against the centre of the NW wall.

A church was established at Inverghiusachan before 1793, but the existing building appears to have been erected by the 2nd Marquess of Breadalbane about the middle of the 19th century and was used both by the Free and the Established denominations.[1]

093400   NN 04 SE   August 1967

250. Chapel, Keil. This chapel (Fig. 128, Pl. 28D) stands within its burial-ground on the W side of the Oban–Fort William road some 10 km SW of Ballachulish. It is a plain oblong building measuring 12·3 m from E to W by 5·6 m transversely within walls about 0·9 m in thickness. Although the walls stand almost to their original height, much of the visible masonry is modern, parts of the N and S walls, as well as the E and W gable-heads, having recently been patched and repaired to assist their preservation. The original masonry is of roughly-coursed local rubble well bonded with pinnings, the quoins and margins being formed of roughly-dressed blocks and slabs of the same material. The interior of the church contains numerous burials, which have considerably raised the level of the floor.

The existing opening towards the W end of the N wall probably occupies the site of an original doorway. Two

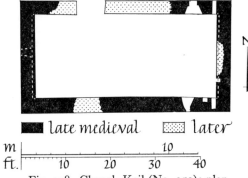

N

■ late medieval   ▦ later

m |_____ 10
ft. |____ 10 ____ 20 ____ 30 ____ 40

Fig. 128. Chapel, Keil (No. 250); plan

slab-lintelled windows (Pl. 28E) stand opposite to one another at the E end of the building, and there is another high up in the centre of the W gable. Other windows may formerly have existed elsewhere in the N and S walls. Both gable-walls are intaken internally a little above the level of the main wall-head. There are two mural aumbries at the E end of the church, one at the S end of the E wall and the other in the S wall. The N and S walls are also pierced by socket-holes which appear to have been designed to carry a horizontal timber beam running across the inside of the E gable-wall. The chapel is probably of late medieval date.

The earliest identifiable reference to this church occurs in 1354, when the lands of the churches of Durobwar (Duror) and Glencown (Glencoe, cf. No. 245) were quit-claimed by John of Lorn to John of Islay.[2] It is not known when the building was abandoned, but a reference to 'a Chappell in that Countrie (i.e. Duror) called

Kilchallumchill'[3] in a topographical account of c. 1630 suggests that the church was still in occupation at that date. The dedication was evidently to St Columba.

FUNERARY MONUMENTS. There are no visible tombstones of a date earlier than 1707, and of the later memorials only the following require mention:

(1) A recumbent slab (Pl. 28B) commemorating Duncan McColl, tenant at Achar, who died in 1822 aged 75. At the foot of the stone there is a relief-carving of a sporting-gun and a hound, while at the head there are carved the conventional emblems of mortality.

(2) A recumbent slab of 1825 (Pl. 28C) commemorating the children of John McDougall at Ballachelish and Rachel McColl his spouse. Above the inscription there is a sunk panel containing carved representations of three children and five infants, each of whom is identified by name. The centre of the panel bears the incised inscription: VIGILATE HORA VENIT ('Watch, for the hour cometh'), while above there is carved a winged angel.

971538   NM 95 SE   September 1970

251. Old Parish Church, Kilbrandon and Kilchattan, Seil. This church was built in 1735 to serve the united parish of Kilbrandon and Kilchattan, and remained in use until the erection of the present parish-church in 1864; the building was subsequently converted into an isolation-hospital and now serves as a private dwelling-house.[4] The shell of the original T-plan church remains, but now incorporates no features of interest apart from a bird-cage belfry which surmounts the W gable.

754143   NM 71 SE   April 1970

252. Old Parish Church, Kilbrandon, Seil. The medieval church of Kilbrandon is now represented only by the W portion of its N wall, 6·4 m in length and 0·8 m in thickness, which stands to a maximum height of 1·1 m, and incorporates on the N side an arched recess over the tombstone of J McLauchlane (*infra*). The church, whose dedication was to St Brendan of Clonfert, an Irish saint of the 6th century, served a parish which comprised Seil and adjoining small islands, and the adjacent portion of the mainland. It was united with Kilchattan at an unrecorded date, probably in the early 17th century, and the church appears to have become ruinous before the end of the 17th century.[5]

FUNERARY MONUMENTS

The following monuments are all situated in the highest part of the burial-ground.

---

[1] *Stat. Acct.*, vi (1793), 179; Name Book, No. 49, p. 111.
[2] *Highland Papers*, i, 77.
[3] *Geog. Coll.*, ii, 157.
[4] S.R.O., Breadalbane Collection, GD 112/40/9, letter from Lord Monzie to Lord Breadalbane, 15 December 1735; *Stat. Acct.*, xiv (1795), 165; *NSA*, vii (Argyll), 79; *Third Stat. Acct.* (Argyll), 202–3.
[5] *Origines Parochiales*, ii, part i, 102.

Medieval

(1) Parallel-sided slab, the bottom of which has broken off; it measures 1·60 m in length by 0·46 m in width. At the top there is a panel which has contained an inscription[1] in Lombardic capitals at least five lines in length. The first three lines read: + HIC IACE/T CALLENU/S PAT[RICII]…('Here lies Colin, son of Patrick…'). Nothing can be made of the other lines, and any decoration that may have existed on the remainder of the slab has been completely obliterated. The fact that the inscription is in Lombardic capitals suggests that the stone was carved before 1500.

(2) Tapered slab, both ends of which are concealed beneath the supports of a later table-tomb. It bears a sword with lobated pommel, and a large thick-stalked plant-scroll. (White, *Knapdale*, pl. xlix, 1). *14th—15th century.*

(3) Tapered slab with bevelled edges, broken across the centre; it measures 1·90 m in length by some 0·50 m in width at the head. There are two plain mouldings on the bevel, and another plain moulding with a row of elongated nail-head ornament inside it round the margin of the upper surface. The decoration within the border is generally similar to that on (2) above. The initials A M D and B L H N have been incised at a later date at the top of the stone. *14th—15th century.*

(4) Tapered slab with bevelled edges, measuring 1·74 m in length by 0·52 m in width at the head. There is a single row of mixed dog-tooth and elongated nail-head ornament on the bevel, and a similar row of ornament between two plain mouldings round the margin of the upper surface. At the top is a pair of shears and a miniature sword, while below these are two animals from whose legs issues a plant-scroll pattern which, apart from a casket at the foot, covers the rest of the surface of the slab. A secondary inscription, reading MR I M, has been incised near the head. (White, *Knapdale*, pl. xlix, 2). *Loch Awe school, c. 1500.*

Post-Reformation

(5) A recumbent slab of schist (Pl. 29D) bearing the incised inscription HIC IACET MR IOHANES MC/LAUCHLANE EVANGELII FIDELIS / PRAECO IN LORNIA INFERIORI AC / MELFORDA QUI AETATIS SUAE SEPTUA/GESIMO OCTAVO OBIIT ANNOQ(UE) / INCARNATIONIS CHRISTI MDC/LXXXV TERTIO NONNOMBR ('Here lies Mr John McLauchlane, a faithful preacher of the gospel in Nether Lorn and Melford, who died at the age of 78 on the 3rd November, 1685'). Above the inscription a shield is carved in relief within a sinuous foliage-border bearing quarterly: 1st, a lion rampant; 2nd, an open book; 3rd, a galley, pennon flying; 4th, a salmon naiant. The upper portion of the slab bears an angel's head and wings and the emblems of mortality, all carved in high relief, and the inscription MEMENTO MORI ('Remember death') incised on a scroll with tasselled terminals. John McLauchlane, who was admitted to the parish of Kilninver and Kilmelford in 1650, was a son of John MacLachlan, minister of Kilbrandon and Kilchattan from 1621 to 1660, and a member of a local family distinguished for Gaelic scholarship.[2]

(6) A sandstone table-tomb bearing a greatly-worn inscription, which appears to commemorate Duncan, brother to Mr John McLachlan, and carved in relief with a shield bearing, quarterly: 1st, a ?lion passant; 2nd, a sinister hand couped fessways holding a cross pattée; 3rd, a galley; 4th, a salmon naiant. The shield is contained within a foliated border similar to that carved on (5), and the two monuments may be by the same craftsman. The table-tomb rests upon end-slabs, of which that at the head bears the initials DM ML, and the date 1745; these slabs are evidently of later date than the main slab, and the person commemorated may be Duncan, son of the Rev. J McLachlan, whose monument is described above, and minister of Strachur and Strathlachlan, who died within a few months of his father, in 1685 or 1686.[3]

(7) Gillies describes a recumbent slab bearing the emblems of mortality and the following marginal inscription: HERE LYES MARGARET CAMPBELL, SPOUS TO ROBERT GRANT OF BRANCHELL, WHO DIED AT OBANE, THE NINTH OF SEPTEMBER 1681. This monument could not be identified at the date of visit. Robert Grant, who is said to have been a factor of Lord Neil Campbell of Ardmaddy, was murdered by the Macleans of Duart.[4]

(8–9) Among the later monuments, the following are of interest:

A recumbent slab (8) of sandstone bearing the emblems of mortality and a worn Latin inscription commemorating Elizabeth, wife of — Sutherland, who was born in 1696 and died in 1726. In the lower part of the slab is an almost totally illegible series of pious verses in English.

A table-tomb (9) of sandstone, erected by Alexander McDougall, 'tacksman of Port Rerrer', to commemorate his brother Allan, son to Allan and Katrin McDougall and 'representiv of the late family of Balichun', who died in 1759 aged 22. Within elaborate mantling there is carved a shield, bearing quarterly: 1st, a lion rampant; 2nd, a castle of three towers; 3rd, a galley; 4th, a dexter hand couped fessways holding a cross-crosslet. For crest there is a dexter hand couped, in pale, holding a cross-crosslet. At the head and foot of the slab there are carved in relief small winged angels' heads.

(10) Gillies[5] describes 'a small, erect slab of red sandstone, bearing the Campbell Arms' which marked a burial-place of the family of Campbell of Calder, who owned land in the parish. This could not be identified at the date of visit.

763166   NM 71 NE   July 1971

253. Old Parish Church, Kilbride. The ruins of this church (Fig. 129, Pl. 29A) stand on the N side of a

---

[1] Steer and Bannerman, *Monumental Sculpture*, inscription no. 68.
[2] Scott, *Fasti*, iv, 88, 96; Gillies, *Netherlorn*, 18–20; *Scottish Studies*, xii (1968), 63, 67; *Argyll Synod Minutes*, ii, 194–5.
[3] Scott, *Fasti*, iv, 44.
[4] Gillies, *Netherlorn*, 21–2.
[5] Ibid., 22.

churchyard which was enclosed shortly after 1794.[1] The existing structure replaced a medieval church dedicated to St Bridget, which first comes on record in 1249, when King Alexander II granted it as a mensal church to the see of Argyll. It is possible that the object of this grant was to expedite the removal of the see from Lismore to Kilbride.[2] Surviving fragments of carved masonry, re-used in the later building, indicate at least two phases of construction which may be assigned respectively to the 13th century and the late medieval period. The parish, comprising the island of Kerrera and the area between Loch Feochan and Loch Etive, was united with Kilmore after the Reformation, but retained its own church.

In 1671 it was reported that the church of Kilbride was 'altogether demolished', and after protracted arguments about the siting of its successor the people

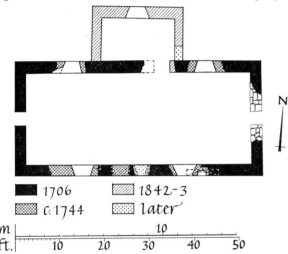

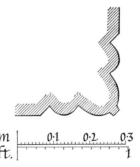

Fig. 129. Old Parish Church, Kilbride (No. 253); plan

of the parish in 1706 'made up a meeting house at Kilbryd wher the old kirk ther was'.[3] This meeting-house may be identified with the oldest part of the existing building, which underwent extensive alterations at two subsequent periods. The first of these, involving the enlargement of all window-openings and the blocking of the S door, may be assigned to c. 1744,[4] while the later restoration was carried out in 1842–3 by Peter MacNab, joiner in Oban, at an estimated cost of £321.[5] At this time a session-house was built at the centre of the N wall, and the window-heads of the S wall were remodelled and the wallhead raised. In 1876 the church was partially demolished, like that at Kilmore (No. 264), to be replaced by a new building at Cleigh.[6]

The original church of 1706 was rectangular on plan, measuring 15·3 m from E to W by 6·1 m transversely within walls 0·7 m in thickness (Fig. 129). Although the arrangement was affected by later alterations, a blocked doorway at the centre of the S wall and two doors, at ground- and gallery-level, in the W gable-wall, are original features. The lower part of another doorway survives in the much-ruined E gable-wall. The masonry

of this period is of random rubble incorporating many fragments of yellow sandstone which bear characteristic medieval tooling-marks. Two fragments, each wrought with a filleted roll clasped between smaller rolls (Fig. 130) were identified in the masonry of the S wall, and at the date of visit part of a window rybat, wrought with a 0·11 m chamfer and an external rebate, was found lying inside the church. The last of these details may be assigned to the 13th century, but the others are probably of late medieval date. A further period of building-activity in the 15th or early 16th century is indicated by the presence of several re-used fragments of green sandstone, from the nearby quarries at Ardentallan or Barrnacarry (Nos. 349, 351); at least four of these pieces are wrought at the arris with a triple roll of meagre dimensions. Towards the E end of the S wall, at ground-level, there is a segmental-arched recess, evidently designed to carry the wall across an existing tombstone, and built into the inner face of the same wall, W of the blocked door, there is a small aumbry.

When the building was remodelled c. 1744, wide windows with shallow-splayed jambs were formed towards each end of the N and S walls. The jambs of these openings, although for the most part built of roughly-squared rubble, also incorporate several re-used blocks of yellow sandstone. The S entrance-doorway was blocked at this time, a small splayed window being formed within the blocking and another immediately to the E, and an external aumbry, whose purpose is uncertain, was inserted E of the SE window. At this period the pulpit may have been moved from the centre of the S wall to a corresponding position against the N wall.

The alterations made by Peter MacNab in 1842–3 comprised the rebuilding of the upper parts of the walls, including the windows, which received elliptical arch-heads, and the construction at the centre of the N wall of a session-house, lit by a large window in its N wall, and

Fig. 130. Old Parish Church, Kilbride (No. 253); carved fragment

[1] *Stat. Acct.*, xi (1794), 129.
[2] *PSAS*, xc (1956–7), 210, 218.
[3] Lorn Presbytery Minutes, i (1651–81), pp. 223–4; ibid., ii (1704–15), p. 74.
[4] *Stat. Acct.*, xi (1794), 121.
[5] Lorn Presbytery Minutes, vii (1839–47), pp. 39, 50, 54, 83–4.
[6] S.R.O., HR 526/5, Kilmore and Kilbride Heritors' Records, Building-Papers.

having at the SE angle doorways to the churchyard and to the interior of the church. All of this work is executed in rubble masonry, laid in regular courses but bonded with mortar of poor quality. A gallery at the W end was a feature of the building until it was dismantled in 1876,[1] and two tiers of put-log holes for the joists of this gallery survive in the W gable-wall.

The MacDougall burial-aisle, situated 2 m SE of the church, is a roofless enclosure of rectangular plan, built by a mason from the township of Barrachrail[2] in 1786, the date incised on the keystone of the elliptical-headed arch in the W gable-wall. Above this arch there is an armorial panel carved in relief with a shield supported by two crowned lions, bearing quarterly, for MacDougall: 1st and 4th, a lion rampant; 2nd and 3rd, a galley, sail furled. The crest is a dexter arm couped holding a cross-crosslet, and the motto is VINCERE VEL MORI ('To conquer or to die').

FUNERARY MONUMENTS

Medieval

The following stones are all in the churchyard, but numbers 11, 14 and 15 could not be found on the date of visit. The descriptions of these three stones are, therefore, based simply on rubbings made for Lord Archibald Campbell at the end of the 19th century, and now at Inveraray Castle.

(1) Tapered slab, 1·79 m long by 0·46 m wide at the head. Although it has been damaged in places by flaking, and by the gouging-out of a pivot-hole, this is a noteworthy stone since it has been more elaborately ornamented than is generally the case with products of the Loch Awe school of carving. The border incorporates a running chevron at the top, and within this the decoration comprises in descending order: (i) a group of motifs consisting of a triquetra, a leaf-spray, and two rosettes, one of which is encircled by four concentric rings; (ii) a pair of wolf-like creatures with further rosettes in the loops formed by their tails; (iii) a sheathed sword flanked by strips of interlacing, partly plant-scroll and partly four-strand plait, which issue from the legs and tails of the animals; and (iv) a foliaceous stem lying parallel to the foot of the slab and enriched with small roundels. The pommel of the sword has been largely destroyed, but was probably of the lobated type, while the quillons are canted; the scabbard resembles one on a stone at Lismore (p. 161, no. 2) in having a narrow band of decoration down the centre. Some of the designs, such as the running chevron, the triquetra, and the plaited strands are not simply blocked out in the normal fashion of the Loch Awe school, but are triple-beaded, and other surface details have no doubt been worn away. *Loch Awe school, 14th—15th century.*

(2) Tapered slab, 1·63 m long by 0·43 m wide at the head. For the most part the decoration consists of a clumsily executed double scroll with short branches ending in leaves or buds. At the top the scroll terminates in an open circle which is surmounted by dragons' heads, while at the foot of the stone there is a casket, standing on end and accompanied by an unidentified object. The border is formed by two plain mouldings. *Loch Awe school, 14th—15th century.*

(3) Tapered slab, 1·84 m long by 0·55 m wide at the top; the surface has been badly damaged by flaking. At the top there is a pair of animals, now headless, and below them a sword, probably similar in form to that on (1) above, flanked by double plant-scrolls. *Loch Awe school, 14th—15th century.*

(4) Tapered slab, 1·76 m long; it is heavily worn and the upper portion of the left-hand edge has broken off. At the top there have been two animals, probably a lion and a unicorn, and below these an unsheathed sword similar to that on (1) above. On one side of the sword there is a single plant-scroll, and on the other a three-strand plait. *Loch Awe school, 14th—15th century.*

(5) Tapered slab, 1·73 m long by 0·60 m wide at the head. At the top, within a border composed of triple plain mouldings, there is a foliated cross. Below this, to the right, is a sword similar to that on (1) above, but with a sword-belt looped round the blade, while to the left is a plant-scroll surmounted by an animal. *Loch Awe school, 14th—15th century.*

(6) Lower part of a tapered slab, 1·17 m long, with a similar border to that on (5) above. At the foot there is a casket and a pair of shears, the rest of the visible decoration consisting of an overall pattern of intertwined plant-scrolls. *Loch Awe school, 14th—15th century.*

(7) Tapered slab, 1·82 m long by 0·50 m wide at the head; very worn. All that is visible is part of an overall pattern of plant-scrolls, of the type used by the Loch Awe carvers, in the central area of the stone. *Loch Awe school, 14th—15th century.*

(8) Tapered slab with bevelled edges, now lacking the foot; it measures 1·45 m in length by 0·48 m in width at the top. There is one row of elongated nail-head ornament on the bevel, and another round the margin of the upper surface. Down the centre is a narrow panel containing a single plant-scroll, the circular volutes of which are filled with clusters of trefoils. *Iona school, 14th—15th century.*

(9) Tapered slab with bevelled edges, 1·91 m long by 0·54 m wide at the head; very worn. There is a row of elongated nail-head ornament on the bevel, and a cable-moulding round the margin of the upper surface. The decoration at the top of the stone has been obliterated, but below this there is a double plant-scroll to the left, and to the right a sword, and a staff of the same length as the sword-blade. The sword has a lobated pommel and relatively short, inclined quillons, while the staff has a round pommel with a long tang-button, and a spike at the foot. A similar staff occurs on an unpublished slab on the floor of St Oran's Chapel, Iona, but the significance of these objects is uncertain. *Probably Iona school, 14th—15th century.*

(10) Tapered slab, 1·84 m long by 0·50 m wide at the head; very worn. On the right there is a sword similar to the one on (9) above, and on the left a double plant-scroll, the upper end of which may have terminated in

---

[1] Ibid.
[2] *SHR*, xvi (1919), 146.

dragons' heads. The border consists of a row of nail-head ornament between two plain mouldings. *14th or 15th century.*

(11) Tapered slab bearing a single-hand sword on the right, and a plant-scroll on the left. *14th or 15th century.*

(12) Parallel-sided slab, pointed at the foot; it measures 1·78 m in length by 0·52 m in width. All that is now visible is the grip and oval pommel of a claymore which have been more deeply recessed into the stone than the rest of the decoration. *c. 1500—1560.*

(13) Parallel-sided slab, the top of which has broken off; it measures 1·50 m in length by 0·59 m in width. There is a single plain moulding round the margin, but within this the only surviving decoration is the grip and pommel of a claymore as on (12) above. *c. 1500—1560.*

(14) Upper part of a slab bearing a foliated cross at the top, and beneath this a claymore with horizontal quillons. To the left of the hilt is a griffin, while on the left side of the blade is a two-line inscription[1] in black letter reading: *h(ic) iacet sallo(m)onu[s]* . . . ('Here lies Solomon . . .'). *c. 1500—1560.*

(15) Lower portion of a cross-shaft displaying double scrolls with formal tri-lobed leaves. *14th—early 16th century.*

(16) Part of a tapered slab with bevelled edges, 1·40 m long. There is a plain moulding on the bevel and a heavy cable-moulding round the margin of the upper surface. Within this border, the only surviving decoration comprises traces of a plant-scroll with five-lobed leaves and a ring-knot. *14th—early 16th century.*

Post-Reformation

(17) The most important of the later funerary monuments, now greatly decayed, is the table-tomb in the MacDougall burial-enclosure commemorating John MacDougall of MacDougall and Dunollie (Iain Ciar), who was forfeited for his part in the Jacobite rising of 1715. The stone bears emblems of mortality and an almost totally illegible inscription which includes his date of death, 1737. Carved in relief is a shield bearing quarterly: 1st, a lion rampant; 2nd, a castle of three towers; 3rd, a galley; 4th, a dexter hand coupled fessways holding a cross-crosslet. For crest there is a dexter arm coupled in pale holding a cross-crosslet, and the supporters are two lions. At the head of the slab are carved the initials I M^cD and M M, for John MacDougall and his wife, Mary MacDonald, a member of the family of MacDonald of Sleat.[2]

(18) A simple recumbent slab of slate in the churchyard, bearing the incised inscription A M^cD PIPER 1773, evidently commemorates one of the MacDougall family, who held a croft at Colagin for their service as hereditary pipers to the MacDougalls of MacDougall.[3]

CROSS. A late medieval disc-headed cross has been re-erected on a modern base about 230 m NNE of the churchyard, close to the S side of the road from Kilbride to Oban.[4] According to local tradition it originally stood beside an old road running south-eastwards from the

coast at Gallanach to the Lowlands, which crosses the modern road about 200 m N of the entrance to the churchyard.[5] By the year 1700, however, it was lying in pieces in the churchyard, and it remained there until 1926 when it was re-assembled and set up in its present position.

The cross, which faces W, has been carved from a single block of greenish-coloured schist and stands 3·13 m high; across the arms it measures 0·69 m. On the front (Pl. 29C) a representation of the Crucified Saviour surrounded by foliage occupies the head and upper portion of the shaft. The head of the Saviour has borne a metal crown. Above the figure is the sacred cypher *i h s*, while below is a black-letter inscription[6] reading *arch/ibald/us ca/mpbel / de lae/rraig / me fie/ri feci/t a(n)no / d(omi)ni m/vxvi* ('Archibald Campbell of Lerags caused me to be made in the year of Our Lord 1516'). Beneath the inscription are an interlace pattern and a unicorn passant guardant, its tail terminating in a foliaceous spray. The initials S M D which have been cut in relief at the foot of the shaft are not part of the original design, but have been added at a later date. On the back of the cross (Pl. 29B) the upper arm displays Archibald Campbell's coat of arms, which is unorthodox according to the rules of heraldry. Upon a field divided gyronny of eight, the following charges are disposed quarterly: 1st and 4th, a galley, sail furled; 2nd and 3rd, a ? boar's head erased. The rest of the decoration consists of two similar plant-scrolls which run parallel up the shaft until they branch out into the horizontal arms of the cross-head.

TOBAR AN EASBUIG (SITE). The officers of the Ordnance Survey were shown this well, 'formerly a fine spring known as the "Bishop's Well", now almost dried up' in 1871[7] and they recorded its position at the SW corner of the field N of the church. There are no visible remains.

857257 (Church)   NM 82 NE   June 1971
857259 (Cross)

254. Burial-ground, Kilbride, Glen Feochan (Site).
There are no identifiable remains of this burial-ground, apart from what appears to be part of a dry-stone wall bounding the S side of the site indicated on the 6-inch O.S. map.

916245   NM 92 SW   July 1968

---

[1] Steer and Bannerman, *Monumental Sculpture*, inscription no. 67.
[2] *Burke's Landed Gentry* (1952 ed.), 1619.
[3] The Commissioners are indebted for this information to Miss H MacDougall.
[4] A full description of this cross is given in *PSAS*, lxi (1926-7), 143-7.
[5] The O.S. 6-inch map records the discovery of a stone cross 550 m NE of the old church, but if this report is correct it must relate to another, otherwise unknown, cross.
[6] Cf. Steer and Bannerman, *Monumental Sculpture*, inscription no. 66.
[7] Name Book, No. 19, p. 106.

255. Chapel, Kilbride, Seil (Site). There are no visible remains, but the site was identified as that of a 'church or chapel' by the local inhabitants in about 1870.[1] The dedication was evidently to St Bridget.

752168   NM 71 NE   April 1970

256. Old Parish Church, Kilchattan, Luing. The ruins of this church (Pl. 30B) stand within a burial-ground about 500 m NW of the village of Toberonochy. It was evidently a small building of oblong unicameral plan measuring about 12·5 m from E to W by 5·3 m transversely within walls varying in thickness from 0·9 m to 1·2 m (Fig. 131), but due to the disappearance of the E wall the precise length of the church cannot now be established. The remaining three walls are practically complete. The masonry is of roughly-coursed local rubble well bonded with pinnings, and the facework incorporates slate flagstones as well as numerous large split boulders. It is uncertain whether or not freestone dressings were

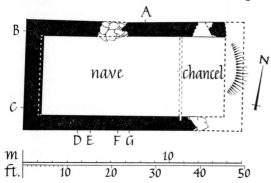

Fig. 131. Old Parish Church, Kilchattan, Luing (No. 256); plan

employed, for none are now visible either *in situ* or amongst the surrounding debris, and the quoins that survive at the NW and SW angles are of slate. A gap in the masonry of the N wall evidently indicates the position of a doorway,[2] while towards the E end of the building there are fragmentary remains of two small splayed windows placed more or less opposite to each other in the N and S walls. A socket-hole, situated immediately to the W of the S window at a height of 1·2 m above the present floor-level, may represent the seating for a timber chancel-screen. The W gable is intaken by 0·2 m at the level of the main wall-head. Except that repairs have at some time been carried out to the lower part of the NW angle, the building appears to be of homogeneous construction. The date of erection is not known, but the building corresponds in plan and overall dimensions to the 12th-century church of Killean, Kintyre,[3] and may tentatively be ascribed to the same period.

This church served the parish of Kilchattan, a district which comprised the islands of Luing, Shuna and Torsa, together with a number of adjacent islets. The parish is now united to that of Kilbrandon, but the date of the

union is not known.[4] The church first comes on record in 1549, and probably remained in use until 1735, when a new church was erected at North Cuan, Seil (No. 251), to serve the united parish.[5] The dedication was evidently to St Cathan.

GRAFFITI

A number of the outer facing-stones of the church bear graffiti, lightly and crudely incised with a knife or other sharp-edged instrument. It seems likely that these

Fig. 132. Old Parish Church, Kilchattan, Luing (No. 256); graffiti (A) (scale 1:5)

graffiti are of pre-Reformation date, since the subjects represented include crosses and also galleys of the type found in the Western Isles in the late medieval period; many of them occur at heights in the wall which suggest that they are the work of children. The positions of the more interesting examples have been marked on the plan (Fig. 131, A–E); details are as follows:

(1) *North Wall* (A). Sketchy outlines of three ships (Fig. 132, Pl. 30C). All resemble medieval West Highland galleys in having centrally-stepped masts and high stems and sterns, while the figure-head of an animal (? a deer) on the stem- or stern-post of one vessel can be paralleled on late medieval tombstones at Iona.[6]

(2) *West Wall* (B). Slight indications of two vessels similar to those on stone A above.

(3) *West Wall* (C). A Greek cross with barred terminals.

(4) *South Wall* (D). An oblong figure with hatching at either end, subdivided by horizontal, vertical and diagonal lines. Around this are other markings including zig-zag lines, a cross and a triangle (Fig. 133).

(5) *South Wall* (E). On a stone adjacent to the last are vague representations of the hulls and rigging of a number of ships similar to those on stone A, and three linear crosses (Fig. 134). One of the crosses has lozenge-

[1] Name Book, No. 9, p. 20; cf. also *NSA*, vii (Argyll), 71.
[2] Muir, *Eccles. Notes*, 21.
[3] *Inventory of Argyll*, i, No. 287.
[4] *Origines Parochiales*, ii, part i, 100.
[5] Monro, *Western Isles*, 52.
[6] Drummond, *Monuments*, pls. xvii, 2 and xxv, 2.

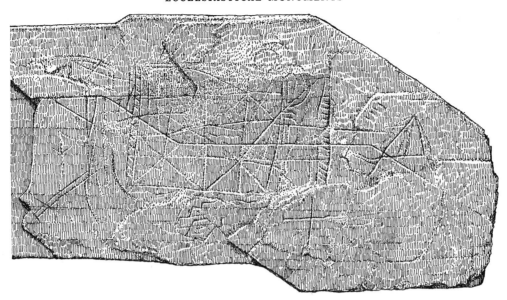

Fig. 133. Old Parish Church, Kilchattan, Luing (No. 256); graffiti (D) (scale 1:5)

shaped figures at the junction and ends of the arms, and a cross-potent set saltire-wise at the centre.

FUNERARY MONUMENTS

The only identifiable monument of a date earlier than 1707 (1) lies inside the church. Several interesting monuments of later date (2–5) are situated in the churchyard.

(1) A recumbent slab bearing the inscription HERE / LAYS / A M L / OF SVNA / I C 1680. This monument evidently commemorates Allan McLean of Shuna and his second wife, Isobel Campbell, who obtained a grant of the island of Shuna in liferent from Lord Neil Campbell in 1679. Both were described as still living in 1691 and the husband died about 1706.[1]

(2) A recumbent slab commemorating Archibald, son of Lachlan Campbell in Ardnamer, who died in 1788. This bears a crudely-incised carving of a boar's head erased, with the motto YOU MON FOLLOW ME.

(3) A large table-tomb (Pl. 30D) commemorating Hugh McDougall, who died at Danna in 1785, and his brother, John McDougall of Lunga, who died in 1809. The stone is carved with a shield bearing, for McDougall: quarterly,

---

[1] S.R.O., Particular Register of Sasines (Argyll), RS 10/1, fol. 297v.; ibid., RS 10/2, fol. 305v.; Sinclair, A M, *The Clan Gillean* (1899), 361.

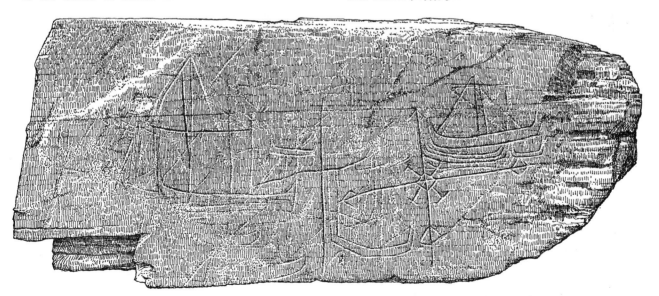

Fig. 134. Old Parish Church, Kilchattan, Luing (No. 256); graffiti (E) (scale 1:5)

1st and 4th, a lion rampant; 2nd and 3rd, a galley, sail furled, pennons flying. The crest is a dexter arm couped, holding a cross-crosslet.

(4) A headstone of slate (Pl. 30E), bearing pious verses in Gaelic and an English inscription commemorating Archibald McArthur, who died in 1826. In the pediment there is a crude relief-carving of two angels blowing trumpets, death with a spear, the sun, the crescent-moon, and a marigold-emblem.

(5) A group of monuments near, or built into, the W wall of the churchyard commemorate Alexander Campbell, founder of a sect which claimed to revive the doctrines of the Covenanters, who died in 1829. A table-tomb bears an inscription beginning: I PROTEST THAT NONE BE / BURIED AFTER ME IN THIS / GRAVE WHICH I HAVE DUG / FOR MYSELF AS JACOB DID / GEN[ESIS] L. 5. A rough boulder, with a lengthy inscription carved by Campbell himself, bears other texts of a similar nature, while two other stones built into the outer face of the churchyard-wall bear inscriptions on the themes of judgment and the covenants.[1]

744090　　　　NM 70 NW　　　　May 1970

257. Kilcheran, Lismore. This building (Pl. 30A) comprises two separate houses linked by a single-storeyed wing which formerly served as a chapel. Each house is a plain oblong gable-ended block of two main storeys, symmetrically planned about a central front door and staircase. The southernmost house, which is the earlier of the two, evidently dates from shortly before the end of the 18th century (*infra*), while its companion belongs to the second decade of the 19th century. The chapel, which is distinguished externally by a bird-cage belfry on the gable-head, is contemporary with the later house. All the interiors have been considerably remodelled and now present no particular features of interest.

In 1803 the Roman Catholic seminary for the Highland District was transferred from Samalaman, in Moidart, to Lismore, where the newly erected house of Kilcheran was purchased from Captain Niall Campbell of Dunstaffnage. Further building was undertaken in about 1815, and the chapel is said to have been completed by September of that year. In 1828 the seminary was transferred to Aquhorthies, and thence to Blairs, and the building at Kilcheran reverted to domestic use.[2]

BURIAL-GROUND. Behind the house there is a small burial-enclosure. This contains a number of tombstones, including those of Bishop John Chisholm, vicar-apostolic of the Highland District, who died in 1814, and of his brother and coadjutor, Bishop Aeneas Chisholm, who died in 1818.

824387　　　　NM 83 NW　　　　June 1970

258. Chapel and Burial-ground, Kilchoan House (Site). This site is now occupied by Kilchoan House, formerly known as Melfort Cottage, a building of mid-19th-century date. When the officers of the Ordnance Survey visited the area in about 1872, they were told that graves containing human remains had been found during the building of the house.[3] Kilchoan, a farm situated about 250 m N of the site, probably derives its name from the chapel; the name appears as 'Kilcongen' in a charter of 1313, the dedication being to St Congan or Comghan.[4]

796133　　　　NM 71 SE　　　　July 1970

259. Parish Church, Kilchrenan. This church served a parish which in the medieval period included land on the E and W shores of Loch Awe, and until the 17th century it was often referred to simply as the church 'of Lochaw'. In 1651 the S portion was disjoined to form a new parish having its church at Dalavich, and although this separation was rescinded ten years later, the additional church remained in use (No. 241). The parish first comes on record in the 14th century, but there is architectural evidence for the construction of a church in the previous century. During the medieval period the church was known as *Ecclesia Sancti Petri Diaconi*. The reference is perhaps to St Peter the Deacon, secretary and companion to St Gregory the Great.[5]

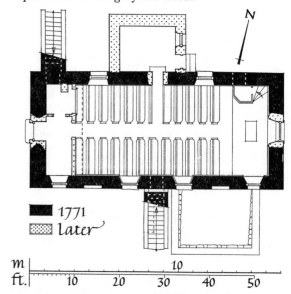

■ 1771
▨ later

Fig. 135. Parish Church, Kilchrenan (No. 259); plan

The dimensions and orientation of the existing building are similar to those of several medieval churches in Lorn, and it is possible that it stands on the foundations, or incorporates some of the masonry, of its 13th-century predecessor. In its present form, however,

---

[1] Several of these inscriptions are given in full in Gillies, *Netherlorn*, 48–9.
[2] MacWilliam, A S, 'The Highland Seminary at Lismore, 1803–1828', *The Innes Review*, viii (1957), 30–8.
[3] Name Book, No. 53, p. 179.
[4] *Origines Parochiales*, ii, part i, 103; Mackinlay, *Non-Scriptural Dedications*, 162–3.
[5] *Origines Parochiales*, ii, part i, 120–1; *Argyll Synod Minutes*, i, 231.

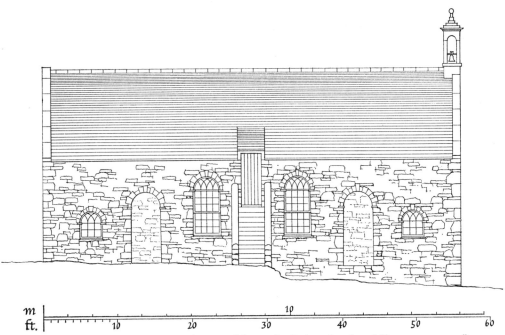

Fig. 136. Parish Church, Kilchrenan (No. 259); S elevation (partially reconstructed)

the structure dates from 1771, when it was rebuilt under the supervision of Donald Campbell of Sonachan, acting on behalf of the heritors. In 1807 the church was said to be in great disrepair, and an estimate of £158 was obtained from Donald MacDougald, 'architect in Craignish', for necessary repairs. Extensive alterations were made to the interior in 1904, and subsequently a vestry was added on the N.[1]

The building (Pl. 31D) stands within a churchyard which slopes gently from W to E and is enclosed by a modern boundary-wall. It is rectangular on plan, measuring 15·1 m from E to W by 6·0 m transversely within walls which vary in thickness from 0·85 m to 1·00 m; a small vestry of recent date projects at the centre of the N wall (Figs. 135, 136). The masonry is of whitewashed rubble, no freestone being employed except in the E and W window-openings and the enlarged W doorway, all of which date from 1904. Built into the existing fabric, however, there are several fragments of window-dressings of 13th-century character, executed in a sandstone similar to that employed at Dunstaffnage Castle (No. 287). One fragment, which at the date of visit was found lying in the churchyard, formed part of the jamb of a window, being splayed internally and having an external rebate; the outer face is wrought with an 0·15 m chamfer bearing dog-tooth ornament (Fig. 137). About 1·4 m below wall-head level there is a distinct change in the alignment and nature of the quoins, which above this point are formed of smaller stones. This change is possibly to be explained by the survival of earlier, perhaps medieval, masonry up to that level, but may, alternatively, be the result of a seasonal break in building-operations.

In the original arrangement of the interior, there were galleries along the S, E and W walls, entered respectively by doorways at the centre of the S wall, and at each end of the N wall. The S and NE doorways were blocked in 1904, and the forestair giving access to the latter has been removed. The church is now entered by a semicircular-headed doorway in the centre of the W gable-wall; this dates from 1904, but replaces a smaller opening in the same position. At the centre of the E gable-wall there is a recess having a width of 0·91 m and a height of 2·13 m, which is probably a blocked entrance-doorway; this opening is not referred to in connection with the alterations of 1904, and may have been blocked during the unspecified repairs of 1807 (cf. supra). Above this recess there is a large semicircular-headed window which was constructed in 1904 to replace a smaller window at a higher level. At the same time a small window above the W entrance-doorway was reconstructed with a sandstone surround. Built into each gable-wall there are fragments of stonework ornamented with dog-tooth, similar to the stone described above.

The principal interest of the exterior is concentrated on the S façade (Fig. 136) which, despite minor alterations in 1904, is a well-preserved and favourable specimen of 18th-century design. Six semicircular-headed openings, each having slightly-projecting imposts and a keystone, are disposed symmetrically on either side of the forestair that led to the doorway of the S gallery. The central openings are tall windows and those at each

[1] S.R.O., Breadalbane Collection, GD 112/9/51, Argyll Rental, Crop 1770–1; GD 112/51/9, Church Papers, estimate by D MacDougald, 1807; HR 478/2, Kilchrenan and Dalavich Heritors' Papers, specification by J Edgar, architect, Lochgilphead, 1904; RHP 8085, plans by J Edgar, 1904.

end of the wall are small windows which formerly lit the spaces below the end-galleries, while the intermediate features are recesses which simulate the appearance of doorways but were probably never used as such. All of the windows contain glazing-bars which conform to the semicircular arch-heads; a 19th-century photograph,[1] however, shows that originally the glazing-bars intersected in the arch-heads. From the same source, it appears that the gallery-doorway rose a short distance above wall-head level and was provided with a catslide roof. The forestair, which rises at right angles to the line of the S wall, is contained within solid stone walls and has treads of slate, two of which bear incised Greek crosses. The W part of the forestair is supported at ground-level by a segmental relieving-arch, as if to carry it across a tombstone, but no such feature is now

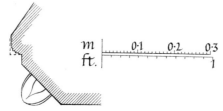

Fig. 137. Parish Church, Kilchrenan (No. 259); carved fragment

visible. Built against the E part of the S wall is a burial-enclosure with a 19th-century tablet commemorating Duncan and Alexander Campbell of Sonachan, who died in 1691 and 1738 respectively, and earlier members of the family. It is stated on the tablet that the enclosure was erected by Donald Campbell of Sonachan in 1779; its walls stand, however, upon substantial footings which may mark the position of an earlier burial-aisle added against the S wall of the medieval church.

A forestair similar to that described above rises to a doorway near the W end of the N wall which gives access to the W gallery. This wall contains two windows with plain semicircular heads. The E gable is surmounted by a bird-cage bell-cot having a stepped roof terminating in a ball-finial, which is probably of 19th-century date.

The existing arrangement of the interior dates from 1904, when the W gallery was rebuilt and the pulpit and communion-table were placed at the E end. It is probable that originally the pulpit was set at the centre of the N wall, where an inserted doorway now leads to the vestry.

FUNERARY MONUMENTS

Medieval

Number 6 is built into the outer face of the E end of the church, while the rest are in the churchyard.

(1) Slab of irregular shape, broken into two pieces; it measures 0·80 m in length by 0·63 m in maximum width. In the upper portion, within a plain border, there is a cross (Fig. 138) which has a head composed of four circles, and a short shaft with a semicircular base. Partly incised and partly in false relief, the cross is crudely executed, presumably by a local mason. No

traces of decoration can now be seen on the rest of the stone. *Late 13th or early 14th century.*

(2) Tapered slab with bevelled edges, measuring over all 1·83 m in length by 0·57 m in width at the head. There is one row of elongated nail-head ornament on the bevel, and another between plain mouldings round the margin of the surface of the slab. Within this wide border there are two panels separated by a running T-fret pattern. In the uppermost is a small effigy of an armed man standing in a niche which is crowned by dragons' heads; he wears a bascinet and an aketon, and carries a sword and spear. The lower panel contains interlacing plant-scrolls and two animals, probably a hound pursuing a stag. (A photograph of this stone is given in Campbell, *Highland Dress*, pl. 37, where, however, it is wrongly attributed to Oronsay). *Loch Awe school, 14th—15th century.*

(3) Tapered slab, the upper corners of which are chamfered; it measures 1·98 m in length by 0·57 m in maximum width and is broken across the centre. At the head there is a strip of decoration consisting of intersecting arcs. Otherwise the surface of the stone is occupied by two panels of roughly equal size which are framed by double plain mouldings enclosing a row of elongated nail-head ornament. The decoration in the upper panel is similar to that on (2) above, except that the dragons' heads are replaced by a pair of four-footed animals. The lower panel contains only plain interlacing. *Loch Awe school, 14th—15th century.*

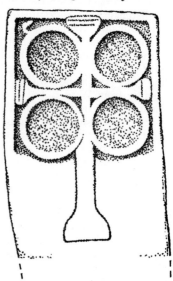

Fig. 138. Parish Church, Kilchrenan (No. 259); fragment of cross-decorated stone (scale 1:15)

(4) Upper part of a tapered slab with bevelled edges, 0·92 m long by 0·60 m wide at the head. Within a single plain moulding it bears an armed man similar to those on (2) and (3) above, standing in a niche crowned by dragons' heads. *Loch Awe school, 14th—15th century.*

[1] In the possession of His Grace the Duke of Argyll, Inveraray Castle.

(5) Fragment of a parallel-sided slab, 0·60 m long, with bevelled edges decorated with a heavy roll-moulding. Down the centre of the stone, within wide plain margins, there is a finely carved double scroll incorporating the palmette ornament. A similar scroll occurs on two slabs at Iona (Drummond, *Monuments*, pls. xix, 2, and xxx, 1). *Iona school, 14th—15th century.*

(6) Tapered slab, pointed at the foot (Pl. 31C). It measures 1·78 m in length by 0·57 m in width at the head, and has a border composed of a row of dog-tooth ornament between plain mouldings. Within this, at the top, there is a four-line inscription[1] in raised black letter which reads: *hic iacet d/(u)gall(u)s makall/ur (et) colin(us) / [a]ngusii co(n)str(uxit)* ('Here lies Dugall MacKellar, and Colinus, son of Angus, made it'). Below the inscription is a claymore flanked by plant-scrolls which are linked to the tails of a lion and a griffin situated on either side of the hilt. An inscribed stone placed at the foot of this slab in 1866 erroneously identifies it as the tombstone of Cailean Mór, progenitor of the Clan Campbell, who was slain in 1294. In fact, however, the claymore and the use of black letter indicate that the slab belongs to the period *c.* 1500–1560. Two other early 16th-century gravestones by the same sculptor are at Taynuilt (p. 165, number 4) and Inishail (p. 136, number 8).

(7) Side of a tomb-chest, 2·24 m long by 0·63 m high. Apart from a plain border along the lower edge, which was sunk into the ground, it is decorated with foliaceous ornament, consisting of a thick-stemmed scroll with circular volutes and large, mainly tri-lobed, leaves. In amongst the foliage at one end of the stone there is a hound pursuing a stag, and another pair of indeterminate animals. *c. 1500—1560.*

(8–9) Two other late medieval slabs at Kilchrenan are illustrated in a series of rubbings made by Lord Archibald Campbell, and now at Inveraray Castle, but the stones themselves could not be found on the date of visit. One (8), which lacks the foot, has a four-petalled cross made of intersecting arcs at the head, with a triquetra and other similar motifs in the spaces between the petals. Below this is a sword with a lobated pommel and a pair of animals, one on either side of the hilt; to the left of the blade is a plant-scroll, and to the right a four-strand plait. The other slab (9) is evidently very worn, all that is visible being an armed man under a canopy with dragons' heads, as on (2) above. Both slabs are of 14th or 15th century date, and (9) is a product of the Loch Awe School.

Post-Reformation

(10) Tapered slab with bevelled edges, measuring over all 1·74 m in length by 0·51 m in width at the head. Within a cable-moulding, the entire surface is covered with decoration, which, apart from a pair of shears, consists of geometric designs, such as barred circles and running chevron patterns, set down in a haphazard fashion and clumsily executed. This is obviously a degenerate descendant of the late medieval carved slabs, made at some time after the Reformation.

(11) Tapered slab similar to the last. The decoration has been almost entirely obliterated.

(12–13) Two monuments commemorate Robert McIntyre, surgeon successively with the 60th and 53rd Regiments, who died at Toulouse in 1815. One (12) is an elegant mural tablet of marble (Pl. 31F), now set against the inner face of the S wall of the church, which bears a lengthy English inscription. The other (13) is a tall Grecian monument (Pl. 31E) in the churchyard, whose pedestal incorporates a tablet bearing an inscription in Latin. A boldly-projecting cornice supports a plinth having acroteria at the angles, from which rises a squat obelisk terminating in a pedimented feature. Carved in relief on the upper part of the obelisk is an oval medallion depicting a mourning female figure seated beside a pedestalled urn. Below this there is an armorial incorporating a shield bearing quarterly: 1st and 4th, an ?eagle displayed; 2nd, a galley, sail furled; 3rd, a dexter hand couped fessways holding a cross-crosslet. For crest there is a dexter hand couped brandishing a sword.

036229   NN 02 SW   August 1970

260. Chapel, Killandrist, Lismore (Site). There are no visible remains of this chapel, which was presumably dedicated to St Andrew.[2]

ST ANDREW'S WELL. Immediately to the S of the site of the chapel a spring issues from the base of a rock cliff overlooking the shore of Loch Baile a' Ghobhainn. The mouth of the spring is protected by a canopy of dry-stone masonry.

858427   NM 84 SE   May 1968

261. Chapel and Burial-ground, Kilmaha (Site). This site, which formerly lay within a Forestry Commission plantation, was severely damaged during the great gale of January 1968, when all the standing timber was uprooted and blown down. Although the trunks of the fallen trees have since been removed, large stumpholes remain and these, together with a thick overburden of brushwood and other vegetation, make effective investigation impossible. Consequently the following account has been prepared mainly from the published account of a site-survey carried out some time between 1954 and 1963.[3]

The site occupies a small promontory, known as Rubha na Fìdhle, situated on the NW side of Loch Awe about 6 km SW of Dalavich. Access was probably obtained by means of a rock gully leading up from the shore of the small bay on the NW side of the promontory. Within an enclosure-wall of dry-stone construction there were the remains of two buildings of sub-oval plan, of which the first measured about 6·5 m from NW to SE

---

[1] Cf. Steer and Bannerman, *Monumental Sculpture*, inscription no. 65.
[2] Name Book, No. 22, p. 92; Mackinlay, *Scriptural Dedications*, 213.
[3] Campbell, M and Sandeman, M, 'Mid Argyll: an Archaeological Survey', *PSAS*, xcv (1961-2), 70-1.

by 2·4 m transversely within walls some 1·4 m in thickness. In the centre of the NE wall there was a doorway having a width of 0·6 m. The second building, which stood at right angles to the first and adjacent to its SW corner, measured about 9·1 m from NE to SW by 3·3 m transversely within walls some 1·5 m in thickness. A little further to the SW, and at a lower level, there were slight traces of a third building.

Nothing is known of the history of this site, but in view of the evidence provided by the associated carved stones (*infra*) it may be ascribed to the Early Christian period. The dedication is said to have been to St Mochoe of Nendrum, but Watson explains the place-name as a corruption of Cill Mo-Thatha, and suggests that it commemorates an Irish saint of the name of Tua. Another possibility is St Kentigern, the Gaelic version of whose nickname was Mochoe.[1]

ROCK-CARVING. On the surface of a rock outcrop situated between the burial-ground and the tip of the promontory, there is a crudely incised Early Christian carving consisting of a 'Maltese' ring-cross with sunken interspaces and a short stem or handle, which is flanked

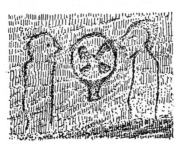

Fig. 139. Chapel and burial-ground, Kilmaha (site) (No. 261); rock-carving (scale 1:15)

by two long-robed figures (Fig. 139). The heads of the figures resemble those of birds rather than of men, but it is uncertain whether this is accidental or deliberate. The carving is difficult to distinguish since the rock is heavily cracked and fissured.

CARVED STONES. Within the burial-ground there are the remains of two carved stones, also of Early Christian date.

(1) The greater part of a cross-decorated stone, which has clearly been intended to stand upright. When complete it measured about 1·9 m in length by 0·47 m in greatest width, and 0·11 m to 0·19 m in thickness. On one face it bore a ring-headed cross with sunk arm-pits, and a shaft defined by deeply-incised lines and open at the foot (Fig. 140). In the centre of the shaft, immediately below the cross-head, there is a cup-shaped depression, while to the right of the shaft is a linked row of circles and bosses of different sizes. Two of the circles enclose central hollows, after the fashion of Bronze Age cup-and-ring markings. The edges and back of the stone are undecorated. The cross-head was broken off during the gale of 1968 and has since disappeared, but photographs of the stone taken prior to that date, on which Fig. 140

is partly based, are preserved in the National Monuments Record of Scotland.

(2) A cross-decorated stone in two pieces (Fig. 141). When complete it measured 2·20 m long by 0·50 m in greatest width and 0·14 m to 0·18 m in thickness. On

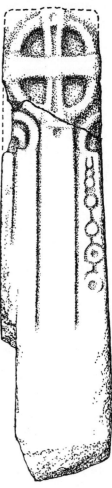

Fig. 140. Chapel and burial-ground, Kilmaha (site) (No. 261); cross-decorated stone (scale 1:15)

one face there is a triple-barred cross in false relief, the shaft and arms being embellished by incised decoration. The opposite face bears a (? ring-headed) cross, the shaft of which is ornamented with interlace, while the spaces on either side are decorated with step patterns.

937078   NM 90 NW   July 1971

262. Church and Burial-ground (possible), Kilmaronag (Site). These remains are situated in a field about 600 m from the S shore of Loch Etive, and about 450 m S of Kilmaronag House. They comprise

---

[1] Ibid; Watson, *Celtic Place-names*, 297–8; Jackson, K H, in Chadwick, N K *et al.*, *Studies in the Early British Church* (1958), 300–3.

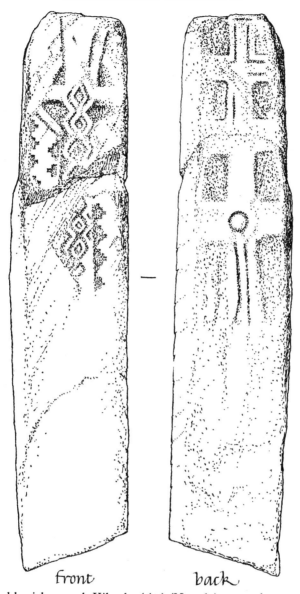

front   back

Fig. 141. Chapel and burial-ground, Kilmaha (site) (No. 261); cross-decorated stone (scale 1:15)

the turf-covered walls of two buildings (A and B on Fig. 142) whose axes run respectively from E to W and from NNW to SSE, and two sub-rectangular enclosures, one of which (C) lies immediately W of the buildings while the other (D) adjoins it to the N.

Building A is sub-rectangular on plan, measuring 23 m from E to W by 9·5 m transversely over walls having a thickness of about 0·9 m. The rounded appearance of the E end of the building may be the result of the collapse or removal of the outer angles of an originally rectangular structure. A section of the outer wall-face is exposed on the N, and a portion of internal wall-face is also visible immediately E of a gap in the S wall which is probably the site of an entrance-doorway. The walls, which stand to a maximum height of about 0·6 m, are built of rubble set in lime mortar and incorporate many granite boulders. Fragments of yellowish-brown sandstone, similar in appearance to that quarried at Ardtornish, were found in the area of the doorway at the date of visit. An apparent cross-passage, and two depressions running W from it along the inner faces of the N and S walls, are probably the results of unrecorded excavation at a comparatively recent date. Within the E end there lies a plain slab of coarse sandstone measuring 1·85 m in length by 0·64 m in width.

Building B is poorly preserved and only the E wall is distinguishable; a few stones remain *in situ* at the NE angle. It appears to have been a rectangular structure

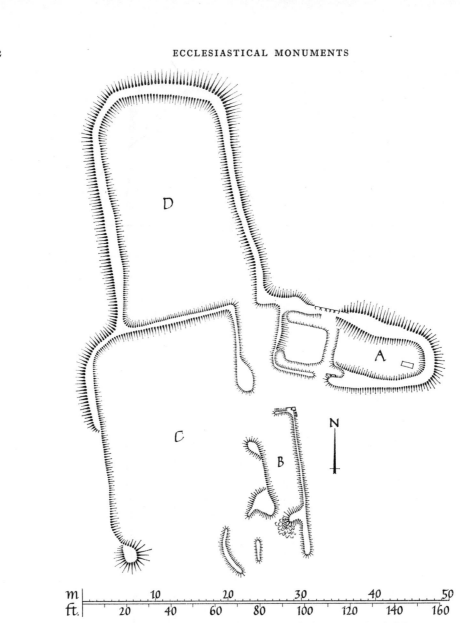

Fig. 142. Church and burial-ground (possible), Kilmaronag (site) (No. 262); plan

measuring 14·3 m from N to S by about 6 m transversely. The side-walls are continued for 5·5 m to form a smaller enclosure on the S, and there is a small D-shaped annexe immediately W of this.

Enclosure C, which measures about 32 m from N to S by about 20 m from E to W, is bounded on the N and W by the turf-covered remains of a substantial rubble wall. There is no surviving boundary on the S. Enclosure D is less clearly demarcated, except on the S, where it is bounded by C. The interior is elevated about one metre above the level of the surrounding field, but the boundary is represented only by a slight mound. The overall dimensions of the enclosure are about 30 m from N to S by about 18 m from E to W, the NE and NW angles being distinctly rounded.

The name 'Kilmaronag' establishes the existence of

an ecclesiastical site dedicated to St Ronan, or else to St Cronoc,[1] and a description of the area, said to have been compiled in the late 17th century, states that 'there yet remain the walls of an old church'.[2] The remains described above were also identified as those of an early church by Cosmo Innes, who suggested that it was the original parish-church of Muckairn, and by the officers of the Ordnance Survey.[3] While the orientation of building A lends some support to this identification, its dimensions are unusually large for a structure of this type, and the other remains are also untypical of ecclesiastical sites. The use of lime mortar and sandstone

---

[1] Cf. Watson, *Celtic Place-names*, 303.
[2] MS belonging to General Campbell of Lochnell, quoted in *NSA*, vii (Argyll), 512.
[3] *Origines Parochiales*, ii, part i, 132; Name Book, No. 23, p. 6.

dressings would indicate a secular building of some importance, which may tentatively be associated with the barony of Kilmaronag, held during the 17th century by the Campbells of Calder.[1]

937341   NM 93 SW   July 1970

263. Parish Church, Kilmelford. This church, which was dedicated to St Maelrubha, first comes on record in the 15th century.[2] The parish, which comprised a hilly area S of Loch Tralaig, was united with Kilninver at an unknown date, possibly in the 16th century. The church was rebuilt in the second half of the 18th century, and thoroughly renovated in 1890.[3] In its present form it is of late Victorian date, although preserving the simple rectangular plan of the earlier building, which had an external stair, probably leading to a gallery, against the W wall.[4]

FUNERARY MONUMENTS AND OTHER CARVED STONES

The first of these stones is in the vestry and the second in the churchyard.

(1) An undecorated cruciform stone of schist measuring 0·72 m in length, 0·34 m in width across the arms, and from 0·06 m to 0·11 m in thickness. The relatively unworn appearance of this stone makes it unlikely that it dates to the Early Christian period, and it is probably of much more recent origin.

(2) A tapered slab, the head of which is concealed by a monument to the Campbells of Melfort. The decoration, which is enclosed by a double plain moulding, consists of a diaper pattern of interlocking plant-scrolls surmounted by a lion and unicorn. *Loch Awe school, 14th—15th century.*

There are no other identifiable funerary monuments in the churchyard of a date earlier than the late 18th century.

849130   NM 81 SW   April 1970

264. Old Parish Church, Kilmore. The ruins of the former parish-church of Kilmore (Fig. 143, Pl. 31B) stand on the N side of its graveyard, at the W end of Glen Feochan and about 1·5 km from the sea-loch of that name. The church, which was dedicated to St Bean, first comes on record at the beginning of the 14th century;[5] the existing structure, however, appears to be of 15th- or 16th-century date. The parish was united with that of Kilbride, probably early in the 17th century, and the building was remodelled at this period. Further alterations were made in 1838, under the direction of an Oban architect named Dalzel,[6] and in 1859. In 1876 the roof and fittings were dismantled and most of the door- and window-openings were blocked; at the same time the upper part of the E gable was removed and the side-walls partially destroyed to create the appearance of a picturesque ruin. In the same year a new church was erected at Cleigh, equidistant between Kilmore and the old church of Kilbride (No. 253), which was partially demolished.[7]

The medieval church was an oblong unicameral building, measuring 17·1 m from E to W by 6·1 m transversely within walls having a thickness of some 0·9 m. The walls are built of roughly-coursed rubble masonry, set in lime mortar and harled both internally and externally, with quoins and window-dressings of coarse-grained green sandstone similar in appearance

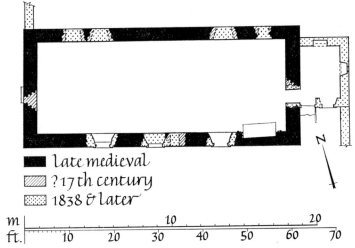

Fig. 143. Old Parish Church, Kilmore (No. 264); plan

to that found at the nearby quarries at Barrnacarry (No. 351) and Ardentallan (No. 349); the latter was specified as a source of freestone for repairs executed in 1859.[8] In the original arrangement the church was entered by a doorway placed near the centre of the S wall; the lower stones of the inner jambs of this opening remain *in situ*. The nave was lit by a single window set eccentrically in the W gable-wall, while the chancel was lit by single-light splayed windows in the N, E and S walls. All of these window-openings have suffered from subsequent alterations, and the SE window has been enlarged by the removal of its E jamb, although some of the original rybats were re-used. The W and NE windows retain their lintelled ingoes. The most notable feature of the interior is a large tomb-recess (Fig. 144, Pl. 31A) of late-medieval date at the E end of the S wall. This has a semicircular arch-head wrought with a deeply-undercut filleted roll-moulding flanked by shallow filleted rolls and hollows, all contained within a filleted hood-mould which has continuous dog-tooth ornament in the soffit. (Fig. 145). The hollows of the outer face of the arch

---

[1] *Origines Parochiales*, ii, part i, 133; cf. Blaeu's *Atlas* (Lorn).
[2] *Cal. Scot. Supp.*, ii, 7; *Origines Parochiales*, ii, part i, 104.
[3] *Stat. Acct.*, x (1794), 321; S.R.O., HR 727/1, Kilninver and Kilmelford Heritors' Minute-book, 1861–1927, minutes of meeting 21 July 1890.
[4] This feature is shown on the 25-inch O.S. map, Argyll, sheet cxxx, 3, surveyed in 1871.
[5] *Cal. Scot. Supp.*, ii, 104; *Origines Parochiales*, ii, part i, 119.
[6] Lorn Presbytery Minutes, vi (1829–39), pp. 358, 410.
[7] S.R.O., HR 526/5, Kilmore and Kilbride Heritors' Records, Building-Papers, *passim*.
[8] Ibid., specification for repairs, 1859.

contain irregularly-spaced ornamental carvings, some in the form of circular rosettes and others square with central bosses; the outer hollow also contains two short sections of dog-tooth ornament, while a further area of stone has been intended for such ornament, but left uncarved. The hood-mould terminates on the E in a carved stop, but the corresponding terminal on the W has been damaged. Set into the back of the recess there

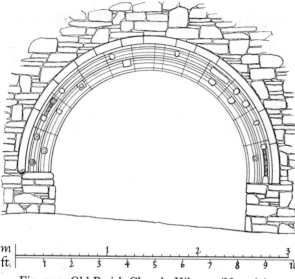

Fig. 144. Old Parish Church, Kilmore (No. 264); tomb-recess

is a mural tablet commemorating Isabella Campbell of Glenfeochan who died in 1844, and below this there is a tomb-chest of similar date. Modern plaster on the wall into which the tomb-recess is set makes it impossible to distinguish whether it was an original feature of the existing building, or whether it was inserted soon after the construction of the church.

In the post-Reformation period the church was adapted for Reformed worship by the insertion of wooden galleries, whose joist-holes are visible in both gable-walls. The medieval window-openings in these walls

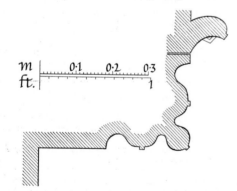

Fig. 145. Old Parish Church, Kilmore (No. 264); profile moulding of tomb-recess

were blocked, and doorways constructed at a higher level to provide access to the galleries. At the same period, the external opening of the medieval window at the E end of the N wall was enlarged and a new window formed immediately to the W, while a new doorway and window were formed at the W end of the same wall. The central doorway and the existing medieval window in the S wall remained in use at this period, and it is possible that an additional window was formed W of the doorway; this opening in its present form, however, is of 19th-century date. Another small window, now blocked, was inserted at a high level immediately E of the doorway. The pulpit was evidently placed at the centre of the N wall. A bird-cage belfry was added to the W gable, probably in the 18th century; although entire in c. 1900,[1] this has now disappeared.

The church retained its 17th-century arrangement until 1838, when the existing door and window in the S wall were enlarged to form tall arch-pointed openings having chamfered jambs, and a similar window was inserted W of the doorway. At the same time an additional doorway was formed in the E gable-wall, causing the removal of most of the blocked medieval E window, and a single-storied extension was built against the N part of this wall to serve as a porch and also a vestry. This building obstructed the upper doorway in the E gable, which was therefore contracted to become a window, and new doorways giving access to the galleries were made at the E and W ends of the N wall. The fore-stair leading to the E gallery obscured the altered medieval N window, which was blocked at this period. In 1859 the S doorway was altered into a window similar to those which already existed in the S wall.

FUNERARY MONUMENTS

Medieval

The following five stones are in the churchyard.

(1) Parallel-sided slab, 1·84 m in length by 0·50 m in width (Fig. 146). At the top, within a double plain border, there is a cross consisting of four circles, and below this the hilt of a sword with a round pommel and canted quillons with expanded ends. There is no sign of either a cross-shaft or sword-blade and it is uncertain whether or not these ever existed. The initials D M C have been added at a later date, probably in the 17th century. *Late 13th—early 14th century.*

(2) Tapered slab, with plain bevelled edges, measuring about 1·80 m in length by 0·59 m in width at the top. The border consists of a row of elongated nail-head ornament between two plain mouldings, and within this there are three panels separated in each case by a two-cord plait. In the uppermost panel there is a figure of a man set in a niche crowned by dragons' heads: he wears an aketon and a conical bascinet, and is armed with a sword and spear. The central panel contains a pair of opposed quadrupeds, and the lower one an overall pattern of foliaceous interlace. *Loch Awe school, 14th—15th century.*

---

[1] Cf. photograph in Faichney, *Oban*, opp. p. 46.

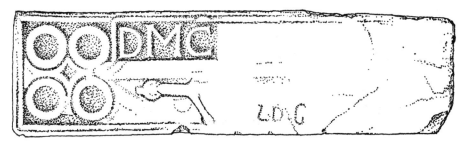

Fig. 146. Old Parish Church, Kilmore (No. 264); cross-decorated stone (scale 1:15)

(3) Tapered slab, 1·86 m in length by 0·56 m in width at the head. The border is unusual, consisting of a double-strand plait between two plain mouldings. At the top there is a quadruped facing left, and beneath this a centrally-placed sword with lobated pommel and canted quillons. Flanking the sword, and linked to the legs and tail of the quadruped, there are asymmetrical plant-scrolls displaying a few variegated leaves. *Loch Awe school, 14th—15th century.*

(4) Tapered slab, 1·94 m in length by 0·52 m wide at the head; very worn. The border is the same as on (1) above. Within this the decoration has been completely obliterated at the top of the stone, but otherwise it consists simply of interlaced plant-scrolls of Loch Awe type. *Loch Awe school, 14th—15th century.*

(5) Tapered slab with pointed base, measuring 1·89 m in length by 0·52 m in width at the head. It is in a very worn condition, the only visible decoration being faint traces of a small figure of a man similar to the one on (2) above. *Loch Awe school, 14th—15th century.*

Post-Reformation

(6) A mural monument, which bears a Latin inscription commemorating James Campbell, minister of Kilmore, who died in 1756 aged 47, and two of his children, is built into the outer face of the W gable-wall, concealing the exterior of the blocked medieval W window. The inscribed tablet is surmounted by a semi-circular pediment carved in relief with an open book and two butterflies.

(7) The most interesting of the numerous 19th-century monuments in the graveyard is a table-tomb commemorating Malcolm McPherson, shepherd, Midmun, who died in 1840; the lower edge of the slab bears the name of the sculptor, D Smith, Oban.

887249   NM 82 SE   June 1970

265. Chapel and Burial-ground, Kilmun (Site). This site is occupied by an enclosure of irregular plan measuring about 30 m by 26 m over all. Within the enclosure, which is surrounded by the scanty remains of a dry-stone wall, there may be seen some traces of a sub-rectangular building, presumably a chapel, measuring about 6·7 m from NW to SE by about 3·5 m transversely within walls some 0·9 m in thickness (Fig. 147). An entrance-doorway appears to have existed towards the NW end of the NE wall. There are no visible tombstones.

This burial-ground is supposed to have been used during the period in which Innis Chonnell Castle (No. 292) was inhabited by the Campbell family. The dedication was evidently to St Munn, who is said to have been the patron saint of the early Campbell lords of Loch Awe.[1]

971145   NM 91 SE   May 1968

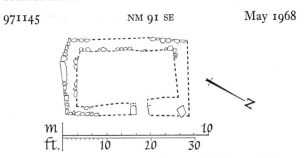

Fig. 147. Chapel and burial-ground, Kilmun (site) (No. 265); plan

266. Parish Church and Burial-ground, Kilninver. The medieval church of this parish, which first comes on record in the middle of the 13th century and was dedicated to St Bean, was situated on a hill-top about 200 m NE of the present church.[2] The parish was united with that of Kilmelford, possibly before the Reformation.[3] In 1783 it was reported that 'the Church at Killninver is in the very worst repair .... It is situated on an eminence exposed much to the storm, and when the wind blows the minister cannot be heard tho' the church be very small'. Some years later John Campbell of Lochend obtained from John Clerk, mason in Oban, a plan for rebuilding the church on its present site, and the building was completed in 1792. It was re-roofed in 1891–2, and at that date a porch and a session-house were added.[4]

The plan of *c*. 1790 shows a rectangular building having internal dimensions of 11·9 m by 5·5 m, with an

---

[1] Name Book, No. 53, p. 142; *SHR*, x (1913), 32–4.
[2] *Origines Parochiales*, ii, part i, 105; *Cal. Scot. Supp.*, ii, 112.
[3] Scott, *Fasti*, iv, 96.
[4] S.R.O., Breadalbane Collection, GD 112/12/1, letter from J Campbell, 3 September 1783; ibid., GD 112/51/15, Church Papers; ibid., GD 112/9/51, Argyll Rental, Crop 1791; Groome, *Ordnance Gazetteer*, 943.

entrance in one gable-wall and another near the pulpit, which is placed centrally against one of the side-walls. The only windows were two large openings flanking the pulpit, and two smaller windows in the same wall below the galleries, which were reached by forestairs at each end of the opposite wall. The dimensions of the existing building are somewhat different, being 11·6 m from NW to SE by 6·5 m transversely within walls 0·6 m in thickness. Although it is probable that the masonry dates from 1792, the existing windows and all of the internal fittings date from 1891 or later.

The site of the medieval church is now marked by a small disused burial-ground. The earliest stone that bears a legible inscription is dated 1721. There are also a number of other 18th-century stones, including a large recumbent slab showing traces of relief-carving and an inscription, now altogether illegible. The burial-ground may formerly have extended a little further to the N, where what seem to be tombstones can be seen beyond the 19th-century enclosure-wall, and this is consistent with the report of 1783 which states that 'the churchyard . . . . has never been enclosed—the dead are buried in the open fields'.[1]

824217 (Church)   NM 82 SW   April 1970
826218 (Burial-ground)

267. Cathedral of St Moluag and Parish Church, Lismore. The remains of the cathedral church of the medieval diocese of Argyll, frequently known as Kilmaluag, are situated partly within a churchyard whose boundaries were defined in 1760[2] and partly in adjacent glebe-land to the W. They comprise a much-restored aisleless choir which serves as the parish church, the site of a NE chapel or sacristy, and the excavated foundations of an aisleless nave and added W tower (Fig. 148, Pl. 32). Although the cathedral probably occupied the site of an earlier church dedicated to St Moluag (or

Lugaidh), an Irish saint who founded a religious community on Lismore in the second half of the 6th century, there are no remains which can with certainty be ascribed to the Early Christian period. It is, however, interesting to note that the field-boundaries to N, E and S of the site conform to the perimeter of a rough circle having a diameter of about 240 m; this may perpetuate the line of a *vallum* comparable with those which enclosed certain early monastic sites.[3]

ARCHITECTURAL DESCRIPTION

The medieval nave and choir had a combined length of some 38 m and a width of 7·2 m within walls having an average thickness, above plinth-level, of 0·95 m. The masonry is of local limestone- and whinstone-rubble, with dressings of sandstone from the Ardtornish quarries, and the excavated footings of the nave-walls incorporate substantial slabs of slate. A thick coat of harling on the outer walls of the choir, and internal plasterwork, conceal much of the medieval masonry, although plaster which had obscured certain medieval features in the S and W walls was removed in 1956–7.

THE CHOIR. In its present form, as the parish church, the choir of the medieval cathedral has internal dimensions of 15·6 m from E to W by 7·2 m transversely, a size which it attained in the late medieval period when a massive stone pulpitum was built at the W end, probably replacing an earlier screen of timber. Without excavation

---
[1] Loc. cit.
[2] Carmichael, *Lismore,* 145.
[3] The Commissioners are indebted to Mr A D S MacDonald for this information. The boundaries recorded on the O.S. maps of the 19th century are identical with those shown in an estate survey of 1778 by G Langlands, preserved in a 19th-century copy in S.R.O., RHP 8180. Cf. Carmichael, *Lismore,* 145, for a reference to the large extent of 'the precincts of the old Cathedral of Lismore'. For circular *valla,* cf. Thomas, C, *The Early Christian Archaeology of North Britain* (1971), 38–43.

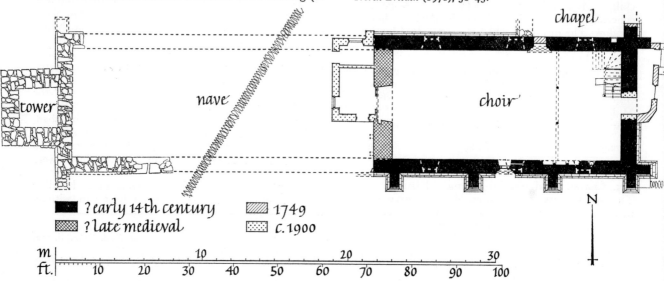

Fig. 148. Cathedral of St Moluag and Parish Church, Lismore (No. 267); plan

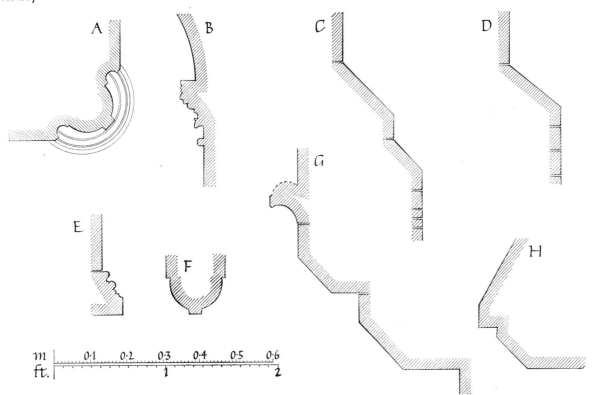

Fig. 149. Cathedral of St Moluag and Parish Church, Lismore (No. 267); profile mouldings: A, F, sedilia shafts; B, sedilia capital; C, choir plinth; D, nave plinth; E, sedilia base; G, north choir doorway; H, window-jamb

in the churchyard, it is not possible to ascertain what proportion of the original building was occupied by the choir, but if the E face of the pulpitum is in the position of the earlier screen, this would explain the existence of a short section of wall left standing to the W of the SW buttress. The height of the side-walls of the choir was reduced by between 1·8 m and 3·1 m about 1749.[1]

The S wall of the choir is divided into three bays by projecting buttresses which have sloping offsets at a height of about 2·0 m above plinth-level; the upper parts are diminished in width, and terminate some 0·6 m below wall-head level. At the NE and SE angles of the choir there are pairs of buttresses of similar form. Although the upper parts of these buttresses were probably truncated and altered during the 18th century, they are original features of the building, and a double-member sandstone plinth (Fig. 149c), which runs along the choir-walls, returns round each one. Because of a rise in the level of the churchyard, this plinth is now concealed below turf-level. Each bay contains one round-headed window of 18th-century date, possibly replacing medieval windows in the same position,[2] while in the central bay there is an original round-headed doorway (Pl. 33A), which remained in use until 1900. This is of two chamfered orders having a filleted hood-mould terminating in greatly-worn human heads; that to the W wears a female head-dress.

The W wall of the choir, which has a thickness of

1·3 m, is pierced by a large semicircular-headed doorway whose dressings are of a greenish sandstone similar in appearance to that found at Barrnacarry and Ardentallan (Nos. 351 and 349). To the S of this opening, at a height of 2·3 m above present ground-level, there are two corbels, one having a moulded lip. A third corbel, which formerly existed near the N end of the same wall, is shown in photographs taken in 1882 (Pl. 32B);[3] its position is now concealed by the roof of the modern boiler-house that is built against the wall. These features probably formed part of a pulpitum which was fitted either with a timber beam carrying a rood, or with a projecting timber gallery.[4] It is probable that there was originally a large opening above the pulpitum, and that this was blocked when the wall became an external one. Until the church was restored in 1900, the doorway in the W wall served as the principal entrance; the gable above contained two rectangular windows lighting a W

---

[1] *Stat. Acct.*, i (1791), 491; Brown, A L and Duncan, A A M, 'The Cathedral Church of Lismore', *TSES*, xv (1957–65), 41–50.
[2] The eccentric position of the window in the W bay may possibly be explained by the retention of one jamb of a narrower medieval window.
[3] Photographs in Erskine Beveridge Collection, N.M.R.S.
[4] Corbels occupying a similar position may be seen in the W face of the W tower-arch at Ross Errilly Friary, Co. Galway (Champneys, A C, *Irish Ecclesiastical Architecture* (1910), pl. xcvii). Cf. also Ardchattan Priory (No. 217).

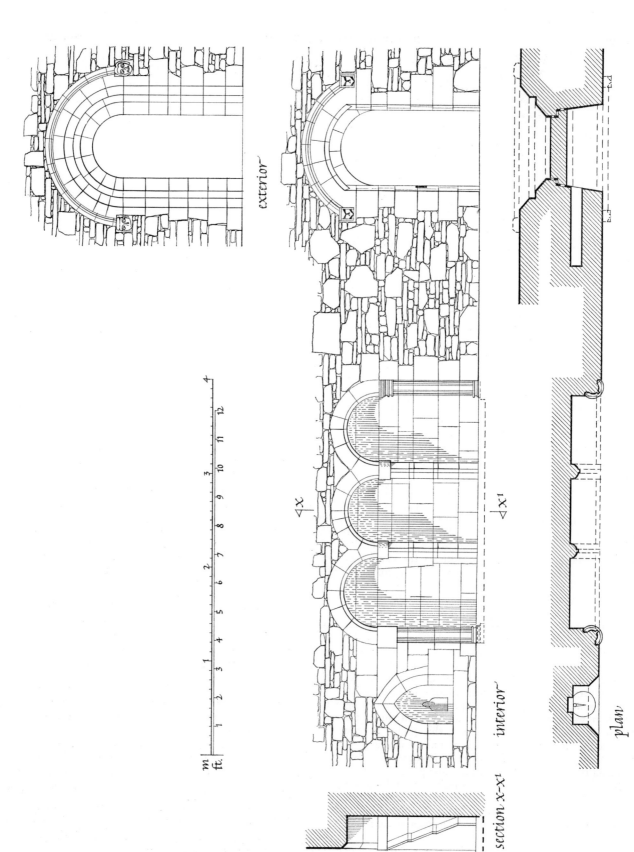

exterior

interior

section x–x¹

plan

m
ft.

Fig. 150. Cathedral of St Moluag and Parish Church, Lismore (No. 267); piscina, sedilia and doorway in S choir wall

gallery, and was surmounted by a bird-cage belfry (Pl. 32B). At the time of the restoration the latter feature was moved to the E gable, while the windows were replaced by a central circular window and the doorway enclosed within a lean-to vestry.

The appearance of the E gable-wall also was altered in 1900. The previous arrangement, which was probably of mid-18th-century date, comprised an open forestair leading to a gallery-door, above which was a round-headed window.[1] At the restoration, a new principal entrance-doorway was formed in the E gable-wall of the church, and the outer walls of the forestair were incorporated into a porch, while the door and window above were replaced by a three-light window within a round-headed recess. Although this restoration provided an opportunity for examination of the remains of the medieval E window that presumably existed in this wall, and indeed for the examination of other parts of the medieval fabric, there is no record of any such investigations.

Except for three round-headed windows which were formed in 1900, the only feature now visible in the N wall is an aumbry, rebated externally, at the E end of the wall. This feature, and a blocked doorway of medieval date inside the choir, have been interpreted as evidence for the existence in this position of a chapel, possibly serving as a sacristy and chapter-house. Excavations conducted in 1950–3 failed to locate the N wall of this chapel,[2] but in 1970 the return of the W wall was exposed by the removal of turf, immediately W of the blocked doorway. The buttress at the E end of the N wall of the choir was identified as the truncated E wall of the chapel, giving an internal length from E to W of 6·3 m. The double-member plinth of the choir returns along the outer faces of both walls of the chapel, which clearly formed part of the original structure.

The existing internal arrangements of the church (Pl. 33B), including a communion-table and pulpit at the W end, and a large E gallery reached by a timber stair in the NE angle, date from the restoration of 1900. The earlier arrangement, which was probably of mid-18th-century date, comprised a long central communion-table with benches, narrow E and N galleries reached by the external forestair against the E wall, and a wider W gallery reached by a stair in the NW angle. The pulpit stood against the S wall, immediately E of the medieval

doorway which remained in use for the minister.[3] Several features of the medieval choir remain *in situ*, notably the piscina and triple sedilia in the S wall (Fig. 150, Pl. 33D), and the N and S doors already referred to, all of which are executed in Ardtornish sandstone. Their architectural detail, which constitutes the principal evidence for dating the building, appears to be derived from common 13th-century types, but displays no connection with known work of that period elsewhere in Argyll, and may best be attributed to the early 14th century. All these features display similar masons' marks (Fig. 151) but their execution varies in quality.

The piscina-bowl, damaged but having its drain-hole intact, is formed in the sill of a broad-chamfered lancet-pointed niche, in whose rear-wall there is a small cusped recess to accommodate the cruets (Pl. 33E). The bays of the sedilia (Fig. 149A, B, E, F) are formed by three chamfered semicircular arches, springing from moulded shafts to E and W, and at the centre from the completely plain capitals of two shafts that separate the bays. These shafts are, in the lower part, simple half-rounds with a broad fillet, but they rise obliquely outwards in three steps which are repeated in the panelling that decorates their sides. The E and W jambs are wrought with filleted rolls set between flanking hollows; the W shaft has a capital whose mouldings are flat and shallow in character, while the capital of the E shaft has probably never been carved. The bases of these shafts are partially obscured because of a rise in the floor-level, which is probably about 0·6 m above its medieval level; the E base is water-holding in type, while the W base is simple in character.[4]

The inner jambs of the medieval S door (Fig. 150, Pl. 33C) are wrought with a sharp arris, but the segmental arch-head is chamfered and the springers are carefully executed. A filleted hood-mould terminates in corbel-stops which, although derived from a purely decorative type common in England in the 13th century,[5] are here treated as formalised faces with eyes, nose and mouth. In the E ingo there is a deep socket for a draw-bar, but no corresponding socket is visible in the W ingo. In contrast to the internal treatment of this door, that in the N wall (Fig. 152, Pl. 34B), which led into the now-vanished sacristy, is of some elaboration, comprising a lancet-arch of two broad-chamfered orders, within a hood-mould (Fig. 149G) similar in profile to that of the S door. The stops of the hood-mould are human heads,

---

[1] This arrangement is shown in a photograph, taken by Dr J Mitchison, in Bodleian Library, MS Top. Eccl. b 33, p. xv, and in a plan of the church dated 1877 (S.R.O., RHP 8188); cf. *Eccles. Arch.*, ii, fig. 668.

[2] *TSES*, xv (1957–65), 48.

[3] The arrangement of the interior before 1900 is shown in S.R.O., RHP 8188, and in two photographs taken in 1882 in the Erskine Beveridge Collection, N.M.R.S.

[4] Traces of red and black paint, visible on the arch-heads of the sedilia and on the head-stops of the N choir-door, are associated with a decorative scheme of mid-19th-century date shown in Beveridge's photographs.

[5] This feature occurs at Dunblane Cathedral in the corbel-tables of the nave, probably dating from the first half of the 14th century.

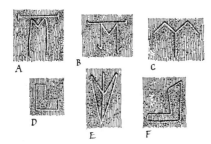

Fig. 151. Cathedral of St Moluag and Parish Church, Lismore (No. 267); masons' marks: A, C, E, south choir doorway; B, north choir doorway; D, sedilia; F, piscina (scale 1:5)

carved in high relief and both somewhat mutilated; that to the W depicts a bishop wearing a low mitre, while the other may represent a cleric with tonsured hair (Pl. 34A, C).

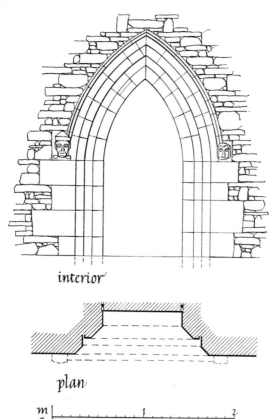

interior

plan

Fig. 152. Cathedral of St Moluag and Parish Church, Lismore (No. 267); N choir doorway

The archway in the late medieval pulpitum (Pl. 33F) that forms the W wall of the present church is slightly splayed internally, having a maximum width of 2·5 m. The soffit of the arch preserves clear marks of the plank-centering employed during its construction. In the S ingo there is a shallow socket of uncertain purpose.

THE NAVE. The excavated remains of the nave (Pl. 33A) are separated from the W wall of the choir by an area of the churchyard, 12·2 m in length on the S side, within which no excavation has been possible.[1] The nave had an internal length, after the construction of the pulpitum which encroached on its E part, of 20·7 m, and a width of 7·2 m, identical with that of the choir. Its S and W walls were preserved to a maximum height of only 0·2 m above the sandstone plinth which, unlike that of the choir, was of a single member (Fig. 149D); at a depth of 0·6 m below the level of the plinth there was a projecting foundation-course of slate. A continuation

of the W gable-wall to N and S formed two buttresses, the only ones to be identified. The S doorway, which had a daylight-opening of about 1·0 m, was of two orders, the outer order having a shallow curved profile; only the lowest stone of the outer order of each jamb remains *in situ*, but the position of the inner order of the W jamb is marked by a patch of mortar. The threshold was formed by large slabs of limestone. During the course of the excavations, a single fragment of a window-rybat, wrought with a 0·12 m chamfer and an external rebate, was discovered in loose debris within the nave; at the date of visit this was lying beside the SW angle of the choir. This detail (Fig. 149H) is characteristic of the first half of the 13th century, and certain other features, notably the differences in the plinths and buttresses, indicate that choir and nave may not be of the same period. The moulding of the S door of the nave, however, is not consistent with a 13th-century date, and it is possible that the variations referred to were due to the hasty or less elaborate construction of the nave after the completion of the choir.

At an uncertain date, probably in the late medieval period, a small tower, measuring 2·6 m square within walls 1·2 m in thickness and having no means of access at ground-level, was erected against the W gable-wall of the nave. When the foundations of this structure were excavated, it was discovered that the adjacent sections of the plinth of the nave-wall had been removed to facilitate the insertion of the tusking of the N and S walls of the tower.

HISTORICAL NOTE

The history of St Moluag's monastic foundation is obscure, depending on stray references in early Irish annals and martyrologies, and a brief life of the saint in the Aberdeen Breviary of 1509. The names of some of his successors as abbot are recorded, the last being of mid-8th-century date. A certain amount is known, however, about the history of the medieval cathedral and diocese, which have been the subject of several recent studies.[2]

The diocese of Argyll was formed from part of the very extensive diocese of Dunkeld between 1183 and 1189, and Lismore was probably selected as the site of the cathedral at that time. As early as 1249 there were proposals that the see should be moved to a more accessible church on the mainland. The endowments of the see were few, and the chapter was not fully organised until the last quarter of the 14th century. Although donations to the fabric of the cathedral church are stipulated as penalties in several transactions during the 14th and 15th centuries,[3] there is little specific informa-

---

[1] For a full account of the excavations of 1950–3, cf. *TSES*, xv (1957–65), 41–50; the Commissioners are indebted to Prof. A L Brown, University of Glasgow, for additional information about the excavations. Portions of the excavated area were re-exposed by members of the Commission's staff in 1970, to facilitate recording.
[2] Ibid.; Carmichael, *Lismore, passim*; *PSAS*, xc (1956–7), 209–10; Watt, *Fasti*, 26–36; Cowan, *Parishes*, 134; *Origines Parochiales*, ii, part i, 159–63.
[3] *Origines Parochiales*, ii, part i, 160.

tion about the buildings and their condition. In 1411 the Pope granted revenues to the cathedral, in response to an episcopal petition reciting that, because of wars, famines and plagues, the church lacked furnishings and required repair.[1]

In the records of the late medieval period, the church's cathedral status is less prominent than its use as the parish church of Lismore. Although a visit by Bishop George Lauder is recorded in 1452,[2] it was claimed by James IV, writing to Pope Julius II in 1512, that the cathedral had seen no capitular life for centuries, and was in ruins. He recommended the transfer of the see to the former Cistercian abbey of Saddell, whose revenues had recently been annexed to the bishopric of Argyll,[3] but nothing came of this proposal. The construction of the pulpitum may possibly be ascribed to this period, and the building certainly remained more intact than is stated in the royal petition. Attention has recently been drawn[4] to a notarial document of 1531 recording the installation of John Makcaw, a royal servant, as archdeacon of Argyll, in the presence of a Gaelic-speaking curate and his parishioners. There is no evidence for the use of the building other than as a parish church in the post-Reformation period, and the nave was probably allowed to become ruinous before the end of the 16th century.

Except for a brief period during the 17th century, the parish of Lismore included the districts of Kingairloch, in N Argyll, and Appin. In practice, however, Appin was served in the medieval period by its own chapel at Keil (No. 250), and from 1641 at latest by a church at Tynribbie (No. 214). The limited resources of the island of Lismore were insufficient to maintain the church in the 17th century, and in 1679 it was 'altogether without a roof'. The minister stated on this occasion that the people of Appin and Duror would not contribute to its repair because they had their own church.[5] A comprehensive remodelling, whose results have been described above, was carried out in 1749, and the limits of the churchyard were defined in 1760. Quantities of dressed sandstone were removed at this period, probably from the ruined nave; such masonry has been identified in the walls of the manse, built in 1750,[6] and can be seen inside the barn that is situated NW of the manse, where one fragment is wrought with a roll-moulding.

Plans for the restoration of the church were prepared by an unnamed architect in 1894,[7] and executed in a less elaborate manner about 1900. The only subsequent alteration has been the removal of modern plaster from the pulpitum archway and from other medieval features of the choir, carried out under the direction of the late Ian G Lindsay in 1956.

Funerary Monuments and other Carved Stones
Medieval

Numbers 3, 4, 5 and 13 are inside the church, number 4 being let into the floor under the stair leading to the gallery at the E end; the remainder are in the churchyard.

(1) Tapered slab, 1·71 m long by 0·39 m wide at the head. At the top a stag with a ?bird perched on its hind-

quarters is being attacked by a hound. Underneath this there is a row of three ring-knots linked together, and then a sheathed sword flanked by double plant-scrolls, while at the foot of the slab is a casket and a pair of shears. The sword has a lobated pommel and canted quillons, and the scabbard ends in a chape. *Iona school, 14th—15th century.*

(2) Parallel-sided slab with bevelled edges, measuring 0·47 m in width over all. It is now only 1·55 m long, the top of the stone, as well as one of the bottom corners, having broken off. A narrow central panel contains a double scroll incorporating the palmette device, while in the right-hand margin there is a sword of Viking ancestry with lobated pommel, a short horizontal guard, and a scabbard decorated with a thin strip of cable pattern. The border and edges of the slab are enriched in each case with a single row of elongated nail-head ornament. *Iona school, 14th—15th century.*

(3) Upper portion of a similar slab to the last, 0·46 m long. The only differences are that the scroll issues from the jaws of an animal and contains clusters of trefoils in place of the palmette, while the sword in the right-hand margin is balanced by a tau-headed stave (cf. (4) below). The tau-head is formed by two dragons which confront one another on either side of the shaft. *Iona school, 14th—15th century.*

(4) Tapered slab, 1·73 m long by 0·46 m wide at the head (Pl. 34D). Beneath a foliated cross there are incised representations of a pair of tau-headed staves, similar to, but more stylized than, the one on (3) above. The shafts expand slightly towards the foot and terminate in long spikes. These liturgical instruments may indicate that the stone marked the grave of one or more 'chantors' (*precentors*) of the cathedral.[8] *Probably Iona school, 14th—15th century.*

(5) Upper half of a slab measuring 0·98 m in length by 0·37 m in width. Within a double plain moulding there is a cross at the top, composed largely of plaitwork, and below this is an overall pattern of interlocking plant-scrolls. *Probably Iona school, 14th—15th century.*

(6) Tapered slab, the bottom of which has broken off. It measures 1·78 m in length by 0·48 m in width at the head. Within a wide border, consisting of two plain mouldings separated by a row of elongated nail-head ornament, there is a sword with a similar hilt to that on (1) above, but longer in the blade. The sword is enclosed by plant-scrolls of simple design, which are linked to the hind-legs and tail of an animal placed above the pommel. *Loch Awe school, 14th—15th century.*

---

[1] *Highland Papers*, iv, 159-61.
[2] Craigie, W A (ed.), *The Asloan Manuscript*, Scottish Text Society (1923-5), i, 222.
[3] Hannay, R K, Mackie, R L and Spilman, A, *The Letters of James the Fourth 1505-1513*, SHS (1953), 245-6. Cf. *Inventory of Argyll*, i, No. 296.
[4] *The Innes Review*, xxi (1970), 80-1.
[5] Lorn Presbytery Minutes, i (1651-81), pp. 319-20; Carmichael, *Lismore*, 137.
[6] Carmichael, *Lismore*, 100-1.
[7] S.R.O., RHP 8182-4.
[8] Cf. the discussion of this and of the previous stone in Steer and Bannerman, *Monumental Sculpture*.

(7) Tapered slab, 2·02 m long by 0·70 m wide at the head; it is broken across and badly worn. The border is enriched with elongated nail-head ornament, but within this all that can be seen is a small effigy of an armed man standing in a niche crowned by dragons' heads, and traces of a pair of indeterminate creatures situated immediately underneath the niche. The man is wearing a pointed bascinet and an aketon, and carries a sword and spear. *Loch Awe school, 14th—15th century.*

(8) Lid of a tomb-chest, parallel-sided and measuring 1·66 m in length by 0·68 m in width (Pl. 34E). Down the centre there is a fine representation of a two-handed sword, or claymore. It has slightly inclined quillons with pierced quatrefoil terminals, a round pommel, and a long langet. Above the quillons are a lion (or dragon) and a griffin, and stemming from their tails is a mass of foliage which fills all the remaining space within the border. The border is enriched with a row of debased dog-tooth ornament. The sculptor who carved this slab was also responsible for (9) below, and for two tomb-chests at Kilmichael Glassary.[1] *c. 1500—1560.*

(9) Lid of a tomb-chest, 1·69 m in length. Although it is slightly tapered, it is too wide at the foot (0·60 m) to have been a recumbent slab. The decoration is heavily worn but has been similar to that on (8) above, which is by the same carver. At the top there is a secondary inscription which contains the date 1661 and a name, possibly M D[O]W. *c. 1500—1560.*

(10) Tapered slab, 1·86 m long by 0·43 m wide at the head. It is broken across, and part of the decoration at the foot has scaled off. Within a niche at the top of the stone there is a small figure of a woman, facing the front and with arms akimbo. She is wearing a close-fitting hood, and an ankle-length kirtle over which is an outer garment, possibly a cote-hardie, with long flaps (tippets) hanging from the elbows. Beneath the niche there is a band of interlace, and then an overall pattern of interlocking plant-scrolls. A crude piece of work by a local carver, the slab presumably dates to within the period 1400—1560.

(11) Tapered slab, 1·60 m long by 0·40 m wide at the head. Broken across, it has lost the top right-hand corner and is badly worn. There is a border consisting of two plain mouldings, but within this all that can now be seen is a small effigy of an armed man, similar to the one on (7) above but not standing in a niche, and, beneath the effigy, some slight traces of an interlace pattern. Like (11), this is the clumsy product of a local carver. *Probably 15th century.*

(12) Fragment of a slab, 1·50 m long. It bears the deeply incised outline of the upper half of a small figure of a man, possibly a priest, standing beneath what may have been intended for a canopy. Another crude local product. *Probably 1400—1560.*

(13) Parallel-sided slab (possibly the lid of a tomb-chest), 1·89 m long and 0·60 m wide. The two longer edges are decorated longitudinally with key- and fret-patterns. The upper surface has a wide plain border and is divided by a label of similar width into two panels of unequal size. The decoration on these panels has been

completely obliterated. There are no parallels for this kind of slab in the Early Christian period, and it may even be of post-medieval date; a local origin seems likely.

(14) Fragment of the side of a similar slab to (13) above. It bears traces of mortar, showing that it has been re-used as building material at some time. In addition to running key- and fret-patterns on the edge, some slight indications of interlacing can be seen on the border. Like the preceding stone it is probably of medieval or later date.

(15) Some 11 m from the SE corner of the churchyard there is a cross-base which may be in its original position since the longer sides face E and W. It is 0·77 m long by 0·59 m wide, and the slot for the cross is 0·34 m long by 0·08 m wide.

Post-Reformation

(16-17) Only two of the post-Reformation memorials call for mention. The first (16) is a much-weathered recumbent slab of sandstone which lies in the churchyard. This incorporates an inscription and an heraldic achievement, both now illegible, together with a representation of two angels sounding trumpets. This stone probably dates from the first half of the 18th century. The second memorial (17) takes the form of a marble panel (Pl. 34F) built into the external face of the E wall of the church. This commemorates James MacGregor of Correctled, who died in 1759, and his wife Marjory, daughter of Alexander Campbell of Airds, who died in 1780. The monument was erected in 1787. At the top of the panel a full armorial achievement is carved in relief, the shield being charged, for MacGregor: a fir-tree surmounted by a sword in bend, on the point an imperial crown in the dexter chief canton.

'FONT'. Near the cross-base there is a rock with an artificial hollow, 0·13 m in diameter, on the top. This is apparently the 'Font' marked on the O.S. map.

CHAPEL (SITE). This chapel is said to have stood immediately to the W of the burial-ground, close to the office-houses of the manse.[2] There are no visible remains.

STANDING STONE, NUNNERY AND SANCTUARY (SITE). The first of these is an erratic boulder of granite roughly shaped in the form of a cross, which stands about 60 m S of the E wall of the cathedral. It measures 0·80 m in height, 0·60 m in width at base, and 0·40 m in width at the top. This stone, called in Gaelic, 'Clach na h-eala' ('the stone of the swan'), is supposed to have marked a boundary in connection with certain rights of sanctuary associated with an adjacent building, of which the site is indicated on the O.S. 6-inch map. Here, the remains of 'some ancient walls' were to be seen in 1841, but these had disappeared by the time that officers of the Ordnance Survey visited the place about thirty years later.[3] There

[1] Drummond, *Monuments*, pls. lxx and lxxiii.
[2] *NSA*, vii (Argyll), 243; Name Book, No. 22, p. 89.
[3] *NSA*, vii (Argyll), 242; Name Book, No. 22, p. 89.

is no evidence of the existence of a nunnery on the island, and the author of the entry in the *New Statistical Account* records only the tradition that the building was a sanctuary 'whither malefactors of every description fled for refuge, during the darkness of past ages'.[1] No confirmation of this tradition has been found.

861435   NM 84 SE   June 1970

268. Old Parish Church, Muckairn, Taynuilt. The fragmentary remains of the former parish-church stand immediately to the S of its early 19th-century successor (No. 269). Parts of the S and N walls remain, together with a substantial portion of the E gable-wall, but the

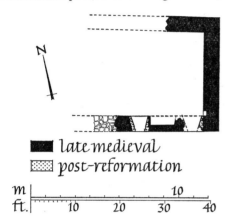

late medieval
post-reformation

Fig. 153. Old Parish Church, Muckairn, Taynuilt (No. 268); plan

entire western portion of the church has disappeared so that its original length cannot now be ascertained. The building measures 5·6 m in width within walls about 1·0 m in thickness (Fig. 153). The masonry is of roughly-coursed local rubble, while the dressings, nearly all of which have been robbed, appear to have been composed of yellow sandstone. The external wall-faces are heavily overgrown with ivy and other vegetation, and this makes examination difficult. The upper part of the E gable-wall is intaken externally by a splayed scarcement, while there are some traces of an internal scarcement at about the level of the main wall-head. According to Howson,[2] the E wall contains a window, but if so this is now concealed by vegetation.

A number of openings occur in the S wall, the most interesting of these being a segmental-arched recess, 1·7 m in width, which probably housed a tomb-chest.[3] To the E of this there was a window and to the W a high-level doorway, which probably gave access to a gallery. Both these openings are probably to be associated with a post-Reformation reconstruction of the building. Part of the splayed jamb of a third window can be seen at the W end of the surviving portion of the S wall. There is also an aumbry in the E wall, close to the SE corner, at a height of about 0·8 m above the present floor-level.

It is not easy to date the church precisely, but if the tomb-recess in the S wall is an original feature, which

seems likely, the building may probably be ascribed to the later Middle Ages. This attribution is supported by the author of an early description of Muckairn, probably compiled in the late 17th century, who states that a church was built on this site 'shortly before the Reformation'.[4]

This church served the former parish of Muckairn, or Kilespickerill,[5] which was united to that of Ardchattan in 1637. It has been suggested that, prior to the construction of the building described above, the parish-church was situated at Kilmaronag, near Connel, where there is some evidence of an early ecclesiastical site[7] (cf. No. 262), but this seems unlikely. Moreover, the existence of an earlier church on the present site, namely Kilespickerill, is recorded in a mid-14th-century charter, and is further vouched for by a local tradition related at about the end of the 17th century.[7]

005309   NN 03 SW   July 1970

269. Parish Church, Muckairn, Taynuilt. This is a plain oblong building measuring 18·2 m from E to W by 7·8 m transversely within walls about 1·0 m in thickness; there is a contemporary two-storeyed outshot at the E end (Fig. 154, Pl. 35B). The masonry is of coursed rubble with buff-coloured sandstone quoins and dressings possibly emanating from Ardtornish. Most of the rubble facework is of grey Bonawe granite, but an igneous rock of reddish hue is also used, particularly in the lowermost courses of the N wall. The roof is gable-ended and slated, the W gable being surmounted by a bird-cage belfry having a stepped roof and ball-finial. The church is lit by large Gothic windows in the side-walls (Fig. 155). These have four-centred arch-heads, and the openings are mullioned and transomed, the small lozenge-shaped glazing-panes being contained within cast-iron frames.

The interior (Pl. 35C) has been recast more than once, but in the original arrangement there was probably a gallery at each end, the pulpit standing against the centre of the S wall. The W portion of the church and the W gallery were entered, as they are today, by means of a centrally placed doorway in the W gable-wall, and an internal stone staircase at the SW corner. The gallery is supported upon timber columns and the front is panelled and corniced. The lower part of the outshot at the E end of the building, now a vestry, probably served as an entrance-porch to the E end of the church, the E gallery being approached by means of a staircase corresponding to the one at the W end. From this gallery, which no longer exists, access was obtained to

[1] Loc. cit.
[2] Howson, *Antiquities*, 94.
[3] Howson (loc. cit.) records the existence of a 'small illegible inscription' above the recess.
[4] *NSA*, vii (Argyll), 512.
[5] The name has been explained as a corruption of 'Cill Easpuig Chaorrail', the dedication being to the Irish saint St Cairrell (*TSES*, v (1915–18), 53; but cf. Mackinlay, *Non-Scriptural Dedications*, 20, and *NSA*, vii (Argyll), 512).
[6] *Origines Parochiales*, ii, part i, 132.
[7] *Highland Papers*, ii, 142; *NSA*, vii (Argyll), 512.

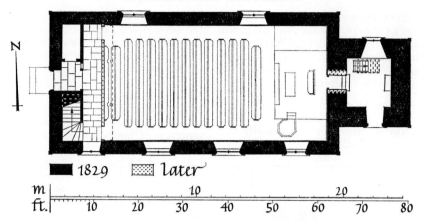

Fig. 154. Parish Church, Muckairn, Taynuilt (No. 269); plan

a small retiring-room situated over the entrance-porch; this is provided with a plain stone fireplace.

The church was erected in 1829 at the expense of General Campbell of Lochnell, the principal heritor, the total cost being £993 14s 6d. The design appears to be a slightly more elaborate version of the one employed by Thomas Telford for the construction of the contemporary 'Parliamentary kirks' in the Highlands (cf. No. 244).[1]

BELL. The present bell seems to be of fairly recent manufacture, but an older bell (Pl. 35F) is preserved within the church. This measures 0·43 m in height and has a diameter of 0·41 m at base; it bears the inscription: GIFTED BY SIR DUNCAN CAMPBELL / R M & COMPY FECIT

EDR 1733. The donor was evidently Sir Duncan Campbell, 7th of Lochnell (cf. No. 330), the bell being cast in the Edinburgh foundry of Robert Maxwell and Company.[2] This bell presumably hung for nearly a century in the old church (No. 268) before being transferred to the present building.

FUNERARY MONUMENTS AND OTHER CARVED STONES
Medieval

Two carved stones (1–2), probably of medieval date, are built into the external facework of the S wall of the

[1] Telford, *Life*, 186–7, 490–1; Telford, *Atlas*, pl. 59; *NSA*, vii (Argyll), 521.
[2] *PSAS*, lxxxiv (1949–50), 102.

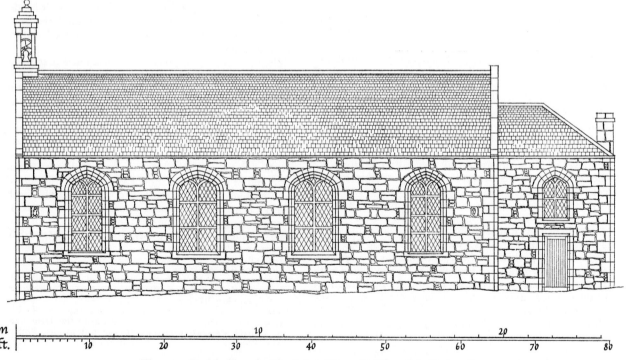

Fig. 155. Parish Church, Muckairn, Taynuilt (No. 269); S elevation

church; both probably emanate from the earlier church (No. 268). The other seven stones described below (3–9) are in the churchyard.

(1) A much weathered carving of buff-coloured sandstone (Pl. 35E) evidently representing a female fertility figure of the type known as a *sheela-na-gig*; it measures 0·41 m in height and about 0·23 m in width.[1]

(2) A dressed block, of similar material, measuring 0·25 m by 0·20 m, carved in high relief with a male human head (Pl. 35D). This stone may originally have been utilized as a gable-skewput.

(3) Tapered slab, 1·84 m long by 0·51 m wide at the head. The bottom corners are slightly chamfered. The decoration, now heavily worn, consists simply of a pair of plant-scrolls similar to those on (4) below. (*PSAS*, xxxv (1900–1), 95, fig. 3). *Probably 1500—1560.*

(4) Tapered slab, 1·62 m long by 0·50 m wide at the head. The top right-hand corner has broken off and the surface of the stone is fairly heavily worn. Within a wide border, which is enriched with debased dog-tooth ornament, there is a claymore flanked by single plant-scrolls bearing large tri-lobed leaves. Disposed around the hilt of the sword are a stag, a hound, and a pair of long-eared creatures (? hares). The tails of all four animals end in leaf-sprays. A poor drawing of this slab is given in *PSAS*, xxxv (1900–1), 95, fig. 2. *c. 1500—1560.*

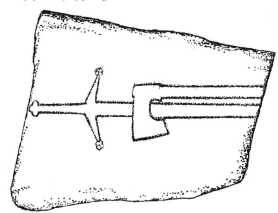

Fig. 156. Parish Church, Muckairn, Taynuilt (No. 269); fragment of grave-slab (scale 1 : 15)

(5) The upper part of a tapered slab, measuring 1·07 m in length by 0·82 m in width at the top, bearing incised representations of a claymore and battle-axe (Fig. 156). A second fragment of the same stone, illustrated in *PSAS*, xxxv (1900–1), 96, fig. 4, is no longer visible. *c. 1500—1560.*

Post-Reformation

(6–8) The most interesting of these is the group of Campbell table-tombs that lies immediately to the E of the old church. The earliest (6) commemorates Donald Campbell of Lossit, late bailie of Muckairn, who died 10 June 172[?9], aged 77. Above the inscription there is a circular panel with a cable-moulded border containing the emblems of mortality, while at the head of the

stone there is carved a full armorial achievement. The shield bears, quarterly: 1st, a hart's head cabossed; 2nd, gyronny of eight; 3rd, a galley, sail furled; 4th, on a chief, ? an unidentified charge. For crest there is a swan.

(7) Nearby there is a similar stone, probably of slightly later date, bearing the same coat of arms, but lacking any legible inscription. The lower part of the stone contains a relief-carving depicting the soul of the deceased being supported heavenwards by angels. This stone may commemorate John Campbell of Lossit, son of the above, and likewise bailie of Muckairn, who died before 1747.[2]

(8) The third stone in this group (Pl. 35A) commemorates Alexander Campbell, bailie of Ardnamorehan (Ardnamurchan), who died 28 March 1751, aged 45. Above the inscription there is carved the full heraldic achievement of the deceased, the shield bearing, quarterly: 1st and 4th, gyronny of eight; 2nd, a boar's head couped; 3rd, a galley, sail furled. For crest there is a ?dexter hand holding a spear. The stone also bears the emblems of mortality, and a representation of the soul of the deceased similar to that on (7). This stone was probably carved by the sculptor responsible for the McLerran stone of 1757 at Dalavich (cf. No. 241).

(9) The only other stone that calls for mention is a table-tomb commemorating Archibald Campbell, innkeeper at Bunaw (Bonawe), who died in November 1704, aged 49, and his wife, Anna Campbell, who died 29 December 1728, aged 72. The stone probably dates from the latter year. Above the inscription there is an oval panel containing the emblems of mortality, while at the head of the stone there is carved a full armorial achievement, the shield bearing, quarterly: 1st and 4th, gyronny of eight; 2nd, a galley, sail furled; 3rd, a ?salmon naiant.

005310   NN 03 SW   August 1970

270. Free High Church, Oban. This church (Pl. 36A) occupies a commanding site at the S end of Rockfield Road, overlooking the town and harbour of Oban. The design has commonly been attributed to the English architect, A W N Pugin,[3] and although David Cousin of Edinburgh furnished and received payment for the plans of the church, and supervised the contract work, there can be no doubt that most features of the building are borrowed from churches illustrated in Pugin's *The Present State of Ecclesiastical Architecture*. This work was published in 1843, three years before the commencement of the church.[4] Despite this derivative character, the

---

[1] Similar figures occur at Kirkwall Cathedral (*Inventory of Orkney and Shetland*, ii, p. 123), St Clement's Church, Rodel (*Inventory of the Outer Hebrides*, p. 33), and Iona Nunnery; there are numerous examples in Ireland (*JRSAI*, lxvi (1936), 107–29), and some in England.
[2] *Clan Campbell*, i, 222, 231, 237.
[3] E.g. Groome, *Ordnance Gazetteer*, 1252.
[4] The design of the tower, and its position within the NW angle, may be compared to St Wilfrid's, Manchester (pls. iii, vii), to which the whole building has a close similarity. The timber roof is of a type used by Pugin at St Mary's, Southport, and St George's Fields, London (pls. x, xii).

building is interesting for its ingenious adaptation of a conventional Gothic Revival design to contain a T-plan of traditional Scottish Presbyterian type.

The church is built of greenish sandstone ashlar, probably quarried at Ardentallan (No. 349) or Barrnacarry (No. 351). It is rectangular on plan, measuring 23 m from E to W by 13 m transversely. Externally it appears as a nave, divided by shallow buttresses into five bays, and a lower N aisle, also buttressed, at the W end of which there rises a square tower divided by offsets into three stages; the tower terminates in a low pyramidal roof. The entrance-doorway, in the W wall of the tower, has an arch-pointed head with a hood-mould, above which there is carved the date 1846. In each face of the third stage of the tower there are elaborate two-light windows in 13th-century style, with nook- and mid-shafts having moulded caps and bases. The W wall of the 'nave' is occupied by a tall triple lancet contained within a hood-mould which has foliated stops. In the gable above there is a small sub-triangular cusped window. Each bay of the S wall contains a single large lancet, while in the E wall of the 'nave' there is a triple lancet similar to that in the W wall.

Internally the W and E bays of the N aisle are occupied respectively by a vestibule and a session-room; the three central bays form an aisle facing the canopied pulpit (Pl. 36B) which is set against the centre of the S wall. The aisle is divided from the main body of the church by an arcade of three round-headed arches which spring from octagonal columns having moulded capitals in Perpendicular style. The body of the church (Pl. 36C) has an open timber roof of five bays, the principal trusses of which spring from the arcade capitals on the N and from moulded corbels on the S. Large arch-braces support collar-beams which carry king-posts and curved struts. The aisle is roofed in a similar fashion.

The site for the church was made available to the Free Church congregation by the 2nd Marquess of Breadalbane. In January 1846 the local minister submitted to the Marquess alternative plans for the building; that preferred by the congregation was by a local architect named McNab. It appears that Lord Breadalbane was personally responsible for commissioning designs from David Cousin at short notice, for in March 1846 he undertook to make good the difference between the cost of Cousin's design and the sum of £600 subscribed by the congregation, 'the details of architecture in the tower and generally being left to his Lordship'. The contract was awarded to William Dalziel, a local builder, and the foundation stone was laid in September 1846. The final cost was about £1624, of which Cousin received £74 11s. for plans and drawings.[1]

860298   NM 82 NE   August 1970

271. Chapel, Port Maluag, Lismore (Site).
The site of the chapel is occupied by a sub-rectangular enclosure measuring about 20 m from N to S by 10 m trans-

versely within a dry-stone wall some 0·8 m in thickness. This may have been a burial-ground, but no tombstones are now visible. Towards the NE corner of the enclosure there is a mound of stones, apparently a field-clearance heap of comparatively modern origin.

WELL. A freshwater spring, known as Tobar na Slainte, issues from the foot of a limestone cliff about 45 m S of the site of the chapel.

This chapel is said to have been erected close to the landing-place by which the relics of St Moluag were brought to Lismore.[2] The well, which was reputed to possess healing properties, was frequented for medicinal purposes until about the second quarter of the 19th century.[3]

871433   NM 84 SE   May 1968

272. Episcopal Church, Portnacroish.
This church (Pl. 36E) was built shortly before 1815 to serve the southern portion of Appin, an area where Episcopalianism was predominant throughout the 18th and

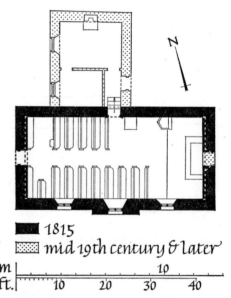

1815

mid 19th century & later

Fig. 157. Episcopal Church, Portnacroish (No. 272); plan

early 19th centuries. It was consecrated in July 1815, when the heads of five of the local Stewart families became trustees. Extensive repairs were executed in 1839, and four years later the vestry was converted into

---

[1] Correspondence and accounts in S.R.O., Breadalbane Collection, GD 112/51/13, Free Church Papers.
[2] NSA, vii (Argyll), 223.
[3] Name Book, No. 22, p. 96.

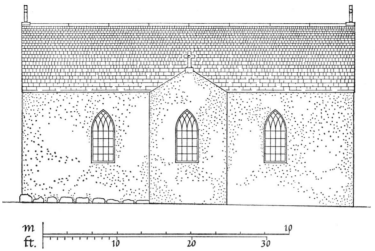

Fig. 158. Episcopal Church, Portnacroish (No. 272); S elevation (partially reconstructed)

a parsonage-house at a cost of £150.[1] A new vestry was built in the 1860s, and the church itself underwent further alterations in 1887.[2]

The church is rectangular on plan (Fig. 157), measuring 13·6 m from E to W by 6·8 m transversely over all; the central portion of the S wall is advanced 0·3 m to form a gabled centre-piece. The vestry is a rectangular block placed towards the W end of the N wall. The masonry is of local rubble, originally harled but now cement-pointed.

The principal, or S, elevation (Fig. 158) is of three bays, each containing one arch-pointed window; the existing Gothic tracery with diamond-shaped panes replaces original square panes whose mullions intersected in the arch-heads. Each of the gable-walls originally contained an entrance-doorway at ground-floor level and an arch-pointed window above, but the W window and the E door are now blocked. The gabled centre-piece of the S wall, and the E gable, are surmounted by cross-finials; that on the W gable, which existed in 1883, has since been replaced by a metal bell-cot.

In the original internal arrangement, the altar stood 'in the side of the church', probably below the central window in the S wall, and a three-decker pulpit was placed opposite, against the N wall.[3] Against the E and W walls there were galleries whose position is indicated by scarcements at a height of 2·1 m. None of the existing interior fittings appears to be original, except for the timber roof which is of three principal trusses, each having a collar-beam bearing a metal-stirruped king-post. The vestry is entered by a doorway centrally placed in the N wall of the church, and by an entrance-doorway in the E wall. It comprises two rooms, the larger of which has a fireplace in the N wall.

927473   NM 94 NW   July 1970

273. Burial-enclosure, Shuna, Nether Lorn. About 100 m N of Shuna farmhouse there is a small rectangular enclosure containing an inscribed tombstone which

commemorates John McLean of Shuna and his wife Mary Campbell, daughter of Angus Campbell of Ardlarach. This is probably the John McLean who died in or about 1787, and was succeeded by his son Alexander McLean, the last member of this family to possess the island[4] (cf. also No. 256).

765076   NM 70 NE   May 1970

274. Burial-enclosure, Sonachan. This small walled enclosure was erected as the private burial-place of the Campbells of Sonachan in 1760, this date being incised upon a stone that forms part of the S wall. The enclosure contains a number of late 18th- and early 19th-century memorials, together with a mural panel bearing the full heraldic achievement of the family (Pl. 36D).

042205   NN 02 SW   April 1968

275. Cross, Taynuilt (Site). A late medieval cross was still standing in 1798 on a hillock a short distance W of the village of Taynuilt.[5] It was subsequently broken, and the fragments dispersed, but the head was later recovered and is now in the National Museum of Antiquities of

---

[1] Craven, J B, *Records of the Dioceses of Argyll and the Isles 1560–1860* (1907), 271, 355–6, 361–2. Early references to this church describe it simply as 'the Episcopal chapel at Portnacroish'. It is named 'St John's' in 1848 and 1896 (ibid., 282, 371). This dedication was recorded by the Ordnance Survey in 1871, on local information (Name Book, No. 22, p. 59) and retained on the 2nd ed. (1900) of the 6-inch map, sheet lvii SW. However, an alternative dedication, to the Holy Cross, was in use for official purposes by 1880, and has remained current up to the present day (*The Scottish Episcopal Church Year Book and Directory for 1972–3*, 114).
[2] 'The Episcopal Church in Appin', *Argyll Diocesan Notes* for April 1962. The appearance of the exterior in 1883 is recorded in a photograph by E Beveridge, in N.M.R.S.
[3] Craven, op. cit., 293; *Argyll Diocesan Notes*, loc. cit.
[4] S.R.O., Abbreviated Register of Sasines (Argyll), 1781–1820, no. 366; Gillies, *Netherlorn*, 59.
[5] Garnett, *Tour*, i, 131. See also *PSAS*, xxiv (1889–90), 143–4.

Scotland. Made of slate, it takes the form of a simple Latin cross and measures 0·80 m in length, 0·62 m in width across the arms, and 0·07 m in thickness. The back and edges are plain, but the front bears a Crucifix carved in false relief. The figure of the Saviour bears a remarkably close resemblance to the one on the Campbell of Lerags Cross of 1516 (p. 143), and this, together with the fact that the three late medieval slabs in the nearby church-yard (No. 269) all appear to have been made within the period 1500–1560, suggests that the Taynuilt Cross was carved by a local craftsman in the early 16th century.

c. 0031   NN 03 SW   April 1970

CASTLES, TOWER-HOUSES AND FORTIFICATIONS

276. Achadun Castle, Lismore. The 13th-century castle of the bishops of Argyll (Pl. 37A, C) occupies the summit of a prominent limestone ridge some 200 m from the W coast of Lismore and 3·9 km from the S point of the island. The main axis of the ridge runs from SW to NE, and from these directions the ground rises evenly to the summit; the NW flank forms a sheer cliff having a maximum height of about 20 m, while the SE flank, although less precipitous, is also extremely steep. Achadun Bay provides a good anchorage, reached by a path which leads SW from the NW entrance-gateway of the castle. A well-worn path, which descends through a gully in the cliff 50 m NNE of the castle, gives access to a spring at the base of the cliff. The structure is ruinous, the SW and SE walls having collapsed outwards; the NE wall and a substantial portion of the NW wall, however, survive to wall-head level, a height of about 6·7 m. Owing to a natural fall in the rock-surface, the SE part of the site is about 1·4 m lower than the NW part of the courtyard, and this area is buried in debris to a considerable depth. Excavations conducted at the site in 1970–3 have clarified some of the problems of interior arrangement.[1]

A curtain-wall varying in thickness from 1·4 m to 2·4 m encloses an area measuring about 22 m square, which has comprised at least two ranges of buildings flanking a small courtyard (Figs. 159, 160). The masonry consists for the most part of small slabs of limestone rubble bonded in lime mortar, with occasional coursed cubical blocks of basalt, quarried locally from dykes, and granite boulders, many of which are split and set on edge. Most of the freestone dressings used in window-, door- and garderobe-openings have been robbed, those that remain being of a coarse yellow sandstone, probably from Carsaig. Masons' marks of three types (Fig. 161) have been identified on the dressed masonry of the SE range during excavation. The walls have been harled internally and externally.

The landward entrance is centrally placed in the NE curtain-wall (Pl. 37D), but the opening has been so damaged that the original form of the arch-head cannot

be ascertained.[2] Some 7·8 m SE of this entrance the curtain-wall returns outwards for 1·5 m to accommodate a garderobe-chamber at first-floor level; this was lit by a window of which one sandstone jamb remains *in situ.* The NW portion of this chamber appears to have been corbelled out above a re-entrant formed by the curtain-wall and the lower portion of the garderobe-projection. The latter returns outward at ground-level about 1·0 m SE of the corresponding point at first-floor level. A small window lighting the passage that gave access to the chamber, and two larger windows at first-floor level NW of the entrance, have been completely destroyed externally. An opening which served to drain the E part of the courtyard penetrates the curtain-wall at ground-level SE of the entrance. The NW curtain-wall returns outwards for a distance of 0·8 m at a point 10·6 m SW of the collapsed N angle, and two garderobes within the corbelled-out upper part of the wall NE of this discharged into the re-entrant thus formed. The stumps of the massive sandstone corbels are still visible, although most of the masonry that they supported has disappeared. Further to the SW there is a second entrance-gateway, equipped with a drawbar-socket in the NE ingo and having an internal width of 1·4 m. Approach from the exterior was facilitated by a stone-built platform which on excavation was found to incorporate a deep pit measuring about 2·2 m square and evidently designed to contain a movable platform or bridge. This forework replaced an original timber platform whose putlog-holes penetrate the curtain-wall (cf. Fig. 159), and are partially blocked by the masonry of the forework. The pit had subsequently been filled in with loose stones, and rough steps were formed against the curtain-wall rising to the threshold-level of the gateway. The greater part of the SW curtain-wall still survived to its full height until about 1890,[3] but since then it has collapsed outwards except for a small portion at the SW end of the SE range, the inner face of which survives to first-floor level. Even this, however, is so ruinous that the original thickness of the wall cannot be ascertained. The SE curtain is even more fragmentary, only the lowest courses of the inner face of the wall being visible.[4] Considerable pieces of masonry lie at the foot of the steep SE slope, and these include the remains of a splayed window-embrasure, probably from a first-floor window lighting the SE range.

Within the entrance-doorway, the lowest courses of the splayed NW ingo and part of a draw-bar socket survive, while on the SE a straight stair (Pl. 37B) rises in the thickness of the wall to give access to the parapet-walk. The curtain-wall is thickened internally to accom-

---

[1] The Commissioners are indebted to Mr D J Turner, BSc, FSA, who directed the excavation, for assistance in preparing this account.
[2] During excavation in 1973, two sandstone rybats which probably formed part of this doorway were found among rubble in the E angle of the courtyard. They are wrought with two chamfered orders, each of 0·13 m, and appear to be of late 13th-century date.
[3] *Cast. and Dom. Arch.,* iii, 76–7.
[4] Excavation in 1971 showed that this curtain-wall had a thickness of 1·5 m above a stepped plinth.

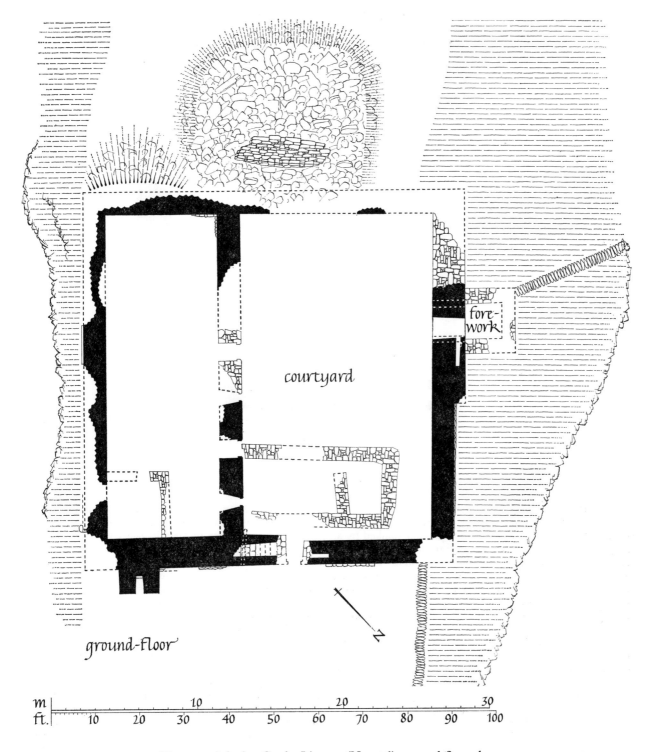

courtyard

fore-
work

ground-floor

m				10		20		30
ft.	10	20	30	40	50	60	70	80	90	100

Fig. 159. Achadun Castle, Lismore (No. 276); ground-floor plan

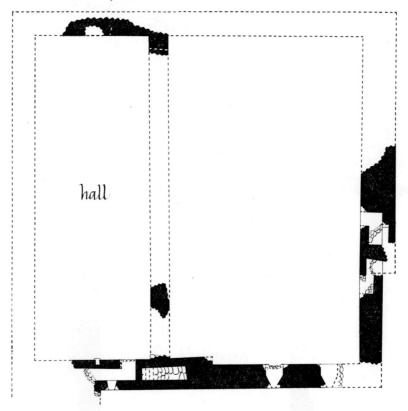

hall

first floor

Fig. 160. Achadun Castle, Lismore (No. 276); first-floor plan

modate this stair and a mural passage leading from the SE range to the garderobe-chamber at the E angle. The courtyard, which was roughly cobbled, was flanked by a substantial SE range measuring 7·6 m in internal width, and possibly by another range in the N angle. The NW wall of the SE range, which measures 1·6 m in thickness at ground-level, is buried under rubble, but still stands to a greatest height of about 2·0 m. Excavation in 1970 revealed a doorway 5·2 m from the NE end of the wall; the dressed masonry of the NE jamb survives to a height of about 1·2 m, being wrought with an 0·10 m chamfer on the external arris and with an 0·03 m chamfer on the arris of the rebate. A second doorway serving the

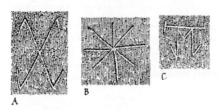

Fig. 161. Achadun Castle, Lismore (No. 276); masons' marks: A, B, south-east range; C, detached fragment (scale 1:5)

SW part of the range was exposed in 1971. The ground-floor was lit by at least two windows, one on each side of the NE doorway; of that to the SW, only the sill survives, but that at the NE end of the wall is almost intact. These windows were vertical slits with daylight-openings of 0·32 m, wrought externally with continuous 0·08 m chamfers and rebated and splayed internally; the inner jambs of freestone have been removed. A separate apartment has been formed within the E angle of the range by a wall some 0·6 m in thickness which is not bonded into the masonry of the NE wall. Little remains of the upper part of this range, the side-walls having completely disappeared. The joists of the first floor, which probably contained the hall, were carried on substantial scarcements of which a fragment survives towards the NE end of the NW side-wall. The position of the first-floor doorway is uncertain; access was probably obtained by a forestair from the courtyard. Set into the existing fragment of the SW gable-wall there is a sandstone block which may mark the position of a former window-opening. A doorway in the NE wall gave access, by a dog-leg passage, to the garderobe-chamber described above; the slab-lintelled roof of the chamber was higher than that of the passage, and it is probable that the floor rose by a short flight of steps. The passage was lit by a small splayed window, and the chamber by a window in the re-entrant angle. At the centre of the NE wall of this range, at a height of about 2·1 m above first-floor level, there is an opening which appears to have been deliberately formed to contain a projecting beam or corbel; its exact purpose is uncertain.

The range that occupied the N angle of the courtyard (Pl. 38A) appears to have been less substantial than that just described; no trace of the inner walls has been revealed by excavation and, if constructed, they may have been timber-framed. Two window-embrasures survive at first-floor level in the NE curtain-wall NW of the entrance-doorway. These embrasures have straight ingoes for a distance of 0·8 m and are then splayed, in the same fashion as a ground-floor window in the SE wall of Castle Coeffin (No. 282). The windows may have been designed to light a NW range whose construction was abandoned as a result of financial difficulties or an episcopal vacancy. The twin garderobe-chambers that project from the NW curtain-wall are entered by two doorways whose thresholds are at a height of about 1·8 m above courtyard-level (Pl. 38B); these may have been entered by steps leading up from the ground-floor of a range, or by a timber gallery running along the courtyard-wall. The chambers themselves are reached by dog-leg passages. The SW wall of the NE chamber is splayed to form one side of a small window, while an obliquely-set window is similarly contrived in the NW angle of the other chamber, which has been rather more spacious. A portion of the ledge supporting the seat of the garderobe remains *in situ* in the SW wall of the latter chamber.

The straight stair that rises from the SE ingo of the NE entrance retains most of its stone treads, and the positions of the timber lintels that originally formed the roof are clearly visible. A portion of the parapet-wall, 0·7 m in thickness, stands to a height of about 1·1 m above the roughly-paved wall-walk in the area near the NE entrance. There is no evidence of the existence of weep-holes.

The remains of a sub-rectangular building of dry-stone masonry, occupying the NE part of the courtyard and partially overlying the NW range, were excavated in 1971. This structure, whose foundations rested on black soil overlying medieval occupation-levels, was evidently of late date; it had subsequently been subdivided by a partition-wall of rubble bonded in clay mortar.

In 1240 two pennylands at 'Achacendune' were among lands in Lismore granted by Ewen, son of Duncan of Argyll, to Bishop William, while in 1304 his grandson granted to Bishop Andrew other property near the bishop's 'castle or manor of Achychendone'.[1] With the exception of the partition-wall in the E angle of the SE range and the forework at the NW entrance, the remains described above may be assigned to the period between these grants. The discovery in 1973, on the quoins of the E garderobe-projection, of masons' marks similar to one which occurs at Lismore Cathedral

in work ascribed to the early 14th century (Fig. 151B), suggests that building was in progress during the last years of the 13th century.[2] Excavation-finds from the site demonstrate recurrent, if intermittent, occupation throughout the late medieval period. The only historical record relating to the castle in this period, however, is the description by a contemporary chronicler of Bishop George Lauder's visit to Lismore in 1452, when he stayed on the island for over a month, probably at 'his castall of Auchindoun'.[3]

The construction by Bishop David Hamilton of his castle at Saddell c. 1508–12,[4] effectively terminated the occupation of Achadun as an episcopal residence, and thereafter it probably fell into a state of decay. Although it has been stated that Sir James Livingstone, who had a grant of the temporalities of the bishopric of Argyll in 1640, resided at Achadun Castle,[5] no authority has been found for this statement. In 1666 the farm of Achadun was in the possession of the 9th Earl of Argyll, who wadset it to Colin Campbell of Lochnell, but there is no mention of the castle in this transaction.[6] If there is any truth in the local tradition that describes Hector Maclaine, last bishop of Argyll prior to the Revolution of 1688–9, as occupying the castle,[7] this must refer to the dry-stone building in the courtyard; the existence of this structure is sufficient proof that no part of the original building remained habitable at the period of its construction, which may be ascribed to the 17th or 18th century. The fabric of the castle, weakened by stone robbing, has continued to deteriorate up to the present day, much of the SW curtain-wall having collapsed since about 1890.

804392   NM 83 NW   August 1973

277. Achallader Castle. This small tower-house (Pl. 38C, D) is situated on the S edge of the Black Mount and Rannoch Moor area, 1·3 km NE of Loch Tulla. It was built by Sir Duncan Campbell, 7th of Glenorchy, shortly before 1600, to protect the northern approaches to his extensive estates, and also to serve as a hunting-lodge. The castle was attacked and burnt by members of the Jacobite army in 1689, and is now fragmentary. While the N and E walls (Pl. 39C) stand almost to their original heights, only a small portion of the W wall survives and the S wall has disappeared completely.

The tower is oblong on plan, measuring 8·7 m from E to W by 6·7 m transversely over walls which vary in thickness from 0·91 m to 1·07 m (Fig. 162). The accommodation comprised three storeys and a garret, the side-walls rising to a height of 9·3 m. The masonry is of

[1] *PSAS*, xc (1956–7), 219; *RMS*, ii (1424–1513), no. 3136.
[2] A fragment of sandstone discovered in the courtyard in 1970 also bore a mason's mark that occurs at Lismore Cathedral (Fig. 161C).
[3] Craigie, W A (ed.), *The Asloan Manuscript*, Scottish Text Society (1923–5), i, 222.
[4] *Inventory of Argyll*, i, No. 313.
[5] Carmichael, *Lismore*, 122; *Origines Parochiales*, ii, part i, 132.
[6] Campbell, *Argyll Sasines*, ii, no. 1321.
[7] Carmichael, *Lismore*, 132.

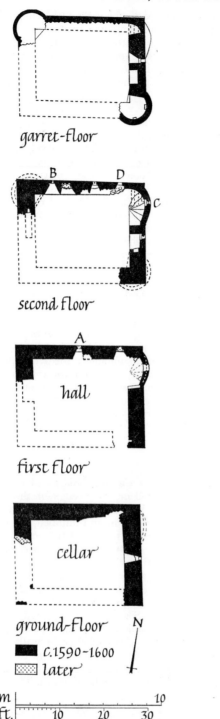

garret-floor

second floor

hall

first floor

cellar

ground-floor   N

■ c.1590–1600
▨ later

m |————————————| 10
ft.| 10   20   30

Fig. 162. Achallader Castle (No. 277); floor-plans

small rectangular openings having round arrises and are splayed internally, and there is also a varied series of pistol-holes (Figs. 163, 164).

Externally the most interesting feature is the rounded stair-projection at the N end of the E wall (Pl. 38D). This is carried on two courses of continuous corbelling at first-floor level, and terminates in a flat roof at wall-head level. There are corner-rounds carried on similar double-member corbel-courses at the SE and NW angles; the latter is now represented only by two stones of the lower corbel-course. The E gable, which originally terminated in a chimney, rises vertically on the S, where it adjoins the corner-round, and is crow-stepped on the N. A small section of a cavetto-moulded eaves-cornice survives near the E end of the N wall.

The principal entrance-doorway was situated at the E end of the S wall, at first-floor level. Sufficient of the E jamb remains *in situ* (Pl. 38E) to establish that it was wrought externally with a rounded arris, and checked internally for a timber door[1] and an iron yett, the latter being secured by a draw-bar. It is probable that the only access to the ground-floor apartment was by means of an internal stair in the NE angle, where the N wall shows signs of disturbance. This apartment, which was unvaulted, was lit by a window in the E wall. The first-floor apartment was probably the hall; in the W wall there survives a portion of the N jamb of a large fireplace, wrought with a rounded arris. In the N wall there is a window (Pl. 38F), originally fitted with an iron grille, whose sill forms the inner lintel of a pistol-hole (Fig. 163A); this opening is splayed internally, while externally it has a small round aperture surrounded by a hollow. Towards the E end of the N wall there is a blocked window-opening which may have lit the head of the stair that led down to the cellar, or else a small closet below the stair that rises to the second floor and is contained within the corbelled projection described above. This stair is served by a pistol-hole in the form of a narrow horizontal slit with slightly expanded terminals.

The second floor also probably formed a single apartment, which may have had a fireplace in the W wall, where traces of the flue of the hall-fireplace are visible. In the E wall there is an embrasure furnished with an aumbry and lit by a small horizontal slit. The N wall contains a splayed recess, of uncertain purpose, and a window, in addition to two pistol-holes. The pistol-hole at the stair-head is a horizontal dumb-bell shaped slit (Fig. 164D, Pl. 39B), while the other has a square aperture splayed internally and externally, the outer face being rebated with two vertical grooves (Fig. 163B, Pl. 39A). A pistol-hole of similar but simpler form is set into the wall of the stair that leads to the garret (Fig. 164C). A roughly-shaped series of corbels carries the gable-wall above this stair, and the thresholds of the angle-turrets are also corbelled above the angles of the chamber below. The SE angle-turret is provided with two pistol-holes at floor-level, which open through the lower external

[1] A door, which is said to have been removed from Achallader in the 18th century, is preserved at Dunans Castle, Cowal.

random rubble laid in lime mortar, with dressings of schist; internally, the stonework displays marks of burning. A limited amount of consolidation has been undertaken during the present century. The windows are

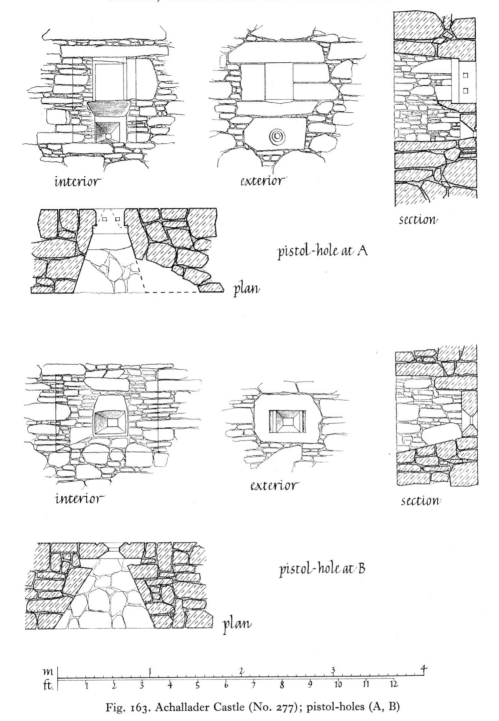

interior   exterior   section

pistol-hole at A

plan

interior   exterior   section

pistol-hole at B

plan

Fig. 163. Achallader Castle (No. 277); pistol-holes (A, B)

corbel-course. In the E gable-wall, close to the entrance of the SE angle-turret, there is a fireplace, the lintel of which has been removed, and N of this there is a window.

Two architectural fragments which evidently derive from the castle are now preserved in the nearby burial-ground (No. 212). One of these is a pistol-hole having a round aperture within a hollow moulding, similar to that at first-floor level in the N wall of the castle (cf. Fig. 163A); this is now built into the outer face of the N wall of the burial-ground. The other fragment is part of a window-jamb, wrought externally with a 0·08 m chamfer and provided with a glazing-groove.

Achallader may have been included in the grant of the lordship of Glenorchy to Sir Colin Campbell in 1432, for the lands granted included the nearby Island of Loch Tulla (cf. No. 288). The earliest mention of a Campbell residence occurs in 1567, when Archibald Campbell received a tack of 'Auchalladour with the keping hous thairof.'[1] The present building, however, dates from the time of Sir Duncan Campbell, 7th of

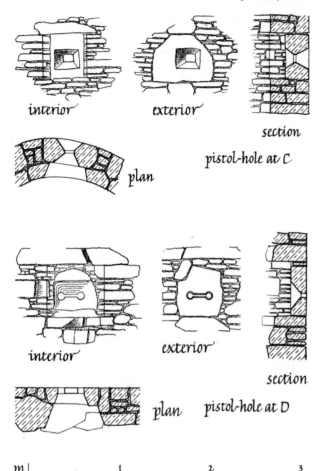

Fig. 164. Achallader Castle (No. 277); pistol-holes (C, D)

Glenorchy, of whom the family chronicler records, 'he biggit the toure of Achalladoure, for the warkmanship of the quhilk he gaiff ane thowsand markis'.[2] Although the date is omitted, the context establishes that it was shortly before 1600. In 1603 or 1604 the building was attacked and burnt by members of the Clan Gregor led by Alastair MacGregor of Glenstrae; he, with many of his companions, was executed for this and other crimes in 1604, and others were convicted between 1611 and 1613.[3]

Throughout the 17th and 18th centuries the nearby township was occupied by members of the M'Inleister or Fletcher family, a sept of the MacGregors. They

were, however, subordinate to a series of tacksmen; one of these was Duncan, a natural son of Sir Duncan Campbell, 7th of Glenorchy, who in 1634 received a tack of the property.[4] The lands of Achallader, with 'the Castle, tour and fortalice', were wadset by the 1st Earl of Breadalbane to John Stewart of Ballachulish in 1680 and were still in his possession in 1693, and possibly later.[5]

Because of its convenient situation, several justice-courts were held at Achallader by the Commission for Pacifying the Highlands in 1683 and 1684, and it is probable that the Commissioners were accommodated in the castle.[6] In 1689 the 1st Earl of Breadalbane successfully argued against proposals to station a garrison at Achallader, which was unable to contain a force sufficiently strong to be useful. It was with particular feelings of outrage, therefore, that he received news of the destruction of the castle at the beginning of October 1689 by a detachment of the Jacobite army, consisting of Stewarts and MacNicols, aided by a number of his own tenants in Glenorchy, and he tried to discover whether the Jacobite leaders had given instructions for this action.[7]

Although the castle was not 'burnt to the ground', as Lord Breadalbane claimed in a letter to the Earl of Melville,[8] no attempt was made to repair the building at that time, and temporary accommodation was provided for the conference between the Earl and the Jacobite leaders in 1691. The Treaty of Achallader, signed on 30 June of that year, was the culmination of Breadalbane's policy of arranging a cessation of hostilities.[9] In 1746, when the disposition of permanent garrisons in the Highlands was being considered, it was suggested that 'a small command might be at the old Castle of Achalader . . . . which might be easily repaired for that purpose', to control Rannoch Moor 'the thoro-

[1] S.R.O., Breadalbane Collection, GD 112/5/4, 'Regester', p. 21. Archibald, said to be a natural son of Sir Colin Campbell, 6th of Glenorchy, was ancestor of the Perthshire family of Campbell of Achalader (*Burke's Landed Gentry* (18th ed., 1965–72), ii, 82).

[2] *Taymouth Bk.*, 35.

[3] Ibid., 38; Pitcairn, *Trials*, iii, 113–14, 232, 249.

[4] S.R.O., Breadalbane Collection, GD 112/10/1.

[5] S.R.O., Particular Register of Sasines (Argyll), RS 10/1, fol. 352 v.; Breadalbane Collection, GD 112/9/33, Rental, 1687–99, *passim*.

[6] *RPC*, 3rd series, viii (1683–4), 533.

[7] S.R.O., Campbell of Barcaldine Collection, GD 170/629/ nos. 14 and 15, letters from Lord Breadalbane to Alexander Campbell, 10, 16 October 1689; in Breadalbane Collection, GD 112/40/3, Letters, there is a wrapper endorsed, in a contemporary hand, 'Coll(onel) Canon's principall order for burning the Castle of Achchalder 1689', but the letter itself is missing. It has recently been stated (Prebble, J, *Glencoe* (1966), 80–1) that the MacDonalds of Glencoe destroyed Achallader; it is, however, evident from the letters cited above that this event occurred before the MacDonalds under Keppoch ravaged Glenlyon 'about the latter end of October, 1689' (Campbell, D, *The Lairds of Glenlyon* (1886), 53).

[8] *Leven and Melville Papers*, Bannatyne Club (1843), 530.

[9] *Papers Illustrative of the Political Condition of the Highlands of Scotland, from the Year MDCLXXXIX to MDCXCVI*, Maitland Club (1845), 21–2.

fare of Thieves', but nothing came of this proposal.[1]
The senior branch of the Fletcher family moved their
residence to Dunans in Glendaruel parish, Cowal, in
about the middle of the 18th century.[2]

322442   NN 34 SW   August 1970

278. Ardfad Castle, Seil. The scanty remains of this
small castle (Fig. 165, Pl. 39D) occupy the summit of an
elongated rocky outcrop close to the N shore of the island
of Seil. The site is bounded by sheer rock-faces rising to a
height of about 7 m on all sides except the SW, where a
natural gully has been widened to form a smoothly-
sloping approach. The summit area, which measures 38 m
from NE to SW by 14 m transversely, has been enclosed
by a curtain-wall of lime-mortared rubble masonry, 0·9 m
in thickness, conforming to the irregular outline of the
perimeter. This wall is best preserved on the NE and E
flanks, where a stretch of revetment remains *in situ* on
the cliff-face; elsewhere the wall is now represented only
by a low scarp, and no remains are visible in the SW
section.

The site has been divided into two unequal portions
by a transverse rectangular building measuring 14·0 m
from NW to SE by 6·7 m in width over walls 0·9 m in
thickness. This structure is now reduced to foundation-
level, except for a fragment of its NW gable which
survives to a height of 1·2 m and incorporates a recess,
perhaps a fireplace or a window-embrasure. At the W
angle there are the foundations of a round tower 2·9 m
in diameter, which perhaps contained a stair. Although
an entrance-passage must have formerly existed, as at
Gylen (No. 291), to provide access to the inner enclosure,
its position cannot be identified. In the SE portion of the
NE wall, which serves as the foundation of a dry-stone
wall of recent construction, there is a splayed return
which possibly formed one side of a doorway. The wall
returned NE at the SE end to form a small chamber,
probably a latrine, at the junction with the curtain-wall.

A large roughly-shaped corbel projects from the outer
face of the NW gable-wall of the building (A on Fig.
165), near its junction with the round tower, and another
similar corbel (B) projects from the base of the curtain-
wall in the NE section. The purpose of these features is
uncertain. A brief description of the castle, published
in 1895,[3] refers to the existence of 'the usual arrow slits',
but none are now visible.

Ardfad has no recorded history, but the plan of the
building is consistent with a date in the late 16th or early
17th century. At this period the N part of Seil was held
by the MacDougalls of Ardincaple, a branch of the
MacDougalls of Rarey, as tenants of the Campbells of
Glenlyon who had been granted the four merklands of
Ardincaple in 1510. The construction of the castle may
be ascribed to John MacDougall, who died shortly before
1615, or to his son of the same name,[4] and it was probably
the principal residence of the family during the 17th
century.

769194   NM 71 NE   June 1971

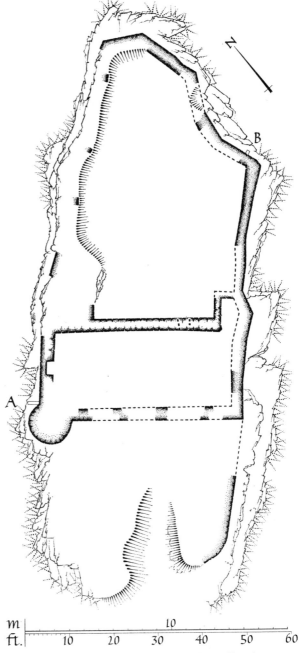

Fig. 165. Ardfad Castle, Seil (No. 278); plan

[1] S.R.O., Breadalbane Collection, GD 112/47/4, Roads
Papers, 'Memorandums concerning the Highlands 1746';
TGSI, xxii (1897–8), 79.
[2] *Burke's Landed Gentry* (18th ed., 1965–72), ii, 205.
[3] *PSAS*, xxx (1895–6), 24.
[4] *Origines Parochiales*, ii, part i, 103; *Burke's Landed Gentry*
(13th ed., 1921), 1161–2; Campbell, *Argyll Sasines*, i, no. 185.

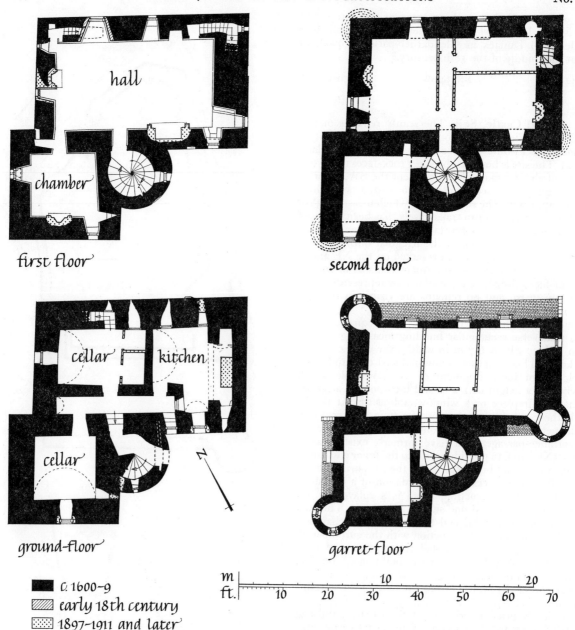

hall

chamber

first floor

second floor

cellar   kitchen

cellar

ground-floor

garret-floor

■ *c.* 1600–9
▨ early 18th century
▥ 1897–1911 and later

m |————————————————10————————————————20——|
ft. |——10——20——30——40——50——60——70——|

Fig. 166. Barcaldine Castle (No. 279); floor-plans

279. Barcaldine Castle. This early 17th-century tower-house (Pls. 1, 40, 41D) stands on the E slope of a low ridge about 500 m from the S shore of Loch Creran and 1·1 km S of South Shian Ferry (No. 367). It commands the original road from Connel to Appin, but is not in a strong position defensively, being overlooked by higher ground on the W. The castle was built by Sir Duncan Campbell, 7th laird of Glenorchy, and was completed in 1609. A number of minor alterations were made to the building in the early 18th century, and after standing roofless during the second half of the 19th century it was restored between 1897 and 1911. Despite this restoration the castle remains a good example of a laird's dwelling of its period, and its interest is enhanced by the survival of an inventory of fittings compiled in 1621.

ARCHITECTURAL DESCRIPTION

The castle stands in gardens enclosed by a modern boundary-wall. It is basically L-shaped on plan (Fig. 166), with the axis of the main block running from ESE to WNW, but it will be described as if that axis ran E and W. The main block measures some 14·5 m from E to W by 8·9 m transversely over walls which vary in thickness from 1·4 m to 1·9 m at ground-level. The wing at the SW measures 7·5 m from E to W by 7·3 m from N to S; it projects slightly beyond the W gable of the main block, and in the SE re-entrant angle there is a circular stair-tower. The building consists of a vaulted ground-storey with two unvaulted storeys and a rebuilt garret above, and the height to the wall-head is 9·8 m. Local rubble, probably quarried from the ridge to the NW of the castle, is used for the walls, which are now harled, with sparse dressings of schist and coarse pink and yellow sandstone. The schist employed for the corbels of the angle-turrets is similar to that used at Kilchurn Castle (No. 293), which was probably quarried in the Loch Awe area.

The entrance-doorway, which is on the E side of the stair-tower, has sandstone jambs with rounded arrises and above it there is an oblong window with an iron grille. Over this there is a schist panel (Pl. 41A) carved in relief, bearing the inscription F/OL/LOV ME 16/09[1] and the initials S D C (for Sir Duncan Campbell) in two places. A shield bears the arms of Campbell of Glenorchy, quarterly: 1st and 4th, gyronny of eight; 2nd, a galley, sail furled, pennons flying; 3rd, checky (in error for a fess checky); it is supported by two stags rampant and surmounted by a helm and crest of a boar's head. In the S wall of the main block, at the same level, is a much-weathered carved panel of similar stone (Pl. 41B) which

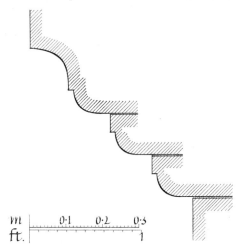

Fig. 167. Barcaldine Castle (No. 279); corbelling of SW angle-turret

bears a shield parted per pale: dexter, Campbell of Glenorchy (as above); sinister, Stewart of Atholl, quarterly: 1st and 4th, paly of six; 2nd, illegible; 3rd, checky (in error for a fess checky). The shield is supported by two male figures (?savages) and surmounted by a helm and illegible crest, and the lower part of it is flanked by the initials [S D] C and L/ I S, for Sir Duncan Campbell and his first wife, Lady Jean Stewart, daughter of the 4th Earl of Atholl. Below the shield is the date

1609; this is remarkable because Jean Stewart died in 1593 and Sir Duncan married Elizabeth Sinclair in 1597.[2] As the method of carving, in relief, makes it improbable that the date was added to an existing stone, the most likely explanation is that there was originally another panel showing the arms of the second wife, so that both were represented. Two other heraldic panels have been built into the outer walls to commemorate the restoration of 1897.

All the window-openings at ground-floor level were originally narrow slits, placed either vertically or horizontally, but two, in the S walls of the kitchen and wing, have been enlarged at or since the restoration. The remaining windows appear to be original, with the exception of that nearest the W end of the N wall at first-floor level. This is larger than the other windows and has sandstone jambs with small rounded arrises; a relieving-arch, the only one in the building, was visible until recent harling.[3] This window was probably formed or enlarged in the early 18th century. The original windows and the internal doors have rounded arrises, although in many of the former these are now obscured by harling. Grooves in the jambs and lintels of several windows indicate that they were originally half-glazed, with shutters below, and the description of window-fittings in the inventory of 1621 confirms this and shows that the glass was originally set in lozenge-shaped panes. Some of the small windows in the mural staircases were completely glazed. Many of the windows have iron grilles, made with interpenetrating bars, as in a yett, fixed into the jambs and lintels. Most of these seem to be replacements dating from the early 20th century, although the grilles of the E windows in the N wall at both first- and second-floor levels appear to be old. Drawings and descriptions[4] made before the restoration of 1897 indicate, however, that similar grilles existed before this date, and the 1621 inventory shows that the windows had 'stanshours' from the beginning.

At the SE and NW corners of the main block, and the SW corner of the wing, there are angle-turrets (Pl. 41C) supported on four courses of continuous moulded corbelling of which two courses project beyond the angle. The corbelling of the turret in the wing (Fig. 167) differs from the others in that the highest course is a cavetto and not an ovolo. Comparison with pre-restoration views[5] shows that the upper parts of these turrets, from the level of the window-sills, have been rebuilt. All three turrets have modern conical roofs. The E and W gables of the main block, and the S gable of the wing, have crowsteps with cavetto skewputs and are surmounted by chimneys whose copings have been renewed. A large chimney rises from the S wall of the main block near

[1] The drawing of this panel by D MacGibbon (*Cast. and Dom. Arch.*, iii, fig. 573) is inaccurate.
[2] *Scots Peerage*, ii, 185, 187.
[3] Unpublished paper by L Grahame MacDougall, p. 9; the Commissioners are grateful to Mr MacDougall for permission to quote this paper.
[4] E.g. *Cast. and Dom. Arch.*, iii, 619 and fig. 572; *PSAS*, xvii (1882–3), 129.
[5] *Cast. and Dom. Arch.*, iii, fig. 572.

the junction with the stair-tower, and the SW corner of the stack is cut away to make room for the conical roof of the tower. The roofs are now covered with slate; they were repaired at various times in the 18th and 19th centuries with Ballachulish slate, and at that period the angle-turrets were roofed partly or wholly with lead.[1]

The timber outer door dates from the restoration, but the 'tirl-pin' and the latch-plate (Pl. 42C), which has a crescent-shaped lower terminal, appear to be old, probably dating from the late 17th or early 18th century. Within the door is an iron yett (Pl. 42A), the lower part of which has perished. It now swings on two hinges, of which the lower is a replacement,[2] and the stump of a third survives in the jamb. The upper part of the yett is fitted with two vertical iron loops which held a sliding iron bolt, and there is a third loop for the hasp (Pl. 42B). A socket in the S jamb indicates that another similar bolt formerly existed at the lower part of the yett. In the N jamb there is a bar-hole 1·7 m deep. A large sandstone lintel separates the embrasure of the doorway from that of the window above it.

A lobby leads to a doorway whose modern door carries a handle and latch-plate made in the shape of a human figure (Pl. 42D), probably of the same period as the fittings of the outer door. Three steps lead down to a vaulted corridor, at the E end of which is the kitchen, an L-shaped apartment with its main E–W vault intersected by a vault running N from the enlarged S window. A fireplace with a segmental arch (Pl. 43B), wrought on the face with a rounded arris, occupies most of the E wall. Within it on the S is an ingle-neuk lit by a small window; a modern cupboard on the N probably replaces an earlier oven. An opening at the E end of the N wall, now blocked externally, appears to represent a slop-sink. To the W of it was a water-inlet, now blocked, whose position is indicated by the broken stump of a stone basin projecting from the wall externally.[3] A service-hatch opening into the corridor probably represents the 'dressing windo' of the 1621 inventory.

The W part of the main block is occupied by a vaulted cellar, sub-divided at the restoration of 1897. A mural service-stair leading to the first floor is entered from the embrasure of a small window in the N wall. An oblong window in the W wall is similar to another in the corridor, which looks towards the outer door. Built into the vault of the cellar there is an iron stump which probably represents one of the meat-hooks described in the 1621 inventory. The apartment in the wing, which has a vault running N and S, is featureless except for an enlarged window in the S wall and a splayed opening in the E wall, now blocked externally, which appears to be a peep-hole or pistol-hole covering the entrance. In 1621 this cellar contained various items of baking equipment. During the restoration of 1897 a prison or pit was discovered below the floor of this apartment.[4] It was entered from the lobby at the foot of the staircase, and the floor was recorded as being 4·0 m below the floor level of the lobby. The pit, which had no window-openings, contained about 0·6 m of water, and the entrance was sealed after examination.

The main stair, described in 1621 as the 'great trumbel', rises from the S side of the entrance. It is spacious in the lower part, the treads measuring 1·6 m from the newel to the wall; above the second floor the average width is 1·3 m. The steps, which are tangential to the newel, are now covered with cement; they are carried above the doorways at ground- and first-floor levels on an arrangement of corbelled slabs. To the W of the window between the ground and first floors there is a small cupboard, now inaccessible, which occupies an original pistol-hole.

The hall (Pl. 43A) occupies the first floor of the main block. The existing panelling, ceiling and fireplaces date from the restoration of 1897–1911, but the large fireplace in the S wall occupies the position of an original one. The arrangement of mural staircases, windows and the fireplace suggests that the dais was at the E end. Two adjacent windows at the SE corner provide an excellent view of the entrance, and a stone bench is preserved on the N side of the embrasure of the window in the E wall. A doorway in the N wall, now concealed behind panelling, gives access to a mural stair leading to the floor above ('the trumbel that gais oub fra the hall'), which is lit by a window in the E wall at the top of the first flight, and by a small window at the top of the second flight. The mural stair from the cellar enters by a doorway at the W end of the N wall; on the N side of the stair-head there is a rebuilt aperture for a lantern. The inventory of 1621 suggests that part of the hall, probably the area near the head of the mural stair lit by the small window in the W wall, was partitioned off to serve as a pantry. The W wall of the hall has undergone various alterations; most of the external evidence has been concealed by recent harling and the following account is based on the plan by MacGibbon and Ross, and a description compiled in 1953.[5] Until the external wall was harled, a large blocked arch was visible, which probably represented one of the four 'great windowis' of 1621. In the early 18th century the hall was subdivided, and the W window was replaced by a large new window in the N wall; the embrasure was filled by a fireplace which had a cupboard to the S, while the outer part of the window was left as an external recess. This was the arrangement at the time when MacGibbon and Ross made their plan, but at the restoration of 1897 the fireplace was rebuilt, the external opening blocked, a new window created where there had been a cupboard, and the 18th-century partition removed.

A door at the W end of the S wall of the hall leads to the 'chalmer des' which occupies the first floor of the wing. In the W wall of the lobby is a closet, originally a close-garderobe, lit by a small window in the lesser re-entrant angle of the wing. At the S end of the E wall there is a splayed opening, blocked externally, which

[1] S.R.O., Campbell of Barcaldine Collection, GD 170/381/3, Building-Accounts.
[2] *PSAS*, xvii (1882–3), 129.
[3] MacDougall, op. cit., p. 10.
[4] Ibid., pp. 16–17.
[5] *Cast. and Dom. Arch.*, iii, 618, fig. 571; MacDougall, op. cit., p. 11.

was probably a peep-hole, and below the window in the W wall is a pistol-hole, also blocked, whose freestone surround survives internally.

The second floor of the main block was described in 1621 as 'a loft lait abuve the hall', and was probably a single apartment. It is now sub-divided and contains no features of interest except for a round-ended close-garderobe at the E end of the N wall which is lit by a small window and provided with a lamp-recess. There is another close-garderobe in the W wall. The apartment in the wing is entered from the main stair at a slightly lower level than the main block. In the N wall is a cupboard.

The garret above the main block was originally lit only by two windows, one in each gable, but when the roof was rebuilt at the restoration of 1897 three dormer-windows were incorporated on the N side. The garret of the wing, which is entered from the main staircase, has an original window in the S wall and a modern dormer-window on the W; in 1621 this apartment was lit by two windows, and it is possible that the dormer-window may replace an earlier opening. The angle-turrets of the main block are floored at a lower level than the garret from which they are entered. Each of the three turrets was provided with a pair of pistol-holes, placed near the junctions of the turrets with the main walls at a height corresponding to the present floor-level, but these are now partly blocked up.

In the grounds to the S of the castle an 18th-century sundial stands on a rebuilt pillar. The copper dial (Pl. 43C) bears the inscription HORA FUGIT 1720, and the Royal Arms of Great Britain, English style, with the motto DIEU ET MON DROIT.

HISTORICAL NOTE

The six merklands of Barcaldine were included in the third of Lorn granted by Colin, 1st Earl of Argyll, to his uncle, Sir Colin Campbell of Glenorchy, in 1470.[1] The existing castle was built by the 7th Laird of Glenorchy, Sir Duncan Campbell, and its construction is recorded in two successive entries in *The Black Book of Taymouth* which state that 'he biggit ane greit hows in Benderloch in Lorne of four hows heicht, the lawest hows thairoff woltit, for the workmanschip quhairoff he gaiff fyve thowsand markis, anno 1601. Item he biggit the howss of Barchaltane in Lorne and endit it anno 1609, for the warkmanschippe quhairof he gaiff ten thowsand pundis, by and attour the plenisching thairof'.[2] The first entry describes the present building so precisely that there can be no doubt that both entries relate to the same house, despite the variation in nomenclature. It is probable that 1601 marked the beginning of building operations; by 1603 they were sufficiently advanced for the six merklands of Barcaldine 'with the tour' to be included in a grant of lands from Sir Duncan Campbell to his fourth son, John Campbell of Auchinryre.[3] In 1609 payment was made to Alexander Jack, slater, 'for thatching (roofing) Glenorchie's house in Lorn', and this probably marks the completion of building at Barcaldine.[4] John Campbell of Auchinryre died in 1618, and three

years later the 'place of Barcaltin' was placed in the custody of Patrick Campbell, 'fear of Delmarglen', a natural son of Sir Duncan Campbell; the inventory compiled on this occasion is unusually informative about the permanent fittings of the building, and is given in full *infra*.[5] Patrick Campbell received a new tack of Barcaldine in 1642, 'provyding that the said manor place of Barchaltan be patent to the said Sir Robert (Campbell, 9th laird of Glenorchy) at all occasiones quhen it sall happin him to resort thairto . . . . and also the said Sir Robert sall uphold and hold watertight the said manor place of Barchaltan upone his owne expenss'.[6] In 1645–6 Patrick Campbell garrisoned the castle on behalf of the Marquess of Argyll, and the Glenorchy family chronicler includes it in the list of 'garisone housis' which 'by the providence of God' were not captured by Montrose.[7]

Although Patrick Campbell occupied Barcaldine Castle as tacksman for over fifty years, both he and his son John continued to be designated by the name of their estate in Perthshire, Invergeldie. When the commander of the garrison at Inverlochy was authorised to garrison the castle in 1678, it was described as 'belonging to the Earle of Caithnes (John Campbell of Glenorchy)', although the estate of Barcaldine, with heritable keeping of the tower, had been sold by the Earl to Patrick Campbell in the preceding year.[8] Alexander Campbell, who as Chamberlain of the Earl of Breadalbane's Argyll estates supervised the extensive building-operations at Kilchurn Castle (No. 293) during the 1690s, was the first member of the family to be styled 'of Barcaldine'.

In November 1698, when work at Kilchurn was almost completed, Lord Breadalbane instructed Andrew Christie, master-mason there, to repair Barcaldine Castle. After detailed examination of the structure, however, the Earl 'receaved a confounded account of that ruineous place of Barcaltin'; the mason reported that the roof and much of the walls were 'totally failld', and estimated the cost of repairs, including the complete replacement of floors and roof, and a new iron gate and window-bars, at almost £3200 Scots. The Earl complained, 'that in effect is to build a new house and to be at the expenss to pull down the old and yet to be tyed to that foundation', and condemned Sir Duncan, his ancestor, for building on such an exposed hill-top. At first, convinced of the need to retain a residence in Benderloch, he gave instructions for materials to be prepared and timber floated down Loch Etive and through the Shian narrows. He quickly changed his mind, however, granting the castle in feu to Alexander

---

[1] S.R.O., Breadalbane Collection, GD 112/5/5, 'Chartulary', p. 23.
[2] *Taymouth Bk.*, 35–6.
[3] S.R.O., Breadalbane Collection, GD 112/5/4, 'Regester', p. 178.
[4] Ibid., GD 112/5/7, 'Inventory of Writs', *sub anno* 1609.
[5] Ibid., GD 112/22/4A; Johnston, *Campbell Heraldry*, i, 63.
[6] S.R.O., Breadalbane Collection, GD 112/10/1, Tacks.
[7] *Dunstaffnage Case*, 173, 176; *Taymouth Bk.*, 100–1.
[8] Tombstone of Patrick Campbell at Ardchattan Priory (*supra*, p. 114, no. 25); RPC, 3rd series, vi (1678–80), 35–6.

Campbell in May 1699, and the only extant account for repairs was paid by the new owner.[1]

The sub-division of the hall described above, was probably carried out soon after this. On the completion of Barcaldine House (No. 313) in about 1724 the senior branch of the family left the castle, and the only building-operations carried out thereafter were minor repairs to the roof. After the sale of the Barcaldine estate in 1842 the castle became ruinous; in 1896 it was bought by Sir Duncan Campbell, 3rd Bt. of Barcaldine and grandson of the last Campbell owner, who carried out an extensive restoration which was completed in 1911.[2]

THE INVENTORY OF 1621. This document[3] is unusual as a detailed list of the permanent furnishings of a Highland castle. The transcript below, which reproduces the original text with the addition only of punctuation, is followed by a modernized version.

Original Text

'The Inwentur of the place of Barcaltin and graith theyrin delyverit be Robert Campbell of Glenfalloche to Patrik Campbell fear of Delmarglene in keiping and custodie the xix of Jannowar 1621 zeir.

Item in the hall of Barcaltin tua lang burdis with thair furmis. Item ane four fittit taffill with ane four fittit scheir. Item in the hall four great windowis with thair stanschouris haill and brottis with thair cacis maskis and bandis. Item tua haill glassin windowis and wthair tua glassin windowis wantis fyf locencis. Item ane tymer fir dour at the end of the hall bund with bandis and ane tymer slott. Item tua littill furmis for the taffell. Item mair ane ?tilk blank of plain trie. Item ane pantrie with dour kay lock and bandis with ane window glass thairin caice and brot without bandis with ane littill ?woie furme and a ?bid burd.

Item the chalmer des, dowbill dour lokit and bandis. Item mair ane standing bed of aik turnit work. Item ane wthair bed of fir with ane trall bed. Item tua windowis with thair caices brotis and bandis and thair glass haill except ane locent. Ane priwie with dour and bandis.

Item ane loft lait above the hall with dour lok bandis and key. Item in the said loft four windowis with caist half brottit with thair stanshouris and maskis and glassit haill.

Item above the said loft layit fyftin jestis of fir. Item above the saidis jestis tua windowis caicit without brottis stanshourit and glassit quhairof ane glassin windo half brokin.

Item ane chalmer above the chalmer des in the jam with dowbill dour lok bandis and key, with ane turnit standing bed of aik and ane wthair standing bed of fir. Tua windois with thair stanshouris brottis caices bandis and maskis, ane of thame haill glassit except a locent, the wthair glassin windo the thrid of it brokin. Ane chalmer furme, ane cut of a blank ane eill lang.

Item the wmost chalmer in the jam with dour lock and bandis, with tua windo caicit half brottit, ane of thame glassit and stanshourit.

Item in the great trumbel, thrie windois with thair caicis stanshouris half brottit except ane and glassit.

Item in the trumbel that gais oub fra the hall, ane windo with stanshour caiceis half brotis and glassit haill.

Item the kitsine dowbill dourit lok and bandis and key, a dressing burd and ane blank, ane dressing windo with brot and bandis. Item in the pend of the kitsin tua great irne glikis for hinging of mertis.

Item ane wthair wount neir the kitsin with ane dour lok and key with tua irin glikis in the pend for hinging of mertis.

Item the wountt of the jame ane dowbill dour with lok key and bandis. Item thairin ane mikill kirnell of fir and ane baiking stuill and tua irin glikis and ane baiking troche.

Item at the entrie of the plaice ane irne yet with ane sloitt and a great irin bar, ane tymer yet withe lok and key of auld irne.

Hameris, ane brokin mell with ane littill hamer. Item mair thrie kistis with lokis, bandis and keyis.'

Modernized Version

'The Inventory of the house of Barcaldine and furnishings therein, delivered by Robert Campbell of Glenfalloch (later 9th laird of Glenorchy) to Patrick Campbell, fiar of Delmarglene (and Invergeldie) in keeping and custody, 19 January 1621.

Item, in the hall of Barcaldine two long tables with their benches. Item, a four-legged table with a four-legged chair. Item, in the hall, four great windows with their stanchions intact and shutter-boards, with their frames, masks and hinges. Item, two intact glazed windows; the other two glazed windows lack five lozenges. Item, a door of fir timber at the end of the hall, fitted with hinges and with a timber draw-bar. Item, two little benches for the table. Item, also, a [?] plank of plain wood. Item, a pantry with door, key, lock and hinges. A glazed window having frame and shutter without hinges. A little [?] bench and a [?] board.

Item, the principal chamber, double door with lock and bands. Item, also a standing-bed of turned oak. Item, another bed of fir with a truckle-bed. Item, two windows with their frames, shutters and hinges, and their glass complete except for one lozenge. A privy with door and hinges.

Item, a loft laid above the hall, with door, lock, hinges and key. Item, in the said loft four windows with frames, half-shuttered, with their stanchions and masks, and glazing intact.

Item, laid above the said loft, fifteen joists of fir. Item, above the said joists, two windows with frames but without shutters, fitted with stanchions and glazed; one glazed window is half broken.

Item, a chamber in the jamb, above the principal chamber, having a double door, lock, hinges and key,

[1] S.R.O., Campbell of Barcaldine Collection, GD 170/629/ nos. 96, 99, 102, letters from 1st Earl of Breadalbane; ibid., GD 170/204, estimate and account of repairs; ibid., GD 170/3, feu charter of Barcaldine Castle.
[2] Johnston, *Campbell Heraldry*, i, 66; MacDougall, op. cit., pp. 6–7.
[3] S.R.O., Breadalbane Collection, GD 112/22/4A. The inventory is written on one side of a single sheet of paper.

with a turned standing-bed of oak and another standing-bed of fir. Two windows with their stanchions, shutters, frames, hinges and masks: one of them completely glazed except for one lozenge, the other glazed window a third of it broken. A chamber-bench. A section of board one ell (1·1 m) long.

Item, the highest chamber in the jamb, with door, lock and hinges, with two windows, framed and half-shuttered, one of them glazed and fitted with stanchions.

Item, in the great turnpike-stair, three windows with their frames and stanchions, half-shuttered except for one, and glazed.

Item, in the stair that goes up from the hall, a window with stanchions, frames, half-shutters and intact glazing.

Item, the kitchen, with double door, lock and hinges and key. A dressing-board and a plank, a serving-window with shutter and hinges. Item, in the vaulted roof of the kitchen, two great iron hooks for hanging marts (beef-carcasses).

Item, another vault near the kitchen with a door, lock and key, with two iron hooks in the roof for hanging marts.

Item, the vault of the jamb, a double door with lock, key and hinges. Item therein, a large meal-chest of fir and a baking-stool and two iron hooks and a baking-trough.

Item, at the entry of the house, an iron yett with a draw-bar and a great iron bar. A timber gate with lock and key of old iron.

Hammers: a broken maul with a little hammer. Item, also three chests with locks, hinges and keys'.

907405   NM 94 SW   May 1969

280. Caisteal nan Con, Torsa. This castle (Fig. 168, Pl. 44A, B) occupies a small rocky eminence on the NE shore of the island of Torsa, overlooking Seil Sound and Ardmaddy Bay. The entire area of the rock summit was enclosed, the upper and landward portion being occupied by a small oblong tower-house or hall-house, and the lower seaward portion by an oblong bailey which incorporated a circular tower at the NE corner. The castle appears to have been approached by means of a footpath leading up to a point on the S side of the bailey. All the buildings are very ruinous and much overgrown with turf, but considerable portions of the external wall-face, both of the tower-house and of the bailey, survive.

The masonry is of local rubble bonded in coarse lime mortar. The facework is variable in character (Pl. 44C) and includes flagstone-slate and split boulders, some of the slabs being set on edge; there is nothing to suggest that freestone dressings were employed. Some portions of the walls are founded upon a plinth, while others rise from scarcements carried down to natural ledges in the rock face. The tower measured about 13·7 m from NE to SW by 8·8 m transversely over all, but the thickness of the walls cannot be ascertained without excavation. Access from the bailey was evidently obtained by means of a doorway in the NE wall, while gaps in the mounds of debris that cover the side-walls probably indicate the

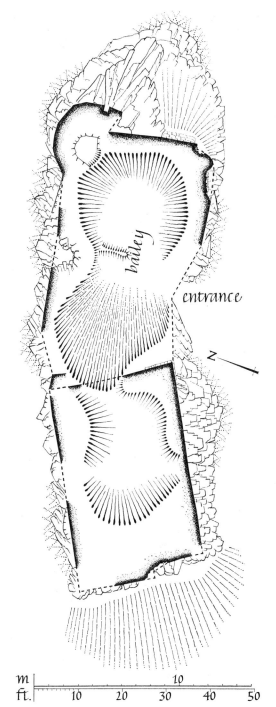

Fig. 168. Caisteal nan Con, Torsa (No. 280); plan

positions of former window-openings. The bailey measured 16·2 m by 10·6 m over all, the NE angle-tower having an external diameter of about 5·5 m. The angle-tower evidently contained a garderobe, of which the discharge-chute is visible in the external wall-face.

About 75 m to the NE of the castle there is a small rocky inlet which probably served as a boat-landing.

It is difficult to estimate the date of this castle, but it may probably be ascribed to the later Middle Ages. The overall dimensions of the tower-house correspond fairly closely to those of Caisteal na Gruagaich, in Morvern, which probably belongs to the 15th century.

The island of Torsa was granted to the Campbells of Lochawe (afterwards Earls of Argyll) in 1313, and the superiority appears to have remained in their possession until the late 17th century, when it passed to the Campbells of Breadalbane. During the first half of the 16th century, and perhaps earlier, the island seems to have been held from the Campbells by the MacDougalls of Rarey, but during the second half of the century Torsa, like Luing, was probably feued by the MacLeans of Duart, from whom the castle may derive its present name of Caisteal nan Con ('the Dogs' Castle').[1]

The island evidently reverted to the MacDougalls early in the 17th century, however, when it was held by Allan MacDougall of Torsa, ancestor of the MacDougalls of Gallanach.[2]

765136   NM 71 SE   June 1971

281. Caisteal na Nighinn Ruaidhe, Loch Avich.

The ruins of this castle occupy a small island situated close to the NW shore of Loch Avich about 7 km E of Kilmelford. The island itself is approximately hour-glass shaped on plan, the central waist, which is lower than the remainder, constituting a convenient landing-place. The W portion of the islet can be reached from the mainland by wading, the distance being about 30 m, and the maximum depth of water at the date of visit 1·0 m.

The castle occupies the E portion of the islet, and the remains comprise an oblong tower-house, or hall-house, standing within a defensive enclosure which contains some remains of outbuildings (Fig. 169). The SE wall of the tower-house stands almost to its full height, but the remaining walls are fragmentary, any surviving portions now being buried beneath rubble and debris, which also fills the interior of the two lower storeys. The building evidently comprised at least three storeys, and appears to have measured about 15·8 m from SW to NE by 11·3 m transversely over walls having a thickness of some 2·3 m at second-floor level. The masonry is of local random rubble well bonded with pinnings. Some of the dressings, including window-jambs, are of a coarse-grained buff-coloured sandstone, possibly derived from Bridge of Awe (No. 354), but the surviving window-sills, the lowermost quoins of the E angle, and the splayed offset-course that forms the uppermost member of a base-plinth which extends along the SE wall, are of schist. This plinth is roughly formed, having an average projection of about 0·5 m, while above it the SE wall rises with a pronounced batter.

Towards the NE end of the SE wall there are the remains of an entrance-doorway situated immediately above the base-plinth. The dressed jambs of the opening have been removed, and the slab-lintelled ingoes blocked with

fallen rubble from within, but a draw-bar tunnel can be seen in the SW jamb with a corresponding socket on the opposite side. This doorway evidently gave access to the basement; its height cannot have exceeded 1·4 m, and the approach must have been made by way of a ladder or timber forestair. The principal entrance was probably situated on the other side of the building, or in the SW gable-wall, at first-floor level. Further SW in the SE wall, and at about the same height as the doorway, there may be seen two latrine-chutes, the NE one probably having served a garderobe at first-floor level, and its neighbour one at second-floor level. There are also two openings at first-floor level towards the NE end of the wall, the SW one being a window and the NE one a latrine-chute serving a second-floor garderobe in the E corner of the building.

The only visible internal feature relating to the two lower floors of the building is a chimneyed fireplace in the centre of the SE wall at first-floor level. There is no evidence to indicate whether or not the basement was vaulted, but the upper floors appear to have been of timber. Two windows remain in the SE wall at second-floor level, the NE one apparently having been provided with bench-seats set within an arched embrasure. The daylight-opening measured 0·45 m in width and the jambs were wrought with plain 0·12 m chamfers. The SW window, which was similarly moulded, had a daylight-opening of 0·35 m; both windows had central iron stanchions. Between the windows there may be seen what appears to be a fragment of a transverse partition-wall, suggesting that at this level the building was sub-divided to contain two main apartments, each served by one of the latrines to which reference has already been made.

Except on the SE side, where the tower-house stands directly above the shore, the E portion of the islet appears to have been enclosed by a stone wall. This is now very ruinous, but some sections show evidence of lime-mortar construction. At the point A on the sketch-plan (Fig. 169) there may be seen what appears to be the jamb of an entrance-doorway, while at B there are the remains of a small sub-rectangular building measuring about 16·1 m from SW to NE by 10·0 m transversely over all. This appears to have been of dry-stone construction and to have comprised two apartments. Lying on the surface of the enclosure-wall near the NE extremity of the island there is a broken millstone of schist measuring 0·81 m in diameter.

Almost nothing is known of the history of this castle, which appears to have been an early stronghold of the Campbells of Craignish. According to a traditional history of the family, the name Caisteal na Nighinn Ruaidhe ('castle of the red-haired maiden') derives from

---

[1] 'It is supposed to have been a hunting-seat of the Lords of the Isles; but more than likely the name is derived from a sobriquet often applied by their enemies to the powerful Clan MacLean—Clann Illeathain nan Con' (Gillies, *Netherlorn*, 58).
[2] *Origines Parochiales*, ii, part i, 101; *Highland Papers*, iv, 221; Skene, *Celtic Scotland*, iii, 438; *APS*, vii (1661–9), 340, 342; *Burke's Landed Gentry* (1952 ed.), 1619.

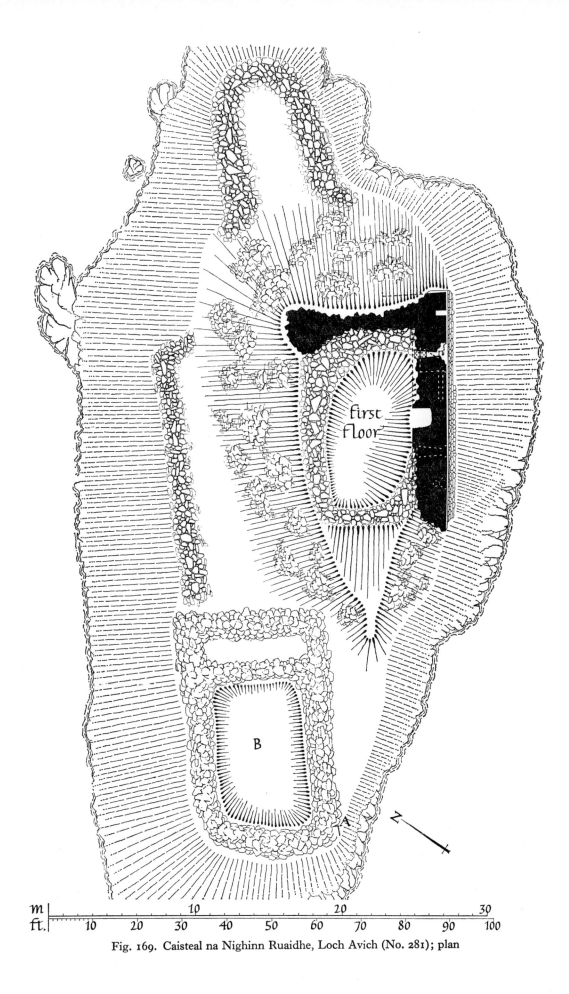

First Floor

B

A

N

m
ft.

10
10   20   30   40   50   60   70   80   90   100

20

30

Fig. 169. Caisteal na Nighinn Ruaidhe, Loch Avich (No. 281); plan

Bridget, daughter of the tòiseach of Loch Avich, by whose marriage to Dugald Campbell of Craignish (*d.* 1220) the lands and castle of Loch Avich came into the possession of the Campbells. The first, and almost the only, reference to the castle in early written record, however, occurs in a charter of 1414 by which Sir Duncan Campbell of Lochawe granted four pennylands of Loch Avich, together with certain other properties, to Ronald Campbell of Craignish, his kinsman. By the terms of this charter Ronald was to become constable of the castles of Craignish and Loch Avich on behalf of Sir Duncan and his heirs, provided that he built up and roofed the two castles. The existing structure is so ruinous that its age is difficult to ascertain, but in size and plan-form the building bears a considerable resemblance to the nearby castle of Fincharn, Loch Awe, which may be as old as the 13th century. The lands of Loch Avich were held by the Campbells of Craignish until at least as late as the 16th century, and an associated office of sergeanty until the 18th century, but nothing more is heard of the castle.[1]

916137   NM 91 SW   June 1971

282. Castle Coeffin, Lismore. The castle (Fig. 170, Pl. 45) stands upon a small limestone promontory on the NW shore of the island, and commands an extensive prospect of Loch Linnhe and the Sound of Mull. To the SE a gently shelving bay affords a convenient anchorage and landing-place directly beneath the castle. The remains comprise an oblong hall-house, which occupies the summit of the promontory, together with an irregularly-shaped bailey enclosing the main entrance-approach on the NE side. All the buildings are now ruinous, and many of the wall-surfaces are ivy-clad, and this makes examination difficult. There are no closely dateable features, but the hall-house may be ascribed to the 13th century on typological grounds, and some portions of the bailey possibly belong to the same period. Most of the bailey appears to be of secondary construction, however, and can be ascribed to the later Middle Ages. There are also indications of the repair and partial reconstruction of the N and W corners of the hall-house, and these alterations may be assigned to the same period.

THE HALL-HOUSE. The building is of irregular oblong plan, measuring about 20·3 m from NE to SW and 10·4 m transversely over walls some 2·1 m to 2·4 m in thickness. The irregularities of the plan are accounted for mainly by the nature of the site, but the rounding-off of the N angle is probably a secondary feature, associated with a reconstruction of the mural staircase in this quarter. The original corner was no doubt square-cut, and the same is probably true of the W corner, although this is now broadly splayed. The splayed section of the wall is thinner than the remainder, and some traces of what appears to be an earlier plinth can be seen beyond it, occupying a position close to the presumed site of the original external angle. The masonry is of roughly-

coursed local rubble, well bonded with pinnings and coarse lime-mortar, and containing numerous granite beach-boulders. Some of these boulders have been split and are bedded on edge. The quoins and dressings are of buff-coloured sandstone, probably quarried from the carboniferous beds at Ardtornish,[2] but most of these have been robbed. There is some evidence to suggest that doorway- and window-embrasures were ceiled with timber lintels.

The building appears to have comprised two main storeys (Pl. 46A), of which the lower was originally provided with three separate entrance-doorways. The principal doorway, which seems to have been equipped with a draw-bar, was situated in the NE gable-wall, and was probably approached from the bailey by means of a forestair. From the entrance-lobby a stair ascended in the N angle of the building to give access to the first floor. This staircase appears to have been contracted in width and partially reconstructed. Beyond the lobby an inner door presumably gave access to the ground-floor apartment, but this opening is now obscured by debris, which fills the lower part of the chamber to a depth of about 1·0 m. A second doorway was situated in the SW gable-wall, and gave access to the tip of the rock promontory upon which the castle stands, and thence to the shore. The SE side of the doorway contains a draw-bar socket. This doorway seems to have been blocked up when the W corner of the building was reconstructed, and traces of rubble-blocking can be seen at the inner threshold. The third doorway, also equipped with a draw-bar socket, is situated towards the centre of the NW wall. Access on this side could hardly have been obtained unless by means of a rope, and it is possible that this opening was utilized as a hoisting-door in connection with the movement of stores. Towards the SW end of the SE wall there are the remains of a steeply-splayed window-embrasure, and there was probably a second window of similar type situated close to the junction of the S wall of the bailey with the hall-house. The ground-floor chamber was ceiled with timber joists at a height of about 2·7 m above floor-level, the NE wall being intaken by a scarcement at this level; there is nothing to suggest that the apartment was sub-divided.

The first floor is incomplete, but the salient features of the plan are still apparent. Access was obtained by means of the staircase in the N corner already described, and the greater part of the floor-area was probably occupied by a single large apartment constituting a hall. This was lit by embrasured windows, of which there appear to have been two in the SE wall and another in the NW wall. To the SW of this latter window there was a garderobe of which part of the mural discharge-chute survives.[3] The SW gable contained a large fireplace, of which one ingo, together with part of the splayed

[1] *Origines Parochiales*, ii, part i, 125; Campbell, A, 'The Manuscript History of Craignish', *SHS Misc.*, iv (1926), 207, 224, 271–2, 292–3; *Dunstaffnage Case*, 353–4.
[2] Information from Mr G H Collins, Institute of Geological Sciences.
[3] It is possible that this chute also served a garderobe at a lower level, entered from the ground-floor chamber.

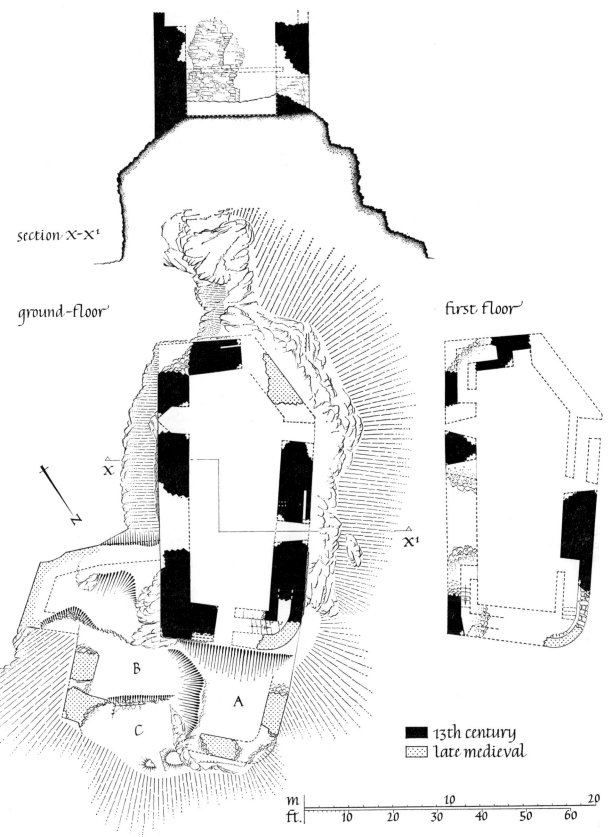

section X-X¹

ground-floor

first floor

X

X¹

N

A

B

C

■ 13th century
⬚ late medieval

m | 10   20
ft. | 10   20   30   40   50   60

Fig. 170. Castle Coeffin, Lismore (No. 282); floor-plans and section

back and rounded chimney, still remain *in situ*. Within the thickness of the S corner of the building there was a chamber, which seems to have been reached by means of a mural passage communicating with a doorway in the SE wall. This chamber was probably a garderobe, and traces of what appear to be vent-chutes are visible externally; the roof of the chamber seems to have been corbel-lintelled. Towards the NE end of the SE wall a mural staircase (Pl. 46B) rises towards a wall-walk, returning at the E corner of the building to pass above the principal ground-floor entrance. One jamb of a small window which formerly lit the staircase can be seen close to this return. Portions of the wall-walk survive on the SE and NW sides of the building, and likewise on the SW gable, where the chimney-flue seems to have passed directly beneath the walk before emerging obliquely through the outer wall-face. The parapet of the wall-walk has a width of 0·71 m. The building was probably covered with a pitched roof rising within the wall-walk, but there is no evidence to indicate whether or not a garret was contained within the roof-space.

THE BAILEY. The masonry of the bailey-walls is in part similar to that of the hall-house, but some sections show an absence of split boulders and a preponderance of small flagstone-rubble of inferior construction. The bailey appears to have been designed mainly to protect the principal entrance to the hall-house, but the precise nature of the defences cannot be deduced from the scanty surface-remains. It is clear, however, that the bailey enclosed the NE gable-wall and part of the SE wall of the hall-house, and contained an entrance on the NE side from which approach-steps rose towards the threshold of the hall-house entrance, some 10 m above. The steps were overlooked by three defensive platforms or chambers, of which the uppermost (A on Fig. 170) retains traces of an opening in the NW wall, while the middle one (B) incorporates a splayed embrasure in the SE wall. Beneath the NE wall of this latter platform there can be seen the upper portion of a lintelled passage or mural chamber, now almost completely filled with debris. This may represent part of an entrance-passage to the bailey, situated at the level of the lowermost platform (C), which retains traces of a splayed opening on the N side. To the S of platform B the bailey-wall returned round the edge of a rock-spur before meeting the SE wall of the hall-house.

There are no signs of a well within the castle, and the nearest visible source of water is a burn which flows into a bay on the N side of the castle. Some traces of buildings, now represented by turf-grown mounds of debris, can be seen in the field that lies immediately to the NE of the castle.

FISH-TRAP. The bay to the SE of the castle contains a tidal fish-trap of unknown age (Pl. 46C). This is approximately U-shaped on plan, and takes the form of a broad dry-stone wall laid directly upon the sea-bed a little below high-water level.

CARVED STONE. Beneath the W corner of the castle there lies a fragment of dressed sandstone which

evidently formed part of a window-jamb (Fig. 171); the arris is wrought with a 65 mm chamfer.

HISTORICAL NOTE. Castle Coeffin was probably erected by one of the MacDougalls of Lorn, within whose lordship the island of Lismore occupied a position of the first political and strategic importance. The site of the castle is one of great natural strength, well placed for seaborne communication within the Firth of Lorn, and lying in close proximity to the diocesan cathedral (No. 267), which is known to have been established on the island some time during the late 12th or early 13th century. Political and topographical considerations alike suggest the probability that this site was

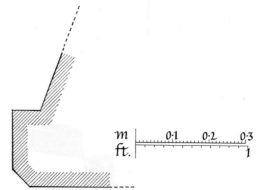

Fig. 171. Castle Coeffin, Lismore (No. 282); carved fragment

occupied by a MacDougall residence (although not necessarily by the present building) prior to the foundation of the nearby episcopal castle of Achadun (No. 276) on lands granted to Bishop William by Ewen of Lorn in 1240. The forfeiture of the MacDougalls in the early 14th century, following their defeat by Robert Bruce, led to the dispersal of their territories, but Lismore seems to have been included among those lands that were regained by John of Lorn during the reign of David II. In 1388 John's daughter, Janet, and her husband, Sir Robert Stewart, sold the MacDougall lordship, including Lismore, to John Stewart of Innermeath, whose family retained it for the next eighty years. In 1469–70, however, an exchange of lands between the Stewart and Campbell families brought the Lordship of Lorn into the hands of Colin, 1st Earl of Argyll, who promptly granted part of Lismore, including the two merklands of the castle of 'Chaben' to his uncle, Sir Colin Campbell of Glenorchy. This is the first identifiable reference to the castle in written record, for it is not included in Fordun's list of island castles, compiled some time during the second half of the 14th century.[1]

In an anonymous account of the Western Isles, written some time between 1577 and 1595, it was reported that

[1] Duncan, A A M and Brown, A L, 'Argyll and the Isles in the Earlier Middle Ages', *PSAS*, xc (1956–7), 192–220; MacDonald, *Argyll*, 138, 159, 174, 233–4; *Origines Parochiales*, ii, part i, 164–5; Fordun, John of, *Chronica Gentis Scotorum*, book ii, chapter x.

in Campbell of Glenorchy's part of the island of Lismore there was 'ane auld castill callit Bealwothar, but is not mantenit'. Pont's map of the early 17th century, however, reverts to the earlier name, which is rendered as 'Castel Kaven', while the author of the *New Statistical Account* of 1841 terms the place 'Castle Coeffin'. (Local tradition holds that this name derives from the legendary Norse prince, Caifean, while the alternative form mentioned above may be related to that of Caifean's supposed sister, Beothail). The castle remained in the possession of the Campbells of Glenorchy until the second quarter of the 18th century, but there is no evidence to suggest that it was inhabited in post-medieval times.[1]

853437   NM 84 SE   July 1970

283. Castle, Castles Farm (Site). This castle is said to have occupied the low flat-topped mound that lies about 60 m NNW of the present farmhouse,[2] but the existing remains in this position appear to be those of a dun (No. 161). Consequently, the site of the medieval castle of Glen Strae is uncertain, but it is possible that it stood about 45 m to the NW of the mound, where there are some slight traces of buildings.

The castle appears to have been a residence of the MacGregors (cf. Nos. 314 and 335), who held the lands of Glen Strae and Stronmilchan from about the beginning of the 15th century until 1624, when Gregor MacGregor, 8th of Glenstrae, sold them to Sir Duncan Campbell of Glenorchy. This property included the two merklands of 'Castill' which are on record in 1519.[3] The castle itself is said to have been burnt by Sir Duncan Campbell in 1611.[4]

137296   NN 12 NW   September 1967

284. Castle Shuna, Appin. This small tower-house (Pl. 46D, E) is situated on sloping ground at the S end of the island of Shuna, about 1·1 km NNW of Castle Stalker (No. 285). A description of the Western Isles, compiled between 1577 and 1595, states that the island at that time belonged to John Stewart, Laird of Appin, while another description of c. 1630, which describes Shuna (wrongly referred to as 'Iona') as 'the most profitable and fertilest (island) in all these Countries', similarly describes it as the property of the Laird of Appin.[5] Neither of these sources refers specifically to the castle; the building is markedly domestic in character, however, and would not have been considered worthy of special notice. On architectural grounds it may be ascribed to about the end of the 16th century; the builder was probably John Stewart, who died in 1595, or his son Duncan Stewart. During the course of the 17th century, a circular stair-tower was added against the SE wall.

The original structure comprises a rectangular block measuring 11·6 m from NE to SW by 7·4 m transversely over walls 1·1 m in thickness (Fig. 172). The vaulted ground-floor remains intact, and the SW and SE walls

stand to second-floor level. The masonry is of local rubble, predominantly limestone, set in coarse lime-mortar, with quoins and window-dressings of schist; many of the latter have been removed since the building became ruinous.

An entrance-doorway near the NE end of the SE wall, now enclosed within the added stair-tower, gives access to the NE compartment of the axially-vaulted ground-storey, which was the kitchen. In the NE gable-wall there was a large fireplace, the rear wall of which has

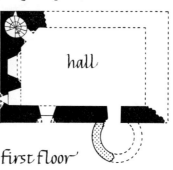

first floor

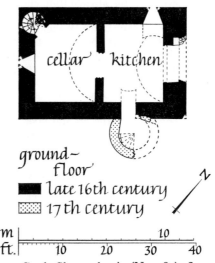

ground-floor
■ late 16th century
▨ 17th century

Fig. 172. Castle Shuna, Appin (No. 284); floor plans

collapsed, having a salt-box in the NW side; the fire-place-arch has disappeared, and its original form cannot be ascertained. This apartment is lit by a splayed window at the NE end of the NW wall, which has a daylight opening of not less than 0·45 m. A substantial

[1] Skene, *Celtic Scotland*, iii, 436; Carmichael, *Lismore*, 74–6; Blaeu's *Atlas* (Lorn); *NSA*, vii (Argyll), 237, 241; Campbell, Lord A, *Records of Argyll* (1885), 324–33.
[2] Name Book, No. 49, p. 141.
[3] *Origines Parochiales*, ii, part i, 138; MacGregor, A G M, *History of the Clan Gregor* (1898–1901), i, 452–3.
[4] *RMS*, viii (1620–33), no. 1076.
[5] Skene, *Celtic Scotland*, iii, 436; *Geog. Coll.*, ii, 155.

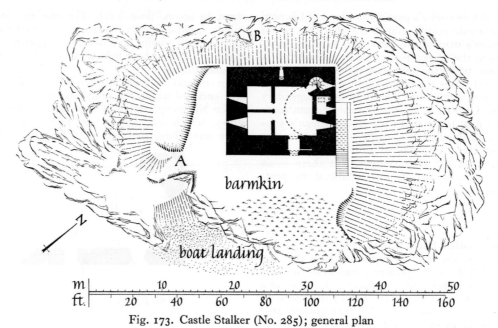

barmkin

boat landing

Fig. 173. Castle Stalker (No. 285); general plan

partition-wall separates the kitchen from another vaulted apartment of similar dimensions, lit by a window in the SW gable-wall, and having in the W angle a narrow spiral stair which leads to the first floor. This stair, which is lit by two small slits, is constructed without a newel, and terminates at first-floor level in a neatly corbelled roof; both of these features can be paralleled in work ascribed to the late 16th century at Breachacha Castle, Coll.[1]

The principal entrance-doorway to the first floor was placed immediately above the ground-floor entrance in the SE wall, and it appears probable that access was originally by a forestair, perhaps of timber, which was subsequently replaced by the existing stone stair-tower. The NE side of this structure has entirely collapsed, but part of the splayed jamb of an entrance-doorway at ground-floor level remains *in situ*. The first-floor apartment, which was evidently the hall, was served by a large segmental-arched fireplace in the SW gable-wall. At the W angle a doorway leads to the service-stair that communicates with the cellar, while to the SE of the fireplace there is an embrasured window, having splayed jambs and a straight lintel. A similar but wider opening is formed near the SW end of the SE wall, and others may have existed in the NW and NE walls, which do not survive to this level. A series of five moulded corbels which carried a runner supporting the joists of the second floor can be seen in the SE wall, while there is a scarcement in the SW wall at a slightly higher level. The original means of access to this floor is uncertain; the walls were not sufficiently thick to include a mural stair, although it is possible that the N angle projected internally to include a small spiral stair. When the external stair-tower was built, it was carried up to a doorway at second-floor level. The only other features that survive at this level are the scanty remains of two small windows

on either side of the chimney-flue in the SW gable-wall, and another window at the SW end of the SE wall.

About 10 m SE of the castle there are the turf-covered foundations of a substantial building. This appears to have measured 20 m from NE to SW by 7·3 m transversely over walls 1·2 m in thickness, which stand to a height of about 1·1 m at the NE end. The masonry is set in clay mortar and is brought to a neat vertical face. The structure appears to have been divided by a partition-wall into two unequal compartments with no internal means of communication, the larger being towards the NE and having a doorway mid-way along its length in the SE wall. A small annexe is built against the outer face of the NE wall. The exact nature of these remains is uncertain, but the plan-form, taken in conjunction with the position of the doorway in the wall furthest removed from the castle, suggests that they may have comprised a house and byre built after the castle ceased to be occupied, and doubtless making use of building-materials removed from it, perhaps in the 18th or early 19th century.

915482   NM 94 NW   July 1970

285. Castle Stalker. This castle stands upon a rocky islet at the mouth of Loch Laich, known as Eilean an Stalcaire, from which it commands an extensive prospect of Loch Linnhe and the Strath of Appin. The existing remains comprise a well-preserved tower-house (Figs. 173, 174, 175; Pls. 47, 48A, B) together with fragmentary traces of an associated barmkin. The tower-house is substantially of mid-16th-century date, but the upper-works appear to have been remodelled about a century

---

[1] *PSAS*, cii (1969–70), 155–87.

later. A certain amount of structural consolidation was carried out during the first half of this century, while a more extensive scheme of reconstruction was begun by the present proprietor in 1965 and is still in progress. The following description and the accompanying drawings relate to the building as it stood in 1966, but some of the photographs are of more recent date.

The usual approach to the castle is from the E, where the islet is separated from the mainland by a shallow stretch of water about 100 m in width. There is no sign of a causeway, and it is likely that access has always been obtained principally by means of small boats. It is sometimes possible to reach the castle at low tide by wading, however, the approach being made either from the E shore of Loch Laich, or from Ardtur Point, by way of Eilean a' Ghaill.

From a landing-place on the sheltered SE shore of the islet the main approach-path appears to have ascended to the barmkin by means of a roughly-constructed staircase (A on Fig. 173), of which some traces are still discernible. The barmkin itself seems originally to have enclosed the tower on all sides except the NW and, in addition to the approach-stair already mentioned, was provided with a postern-doorway adjacent to the W corner of the tower-house. Part of the jamb and arch-springer of this doorway (Pl. 50D) can be seen wrought upon the quoin-stones of the tower, while immediately to the SW of the doorway the footings of the barmkin-wall survive for a length of at least 3·0 m. Elsewhere there are no visible remains of the barmkin-wall, except at the N corner of the tower, where there may be seen a number of projecting bond-stones whose disposition indicates that the wall had (or was intended to have) a maximum thickness of 1·5 m and a height of about 3·9 m. The barmkin is not indicated in the 18th-century ground-plan of the castle reproduced in Pl. 48C, and is unlikely to have been in existence at that time. Just below the postern-doorway there is a small rock-cut pool (B on Fig. 173), which seems to have served as a catchment-point for rain-water discharged from the parapet drain-spouts on the NW side of the tower. This appears to have constituted the only source of water supply for the castle.

The tower-house is of oblong plan and measures about 14·8 m from NE to SW by 11·8 m transversely over walls some 2·7 m in thickness. It rises to a height of three storeys and a garret, and is strongly constructed of rubble masonry with quoins and dressings of fine-grained variegated sandstone obtained from the Inninmore Bay quarries in Morvern.[1] The original masonry of the 16th century is characterized by the excellence and regularity of its construction and by the widespread use of relieving-arches. Most of the openings of this period have chamfered arrises, and the windows have been glazed and barred (Pl. 50B). The majority of the 17th-century openings, on the other hand, show roll-moulded arrises and only the larger windows appear to have been glazed.

The ground-floor of the tower-house (Fig. 174) is entered by means of a round-headed doorway situated towards the centre of the SE wall (Pl. 50C). The doorway is wrought externally with a bold quirked edge-roll (Fig. 176C); it has provision for two doors, of which the inner, probably an iron yett, was secured by a draw-bar. The doorway is also protected by a box-machicolation corbelled out at parapet-level. A second doorway, situated on the inner side of the wall, and having a lintelled head and chamfered arrises, leads into the largest of the four apartments that occupy the ground-floor. This was formerly lit by a small window in the NE wall, but the window is now obscured by the forestair that rises to the principal entrance-doorway at first-floor level. A doorway in the N corner opens into a turnpike-stair, which rises to the full height of the building and provides the only means of access to the two uppermost floors. Two doorways in the SW wall lead into smaller rooms, of which that to the SE is lit by a small window, and that to the NW by a loop of inverted-keyhole shape (Pl. 50E). All three cellars are roofed by a continuous barrel-vault springing from NW to SE.

The fourth apartment at this level is a pit-prison, contrived within the thickness of the NE wall, to which the only access is by means of a hatch (Pl. 51G) formed within a first-floor window-embrasure. The prison, which is ceiled with a pointed barrel-vault (Pl. 50F), measures about 2·4 m by 1·3 m and has a depth of 3·6 m; in the NE wall there is a garderobe, together with a slit-window, now obscured by the forestair.

The principal entrance-doorway to the castle (Pl. 50A) is situated in the NE wall at first-floor level, and gives access, by means of an inner doorway, to the single large apartment that occupies this level. In the original arrangement the entrance-doorway was probably reached by means of a timber forestair and gang-plank, but subsequently a drawbridge was constructed spanning an open timber framework founded upon a stone base. The stone base, which incorporated a splayed plinth, was situated immediately beneath the entrance-doorway and thus obscured the slit-window of the prison. Initially the drawbridge appears to have been approached by means of the timber forestair, but in or before the early 18th century this was replaced by a stone forestair, an alteration which led to the blocking-up of the cellar-window in the NE wall of the tower. This is the arrangement depicted in a Board of Ordnance drawing of about the first half of the 18th century[2] (Pl. 48C), and, to judge from the wording of a document of 1684,[3] the draw-bridge in use at this period was designed to hinge downwards into a 'pit' formed within the supporting timber framework when the castle was prepared for defence. Some time later, probably during the late 18th or early 19th century, the drawbridge went out of use and the timber framework was removed and the pit built up with masonry, but two of the socket-holes associated with the framework were still visible in 1889.[4]

As it stands today, therefore, the column of masonry that supports the entrance-platform is of three distinct

---

[1] Information from Mr G H Collins, Institute of Geological Sciences.
[2] B.M., King's Maps, XLIX 40.
[3] *RPC*, 3rd series, x (1684–5), 367–8.
[4] *Cast. and Dom. Arch.*, iii, fig. 102.

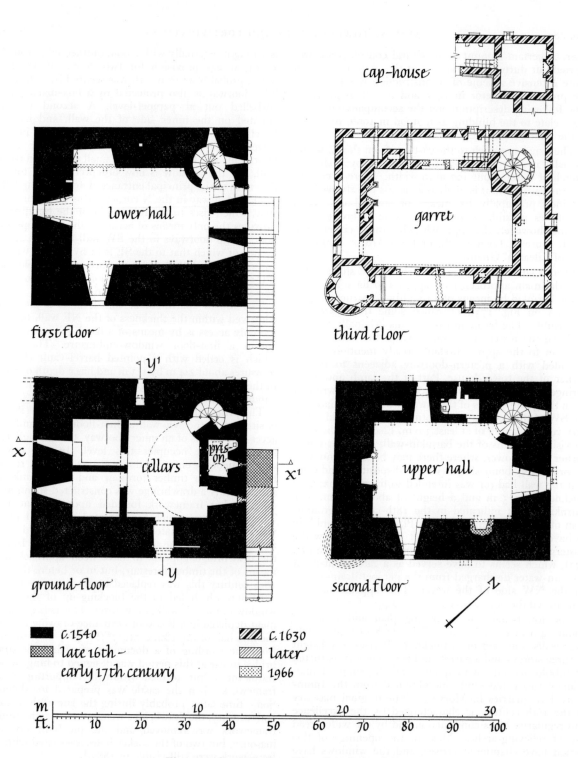

cap-house

lower hall

first floor

garret

third floor

cellars

pris on

ground-floor

upper hall

second floor

Y¹

X

X¹

Y

■ c.1540
▨ c.1630
▩ late 16th –
early 17th century
▤ later
▨ 1966

m
ft.   10   20   30   40   50   60   70   80   90   100
                    10   20   30

Fig. 174. Castle Stalker (No. 285); floor-plans

190

building-periods, the uppermost portion being of recent origin, the central portion of late 18th- or 19th-century date, and the lowermost portion, which is distinguished by its sandstone quoins and base-plinth, of late 16th- or 17th-century date. The straight joint that separates the stone base and former drawbridge-pit from the later stone forestair is clearly distinguishable. An ornamental device is carved in high relief upon one of the E quoin-stones of the tower, being so placed as to be visible to anyone ascending a forestair. This device (Pl. 50G), evidently an original feature, is greatly worn, but may represent the head and foreparts of a dragon or lizard.

The entrance-doorway itself is wrought with a continuous quirked edge-roll. The head is pointed, but the central voussoirs have evidently been restored within recent times and there is little doubt that the doorway was originally round-arched[1] (Pl. 49A). The doorway has no provision for an inner door or for a draw-bar, but was defended from parapet-level by means of a box-machicolation similar to that above the ground-floor entrance. Immediately over the doorway there is an heraldic panel set within a boldly projecting frame carved in relief with foliaceous and tendrilled decoration within a ribboned edge-roll. The panel, which is much weathered, appears to have borne the full heraldic achievement of the sovereigns of Scotland. The shield is charged with a lion rampant and is supported by unicorns, while above there are traces of a helm in profile surmounted by a crown.

The first-floor apartment, or lower hall (Fig. 174), is lit by large windows in the SE and SW walls, as well as by a smaller low-level window in the NE wall. The embrasures of the larger windows are provided with stone bench-seats. The lintel of the SW window is carved externally with a shield bearing a coat of arms. The carving is very worn, but the shield appears to bear: quarterly, 1st, gyronny of eight; 2nd, ?a galley, sail furled; 4th, ?a hart's head cabossed; on a chief, ?a buckle between two mullets. The 3rd quarter is indecipherable. These are probably the arms of the Campbells of Airds, in which case the carving is likely to date from the first half of the 17th century.

In the W corner of the apartment there are the remains of a large segmental-headed fireplace wrought with a cavetto-moulded arris. The greater part of the arch-head is missing, but the cavetto-moulding of the remaining springer shows traces of relief decoration. Within the SW jamb of the fireplace there has evidently been a low bench-seat or shelf, while between the fireplace and the SW window-embrasure a mural socket-hole occurs at a height of 1·3 m above floor-level. Since the tower-house is not provided with an internal kitchen it is possible that this fireplace was used for culinary purposes. The ceiling-joists of the apartment are supported upon runners carried by moulded stone corbels, an arrangement which is repeated on the floor above. The roughly-cobbled floor is of comparatively recent date.

From the stair-landing separate doorways (Pl. 51G) give access to ascending and descending flights of the stair, while the partition-wall separating the two openings incorporates a relieving-arch buttressed by a splayed expansion of the newel (Pl. 51E). Notwithstanding the fact that the 18th-century Board of Ordnance drawing (Pl. 48C) represents only a single doorway in this position, the existing arrangement is likely to be original. It is evident, however, that the outermost section of the partition-wall, together with the threshold of the upper doorway, has been reconstructed at a comparatively recent period. The window lighting the stair-landing (Pl. 50B) was formerly provided with a sink or laver in its breast, and although the sink itself has been removed or built up the outlet-spout remains.

In the original arrangement the second floor (Fig. 174) probably contained a single large apartment serving as an upper hall, but sub-dividing walls of timber were introduced before the middle of the 18th century (cf. Pl. 48C). Today there is again a single room, and this is lit by means of three windows, of which those in the NE and SE walls are provided with bench-seats within their embrasures. Towards the NE end of the NW wall there is a spacious mural garderobe provided with a window and a vent-shaft whose external outlet, rebated for a door-frame, can be seen at the foot of the wall (Pl. 51A). This vent-shaft is joined at second-floor level by a similar descending shaft, which must have served a third-floor garderobe subsequently removed during the early 17th-century alterations to the castle.

The large fireplace in the centre of the SW wall has been richly decorated, but now lacks its lintel, together with the greater part of one of the jambs. The remaining jamb comprises a high scalloped base of semi-octagonal plan, from which a column rises to support a scalloped capital (Fig. 176A, B, D; Pl. 51F). The column is carved in bold relief with a costumed male figure flanked by cable ornament. The figure appears to be kneeling, his hands clasping a waist-belt from which a sword or dagger hangs at his right side. The base of the opposite jamb is similar to the one already described.[2] Immediately above the site of the lintel there is a segmental-headed relieving-arch of ashlar. The fireplace in the SE wall appears to have been roughly reconstructed at a comparatively recent period, but part of what seems to be an original sandstone rybat survives at the base of the SW jamb. This fireplace was probably inserted when the apartment was sub-divided.

The existing upperworks of the tower, including the round at the S angle, the corbelled machicolations and garderobes, and the garret-chamber itself, appear to be substantially of early 17th-century date, and the original arrangements are uncertain. As it stands today the third floor (Fig. 174) comprises a garret-chamber surrounded by an enclosed parapet-walk. The chamber is entered from doorways in the NE and SW parapet-walks, the former opening displaying chamfered arrises and the latter roll-moulded arrises. The room was lit by means

---

[1] Cf. Pococke's drawing of 1760 (Pococke, *Tours*, 96), and *Cast. and Dom. Arch.*, iii, fig. 102.

[2] The scalloped capital of this jamb was recovered from the island foreshore in 1968 and has since been replaced in position.

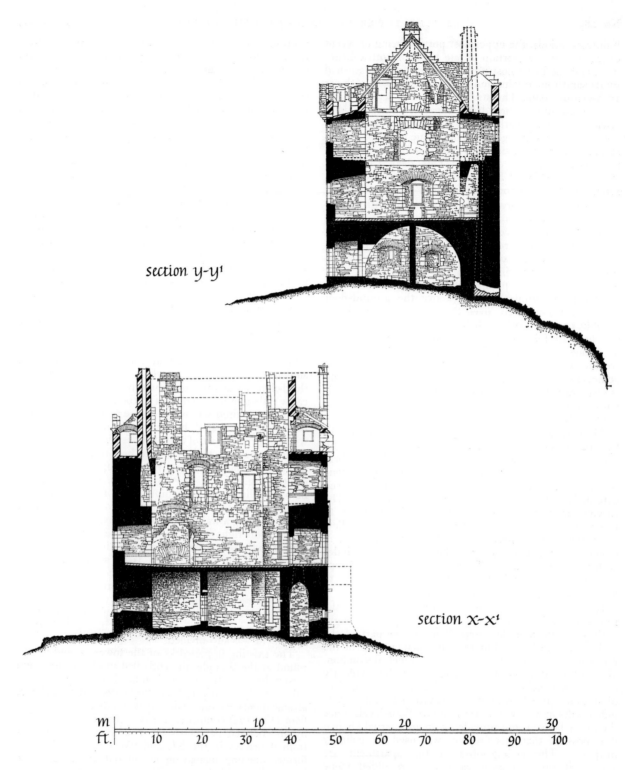

section Y-Y¹

section X-X¹

m 10 20 30
ft. 10 20 30 40 50 60 70 80 90 100

Fig. 175. Castle Stalker (No. 285); sections

192

of dormer-windows in the two long walls, but the precise arrangements are uncertain. At the time when the 18th-century Board of Ordnance drawings were made the apartment was evidently sub-divided by a timber partition (Pl. 48C).

Towards the NW end of the SW wall there is a fire-place (Fig. 176E) incorporating high moulded bases with ribbon-moulded neckings, plain jambs of square section, and cavetto-moulded capitals having neckings carved in relief with a double row of dog-tooth ornament. Both capitals are somewhat mutilated, but the NW one appears to have been carved in relief with a foliaceous

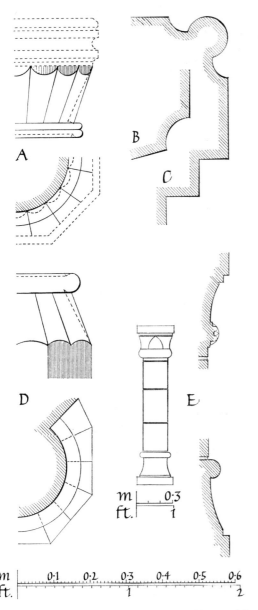

Fig. 176. Castle Stalker (No. 285); profile mouldings:
A, B, D, second-floor fireplace; C, ground-floor entrance;
E, third-floor fireplace

design incorporating thistles, a rose and a leaf. A lobe-shaped central panel bears an incised seven-spoked figure.

The staircase in the N corner terminates at a landing from which segmental-arched openings give access to the adjacent parapet-walks. These are lit from windows in the external walls and are provided with a variety of gun-loops and pistol-holes (Pl. 51D). The NW walk incorporates a garderobe corbelled out from the external wall-face, while the SE walk terminates in a round corbelled out from the S angle upon a moulded corbel-course of four members (Pl. 51C). The round is equipped with three circular-mouthed gun-loops and is lit by means of a window having chamfered arrises; one of the external jambs of the window is carved with a human head in bold relief (Pl. 51B). There is no communication between the SE and SW parapet-walks. At the NE end of the NW walk a narrow stone staircase rises to give access, by means of a roll-moulded doorway, to a cap-house situated above the stair-head. The cap-house has a roll-moulded fireplace and two windows in the NE gable-wall, while in the NW wall there is a corbelled garderobe similar to the one on the parapet-walk below. The rectangular sockets seen in the external gable-wall of the cap-house were probably intended to serve as scaffolding-holds.

The roofing-arrangements were unusually compli-cated. The NE and SW parapet-walks had lean-to roofs carried upon corbelled runners, while the NW and SE walks were provided with pitched roofs. The valleys formed between these latter roofs and the pitched roofs of the garret itself were drained by means of stone gutters discharging through the walls of the garret-chamber and across the floors of the parapet-walks, whence they issued externally by means of stone spouts. The round at the S angle was presumably intended to be roofed, but was evidently roofless in the second half of the 18th century (Pl. 49). The gable-walls of the garret-chamber are crow-stepped.

HISTORICAL NOTE

Castle Stalker was an early residence of the Stewarts of Appin who, as descendants of the former Stewart lords of Lorn, acquired extensive rights and possessions in Upper Lorn during the late 15th and early 16th centuries. Eilean an Stalcaire ('Hunter's Island') was granted to Duncan Stewart, 2nd of Appin, in 1501,[1] but the castle itself seems not to have been built until the time of Duncan's son, Alan, who succeeded to the estate in or before 1513 and died in about 1562.

No contemporary evidence relating to the erection of Castle Stalker has so far come to light, and the earliest account of its foundation appears to be that put forward during a late 17th-century lawsuit. This account, which seems to have been accepted by both parties to the dispute, relates that the castle was built by James V for the Stewarts of Appin and remained in the hands of that family until the time of Duncan Stewart, 6th of

[1] *Origines Parochiales*, ii, part i, 167.

Appin.[1] Further details are supplied by an inscription on a mid-18th-century Board of Ordnance drawing,[2] which refers to the building as 'one of the Castles built by Order & at the Expence of King Iames the 5th of Scotland, after His Voyage in these Parts, to Suppress the Disorders in the Highlands'. Since James V's expedition to the Western Isles took place in 1540, two years before the king's death, the erection of the castle must have occurred, on this showing, in about 1540–2.

Notwithstanding the fact that certain later writers have ascribed the castle to Duncan Stewart, 2nd of Appin, the earlier account is to be preferred. Moreover, the architectural character of the building is consonant with a date in the second quarter of the 16th century. That the castle was erected at the direct expense of the Crown is improbable, however, and there is no record of any royal expenditure for such a purpose. It is known, however, that the Stewarts of Appin strongly supported James IV and James V in their efforts to subjugate the Western Isles, and that this loyalty was rewarded by various royal grants of lands and offices. In 1538, for example, Alan Stewart was granted a feu-farm charter of lands in Duror,[3] while four years later, just about the time when the castle is supposed to have been built, payment was made to him of the ferms of Sunart by royal command.[4] It was, no doubt, in token of such favours received, no less than of the family's somewhat distant kinship with the sovereign, that the Stewarts of Appin displayed the Royal Arms so prominently upon Castle Stalker.

In or about the third decade of the 17th century the castle passed into the hands of Sir Donald Campbell of Ardnamurchan and Airds (cf. No. 304) under circumstances that cannot now be fully ascertained. The account of the matter put forward by the Stewarts during the late 17th-century lawsuit mentioned below was to the effect that Duncan Stewart, 6th of Appin, was forcibly dispossessed of Castle Stalker by the Marquess of Argyll, but later writers have maintained that the Campbells of Airds obtained the castle by purchase or barter.[5] Moreover, there is record of the sale of the lands of Appin by Duncan Stewart in 1620, and of Donald Campbell of Ardnamurchan's sasine therein (specific mention being made of Castle Stalker) in 1627.[6] In any case, there can be little doubt that the early 17th-century alterations to the upperworks of the castle were carried out by the Campbells, and the author of the *New Statistical Account* states specifically that the building was 'new-roofed and floored by Sir Donald Campbell of Ardnamurchan in 1631'.[7]

The Campbells appear to have retained possession of Castle Stalker until the downfall of the 9th Earl of Argyll in 1681. In the following year, however, John Stewart of Ardsheal, taking advantage of the current political difficulties of the Campbell family, raised an action for the restoration of the castle on behalf of his ward, Robert Stewart, 8th of Appin, who was then still a minor. The petition was opposed by John Campbell, 3rd of Airds, who successfully maintained his case until December 1684, when the privy council ordered delivery of the

castle to Robert Stewart. Campbell, however, continued to garrison the building and refused entry despite besiegement by a force of Stewart's adherents which he claimed numbered more than one hundred and twenty men. Moreover, when James Guthrie, Dingwall Pursuivant, was sent from Edinburgh to execute the council's orders, he was waylaid on his return by Campbell and his followers, 'who fell upon and did most cruelly beatt, bruise and wound (him) and broke his trumpet'.[8] The Stewarts finally obtained possession of the castle some time in 1686, but their triumph was short-lived, for in consequence of their support of the Jacobite cause the family was forfeited after the Battle of Killiecrankie, Castle Stalker itself surrendering upon terms in October 1690.[9]

The castle was garrisoned by Hanoverian troops during the Forty-five,[10] and in 1748, when the government were again considering the policy of garrisoning certain Highland strongholds, Castle Stalker was visited by David Watson, Engineer to the Board of Ordnance, who reported that the walls were 'very sufficient', and that if £500 were to be spent upon repairs the building would be able to accommodate forty men.[11] This scheme does not seem to have been put into effect, but it was probably at this time that the two surviving Board of Ordnance drawings of the castle were made. The castle was evidently still occupied when Pococke visited the site in 1760,[12] but became roofless shortly before 1841.[13]

920473   NM 94 NW   September 1966

286. Dunollie Castle. This castle (Pl. 52A) is superbly situated upon the summit of a rock promontory towards the N end of Oban Bay, from which it commands a prospect of the islands of Kerrera and Lismore and of the Sounds of Kerrera and Mull. On its S and W sides the promontory terminates in a sheer rock face some 24 m in height, but elsewhere the ground falls away somewhat less steeply, the natural line of approach being from the NE. The existing remains (Fig. 177) comprise a tower-house with an associated bailey, or courtyard, standing upon the SW portion of the promontory, together with

---

[1] *RPC*, 3rd series, vii (1681–2), 505.
[2] Negative preserved at Courtauld Institute of Art (Wren Drawings, K.12).
[3] *RMS*, iii (1513–46), no. 1866.
[4] *Exch. Rolls*, xvii (1537–42), 541. At this period the chamberlainship of Sunart, and of other territories in Argyll, was held by Alan's son, Duncan.
[5] Stewart, J H J and D, *The Stewarts of Appin* (1880), 113.
[6] Argyll MSS, Inveraray Castle, Vault, portfolio V6.
[7] *NSA*, vii (Argyll), 241.
[8] *RPC*, 3rd series, vii (1681–2), 505, 536–7, 590; x (1684–5), 57, 93, 100–1, 170, 361, 367–8, 370; xi (1685–6), 275, 282.
[9] *APS*, ix (1689–95), appendix, 61; *Hist. MSS. Comm.*, 6th Report (appendix), 702; *Memoirs of Sir Ewen Cameron of Locheill*, chief of Clan Cameron, Abbotsford and Maitland Clubs (1842), 302; Dunbar, J G, 'A Siege of Castle Stalker', *The Stewarts*, xiii (1968), 29–32.
[10] Fergusson, *Argyll, passim.*
[11] Nat. Lib. of Scot. MS 1648.Z.3/nos. 28–9.
[12] Pococke, *Tours*, 95–6.
[13] *NSA*, vii (Argyll), 241.

fragmentary traces of an outer enclosure, which embrace the remaining area of the summit. The tower occupies the most vulnerable, or NE, portion of the courtyard, the remainder of which is enclosed by a curtain-wall and contains traces of internal buildings. Most of the external wall-surfaces are densely covered with ivy, which may conceal certain features of architectural interest. The greater part of the castle may be ascribed to the 15th century, but some portions of the curtain-wall appear to be of later date.

THE TOWER-HOUSE. The tower (Pls. 52B, 53) is almost square on plan and measures 12·0 m from E to W[1] by 11·3 m transversely over walls some 2·7 m in thickness. The masonry, which is of superior construction, is of roughly coursed local rubble, well bonded with pinnings and coarse lime-mortar. The freestone dressings at quoins and margins appear to have been composed mainly of fine-grained greenish-grey sandstone but some are of coarse-grained purple sandstone. Both stones probably emanate either from the Ardentallan area (cf. Nos. 349 and 351), or from the S shore of the island of Kerrera (cf. p. 217). The great majority of freestone dressings, however, both from the tower itself and from elsewhere in the castle, have been systematically pillaged for later building-purposes, some of them having probably been re-used in the construction of the court of offices at Dunollie House (No. 318). The only visible window-opening that remains intact is wrought on its outer arrises with a plain 0·07 m chamfer, and at least two of the internal doorways appear to have been dressed in the same way.

The tower-house incorporates four main storeys, each of which comprises a single apartment. The lowest of these is a barrel-vaulted cellar which contains an entrance-doorway in the W wall, now somewhat restored, together with a deeply-splayed window in each of the W and S walls. The soffit of the barrel-vault bears the imprint of the wicker-centering used in its construction (Pl. 54B).[2] Immediately inside the entrance-doorway a right-angled staircase within the thickness of the W and S walls rises to give access to the first floor. The stair continues upwards in the same manner to second-floor level, above which it rises as a turnpike in the SW angle. The lower flights are spacious, having a width of 1·1 m, and are roofed with slab-lintels.

The first-floor apartment (Fig. 178, Pl. 54A) is provided with its own external entrance-doorway in the W wall, which must formerly have been reached from the courtyard by means of a ladder or forestair. In 1887 this doorway still retained a socket-hole for a draw-bar,[3] but this feature has since been obliterated. The apartment was lit from windows in the N and E walls, while towards the E end of the S wall there are the remains of a fireplace. The window-embrasures, in common with those elsewhere in the tower, have well-constructed voussoired arch-heads. Towards the W end of the N wall there are the remains of a garderobe, one of a pair disposed vertically to each other in this quarter of the tower. Both are roofed with corbelled slabs (Pl. 54E) and were formerly provided with external discharge-chutes. The

ceiling of the main apartment consisted of timber joists carried upon sandstone corbels, an arrangement which also obtained on the upper floors of the tower.

The second-floor chamber (Fig. 178), evidently a hall, was lit by means of large embrasured windows in the W, E and S walls, each one having been provided with stone bench-seats in the ingoings. To the E of the window in the S wall there are the remains of an aumbry. In the N wall there is a large fireplace, and to the W of it a garderobe of the same type as that on the floor below. The third-floor chamber was a garret and probably had a pitched roof rising within a surrounding parapet-walk. There is no fireplace, and lighting must have been obtained from dormer- and gable-windows. The stair terminates at this level with a lintelled ceiling, and access to the parapet-walk was presumably contrived by means of a stair or ladder from the garret-chamber. The entire wall-head of the tower is now overgrown with ivy, but traces of the parapet-walk can be seen on the N side, where there are also the remains of an external corbelled projection, perhaps a garderobe. The tower has an overall height of about 14·3 m.

THE COURTYARD. The courtyard measures about 24·4 m square, and was formerly completely enclosed by a curtain-wall. This is now reduced to its lower courses, except on the N and E sides, where it rises to an average height of about 4·6 m. The masonry is similar in character to that of the tower-house, with which the greater part of the curtain is evidently contemporary in date. The N and E sections of the wall, which overlook the more vulnerable sides of the promontory, have a thickness of about 2·3 m, while the W and S sections vary in thickness from 1·5 m to 0·6 m. Here the wall is constructed upon the extreme edge of the rock summit, being strengthened at the angles by splayed buttresses. The N and E curtains may formerly have carried wall-walks, but no visible traces of such features now survive. The E curtain (Pl. 52B) incorporates a much-restored entrance-gateway formerly secured by a draw-bar. Above the doorway there may be seen fragments of two moulded corbels, which probably supported a box-machicolation. There is some evidence of the former existence of buildings along the inner face of this curtain.

A second entrance, in the form of a postern-doorway of zigzag plan, formerly pierced the N curtain (Pl. 53C), but is now sealed off by a cross-wall. The central arm of this doorway appears to have been lit by a slit-window overlooking the courtyard. To the W of the doorway a large cavity in the internal wall-face may indicate the site of a first-floor fireplace serving a building situated within the NW corner of the courtyard. The ground-floor area of this building was lit by a splayed window in the W curtain. A little to the S of this window the W curtain returns outwards at right angles, before continuing southwards to the SW angle of the courtyard. This portion of the curtain appears to be of later date than the

---

[1] The cardinal points are used here for convenience of description; the true orientation is shown on Fig. 177.

[2] This feature also occurs at Castle Tioram, in Moidart.

[3] *Cast. and Dom. Arch.*, i, fig. 234.

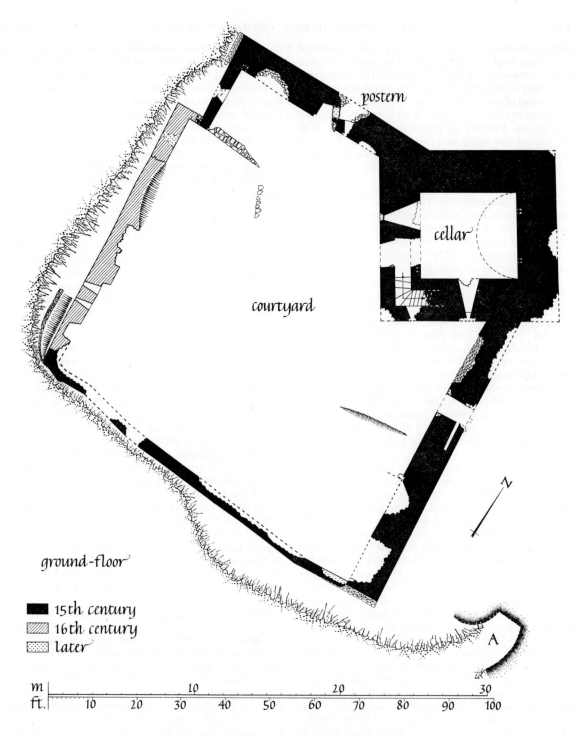

postern

cellar

courtyard

ground-floor

N

■ 15th century
▨ 16th century
⠿ later

A

m | 10 20 30
ft. | 10 20 30 40 50 60 70 80 90 100

Fig. 177. Dunollie Castle (No. 286); general plan

196

second floor

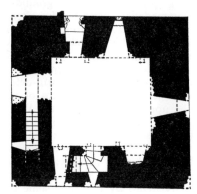

first floor

Fig. 178. Dunollie Castle (No. 286); first- and second-floor plans of tower-house

remainder, and may probably be ascribed to the 16th century. It contains a number of ground-floor openings, which indicate the former existence of buildings along its inner face, while the NW return (Pl. 54C, D) still rises to a height of three storeys and contains a number of small round-arrised windows, formed mainly of reddish-brown sandstone. The northernmost ground-floor apartment contained a garderobe whose discharge-chute pierces the base of the curtain-wall. The S curtain is ruinous and overgrown, and presents no features of interest.

OTHER REMAINS. About 9 m E of the SE angle of the courtyard a natural defile, which provides a possible way of ascent to the summit, has been sealed off by a well-constructed wall of rubble and lime mortar (A on Fig. 177). Traces of a rampart can also be seen on the N side of the castle, where 'the remains of Earth works' were reported in 1870.[1] This rampart does not appear to be associated with the existing castle and it may have formed part of the defences of the Dark Age fortress referred to below.

CARVED FRAGMENTS. Two fragments of light-grey sandstone recently recovered during repairs at Dunollie

House, and now preserved there, probably derive from the castle. Both appear to have formed part of an arched window wrought with a shallow roll-and-hollow moulding flanked by bands of nail-head ornament (Fig. 179, Pl. 54F). They can be ascribed to the 16th century.

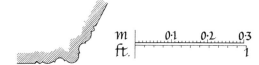

Fig. 179. Dunollie Castle (No. 286); carved fragment

HISTORICAL NOTE. Dunollie first comes on record about the turn of the 7th and 8th centuries, as the chief stronghold of the Lorn kings in Northern Dalriada. The fortress is said to have been captured and burnt by Irish adversaries in 698 and afterwards rebuilt by Selbach, ruler of Northern Dalriada.[2]

During the early Middle Ages the lands of Dunollie formed part of the extensive MacDougall lordship of Lorn, of which the principal castle appears to have been Dunstaffnage (No. 287), situated only 5 km away. There is no record of the existence of a castle at Dunollie at this period unless, as has been suggested, it was one of the three unnamed castles mentioned in a document of c. 1308 as being under the control of John Bacach of Lorn.[3] Following the defeat of the MacDougalls by Robert I in 1309 their lands were forfeited, and in 1321 or 1322 there is record of a royal grant of a penny-land of Dunollie, and 3 pennylands of Ardstofniche, near Dunollie, to a kinsman of Colin Campbell of Lochawe, Arthur Campbell, who also became constable of Dunstaffnage Castle.[4]

During the reign of David II the MacDougalls were able to regain some of their former estates including, in all probability, Dunollie itself and the coastal area of Nether Lorn.[5] In 1388 these lands passed to John Stewart of Innermeath, brother-in-law and husband respectively of the two daughters and co-heiresses of John (MacDougall) of Lorn, and remained in the possession of the Stewarts until the middle of the 15th century. In 1451, however, John Stewart, lord of Lorn, made a grant of Dunollie and certain neighbouring lands, including much of the island of Kerrera, together with the office of bailie of the lordship of Lorn, to John MacDougall, an indirect descendant of the earlier MacDougall lords of Lorn.[6] This grant evidently marked the re-establishment of the MacDougall family at Dunollie, and may well have provided the incentive

---

[1] Name Book, No. 19, p. 33.
[2] MacDonald, *Argyll*, 38–9; Anderson, *Early Sources*, i, 193, 205, 207, 215, 232.
[3] *Cal. Docs. Scot.*, iii (1307–57), no. 80; MacDonald, *Argyll*, 135.
[4] *Highland Papers*, iv, 195–6.
[5] MacDonald, *Argyll*, 160.
[6] Ibid., 174; S.R.O., Breadalbane Collection, GD 112/5/4, 'Regester', p. 1.

for the erection of the present castle. Thereafter Dunollie remained the principal residence of the MacDougalls, who retained the bailiery of Lorn following the transference of the lordship of Lorn from the Stewarts to the Campbell Earls of Argyll in 1469–70. During the covenanting rebellion the castle was successfully attacked by the Marquess of Argyll, and John MacDougall was forced to surrender his estates, to which he was restored in 1661.[1] Fourteen years later the 9th Earl of Argyll garrisoned the castle against the MacLeans.[2] John MacDougall, 22nd of Dunollie, was forfeited for his part in the 1715 rebellion, but the estate was subsequently restored to his son Alexander, during whose lifetime the castle appears to have been abandoned as a residence in favour of a new dwelling-house on an adjacent site (No. 318).

852314   NM 83 SE   July 1968

287. Dunstaffnage Castle. This castle (Pls. 55, 56, 57A) stands at the mouth of Loch Etive, about 5 km NE of Oban. It occupies the summit of a prominent outcrop of conglomerate rock, some 6 to 9 m in height, situated close to the extremity of a peninsula which extends north-eastwards from the southern shore of the loch and partly across its mouth. Thus, the castle is ideally placed to command the seaward approach to Loch Etive and the Pass of Brander, whilst also exercising surveillance over the Firth of Lorn and the eastern entrance to the Sound of Mull. Moreover, there is an excellent anchorage close at hand in Dunstaffnage Bay, which lies immediately to the SE of the castle, sheltered from the prevailing westerly winds. The landward approach is made by way of the peninsula, which narrows to a width of about 160 m some 500 m SW of the castle before broadening again to take in a low wooded knoll, known as Sean Dun (No. 182), beyond which lie the chapel (No. 243) and the castle itself.

SUMMARY

The castle incorporates work of several building-periods, the principal stages in the evolution of the fabric apparently being as follows. The original castle was built by one of the MacDougall lords of Lorn about the middle of the 13th century, and comprised a massive curtain-wall whose outline was dictated largely by the configuration of the underlying rock-summit. At the western and northern angles of the roughly quadrangular enclosure thus formed the curtain was punctuated by cylindrical towers of slight projection, while at the eastern angle, where a rock-fissure falls away from the summit, there was an entrance-gateway. Within the enclosure two-storeyed ranges of domestic buildings stood against both the NW and the E curtain-walls, while additional accommodation was provided in the two adjacent angle-towers. The SW and SE curtain-walls, overlooking the vulnerable landward approach, were equipped with a series of slit-embrasures, while the entire curtain-wall was crowned by a parapet-walk which communicated with the upper floors of the angle-towers to provide a continuous circuit of the walls.

The first major alteration to the castle that can now be traced appears to have been carried out in the late 15th or early 16th century, following a transfer of ownership to the Campbell Earls of Argyll, on whose behalf it was subsequently held by a series of hereditary captains. This alteration comprised the reconstruction of the entrance-gateway, the new entrance being contained within a broad frontal projection set forward up to 2·0 m in advance of the original line of the curtain-wall. A second major phase of rebuilding took place towards the end of the 16th century, when the gatehouse was again altered, this time by a complete reconstruction of the upperworks. At or about the same time the NW courtyard-range was drastically remodelled, new kitchen-quarters being provided on the ground-floor with domestic accommodation above. Further alterations were evidently made to the castle during the first half of the 17th century, and to this period may be ascribed the sub-division of the ground-floor of the gatehouse, the conversion of the slit-embrasures in the SW and SE curtain-walls to equip them for firearm-defence, and a similar reconstruction of the defences of the curtain-parapets. The uppermost storey of the W angle-tower seems also to have been rebuilt at this time.

Minor alterations and repairs are known to have been carried out during the late 17th and 18th centuries (*infra*), and in 1725 the NW range was again remodelled, this time to form a self-contained two-storeyed dwelling-house at the NE end. By this time some parts of the castle, including the two angle-towers, were becoming ruinous, but repairs were made to a sizeable breach which had developed at the N end of the E curtain, and some work was also carried out on the E range itself. Following the gutting of the gatehouse by fire in 1810 the castle ceased to be the principal family-residence of the captains of Dunstaffnage, but their tenants continued to occupy the place from time to time up to about the end of the 19th century. During this period a number of repairs were carried out, and these were continued intermittently throughout the opening decades of the present century. In 1962 the greater part of the castle passed into the guardianship of the Department of the Environment, who began a further and more extensive programme of repair and consolidation which still continues. The erection of scaffolding in connection with these latter operations, and the progressive clearance of debris and vegetation, has enabled the fabric to be inspected more closely than was possible at the time when either of the two main existing accounts of the castle were prepared,[3] and the conclusions now put forward differ in some respects from those of earlier writers. Certain problems of analysis and interpretation remain unsolved, however, while others (and in particular those relating to the N angle-tower) must await the completion of further clearance-operations.

---

[1] *APS*, vii (1661–9), 337–43.
[2] *RPC*, 3rd series, iv (1673–6), 484.
[3] *Cast. and Dom. Arch.*, i, 85–93; Simpson, *Dunstaffnage*.

ARCHITECTURAL DESCRIPTION

GENERAL. The castle is of irregular quadrangular plan and measures about 35 m from SW to NE by 30 m transversely over walls that vary in thickness from 2·6 m to 3·3 m (Figs. 180, 181, 182). Except at the gatehouse, where the masonry rises almost from ground-level, the walls stand upon the edge of the rock-summit, being founded in places upon a rough scarcement. The rounded S angle of the curtain-wall, and the N angle-tower, are supported by irregular base-plinths. The height of the parapet-walk above the courtyard varies from about 6·1 m to 8·2 m, while the W tower rises to a height of about 9·7 m, being 18·6 m above the external ground-surface. At the base of the curtain-wall there may be seen a number of drainage-outlets which discharge surface-water from the courtyard. The masonry is generally of local rubble brought to courses and well bonded with pinnings. This coursing is most evident in the external faces of the curtain-walls, which contain numerous large blocks and split boulders set on edge. Towards the SE end of the SW curtain the coursing is interrupted as if by a former breach measuring some 2·0 m in width, which extends upwards almost to the full height of the wall. Since there is no reason to suppose that such a breach was made during the lifespan of the castle, it seems likely that this opening was deliberately formed during the initial period of construction in order to facilitate the passage of building-materials, and thereafter sealed up. At the junction of the W tower with the curtain-wall the NW and SW curtains return inwards for a short distance before swelling into the curve of the tower. The external angles of the returns are emphasized by freestone quoins, those on the NW side apparently lacking any good bond with the masonry of the tower itself. This suggests that the adjacent section of the NW curtain was completed before work began on the tower, although both evidently formed part of the same scheme of building-operations.

All the dressings used in the castle are of sandstone, but there is considerable variation in colour and texture. Most of the 13th-century dressings are formed of a rather coarse-grained stone of iron-stained buff colour, similar in character to that seen in the adjacent chapel (No. 243), and probably deriving from the Ardtornish area. Here and there in the early work, however, and more extensively in the later, a finer-grained stone of greenish-yellow hue is found, and this may derive from the Carsaig beds in Mull.

THE GATEHOUSE. The gatehouse (Pls. 57B, 59A) stands on the E side of the castle, apparently occupying the site of a natural fissure which may originally have provided a means of access to the summit of the rock. As it stands today the building constitutes a massive frontal projection, centrally placed between the SE and E curtain-walls, and rising from a solid base built over the rock fissure. In the E wall of the gatehouse, which is slightly bowed on plan, an arch-pointed recess stands at a height of 5·3 m above ground-floor level. Within this recess, and situated a little to the S of centre, there is a round-arched doorway which forms the present entrance. The lower part of the S jamb of the outer arch

seems to have been patched up following the removal of the original freestone-dressings. Some of the dressings of the doorway itself have recently been replaced, and the remaining original dressings are greatly worn. It is clear, however, that the jambs and arch-head were originally carved with a continuous bold outer rebate wrought with a narrow chamfer on the arris; the inner rebate is roll-moulded (Fig. 183B).[1]

All this work can be ascribed to the late 15th or early 16th century, apart from the upper storeys of the gatehouse, which appear to be of late 16th-century date. The nature of the original entrance-arrangements is uncertain, but some inferences can be drawn from the structural evidence now to be described. Thus, at the junction of the lower portion of the gatehouse with the E curtain-wall there is an unbonded masonry-joint, beyond which the curtain appears originally to have extended at least 1·5 m on the same alignment behind the present external wall of the gatehouse. Similarly, on the S side of the gatehouse, which is linked to the main SE curtain by means of a quarter-round curve, a straight joint can be discerned at the junction of the curve with the S return-wall of the gatehouse. This suggests that the curved face originally continued on a similar arc to meet the E curtain-wall at a point just inside the present gatehouse. Partial confirmation of this theory, which was first put forward by Hugo B Millar in 1962,[2] was provided by a trial excavation carried out by the Commission's officers in 1970. This revealed what appeared to be the external scarcement of the former curtain-wall beneath the floor of the guard-chamber on the N side of the transe. Thus it may be supposed that the original entrance-doorway stood close to the junction of the extended E curtain, with a half-round tower of shallow projection in the area now occupied by the E end of the gatehouse-cellar (cf. Fig. 180).

Returning to a consideration of the present entrance-arrangements, it may be noted that most earlier writers have sought to differentiate the outer arch-pointed recess from the round-headed doorway within it, maintaining that the latter has been inserted within a wider arch-pointed opening of earlier date.[3] The arguments advanced in support of this theory are based partly on the fact that a very similar arch-pointed opening formerly existed at the inner end of the gatehouse-transe, and partly on the allegedly 13th-century character of the two arches themselves. Against this, however, it may be argued that the lower part of the gatehouse-façade appears to be homogeneous up to first-floor level, where

---

[1] A timber-lintelled doorway, probably dating from the later 17th century, which formerly stood within the round-arched opening (Simpson, *Dunstaffnage*, pl. 9), has been removed by the Department of the Environment during the course of the present restoration. Above this doorway, and immediately beneath the keystone of the round-arched opening, there was a square hole housing a drawbridge pulley-beam of timber (ibid., 76). The pulley-beam, together with an associated framework comprising a timber lintel and side-posts, are now in the custody of the Department of the Environment.

[2] *TGAS*, new series, xv (1960–7), 53–7.

[3] *Cast. and Dom. Arch.*, i, 86; Simpson, *Dunstaffnage*, 75–6; Millar, op. cit., 56.

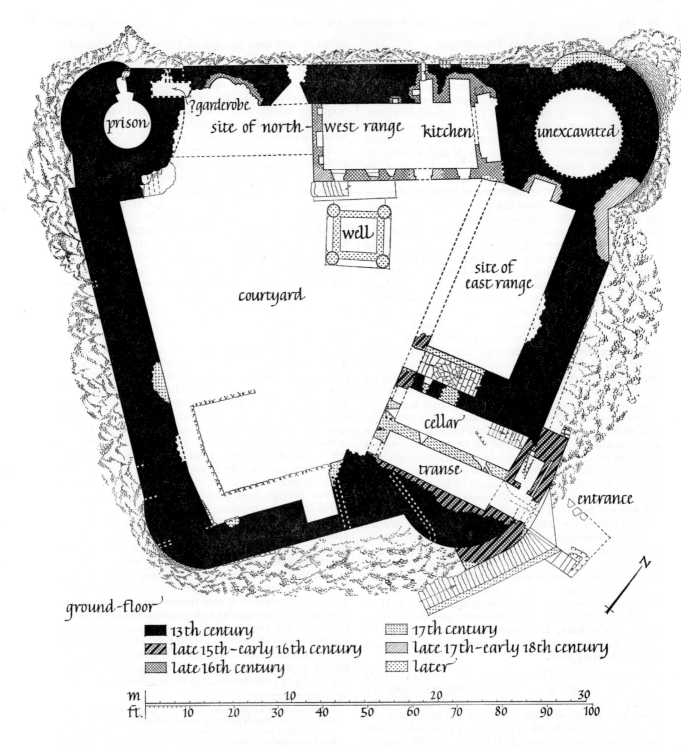

prison

?garderobe

site of north—west range

kitchen

unexcavated

well

courtyard

site of
east range

cellar

transe

entrance

N

ground-floor

13th century

late 15th–early 16th century

late 16th century

17th century

late 17th–early 18th century

later

m		10		20		30

ft.	10	20	30	40	50	60	70	80	90	100

Fig. 180. Dunstaffnage Castle (No. 287); ground-floor plan

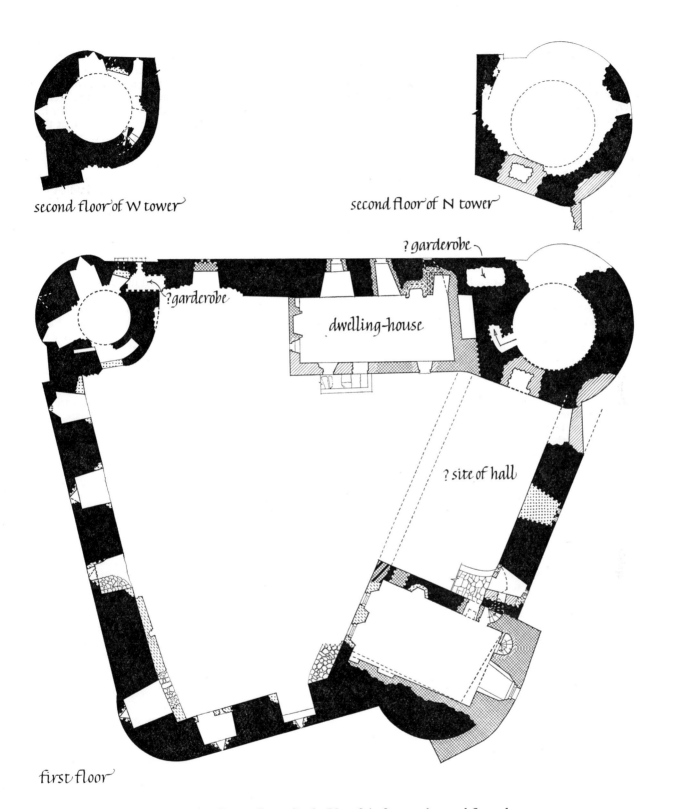

second floor of W tower

second floor of N tower

?garderobe

?garderobe

dwelling-house

?garderobe

?site of hall

first floor

Fig. 181. Dunstaffnage Castle (No. 287); first- and second-floor plans

a change in the treatment of the facework and quoins marks the beginning of late 16th-century work, and that there is no evidence to suggest that the outer arch-pointed recess ever formed an opening in the wall.[1] Moreover, it has already been shown that there are good grounds for supposing that the existing entrance-arrangements superseded the original ones of the 13th century. On this showing, then, the dating of the lower portion of the existing gatehouse-façade depends very largely upon the character of the round-arched doorway, which may most plausibly be ascribed to the late 15th or early 16th century.[2] It is noticeable that the voussoirs of the rear-arch of the doorway are not truly radial, a peculiarity which also occurs in the 15th-century tower-house of Dunollie (No. 286).

The entrance-doorway is today approached by means of a stone forestair built against the S part of the gatehouse-façade, and the area between the top of the forestair and the entrance-threshold is spanned by modern timber decking. The forestair is said to have been constructed during the third quarter of the 19th century,[3] but probably replaces an earlier stairway occupying a similar position. The area now occupied by decking was formerly spanned by a drawbridge, but the precise means of operation is uncertain, except during the last phase of military activity in the late 17th and 18th centuries, when the bridge was evidently raised by the pulley-mechanism mentioned above. It is possible, however, that at an earlier period the drawbridge was operated from the first floor of the gatehouse, the bridge being housed, when in a raised position, within the arch-pointed recess already described. The lower part of the buttress that supports the forestair appears to be older than the remainder, and probably represents part of the S wall of a drawbridge-pit. The foundations of a corresponding N wall are also visible, together with some associated masonry-tusking, situated immediately beneath the N jamb of the arch-pointed recess. A drainage-channel lying beneath the gatehouse-transe discharges into the drawbridge-pit. At the NE angle of the gatehouse there may be seen part of a low wall, built over the steeply sloping face of the rock outcrop. This wall appears to have run northwards, parallel to the E curtain, but it is uncertain how far it extended or what purpose it served. The wall is evidently of later date than the gatehouse itself.

The entrance-doorway is rebated externally for double-leafed doors secured by a draw-bar. Immediately within the doorway a low lintelled doorway on the N gives access to an unlit guard-chamber having a small aumbry in its N wall. The chamber is ceiled with slate slabs, and the threshold, made of similar material, contains a socket for a door swivel-pin. Beyond the guard-chamber a timber-roofed transe rises to give access to the courtyard by means of a square-headed doorway wrought with a plain chamfer on jambs and lintel. The N wall of the transe is equipped with two defensive slits and a gun-port, all manned from the cellar within. This wall, and possibly the courtyard-doorway itself, are of 17th-century date, the lower floor of the

gatehouse having previously been undivided, thus forming a transe of considerably greater width than the present one. This earlier transe gave on to the courtyard by means of the arch-pointed opening to which reference has already been made. The outline of the arch can be seen in the W wall of the gatehouse, indicating that the opening had a width of about 3·0 m. This opening seems to have been the only source of light for the transe, and there is no evidence to suggest that it was equipped with gates. When the ground-floor of the gatehouse was sub-divided in the 17th century the opening was infilled by a screen-wall containing two windows of different sizes, and a doorway so constructed as to take advantage of the N jamb of the earlier opening. This doorway gives access to a cellar whose floor originally lay 1·0 m or more beneath the level of the present earthen floor. In the N wall of the cellar there may be seen the external aperture of a splayed slit, now partly blocked up, and the outline of a blocked doorway, both openings being formed with sandstone dressings. These openings formerly communicated with the main E range of the castle, and are probably as old as the 13th century, much of the N wall of the gatehouse apparently being of this period. Above the openings there is a row of stone corbels carrying the runner for the first-floor joists, while against the E section of the same wall a stone staircase rises to give access to the first-floor apartment. This staircase is probably of late 17th- or early 18th-century date, but has subsequently been repaired. Beneath the stair there is a vaulted opening containing a small aumbry.

The main access to the first floor of the gatehouse is provided by a doorway at the E end of the N wall, now approached by means of an open ramp bounded on its N side by a retaining-wall. Prior to the destruction of the E range, however, this doorway (or an earlier one in the same position) no doubt provided direct internal communication between the gatehouse and the E range at first-floor level. At one time the gatehouse may also have communicated directly with the courtyard by means of a forestair at the SW corner, the forestair perhaps continuing upwards to give access to the SE parapet-walk. The ragged mass of masonry now visible at the inner re-entrant angle of the gatehouse and the SE curtain-wall may represent the lower portion of such a stair, of which the remainder is likely to have been demolished when the ground-floor of the gatehouse was sub-divided and a new inner doorway to the transe formed during the 17th century.

As it stands today the first-floor apartment of the gatehouse (Fig. 181, Pl. 58c) is mainly of late 16th-century and subsequent date. It is noticeable that the alignments of the E and N walls differ somewhat from those of the corresponding walls beneath, but there is no discrepancy in the alignment of the N wall, which is

---

[1] Recent investigation of the masonry of the arch-head has revealed no indications of a straight joint piercing the thickness of the wall.

[2] The doorway bears a considerable resemblance to the entrance-doorway of the early 16th-century forework at Rothesay Castle.

[3] Simpson, *Dunstaffnage*, 23.

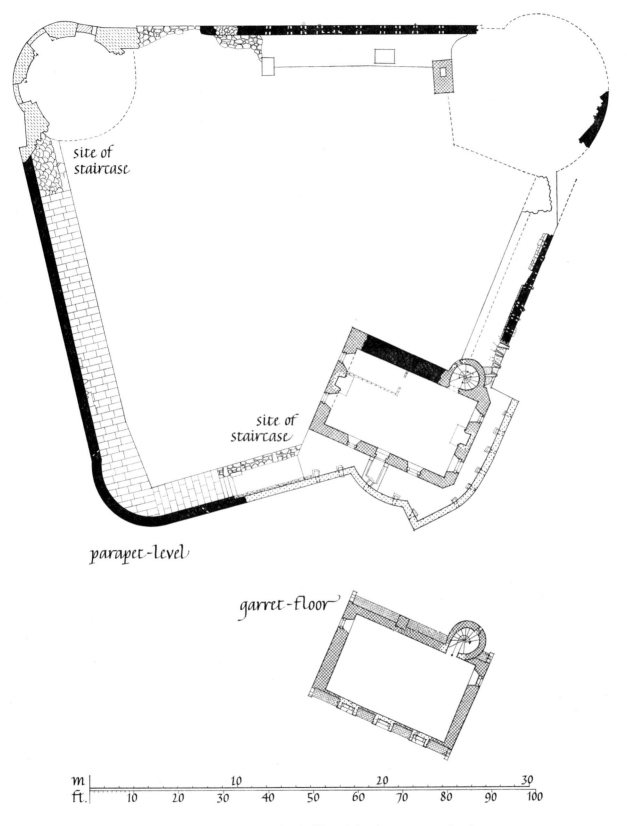

site of
staircase

site of
staircase

parapet-level

garret-floor

m
ft.

Fig. 182. Dunstaffnage Castle (No. 287); plan at parapet-level

203

probably for the most part of 13th-century date. So much at least is suggested by the existence of a blocked opening high up at the W end of the N wall. This opening is not related to the existing floor-levels within the gatehouse, and one of the corbels that support the second-floor runner is integral with the blocking of the opening. Possibly the opening represents a doorway giving access to a loft or gallery in the adjacent apartment of the former E range, which may have been a hall (*infra*). The lintelled fireplace situated in the N wall appears to have been reconstructed fairly recently, but probably occupies the site of an earlier fireplace. The S wall incorporates a lintelled recess and an aumbry, while in the W wall there are two recently restored chamfer-arrised windows which probably date from the 17th century. In the E wall there is a large segmental-arched window-embrasure (Pl. 58D) equipped with stone side-benches. The window-opening is square-headed and the jambs and lintel are chamfer-arrised; the opening was formerly secured by an iron grille. The embrasure is probably of 16th-century date, but the window-opening itself may have been reconstructed in the 17th century. To the N of the embrasure there is a doorway communicating with the cellar-staircase, while in the adjacent section of the N wall another doorway gives access to a stair-turret corbelled out in the re-entrant

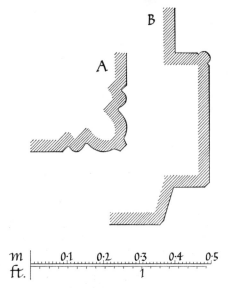

m | 0·1   0·2   0·3   0·4   0·5
ft. | 1

Fig. 183. Dunstaffnage Castle (No. 287); profile mouldings: A, fireplace in east range; B, entrance-doorway

angle between the gatehouse and the E curtain. The jambs of this doorway are round-arrised, most of the openings on the two uppermost floors of the gatehouse being treated in the same way.

The second floor of the gatehouse (Fig. 181) was evidently sub-divided to form two rooms of similar size, each provided with a fireplace in one of the gable-walls. The existing fireplaces have moulded stone jambs of 18th-century date, but the jambs of an earlier fireplace of larger dimensions are traceable in the eastern one, which

also has a timber surround of fairly recent origin. Some of the windows show traces of stanchion-sockets and glazing-grooves. The N wall is thicker than the other walls and may incorporate some 13th-century masonry. A doorway in the S wall gives access to the parapet-walk.

The garret-chamber presents few features of interest. The existing dormer-windows in the S wall are modern, but traces of earlier dormers can be seen below. The pediments of the three dormer-windows (Pl. 58E) (visible externally from the parapet-walk) have been removed from the 18th-century dwelling-house on the NW side of the courtyard.[1] The eastern and central ones are ogival-headed, the former being carved in relief with swags and fruit issuing from a central scallop-shell, while the latter bears the date 1725 and the initials A E C and D L C, for Aeneas (Angus) Campbell, 11th Captain of Dunstaffnage, and his wife, Dame Lillias Campbell, a daughter of Sir James Campbell of Lawers. The westernmost dormer is triangular in shape and incorporates an armorial shield flanked by the initials A C, for Aeneas Campbell, and the inscription LAUS DEO ('Give praise to God'). The shield is considerably worn, but appears to bear: quarterly, 1st and 4th, gyronny of eight; 2nd and 3rd, a galley, sail furled.

The crow-stepped gables, chimney-heads and roofs of the gatehouse and its associated stair-turret are all of fairly recent construction, and the same may be said of the upper part of the parapet-wall and its coping on the E and S sides of the gatehouse. The NE and SE angles of the gatehouse are splayed back at this level to facilitate access along the parapet-walk, returning to the square immediately beneath the eaves by means of moulded corbel-courses of four and three members respectively.

THE EAST RANGE AND EAST CURTAIN-WALL. Little now remains of the E range, the inner, or W, wall having almost completely disappeared, while the lower part of the interior is partly filled with debris. The survival of the E curtain-wall, however, which contains a number of openings associated with the adjacent range, enables the main features of the original arrangement to be deduced with some confidence. As first erected in the 13th century, the E range occupied the area between the N angle-tower and the gatehouse, being some 14 m in length and 6·7 m in width internally. It comprised two main storeys, of which the upper was set over a broad scarcement, considerable traces of which can be seen at the foot of the inner face of the curtain-wall. The first-floor chamber, which was probably a hall, was lit by two pairs of lancet-windows set within arch-pointed embrasures piercing the curtain-wall. Further windows were no doubt provided in the W wall of the range, which may also have incorporated a forestair giving access to a first-floor doorway. From the hall direct access could have been obtained to corresponding chambers in the N tower and gatehouse. The ground-floor may also have communicated with the N tower, as it certainly did with the gatehouse-transe by means of the doorway and splayed slit already described (p. 202). Unfortunately, any

[1] *Dunstaffnage Case*, 58.

openings formerly communicating with the N tower at either level have been built up or otherwise obscured by the construction of a large ground-floor fireplace and associated chimney-flue at the N end of the range. The fireplace and flue incorporate numerous sandstone blocks evidently quarried from Dunstaffnage Chapel, while the quirked and keeled roll-mouldings (Fig. 183A) forming the jambs may derive from earlier work within the castle itself. This fireplace was probably constructed some time during the late 17th or 18th century, perhaps about the year 1740, when a considerable quantity of dressings became available for re-use following the dismantling of the E window of the chapel and the erection of the Campbell of Dunstaffnage burial-enclosure (cf. p. 124).

The two double-lancet window-embrasures in the E curtain have been much altered, and only the S one (Fig. 184) is now accessible internally. This was formerly entered from the hall by a wide arch-pointed opening formed with sandstone voussoirs, and was ceiled with a pointed barrel-vault, except at its inner extremity, where it appears to have been spanned by a massive timber lintel. In the E wall there was originally a pair of lancet-windows having daylight-openings some 0·28 m in width, and rebated internally for glazing- or shutter-frames. The heads and jambs of the windows are wrought with 0·13 m chamfers, the jambs of the southernmost also being carved with bold dog-tooth enrichment. The embrasure has been remodelled on at least two occasions. During the first alteration, which may be ascribed to the 17th century, the lower part of the N window and the whole of the S window were blocked with masonry and the central mullion was removed. About half-way down the line of the former mullion there was inserted a small inverted keyhole-shaped opening similar in character to those that were inserted in the slit-embrasures of the SW curtain during this period. It is hard to say whether this opening should be interpreted as a rudimentary gun-port or a damaged slop-sink, but there are certainly no grounds for supposing it to be a piscina-bowl.[1] Some distance beneath this opening there is a drain-outlet of uncertain date. During the second major phase of alterations the embrasure was contracted in width on the S side, while a screen-wall containing a lintelled doorway was built across the mouth of the original arched opening. This screen-wall was provided with a small splayed window or peep-hole looking into the adjacent apartment of the E range, while the new S wall of the embrasure was equipped with an aumbry. These alterations were probably carried out during the late 17th or early 18th century.

The N window-embrasure (Fig. 185) is now inaccessible, the arched opening that probably existed in the original arrangement having been removed and the opening subsequently blocked up with masonry. In the external face of the E curtain, however, there may be seen the remains of a mullioned double-lancet window similar in character to the one in the southern embrasure, although apparently devoid of dog-tooth enrichment. The window is blocked externally with roughly-made bricks, suggesting that this alteration dates from the later 18th century.

Above the window-embrasures, socket-holes for the ceiling-joists of the former E range can be seen in the inner face of the curtain-wall immediately beneath the level of the parapet-walk. The wall-head is now grass-grown, but the walk appears to have had a width of 1·4 m between inner and outer parapet-walls 0·61 m in thickness. Little remains of the inner parapet, while the outer survives only to an average height of about 0·76 m above the walk. The walk is drained by spout-stones, some of which are roughly formed of slate, while others are composed of purple-brown sandstone of a type that occurs infrequently in the castle.

Shortly before it meets the N tower the external face of the E curtain-wall is sharply intaken, and above the level of the ground-floor scarcement of the E range the wall is reduced to a thickness of about 1·0 m. Moreover, the external facework of this section of the curtain contains a considerable number of re-used freestone dressings apparently deriving from Dunstaffnage Chapel. The adjacent section of facework of the N tower also shows clear signs of patching and partial reconstruction. All this indicates that at some time, and probably during the course of the 18th century, an extensive breach occurred at the junction of the curtain-wall with the N tower, and that this breach was subsequently made good by patching in the manner described. There are also indications that before the development of the breach the E curtain extended northwards upon its main alignment for a distance of 1·0 m or so more than it does today, and that it originally returned to meet the N tower by means of a shallow inset, as do the NW and SW curtain-walls at their junctions with the W angle-tower.

Towards the S end of the E range there lies a large boulder incorporating the remains of a two-pronged iron beacon-stand. This formerly stood on the parapet-walk close to the NE angle of the gatehouse.[2]

THE NORTH TOWER. The N tower (Pl. 55A) is much the larger of the two angle-towers, having an internal diameter of about 5·8 m within walls some 2·4 m in thickness at first-floor level. The size of the tower and its position in relation to the E range, which probably housed a first-floor hall (p. 204), suggest that the tower contained the principal private apartments of the castellan. Unfortunately, the tower has suffered very considerably, having been breached not only at its junction with the E curtain, as described above, but also on the NW side, where a substantial section of wall, extending to the base of the tower, has collapsed and subsequently been rebuilt. Moreover, much of the interior of the tower is now filled with debris, and this makes full examination of the lower floors impossible.

The tower probably contained four floors, but the existence of a ground-floor apartment cannot be confirmed until the interior is cleared of debris. At first-floor level part of the inner wall-face of the tower is visible,

[1] Cf. Simpson, (Dunstaffnage, 82–3), who identifies the embrasure as an oratory.
[2] Ibid., 73, 81.

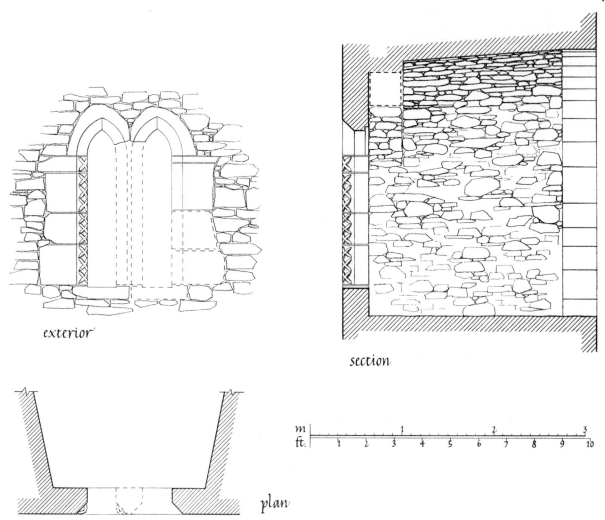

exterior

section

m
ft.

plan

Fig. 184. Dunstaffnage Castle (No. 287); S window-embrasure in E curtain

and there are traces of a mural staircase ascending in a clockwise direction on the SW side of the chamber. No window-openings are visible in the surviving portions of external facework at this level. The apartment was probably entered directly from the E range by means of a doorway situated in the area now occupied by the inserted chimney-flue described above. The second-floor apartment was reached from the mural staircase already mentioned, while at the stair-head there appears to have been a mural chamber, probably a garderobe which discharged in the re-entrant angle between the tower and the NW curtain-wall. The garderobes serving other levels in the tower were probably housed in the NW curtain-wall, being reached by means of mural passages. A double garderobe-chute, recently restored by the Department of the Environment, which can be seen projecting from the adjacent section of the curtain, was probably utilized in this manner. The only surviving window at second-floor level in the tower is a splayed

opening on the E side, now robbed of dressings. Little can be said of the uppermost chamber of the tower, except that it is likely to have communicated with the parapet-walks of the E and NW curtain-walls, the floor of the chamber lying somewhat above the level of the former, but below that of the latter. The only surviving feature in the chamber itself is the fragment of a window on the E side. There are no visible remains of fireplaces or original chimneys within the tower.

THE NORTH-WEST RANGE AND NORTH-WEST CURTAIN-WALL. The most conspicuous surviving feature of the NW range is the dwelling-house that was formed at the NE end in 1725. The building (Pl. 58B) formerly comprised two main storeys and an attic, but is now roofless and unfloored. Although entirely re-modelled in 1725, the dwelling-house appears to incorporate substantial remains of a late 16th-century kitchen standing in the same position, together with more fragmentary remains of earlier date. The dwelling-house is entered from the courtyard by means of a round-arrised lintelled doorway which evidently replaces two closely-spaced 16th-century doorways occupying a similar position. The ground-floor area now comprises a single apartment, but seems formerly to have been partitioned. Two windows look out towards the courtyard, one at each end of the building, while between them there are two other windows blocked externally by the forestair that was built in 1725

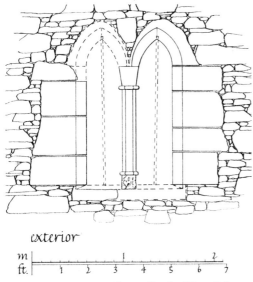

exterior

Fig. 185. Dunstaffnage Castle (No. 287);
N window-embrasure in E curtain

to give access to the first floor of the dwelling-house. In the NE wall there is a large segmental-arched kitchen-fireplace of 16th-century date, formed with round-arrised sandstone dressings and having a salt-box recess within the NW chimney-breast. This fireplace (Pl. 58A) evidently remained in use during the lifetime of the dwelling-house. In the NW wall there are two segmental-arched recesses, probably of 16th-century date, of which the one to the SW contains a slop-sink discharging through the curtain-wall. This recess has an aumbry in the SW ingo, and there is a second aumbry in the main wall a little further to the SW. The SW wall of the building contains another aumbry, together with an inserted fireplace of late 18th- or 19th-century date, whose flue discharges by means of a roughly formed vent about 2·0 m above ground-level.

Access to the first floor of the dwelling-house was obtained by means of the stone forestair already mentioned. The area within was divided into two main apartments, an arrangement which evidently repeated that of the 16th century. The NE apartment was lit on the courtyard-side by means of a dormer-window, and from the NW by means of a recently restored window which pierces the curtain-wall. Immediately to the NE of this latter opening there is a fireplace having a segmental-headed relieving-arch and round-arrised jambs of yellow

sandstone; the lintel is missing. This fireplace is evidently of late 16th-century date, but it was contracted in width in 1725, when a bolection-moulded chimney-piece was inserted within the earlier opening. The jambs of this chimney-piece remain, but in this case also the lintel is missing. A little further to the NE there is a cupboard-recess, and above it a segmental-headed window-embrasure of which the daylight-opening is blocked with masonry. The floor-level of the window-embrasure lies about 0·7 m beneath the garret floor-level of the dwelling-house, which is indicated by joist-holes in the adjacent wall-face. Presumably, therefore, the window is a relic of a 16th-century arrangement in which the garret-floor lay at a level corresponding with the lower of the two scarcements by which the NE wall is intaken to accommodate the kitchen-flue. After the daylight-opening was blocked in 1725 the upper part of the window-embrasure probably served as a cupboard in the newly-formed garret of the dwelling-house. The freestone dressings of the blocked external opening, which are wrought with a quirk-and-chamfer moulding, have recently been renewed.

The sequence of alterations in the large segmental-headed window-embrasure that lights the adjacent SW apartment from the NW is even more complex. In its original form this opening probably represents a 13th-century window relating to a floor-level about 1 m above that of the 16th- and 18th-century floor. Evidence for this view is provided by the broken-off sandstone stumps of a bench-seat that can be seen on each side of the embrasure at a height of about 1·8 m above the present floor-level of the embrasure. When the NW range was remodelled in the later 16th century the embrasure was reconstructed to comply with a lower first-floor level, and a new daylight-opening was formed, comprising a square-headed window wrought with a quirk-and-chamfer moulding. The upper part of the embrasure probably served as a cupboard for the garret, and this arrangement continued after the adjustment of the garret floor-level in 1725. In the SW wall of the apartment there is a centrally-placed fireplace of 16th-century date similar to the one in the adjacent apartment, and beside it a mural recess and aumbry of the same date. On the SE side of the fireplace there is an 18th-century window (Pl. 58F), whose lintel is carved with the worn initials A E C and L C flanking an ornament resembling a cross-pattée. The initials are those of Aeneas Campbell, 11th of Dunstaffnage, and his wife Lillias Campbell. On the courtyard-side the apartment was lit by a dormer-window, of which the pediment, together with the pediments of the adjacent doorway and of the remaining dormer, are now re-utilized in the gatehouse-garret (cf. p. 204).

The remaining portion of the NW range, lying between the 18th-century dwelling-house and the W tower, has probably been roofless since the 18th century and the SE wall has completely disappeared. In the original arrangement of the 13th century, however, this part of the range, at least, seems to have measured only about 3·3 m in width, this curtailment of width being made necessary by the proximity of the adjacent fore-stair giving access from the courtyard to the W angle-tower. The roof-raggle visible on the NE face of this tower indicates that the range originally rose to a height of two storeys. The only original opening visible at ground-floor level is an arched aperture in the NW wall having deeply-splayed jambs and a sloping head. The exterior of the aperture has subsequently been enlarged to form a sizeable opening in the curtain-wall, but the original opening was probably quite small, and is more likely to have been a sink-outlet than a doorway.[1] Between this opening and the W tower there is a large round-backed fireplace whose flue is carried up in the masonry of the curtain-wall. This fireplace is clearly an insertion, and may probably be ascribed to the 16th century. The upper part of the flue is carried through a 13th-century window-embrasure, whose floor-level corresponds approximately with that of the contemporary embrasure in the NW wall of the dwelling-house mentioned above. Within the embrasure there may be seen traces of what appear to have been bench-seats, while externally there remains a blocked double-lancet window wrought with a plain chamfered arris. The only other external feature of interest in the NW curtain not so far described is the projecting garderobe-chute situated a little to the SW of the double chute that is thought to have served the N tower. This chute, now very much restored, probably served the 13th-century first-floor apartments situated at this end of the range. The SW end of the range appears to have been served by a garderobe, or garderobes, situated in the return-wall lying between the main NW curtain and the W tower. This section of wall also housed garderobes serving the tower itself, and although the remains of not less than five and not more than seven vent-chutes are now visible externally in this area it is not possible to relate each vent to the appropriate chamber within. So far as the NW range is concerned, however, it is likely that this was served by a garderobe whose vent can be seen at the base of the wall about 0·6 m SE of the sandstone quoins that mark the return of the curtain-wall. This garderobe was evidently lit by the window whose sill and lowermost rybats can be seen immediately above the vent. The masonry has been very much patched in this area, but the arch-head of the window-ingo can be seen protruding through the facework at a slightly higher level. The window appears to have had a daylight-width of 0·18 m.

The parapet-walk of the NW curtain is now largely covered by concrete and the width of the walk cannot be ascertained, nor is there now any trace of an inner parapet. The outer parapet has a width of 0·6 m and is preserved to a maximum height of 0·6 m. The walk is drained mainly by steeply canted sandstone spouts discharging through the parapet.

THE WELL. Immediately outside the NW range there is a rock-cut well having a modern superstructure. The well is about 2·4 m square at the mouth, and at the date of visit the water lay about 3·6 m beneath the level of the courtyard.

THE WEST TOWER. This tower (Pls. 56B, 57A) comprised four storeys, all the floors having been of timber. It was entered from the courtyard by means of a forestair on the E side, of which considerable traces still remain. This stair gave access to a doorway at first-floor level, beyond which there was a lobby containing an inner door secured by a draw-bar, which admitted to the first-floor chamber. The apartment measured about 3·5 m in diameter and was furnished on the NW and SW sides with timber-lintelled slit-embrasures similar in character to those in the SW and SE curtain-walls. These embrasures contained tall arrow-slits having steeply-splayed sills and fish-tail bases (Fig. 186). The lower parts of the slits have subsequently been built up, but originally extended some 0·76 m beneath the floor-level of the chamber. Midway between the two slits the lower part of a third and similar slit can be seen in the external wall-face, the aperture apparently having been blocked with masonry from within. A consideration of the plan of the first-floor chamber makes it quite clear that a third slit-embrasure can never have existed in this position, and it seems likely that the lower portion of the slit was built in error, the mistake becoming apparent only when the tower was carried above first-floor level. In the N side of the tower there was formerly an opening which probably gave access to a garderobe, but the garderobe itself is now concealed by patching. In the external wall-surface at this point, but at a slightly higher level, there can be seen part of a corbelled garderobe-chute which seems originally to have contained at least two separate vents. One of these vents may have served the garderobe mentioned above. Beneath the first-floor chamber, and presumably reached by means of a trap-door, there was an unlit prison measuring 3·2 m in diameter. On the NW side of the prison there are the remains of a garderobe whose vent-shaft discharged at the base of the wall.

From the entrance-lobby a lintelled staircase ascends in an anti-clockwise direction to give access to the second-floor chamber by means of a doorway secured internally by a draw-bar. This apartment measures 4·6 m in diameter and is provided with two slit-embrasures similar in character to those on the floor below, but without plunged sills. A door on the N side of the chamber formerly gave access to a mural garderobe, but the doorway itself has disappeared together with much of the adjacent internal facework. The garderobe was lit by means of a slit-window in the NW wall, now considerably mutilated, and its discharge-chute appears to have been carried downwards to join the corbelled garderobe-chute already mentioned. The uppermost floor of the tower appears to have been reached only from the parapet-walks, with which it communicated on each side. This storey of the tower was probably reconstructed in the 17th century, and the walls are much thinner than they are below, the chamber having a diameter of about 6 m. Another indication that the upper part of the tower has been remodelled is the existence of

---

[1] Cf. Simpson (*Dunstaffnage*, 85), who identifies the opening as a postern.

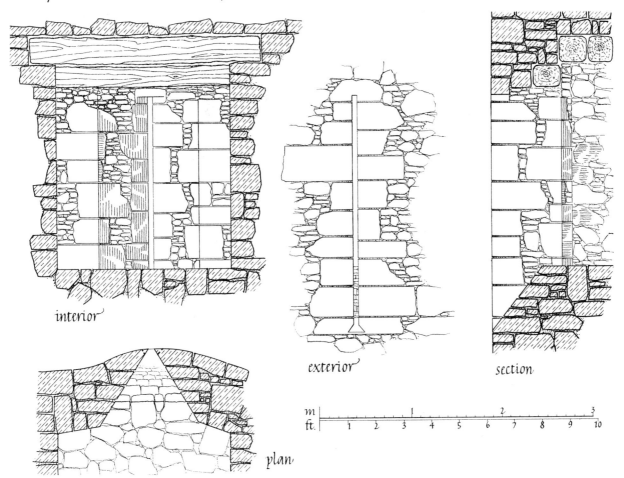

interior

exterior

section

plan

| m | | | | | | 1 | | | 2 | | | 3 |
| ft. | 1 | 2 | 3 | 4 | 5 | 6 | 7 | 8 | 9 | 10 |

Fig. 186. Dunstaffnage Castle (No. 287); arrow-slit in W tower (partially reconstructed)

a garderobe-vent in the NW wall. This vent must formerly have served a latrine at this level, of which no other remains now survive. In the N and W sectors of the tower there are the remains of three straight-sided embrasures measuring some 1·3 m in width. These are rebated for internal timber frames, and may have been designed for firearm-defence, as well as serving as windows. The N embrasure has subsequently been contracted in width, a smaller window having been formed within the daylight-opening. There are now no traces of any fireplaces or chimney-flues within the tower.

THE SOUTH-WEST AND SOUTH-EAST CURTAIN-WALLS. These two sections of the curtain-wall (Pl. 59B) contain a series of slit-embrasures, of which there are four in the SW wall and two in the SE wall. In the original arrangement each of these embrasures contained a deeply-splayed arrow-slit of the type found in the W tower (Fig. 186). The embrasures themselves were timber-lintelled, and those on the SW side were probably manned from a timber platform supported upon a continuous stone scarcement running along the base of the wall. During

the 17th-century alterations the embrasures were partially reconstructed, most of the slits being replaced by smaller inverted-keyhole shaped or circular gun-loops. At the same time the mouths of the two embrasures adjacent to the S corner of the courtyard were sealed off by screen-walls, an alteration which may have been associated with the erection of a courtyard-building in this area. When this part of the castle was restored the embrasure-heads were arched over with stone,[1] except in the case of one of the embrasures of the SE curtain-wall, in which traces of the original timber lintels can still be seen.

Above the present arch-head of the NW embrasure the inner face of the SW curtain-wall is intaken at its junction with the W angle-tower. A good deal of restoration has evidently been carried out in this area, but it seems likely that in the original arrangement the forestair giving access to the tower continued upwards within the thickness of the SW curtain to provide access to the parapet-walk. The third embrasure from the NW in the same curtain contains an inserted 17th-century

---

[1] *Dunstaffnage Case*, 53–4, 59.

window instead of a gun-loop. Between this embrasure and the one to the SE the original mural scarcement at the base of the curtain seems to have been extended upwards in the 17th century, and the facework has been roughly cut away at one point as if to accommodate a fireplace and chimney-flue serving a building in this corner of the courtyard. Further evidence pointing to the former existence of a building in this area is provided by surface-indications of a rough three-sided foundation measuring about 5·8 m by 4·5 m internally, and by the presence of a garderobe-shaft within the screen-wall that seals off the SE embrasure. This embrasure, and the adjacent one in the SE curtain, were evidently entered latterly by means of doorways in the screen-walls. The screen-wall of the embrasure in the SE curtain also contains a small circular peep-hole looking towards the courtyard.

In the original arrangement the SW and SE curtain-walls were surmounted by a continuous parapet-walk, to which access from the courtyard was probably obtained by means of staircases adjacent to the W angle-tower and to the gatehouse, as already described. The walk also communicated, by means of steps, with the uppermost floor of the W tower, while communication with the wall-walk of the E curtain was probably obtained, as it is today, by means of a walk passing round two sides of the gatehouse-garret. During the 17th-century alterations the wall-walk was raised in height by about 0·3 m to 0·6 m, and the parapet was correspondingly heightened and at the same time provided with splayed wide-mouthed embrasures for musketry-defence. The walk has recently been restored to its original level by the Department of the Environment and most of the paving visible today is modern. Here and there, however, there can be seen a number of older flagstones of yellow sandstone (Pl. 59C), which may be of 13th-century date, while at the end of the SE walk there are the remains of sandstone steps (Pl. 59D) which carried the walk downwards towards the adjacent courtyard-staircase. No clear trace of an inner parapet-wall was found during the recent restoration, and the width of the walk remains uncertain. The 17th-century walk was composed of roughly-placed slate slabs. In the outer parapet-wall, which has a thickness of about 0·6 m, a ragged offset-course indicates the level above which the wall was reconstructed during the 17th century. The parapet has subsequently suffered considerable decay, but the remains of two musketry-embrasures can still be seen. Nothing can be seen, however, of the drain-spouts or weep-holes that must have drained both the original and later walks.

HISTORICAL NOTE

The available facts relating to the history of the castle have been set out at some length elsewhere,[1] and do not require detailed reiteration. No contemporary record of the erection of the castle survives, but the structure may be ascribed on architectural grounds to about the second quarter of the 13th century. It is probable, therefore, that the builder was either Duncan, lord of

Lorn, the founder of Ardchattan Priory (No. 217), who died some time between 1237 and 1248,[2] or his son and successor, Ewen, whose death appears to have occurred before 1275.[3]

During the Wars of Independence Alexander of Lorn and his son, John Bacach, were allies of the king of England in opposition to the claims of Robert Bruce. In 1309, however, Robert Bruce defeated the MacDougall forces at a battle in the Pass of Brander and captured Dunstaffnage Castle after a short siege. The MacDougall leaders were forfeited, and their extensive territories were divided among Bruce's supporters, most of the mainland portions of the lordship passing to the Campbells. Dunstaffnage itself probably remained in the king's hands for a considerable period, custody of the castle, together with a grant of the surrounding lands, being given to Arthur Campbell, a kinsman of the Campbells of Lochawe, in 1321 or 1322.

Part of the lordship of Lorn was restored to John Bacach's grandson, John, during the reign of David II, and thereafter passed by marriage to John Stewart of Innermeath, who received a crown charter of lands in Lorn, Benderloch, Appin and Lismore in 1388. Little is heard of Dunstaffnage during this period, and it is not until the lordship of Lorn was transferred by agreement from the Stewarts to the Campbell Earls of Argyll in 1469–70 that references to the castle become more numerous. As in the case of certain other major strong-holds that came into their possession (cf. No. 292), the earls of Argyll entrusted the custody of the castle to a resident warden or captain, and this office became hereditarily established in a family of kinsmen, known as the Campbells of Dunstaffnage. During the 16th and 17th centuries the castle was frequently used, both by the Argyll family and by the government, as a base from which to mount expeditions against enemies in the Western Isles, and as a defensive stronghold of consider-able strategic importance. Thus, Dunstaffnage was garrisoned during the Civil War and throughout the Commonwealth occupation, while following the rebel-lion and forfeiture of Archibald, 9th Earl of Argyll, in 1685, the castle was burnt by forces under the command of the Marquess of Atholl. A proposal to erect a large fort at Dunstaffnage in 1689–90[4] came to nothing, but the castle was again garrisoned by government troops during the two Jacobite rebellions, after which it con-tinued to be occupied by the captains of Dunstaffnage until 1810, when the gatehouse was accidently gutted by fire.

No record survives of the alterations that appear to have been made to the gatehouse by the Campbell Earls of Argyll following their acquisition of the property, nor of the more extensive remodelling of the castle under-

[1] Macphail, J R N, 'Dunstaffnage Castle', *SHR*, xvii (1919–20), 253–271; Simpson, *Dunstaffnage*, 15–68.
[2] Information from Prof. A A M Duncan, revising *PSAS*, xc (1956–7), 207.
[3] MacDonald, *Argyll*, 113.
[4] Mackay, H, *Memoirs of the War carried on in Scotland and Ireland MDCLXXXIX–MDCXCI*, Bannatyne Club (1833), 80.

taken towards the end of the 16th century. A number of references do exist, however, concerning building-operations carried out in the 17th and early 18th centuries. Warrants for repair were issued by Lord Lorn, afterwards 8th Earl and 1st Marquess of Argyll, in 1625 and 1636,[1] while in 1681 it was agreed that £2000 Scots should be expended upon the 'building and repairing' of the castle, the cost being shared equally between the 9th Earl of Argyll and the 10th Captain of Dunstaffnage.[2] It is not known whether these building-operations were, in fact, completed, and the nature of the proposed work is not specified. Some information about subsequent events is contained in a document drawn up on behalf of Angus Campbell, 11th Captain of Dunstaffnage, in 1706. This relates that: 'The Castle of Dunstafnadge . . . was brunt by the Marquiss of Athole's order in the time of the troubles 1685, and about the time of the Revolution the late Duke of Argyle (considering this was the eldest ffortification in Scotland, and the only one in Argyleshyre, and it being then very usefull for him in respect of his Mull business) was pleased to procure Money from the Publick, and causd put a Roof upon the prin(cip)le Tower (?the gatehouse),[3] but the other two Towers and the office-houses were still left Ruinous, and continow soe; And since that time much of the outter wall (being very old, and long since it was lymed) is riven and fallen in many places, and the whole Trench-Wall (?parapet-wall) of the Castle will certainly in a short time turn to ruine, if it be not speedily repaired'.[4] No record of any ensuing repairs is preserved, but in 1725 the Captain seems to have undertaken some work on his own account, as evidenced by the inscriptions associated with the two-storeyed dwelling-house at the NE end of the NW range of courtyard-buildings (*supra* pp. 204 and 207). The contractor employed in the reconstruction of this house appears to have been James Duff, mason in Dunblane, who is known to have been working at Dunstaffnage in 1724.[5]

An inventory of furniture compiled in 1767 indicates that the only parts of the castle in occupation at that time were the 'old tower' (? the gatehouse) and the 'new house' (the dwelling-house of 1725).[6] This is confirmed by an account of a visit made to the castle at about the end of the 18th century by Philip Ainslie, who wrote: 'the portion of (the castle) which was habitable was very limited, situated on the north side of the interior square, consisting of a sitting-room and bedroom; and, on the east side, were some habitable bedrooms, overhanging the battlements, to which you ascended by a circular stair'.[7]

In 1835 plans and estimates for a partial restoration of the castle were obtained from the Edinburgh architect George Angus, but it was decided, on grounds of expense, not to proceed with this scheme.[8] Repairs were made, however, from time to time, and parts of the NW and E curtain-walls are said to have been rebuilt or consolidated at about the end of the 19th century.[9] In 1903–4 the gatehouse was partially restored on the initiative of the 9th Duke of Argyll, and following the conclusion of the Dunstaffnage lawsuit in 1912[10] further

work was carried out by Angus, 20th Captain of Dunstaffnage, up to the outbreak of the Second World War.

882344   NM 83 SE   August 1970

288. Fortified Dwelling, Eilean Stalcair, Loch Tulla (Site).

This island lies near the centre of Loch Tulla, almost opposite the outlet of the River Orchy; it is approximately circular on plan and has a diameter of about 21 m. Superficially the island appears to be composed entirely of small boulders. There is no sign of any kerb or revetment, and the loch shelves steeply on all sides except the SW, where there is a shallow beach. At the top of this beach the stumps of five horizontally-disposed logs lay exposed at the date of visit, which was made at a time when the surface-level of the loch lay about 0·3 m beneath its usual level. The logs, which are spaced at intervals of about 0·8 m, vary somewhat in size, the largest having a diameter of about 0·4 m. All appeared to be composed of coniferous timber, probably Scots pine. Beneath these logs there could be seen some traces of a second and lower layer of similar timbers running parallel to the first. The remaining portions of the logs evidently lie buried beneath the boulders that compose the main core of the island, which, on this showing, must be at least partly artificial in origin. The summit of the island lies about 1·5 m above the usual surface-level of the loch, but contains no structural remains, apart from a modern duck-shooting hide. On the NE side of the island there is a small inlet which has probably been utilized as a boat-landing.

The island of 'Elanelochtollyff' formed part of the lands of Glenorchy granted to Colin Campbell in 1432 by his father, Duncan Campbell of Lochawe.[11] An account of the island prepared in about 1866 mentions that some years previously a local forester had observed 'on a calm summer day, a few feet below the surface of the water, the ends of logs of wood laid horizontally under the stones'.[12]

290425   NN 24 SE   August 1971

---

[1] *Dunstaffnage Case*, 159–160.
[2] Ibid., 184–5. The original contract was drawn up in 1667, but no work appears to have been carried out prior to 1681.
[3] Cf. account for slating house of Dunstaffnage, 1691 (Argyll MSS, Inveraray Castle, Vault, portfolio V 28).
[4] *Dunstaffnage Case*, 213–4.
[5] S.R.O., Campbell of Barcaldine Collection, GD 170/834/1, letter from James Duff to Patrick Campbell of Barcaldine, dated 31 July 1724, mentioning the supply of building-stone from quarries in Morvern; cf. also Nos. 215 and 313.
[6] *Dunstaffnage Case*, 225–7.
[7] Philo-Scotus, *Reminiscences of a Scottish Gentleman, commencing in 1787* (1861), 109.
[8] *Dunstaffnage Case*, 251–3.
[9] Ibid., 63.
[10] This lawsuit re-established the position of the captains of Dunstaffnage as hereditary keepers of the castle on behalf of its proprietors, the Dukes of Argyll.
[11] *Highland Papers*, iv, 199.
[12] *PSAS*, vi (1864–6), 173.

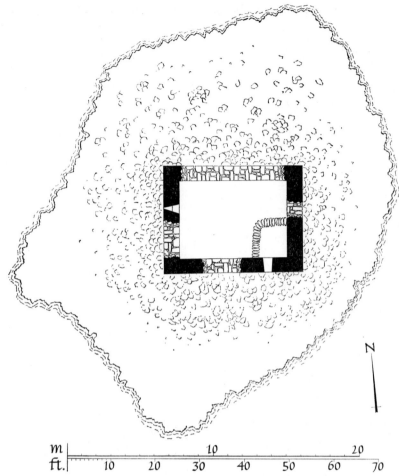

Fig. 187. Fortified dwelling, Eilean Tighe Bhàin, Loch Tromlee (No. 289); plan

289. Fortified Dwelling, Eilean Tighe Bhàin, Loch Tromlee. This small natural island situated 200 m from the SE shore of Loch Tromlee contains the overgrown ruins of a building which is traditionally said to have been the residence of the family of MacCorquodale of Phantilands, until it was sacked by the army of Alasdair Colkitto MacDonald in 1646.[1] The island is almost circular, having a diameter of about 25 m, and rises to a height of about 2·0 m above the water-level of the loch. Although parts of the loch are very shallow, there is no evidence for the existence of a causeway.

The remains are those of a rectangular structure measuring 9·5 m from E to W by 7·0 m transversely over walls varying in thickness from 0·9 m to 1·1 m, and standing to a maximum height of 2·7 m (Fig. 187). The remainder of the island is covered by a mass of fallen stones, and the building may have comprised two storeys, but there is no unambiguous evidence for this. The walls are built of local rubble-masonry containing much schist and bonded with clay mortar; no dressed stones are visible either *in situ* or in the surrounding debris, but part of a broken millstone, having a diameter of about 0·7 m, and doubtless re-used as building-material, was found lying on the N wall. In the W wall there is a small splayed slit having a daylight-opening of 0·08 m and a height of 0·31 m, whose internal sill is stepped. Similar openings may have existed in the E wall, where there is a break in the masonry, and in the side-walls, portions of which have collapsed. Near the E end of the S wall there is an opening measuring 0·7 m in width and having its sill at least 1·2 m above ground-level; this may have been a raised entrance-doorway. The building may be ascribed to the late 16th or early 17th century.

In the SE angle of the building there is a small enclosure formed by a curving dry-stone wall; this is of recent date, and may have been constructed for the purposes of duck-shooting.

043249   NN 02 SW   July 1971

290. Castle, Fraoch Eilean. Fraoch Eilean is one of a group of islands situated at the N end of Loch Awe towards the mouth of the Pass of Brander, and lies about 1 km NE of Inishail, the largest member of the group.

[1] *Highland Papers*, ii, 156; *The Scottish Genealogist*, xi (1964), 14–15.

The island, which is roughly Y-shaped on plan with its long axis running from NE to SW, measures about 200 m in length and up to 120 m transversely; it comprises two rocky eminences separated by a central area of low-lying ground, and has a total extent of about 0·81 ha (2 acres).

The castle (Fig. 188, Pls. 60, 61) occupies the plateau summit of the larger, or NE eminence, which affords a strong defensive position about 0·10 ha (¼ acre) in extent. The existing remains appear to comprise work of four main periods, of which the earliest may be ascribed to a date within the 13th century. During this first period of building-activity a substantial stone hall-house was erected towards the E end of the site, the remaining area of the plateau probably being utilized for the construction of ancillary buildings of turf and timber. At some later date within the medieval period this remaining western portion of the summit was enclosed by a stone curtain-wall incorporating an entrance-gateway on the S side and a round tower at the SW angle. This curtain-wall may have superseded an earlier defence of stone or timber. The N and S sections of the curtain-wall returned to meet the hall-house, to which the area thus enclosed formed a bailey. Some time towards the end of the Middle Ages the castle appears to have gone out of use, remaining unoccupied long enough for the hall-house to become derelict. About the beginning of the 17th century, however, the place was re-occupied, a small dwelling-house being constructed within the NE corner of the original hall-house. At the same time the remaining portion of the hall-house, now roofless, was adapted for use as an inner courtyard. A final reconstruction took place sometime during the latter part of the 17th century, when the small house in the NE corner of the hall-house was enlarged by extending it southwards to take in the SE corner of the hall-house as well. The castle appears to have been abandoned for use as a private residence some time before 1769.[1] The buildings were for long overgrown with a dense covering of trees and other vegetation, much of which has been removed by the proprietor within recent years to permit inspection and repair of the fabric. Exploratory excavations were carried out in 1969–73 under the direction of Dr Francis Celoria, University of Keele.[2]

THE HALL-HOUSE. The hall-house is oblong on plan and measures about 21·7 m from W to E by 12·6 m transversely (Figs. 188, 189).[3] The W and S walls measure 1·7 m in thickness, but the N wall, which is founded upon a stone plinth, has a thickness of nearly 2·1 m. The E wall has a thickness of 2·4 m on the ground-floor, where it incorporated a staircase, but may have been of lesser thickness at the upper levels. The walls stand to an average external height of about 4·6 m, the N wall, however, which is founded at a lower level than the remainder, surviving to a height of about 9 m.

The masonry facework is composed of roughly-coursed split boulders bonded with an abundance of small pinnings and good-quality lime-mortar; some of the boulders are of considerable size. Most of the masonry is of local schist and granite, the former

probably having been derived in part from the island itself, where quarrying may have taken place along the W and S sides of the rock eminence upon which the castle stands. Freestone was employed very sparingly, apparently having been used mainly for external quoins and for doorway- and window-rybats. The material in question is a coarse-grained sandstone varying from light pink to purple in colour, which probably derives from Bridge of Awe (No. 354). Timber was utilized extensively for the construction of doorway- and window-lintels, and for the ceilings of window-embrasures, mural passages and stairs. Stone relieving-arches do not appear to have been employed above doorway- and window-openings, the only visible surviving relieving-arch being situated immediately above plinth-level towards the W end of the N wall, where it probably spans a fissure in the underlying rock. The external wall-surfaces were harled.

The hall-house appears to have contained two main storeys, but there may also have been a garret-floor or loft at one or both ends of the building. The arrangement of the ground-floor is uncertain, but the provision of two separate entrance-doorways in the S wall suggests that the undercroft was divided transversely into two main apartments. Both doorways seem to have been provided with three draw-bars, but in the case of the E doorway, at least, only the middle bar was long enough to extend across the full width of the door, the upper and lower bars presumably having fitted into brackets attached to the door. The undercroft was also divided axially by a stout timber beam, one of the socket-holes for which is visible midway along the inner face of the W gable. This beam may have been supported by intermediate posts of stone or timber and by the transverse partition-wall already mentioned. The transverse joists supporting the floor above were probably notched into the axial beam, which lay about 2·0 m above the original floor-level. The undercroft was evidently lit by four principal windows, two in the N wall and two in the S wall, but all have been mutilated to a greater or lesser extent. There is evidence to suggest, however, that these windows were of uniform size, with daylight-openings about 0·71 m square wrought externally with plain 0·17 m chamfers.

The original arrangements at the E end of the undercroft are not altogether clear, but it would appear that a doorway centrally placed in the E wall gave access to a lobby from which a mural stair descended to a prison in the NE corner. The doorway, which was equipped with a draw-bar socket, was blocked up in the late 17th century. The stair is lit by a small window in the E wall. The prison itself, which measures 2·2 m by 1·4 m by 1·6 m in height, is unlit, but is provided with a latrine in the N wall. The door opening into the prison from the staircase was secured by three draw-bars. It was no

---

[1] Pennant, *Tour (1769)*, 238.
[2] Celoria, F, 'Fraoch Eilean Castle, Loch Awe, Argyll' (typescript reports for private circulation, 1969 and 1974).
[3] The cardinal points of the compass are used here for convenience of description; the true orientation is shown on Fig. 188.

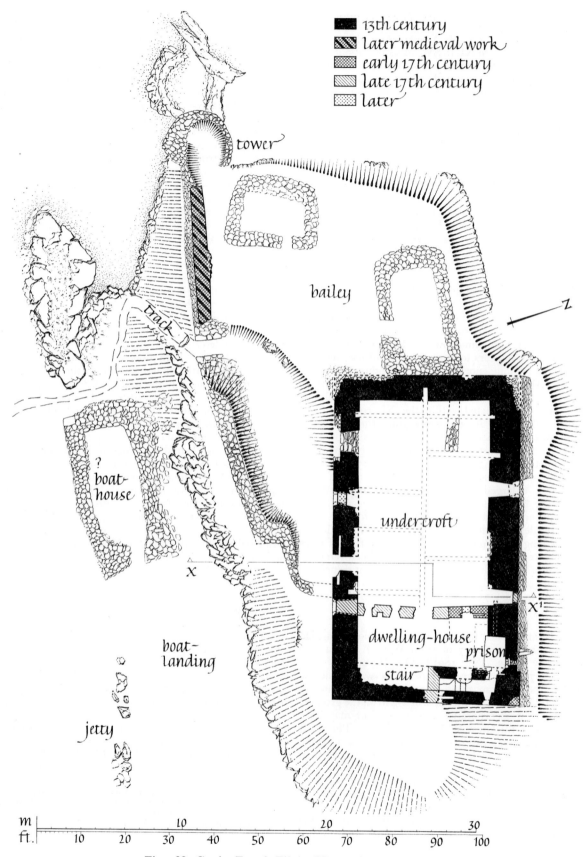

13th century
later medieval work
early 17th century
late 17th century
later

tower

bailey

Z

track

? boat-house

undercroft

X

X¹

boat-landing

dwelling-house

prison

stair

jetty

m | 10 | 20 | 30
ft. | 10 | 20 | 30 | 40 | 50 | 60 | 70 | 80 | 90 | 100

Fig. 188. Castle, Fraoch Eilean (No. 290); general plan

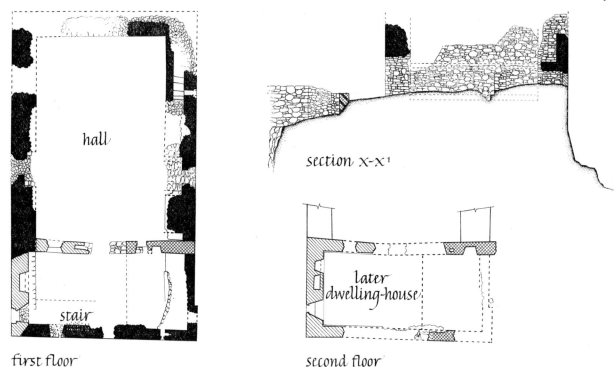

Fig. 189. Castle, Fraoch Eilean (No. 290); upper floor-plans and section

doubt as a result of the decision to incorporate mural chambers in this corner of the building, both at ground- and at first-floor levels, that it was found necessary to strengthen the external NE angle of the hall-house by a pilaster-buttress rising from the base-plinth of the N wall (Pl. 62B). There is no evidence for the existence of a corresponding buttress at the NW angle of the building.

From the lobby the mural stair also rose southwards to give access to the floor above. The sockets for the timber stair-treads survive, and there are some remains of a small window-opening. At first-floor level (Fig. 189) the building appears to have contained a single large apartment, evidently a hall, measuring up to 17·5 m in length and 8·8 m in width, but it is possible that the E portion was divided off by a timber partition to form a solar. The embrasured windows in the N and S walls were provided with bench-seats and had daylight-openings some 0·9 m in width. There is evidence of two such windows in the N wall, and of another, or more probably of two more, in the S wall, the openings being placed more or less opposite to one another. A gap in the masonry of the S wall immediately above the W ground-floor doorway may represent the site of a first-floor entrance approached by means of a forestair. Towards the W end of the N wall a doorway gave access to an ascending mural staircase (Pl. 62D) which presumably led to a wall-walk and perhaps also to a loft above this end of the hall. In the absence of any evidence to indicate that the hall was equipped with a mural fireplace, it may be inferred that it contained a central hearth from which the smoke rose to a roof louver.

The E end of the building communicated with the undercroft by means of the mural stair in the E wall already described. There was also a mural chamber in the NE corner lit by a small window in the E gable-wall. This window is rebated for a shutter, which was secured by a draw-bar; the arrises of the daylight-opening are wrought with plain 0·15 m chamfers.

There is little evidence to indicate the nature of the arrangements above first-floor level, but it is likely that the wall-head was surmounted by an open parapet-walk. The existence of a sandstone corbel situated immediately to the W of the pilaster-buttress at the NE angle suggests that the parapet-walk was equipped with a garderobe at this point. The roof was probably double-pitched, and the bays over the hall, at least, were presumably of open-timber construction. Since the building is of considerable width the roof must have been substantially framed with timbers of large scantling.

THE DWELLING-HOUSE. The early 17th-century dwelling-house (Pl. 62C, E) was formed by enclosing the NE corner of the hall-house to form a building measuring about 6·5 m from E to W by 4·6 m transversely over all. The masonry of this building is noticeably inferior to that of the hall-house, and apart from one or two re-used fragments of sandstone no freestone is employed; the openings are spanned with slab-lintels. The house rose to a height of three storeys, and was covered with a roof pitched from N to S, the NW angle being roughly corbelled out to correspond with the projection of the original buttress at the NE angle of the hall-house. The building was probably entered at ground-floor level by means of a doorway in the S wall. The ground-floor area comprised a single main apartment and, at a lower level, the former prison in the N wall reached by means of the mural stair. The main apartment was lit by means of a window in the W wall; the embrasure is equipped with a draw-bar socket. The first floor was occupied by a single apartment of which the N portion was formed by taking in the original mural chamber of the hall-house. There was a window and a fireplace in the W wall and, presumably, another window and an upper entrance-doorway in the S wall. Above, there was a garret-chamber provided with a fireplace and probably reached by means of an internal timber staircase.

When this dwelling-house came to be enlarged in the later 17th century, the S wall was removed and the W wall extended southwards to meet the S wall of the hall-house. Within the area thus formed there was constructed a four-storeyed building having its roof pitched from E to W. The original walls of the hall-house were repaired and heightened at each end to form gables, of which the southern one still survives intact, rising to a height of 10·9 m above the external ground-level. Like its immediate predecessor, the late 17th-century dwelling-house was approached through the shell of the hall-house, whose walls now formed an open courtyard.

The masonry of the late 17th-century dwelling-house is superior to that of its early 17th-century predecessor and some of the openings incorporate dressed rybats and lintels of schist. The window-openings are rebated and the arrises are wrought with plain 0·05 m chamfers. Purple sandstone, probably derived from Bridge of Awe (No. 354), also appears to have been employed at this period to repair the external SE corner of the hall-house.

At ground-floor level the enlarged dwelling-house appears to have been entered by means of a doorway in the W wall. The apartment, or apartments, within were lit mainly from windows overlooking the courtyard to the W. At first-floor level there is evidence for another entrance-doorway, secured by a draw-bar, in the W wall, for windows in the W and S walls, and for a lintelled fireplace in the centre of the S wall; the doorway was presumably approached by means of a forestair. The

arrangements at second-floor level were similar, communication between these two levels perhaps having been obtained by means of a staircase situated within the area formerly occupied by the early 17th-century house. Both these floors were probably divided into two main apartments by means of transverse partitions. Communication between ground- and first-floor levels was obtained by means of a timber staircase occupying the site of the original 13th-century stair against the E wall. The floors both of the early 17th-century and of the later 17th-century dwelling-houses were joisted.

Some time during one of these later periods of occupation a building appears to have been erected against the interior of the W gable-wall of the hall-house, but this structure is now so fragmentary that its nature cannot be determined.

THE BAILEY. The bailey was enclosed by a curtain wall some 1·3 m or more in thickness, which now survives to a considerable extent only on the S side (Pl. 62A), where it attains a maximum height of about 3·0 m. The curtain was evidently designed to guard the entrance-doorways of the hall-house, as well as to give protection to ancillary buildings standing at the W end of the rock summit. The masonry is of local rubble laid in lime mortar. The W section of the S curtain is of inferior construction to the E section and shows a pronounced batter, differences which suggest that this portion of the wall was at some period reconstructed. At the SW angle of the bailey there are the remains of a roughly circular tower of bold projection.

Within the bailey (Fig. 188) there may be seen traces of two small sub-rectangular buildings of dry-stone construction, both of which probably belong to the latest period of occupation of the site. The bailey is approached by a path leading up the southern slope of the rock plateau to a doorway in the S curtain-wall some 1·1 m in width.

BOAT-LANDING. Below the SE corner of the rock summit upon which the castle stands there are the remains of a boulder jetty bounding the S side of a small gently-sloping beach. This is presumably a boat-landing, and since there is some evidence to suggest that the level of the loch was formerly somewhat higher than it is today,[1] boats may have been drawn up immediately beneath the castle. The jetty terminates on its landward side a little to the E of a sub-rectangular building of dry-stone construction measuring about 10·9 m from W to E by 5·5 m transversely over all. This may have been a boat-house.

CARVED STONE. During the excavations of 1969 a fragment of buff-coloured sandstone, possibly deriving from the Ardtornish area, came to light among debris lying within the NW interior of the building. The stone (Fig. 190, Pl. 62F), which is wrought with a filleted roll

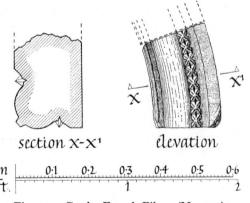

section X-X¹   elevation

m | 0·1   0·2   0·3   0·4   0·5   0·6
ft | 1   2

Fig. 190. Castle, Fraoch Eilean (No. 290); carved fragment

[1] *NSA*, vii (Argyll), 99; *PSAS*, vii (1866-8), 235. A late 18th-century water-colour painting by W H Watts in the possession of Mr Ian M Campbell suggests that the low-lying central area of the island was wholly or partially submerged at that period.

between hollows containing well-executed dog-tooth ornament, probably formed part of an arched window-head, or similar feature, of 13th-century date.

HISTORICAL NOTE

The castle first comes on record in 1267 in a charter of Alexander III to Gillechrist MacNachdan, a member of a prominent local family of baronial status. By the terms of this charter the Macnaughtons were granted '*custodiam castri nostri et insulae de Frechelan, ita quod dictum castrum sumptibus nostris construi faciant et reficiant quotiens opus fuerit et salvo custodiant ad opus nostrum*'[1] ('custody of our castle and island of Frechelan, so that they should cause the said castle to be built at our expense and repaired as often as necessary, and should keep it safely for our use'). The charter is open to more than one interpretation, and its authenticity is not beyond dispute, but if genuine it is probably to be construed as a grant of custody relating to a castle then in course of erection, or about to be erected, rather than to one already in occupation.[2] Such a grant, to an established local landowner, would have been in complete accordance with the policy of consolidation of royal power in the Western Highlands pursued by Alexander III following the Treaty of Perth in 1266.[3] Moreover, the architectural characteristics of the castle, as described above, are consonant with a date in the third quarter of the 13th century, a close parallel being provided by Greencastle, County Down, a structure of very similar size and form, which is known to have been built in about the middle of the 13th century.[4]

Nothing is known of the history of the castle in the later Middle Ages, during which period the Macnaughtons appear to have become vassals of the Campbells, latterly establishing themselves at Dundarave, on Loch Fyne. At some date now unknown Fraoch Eilean passed into the possession of the Campbells of Inverawe, a cadet branch of the house of Argyll, and it was no doubt this family that was responsible for the 17th-century reoccupation and reconstruction of the castle. In 1765 the island was sold to Robert Campbell of Monzie, subsequently passing to the Campbells of Dunstaffnage, but in 1960 it was repurchased by a member of the Inverawe branch of the family, Ian M Campbell, WS, who has since taken steps to preserve the fabric of the castle.[5]

108251   NN 12 NW   August 1970

291. Gylen Castle, Kerrera. This small tower-house, probably completed by Duncan MacDougall of MacDougall and Dunollie in 1582, is dramatically situated at the SW extremity of a rocky promontory near the S shore of the island of Kerrera (Pls. 63, 64A, B). Cliffs of agglomerate, rising sheer to a height of about 17 m, surround the site on all sides except the N and NE where steep grass-covered slopes permit access to an outer bailey (Fig. 191). The highest point of this bailey is about 3·5 m above the level of the SW part of the promontory, to which it is linked by a narrow neck of ground whose entire width is occupied by the tower-house and a defensive forework. The area SW of the tower was enclosed by a stone wall measuring some 0·9 m in thickness; it shows traces of ridges running from SE to NW and may have been used as a garden. The extreme SW point of the promontory, which is penetrated at ground-level by a natural archway, appears not to have been included within the defensive system.

The tower-house is a homogeneous structure which was occupied for a period of only 65 years before being destroyed by fire, and has undergone no alteration. Despite fears for its survival expressed in 1887, only one small section of the upper part of the W wall has collapsed since that date.[6] Certain important carved stones were removed to Dunollie House for preservation during the 19th century, and in 1913 HM Office of Works undertook a limited programme of consolidation.

ARCHITECTURAL DESCRIPTION

The masonry of the tower-house consists of rubble comprising whinstone, rounded boulders derived probably from the agglomerate upon which the castle stands, green sandstone which appears to be from the quarries at Ardentallan (No. 349), and a purple-brown sandstone of local origin. This last stone, probably quarried from the sandstone beds that outcrop at Port Dubh (NM 790268) and elsewhere along the S shore of Kerrera,[7] is freely utilized for quoins and door- and window-dressings. There are slight differences in the composition of the masonry at different levels, that in the lowest part being predominantly of green sandstone, and it is probable that the work of building was spread over several seasons. Originally the masonry was covered with harling, some of which still adheres to the SW part of the NW wall. Most of the door- and window-openings are constructed with relieving-arches and the vaults at ground-floor level are neatly executed. With a few exceptions window- and door-jambs are wrought at the arris with a 0·08 m chamfer returned across the lintel. The sills of the larger window-openings are chased to receive wooden frames fitted behind the check, and grooved to allow the seepage of moisture from below the frames (Pl. 65A); these windows were fitted with vertical and horizontal metal bars. The smaller windows of the stair-tower are wrought with continuous glazing-grooves.

[1] *Highland Papers*, i, 107.
[2] But cf. the interpretation put forward by H B Millar in 'The Castle of Fraoch Eilean, Loch Awe, Argyll' (*TGAS*, new series, xv (1960–7), 111–28).
[3] Duncan, A A M and Brown, A L, 'Argyll and the Isles in the Earlier Middle Ages', *PSAS*, xc (1956–7), 216–7.
[4] *An Archaeological Survey of County Down* (1966), 211–9.
[5] *Inchaffray Chrs.*, lxxxiii–iv; Douglas, *Baronage*, 418–20; Campbell, I M, *Notes on the Campbells of Inverawe* (1951), 9–16, 39, and 'Notes about two Loch Awe islands' (privately circulated, 1966); Wimberley, D, *Memorials of the Family of Campbell of Kilmartin and some notes on the Family of Campbell of Inverawe* (1894), 5; Macnaghten, A I, *The Chiefs of Clan Macnachtan* (1951), 54–5.
[6] *Cast. and Dom. Arch.*, ii, 70–4.
[7] Lee, G W and Bailey, E B, *The Pre-Tertiary Geology of Mull, Loch Aline, and Oban* (1925), 39–40, 125.

R   217

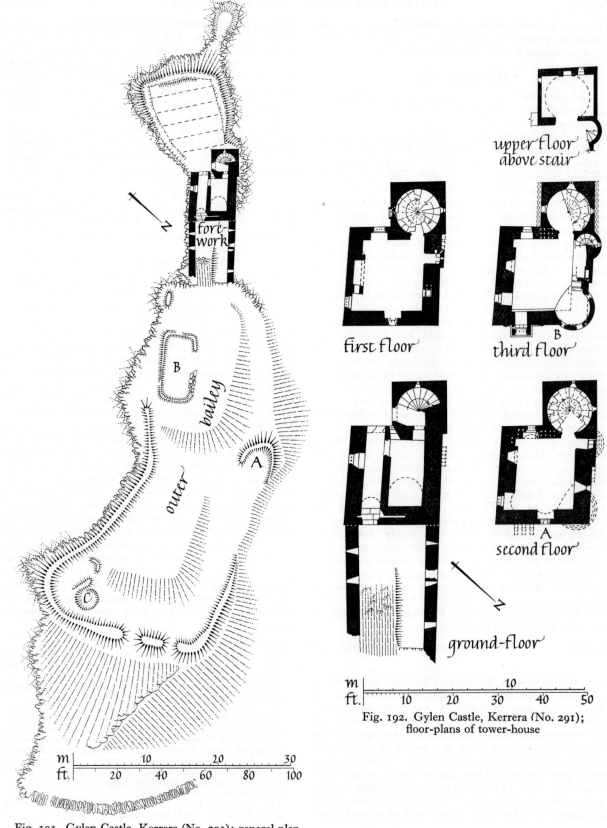

fore-
work

B

outer   bailey

A

C

N

m | 10   20   30
ft.| 20   40   60   80   100

Fig. 191. Gylen Castle, Kerrera (No. 291); general plan

upper floor
above stair

first floor

third floor

B

second floor

A

ground-floor

N

m | 10
ft.| 10   20   30   40   50

Fig. 192. Gylen Castle, Kerrera (No. 291);
floor-plans of tower-house

The tower is L-shaped on plan (Fig. 192), the main block measuring 6·4 m square and the stair-tower at the W angle measuring 3·7 m by 2·8 m over walls varying in thickness from 0·9 m to 1·2 m at first-floor level. It comprises four storeys, with an additional chamber, reached by a corbelled stair-turret, above the stair-tower, the height to the wall-head of the principal block being 9·4 m and to the wall-head of the stair-tower some 11·6 m. The ground-floor contains a vaulted pend linking the two parts of the promontory, and a vaulted cellar parallel to the pend, while each of the upper floors comprised a single apartment equipped with a garderobe.

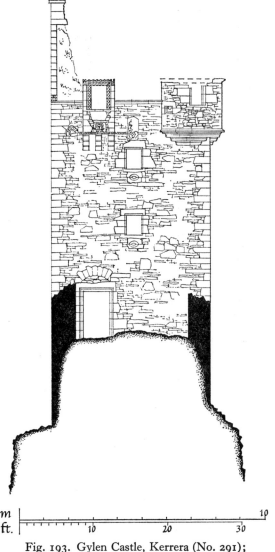

Fig. 193. Gylen Castle, Kerrera (No. 291);
NE elevation

The upper part of the NE, or entrance, façade (Fig. 193, Pl. 64A) is a composition of considerable elaboration. The doorway giving access to the pend, at the SE end, is wrought with a 0·13 m semicircular moulding (Fig.

194B), returned across the lintel and stopped above the threshold. The first- and second-floor apartments are each lit by a centrally-placed window having an outward-splayed horizontal gun-loop (Fig. 195A) beneath the sill.

At the wall-head immediately above the entrance-doorway there projects a feature (Fig. 196, Pl. 64C), unique among the surviving architecture of the West Highlands,[1] which combines the functions of an oriel-window and a box-machicolation. This is carried on three triple-membered corbels having moulded lips. Above the central corbel there is carved in relief a female head whose tresses return as a cable-moulding along the base of the oriel and on to the wall of the tower, where the moulding terminates at either end in a sculptured panel. That to the SE is carved in high relief with the head and bust of a man, wearing a ruff and a pleated skull-cap, who pulls the cable across his chest. The other panel, which has suffered from flaking of the surface, apparently depicted a kneeling man holding one strand of the cable in each hand.

Below the window-sill there is a panel bearing the following inscription in capital letters, carved in relief.

    TR[?V]ST · IN · T[?IL] / GOD · AND · IN · / NE · ME · MY · / SIN · DO · VEIL · / & · LAT · THAME · SAY

The final word is carved on a separate smaller stone, and each word is divided by a raised point. The third letter of the first word appears to be V, although the form 'traist' would be more normal orthography for 'trust' in 16th-century Scots. Another abnormal form occurs in the words 'ne me', probably intended to represent 'nae mae' ('no more'), while 'sin' in the fourth line is perhaps an error for 'son', resulting from confusion with 'sin', mistakenly written 'in', in the second line.[2] Emended thus, the couplet would mean 'Trust unto God, and sin no more (or alternatively, 'in no other'); my son, do well, and let them say'. This is a concise summary of Proverbs, chapter three, with the Scots tag 'let them say' appended to the moral injunction, 'do well', with which it was familiarly associated.[3]

The chamfered jambs and lintel of the oriel-window are wrought with billet-ornament, within a roll-moulded surround (Fig. 194C), while the hood-mould is carved with a continuous pattern of hollow lozenges, and terminates in grotesque animal-heads of decidedly Romanesque character. When John Leyden visited Gylen in 1800 he saw the date 1587 in this part of the castle;[4] this undoubtedly refers to the date-stone preserved at Dunollie (*infra*) which, with another fragment bearing initials, probably formed the pediment of the oriel-window. A crude figure of an angel, carved on the NE skewput of the SE gable, completes the sculptural decoration of this area. Much of this ornament

---

[1] A similar feature occurs at Amisfield Tower, built in 1600 (*Inventory of Dumfriesshire*, No. 578). Cf. also Baltersan, Ayrshire (*Cast. and Dom. Arch.*, iii, 503).
[2] The Commissioners are indebted to Professor J MacQueen, University of Edinburgh, for discussion of this inscription.
[3] Cf. the inscription 'Do you weill, and lat them saye', recorded on a house in Peterhead (Findlay, J T, *A History of Peterhead* (1933), 63).
[4] Leyden, *Tour*, 120.

bears a strong resemblance to the decoration of the entrance-doorway at Dundarave Castle, Mid Argyll, dated 1596, and although the two buildings differ in design and architectural characteristics, it is probable that one of the Gylen masons was subsequently employed in a subordinate capacity at Dundarave.[1] The sculptural decoration of both of these castles appears to be connected with that of a group of buildings in SW Scotland. Fragments built into the court of offices at Blairquhan Castle, Ayrshire, include grotesque figures, some closely resembling those at Gylen, associated with cable-mouldings, and similar work exists at Kenmure Castle, Kirkcudbrightshire, and Haggs Castle, Renfrewshire.

At the wall-head is a cavetto-moulded eaves-cornice (Fig. 194D) which is not continued beyond the junction of the wall with a corbelled turret at the N angle. This

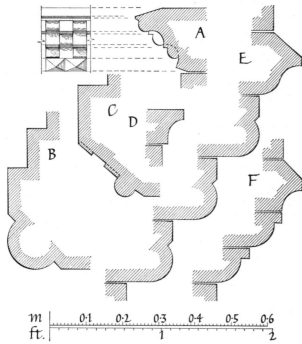

Fig. 194. Gylen Castle, Kerrera (No. 291); profile mouldings and details: A, E, north angle-turret; B, entrance-doorway; C, oriel-window; D, eaves-cornice; F, corbelling of chamber above stair-tower

turret (Pl. 64D), carried on a corbel-course of four members, the uppermost of which is of ogival section (Fig. 194E), was originally roofed and was lit by a single window facing NNE. At the points where the turret merges with the NE and NW walls there are pistol-holes (Fig. 195B) of redented type. Most of the cornice that was illustrated in 1887[2] has disappeared, but a small portion remains intact on the NW (Fig. 194A); it comprises a narrow band of faceted ornament surmounted by three rows of miniature corbels arranged in chequer pattern.

On the NW the tower-house rises directly from the

cliff-face, and there is considerable under-building at the NE end of this wall. At ground-level the SW portion that contains the stair-tower returns outward for a distance of 0·33 m; to the NE of this re-entrant there is a series of corbelled-out garderobe-shafts serving the three upper floors, and these merge so as to bring the greater portion of the upper wall-face into line with the stair-tower. The garderobe-chambers are lit by small openings, one of those at first-floor level being cut obliquely through the angle of its projecting shaft in a manner characteristic of buildings of the late medieval period in Ireland.[3] At second-floor level there is an inconspicuous horizontal gun-loop commanding a boat-landing to the NW. The projection containing the stair that led to the chamber above the stair-tower is carried out on four courses of corbelling, and the chamber itself is supported on continuous corbelling of three courses (Fig. 194F).

The SE gable-wall, which also rises sheer from the cliff-face, contains a single window in each storey and terminates in crow-steps surmounted by a chimney-stack. Within the courtyard, the archway leading from the pend is a simple round-headed opening (Pl. 65F), above which are windows lighting each floor of the tower, that at third-floor level having been a dormer. In the re-entrant angle between the principal block and the stair-tower, at ground-floor level, is an obliquely-set window lighting the vaulted cellar, and close to this is a doorway giving access to the stair-tower. Above the doorway is a recess, evidently designed for an armorial panel and having a roll-moulded surround. The stair-tower with its chamber was lit by windows in the NW, SW and SE walls, and the crow-stepped SW gable originally terminated in a small chimney.

The entrance-doorway, protected by the machicolated oriel-window above, evidently formed the principal defence of the castle. Internally it has a double rebate for a timber door and a yett, which were secured by a draw-bar, housed in the NW jamb. The butt of the draw-bar fitted into a socket in the SE jamb, in whose base there is a smaller vertical socket designed to receive a staple fixing the draw-bar in position. At the SW end of the NW wall of the pend there is a doorway leading into the cellar, which also communicates directly with the lobby at the foot of the principal stair. The spiral stair (Pl. 65C), lit by three windows on each flight, survives intact to first-floor level; above that level the newel has been destroyed and only fragments of the treads remain *in situ*.

Each of the three upper storeys is similar in arrangement, having a garderobe-chamber in the NW wall and

[1] *Cast. and Dom. Arch.*, iii, 617–8; Leyden (*Tour*, 119–20) records seeing 'the figure of a bagpiper playing' above the gateway at Gylen, and if correct this would reinforce the suggested link with Dundarave where a figure playing a long chanter is inserted on the E side of the entrance-doorway. There is, however, no obvious position for such a figure at Gylen, and it seems likely that Leyden misinterpreted one of the carvings described above.
[2] *Cast. and Dom. Arch.*, ii, 73.
[3] Leask, H G, *Irish Castles and Castellated Houses* (1964), 96–8.

windows in the other walls, with a fireplace and cupboard-recess in the SE wall. The fireplace of the first-floor apartment (Pl. 65B), which evidently served both as kitchen and hall, is some 1·7 m in width; the lintel, a thin vertically-set slab, has disappeared, but the segmental relieving-arch remains intact.[1] An aperture some 0·4 m square, rebated externally for a wooden door opening into the adjoining window-embrasure, penetrates the NE jamb of the fireplace. This may have been, as has been suggested,[2] a salt-box, perhaps divided from the fireplace by a stone slab fitted into the two

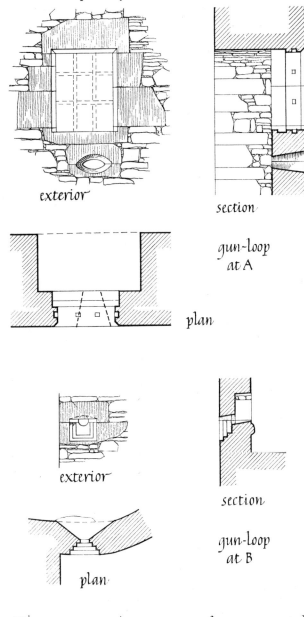

exterior

section

gun-loop at A

plan

exterior

section

gun-loop at B

plan

m
ft.

Fig. 195. Gylen Castle, Kerrera (No. 291); gun-loops

chases that are formed in the sides of the opening at the SW end. Towards the NE end of the NW wall there is a recess which was described in 1887[3] as a sink draining into the shaft of the adjacent garderobe; the bottom is now covered with mortar and no outlet is visible. It is rebated externally for a door and internally for a horizontal frame, having at the SW end two vertical chases for a small sluice-gate to control the flow of water into a smaller recess set low in the SW side. The garderobe-chamber is lit by two small windows, one of them being the oblique opening described above, and has an aumbry or lamp-recess in the SW wall. The embrasures of the first-floor windows were originally roofed by shallow vaults similar to those of the second-floor apartment; the scars left by their collapse have been patched, and the window-lintels were repaired with concrete in 1913. Much of the masonry at this level bears marks of fire, evidently resulting from the conflagration of the floor-timbers when the castle was destroyed in 1647.

The fireplace of the second-floor apartment is of modest size. Near the NE end of the NW wall is a splayed embrasure having a flat sill but roofed by a stepped series of lintels; this contains the horizontal gun-loop described above. The joists of the third floor were fixed into socket-holes in the SW wall, and received support from a runner. The other ends of the joists were supported partly by a scarcement in the NE wall, and partly by socket-holes built into the masonry of the segmental arch that spans the N angle to give additional floor-space to the corner-round.

The oriel-window at third-floor level has no provision for a door separating it from the main apartment; it is equipped with a pistol-hole in the SE side-wall, covering a small bay to the E. Immediately SW of the N angle-turret there has been an aumbry of unusual form, having two doors opening respectively into the turret and into the main apartment; only the lowest stones remain *in situ*. A short mural passage gave access to the garderobe-chamber and to the newel-stair that led to the upper chamber in the stair-tower. Although the inner wall of this passage has collapsed and the exact position of the doorway cannot be identified, the general arrangement is evident.

The SE portion of the principal wing of the tower-house was covered by an open timber roof without tie-beams. Sockets for the rafters, sole-pieces and ashlar-pieces are visible in the SW wall, and the crow-steps of the SE gable are grooved to receive the roof-covering. The form of the roof-structure at the NW gable, and the way in which access was gained from the stair-turret to the door of the upper chamber, whose NW jamb remains *in situ*, is not certain, but a wooden landing probably bridged the intervening space. The chamber was provided with a small fireplace in the SW gable-wall, and was lit by windows in the SW and NW walls.

---

[1] An iron fire-basket, traditionally said to have been removed from Gylen, is preserved at Dunollie House.
[2] *Cast. and Dom. Arch.*, ii, 72-3.
[3] Ibid., ii, 72.

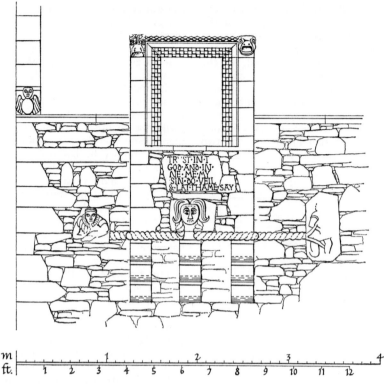

Fig. 196. Gylen Castle, Kerrera (No. 291); oriel-window

THE FOREWORK. The NE portion of the narrow neck of ground upon which the tower-house is built is enclosed by two parallel walls measuring some 0·9 m in thickness and standing to a maximum internal height of about 2·0 m. The masonry of these walls is not bonded with that of the tower-house, but it closely resembles the material of the upper part of that structure and may be ascribed to the same date. This forework serves no defensive purpose in relation to the direct approach to the tower-house, but the walls are penetrated by musket-loops covering the two small bays, to E and NW respectively, that provide possible boat-landings at certain states of the tide. There are no visible remains of the 'ruins of offices' that MacGibbon and Ross recorded as existing against the NW wall.[1]

THE OUTER BAILEY. The outer bailey measures some 48 m from NE to SW by 18 m transversely and was formerly enclosed by a wall which survives only as a low turf-covered mound. At the mid-point of the N flank, where access is possible from the boat-landing below, the wall appears to have returned to form a small tower (A on Fig. 191), perhaps associated with a postern-gate. In the SW part of the bailey there are the turf-covered remains of a sub-rectangular building (B) of dry-stone masonry measuring some 10 m by 5 m over all and apparently having a single doorway in the NW wall. Within the E angle of the bailey there is a depression (C), partially rock-cut, which evidently served as a catchment-basin for rain-water.

CARVED STONES. The following items were removed during the 19th century from Gylen to Dunollie House (No. 318), where they are preserved in the porch. All are carved in green sandstone, identical in appearance with that quarried at Ardentallan (No. 349).

(1) A fragment (Pl. 65D), measuring 0·33 m in width at the base, carved in relief with the date 1582.[2] This stone evidently formed the upper part of the pediment of the elaborate oriel-window described above.

(2) A stone (Pl. 65E), now broken obliquely into two pieces, whose upper edge has a width of 0·38 m; this originally formed the lower portion of the same pediment. It bears the initials D M D F ?O ?F D / V B M. The upper line should probably be expanded as 'D(uncan) M(ac)D(ougall), F(iar) OF D(unollie)', the title by which the builder of Gylen Castle was invariably known until the death of his elder brother.[3] The significance of the letters V B M is obscure, bearing no obvious relationship to Duncan MacDougall.[4]

---

[1] *Cast. and Dom. Arch.*, ii, 71.
[2] Leyden read this date as 1587 (*Tour*, 120); the lower edge of the stone has been damaged, but the final numeral is undoubtedly a Z-shaped 2.
[3] *RPC*, 1st series, iv (1585–92), 211 and *passim*; Nat. Lib. of Scot. MS 2129, pp. 96–7.
[4] His wife, who appears on record in 1581 and 1589 (Nat. Lib. of Scot. MS 2129, pp. 78–80, 96–7), was Margaret McLean of Duart. The interpretation V(irgo) B(eata) M(aria), suggested by A A MacGregor (*Skye and the Inner Hebrides* (1953), 116), assumes that a family having no known Roman Catholic sympathies at this period would employ an unusual, perhaps unique, form of this sacred monogram.

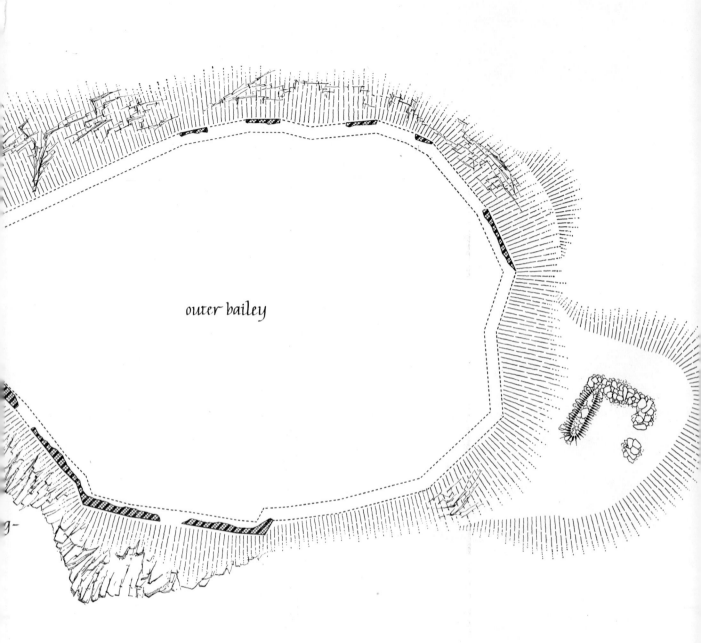

outer bailey

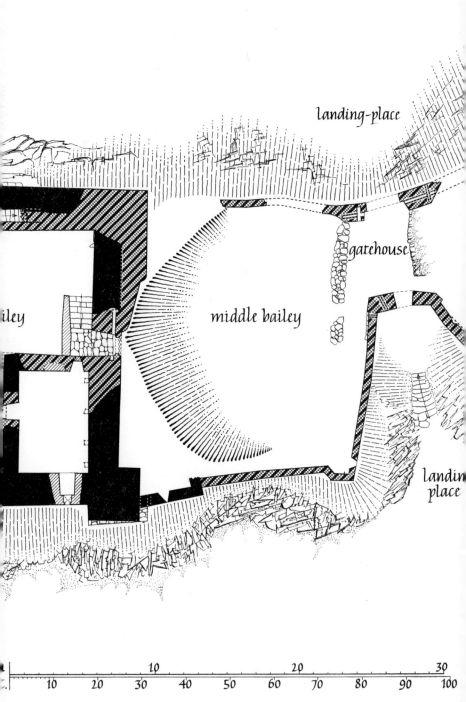

landing-place

gatehouse

iley

middle bailey

landing place

10   20   30

10   20   30   40   50   60   70   80   90   100

Fig. 197. Innis Chonnell Castle (No. 2

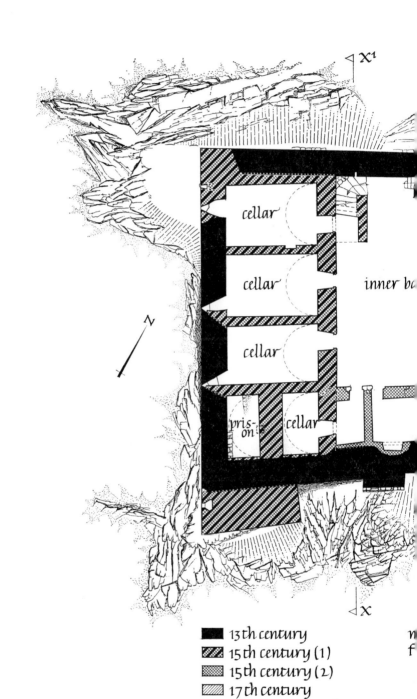

X¹

cellar

cellar

inner b

cellar

pris-
on | cellar

N

X

13th century
15th century (1)
15th century (2)
17th century
restoration work

(3) A standing figure (Pl. 65G), apparently female, carved in the round; the lower part is broken, and the surviving portion has a height of 0·53 m. It portrays a woman with long hair who wears a pleated dress having long sleeves and tight cuffs, gathered at the waist with a rope-like belt. Above the dress she wears a pleated ruff and a cloak which is fastened at the breast by a large annular brooch, apparently having a cross-bar to which the pins are attached.[1]

HISTORICAL NOTE

The lands of Gylen, extending to six merklands, were set in tack by Dougall MacDougall of Dunollie to Duncan, his brother and heir, in 1581.[2] It is evident from the inscriptions recorded above that the castle was built by Duncan, as his personal residence, during the lifetime of his brother. In sources of the second quarter of the 17th century it appears as 'Doun Donacky', or 'Dundouchie', ('Duncan's Castle').[3] Relations between the two brothers became strained, and between 1587 and 1589 the Privy Council took numerous bonds of caution from Duncan and his retainers, on the one part, and Dougall and Allan MacDougall of Rarey, on the other, to restrain a potential feud; one of these bonds was executed by Duncan at 'the Gillinge' in 1588.[4]

Thereafter the castle has no recorded history until its destruction in 1647, when its Royalist garrison was attacked by a detachment of the Covenanting army of David Leslie. The besiegers, who had completed successful campaigns in Kintyre and Islay, 'threatned those that wer therin with hanging to death if they did not burne the same', and, doubtless mindful of the fate of their kinsmen who had suffered in the massacre of Dunaverty, the garrison complied with this order. The 'Brooch of Lorn', a celebrated MacDougall heirloom which had been sent to Gylen for safekeeping, was removed by Campbell of Inverawe, one of the attacking force.[5] The castle was probably never reoccupied after this catastrophe.

805264   NM 82 NW   June 1971

292. Innis Chonnell Castle. This castle (Pl. 66A, C, E) takes its name from a small rocky island situated close to the SE shore of Loch Awe, about 14 km NE of Ford and directly opposite the village of Dalavich. The island is approximately hour-glass shaped on plan (Fig. 197), and the castle occupies almost the entire area above the shoreline, an outer bailey to the E being separated from middle and inner baileys to the W by an entrance-gatehouse which straddles the narrow central neck of the island.

SYNOPSIS

The existing buildings belong to several different periods, the main stages in the architectural evolution of the castle apparently being as follows. The earliest surviving building is the inner bailey, which was erected in or about the first half of the 13th century as a small rectangular castle of enceinte having one or more square

angle-towers of shallow projection. Within the interior of this castle there were a number of buildings grouped round a small central courtyard, the entrance-doorway probably being situated on the E side.[6] Some time during the first half of the 15th century the castle was drastically remodelled, a new SW tower and courtyard-buildings, including a spacious first-floor hall, being erected; at the same time a new entrance-doorway was formed in the E curtain and the NW and NE corners of the enceinte were rebuilt without angle-towers. The wall-head was crowned with an almost continuous parapet-walk reached from the courtyard by means of a stone forestair rising against the N curtain-wall.

The last main series of building-operations appears to have been carried out at some time during the 17th century, when the service-area of the 15th-century hall was remodelled to incorporate a new kitchen-fireplace, while musketry-loops were formed in the S parapet and elsewhere, and a stone forestair was constructed to replace a timber forestair giving access from the courtyard to the entrance in the E curtain. After it became unoccupied in the 18th century the structure was allowed to deteriorate, and when MacGibbon and Ross visited the site shortly before 1889 many features were evidently obscured by debris and vegetation.[7] This damage was relatively superficial, however, and as a result of a programme of clearance and consolidation, apparently carried out early in the present century, the inner bailey, at least, is now in fairly good repair, although little remains of the gatehouse, or of the middle and outer baileys. Considerable clearance of ivy was carried out by the Commission's officers before the present survey was begun.

ARCHITECTURAL DESCRIPTION

THE INNER BAILEY. Although extensively remodelled during the 15th century, the inner bailey (Figs. 198, 199, 200) retains a good deal of earlier work, and its general plan and overall dimensions (25·7 m by 25·1 m) evidently correspond approximately with those of the 13th-century castle. The early masonry is most conspicuous externally, as for example in the central portions of the N and W walls, where it is seen to comprise split boulders of varying size, roughly coursed and bonded with numerous small pinnings. This masonry contrasts sharply with that of the remodelled NW, NE and SW angles, where uncoursed flagstone-rubble predominates. The 15th-century masonry itself, however, varies widely both in quality and character, the NW and NE angles,

---

[1] Cf. the Glenlyon brooch, now in the British Museum (Wilson, D, *Prehistoric Annals of Scotland* (2nd ed., 1863), ii, 314 and pl. xx). For information about the costume of this figure the Commissioners are indebted to Mr S Maxwell, National Museum of Antiquities of Scotland.
[2] S.R.O., Register of Deeds, xix, fols. 128–35.
[3] Blaeu's *Atlas* (Lorn); *Geog. Coll.*, ii, 175.
[4] *RPC*, 1st series, iv (1585–92), 315 and *passim*.
[5] *APS*, vii (1661–9), 340; *NSA*, vii (Argyll), 526.
[6] The cardinal points of the compass are used for convenience of description. The true orientation of the building is indicated in Fig. 197.
[7] Cf. the account given in *Cast. and Dom. Arch.*, iii, 87–90.

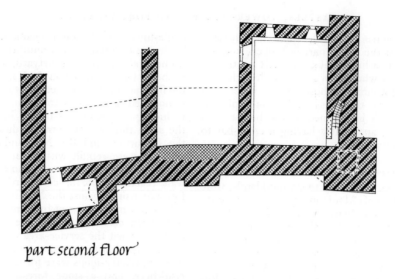

part second floor

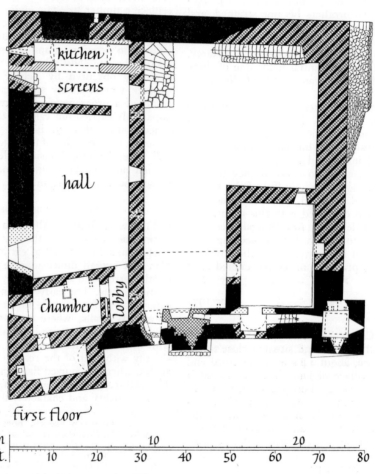

kitchen

screens

hall

chamber

lobby

first floor

m   10   20
ft.   10   20   30   40   50   60   70   80

Fig. 198. Innis Chonnell Castle (No. 292); inner bailey, first- and second-floor plans

for example, being of inferior construction to the SW angle-tower, while within the courtyard large split boulders predominate in the E wall of the hall-range, while the adjacent S range exhibits both split boulders and flagstone. Dressings are used sparingly in the 13th-century work, but where they do occur, as for example in the arrow-slits of the SE angle-tower, they are composed of fine-grained yellow sandstone possibly quarried from the Jurassic beds at Ardtornish.[1] In the 15th-century work, however, dressings are in general use, being for the most part of epidiorite, but occasionally of a coarse-grained pink sandstone which also occurs at Fraoch Eilean Castle (No. 290); many of these dressings bear masons' marks (Fig. 201B–D). Another characteristic of the 15th-century masonry is the varied treatment of doorway- and window-openings. Plain lintelled openings are most common, but round-headed doorways also occur, some being voussoired and others lintelled, while there are also single examples of the semi-hexagonal and of the 'round-cornered' lintel. The jambs of these openings are invariably wrought with chamfered arrises. The external wall-surfaces appear to have been harled, and considerable traces of harling still survive on the S curtain. Latterly, at least, the roofs were slated, the slates used resembling those from the Easdale quarries (No. 356).

THE ENTRANCE-GATEWAY. The inner bailey is entered by means of a lintelled doorway (Pl. 66D, F) in the E curtain, of which the jambs and lintel are wrought with a quirk and double-chamfer moulding (Fig. 202A). The dressings are clumsily worked, the lintel, in particular, being of insufficient span for the opening below. The doorway was equipped with inner and outer doors and with two draw-bars. The rear-arch of the doorway is set at a higher level than the external opening and is slightly pointed. The doorway is situated about 2·4 m above the level of the courtyard, which itself corresponds approximately with that of the middle bailey. Here the doorway is approached by means of what seems to be an artificial earth-ramp, while internally a stone forestair built against the E curtain leads down to the courtyard. The landing of the forestair obscures a 15th-century window in the adjacent S range, indicating that access to the courtyard must formerly have been obtained by means of an open timber forestair. The height at which the doorway is placed is difficult to account for unless either the approach-ramp is of modern origin, and replaces an earlier stair and simple drawbridge, or, less probably, the E curtain stands upon a rock ridge which makes access at a lower level impracticable. The existing doorway can be ascribed to the 15th century, but the original entrance probably occupied a similar position, and may now lie concealed beneath the ramp and forestair.

THE SOUTH RANGE AND SOUTH-EAST TOWER. This part of the castle contains a good deal of early work, the S elevation, in particular, being predominantly 13th-century in character. Here there may be seen the E and S walls of the SE angle-tower (Pl. 66B) standing upon

a rough plinth and incorporating original archer-slits on each face, while further along the S curtain a pilaster-buttress containing a similar slit rises from a high stepped plinth to a weathered coping situated a little above the level of the parapet-walk. Similar angle-towers may originally have existed at the three other corners of the inner bailey, but no visible traces of these now remain. The mid-buttress, on the other hand, was probably a unique feature, since the 13th-century masonry of the central portions of the W and N curtains appears to be undisturbed.

The existing courtyard-buildings (Pl. 67A) of the S range, however, are almost entirely of 15th-century date. They comprise a substantial four-storeyed block, which occupies the SE corner of the courtyard, together with an adjacent three-storeyed block of considerably smaller size, this last apparently being of slightly later date than its neighbour. Parts of the W and N walls of the SE corner-block may be of 13th-century date, however, since they differ somewhat from the remainder both in alignment and in masonry treatment. The setting-out of the NW corner is particularly irregular, the upper quoins overriding those at the base of the wall. It should be noted, however, that identical 15th-century masons' marks (Fig. 201B–D) occur both above and below this change of alignment.

The SE corner-block (Pl. 67B) contained a single apartment at each level, all the floors being joisted. The ground-floor room, which is entered from a doorway in the W wall, contains a blocked-up fireplace in the N wall, together with a window, which was converted into a cupboard when its daylight-opening was blocked by the erection of the present entrance-forestair. In the S wall another window pierces the curtain-wall, and beneath the window-sill there is a double-splayed musketry-loop (Fig. 203, Pl. 67E). This opening is probably an insertion of the 17th century, but there is some evidence to suggest that the loop has been contrived within the outlet-shaft of an earlier latrine-chute. Latterly, at least, the first-floor room was reached by means of a doorway communicating with the adjacent apartment to the W, but in the original arrangement access was probably obtained by means of a timber forestair against the W wall, and a corbel which may have supported the landing of this stair still survives. The doorway itself has been consolidated and partially restored in fairly recent times. The apartment is provided with a segmental-headed lintelled fireplace, of which the flue is now blocked, in the E wall, and is lit by means of a narrow window in the N wall, as well as by an embrasured window which pierces the S curtain. The jambs and head of this embrasure have been restored, but the 15th-century window-opening is well preserved, as are the narrow mural passages that open off each side of the embrasure.

These passages are of 13th-century date, having originally communicated with a contemporary S range of courtyard-buildings. The E passage leads to a small

---

[1] Information from Mr G H Collins, Institute of Geological Sciences.

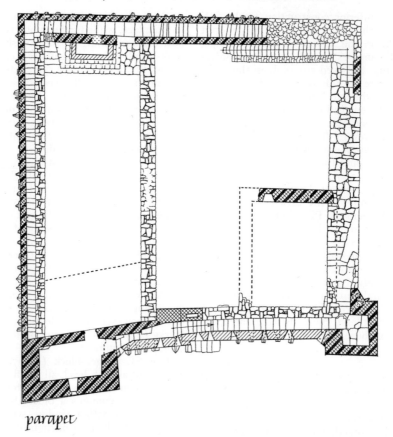

parapet

Fig. 199. Innis Chonnell Castle (No. 292); inner bailey, plan at parapet-level

chamber in the SE angle-tower equipped with archer-slits in the E and S walls, and with an aumbry in the N wall, where there is also a roughly-formed opening of late date. The floor of the chamber has been stone-flagged, but the ceiling was of timber. The disappearance of this ceiling has revealed the outline of an upper chamber slightly smaller in size than the one already described, but this was evidently filled with masonry when the present parapet-walk was constructed in the 15th century. The former existence of a loft is suggested by the presence of small circular joist-holes at an inter-mediate level, but this may not have been an original feature. The archer-slits themselves are not completely preserved, but from what survives of them here, together with the evidence provided by the slit in the mid-buttress, it is possible to reconstruct their original appearance with some confidence (Figs. 201A, 204). The slits appear to have been of fairly uniform size, measuring about 1·5 m in height and having an internal width of 1·2 m splaying outwards to a daylight opening of 0·05 m. The bases of the slits are sharply plunged and have fish-tail terminations. Similar slits occur at Dunstaffnage Castle (No. 287).

The W passage runs only about 2·0 m before it is blocked by the inserted 15th-century chimney-flues of the adjacent three-storeyed range, but in the original arrangement it must have extended a good deal further, communicating with a small chamber in the mid-buttress (now represented only by the external evidence of the archer-slit), and perhaps continuing to a tower at the SW angle.

The second-floor chamber in the SE block was lit by means of two small windows in the N wall together with a large mullioned window looking W; there does not appear to have been a fireplace at this level. The access arrangements are not very satisfactory, the only entry being by means of a mural staircase, in places only 0·46 m wide, which leads down from the E parapet-walk. The uppermost chamber, which was a mere garret, was probably entered from a doorway leading off the S parapet-walk. The lower portion of the N gable survives and contains the remains of a fireplace and of a window.

The three-storeyed portion of the S range appears to be somewhat later in date than the four-storeyed portion described above, its N wall being sandwiched awkwardly between the ground- and first-floor doorways of the adjacent SE block. The ground-floor area is sub-divided to form two apartments, of which that to the W is a lobby communicating with one of the cellars of the W range. The E apartment has a fireplace and was lit by means of a window in the N wall. At first-floor level there was a single apartment, which was presumably

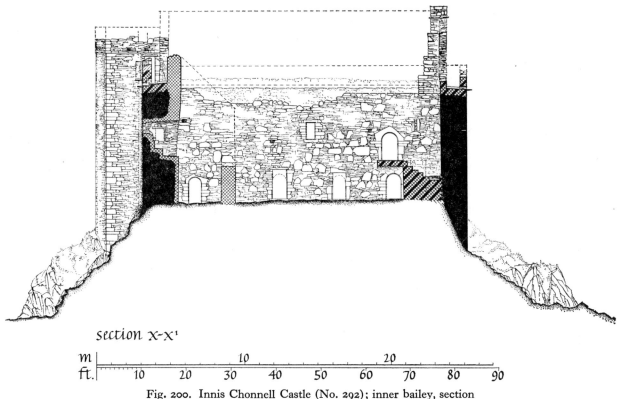

section x-x¹

Fig. 200. Innis Chonnell Castle (No. 292); inner bailey, section

entered by means of a forestair leading to a doorway in the N wall, of which nothing now remains at or above this level. In the S wall there is a fireplace and an embrasured window. Each side of the window-embrasure contains an aumbry, that to the E apparently having been formed within a larger opening which seems to represent a continuation of the 13th-century mural passage mentioned above. The floor of the embrasure is stepped, and beneath the inner portion of the floor there is a small rectangular cavity now partially filled with debris, but apparently having a depth of at least 1·2 m. This may be an early latrine-chute or chimney-flue which went out of use when alterations were carried out in this part of the castle during the later 15th century. The second-floor apartment was nothing more than a loft, roofed with a lean-to roof, and probably reached by means of a trap-door from the room below.

THE WEST RANGE AND SOUTH-WEST TOWER. As re-constructed during the 15th century, this comprised a hall and kitchen set over a range of vaulted cellars, together with a large square angle-tower containing a series of small private rooms. This angle-tower is of very sub-stantial construction, and is founded upon a solid base, from which it rises by means of a number of narrow inset courses to a total height of 14·6 m at the level of the parapet-walk. The tower projects only on the S side of the castle, the W face being flush with the outer face of the W curtain-wall. Evidence of earlier work survives

mainly in the central portion of the W curtain, where two slit-windows indicate the existence of an original 13th-century range in this quarter.

At ground-floor level there are four barrel-vaulted cellars, each having its own entrance-doorway opening off the courtyard. All these doorways were probably round-headed (Pl. 67F), but the two central ones lack their original heads and are now roughly lintelled. Each of the cellars except the southernmost is lit by a slit-window in the W curtain-wall, and in the case of the two central cellars these slits are partially obscured internally by the 15th-century partition-walls, indicating that the windows have been adapted for secondary use. The northernmost cellar incorporates a partially-blocked opening in the S wall. This may have been designed to serve as a fireplace, but it is difficult to see how its flue could have been carried up through the hall above; nor does the opening appear to have been suitable for use as a hatch. The southernmost cellar is smaller than its neighbour, owing to the existence of a prison immediately to the W of it (*infra*). In the E wall there are the remains of what seems to be a splayed opening blocked by the adjacent partition-wall. This is hard to explain, except as an abortive 15th-century window-opening.

The hall is approached from the courtyard by means of a stone forestair leading up to a wide, but rather low, round-headed doorway (Pl. 67D). In the original arrange-ment this doorway appears to have opened into a screens-passage, of which the footing of the S wall and part of the tusking of the N wall remain *in situ*. The hall itself (Pl. 67C) measured 6·6 m in width and about 10 m in length, and was lit by means of a single window in each of the W and E walls. The W window, which is a large embrasured opening commanding a fine view down Loch Awe, may have been provided with window-seats, but if so these have disappeared, in common with most of the other internal and external dressings; the window has subsequently been restored. There is no evidence of a mural fireplace in the hall, which was probably heated by means of a central hearth, the smoke rising to a louver in an open timber roof.

The original kitchen at the N end of the hall measured only about 2·0 m in length, and was lit by windows in the W and E walls, the former having a well-formed slop-sink below its sill. The greater part of this area was presumably occupied by a fireplace (Pl. 67C), but this must have been replaced by the present fireplace in the 17th century, when the N wall of the screens-passage was demolished to increase the size of the kitchen. The existing fireplace has a massive stepped flue very similar in character to the one at Loch Dochart Castle, Perthshire.[1] The arrises of the jambs appear to have been chamfered both internally and externally, but only the lowest courses now remain *in situ*; the segmental-arched head is probably a modern reconstruction. The E abutment of the arch blocks the earlier window looking into the courtyard. High up in the rear-wall of the flue there is a small doorway, rebated externally, but now blocked with masonry. This opening, to which access was gained from the N parapet-walk, was presumably intended to facilitate chimney-sweeping and maintenance-operations, and probably served the original 15th-century fireplace as well as the present one. Above the screens-area and kitchen there was a room or gallery lit by means of a

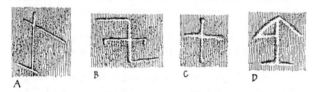

Fig. 201. Innis Chonnell Castle (No. 292); inner bailey; masons' marks: A, arrow-slit in south-east angle-tower; B, C, D, south-east tower (scale 1:5)

window in the N wall. This evidently continued in use after the 17th-century alterations, access at this period being gained by means of a roughly-formed flight of steps cantilevered out from the W wall and lit by a contemporary inserted window.

At the S end of the hall a doorway gave access to a lobby (Pl. 68A) from which a second doorway, equipped with a draw-bar, led into a small chamber lit by a window in the W wall. The N wall of this room incorporated a canopied fireplace with a corbelled lintel (Pl. 68B), but only the moulded corbels themselves now remain (Fig. 202B). Immediately in front of the fireplace a hatch in the floor provides the only means of access to a barrel-vaulted prison below. This measures 4·2 m in

length and 2·2 m in width, and rises to a maximum height of about 3·0 m; there is no provision either for ventilation or light. The rough stone seatings visible along the side-walls may have served as benches, but they are now largely obscured by debris. A doorway in

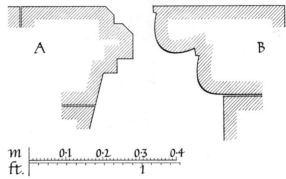

Fig. 202. Innis Chonnell Castle (No. 292); inner bailey; profile mouldings: A, entrance-gateway; B, lobby fireplace in west range

the S wall of the upper room gave access to a small barrel-vaulted chamber in the SW angle-tower. This is equipped with a latrine having a mural discharge-chute whose outlet is rebated to receive a door or shutter; there is a window in the S wall.

Within the lobby a timber stair formerly rose to give access to an apartment situated immediately above the chamber at the S end of the hall, and presumably lit by borrowed light. A doorway in the S wall of this room led into a barrel-vaulted chamber in the SW angle-tower lit by a window in its S wall. Above this level there was a third pair of chambers of similar size, the one in the SW tower being entered from a doorway leading off the S parapet-walk. This room was lit by a window in the S wall, while in the opposite wall a doorway led into the adjacent chamber, which in turn appears to have communicated with the W parapet-walk by means of a doorway in the SW corner.

THE NORTH AND EAST CURTAIN-WALLS. Except at the extremities, and above parapet-walk level, the external facework of the N curtain appears to be of 13th-century date, and evidence for the existence of contemporary internal buildings can be seen towards the W end, where there is a latrine-chute and an associated slit-window, both now blocked from within. This latrine-apartment was evidently situated immediately behind the present kitchen-fireplace, and presumably served an original W or N range of courtyard-buildings. The easternmost section of the N curtain, and a considerable portion of the E curtain, were evidently rebuilt in the 15th century, the NE angle being strengthened on its E side by a massive buttress clumsily weathered back into the adjacent facework. The crudity of this work contrasts markedly with that visible in the SW tower, apparently constructed at the same period. Against the internal face

---

[1] Illustrated in *PSAS*, xl (1905–6), 368.

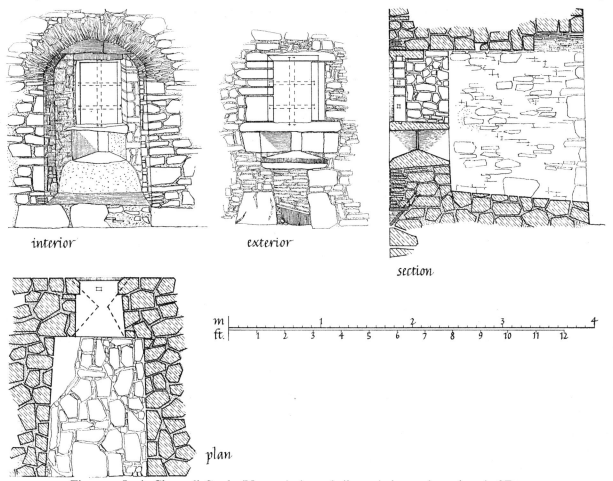

interior   exterior   section

plan

Fig. 203. Innis Chonnell Castle (No. 292); inner bailey; window and gun-loop in SE tower

of the N curtain there rises a stone forestair (Pl. 68c) of 15th-century date which may replace an earlier staircase situated in a similar position. Some remains, perhaps those of such an earlier staircase, can be seen about 1·2 m to the S of the inner junction of the present forestair with the E curtain, from whose facework there protrude several tusks of masonry.

THE PARAPET-WALKS. The existing layout at parapet-walk level (Fig. 199) dates mainly from the 15th century, but the S parapet itself appears to have been partly reconstructed during the 17th century. Nothing is known of the original arrangements at this level, but there is some evidence to suggest that in the 13th century the curtain-walls were at least as high as they are today, the present maximum height of the wall-walk above the external ground-level being about 7·9 m, 9·1 m, 10·7 m, and 10·4 m on the E, S, W and N sides respectively. Since the 15th century the principal, and probably the only, means of access to the parapet-walk has been by way of the forestair in the NE corner of the courtyard already described. At the top of the forestair there are the remains of a splayed embrasure overlooking the middle

bailey, and from this level steps within the thickness of the E and N curtain-walls formerly led upwards to the adjacent wall-walks.

The E walk survives only at the S end, where a narrow flight of steps, situated between the former E wall of the adjacent garret-chamber of the SE courtyard-block and the narrow staircase that descends to the room below, evidently rose to give access to the southernmost section of the walk, which was at a slightly higher level than the remainder. The S walk (Pl. 68D) is well preserved, being floored with large slabs shaped as ridges and runnels, these latter being drained by external spouts. From a stance within the SE angle-tower, which may have served as a look-out post, the walk descends slightly as it runs westwards, and about midway along its length a flight of steps carries it down to a lower level which is maintained as far as the SW angle-tower. The parapet, which has a width of about 0·6 m and a height of about 1·9 m, is carried across to the angle-towers by means of corbelling; it contains a number of splayed musketry-loops situated at a height of about 1·2 m above the level of the walk. These loops were evidently inserted during the 17th century to enable fire to be directed upon the main-

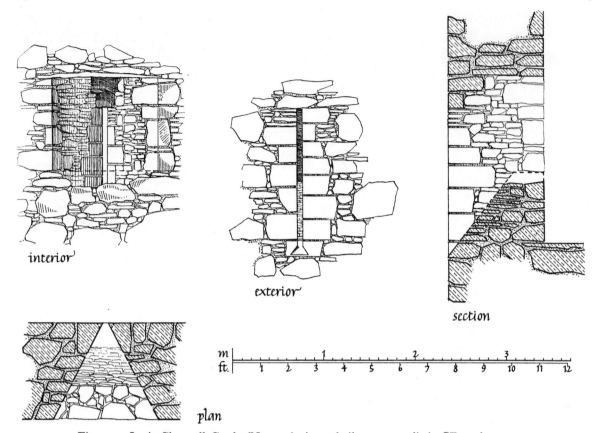

interior

exterior

section

plan

Fig. 204. Innis Chonnell Castle (No. 292); inner bailey; arrow-slit in SE angle-tower

land shore opposite this side of the castle. The SW tower was provided with a separate walk, probably reached from the floor below by means of a ladder. The W parapet-walk (Pl. 68E) is well preserved, but the parapet, which appears originally to have had a height of about 1·7 m, is now incomplete, and it is uncertain whether it incorporated any defensive openings. The same can be said of the N parapet, which now rises to a maximum height of about 1·2 m; the walk on this side, too, is well preserved.

THE GATEHOUSE AND MIDDLE BAILEY. The gatehouse is approached from landing-places situated almost opposite to each other on the N and S sides of the island, and at its narrowest point. To judge from the comparative widths of the doorways, the principal approach was from the N, but the S approach is the better preserved. This comprises a roughly-built stone staircase which rises between the converging walls of the middle and outer baileys to give access to a doorway some 1·1 m in width. This doorway appears to have been restored at a comparatively recent date, and now incorporates neither bar-holes nor door-checks. The N doorway, too, may have been partially restored; it has a width of 2·4 m, and was presumably equipped with double doors. The slab-lintel does not span the full width of the opening, but is

supported at each end on rough stone corbels; a similar expedient was adopted for the rear lintel of the S doorway. The door was secured by two pairs of draw-bars, the uppermost socket in the W jamb having a depth of 1·5 m and its neighbour on the E a depth of about 2·3 m. Of the lower sockets, the W one has a depth of 0·46 m, while the E one is not now accessible for measurement. Above the uppermost socket on the W side there is a T-shaped putlog-hole, while other putlog-holes occur in the S wall of the gatehouse and in the walls of the middle and outer baileys; some of these latter openings, however, may have been formed rather for purposes of drainage.

The gatehouse itself appears to have been a single-storeyed building comprising a transe some 5·8 m in length and 4·3 m in width, from which doorways in the W and E walls opened on to the middle and outer baileys respectively. The doorway giving access to the middle bailey seems to have led into a short passage running parallel to the E bailey-wall. The gatehouse was roofed with timber and was equipped with parapet wall-walks on the N and S sides, overlooking the entrance-doorways below. The S walk, which is the better preserved, measures 0·6 m in width; the parapet rises to a maximum height of 1·4 m and incorporates at the centre a crenelle measuring 1·0 m in width. The parapet-walks were

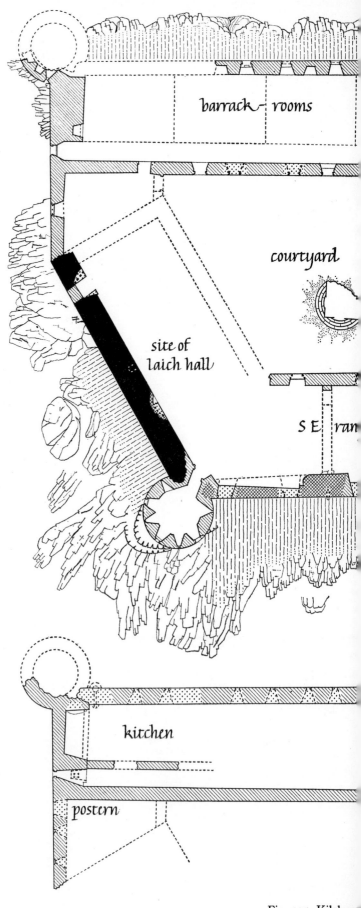

barrack-rooms

courtyard

site of
laich hall

S E ran

kitchen

postern

Fig. 205. Kilchur

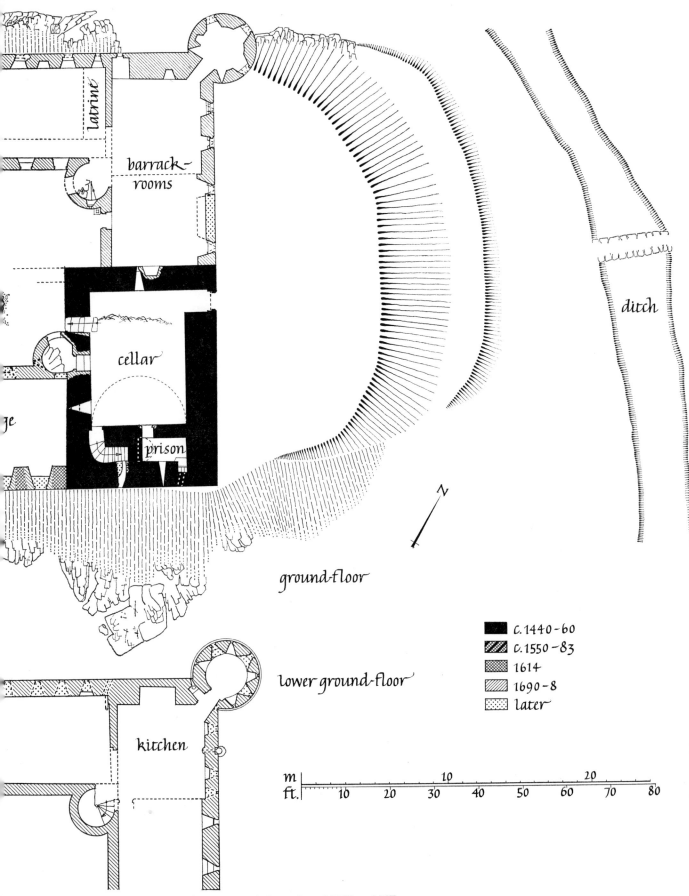

latrine

barrack-
rooms

cellar

prison

ge

ground-floor

lower ground-floor

kitchen

ditch

N

■ c.1440-60
▨ c.1550-83
▦ 1614
▧ 1690-8
▨ later

m
ft.

10 20

10   20   30   40   50   60   70   80

Castle (No. 293); general plan and lower ground-floor plan of NW and NE ranges

drained by weepers. The masonry of the gatehouse, like that of the middle- and outer-bailey walls, is of random rubble with numerous pinnings.

The wall of the middle bailey is best preserved on the S and E sides, where it rises to a maximum height of about 2·4 m. The wall has a width of 0·6 m, except at the W end of the S curtain, where it has a width of 0·8 m. This latter section of wall is older than the remainder and may be of 13th-century date. It evidently returned northwards at a point about 4·3 m E of the SE angle-tower, and may have formed part of an original bailey somewhat smaller in size than the present one. This earlier section of wall incorporates a splayed slit having a daylight-opening of about 0·08 m. A little to the W of this slit a drainage-outlet pierces the base of the wall. This may have drained the bailey itself, or may have been associated with a latrine in the SW angle-tower, of which no other traces now remain. There is no trace of the 'very thick wall' on the N side of the bailey mentioned by MacGibbon and Ross,[1] but the existing wall presumably abutted the E curtain of the inner bailey close to its external NE angle. At the SE corner of the bailey the wall returns to form a stance overlooking the S entrance-approach and adjacent curtain. This is equipped with a splayed embrasure looking on to the foot of the entrance-staircase.

THE OUTER BAILEY. The outer bailey is roughly oval in plan and measures about 38·4 m from W to E by 26·0 m transversely within an enclosing wall 0·9 m in thickness. This wall is now ruinous and incomplete, the best pre-served sections being situated to the SE of the gatehouse, where it rises to a maximum height of about 2·4 m. The wall is founded upon the perimeter of a rock summit whose upper surface is fairly level, but whose sides fall steeply to the surrounding shore. A little below the SE extremity of the main summit-area, and beyond the bailey-wall, there is a natural platform upon which there may be seen the remains of a small dry-stone building of sub-rectangular plan and indeterminate date. There are no traces of any buildings on the summit itself, apart from those of recent erection.

HISTORICAL NOTE

The castle has little recorded history. It was probably built by a founder member of the Campbell family of Loch Awe, of whose origins little is known prior to the appearance on record of Sir Colin Campbell at the end of the 13th century. The castle itself is first speci-fically mentioned in October 1308, when it was being held by John of Lorn on behalf of Edward II, but it was almost certainly one of the three MacDougall castles mentioned, but not named, by John in a well-known letter written to Edward probably in the spring of the same year.[2] Following the defeat of the MacDougalls, the lordship of Loch Awe reverted to the Campbells, being confirmed in free barony to Sir Colin Campbell, son of Sir Neil Campbell, by Robert I in 1315.[3] There-after Innis Chonnell seems to have remained the chief stronghold of the family until the time of Colin Campbell,

1st Earl of Argyll (1453–93), who made Inveraray his principal residence. The earlier 15th-century recon-struction of the castle may probably be ascribed to the 1st Earl's grandfather, Sir Duncan Campbell of Loch Awe, a prominent royal supporter and the founder of Kilmun collegiate church, who died in 1453.

During the 16th and 17th centuries Innis Chonnell was frequently used by the Campbell Earls of Argyll as a place of captivity for political and criminal prisoners, the custody of the castle being entrusted to a series of hereditary captains. During the late 16th century this office was held by the MacArthur family, but passed to the MacLachlans following the conviction of Duncan MacArthur for theft in 1613.[4] The captains of Innis Chonnell were proprietors of the small estate of Ardchonnell, situated on the adjacent SE shore of the loch, and the office carried with it an obligation to maintain the roofs of the castle in a watertight condition.[5] As late as 1801 the 5th Duke of Argyll confirmed a charter of 1767 by which Donald MacLachlan of Innis Chonnell had disponed his hereditary privileges and duties to Colin MacLachlan of Craiginterve,[6] but an estate plan of 1806 indicates that the castle had become ruinous by this date.[7] The date at which the castle was abandoned for occupation is not recorded, but the MacLachlans are known to have built a small mansion-house on their Ardchonnell estate in 1704,[8] and it seems likely that they took up residence on the mainland at that date. The last member of the family to own Ardchonnell was Patrick MacLachlan, who sold the property to Neil Malcolm of Poltalloch in 1815.[9]

976119   NM 91 SE   August 1969

293. Kilchurn Castle. The castle (Pls. 69, 70, 71) stands upon a low peninsula at the NE extremity of Loch Awe, and commands an extensive prospect embracing the upper part of the loch, Glen Strae and the Strath of Orchy. The site itself (Fig. 205) is a small rocky eminence surrounded by marshy ground, and further delimited on the landward side of the peninsula by an artificial ditch having a width of about 4·5 m and a present depth of about 0·6 m. When the level of the loch is high the site is virtually insulated, and at least one early writer states that the castle stands upon an island.[10] Moreover, the remains of what appears to be a small jetty, or boat-landing, composed of boulders, can

[1] *Cast. and Dom. Arch.*, iii, 88.
[2] *Rotuli Scotiae*, i (1814), 58; *Cal. Docs. Scot.*, iii, no. 80; Barrow, G W S, *Robert Bruce and the Community of the Realm of Scotland* (1965), 254–5.
[3] *Origines Parochiales*, ii, part i, 122.
[4] *SHS Misc.*, iv (1926), 287; *Highland Papers*, iv, 26, 53.
[5] *Dunstaffnage Case*, 335–7.
[6] Ibid., 361–2.
[7] S.R.O., RHP 189.
[8] Ibid. The plan of Ardchonnell House and offices shows 'the old Mansion House built in 1704 taken down by Major McLachlan to rebuild.'
[9] Information from Mr J S Scott, Eredine House, quoting title-deeds of Eredine.
[10] Pococke, *Tours*, 68; but cf. Stoddart, *Local Scenery*, i, 269.

be seen on the SE side of the castle, It is known, however, that some clearance of the river bed at the outflow into the Pass of Brander was carried out in 1817, and this probably resulted in a general lowering of the level of the loch.[1]

SYNOPSIS

The castle (Figs. 205, 206) comprises a series of buildings ranging in date from about the middle of the 15th century to about the end of the 17th century. The earliest of these is a five-storeyed tower-house standing at the E corner of the castle, which is known to have been erected by Sir Colin Campbell, 1st of Glenorchy, who died in 1475. Immediately to the SW of the tower-house there was probably a small courtyard or barmkin, enclosed by a curtain-wall of which considerable remains appear to survive on the S and SE sides. The main entrance to the courtyard lay through the ground-floor of the tower-house, but there was also a postern in the S section of the curtain-wall. The courtyard probably contained a number of ancillary buildings.

The next building to come on record is the 'laich hall', which was constructed by Sir Duncan Campbell, 2nd of Glenorchy (1475–1513). Later documentary information suggests that this structure stood against the inner face of the S curtain, where the foundations of a substantial stone building lie just beneath the turf. Sir Colin Campbell, 6th of Glenorchy (1550–83), reconstructed the upper storey of the tower-house and added corbelled angle-rounds. He was also responsible for the erection of a building known as the 'north chalmeris', which presumably stood on the NW side of the courtyard, but of this no traces now remain. It is recorded that in 1614 the laich hall, together with a kitchen which seems to have occupied the S corner of the courtyard, was rebuilt and raised to a height of two storeys, while two years later a range of buildings comprising two cellars, a loft and a chapel, was erected on the SE side of the courtyard. Further extensive repairs are known to have been made to the laich hall and tower-house in 1643. The last major phase of building-operations was carried out during the period c. 1690–98, when John, 1st Earl of Breadalbane, remodelled much of the castle, and enlarged it by the construction of cylindrical angle-towers and of two ranges of four-storeyed barrack-blocks situated on the NW side of the courtyard.

The castle appears to have been abandoned as a residence about the middle of the 18th century and was unroofed in about 1770, after which the fabric deteriorated rapidly.[2] Some time after MacGibbon and Ross made their survey of the castle in c. 1887,[3] the building appears to have been extensively patched and consolidated, an operation which unfortunately led to the obliteration or alteration of a number of original structural features.

ARCHITECTURAL DESCRIPTION

The castle is constructed of local rubble masonry with dressings of calc-epidote-chlorite schist probably quarried locally. Many of the original stone dressings of the tower-house bear masons' marks (Fig. 207A–H), but these are seldom found in the original dressings of the work of c. 1690–98 (but cf. Fig. 207J, K). It is evident, however, that much of the dressed stonework utilized during this latter period of construction was quarried from earlier buildings altered or dismantled during the course of building-operations. A good example of such re-use of earlier materials is provided by the courtyard doorway of the NE barrack-range, of which the jambs are formed largely of arch-voussoirs, while the lintel has been quarried from a large window-opening. The masonry of the NE chimney-stack of the tower-house contains a number of re-used edge-roll mouldings of 16th-century character, together with some fragments of coarse-grained pink sandstone wrought with chamfered arrises. These latter dressings, which seem to be the only fragments of sandstone in the castle masonry, appear to be identical with the 13th-century dressings at Fraoch Eilean Castle (No. 290), some 3 km away, whence they may have been derived in c. 1690–98.

THE TOWER-HOUSE. The tower-house (Pl. 72A) is oblong on plan, measuring 14·7 m from NW to SE by 10·4 m transversely over all. The exposed NE wall is somewhat thicker than the others, which have an average width of 1·7 m. The height of the tower from the parapet-walk to the external ground-surface on the SE side is 15·4 m, and to the level of the courtyard on the SW side 12·7 m. The original internal arrangements are not altogether clear, but there is evidence to suggest that the main entrance-doorway was situated in the SW wall at first-floor level, access to the second and third floors being obtained by means of a mural stair rising in the SW and NW walls. The original arrangements at parapet-level are also uncertain. The ground-floor of the tower-house was provided with a separate entrance-doorway situated close to the N angle, internal access to the first floor being obtained by means of a service-stair in the opposite corner. The placing of this doorway in the exposed NE wall of the tower-house, rather than in one of the walls facing into the courtyard, is possibly to be accounted for by supposing that the doorway was designed to serve as the principal entry to the courtyard itself, to which no other convenient means of access existed because of the steep surrounding rock-face. On the two lower storeys the tower-house incorporated a single main apartment together with an associated series of mural chambers and latrines, but the third and fourth storeys appear to have been sub-divided. Most of the original doorways and windows are wrought externally with broad chamfered arrises, but some of the smaller openings are sharp-arrised. Of the numerous alterations made to the tower-house subsequent to its erection, the most important were the remodelling of the upperworks in the second half of the 16th century, and the construction of a turnpike-staircase on the SW side in 1691, thus supplementing the original means of access to the upper floors.

[1] PSAS, vii (1866–8), 235.
[2] NSA, vii (Argyll), 88; Pennant, Tour (1769), 237.
[3] Cast. and Dom. Arch., i, 382–4.

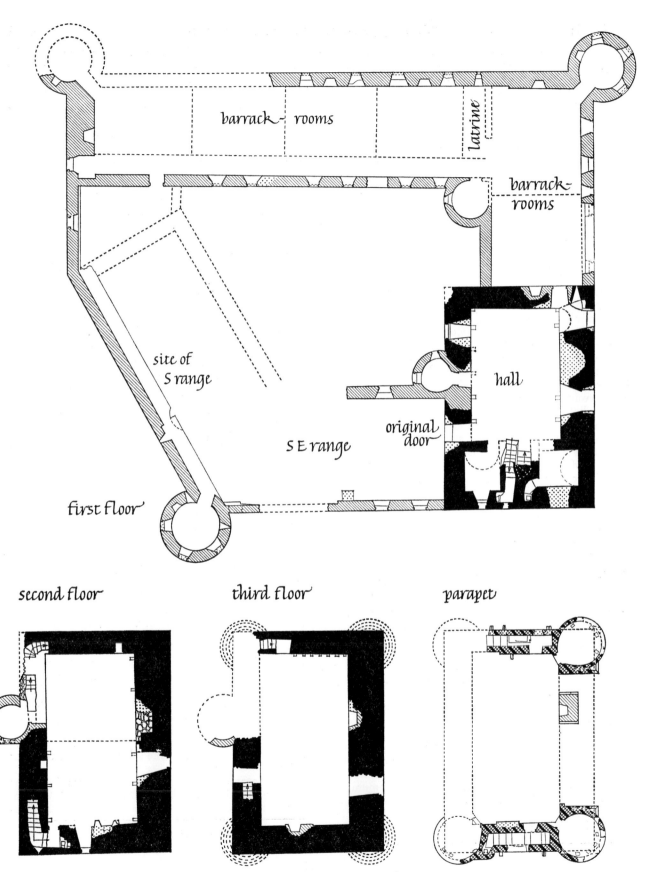

barrack - rooms

latrine

barrack-
rooms

site of
S range

hall

original
door

S E range

first floor

second floor

third floor

parapet

Fig. 206. Kilchurn Castle (No. 293); first-floor plan and upper floor-plans of tower-house

The tower-house is entered by means of the ground-floor doorway in the NE wall already referred to. The doorway is rebated to receive two doors, of which one was no doubt an iron yett; there is no visible evidence of a draw-bar socket. The external lintel of the doorway (Pl. 72F), which was renewed during the late 17th-century alterations, is carved in relief with an armorial shield flanked by the date 1693 and the initials E I B and C M C, for John, 1st Earl of Breadalbane and his second wife, (Countess) Mary Campbell, whom he married in 1678 and who died in February 1691. The shield is charged: quarterly, 1st and 4th, gyronny of eight; 2nd, a galley, sail furled, oars in action and pennon flying; 3rd, a fess checky. Beneath there is a label bearing the motto: FOLLOW ME. The shield and both sets of initials are surmounted by earl's coronets, and the whole is flanked by scrollwork. Above the lintel there is a cavetto-moulded drip-course.

The ground-floor chamber, which is barrel-vaulted, probably served as a cellar. Access to the courtyard is obtained by means of an original doorway in the SW wall, but this has been contracted in width and otherwise altered during the late 17th-century building-operations. Immediately to the SE an inserted doorway gives access to the turnpike-staircase. This staircase, which served all the upper floors of the tower-house, also has an entrance-doorway (Pl. 72A) giving directly on to the courtyard. The lintel of this latter doorway bears the incised date 1691, and above the lintel there is a housing for an inscribed panel or coat of arms. The small low-level window on the SW side of the staircase appears to be an error of design, and was evidently built up when the stair-treads were installed. The cellar was lit by two windows, of which that in the SW wall must have been blocked up when the SE courtyard-range was erected in 1616, while that in the NW wall appears to have been somewhat contracted in width during the late 17th-century alterations. In the SE wall of the cellar a high-level doorway gives access to a vaulted prison measuring 3·1 m by 1·6 m internally. The lower part of the prison is now choked with debris, but the floor-level probably corresponded approximately to that of the cellar, giving a height to the crown of the vault of about 3·5 m. The prison is lit by a slit-window placed high up in the SE wall and beside it there is a latrine having a mural discharge-chute. A doorway in the S corner of the cellar gives access to the service-stair, which appears to have been lit by a small window, now greatly mutilated, in the SE wall.

In the original arrangement the first-floor apartment (Fig. 206, Pl. 72D, E), probably a hall, appears to have been entered from the external doorway in the SW wall already mentioned, the doorway itself being reached from the courtyard by means of a forestair. With the completion of the SE courtyard-range in 1616, however, this opening became an internal doorway communicating with the first floor of the new range. At the same time an alternative means of access appears to have been provided by means of the erection of a staircase occupying much the same position as the existing turnpike-staircase of 1691 (*infra* p. 236). The outer part of the doorway has been mutilated, but the ingo and vaulted ceiling remain entire. To the NW of the doorway an inserted opening gives access to the turnpike-staircase of 1691, but originally this opening must have communicated with the ascending mural stair that partly survives in this section of the SW wall. The hall was lit by large splayed windows in the SW and NE walls, of which the former survives in part, while the latter is represented only by a heavily-restored arched embrasure. In the N corner of the apartment there was a vaulted mural chamber lit by a slit-window in the NW wall, and equipped with a small aumbry. During the 17th-century alterations this chamber was dispensed with, a doorway being broken through the NW wall to give access to the NE range of barracks, and a window formed in the NE wall to improve the lighting of the hall. The hall-fireplace was evidently situated immediately to the SE of the mural chamber just described,[1] but the opening has been obliterated by repair and patching. The hall had a joisted timber ceiling carried on runners which rested upon moulded corbels (Fig. 208A), most of which survive. The arrangements at the SE end of the hall (Pl. 72D) are somewhat unusual, the S and E corners of the building at this level being occupied by spacious barrel-vaulted chambers entered from the main apartment; these probably served as private rooms for sleeping-purposes. Both chambers appear to have been lit by windows in the SE wall, but that serving the E chamber has been obliterated by patching.[2] This latter chamber also incorporates a latrine having a mural discharge-chute. Centrally placed between these two mural chambers there are two narrow staircases, one of these being the service-stair already described, while the other rises to a latrine provided with a small window-opening.

The second floor was originally reached by means of the mural stair in the SW wall already described, but the section of wall containing the doorway, as also that incorporating the later opening from the turnpike-stair, has largely collapsed. At this level the tower appears to have been divided by a mid-partition to form two main rooms each having a large embrasured window, a fireplace and a shelved aumbry. The NW room was lit by a window in the SW wall, of which the arch-springer alone survives, but the window of the SE room, situated in the opposite wall, is better preserved and shows a dressed voussoired arch-head. This window (Pl. 72D) may have had a bench-seat in the NW ingo. Little remains of either of the fireplace-openings. The one serving the NW room was situated in the NE wall, while that serving the adjacent apartment was in the SE wall, where there is another original window. The second floor was ceiled in the same manner as the floor below.

Each second-floor room had separate access by means of a mural stair to the third floor, while the NW room also communicated with the late 17th-century turnpike-

---

[1] *Cast. and Dom. Arch.*, i, fig. 331.
[2] Ibid.

stair. The mural stair serving this latter room, and now largely destroyed, was a continuation of the one rising from the floor below.

The mural stair serving the SE room rises from an original doorway in the S corner of the building, and is lit by means of a slit-window in the SE wall. Within the doorway a latrine opens off the foot of the stair. The mural discharge-chute of this latrine connects with a similar chute which formerly discharged from an upper level, but is now blocked up. This presumably served an original latrine, situated at third-floor or parapet-level, which was removed during the 16th-century alterations to the upperworks. The arrangements on the third floor appear to have been similar to those on the floor below (Fig. 208c). The existing fireplaces are probably of 16th- or 17th-century date.

It is uncertain how access from the third floor to the fourth floor was obtained before the construction of the late 17th-century turnpike-staircase, unless a mural stair existed in that portion of the SW wall which has now collapsed. The existing layout at this level, which comprises a garret-chamber with associated angle-rounds and parapet-walks, can be ascribed mainly to the period 1550–1583. The garret-chamber was presumably lit chiefly from dormer-windows, none of which survive. The fireplace in the NE wall, together with the chimney-stack above it, are probably of late 17th-century date. At each corner of the room a doorway appears to have led into an associated angle-turret (Pl. 72B, c), substantial remains of all but one of which survive in situ. The W turret lies upside down in the courtyard below, the tenacity of its construction having enabled it to remain partly intact. These turrets are of unusually bold projection, being carried on continuous moulded corbel-courses of four members (Fig. 208B); the internal diameter is about 3·0 m. In the floor of each turret a series of deeply-plunged pistol-holes pierces the lowermost corbel-course to enfilade the lower corners of the tower-house and other vulnerable parts of the building, including the original first-floor entrance in the SW wall; other pistol-holes (Fig. 209A, Pl. 72G) exist in the walls of the turrets. The turrets formerly contained windows, and were evidently roofed. The roof of the

garret itself extended to the outer wall-face on the NE side, and probably on the SW side also, although here the top of the turnpike-stair is likely to have projected above the roof as a cap-house. On the NW and SE sides, however, the gables rise within open parapet-walks entered not from the angle-turrets, but from the main apartment. These walks are paved with slabs of schist and slate, and are drained by shaped water-spouts. The NW parapet-walk is corbelled out internally upon individual moulded stone corbels, some of which bear incised masons' marks (Fig. 207A–H). The parapet appears to have had a height of at least 1·7 m and contains a doorway, now blocked, which may formerly have given access to a bretasche. The SE parapet-walk is furnished with a latrine having a corbelled discharge-chute. Beside this shaft there is an additional corbel whose function is uncertain, unless it was designed to support a bretasche on this side of the tower. The parapet itself rose to a height of at least 1·5 m, but neither here, nor on the opposite side of the tower, is there any evidence to show whether or not the parapets were crenellated.

THE COURTYARD BUILDINGS. The existing courtyard-buildings are mainly of late 17th-century date, although portions of an older curtain-wall survive on the S and SE sides. It is possible that the original courtyard was somewhat less extensive on the NW side than is the present one, an earlier NW range perhaps having returned to join the W corner of the tower-house. The courtyard-buildings appear to have been provided with a roof-drainage system incorporating down-pipes, for a gutter is visible beside the stair-tower at the N re-entrant angle, and there is also a drain-outlet in the base of the S angle-tower, which probably served the adjacent section of the courtyard. Most of the original openings of the late 17th century are wrought with plain 0·05 m chamfers.

The SE range is now very ruinous and there are no identifiable remains of the two cellars, loft and chapel that are known to have been constructed in 1616 (p. 239). The SE curtain itself (Pl. 73c) has a thickness of about 1·5 m at ground-floor level, except at the SW end, where it appears to have been thinned, either in the late 17th century or during subsequent repair-operations.[1] At the junction of the curtain with the S angle of the tower-house there are no quoin-stones and the masonry is well-bonded, facts that suggest that the lower portion of the curtain, at least, is contemporary with the tower-house. The main window-openings in the curtain, some of which have been furnished with iron grilles, probably date from the late 17th-century remodelling of the SE range, but the sill and NE jamb of a window visible externally at an intermediate level, and the two adjacent projecting drain-spouts, are evidently relics of an earlier arrangement. In the late 17th century the SE range was sub-divided by a mid-partition, the NE portion being

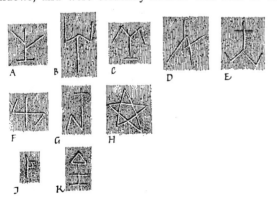

Fig. 207. Kilchurn Castle (No. 293); masons' marks: A-H, tower-house (c. 1440–60); J, K, tower-house door-lintel (1693) (scale 1:5)

[1] MacGibbon and Ross's plan (ibid.) shows three blocked-up windows in this section of the curtain, but today there is evidence only of two.

three-storeyed and the remainder probably two-storeyed. The uppermost storey was lit by dormers and the wall-head was surmounted by a cavetto-moulded eaves-course. Access to the ground- and second floors was obtained from the turnpike-staircase of 1691, while the first floor was entered from the tower-house by means of the old external entrance-doorway already described.

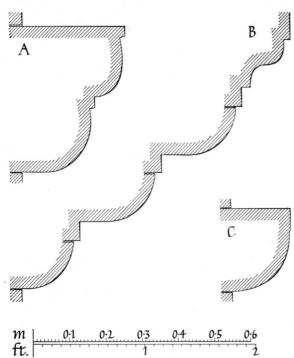

Fig. 208. Kilchurn Castle (No. 293); tower-house; profile mouldings: A, first-floor corbel; B, angle-turret corbels; C, third-floor corbel

The two lower floors probably communicated also with the S range and thence with the S angle-tower. The surviving portion of the NW wall appears to be contemporary with the turnpike-stair of 1691.

The S angle-tower of c. 1690–98 is founded upon a massive base-plinth of irregular plan, above which the walls rise to a height of two storeys and terminate in a cavetto-moulded eaves-course (Pls. 70B, 73A). Each floor was entered from a doorway in the gorge of the tower, which communicated with the S range of courtyard-buildings. At each level the tower contained a single apartment well furnished with windows and figure-of-eight shaped gun-loops (Fig. 209B), those in the first floor often being incorporated beneath the window-sills. The first-floor room was also equipped with a fireplace. As in the other angle-towers the floors were of timber.

The S curtain (Pl. 73B) has a thickness of about 1·8 m at ground-floor level, but above this point the wall appears to have been reconstructed in the late 17th century, and has a thickness of only 0·8 m. The only opening of which there is evidence at ground-floor level is the postern-doorway situated towards the W end of

the curtain, and this is now blocked up externally. Traces of an external relieving-arch are visible within the court-yard ingoes. The S range, initially comprising the laich hall and kitchen, appears to have had an internal width of about 6·2 m and rose to a height of two storeys, of which the upper seems to have been a mere garret. Traces of what appears to be a curved wall-face, perhaps part of a staircase, can be seen set into the internal face of the S curtain, and above it there are the remains of a small window at first-floor level.

The SW range of c. 1690–98 formed an irregular-shaped annexe to the main NW barrack-block, from which it was entered at each of its three main floor-levels. Another doorway gave access from the courtyard at ground-floor level. Within the ground-floor chamber, steps against the NW wall probably led down to a basement, from which access was obtained to the postern-doorway, now blocked, that may be seen in the SW curtain, as well as to a pair of elliptical-mouthed gun-loops placed a little to the SE of the doorway. This postern presumably superseded the one in the S curtain already described. The upper floors of the annexe, each of which probably comprised a single small room lit by a window in the curtain-wall, may have served as officers' quarters.

The late 17th-century NW range and its associated angle-towers are fairly well preserved (Pls. 70A, 74A, 75B), much of the masonry standing almost to wall-head level. The lowest of the four storeys is a basement situated below the level of the courtyard and reached by means of a turnpike-staircase constructed in the N re-entrant angle of the courtyard. The basement served as a kitchen and service-area, and incorporates a large segmental-headed kitchen-fireplace in the SW gable-wall. In the NW jamb of this fireplace there are traces of a blocked-up opening, while immediately to the NE of the fireplace there may be seen the remains of a water-inlet. The service-area may have been sub-divided by stone or timber partitions to form a series of separate apartments entered from a corridor, of which some traces remain, running along the SE side of the range. This corridor was lit from a window at its SW end, and beneath the window there is a slop-sink. The other rooms were lit by a number of small square windows in the NW wall, all of which are now blocked up. At the NE end of the range a pair of drainage-chutes pierce the NW wall near its base. These probably served a series of latrines situated on the upper floors at this end of the range, the latrine-apartments being identifiable externally by their small window-openings. The upper floors are symmetrically planned and the arrangement of the various openings suggests that each floor was sub-divided by timber partitions to incorporate four main barrack-rooms of similar size, together with a corridor running along the full length of the SE wall. Each barrack-room seems to have contained a fireplace and two window-openings in the outer wall, while the corridors were lit by a series of windows overlooking the courtyard, and by others in the SW gable-wall, where there is an additional fireplace at each level. The arrangements at this end of the range are rather uncertain owing

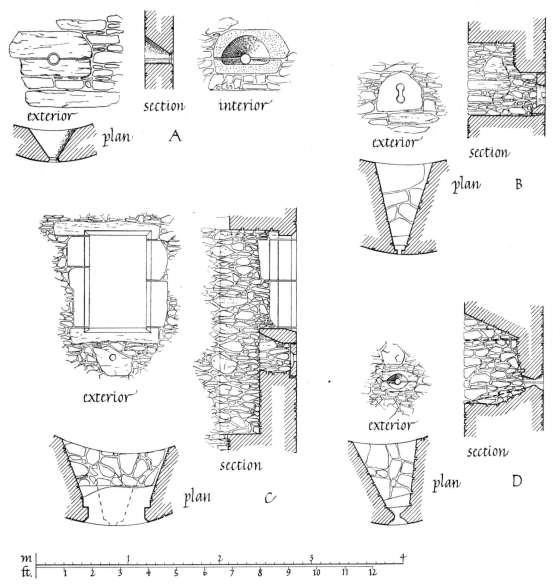

Fig. 209. Kilchurn Castle (No. 293); gun-loops and pistol-holes: A, south angle-turret of tower-house; B, south angle-tower; C, D, north angle-tower

to the disappearance of the upper portion of this section of the NW wall. Possibly the SW barrack-rooms were further sub-divided to form officers' or NCOs' quarters. All the floors were joisted. Access to each floor was obtained by means of the turnpike-stair at the N re-entrant angle of the courtyard, while the first-floor corridor seems to have had an additional doorway approached from the courtyard by means of a forestair.

The W angle-tower evidently rose to a height of three storeys above a solid basement, but only a fragment now survives. The ground- and first floors were provided with fireplaces, and the lower floors, at least, were equipped with gun-ports, of which a single example, having an

elliptical mouth, survives at ground-floor level. Access was obtained at each level from the NW range.

Like the NW range, the NE range (Pls. 74B, C, 75A) comprised a basement and three upper storeys, all entered by means of the turnpike-staircase in the N corner of the courtyard. In addition the ground-floor had separate access from the courtyard. The basement formed a kitchen and service-area, and there is a kitchen-fireplace in the NW gable-wall. MacGibbon and Ross's plan of c. 1887[1] indicates the existence of an oven in the SW jamb of this fireplace, but no traces of this are

[1] Loc. cit.

visible today. The basement was sub-divided by a stone partition, each apartment being lit by means of two small square windows in the NE wall, some of which are now blocked with masonry. The kitchen itself had an additional slit-window, together with a water-inlet (Pl. 75D), a feature which suggests that the main source of water-supply lay outside the castle. The three upper floors appear to have been sub-divided in the same way as the basement, each storey comprising two barrack-rooms of approximately equal size. These were lit from windows in the NE wall, and provided with fireplaces situated in one or other of the end-walls. The rooms at the NW end appear to have communicated with the adjacent NW range. These rooms also communicated with the N angle-tower, which rose to the same height as the NE range, the basement being founded upon a high plinth. Within the W ingo of the basement-chamber of the tower there is a latrine equipped with a mural discharge-chute and a slit-window, while in the opposite ingo there is a second slit-window, now blocked up. The basement-chamber itself was lit by two small square windows, each of which has a circular-mouthed gun-loop beneath its sill (Fig. 209D), while a further series of elliptical-mouthed gun-loops (Fig. 209C) is interspersed midway between the windows. Each of the three upper floors contained a well-lit room, those on the first and second floors being equipped with fireplaces. The first-floor room is provided with a further series of circular-mouthed gun-loops, three of which are placed beneath the window-sills.

CARVED STONES. Preserved within the courtyard there are a number of architectural fragments, mainly portions of window- and door-jambs. There are also parts of two dormer-window pediments, of which the better preserved (Pl. 75C) is carved with fleur-de-lis finials, and incorporates in the tympanum the monogram initials s D C, evidently for Sir Duncan Campbell, 7th of Glenorchy (1583–1631). The other pediment is carved in relief with a chevron-pattern. Both stones probably derive either from the reconstructed laich hall of 1614 or the SE range of 1616 (p. 235).

HISTORICAL NOTE

'Elankylquhurne' formed part of the lordship of Glenorchy which was granted by Duncan Campbell of Lochaw to his son, Colin, in 1432.[1] The exact date of the construction of the castle is uncertain. The 17th-century family chronicler ascribes it to the period after Sir Colin Campbell became guardian to his nephew, the future 1st Earl of Argyll, in 1453. An earlier date is indicated, however, by a carved stone recorded at Taymouth Castle in the 19th century, which was said to have come from Kilchurn and to be inscribed with the initials s C C 1440. Inscriptions of this type do not commonly occur before the 16th century and this stone was probably a commemorative carving of later date, but the existence of buildings at Kilchurn before 1450 is made probable by a charter of John Stewart, lord of Lorn, dated 'apud Castrum de Glenurquhay' in March

1449.[2] The earliest buildings are obviously represented by the existing tower-house and its associated barmkin. The first recorded addition was made by Sir Duncan Campbell, 2nd laird (1475–1513), who 'biggit the laich hall of Glenurquhay'. This was a single-storeyed building associated with a kitchen, which in the 17th century was separated from the great tower by a new range of buildings on the S (i.e. SE) side of the courtyard. The 'laich hall' may therefore be identified with the demolished building that abutted the SW curtain.[3]

During the first half of the 16th century Kilchurn was the principal home of the Campbells of Glenorchy, and the 3rd and 4th lairds died there in 1523 and 1536 respectively. Several keepers or constables of the castle are recorded during the 16th century. Most of them were members of the Clan Gregor, and in 1550 John Campbell, 5th of Glenorchy, set in tack to John M'Conoquhy V'Gregour land at Kincraken and the office of keeper of the castle, on condition that he provided a watchman and kept the tower-head clean. The parapet-walk, whose importance was thus recognised, was remodelled by Sir Colin, 6th laird (1550–83), who built the four 'kirnellis' (angle-turrets) of the tower-house. He also erected a building described as 'the north chalmeris', which probably contained additional accommodation for guests and retainers.[4]

Despite these improvements, Kilchurn became relatively less important during the second half of the 16th century as the lairds of Glenorchy concentrated their resources on their estates in Perthshire. Sir Colin built the house of Balloch (Taymouth), at the NE end of Loch Tay, and his son, Sir Duncan (1583–1631), built Finlarig Castle at the SW end of the same loch. Various inventories of plenishings, the earliest of which was compiled in 1598, show that from the end of the 16th century these castles were the principal residences of the lairds of Glenorchy. Although Kilchurn thus lost its pre-eminent position among the family castles, it was not neglected by Sir Duncan, an energetic landowner who built new castles at Achallader and Barcaldine (Nos. 277 and 279), and at Loch Dochart in Perthshire, as well as at Finlarig. Before the end of the 16th century he 'reparit the castell . . . inwardlie and outwardlie', spending an unspecified sum of money on this work.[5]

The violent conflict waged between Sir Duncan Campbell and the MacGregors of Glenstrae in the first decade of the 17th century may have been responsible for the neglect of the domestic buildings at Kilchurn at this period, for it is stated that the laich hall was 'ruined' when Sir Duncan began extensive alterations in 1614. These operations are described by a contemporary writer as follows: 'The auld laich hall of Glenurquhay and kitchin thairof, bot ane hous hight, being ruined, it was

[1] *Highland Papers*, iv, 199.
[2] *Taymouth Bk.*, 13; *Origines Parochiales*, ii, part i, 145; S.R.O., Breadalbane Collection, GD 112/1/1/7, Mounted Documents.
[3] *Taymouth Bk.*, 16, 44, 46.
[4] Ibid., 17–18, 22, 405–8; *Origines Parochiales*, ii, part i, 146.
[5] *Taymouth Bk.*, 35, 319–51; S.R.O., Breadalbane Collection, GD 112/22/4, Inventories.

reedifiet and reparyt to tua hous hicht, with ane chymnay on the syde wall thairof . . . for the warkmanschip quhairof he gaif thrie thousand merkis money'. The rebuilt SW range was linked to the tower-house by further building-operations which necessitated the rebuilding of most of the SE curtain. 'Upone the south syd of the clos betuix the great toure and kitchin of Glenurquhay, the tua laiche sellaris with ane loft abone thame and ane capell abone the loft wer compleit in Mairche in anno 1616 zeiris, the expens quhairof . . . is fywe hundreth pundis money, at quhilk tyme the stair going frome the clos to the said tour wes biggit'. This last operation was necessary because the original first-floor entrance to the tower-house was enclosed within the new SE range.[1]

In 1643 Andrew Scott of Perth, wright, was employed to re-roof the great tower and angle-turrets, and to repair the laich hall. During the disturbances of the two following years the castle was garrisoned on behalf of the Marquess of Argyll, but it was not attacked.[2] The only recorded siege of Kilchurn took place in July 1654, when Sir John Campbell of Glenorchy and the Marquess of Argyll were besieged there by General Middleton. The royalist force 'had not time to take it in' before General Monck approached from the E, and Middleton abandoned the siege after two days.[3]

On 20 May 1685, the day when the 9th Earl of Argyll, in rebellion against James VII and II, landed in Kintyre, John, 1st Earl of Breadalbane, offered his services to the government, announcing his intention to provide a rallying-post for the loyal Highlanders at Kilchurn, 'near a strong castle . . . befor uhich ther is a plane . . . invirond on tuo sids with deep rivers, and a ditch and trench befor it'. The castle was used by the Marquess of Atholl as a base for the pacification of the Inveraray area, but Argyll's small force remained on the Firth of Clyde.[4]

The Highland War of 1689, and the depredations that accompanied it, made the southern Highlands extremely insecure; the Breadalbane estates were especially vulnerable and the 1st Earl was justifiably anxious about his situation. His house at Finlarig was garrisoned by government forces in the autumn of 1689 and he vigorously opposed proposals to station a further garrison in Kilchurn. Breadalbane argued that the government troops were ineffective and merely attracted counter-attacks, that 'a garison in Bara or in Hirt (St Kilda) is as usfull to the Government as wher they are named', and described Kilchurn as 'that usless house'.[5] Although the government took no action, and Breadalbane was striving to achieve a negotiated peace with the Highland Clans, a major reconstruction of Kilchurn was begun in 1690. This involved alterations to the tower-house and the SE range, and it is probable that the 16th-century 'north chalmeris' were removed at this period to allow the construction of a large block of barracks, suitable for the accommodation of a private army. The master-mason was Andrew Christie, described as 'mason in Balloch', who is first mentioned in connection with Kilchurn in August 1690, and who signed a contract, which has not survived, in November of that year. Alexander Campbell of Barcaldine supervised the work

in his capacity as Lord Breadalbane's Chamberlain of Lorn, and his papers contain many records of payments to the workmen, but little specific information about the work in progress. In July 1693 'ane iron yeatt weighting fortie aught ston' was made by James Smith, hammerman in Glasgow, and transported by sea to Bonawe. In November of that year Thomas Williamson, slater, was paid for mending the hall, probably the laich hall which was retained at this period, as is shown by a roof-raggle on the N face of the S angle-tower. In 1694 Andrew Christie was instructed to bring from the Lowlands, at the start of the building-season, six masons, four barrow-men and three wrights. Work in the SW range was probably completed in that year, for John Kelly, plasterer, submitted an account for plain plaster-work and moulded cornices executed during the winter of 1694–5 in various rooms in 'the chapel' and also in 'the old hall'. Surviving records contain no reference to the barrack-blocks; it is probable that work on them was well advanced by 1696, when slates were being quarried in Easdale by Thomas Williamson. In July of the next year a contract was made for the supply of laths for plastering the rooms in the castle, and 1698 is the last year for which substantial payments are recorded.[6]

Little use was made of this new and expensive accommodation for many years. When it was suggested that Kilchurn might be garrisoned during the abortive French invasion of 1708, Lord Breadalbane protested that it was useless for the purpose, in terms similar to those that he had employed in 1689. A government force occupied the castle in 1715, during the period when Lord Breadalbane was providing military assistance both to the government and to the Jacobites.[7] In 1733 the 2nd Earl of Breadalbane ordered the ironwork of the 'new work' to be inspected, and it was reported that twenty-six windows in the lower storey of the new work were fitted with 'cross stenchers', and that some of the windows of the next storey had cross-bars or gratings, but that seven large gratings which had not been fitted were stored in the tower. 'Some old people here who were imployed about the work (stated) that three stories in that part of The Castle called the Chapel and some windows in the old Tower were likewise planted with strenchers (sic) in the late Earle's time, besides two Iron gates', but these were not reckoned as part of the new work.[8] The sockets for this late 17th-century ironwork can still be seen in the SE wall of the SE range and the tower-house.

[1] *Taymouth Bk.*, 44, 46.
[2] Ibid., 99–100; receipts in S.R.O., Breadalbane Collection, GD 112/20/5; *Dunstaffnage Case*, 169–70.
[3] *Letters from Roundhead Officers*, Bannatyne Club (1856), 83; Firth, C H, *Scotland and the Protectorate*, SHS (1899), 152.
[4] Fraser, W, *The Earls of Cromartie* (1876), i, 44–5.
[5] S.R.O., Breadalbane Collection, GD 112/40/4, Letters. For the unsettled condition of the area, cf. *Leven and Melville Papers*, Bannatyne Club (1843), 353–4, 530.
[6] S.R.O., Campbell of Barcaldine Collection, GD 170/203/6, Building-Papers; GD 170/203/nos. 2–4, Rentals; Breadalbane Collection, GD 112/9/nos. 3, 5, 39, Rentals.
[7] Fraser, W, *The Melvilles* (1890), ii, 219; *Highland Papers*, iv, 232.
[8] S.R.O., Breadalbane Collection, GD 112/40/9, Letters, John Campbell to Lord Breadalbane, 7 September 1733.

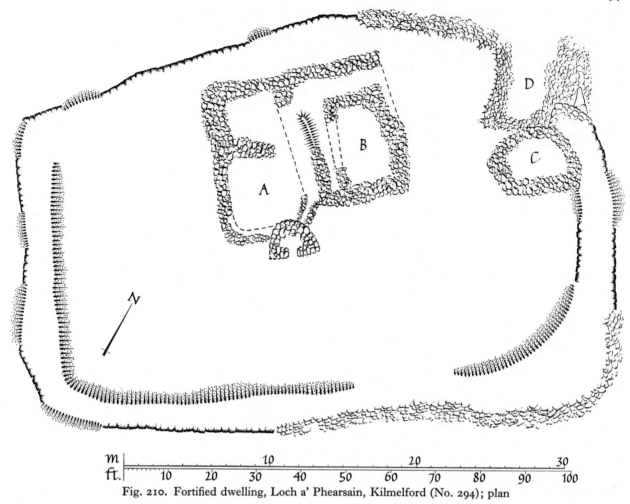

Fig. 210. Fortified dwelling, Loch a' Phearsain, Kilmelford (No. 294); plan

At this period the building was used mainly by the fishermen who leased salmon- and trout-fishing rights on Loch Awe; they were allowed to use the 'fish sellar' at Kilchurn to store salt and preserved fish.[1]

During the Jacobite rebellion of 1745–6 the castle, which was considered to be 'a very proper post', was garrisoned by a force of twelve officers and two hundred militiamen under the command of Captain Colin Campbell of Skipness. Their main duty was to prevent the movements of Highlanders who might be travelling to join the rebel army, and so useful was the castle for this purpose that in 1747 Lord Glenorchy considered the possibility of selling it to the government for use as a permanent garrison.[2] Nothing came of this proposal, and the building was struck by lightning shortly before Pennant visited it in 1769. Thereafter it decayed rapidly; drawings made in 1808 by an English visitor show that the castle was then in the same condition as when it was surveyed by MacGibbon and Ross eighty years later.[3] The castle passed into the guardianship of The Department of the Environment in 1953.

132276   NN 12 NW   July 1969

294. Fortified Dwelling, Loch a' Phearsain, Kilmelford. The small island that lies towards the S end of Loch a' Phearsain is enclosed by a substantial dry-stone wall within which there may be seen some remains of buildings of dry-stone construction (Fig. 210). The wall is fairly well preserved for much of its length, and rises to an average height of 1·2 m. Part of an inner face is visible on the E side, where the wall appears to have had a thickness of 2·7 m, while traces of what is probably a similar face, now largely concealed by debris and vegetation, can be seen on the W and S sides. There are no signs of an inner face on the N side, however, where the wall may have been no more than a revetment.

Towards the centre of the N side of the enclosure there are the remains of two buildings of sub-rectangular plan. Building A measures 10·7 m from NW to SE by 7·0 m transversely over walls about 1·0 m in thickness, and appears to have been sub-divided by a stone partition-

[1] Ibid., GD 112/10/1, Tacks.
[2] Fergusson, *Argyll*, 52, 75, 82; *TGSI*, xxii (1897–8), 78, 81.
[3] Pennant, *Tour* (1769), 237; Bodleian Library, MS Top. Gen. b 49, fols. 51–2.

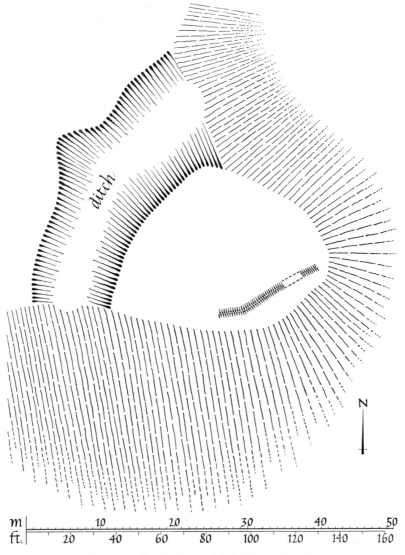

Fig. 211. Castle, Rarey (site) (No. 297); plan

wall. The small hut that overlies the SE end of the building is probably a modern duck-shooting hide. Building B lies parallel and adjacent to A; in its original form it appears to have measured 9·4 m by 6·1 m over walls about 1·0 m in thickness, but in a secondary phase of construction the building was considerably reduced in size. A third building (C), which abuts the inner face of the NE section of the enclosure-wall, measures 5·8 m from NE to SW by 4·3 m transversely over walls about 1·0 m in thickness. Immediately to the NW of Building C the enclosure-wall returns round a small inlet (D), which was probably utilized as a boat-landing. No traces of a causeway were observed at the date of visit.

It is difficult to estimate the age of these remains, but they may probably be ascribed to the late medieval or post-medieval period. Pont's map of the early 17th century indicates that the site was occupied at that date, but by 1843 the buildings were ruinous.[1]

855135   NM 81 SE   June 1971

295. Castle, Loch na Sreinge (Site). There are no visible remains of this castle, which is said to have stood upon the principal island in the loch.[2] A little to the W of the site indicated on the 6-inch O.S. map, however, there may be seen the ruins of a small sub-rectangular building of indeterminate age; this appears to have been constructed of dry-stone masonry.

926169   NM 91 NW   July 1968

[1] Blaeu's *Atlas* (Lorn); *NSA*, vii (Argyll), 65.
[2] *NSA*, vii (Argyll), 68; Name Book No. 53, p. 120.

296. Fortified Dwelling, Loch Nell (Site). This site occupies a small unnamed island situated towards the N end of Loch Nell. The island is probably partly or wholly of artificial origin, but the surface, which appears to be composed mainly of loose boulders, is now much overgrown, and there are no visible traces of buildings. The island is mentioned in two 14th-century charters, and again in 1527, when Archibald Campbell of Lerags had a fee for 'the keeping of the isle of Lochnell'.[1] It may have been a dwelling-place of the Campbells of Lochnell before the family transferred the name to their Benderloch property of Ardmucknish, which became their principal residence some time during the 17th century (cf. No. 330). Pont's map of the early 17th century indicates that the island was occupied at that date.[2]

Three other artificial islands are reputed to exist in Loch Nell,[3] but only one of these, situated at the S extremity of the loch, was visible at the date of visit, and this contains no identifiable traces of buildings.

898280   NM 82 NE   July 1968

297. Castle, Rarey (Site). A small earthwork is situated some 120 m NE of the 18th-century laird's house at Rarey (No. 333). A natural promontory, which falls steeply on the E to the rocky gorge of the River Euchar, 28 m below, is separated from level ground on the NW by an artificial ditch. The summit-area is irregular, measuring about 30 m by 22 m, and the ditch itself has an average width of about 11 m and a depth of about 1·8 m (Fig. 211). The turf-covered foundations of a dry-stone wall can be traced for a distance of about 14 m in the SE sector; this wall does not conform to the edge of the summit, and its date and purpose are uncertain.

Small-scale excavations conducted at this site in 1957 failed to identify the position of any structures; a thick deposit of charcoal was found and was thought to indicate the former existence of timber buildings that had been destroyed by fire. Finds included a small quantity of glazed pottery, and a copper belt-buckle, all of which are probably of 16th- or 17th-century date.[4]

Local tradition, as recorded in the 19th century, named this site 'Tom a Chaisteil', or the Castle Hill, and identified it as 'the mansion of the ancient and brave McDougall's of Raray'.[5] The excavated finds afford evidence of occupation during the period when this family were important landowners in Nether Lorn (cf. p. 251), but Rarey is shown as an unfortified dwelling on the Pont–Gordon map of the second quarter of the 17th century,[6] in contrast to Ardmaddy Castle (No. 310), which was probably the principal residence of the family at this period. The origins and early history of the site are obscure. Rarey was included in a grant of lands by Robert I to Dugall Campbell of Lochaw in 1313, and it is not known when the MacDougalls regained possession of the estate.[7]

831206   NM 82 SW   June 1970

THE BURGH OF OBAN

298. The Topography of the Burgh. The excellence of the anchorage in Oban Bay was first recognised by a Renfrew company which established a trading station there in the first quarter of the 18th century. The development of the town was stimulated by the construction of a custom-house c. 1760,[8] and by the enterprise of the brothers Hugh and John Stevenson who, in the last quarter of the century, established a distillery and a ship-building yard and were widely employed as masons.

Until the beginning of the 19th century the expansion of the town was most rapid in the area owned by the Duke of Argyll, S and W of the Black Lynn. A plan of 1803[9] shows that by that date considerable numbers of slated houses had been built at the NE ends of Shore Street and Albany Street, and on the S side of Argyll Square. Campbell of Dunstaffnage, proprietor of the area N of the Black Lynn, commissioned a 'plan of an intended village' from George Langlands in 1791,[10] but the first feus were not granted until c. 1804, and the main development of this part of the town occurred after it had been purchased by Charles Campbell of Combie c. 1809 (Pls. 76, 77A). The plan adopted was a simple grid-pattern based on a principal N–S thoroughfare, George Street, but the execution of the E section of this plan was hindered by the existence of the distillery and by the irregular nature of the terrain.[11] The buildings of this period, as shown in early photographs,[12] were simple two- and three-storeyed structures; some still survive, although much altered, in George Street.

Oban was erected into a burgh of barony by the Duke of Argyll and Campbell of Combie in 1820, after an earlier charter of 1811 had been set aside, and in the following year a church, now rebuilt, was erected at the S end of Combie Street. The ownership of the S and N parts of the town were transferred respectively to Robert Campbell of Sonachan in 1821 and to the 2nd Marquess of Breadalbane in 1837.[13]

In the following articles, one of the more important

[1] *Highland Papers*, iv, 17–18, 195.
[2] Blaeu's *Atlas* (Lorn).
[3] *PSAS*, xlvii (1912–13), 286–7.
[4] The Commissioners are indebted to Captain J D Inglis for information concerning the excavation, and for access to the finds.
[5] Name Book, No. 53, p. 50; *NSA*, vii (Argyll), 65.
[6] Blaeu's *Atlas* (Lorn).
[7] *Origines Parochiales*, ii, part i, 106.
[8] Pococke, *Tours*, 71. This building, which was demolished to make way for the railway in 1880, is shown in an early photograph reproduced in Black, A D, *Oban of Yesterday* (n.d., c. 1969), 11.
[9] Argyll MSS, Inveraray Castle, Map Cabinet, drawer 5.
[10] A copy made by Alexander Langlands in 1811 is in S.R.O., Breadalbane Collection, GD 112/10/6.
[11] Cf. Robert Stevenson's plan of 1846, preserved in Oban Burgh Museum (Pl. 76).
[12] Black, op. cit., 9, 17.
[13] Ibid., *passim*; Faichney, *Oban*, 70–93; Shedden, *Lorn*, 201–51; *Stat. Acct.*, xi (1794), 132–5; Groome, *Ordnance Gazetteer*, 1251–4; *NSA*, vii (Argyll), 532–3.

monuments in the burgh is described separately, and the remainder are grouped together under the names of the streets in which they occur (cf. also No. 270).

8529, 8629   NM 82 NE
8530, 8630   NM 83 SE

299. Back Combie Street, Oban. A plain two-storeyed block of late 18th-century date stands at the foot of Star Brae, NE of and parallel to the 19th-century frontage of Combie Street, The rubble masonry and dressings are of purple sandstone of local origin, similar to that visible in the cliff face SE of the Oban Distillery. A central passage gives access to the rear, where there is a forestair serving the first floor.

8629   NM 82 NE   September 1971

300. Cawdor Place, Oban.

SOUTH-EAST SIDE. *1–7 Cawdor Place*, the SW continuation of Shore Street, is a two-storeyed block of early 19th-century date. The masonry is of rubble, with window- and door-dressings of drafted ashlar. The principal feature of the frontage is a Doric portico with massive half-engaged columns, now set at the entrance-doorway of number 5, but originally forming the entrance to number 4, the central house in the block.[1]

8529   NM 82 NE   September 1971

301. Piermaster's House, South Pier, Oban. The South Pier and the adjacent piermaster's residence were constructed by the Duke of Argyll, proprietor of South Oban, c. 1814, at the period when Henry Bell's pioneer steamship, 'The Comet' was establishing a regular service between Glasgow and Oban. The house (Pl. 77B) is a small single-storeyed building of whitewashed rubble masonry, having a slated roof of hipped form, which is given some architectural distinction by a small round tower at either end of the N gable-wall. Each tower is lit by a single arch-pointed window and has a conical roof. At the centre of the N wall there is a recess which formerly housed a notice-board, and attached to the NE tower there is a wrought-iron bracket for a guiding-light. A modern extension has been built against the W wall.

The interior is divided by a corridor, the S portion comprising the kitchen and a bedroom and the N portion forming a single large room. There are no original fittings of any consequence.

854297   NM 82 NE   September 1971

DOMESTIC ARCHITECTURE FROM THE 17TH TO THE 19TH CENTURY

302. Achlian. This late 18th-century tacksman's house (Pl. 78A) is situated on a hillside 600 m from the E shore of Loch Awe, enjoying a fine view across the loch to the Pass of Brander. It was probably built by Alexander Campbell, who received tacks of Achlian from Duncan Campbell of Inverawe and his successor, Robert Campbell of Monzie, in 1756 and 1789.[2] The traditional story that connects the building of the house with Dugald Campbell, a nephew of Duncan Campbell of Inverawe,[3] ascribes no date to the events recorded, and stylistic considerations suggest that the present building existed by the time that Alexander Campbell received his second tack. Renovation in 1953 included the remodelling of the interior, but the original gound-floor plan was retained.

The house is built of harled rubble with exposed sandstone-dressings and a slated roof. On plan it is a rectangle, measuring 13·7 m by 8·2 m, with a rounded stair-projection at the rear, and consists of two storeys and a garret. The principal elevation, which faces NW, is symmetrical, having a central entrance-doorway flanked by three-light windows with narrow side-lights. The doorway (Pl. 78B) has a moulded architrave flanked at the upper corners by consoles, which support an undecorated frieze and moulded cornice. The SE elevation is dominated by the stair-tower, which rises above the main wall-head of the house. This is lit by two windows whose margins are undressed except for sandstone sills. The entrance-doorway leads through a lobby to the hall, which is flanked by the main reception-rooms. On the NE is the drawing-room (Pl. 78C), which retains two elliptical-headed alcoves flanking the remodelled fireplace in the NE wall, and a moulded chair-rail. A wide elliptical-headed arch in the SE wall formerly contained book-cases, but now opens into a narrow apartment which was originally a closet or study entered from the hall. The dining-room and kitchen on the SW of the hall have been entirely remodelled. Below the stair is a blocked door which gave access to the out-buildings. The staircase (Pl. 78D) has wooden treads built round a long stone pillar, and continues at full width to the garret. The upper floors have been entirely rebuilt.

121242   NN 12 SW   September 1969

303. Achnaba. The existing farm-buildings incorporate what appears to be a small laird's house and offices of 18th-century date grouped round three sides of a courtyard. The old dwelling-house, now adapted for use as a byre, is a long single-storeyed building occupying the N side of the courtyard. This may date from the first half of the 18th century, and traces of the original window-

[1] Black, op. cit., 11.
[2] *Clan Campbell*, iii, 136, 171.
[3] Campbell, Lord A, *Records of Argyll* (1885), 166.

openings can be seen in the walls. The W and E sides of the courtyard were formerly occupied by single-storeyed ranges of offices containing dummy Venetian windows in the end-walls, and probably dating from about the end of the 18th century. The E range remains in use as a barn, but the W range has been remodelled and now constitutes the dwelling-house.

FIREBACK. A cast-iron fireback, recently removed from one of the rooms in the W range of the courtyard, is in the possession of the proprietor, Mr W B Buchanan. It measures 0·84 m in height and 0·46 m in width and bears in relief the initials S D C, the date 1732 and a mullet (Pl. 78E). These appear to be the initials of Sir Duncan Campbell, 7th of Lochnell, one of the partners in the Glen Kinglass Ironworks (No. 358). Since there is some evidence to indicate that firebacks were occasionally manufactured at early Scottish ironworks,[1] it is possible that this example was cast at Glen Kinglass.

Achnaba was the residence of the Campbells of Achnaba, cadets of the Campbells of Barcaldine. The most prominent member of this family was Colin Campbell, the mathematician and astronomer, who became parish minister of Ardchattan and Muckairn in 1667 and who died in 1726.[2]

945364   NM 93 NW   July 1970

304. Airds House. This well-preserved early-Georgian house (Fig. 212, Pls. 79, 80) occupies an attractive situation at the head of Airds Bay, looking towards the island of Lismore and the mountains of Morvern and Mull. It comprises a three-storeyed main block of which the principal, or SW, façade is linked by quadrant corridors to flanking pavilions two storeys in height. A number of minor alterations and additions have been made to the house at different periods, while in 1858 a billiard-room and additional service-accommodation were constructed at the rear of the SE pavilion and its associated corridor.

The masonry is of harled rubble with exposed free-stone dressings, those of the Georgian period being of a fine-grained greyish-green sandstone; the quoins of the main block are rusticated. Most of the window-openings have plain surrounds wrought with rounded arrises, but few retain their original glazing-bars. The chimney-stacks, which have moulded copings, appear to have been renewed sometime during the 19th century.

The central portion of the main block is advanced and rises to a triangular pediment surmounted by ornamental urn-finials (Pl. 80). The tympanum of the pediment contains a bold relief-carving representing the full armorial achievement of the Campbells of Airds, set between moulded bull's-eye windows (Pl. 81A). The shield is charged: quarterly, 1st, a hart's head cabossed; 2nd, gyronny of eight; 3rd, a galley, sail furled, oars in action and pennons flying; 4th, on a fess three buckles. For crest there is a swan, and the motto is BE MINDFULL.

The entrance-doorway (Pl. 81C), which is centrally placed at ground-floor level, is flanked by shallow pila-

sters which support a plain frieze and segmental-headed pediment. Within the tympanum of the pediment there is a panel bearing a shield carved with a fess and inscribed with the date 1738. This doorway may have been remodelled sometime during the 19th century, and the carved shield, whose armorial significance is uncertain, appears to be of this period, but the date may have been copied from an earlier inscription. The central window-openings on the two upper floors are more elaborately treated than the remainder, that at first-floor level being a round-headed keystoned opening framed by pilasters and a triangular pediment, while that at second-floor level has a lug-moulded and keystoned surround. In contrast to these is a series of small windows, contrived in the side-walls of the advanced central bay, which admit light to the service-stair and to mural closets. The wall-head is crowned with an eaves-course of two principal members, and this continues in a simplified form around the remaining three sides of the main block. These other elevations are quite plain, the central portion of the NE façade, however, being defined by vertical bands of rustication. The two bay-windows on the ground-floor on this side of the house are additions.

The quadrant-walls incorporate centrally-placed doorways with semicircular heads and rusticated architraves (Pl. 81D), but these have been remodelled to serve as windows. The wall-heads are surmounted by moulded cornices, each of which carries a central ball-finial. The pavilions (Pl. 81B), which are treated very simply, rise to pedimented gables and those in the NW pavilion contain central bull's-eye windows. The existing chimney-stacks appear to be of 19th-century date. The S angle of the SE pavilion incorporates two stone panels evidently designed to serve as sundials, but lacking any carved numeration. The SE service-wing has no features of special interest apart from an arched entrance-doorway at the rear, whose keystone bears the incised date 1858.

Although remodelled on more than one occasion, the interior still retains a good deal of its original character (Pl. 82F). The main block is of simple tripartite plan, the central division accommodating the principal staircase, while the two outer divisions contain a single main room at both ground- and first-floor levels. The chimney-flues are gathered into the two main internal partition-walls, one of which also incorporates a narrow turnpike service-stair. This is of stone construction and the treads have moulded nosings. The principal staircase (Pl. 82A), which is approached directly from the entrance-hall (Pl. 82B), is of geometric plan, the lowest flight being of stone and the remainder of timber. The stone treads are sunken and have moulded nosings which return at the outer margins. The timber-work is mainly of oak, with twisted balusters and moulded handrails with turned knops. Elsewhere in the house there are a considerable number of panelled doors and

---

[1] *PSAS*, xxi (1886–7), 110, quoting Pennant, *Tour* (1772), i, 384.
[2] *NSA*, vii (Argyll), 487–9; Scott, *Fasti*, iv, 81; Fraser, A C. *The Book of Barcaldine* (1936), 41–9.

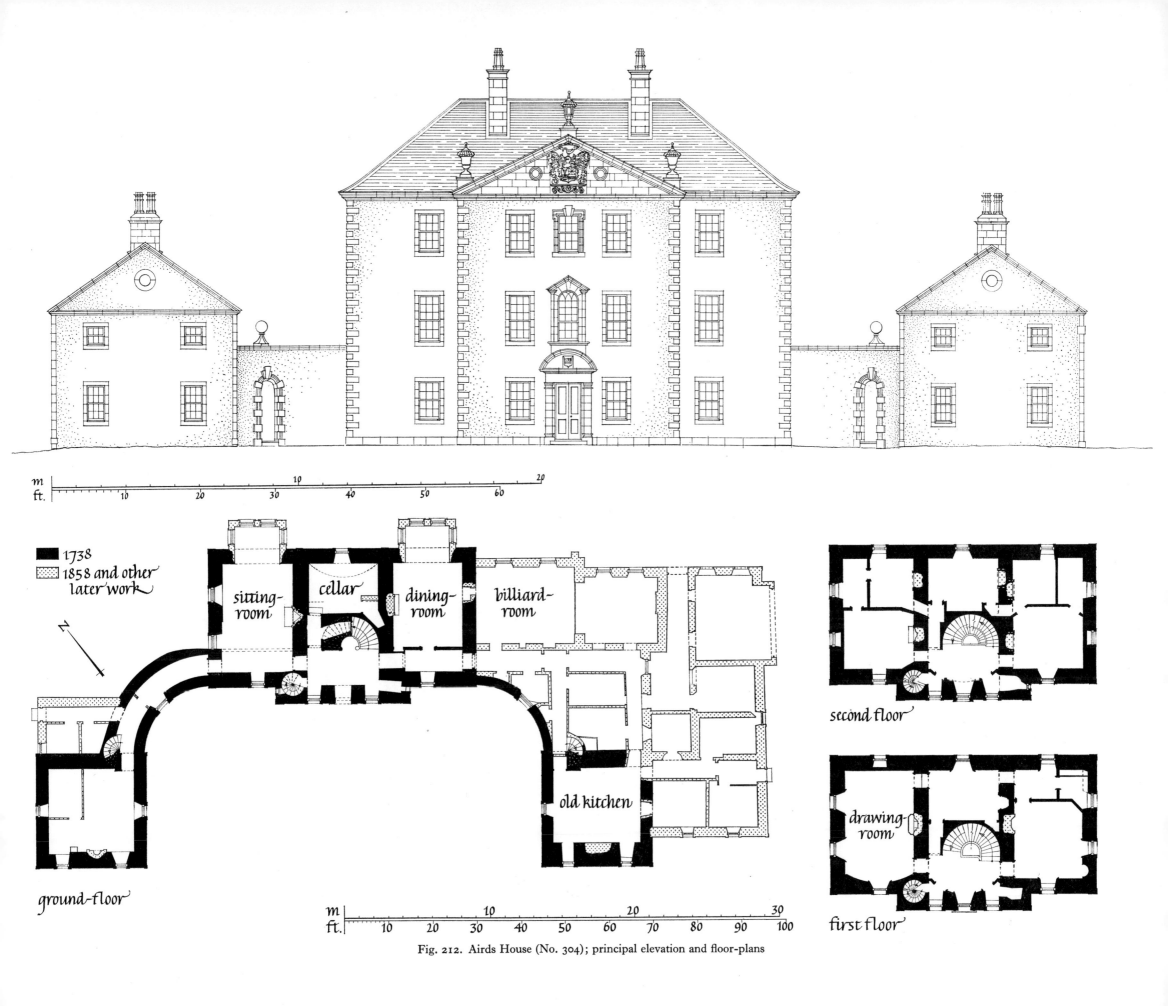

1738
1858 and other later work

sitting-room   cellar   dining-room   billiard-room

old kitchen

ground-floor

second floor

drawing room

first floor

Fig. 212. Airds House (No. 304); principal elevation and floor-plans

Fig. 212. Aisle House (No. 104), principal elevation and floor-plans

shutters of pine, one or two of which retain their original brass furniture.

In addition to the staircase-hall and a barrel-vaulted cellar to the rear, the ground-floor comprises a sitting-room and a dining-room, of which the latter incorporates a timber-and-stucco chimney-piece of late 18th-century date. This room has a heavy moulded plaster ceiling-cornice, one of the few examples of original plasterwork that now remain in the house. The first-floor drawing-room, which occupies the NW division of the main block at this level, appears to have been remodelled fairly recently, when the present ceiling was evidently installed, but some traces of earlier decorative plaster-work are still apparent. This room now contains a pine-and-stucco chimney-piece of late 18th-century date (Pl. 82C), formerly at Smeaton, East Lothian. At second-floor level each of the outer divisions of the main block contains three rooms, another being accommodated behind the staircase. One of the rooms in the NW division retains some 18th-century panelling, together with an original bead-moulded stone chimney-piece (Pl. 82D). From the second floor the principal staircase continues upwards to give access to an attic storey contained within the roof-space and lit by skylights. In the original arrangement this probably accommodated servants.

The interiors of the pavilions have been remodelled and now contain no features of special interest. The ground-floor of the SE pavilion originally housed the kitchen, whose large fireplace and flue were evidently housed within the thickness of the SW wall. Beneath the NW pavilion there is an unvaulted cellar.

HOME FARM. The home farm, which lies a little to the N of the house, appears to be of late 18th-century date. The principal front incorporates a pedimented central bay flanked by segmental-arched windows (Pl. 82E).

GATELODGE. The gatelodge at the NE end of the former main drive to the mansion is probably of late 18th- or early 19th-century date. It is a plain single-storeyed rectangular structure of harled rubble, having a semi-hexagonal bay facing the approach from the public road (Pl. 82G).

BURIAL-ENCLOSURE. This burial-place, which lies about 230 m E of the house, appears to be of 19th-century date. It comprises a small rectangular enclosure entered through heavily rusticated gatepiers; two of the external angles have rusticated quoins. The interior is densely overgrown and the earliest identifiable tomb-stones commemorate late 19th-century members of the family of MacFie of Airds (*infra*).

FISH-TRAP. About 75 m below high-water mark, part of the SE shore of Airds Bay is enclosed by a low barrier of boulders, thus forming a roughly circular fish-trap some 45 m in diameter.

The estate of Airds was purchased by Sir Donald Campbell of Ardnamurchan, a natural son of Sir John Campbell of Calder, sometime during the second quarter

of the 17th century. On Sir Donald Campbell's death in 1651 Airds passed to his nephew, George Campbell, and subsequently descended to Donald Campbell, 5th of Airds, who built the present house. Few documents concerning the erection of the house have so far come to light, and the identity of the architect is unknown. It is recorded, however, that freestone was being quarried in 1737, while in September of the following year Donald Campbell reported that 'the season has proved so cross that I have no expectation of getting the Rooff on my house this year, all I propose is to be sidewall height'.[1] The Campbells continued to hold Airds until about the middle of the 19th century, and in 1852 it was acquired by Robert MacFie, 3rd of Langhouse.[2] This new owner was responsible for the alterations and additions made to the house in 1858, and his family continued in posses-sion of the property until early in the present century.[3]

9°9449   NM 94 SW   July 1968

305. Appin House. This house occupies an attractive site above the eastern shores of Loch Linnhe about 5 km NE of Port Appin, and directly opposite the island of Shuna. Before a major scheme of reconstruction was begun about the year 1965, the building incorporated work of two main periods. The earlier portion comprised a small classical mansion of the first half of the 18th century, which occupied the W corner of the site. In about 1831 additional accommodation was provided by

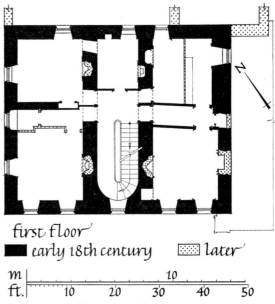

first floor
■ early 18th century   ▨ later

Fig. 213. Appin House (No. 305); first-floor plan

[1] S.R.O., Campbell of Barcaldine Collection, GD 170/765/ nos. 8 and 13.
[2] S.R.O., Abbreviated Register of Sasines (Argyll), 1851–5, no. 304.
[3] G.E.C(okayne)., *Complete Baronetage*, ii (1625–49), 341–2; *Burke's Peerage* (1963 ed.), 422–3; *Burke's Landed Gentry* (1952 ed.), 1624.

the erection of a SE wing, and at the same time the original house was remodelled externally in an attempt to bring it into harmony with the new work. Behind the house there stood a court of offices of 18th- and 19th-century date. Since 1965 the older portion of the house has been entirely demolished[1] and a new building is in course of erection upon the same site, but it is understood that the SE wing and certain portions of the court of offices are to be retained. The present account describes the house as it was before the start of these alterations (Pl. 83A).

The original house was a simple rectangular block measuring about 15·5 m by 12·5 m over walls which had a thickness of 0·9 m and rose to a height of three storeys.[2] The building stood on a NW to SE axis and the principal façade faced SW. The masonry was of rubble and was latterly cement-rendered although no doubt originally harled; some of the dressings were of slate and others of yellow and red sandstone. The windows had chamfered arrises, those on the principal façade having at some time been cut back to admit more light. The roof was hipped and slated.

The principal façade was symmetrically disposed and incorporated three ranges of windows together with the main entrance-doorway, which was centrally placed at ground-floor level. The architrave of this doorway was wrought with a thin roll-and-hollow moulding (Fig. 214A). The entrance-porch, and the balustraded parapet and pinnacles that surmounted the façade, were additions of the early 19th century, but the ovolo-moulded eaves-cornice beneath the parapet was probably original. The central pinnacle incorporated the carved armorial achievement of Robert Downie of Appin (infra), the shield being charged: a fess between three boars' heads couped. For crest there was a cock, and on the upper part of the pinnacle was a dexter hand grasping a dagger; beneath the shield a label bore the motto: COURAGE.

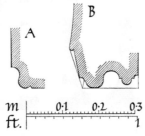

Fig. 214. Appin House (No. 305); profile mouldings: A, entrance-doorway; B, fireplace

The plan was a symmetrical one, the house being divided into three main structural divisions by two partition walls which rose to the full height of the building and contained the flues (Fig. 213). Within the central division a cantilevered geometric stair rose to give access to the two upper floors, the lower flight being of stone and the upper of wood (Pl. 83 C). The treads had moulded nosings returned round the inner ends, and there was a plain wrought-iron balustrade with a mahogany hand-rail. In the original arrangement the two outer divisions

both contained two main rooms on each storey, a fifth and smaller apartment being centrally placed behind the staircase. The arrangement on all three floors was thus very much the same, although certain minor modifications had been introduced during the course of the 19th century. On the ground-floor the small central apartment behind the staircase was vaulted in stone, having no doubt been designed as a strong-room or wine-cellar. Latterly, at least, it was used as a wine-cellar, but the brick bins were evidently insertions for they appeared to block an original doorway giving access from the entrance-hall. The apartment in the E angle may originally have been a kitchen, the disparate thickness of the SE wall suggesting the former presence of a large fire-place and flue. The first floor (Fig. 213) contained the principal apartments and the second floor was occupied by bedrooms.

Some of the rooms contained original pine panelling, shutters, built-in cupboards (Pl. 83B), and other timber fittings, together with brass door-furniture. Most of the rooms also retained their original, heavy, plaster ceiling-cornices, but the ceilings themselves were quite plain. The most interesting of the fittings, however, were four stone fireplaces (Pl. 84A–C), of which one was situated on the ground-floor and three on the first floor. These were all of similar design, having concave ingoings and continuous roll-and-hollow mouldings (Fig. 214B) which curved round the upper angles of the surrounds; two of the fireplaces incorporated false keystones carved respectively with a thistle and a fleur-de-lis.

The SE wing is single-storeyed and has a semi-octagonal projection in the centre of the main front. The angles are defined by square turrets surmounted by pinnacles, and the front parapet is balustraded. The interior contains no special features of interest. The court of offices at the rear is mainly of late 18th- and 19th-century date, but the SE range adjacent to the dwelling-house incorporates some earlier 18th-century work.

The original house was presumably erected by one of the Stewarts of Appin, a family which had held the property since at least as early as the 15th century. The exact date of erection is unknown, but the architectural

[1] Two stone chimney-pieces and a number of pine doors have been preserved with the intention of re-utilizing them in the present scheme of work.

[2] Evidence is said to have come to light during the course of the present building-operations indicating that the house originally comprised two storeys and an attic, and incorporated a central pediment (DES (1966), 11). This theory is in part confirmed by the evidence of two early engravings, of which the first, after Paul Sandby, published in 1781 (Sandby, P, *A Collection of One Hundred and Fifty Select Views in England, Scotland, and Ireland* (1781), ii, pl. lvi), depicts what seems to be a two-storeyed house with attic-windows protruding through the roof, while the second, published in 1810 (*The Scots Magazine and Edinburgh Literary Miscellany*, lxxii (1810), p. 643), shows a three-storeyed block without attic-windows. The proprietor most likely to have carried out such alterations would seem to have been Hugh Seton of Touch, who acquired the estate in 1765 (infra). Mrs Grant of Laggan, writing in 1773 (*Letters from the Mountains* (1807 ed.), i, 70), states that this owner had recently carried out numerous improvements, including the erection of a 'stately mansion'.

evidence suggests that the house was built quite early in the 18th century, in which case it may be ascribed to Robert Stewart, 8th of Appin, who succeeded to the estate as a minor before 1685, and was subsequently forfeited for his part in the 1715 rebellion. He is said to have spent much of the remainder of his life abroad, but appears to have been restored to his Appin estates before his death, which took place some time between 1735 and 1739.[1] In 1724 James Duff supplied concave stone fireplace-surrounds from quarries in Morvern (probably at Ardtornish) for the laird of Appin, which suggests that the house was approaching completion in that year.[2]

In 1765 Robert's son Dugald, 9th of Appin, sold the property to Hugh Seton of Touch, from whom it passed to the Marquess of Tweeddale in 1788.[3] In or about 1816 the estate was acquired by Robert Downie, a retired Bengal planter of ample fortune, who was responsible for the erection of the SE wing and for certain other alterations to the house as mentioned above. These alterations seem to have been carried out in or about 1831.[4] Robert Downie died in 1841, but his indirect descendants retained the property until within recent years.[5]

932494   NM 94 NW   July 1970

306. Appin Post-office, Tynribbie. This is a plain two-storeyed building of oblong plan having a single-storeyed byre attached to one of the gable-walls (Pl. 84D). The masonry is of limewashed rubble, and the roof is hipped and slated. The windows are widely spaced, and a number of them retain their original glazing-bars. The interior has been remodelled and contains no features of special interest. The building appears to be of 18th-century date.

937462   NM 94 NW   July 1968

307. Ardanaiseig. This extensive mansion, formerly known as New Inverawe, is situated about 100 m from the W shore of Loch Awe and 5·5 km ENE of Kilchrenan. It was built for James Archibald Campbell, a descendant of the family of Campbell of Inverawe.[6] The architect was William Burn, of Edinburgh, whose original drawings (Pl. 85A), which are dated 1833,[7] show that the design was modified at an early stage. A tall stair-tower in the centre of the main block was omitted, and the garret space, which was originally designed to contain additional accommodation, was not used; the roof-line was lowered, and some alteration made to the form of the gables. Externally the building remains almost unchanged; the interior, however, was extensively remodelled early in the 20th century.

The principal apartments form a squarish block at the SE corner of the site, containing a basement and two floors. This is connected by a N wing to a stable-court which occupies three sides of a square. The walls are built of stugged granite, with abundant dressings and ornamental stonework executed in a greenish

sandstone. The entrance is in the W front, which is elaborately asymmetrical with a profusion of gables, projecting chimney-breasts, dormers, stair-turrets and false slit-windows. The entrance-doorway (Pl. 86A) is in the Jacobean style; it has a panelled and moulded architrave, surmounted by a blank panel enclosed in strapwork. The S and E façades (Pls. 85B, 86B) are less elaborate, the main decorative feature of each being a bay-window. That at the W end of the S façade is one storey in height and terminates in a strapwork balustrade, while that at the S end of the E façade rises through two storeys and has a moulded cornice.

The entrance gives access through a lobby to a large staircase which has been completely rebuilt. Two rooms, each lit by a bay-window and linked by a wide doorway, occupy the S part of the main block, and a third room occupies the remainder of the E side. In the W wall of this room there is a modern fireplace, which incorporates a spirally-fluted wooden column decorated with continuous foliage in the fluting and having a moulded base and a Corinthian capital. This column appears to be of 17th-century date, and may be Scottish in origin. The remaining rooms present no features of interest, except for the laundry which is situated below the E wing of the stables. This is a stone-floored apartment, 4·9 m square, with a central pillar supporting a stone groin-vault.

088249   NN 02 SE   September 1969

308. Ardencaple House, Seil. This small laird's house of late 18th-century date is oblong on plan and comprises two main storeys in height. The building is symmetrically planned about a central passage and turnpike-staircase, which is extruded at the rear in a semicircular bay (Pl. 86C). The masonry is of harled rubble and the roof is of slate. The house has been altered on several occasions, and a number of external features, including the entrance-porch and dormer-windows, are evidently additions. The interior has been completely remodelled, but in the original arrangement the ground-floor probably contained two rooms on each

[1] A letter of submission to the King was sent to General Wade by Mr Robert Stewart of Appin in August 1725 (Burt, E, *Letters from a Gentleman in the North of Scotland to his friend in London. . . .* (5th ed., by Jamieson, R, 1822), ii, 328–9).

[2] S.R.O., Campbell of Barcaldine Collection, GD 170/834/1. James Duff, mason in Dunblane, undertook the building of the old parish-church of Ardchattan in 1731 (cf. No. 215).

[3] Stewart, D H J and D, *The Stewarts of Appin* (1880), 116–25; *Burke's Landed Gentry* (1952 ed.), 2410–12; S.R.O., Particular Register of Sasines (Argyll), RS 10/7, fols. 24 and 194v.

[4] S.R.O., Campbell of Barcaldine Collection, GD 170/2417/2, letter from Robert Downie to Duncan Campbell giving dimensions of new dining-room at Appin House, 18 May 1831.

[5] S.R.O., Abbreviated Register of Sasines (Argyll), 1781–1820, nos. 2430, 2593–4, 2752, 2905; *The Gentleman's Magazine,* new series, xvi (1841), 547; *Burke's Landed Gentry* (1952 ed.), 1510.

[6] Johnston, *Campbell Heraldry*, ii, 53–4.

[7] Preserved in N.M.R.S.

side of the central area, while on the floor above there seem to have been two small rooms on one side, and a single large drawing-room on the other. The chimney-piece from this latter room, now in secondary use on the ground-floor, incorporates a plain grey marble surround framed within a pine-and-stucco architrave (Pl. 86D). The kitchen-wing on the SW side of the house appears to be contemporary with the main building, but has subsequently been raised in height.

Ardencaple was the residence of the MacDougalls of Ardencaple, and the present house was probably built by John MacDougall, who was seised in the estate as heir of his father, Coll MacDougall, in 1792.[1]

763193   NM 71 NE   April 1970

309. Ardlarach, Luing. This tacksman's house (Pl. 86E) is situated about 350 m NE of Black Mill Bay on the W coast of Luing. Although much altered internally, the house is interesting as an early dated example of the improved farmhouses, of two storeys with slated roofs, that were constructed in large numbers in Nether Lorn during the late 18th and early 19th centuries. The original rectangular house was built in 1787; an additional wing, which makes the building L-shaped on plan, is probably of early 19th-century date.

The original block, which measures 7·1 m by 12·5 m, faces S and is of three bays with a central doorway, now enclosed within a later porch. Between two of the first-floor windows there is a slate panel bearing the inscription: BUILT BY / PATRICK MCDOUGALL / 1787. The N elevation is lit by several irregularly-placed windows of varying sizes; a central doorway gives access to the yard and steading. In the original arrangement of the interior it is probable that a central staircase was flanked by two rooms on each floor. A later wing has been added on the E, with its S wall continuing the line of the original block. This addition has a door in the S wall, and windows larger in size than those of the original building.

736089   NM 70 NW   May 1970

310. Ardmaddy Castle. This mansion (Pl. 87A, C) occupies the summit of a rocky knoll at the head of Ardmaddy Bay, some 6·9 km SW of Kilninver. The lowest storey of a late medieval tower-house, a residence of the family of MacDougall of Rarey, was in 1737 incorporated into a house of Palladian type built by Colin Campbell of Carwhin, chamberlain of the Breadalbane estate in Argyll. This was extended in 1790 by the construction of a separate wing, linked to the original building by an archway with a passage above. Designs for the rebuilding of this addition were prepared by James Gillespie Graham in 1837, but remained unexecuted until 1862, when David Bryce supervised the construction of part of Graham's design, an L-shaped block in Jacobethan style. The house overlooks a walled garden with an ornamental bridge of mid-18th-century date,[2] and the court of offices, built to the designs of

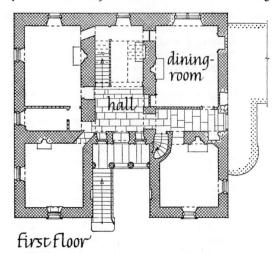

first floor

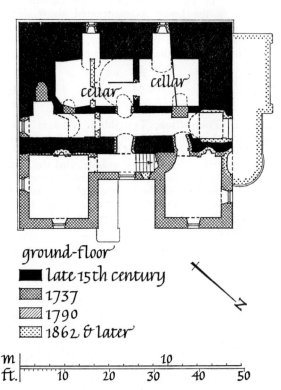

ground-floor

■ late 15th century
▨ 1737
▨ 1790
▨ 1862 & later

m |_____10_____
ft.|____10____20____30____40____50

Fig. 215. Ardmaddy Castle (No. 310); ground- and first-floor plans of early Georgian house

[1] S.R.O., Abbreviated Register of Sasines (Argyll), 1781–1820, no. 703; *NSA*, vii (Argyll), 73–4.

[2] An extensive garden is indicated on Roy's Map of *c.* 1750. The garden is shown in its present form in an unpublished drawing (Pl. 88A) made for Thomas Pennant in 1772 (National Gallery of Scotland, D 208), and in Alexander Langlands's estate-map of Nether Lorn, compiled in 1809 (S.R.O., RHP 720).

James Gillespie Graham in the years 1837–9, is also of interest.

The early building (Fig. 215), which occupies the SE portion of the site, comprises a vaulted ground-floor of late medieval date surmounted by a first floor and garret of 1737. In its present form the house appears as a block measuring 14·5 m from NW to SE by 13·6 m transversely, the central part of the NE façade being deeply recessed. The medieval tower-house measured 14·5 m from NW to SE by 8·7 m transversely over walls varying in thickness from 2·3 m to 2·4 m, except for the NE wall which was 1·2 m in thickness; the walls of the building of 1737 vary in thickness from 0·7 m to 0·8 m. On plan, the lowest stage of the tower comprised an axially vaulted cellar divided by a cross-wall into two compartments, which were entered by separate doors from a vaulted passage running along the NE side of the building. In 1737 the house was extended towards the NE by the construction of two wings, each containing one apartment, linked by a vestibule. At first-floor level the central portion of the house (Pl. 88B) is occupied by a pillared portico and staircase-hall, flanked on each side by one large and one smaller room. The masonry of both periods consists mainly of rubble, harled and whitewashed. Slate is freely used in the barrel-vault of the medieval cellars. Extensive use is made of freestone dressings in the work of 1737; these are of a fine-grained whitish sandstone but are painted over. The hipped roofs have a slight bell-cast; they are covered with local slates, fastened by wooden pegs to sarking-boards which are mostly of 18th-century date. Many of the windows retain thick glazing-bars of the same date, chamfered externally and ovolo-moulded within.

The castle is approached from the S by a drive which passes through a 19th-century archway linking the Georgian and Victorian buildings, and gives access to a terrace in front of the principal or NE façade of the Georgian house (Fig. 216). This is an elegant composition, having a three-bay Ionic portico at first-floor level set between projecting wings which have painted quoins and a heavily moulded cornice. Each wing has a centrally-placed window within a lugged and moulded architrave at ground-floor level, and a larger semicircular-headed window having a Gibbsian surround at first-floor level (Pl. 87B); in the side-walls flanking the portico there are mock windows at first-floor level, having painted freestone margins and imitation glazing-bars. A rebuilt forestair rises against the NW wall of the SE wing. In the original arrangement there was a central doorway at ground-floor level and a small window beside it; in 1879 these openings were blocked and another window formed within the doorway.[1]

The portico is formed of two free-standing and two engaged unfluted columns supporting an entablature of which the cornice is continuous with that of the wings, and returns to enclose a triangular pediment (Pl. 88C). Within the latter there is carved the incised date 1737, together with a spirited rendering in high relief of the armorial achievement of the Earls of Breadalbane, the shield bearing quarterly: 1st and 4th, gyronny of eight;

2nd, a galley, sail furled, oars in action and pennon flying; 3rd, a fess checky. The supporters, two stags, stand upon a scroll bearing the motto FOLLOW ME, and above the shield there are an earl's coronet and helm, and for crest a boar's head erased. Access to the portico from the forestair is obtained through the SE bay of the colonnade; the other bays contain a low stone balustrade of 18th-century date. Within the portico there is a semicircular-headed doorway with a fanlight, flanked by windows having lug-moulded architraves.

The other elevations of the Georgian house are extremely plain. Most of the NW wall is concealed by a block erected in 1862 to contain corridors and a circular stair-tower, and it is possible that the windows towards the NE end of this wall were moved to their present position at that time to make way for the stair-tower. Below the first-floor window there is a re-set stone panel (Pl. 88D) carved in relief with the date 1671 and a monogram of the letters L N C and V K, for Lord Neil Campbell, younger son of the Marquess of Argyll, and his first wife, Vere Ker, daughter of the 3rd Earl of Lothian[2] (infra, p. 252). At the base of the SW and SE walls there is a high plinth with a freestone coping. This may represent an original feature of the medieval tower-house, imitated in the 18th-century portion of the SE wall; a thick hedge and recent harling, however, make detailed inspection impossible, and it must be noted that the Victorian building has a plinth of similar character. Furthermore, two original medieval windows in the SW wall, lighting the ground-floor of the tower-house, where their position can be distinguished internally, would be cut by the top of the plinth. These windows have been replaced by two small rectangular openings occupying the same embrasures. At first-floor level in this wall there are three windows, of which that towards the NW was altered into a double window in 1924, the date carved on a panel above. Three skylights illuminate the roof-space, and although these are of recent construction, they occupy the position of earlier skylights, shown in an architectural drawing of 1790.[3] This drawing also establishes an 18th-century date for the four panelled chimney-stacks, of which two surmount the ridge of the main roof and one each of the wings.

In the original arrangement of 1737, the lowest storey of the house was entered by a door in the recessed portion of the NE wall, within which a stair on the NW provided the only means of communication with the upper floors; a door forced through the NE wall of the medieval tower led into the axial vaulted passage. In 1862 part of the medieval wall at the NW end of this passage, measuring 2·3 m in thickness, was removed to provide access to an added block containing a ground-floor doorway and an additional stair. Subsequently the original doorway in the NE wall was contracted to form

---

[1] These features are visible in Pennant's drawing of 1772, and in a plan at Ardmaddy Castle showing the alterations of 1879.

[2] Scots Peerage, i, 360.

[3] Drawing by J Campbell of Lochend for proposed addition, in S.R.O., Breadalbane Collection, GD 112/51/15, Schools correspondence.

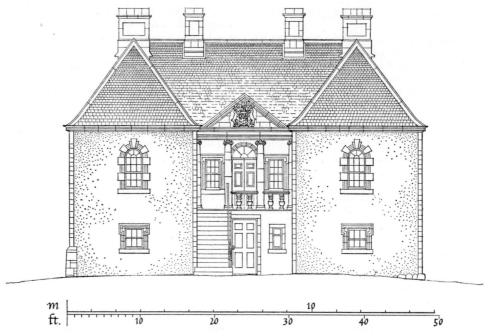

Fig. 216. Ardmaddy Castle (No. 310); principal elevation of early Georgian house (partially reconstructed)

a window. The segmental barrel-vault of the passage is now plastered, and a door was inserted in 1862 when the SE portion became a gun-room. The vault in this area has been removed; it is probable that the 18th-century window in the SE wall occupies the position of the medieval entrance-doorway, and that a mural stair to the upper floors rose on the SW, where there is now a recess. The cellars were originally two separate compartments, entered independently from the passage by doorways placed towards their respective end-walls; the jambs of these doorways, and the small vaults that intersect the principal vault, are visible inside the cellars. These entrances were blocked, probably in 1737, when a new doorway was formed opposite the inserted opening in the medieval NE wall; this door leads into the SE cellar, originally the larger of the two although now sub-divided by a 19th-century wall, and thence by an inserted opening in the medieval partition-wall into the NW cellar. Each apartment was lit by a small splayed window occupying a vaulted embrasure in the SW wall. No details survive in these openings, and they have been superseded by small rectangular windows at a higher level. The room in the SE wing, which was originally used as the kitchen, is entered by a door from the vestibule within the 18th-century entrance, while the corresponding apartment in the NE wing is entered from the vaulted passage by a doorway forced through the medieval NE wall. Neither of these rooms contains any features of interest other than their original windows.

The principal apartments are situated on the first floor and have retained most of their 18th-century fittings. These include wooden panelling and six-panelled doors having, in some cases, brass handles and rim-locks with sliding catches (Pl. 89E). There is also a series of moulded fireplaces having quarter-round curves at the junctions of jambs and lintels; these are carved from marble obtained from a quarry about 660 m S of the castle (No. 355). The central division of the building contains the stone-flagged hall. Against the SW wall there rises a wooden staircase which, although of recent date, probably occupies the position of an original stair, and in the NW wall there is a fireplace of black and white marble having slips of red marble at the bases and imposts, and decorated with panelling. A doorway at the NE end of this wall opens into a corridor whose NW end-wall was removed in 1862 to give access to the re-constructed NW building. In the NE wall of the corridor there are doorways serving the stair that descends to the ground floor, and the room in the NE wing. The latter, which is panelled throughout, has a moulded plaster cornice incorporating a shallow cove. In the S angle of the room there is an octagonal projection which accommodates the stair, and the W angle is bevelled to correspond with this. The fireplace in the SW wall is of painted marble decorated with a continuous bead-moulding. The apartment on the SW side of the corridor was in use as the dining-room in 1790 (*infra*, p. 252); it has a panelled dado and plastered walls having a slightly-coved cornice. In the centre of the SE wall there is a red marble fireplace having plain rebated jambs and a panelled lintel (Pl. 89c). At each end of this wall there is a tall cupboard with a moulded architrave; that at the SW end, which has a six-panelled door, was originally a doorway providing direct access to the staircase-hall. Opposite this, at the SW end of the NW wall, there is another cupboard having a door of similar design but slighter construction; this opening was created in 1790 as a doorway communicating with the drawing-room in the new NW building, and was probably blocked in 1862 when this building was reconstructed and alternative means of access provided.

The SE division of the house is planned somewhat differently; there is no corridor, and both apartments are entered directly from the hall. A passage cut obliquely through the wall at the E angle of the hall leads to the room in the SE wing. This retains no 18th-century features other than its windows and an ogee-moulded plaster cornice; the fireplace in the SW wall is of 19th-century date. The NE portion of the large SW room is sub-divided to form a lobby and bathroom. Although of recent date, these features may replace an earlier closet, for they are entered by a doorway adjoining the entrance to the SE wing. The room itself is entered by a doorway at the foot of the staircase. In the NW wall there is a painted marble fireplace having a bead-and-cavetto moulding and flanked in the panelling by pilasters which rise into the coved cornice (Pl. 89D).

At garret-level the central division of the house is occupied by the stair-well and a landing; in each of the side-divisions there are two rooms, some of which retain 18th-century panelling, divided by an irregularly-shaped lobby. During alterations carried out in May 1970, a re-used stone dressing bearing a plain 0·08 m chamfer was exposed in a door-jamb at the NW end of the landing. The timber roof is of coupled rafters into which collar-beams are halved.

The NW extension of the castle, as designed by Graham in 1837, was probably intended to form three ranges enclosing a courtyard. Only the SW and NW ranges were built in 1862, and the latter is incomplete. The building comprises two storeys and garrets, the principal apartments being at first-floor level in the SW range. These apartments are lit by two elaborate bay-windows in the SW façade (Pl. 87C), above which rise shaped gables surmounted, somewhat incongruously, by small triangular pediments. At the NW end of this façade there is a small octagonal tower which rises above the general roof-level and terminates in a pinnacled parapet. The tall chimneys are spirally fluted or panelled. The NW range incorporates the late 18th-century kitchen as remodelled in 1837.

THE COURT OF OFFICES. This comprises three irregularly-shaped two-storeyed ranges grouped round three sides of a courtyard, the E side being open. The walls are of harled rubble, but green sandstone, quarried at Barrnacarry (No. 351), is used extensively for quoins and door- and window-dressings. Many of the doors and windows have shouldered lintels, and the gables are crow-stepped. A three-storeyed tower at the NW angle terminates in a heavy crenellated parapet which is carried upon a course of double-membered corbels. The coach-house, which occupied the centre of the W range (Pl. 89F), was entered by a large archway, now blocked, in the W wall and by a double arch from the courtyard; each of these openings has a four-centred arch-head wrought with an edge-roll moulding. The N range is occupied by stables while the S range contains work-rooms and domestic accommodation.

BRIDGE. At a point about 240 m NE of the castle a substantial stone-built bridge (Pl. 89B) spans the Allt Dallermaig. A bridge of similar form is depicted in this position in Pennant's drawing of 1772, and the structure may be ascribed to about the middle of the 18th century. The segmental arch has a span of 4·4 m and a height above water-level of 2·5 m; the width of the structure is 4·9 m. The bridge is ornamented by six pylons of harled rubble set above the abutments and the keystone of the arch on each side. Those at the centre are of truncated conical shape, while the others are pyramidal. Pennant shows a low balustrade joining these pylons, but there is now only a very low parapet, 0·15 m in height.

JETTIES AND BOAT-HOUSE. On the E shore of Ardmaddy Bay, about 900 m SSW of the castle, there are two stone-built jetties. One of these may be the pier known to have been built in 1748 by the company that worked the near-by marble quarry (No. 355), and both are shown in an estate survey of 1787,[1] but they have been greatly altered. In the cliff-face immediately to the SE there is a rectangular opening enlarged by quarrying, measuring 8·5 m in width by 11·7 m in length, within which a boat-house was constructed c. 1790. As shown in an architect's drawing of that period,[2] it comprised a stone screen-wall in a simplified Gothic Revival style, behind which four pairs of timber columns supported tie-beam trusses carrying a slated roof. Only the screen-wall now survives (Pl. 89A); it is constructed of rubble masonry ornamented with courses of projecting stones, and has a height of 5·5 m. At the centre there is an opening 4·9 m in height and having an arch-pointed head, which originally contained a fixed wooden tympanum and double doors. The boat-house was lit by two slit-windows, splayed internally and intersected externally by mock cross-lights giving them the form of Greek crosses.

HISTORICAL NOTE. Ardmaddy Castle first appears on record in the late 16th century as a property of the MacDougalls of Rarey, at that time the principal landowners of Nether Lorn.[3] The family became important in the second half of the 15th century,[4] and since the existing remains of the tower-house may be attributed to this period it is probable that it was built by the MacDougalls, who by this time probably considered Ardmaddy rather than the earthwork at Rarey (No. 297) to be their principal residence. In 1595 evidence concerning the murder of Campbell of Calder was heard at 'the place of Ardmadie' in the presence of MacDougall of Rarey.[5]

[1] S.R.O., RHP 975/1, Map of Seil and Luing by G Langlands, April 1787.
[2] S.R.O., Breadalbane Collection, GD 112/20/5, Ardmaddy Building-Papers.
[3] APS, iii (1567–92), 466; ibid., vii (1661–9), 342–3; Geog. Coll., ii, 150, 514.
[4] A charter of various lands in Nether Lorn was granted by Sir Duncan Campbell, 2nd of Glenorchy, to John McDowgall in 1479, S.R.O., Breadalbane Collection, GD 112/5/4, 'Regester', p. 2a.
[5] Highland Papers, i, 159.

MacDougall ownership came to an end in 1648 or 1649, when the aged John MacDougall of Rarey was imprisoned at Inveraray by the Marquess of Argyll, and forced to resign his house and estate of Ardmaddy. In 1650 Argyll appointed Duncan Campbell of Jura as keeper of the 'house of Ardmaddie with the tower and fortalice thereof'. Three years later he granted the castle and the entire Nether Lorn estate to his younger son, Lord Neil Campbell, and despite condemnation of the seizure of MacDougall property which was voiced in the Parliament of 1661 a similar grant by the 9th Earl of Argyll was confirmed by Charles II in 1666.[1] Although no work of this period survives, the existence of the carved stone dated 1671 (*supra*) suggests that Lord Neil Campbell may have altered or extended the medieval building. After his death in 1692, the entire Nether Lorn estate was sold by his eldest son for £20,000 Scots to the 1st Earl of Breadalbane, who undertook settlement of Lord Neil's outstanding debts, and Ardmaddy subsequently became the residence of the chamberlain of the Breadalbane estate in Argyll.[2]

Despite the expenditure of £516 Scots on buildings in 1705, it was reported in 1728 that 'the house of Ardmaddie is quit ruinous . . . it is not more lodgable than a barn'.[3] In 1730, Colin Campbell of Carwhin, a great-grandson of the 4th laird of Glenorchy, became chamberlain. He built the existing house in 1737, largely at his own expense although a bond for £66 was assigned to him by the trustees of the Breadalbane estate, who considered the house 'convenient for the proprietor when visiting the estate'.[4]

Pennant's drawing of 1772 shows two outhouses forming an L-shaped block in the area immediately NW of the castle, and in 1790 one of these buildings, the milk-house, was heightened to provide additional public rooms, while the other became a kitchen. The chamberlain, John Campbell of Lochend, submitted his own designs for a two-storeyed block of the same height as the existing house, linked to the latter by a double archway having a passage above. This was to lead from the dining-room in the NW portion of the existing building to a drawing-room in the SE part of the addition; the remainder of the first floor was to be occupied by an estate-office entered from an outside stair. Work was completed in 1791 at a total cost of £303, which was paid by Campbell and claimed by him from the 4th Earl of Breadalbane when he was dismissed seven years later. The Earl was a son of Campbell of Carwhin and intended to reside frequently at Ardmaddy where he had spent his childhood.[5]

In 1837 James Gillespie Graham, who was then acting as architect for the alteration of Taymouth Castle for the 2nd Marquess of Breadalbane, was commissioned to design a new court of offices and to rebuild the added wing of 1790. The offices were completed in 1839 at a total cost of about £3,400, after the tower had collapsed because of inadequate foundations and been rebuilt, a disaster which, Graham declared, 'never happened during my practical experience of 38 years'.[6] Although working-drawings and a specification were produced

for the rebuilding of the wing of the mansion, and estimates were obtained, the lowest being £4,000, the work was not carried out at this time, but minor alterations were made to the existing buildings, especially the kitchen, under Graham's supervision. In 1862, however, the 2nd Marquess of Breadalbane began to rebuild the addition using Graham's plans as modified by himself; David Bryce was employed as consulting architect. The building was executed in a Jacobethan style, similar in its details to that employed by Graham at New Murthly Castle, Perthshire, built in 1838. An intended NE wing was not erected, and it is probable that work was brought to a premature conclusion by the death of the 2nd Marquess of Breadalbane in November 1862. Ardmaddy continued to be a principal residence of the Breadalbane family until the sale of the estate in 1933.

785164 (Castle)   NM 71 NE   May 1970
787166 (Bridge)
783155 (Boat-house)

311. Ballachulish House. This house comprises a two-storeyed main block, a N wing of the same height, and a S kitchen-wing incorporating one main storey and a garret. All the buildings are of plain harled rubble with slate roofs. The main block comprises two distinct ranges of buildings roofed independently of each other. Both measure 16·5 m in length over all, but whereas the E range has an internal width of about 4·3 m, the W range has a width of 5·5 m. The E range evidently forms the nucleus of the present house and probably dates from about the middle of the 18th century, perhaps from 1764 (*infra*). Only the E wall is now exposed, and this incorporates a central doorway and two rows of symmetrically-placed windows, most of which have been enlarged. The W range (Pl. 90A), which appears to have been under construction in 1799,[7] has a similar five-window front and doorway. The N wing and the S kitchen-wing probably date from the first half of the 19th century.

The interior has been considerably remodelled. The original house probably comprised two main rooms on each floor flanking a central staircase, but the present staircase in this position (Pl. 90B) belongs to the second building-period and serves both portions of the main block. The lowest flight of the stair is of stone with a

[1] *APS*, vii (1661–9), 339; S.R.O., Campbell of Jura Collection, GD 64/3/153, Genealogical documents; Campbell, *Argyll Sasines*, ii, no. 821; *RMS*, xi (1660–8), 488.
[2] *Scots Peerage*, i, 360; S.R.O., Breadalbane Collection, GD 112/2/51, Nether Lorn titles, *passim*.
[3] S.R.O., Breadalbane Collection, GD 112/9/1, Nether Lorn Rental, 1705; ibid., GD 112/40/9, letter from Dugald Campbell to Lord Breadalbane, 10 December 1728.
[4] Ibid., GD 112/20/5, Ardmaddy Building-Papers, memorandum dated 30 December 1738.
[5] Ibid., GD 112/48, letter from J Campbell to Lord Breadalbane, 18 February 1790; ibid., GD 112/51/15, Schools correspondence, architectural drawing; ibid., GD 112/20/5, Ardmaddy Building-Papers.
[6] Ibid., GD 112/20/5, Ardmaddy Building-Papers, letter from J G Graham to Lord Breadalbane, 28 January 1839.
[7] Stoddart, *Local Scenery*, ii, 25.

plain wrought-iron balustrade and mahogany hand-rail. The arrangement of the W portion of the main block is similar, but the greater width makes the rooms considerably more spacious. The present drawing-room, occupying the N end of the main block, contains two marble chimney-pieces of early Victorian date.

CARVED STONE. The bothy that lies immediately to the SE of the house incorporates a window-lintel bearing an incised heart flanked by the initials I S and M W and the date 1764. These are evidently the initials of John Stewart, 5th of Ballachulish, and his wife Margaret, daughter of William Wilson of Murrayshall.[1] John Stewart succeeded his father in the Ballachulish property in 1774 and died in 1794. It seems likely that the lintel was formerly incorporated in the adjacent house, whose date of erection it may commemorate.

048592   NN 05 NW   June 1971

312. Balliveolan (Druimavuic). This is a small laird's house of the second half of the 18th century, to which considerable additions and alterations have been made at later periods (Pl. 91A). The original house, which was symmetrically planned, incorporates a three-windowed front having a central entrance-doorway; it comprises two main storeys and an attic, and the masonry is of harled rubble. The interior has been remodelled and now contains little of interest, apart from a Gothic-moulded sideboard-recess in the dining-room. In the original arrangement both main floors probably comprised two rooms grouped on each side of a central staircase, which may have been extruded in a bay at the rear.

The house formerly belonged to the Campbells of Balliveolan, a cadet branch of the Campbells of Barcaldine,[2] and the original portion is probably the structure referred to in a building-contract for the erection of a new house at a cost of £290, entered into by John Campbell of Balliveolan and John Menelaws, mason in Greenock, in 1768.[3]

008448   NN 04 SW   April 1967

313. Barcaldine House. This mansion (Pl. 90C) is situated about 6 km E of Barcaldine Castle (No. 279), which it replaced as the home of the family of Campbell of Barcaldine in the early 18th century. Until about the end of that century it was commonly described by its original name, Dalfuir. A house appears to have been built on this site for Patrick Campbell by James Duff, mason, shortly before 1724, and the same workman built a kitchen-wing in 1733.[4] The earliest building now identifiable, however, is a three-storeyed block, originally rectangular, measuring some 15·5 m from E to W by 8·0 m transversely over all, which forms the nucleus of the existing house. This appears to be of mid-18th-century date, and was probably built c. 1759, when extensive alterations took place.[5] It was subsequently altered by the construction of a three-sided bay at the

E end of the S elevation and, probably at about the beginning of the 19th century, by a segmental bow at the centre of the N façade. The principal entrance was probably situated in this bow at ground-floor level; this area, however, was subsequently included within a large drawing-room, possibly created in 1815 when extensive alterations were undertaken by John Drummond, an Oban mason.[6]

Alternative designs for a large extension to the N and W of the original building, in both the 'Castle' and 'Priory' styles, were prepared by James Gillespie Graham in 1814, but these remained unexecuted, as did another design for an 'intended castle', commissioned from the same architect in 1821. The court of offices which adjoins the house on the E, and is now greatly altered, was built by John Drummond to Graham's design in 1815.[7] Further building-work recorded in 1831 and 1838 probably comprised the two-storeyed library-wing, in a simple Jacobethan style, at the SE angle of the original building, and a lower two-storeyed wing containing bedrooms which lies to the N of the library and forms the W side of the court of offices. A three-storeyed block was constructed in the angle between the bedroom-wing and the original house in the early years of the present century; this contains the principal entrance and stair-case.

The original arrangement of the interior has been obscured by subsequent alterations. The large drawing-room that occupies the W portion of the ground-floor of the original house, as remodelled in the early 19th century, is decorated on walls and ceiling with elegant Adam-style plasterwork which incorporates medallions of *putti* playing musical instruments. This motif is repeated on the central panel of a pine chimney-piece enclosing a beaded marble fireplace-surround. The dining-room, situated at first-floor level, has a chimney-piece of dark marble (Pl. 90D), incorporating rosettes at the junctions of the fluted jambs and lintel. Each storey of the library-wing of c. 1831 comprises one large apartment, having a small study at the SE angle. The ground-floor room has a massive coffered ceiling, while the library, at first-floor level, has a coved and panelled ceiling springing from a rich classical cornice. The library chimney-piece (Pl. 90E), which is of white and coloured marble, has a central plaque depicting Cupid and Venus who holds his bow.

964413   NM 94 SE   August 1970

---

[1] Stewart, J H J and D, *The Stewarts of Appin* (1880), 181–2.

[2] *NSA*, vii (Argyll), 492–3.

[3] S.R.O., Campbell of Balliveolan Collection, GD 13/82.

[4] S.R.O., Campbell of Barcaldine Collection, GD 170/834/1, letter from J Duff to P Campbell, 31 July 1724; ibid., GD 170/235, Building-Accounts.

[5] Ibid., GD 170/274, Building-Accounts; *TGSI*, xxiv (1899–1901), 35.

[6] S.R.O., Campbell of Barcaldine Collection, GD 170/514/5, Building-Accounts.

[7] Ibid., GD 170/2451/2, letter from J G Graham to Duncan Campbell, 17 June 1814. Two sketch-plans, which probably reproduce Graham's designs of 1814, are preserved in RHP 12343/nos. 6 and 7.

314. Bothan na Dige, Stronmilchan (Site). There are no visible remains of this structure, which is said to have been a residence of the MacGregors of Glen Strae (cf. Nos. 283 and 335). The building is reputed to have comprised a clay and wicker superstructure resting upon stone foundations, and surrounded by a moat; it was demolished early in the 19th century.[1]

153278   NN 12 NE   September 1967

315. Dalmally Manse. This is a plain hip-roofed oblong block built of harled rubble with painted freestone dressings (Pl. 91B). A porch has subsequently been added at the front, and other additions made to the rear. The central portion of the front is advanced and rises to a gablet, beneath which there is a Venetian window. Two similar windows flank the central entrance-doorway on the ground-floor. The interior has been remodelled and now contains no features of interest, but the original layout, in which the principal rooms are grouped on each side of a central staircase, is preserved.

This manse was built in 1804–5 by John Stevenson, architect at Oban, at a cost of £730 sterling.[2]

167275   NN 12 NE   April 1968

316. Degnish. This is a plain oblong house two storeys and an attic in height (Pl. 91F). The masonry is of harled rubble and the roof is gable-ended with coped gables and moulded skewputs. The plan is conventional, a central staircase of timber being flanked at ground- and first-floor levels by a single large room, whilst a third and smaller room is situated immediately to the rear of the staircase. The parlour is on the first floor. None of the rooms now presents any particular features of interest.

A carved panel is built into the external face of the front wall towards one end of the building. This panel may originally have occupied a central position above the entrance-doorway, and have been removed to its present position when the porch was erected. The panel has a moulded border, the upper margin taking the form of a broken pediment which incorporates a scallop-shell flanked on each side by a boar's head ?erased. Beneath, there is the inscription: BUILT BY / NIEL CAMPBELL / [BRO]THER TO MELL[?FORT] / [   ] 1786. Neil Campbell was a younger son of Archibald Campbell of Melfort, and brother to John Campbell of Melfort; he died in 1798.[3] He appears on record in 1789 as Captain Neil Campbell of Degnish,[4] a property which he probably held in tack from the Earl of Breadalbane, whose Nether Lorn estate included the whole of the Degnish peninsula.

782126   NM 71 SE   May 1970

317. The Manor House, Dungallon. This small late-Georgian mansion (Pl. 91C) stands beside the Gallanach road on the southern outskirts of Oban. It comprises an oblong two-storeyed main block with advanced flanking wings a single storey and an attic in height; minor additions, including an entrance-porch, have been made

at later dates. The external appearance of the building is extremely plain, the unharled masonry being composed of large blocks of dark-coloured rubble roughly brought to courses, with offset dressings of light brown sandstone. The roofs are of slate, that of the main block being gable-ended, while those of the wings are hipped. The interior has been considerably altered, but the timber staircase with cast-iron balustrade and mahogany handrail appears to be an original feature, as do some fragments of decorative plasterwork in the Gothic style. The outer doorway of the E wing is equipped with a heavy timber draw-bar. In the garden behind the house there are two barrel-vaulted structures, one formerly serving as a larder and the other as a boat-house; these appear to be of the same date as the house.

This house is said to have been built as the principal residence of the Duke of Argyll's Oban estate, and was evidently in existence by 1789.[5] Between 1826 and 1830 the building was utilized as a bank, but subsequently reverted to domestic occupation.[6]

853297   NM 82 NE   September 1969

318. Dunollie House. The house comprises four main ranges of buildings grouped round a small covered area. Apart from the E range, part of which may be as old as the 17th century, the earliest portion of the house appears to be the N range. This is said to have been erected in 1746,[7] and comprises a plain two-storeyed block of T-plan with symmetrically disposed window-openings and a gabled roof. The S and W ranges, which are no less plain in appearance (Pl. 91E), were added in about 1834–5.[8]

CARVED STONES ETC. Preserved within the entrance-porch there are a number of items from Gylen Castle, Kerrera, which are described under No. 291.

853315   NM 83 SE   July 1968

319. Old Schoolhouse, Ferlochan. This is a long single-storeyed building formerly incorporating a schoolroom and schoolmaster's house (Pl. 91D). It is strongly constructed of rubble masonry with granite dressings, and the roof, which may originally have been thatched, is slated. The chimney-stacks are oval in plan

---

[1] Papers by Archibald Smith, Nat. Lib. of Scot. MS 2128, fols. 59–60; *NSA*, vii (Argyll), 97.
[2] Glenorchy and Inishail Kirk Session Records preserved in the manse, entry dated 5 September 1805. An elevation, plan, specification and estimate for Glenorchy manse were supplied by John Simpson in 1802–3 (S.R.O., Breadalbane Collection, GD 112/9/3).
[3] Campbell, M O, *A Memorial History of the Campbells of Melfort* (1882), 19.
[4] *Clan Campbell*, iii, 168.
[5] The house is depicted in an engraving of Oban by John Beuge, after a drawing by Lieut. John Pierie, RN, published 1 July 1789.
[6] Shedden, *Lorn*, 226, 236.
[7] Information from Mr L Grahame MacDougall.
[8] Ibid.

and rise to a considerable height. The schoolmaster's house, which occupied the W end of the building, formerly comprised two main rooms flanking a central entrance-doorway, access to the loft having been obtained by means of a ladder.

The building appears to date from the first half of the 19th century, a period when a number of new school-houses are known to have been erected in the parish of Ardchattan.[1]

930407   NM 94 SW   April 1967

320. Gallanach. This house was erected for Dugald MacDougall of Gallanach in 1814–17 to a design of William Burn. Considerable alterations were carried out under the direction of Sir John J Burnet in about 1903,[2] the offices being remodelled and a substantial residential wing added to the rear of the main block.

The original house is a symmetrically-planned block of two main storeys above a sunk basement. The masonry is of rubble with dressed sandstone margins, but nearly all the facework is now concealed by a cement cladding. The principal, or NW, elevation (Pl. 92A, C) is a conventional castellated design incorporating a square-turreted centre-piece, circular angle-towers and battlemented parapet. In the original conception (Pl. 93A) the side-elevations were to have been treated in the same manner, but with bowed centre-pieces, but the omission of the entire rear portion of Burn's design converted the bows into terminal features and introduced an element of irregularity into the composition. The detail is very restrained. Most of the windows have four-centred arch-heads, those on the principal floor being surmounted by corbelled hood-moulds, a feature which is echoed in the entrance-doorway.

Burn's original plan (Pl. 93A) incorporated an oval central saloon, two storeys in height, flanked by two spacious open-well staircases, of which that to the SW was primarily a service-stair. At the front of the house the principal floor was to comprise a dining-room and drawing-room, flanking the entrance-hall, while at the rear there were to be four smaller rooms, including a library. The upper floor allowed for eight sizeable bedrooms, most of which had their own dressing-rooms, while the half-sunk basement was to lie beneath the rear portion of the house. With the reduction of the plan in execution, however, the entire rear portion of the design was omitted and the basement brought forward towards the front of the house. The two open-well staircases were eliminated and the saloon sacrificed to accommodate a single geometric cantilevered stair (Pl. 93C), which gains considerably in dramatic effect, if not in facility, from its restricted position. The stair retains its original cast-iron balustrade and mahogany hand-rail, but the bottom newel-post has been renewed. The drawing-room and dining-room were built as planned, although their functions are now reversed. Both rooms have shaped inner ends incorporating carved doors, and both retain their original marble chimney-pieces (Pl. 93B).

The addition of c. 1903 comprises a three-storeyed tower-block built out from the E corner of the original house. This incorporates a billiard-room on the ground-floor with bedrooms above, and although the tower somewhat overwhelms the earlier house in scale, the detail is sympathetic.

The lands of Gallanach were acquired in about the middle of the 17th century by John MacDougall, a member of the family of MacDougall of Rarey and Torsa, and the property has remained in the possession of his descendants until the present day.[3] A drawing of Gallanach,[4] dated 1800, shows the dwelling-house of that period as a plain 'laird's box' flanked by thatch-roofed offices (Pl. 92B), and it was presumably this building that Dugald MacDougall decided to replace when he succeeded to the estate in 1809. Plans and estimates for a house in the Gothic style (Pl. 94) were commissioned from James Gillespie Graham, architect, in 1812, but this scheme evidently fell through, for in April 1814 fresh designs were prepared by William Burn, who appears to have been a personal friend of the laird. The estimated cost of the house was £1260, but the actual sum expended by the contractor, Mr Spottiswoode, seems to have exceeded £1600, excluding the cost of marble (perhaps for chimney-pieces) supplied by the architect's father, Robert Burn, in 1815–16.[5] Plans for alterations and additions to the house were prepared by John Watherston & Son, the Edinburgh builders, in 1888,[6] but these were evidently superseded by Burnet's proposals of c. 1903.

827260   NM 82 NW   June 1971

321. Glenstockdale. This small laird's house, which appears to date from c. 1800, is situated on the SE side of Glen Stockdale, 2·6 km NE of Portnacroish, overlooking a level area which retains traces of rig-cultivation. It is now roofless and overgrown by vegetation, but the external walls are intact (Pl. 96B). The building comprises a basement and two storeys; it is oblong on plan and is constructed of random rubble, formerly harled. Massive slabs of schist are used as window- and fireplace-lintels.

The principal, or NW, façade, and also the SE façade, are symmetrical, having three openings at each level. The entrance-doorway in the centre of the NW façade has jambs of dressed schist, very slightly rounded at the arris; the threshold of this doorway is about 0·6 m above present ground-level, but the steps leading up to it have completely disappeared. At the NW end of the NE wall

[1] *Stat. Acct.*, vi (1793), 179; *NSA*, vii (Argyll), 501, 507.
[2] Information from Major J Williamson of Gallanach.
[3] *Burke's Landed Gentry* (1937 ed.), 1462.
[4] Preserved at Gallanach.
[5] MacDougall of Gallanach Papers, Gallanach, bundle 11, letter from James Gillespie to Dugald MacDougall, 19 August 1812; bundle 29, letter from William Burn to Dugald MacDougall, 6 January 1818; small bound book of plans entitled 'Plans of Gallanach' (unsigned and undated, but probably by Gillespie Graham, 1812) (Pl. 94); plans of basement, principal and upper floors, William Burn, Edinburgh, 1814.
[6] Copies in N.M.R.S.

a window which formerly lit the stair rises through two storeys. Chimney-stacks with roughly-formed copings surmount the gable-walls.

Although no internal partitions have survived except at basement-level, the general arrangement can be deduced from the position of fireplaces and of the stair-window; the latter indicates that the stair was situated in the N angle. The NE part of the basement was occupied by a room, evidently the kitchen, having a large fireplace in the NE wall. The remainder of the basement was divided by substantial stone walls into three small apartments of which that in the S angle contained a fireplace. On each of the upper floors there were three apartments, the principal one being in the E angle. The NW room at ground-floor level was provided with a mural cupboard; the adjoining room, probably a small closet, had an inserted fireplace in the SW angle. At first-floor level the two rooms in the SW part of the building were probably separated by a corridor lit by a small window, now blocked, in the SW wall.

Glenstockdale formed part of the estate of Kinlochlaich (cf. No. 327), which passed from the ownership of the Stewarts of Appin into that of the Campbells of Combie during the course of the 18th century. The house is traditionally said to have been a dower-house of the Stewart family,[1] but this must refer to a period earlier than the construction of the present building. The estate was sold in 1803 by David Campbell of Combie to John Campbell of Lochend, son of a former chamberlain of the Breadalbane estate in Argyll, who granted Glenstockdale to his mother, Margaret Campbell; the house may have been built at this date for her use. It was derelict by the end of the 19th century.[2]

946485   NM 94 NW   June 1970

322. Glenure. This mid-18th-century laird's house (Fig. 217, Pl. 95A) is situated on level ground at the SE side of Glen Creran, close to the junction of that glen with Glen Ure. The building comprises a principal block built by Colin Campbell of Glenure c. 1740 and furnished by him after his marriage in 1749, and a free-standing SW wing containing a kitchen, erected in 1751 to the designs of Duncan Campbell, a Stirling mason. Despite alterations during the present century, the house is the best-preserved example of its class to be described in the present volume; it derives additional interest from the tragic circumstances of the death of its builder, victim of the 'Appin Murder' in 1752 (cf. No. 213).

The original house of c. 1740 comprises two storeys and a garret and is rectangular on plan, measuring 14·5 m from NE to SW by 7·2 m transversely over walls which vary in thickness from 0·9 m to 1·1 m. The masonry is of rubble, harled and whitewashed, and the roof is of slate. The NW façade is of five bays, having at ground-floor level a central doorway which is now enclosed by a modern porch. At first-floor level the window-openings are considerably smaller than those of the ground-floor; at both levels the surrounds have been altered during the present century, but the original dimensions have been preserved. The NE gable-wall contains no original

openings, and the SE elevation is also extremely plain, the only original features being a window towards the centre at ground-floor level, two small windows at first-floor level, and a chimney-stack which rises from the wall-head at the centre of the façade. Remodelled chimney-stacks also surmount the NE and SW gables.

Within the porch the original entrance-doorway is concealed behind panelling of recent date; in the SW jamb, however, there is a deep wood-lined socket containing a draw-bar having a length of 1·5 m. As completed in 1751, the house contained on each floor two principal rooms separated by a central staircase having a smaller room behind it.[3] The lower flight of the wooden staircase (Pl. 95C) is of geometric type and was constructed by George Paterson, an Edinburgh wright; it is probable, however, that he was working to a design by the mason, Duncan Campbell, for sketch-plans of this stair appear on a drawing for the kitchen which is signed by the latter.[4] The existing cast-iron balustrade and wooden handrail are of 19th-century date, as are most of the fittings throughout the building, with the exception of some doors and the panelling of the first-floor apartments. The large room that occupies the SW division of the ground-floor was used throughout the 18th century as the dining-room, and the alcove in the SW wall beside the fireplace is a remodelling of an original feature. This apartment is now L-shaped; originally, however, the area SE of the staircase formed a separate small room, described in 1779 as the drawing-room. A modern fireplace occupies the position of an original one in the SE wall, and under the stair there is a built-in cupboard. The remainder of the ground-floor is occupied by a room which in 1749 was 'the laich bedroom'. It retains no original features except for a simply-moulded plaster cornice which is also employed in the dining-room; it is probable that these rooms were never panelled.

The original disposition of rooms at first-floor level was similar to that described, except that the SE portions of the two principal rooms were partitioned to form closets, and the 'Upper Mid Room' was reached by a short passage NE of the garret-stair. The latter apartment had its own fireplace, but this has now been blocked and the room has been altered, along with the NE and SE closets, to form a bathroom and a passage leading to the adjoining wing. Both of the principal rooms retain their original appearance almost unaltered, except for the renewal of their fireplaces (Pl. 95D). They are fitted throughout with large fielded panels of pine and moulded

---

[1] MacDonald, T D, *Appin, and its Neighbourhood* (n.d., c. 1910), 41.

[2] Ibid.; S.R.O., Abbreviated Register of Sasines (Argyll), 1781–1820, nos. 1474–5.

[3] These rooms are described and named in an inventory of furnishings taken in 1759 (S.R.O., Campbell of Barcaldine Collection, GD 170/404/4, Household Inventory, 8 May 1759), and a detailed list of dimensions compiled in 1779 (ibid., GD 170/381/8), as well as in the various building-accounts referred to *infra*.

[4] Ibid., GD 170/310; S.R.O., RHP 12331. It is interesting to note that a staircase of identical design, executed in stone, exists at Mains of Glins, Stirlingshire, which was built in 1743 (*Inventory of Stirlingshire*, ii, No. 334).

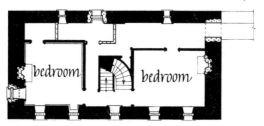

first floor

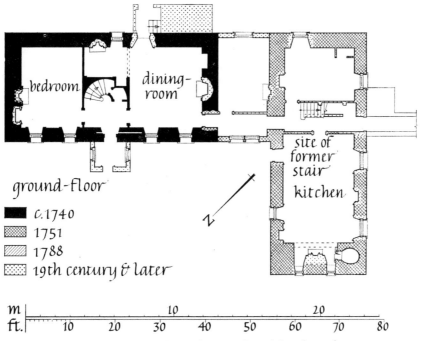

ground-floor

■ c.1740
▨ 1751
▨ 1788
▨ 19th century & later

Fig. 217. Glenure (No. 322); ground- and first-floor plans

wooden cornices, with substantial six-panelled doors having moulded architraves. In the NE wall of the NE room there is a window which has been formed within an original cupboard; the architrave and the lower part of 'the pres dor', mentioned in 1779, remain *in situ.* A straight stair leads to the garret, which was originally lit by two small windows in the gables; both of these are now blocked externally. The timber roof is of coupled rafters into which collar-beams are halved and pegged.

When the kitchen-wing was built in 1751, at right angles to the axis of the original house and 3·4 m to the SW of it, the two buildings were linked by a single-storeyed corridor having on the NW a three-bay colonnade which continued the line of the principal façade of the original house. The SE gable-wall of the kitchen was on the same line as the SE side-wall of the house; during the present century the intervening space has been filled by a wall and the existing NW wall heightened, to form a two-storeyed extension having steeply-pitched gables to NW and SE. The kitchen-block itself was designed as an independent house of conventional plan, having a straight central staircase with a large kitchen on the NW, and three bedrooms at first-floor level. A door in the NE wall opened from the linking colonnade into a transverse corridor SE of the staircase, behind which was an external door placed centrally in the five-bay SW façade. In 1788 the staircase was replaced by another, having two quarter-turns, at the SE side of the transverse corridor; at the same time, doors were formed from existing windows at the SW end of the transverse corridor and at the centre of the NE wall. The colonnade-entrance, however, was retained for use in bad weather. Further extensive alterations have been undertaken during the present century.[1]

The kitchen is a rectangular building of two storeys, somewhat lower and with less steeply-pitched gables

---

[1] An untitled plan which relates to the remodelling of the kitchen in 1788 is preserved in S.R.O., RHP 12343/9; accounts for this work are in S.R.O., Campbell of Barcaldine Collection, GD 170/444/5.

than the original house, measuring 16·0 m from NW to SE by 6·6 m transversely over all. Most of the window-openings in the SW elevation have been altered, and both façades have been affected by adjacent buildings of recent date. The NW portion of the ground-floor forms a single room which combines the original staircase-hall and kitchen, having in the NW gable-wall a massive kitchen-fireplace (Pl. 95B). The depressed segmental arch of this opening is drawn in elevation on the original mason's plan of 1751, which also demonstrates the former existence of a slop-sink penetrating the SW wall. Built into the SW side of the fireplace there is a large brick-lined oven. The stair that leads to the first floor occupies the position of that built in 1788, but rises in the reverse direction; the first floor has been completely remodelled during the present century, and the roof-space has never been utilized for domestic purposes.

The estate of Glenure was granted in feu by the 2nd Earl of Breadalbane to Patrick Campbell of Barcaldine in 1719, and was settled by the latter upon Colin Campbell, the eldest son of his second marriage, in 1738.[1] Accounts are extant for considerable building-operations in 1740 and 1741, when floors were built and windows constructed for the existing openings of the NW façade by William Thompson, joiner in Inveraray.[2] Glenure's marriage to Janet Mackay of Bighouse in May 1749 was the probable reason for a resumption of building-activity in that year. A mason, Robert Smeeton in Beath, Fife, was employed for a period of eight months, and George Paterson, wright in Edinburgh, prepared the ground-floor rooms for plastering while a quantity of Dutch fireplace-tiles was purchased in Edinburgh. A contract to build the kitchen-block was made with Duncan Campbell, mason in Stirling, by Glenure's brother Robert, a merchant of that town, in May 1750, but work did not begin until a new contract had been signed a year later. Duncan Campbell engaged four journeymen and four labourers, and was himself only required to attend for four days; as he explained when rendering his account, however, 'you kept me nine days drawing plans and giving directions'. Construction began in June 1751, and the building was roofed with slate in September of that year.[3]

Colin Campbell of Glenure was murdered in May 1752, and after the birth of his posthumous child, a daughter, the estate passed to his brother, Duncan, and subsequently, along with Barcaldine House (No. 313), to the latter's son, Alexander Campbell, who leased it to his brother, Captain Colin Campbell. Various alterations were carried out by this tenant in 1788, when he employed James Morrison, wright, to remodel the interior of the kitchen-block at an estimated cost of £51 sterling.[4] The Glenure estate was sold by Duncan Campbell of Barcaldine to A Mackenzie Grieve in 1818; twenty years later the buildings were 'falling into a dilapidated state'.[5] At about the beginning of the present century the house was restored for use as a shooting-lodge, a purpose which it still serves.

BARN. This building, which is probably of early 19th-century date, is situated 100 m N of the house. It comprises a two-storeyed rectangular structure of harled rubble-masonry, measuring 32·3 m from NW to SE by 6·7 m transversely over all, and contains at the SE end a stable and byre, while the NW portion is a dwelling-house. The central part of the building, which forms the barn proper, is entered by two large arched doorways in the side-walls; these are flanked by a series of tall round-arched openings, originally fitted with louvers for ventilation. The upper part of the walls contains a continuous series of tall slit-windows, splayed internally and divided horizontally by large slabs at the level of the loft-floors. An added stone forestair built against the SE gable gives access to the loft above the stable.

BRIDGE. A rubble-built bridge spans the gorge of the River Ure about 140 m SE of the house. This is evidently the 'Bridge of Jure' which was built for Duncan Campbell of Glenure by John Tainsh, mason in Innerpeffray (Perthshire), in July 1773.[6] The structure incorporates a single segmental arch having a span of 10·1 m and a height above water-level of 4·7 m; the width of the roadway is 4·2 m within parapets having a thickness of 0·4 m.

044480 (House), 044482 (Barn),
045480 (Bridge)   NN 04 NW   June 1970

323. Hayfield. This small ruined mansion, of late 18th-century date, stands on sloping ground about 250 m from the NW shore of Loch Awe. The building was gutted by fire about 1912 and is now roofless and overgrown by vegetation.

The house consists of a partly-sunk basement and two upper floors; it is rectangular on plan and measures 20·0 m by 8·3 m over walls 0·74 m thick. The principal elevation faces SE and has a frontispiece 7·3 m in width which projects 0·48 m from the main wall-face. The walls are built of local rubble, originally harled. At basement-level the quoins and window- and door-dressings are of pinkish sandstone. Polished schist is used for two horizontal bands at ground-floor level, and for the eaves-cornice. The remaining dressings consist of alternate blocks of sandstone and polished schist.

A curved forestair with iron handrails rises to the entrance-doorway; this has a moulded architrave and a pulvinated frieze and cornice, and is flanked by two tall narrow windows. Two horizontal bands run across the façade at threshold- and sill-level. At first-floor level there is a large semicircular three-light window, and the

---

[1] S.R.O., Breadalbane Collection, GD 112/2/40, Glenure Titles.
[2] S.R.O., Campbell of Barcaldine Collection, GD 170/310, Building-Papers. It is possible that an earlier house existed on the site, and was reconstructed at this time, for there are references to painting 'old windows in the backside of the house'; no earlier work is now identifiable.
[3] Ibid.; *TGSI*, xxii (1897–8), 102.
[4] S.R.O., Campbell of Barcaldine Collection, GD 170/444/5, Building-Papers; ibid., GD 170/1628/53, letters dated 19 February, 18 March 1788.
[5] *NSA*, vii (Argyll), 473.
[6] S.R.O., Campbell of Barcaldine Collection, GD 170/381/5, Building-Papers.

frontispiece is surmounted by a triangular pediment containing a circular window. The side bays of the SE façade contain one window in each storey. An early photograph[1] shows a hipped roof with two tall chimneys.

The interior is extremely ruinous. The central portion of the ground-floor contained an entrance-hall with a fireplace, divided by a cross-wall from the staircases, one of which led down to the service apartments in the basement and the other up to the first floor. On either side there was one large room on the ground-floor, and two rooms on the first floor. Each room had a fireplace, but none of the surrounds remain intact.

A single-storeyed block containing two apartments, one of which was a kitchen or bakehouse, is built against the centre of the NW wall and is contemporary with the house. In the early 19th century this block was extended and other ranges added to form a courtyard behind the N corner of the house; this is entered by an arched pend in the NW range. The NE range contained domestic accommodation, and its SE wall is linked to the house by a screen-wall. Probably at the same period, a large steading (Pl. 96E) was built 220 m NW of the house.

Hayfield was originally known as Tirevadich, and during the 16th and 17th centuries it was the principal seat of the MacArthurs 'of Inistrynich'.[2] In the last quarter of the 18th century it was owned by Allan MacDougall, W S, a member of the family of MacDougall of Gallanach. The mansion was built before 1785 when Thomas Newte described it as 'a well-built modern house called Hayfield'. He also states that it 'formerly belonged to a Mr. Campbell who had a castle upon one of the islands', apparently a reference to Campbell of Monzie, owner of Fraoch Eilean (No. 290). In 1803 the estate, which included the island of Inistrynich, was sold to William MacNeil, a Glasgow merchant, who owned it for about 30 years.[3] Thereafter the house was occupied by Sir Richard Grierson, 7th Bt. of Lag, and for some time it was known as 'Inistrynich House'. At that period the only building on the island of Inistrynich, 3 km to the E on the opposite bank of Loch Awe, was a small *cottage orné*, whose remains are now incorporated within later buildings. The name 'Hayfield' was revived about 1865, after the enlargement of Inistrynich House, and the mansion continued to be occupied until about 1912 when it was destroyed by fire.[4]

076235   NN 02 SE   September 1969

324. Inverawe House. Although this site appears to have been occupied by a laird's residence at least as early as the beginning of the 17th century,[5] the existing house is mainly of 19th- and 20th-century date. An examination of the ground-plan suggests that the nucleus of the present structure is a small oblong block of about the first half of the 18th century, and this conjecture gains some support from the manner in which the property is represented in Roy's Map of about 1750. The house was altered and extended in the Scottish Baronial style some time during the Victorian period, and was sub-

sequently remodelled by Sir Robert Lorimer in 1913–14,[6] and by L C Norton in 1953–4,[7] when it was considerably reduced in size.

CARVED STONE. Built into the W wall of the house there is an inserted stone panel bearing, within a moulded border, the inscription FEAR / GOD / OBEY / THE / KING and the date [?17]54. The inscription has evidently been partially re-cut, and repaired with cement, when the stone was inserted in its present position. The panel is said locally to have been brought from Fort William in about 1890, when the fort was partially destroyed by the formation of the railway.

This property was held by the Campbells of Inverawe from at least as early as the 16th century until 1765, when it was sold to Robert Campbell of Finab and Monzie. Inverawe subsequently passed by descent to Jane Campbell, wife of Alexander Campbell, 19th of Dunstaffnage, and in 1912 was purchased by James Currie.[8]

022315   NN 03 SW   May 1968

325. Kilbrandon House, Seil. This is a substantial two-storeyed rectangular block constructed of rubble with freestone dressings, the main front now being cement-rendered; the roof is gable-ended (Pl. 96A). The entrance-porch, the dormer-windows, and a number of the gable-windows appear to be additions. The plan is conventional, the principal rooms being disposed on each side of a central staircase-hall. The depth of the house is such that there is space for two main rooms on each side of the staircase on the ground- and first floors, and the main reception-room is on the first floor. The internal arrangements have been somewhat altered, but most of the rooms retain their original doors and window-shutters, and some have contemporary moulded fire-place-surrounds of timber. The stair is of timber with a mahogany hand-rail and a cast-iron newel-post. The house seems originally to have incorporated a single-storeyed service-wing centrally placed at the rear. This has subsequently been extended in size and raised to a height of two storeys, while another single-storeyed range has been added on the W.

Kilbrandon House was built in 1827 to serve as a

[1] In the possession of Mrs W Macleod, Hayfield Cottage.
[2] *Highland Papers*, iv, 53–4; Campbell, *Argyll Sasines*, ii, no. 260.
[3] S.R.O., Particular Register of Sasines (Argyll), RS 10/16, fol. 88; ibid., Abbreviated Register of Sasines (Argyll), 1781–1820, no. 276; *Stat. Acct.*, viii (1793), 354; Newte, *Tour*, 86.
[4] *NSA*, vii (Argyll), 86, 98; New Register House, Census of 1841, Glenorchy and Inishail Parish, book 6, p. 11; Name Book, No. 54, p. 53. A detailed report on Inistrynich House has been deposited in the N.M.R.S.
[5] Blaeu's *Atlas* (Lorn).
[6] Plans in the possession of the present proprietrix, Mrs G P Campbell-Preston.
[7] Ibid.
[8] Campbell, I M, *Notes on the Campbells of Inverawe* (1951), 39.

manse for the united parish of Kilbrandon and Kilchattan, but has recently passed into private ownership.[1]

766154   NM 71 NE   May 1970

326. Kilmore House. This building (Fig. 218, Pl. 96c, D) is pleasantly situated overlooking water-meadows on the E bank of the River Nell, about 750 m NW of the former parish-church of Kilmore (No. 264). It was built in 1828 as the manse of the united parish of Kilmore and Kilbride, being designed and constructed by John Thom, an Oban builder.[2] Since 1965 the house has been occupied as a private dwelling.

The house, which comprises a partly-sunk basement and two storeys, is rectangular on plan, measuring 17·5 m from NNW to SSE by 8·7 m transversely over all. The central portion of the principal, or E, façade is advanced, while the corresponding portion of the W façade projects to form a segmental bay. The masonry is of coursed rubble, with freestone margins and quoins, and the roof is hipped and slated.

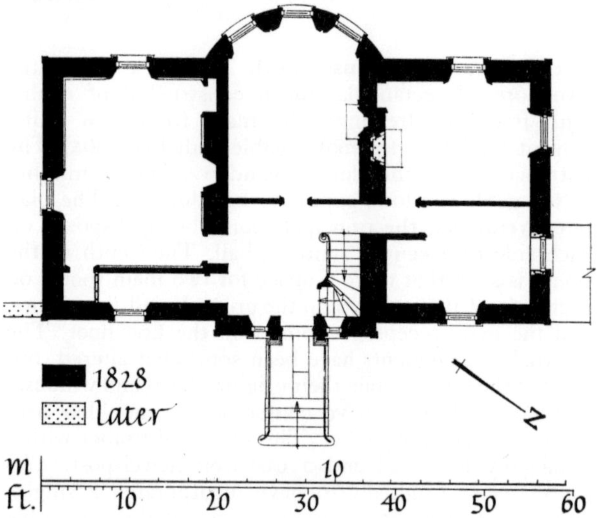

■ 1828
▨ later

m |_____ 10 _____|
ft. |___ 10 ___ 20 ___ 30 ___ 40 ___ 50 ___ 60

Fig. 218. Kilmore House (No. 326); ground-floor plan

The entrance-doorway, in the advanced portion of the E wall, is reached by a forestair. It is framed within pilasters whose moulded capitals support a full entablature, and is flanked by narrow windows. A plain ashlar eaves-course runs round the whole building, and is carried across the frontispiece to define the base of a triangular pediment, within which there is a plain shield. The E elevation is flanked by low crenellated screenwalls which appear to be of mid-19th-century date. The large bay centrally placed in the W façade has three window-openings at each level, but at basement- and first-floor levels the flanking openings are mock windows with painted glazing-bars.

The internal plan is that of a typical small late-Georgian mansion, being divided into three portions by thick walls containing fireplaces. At ground-floor level the central division is occupied by the stair-hall and a room which projects into the rounded bay, while the S division contains a large room, probably the original parlour, and a narrow closet, now sub-divided. These apartments retain wooden fireplace-surrounds of early 19th-century type, and the house is furnished throughout with panelled doors and shutters, while many of the doors, cupboards and windows have moulded architraves. The N division of the ground-floor is occupied by two rooms; that in the NE angle is lit by a modern window in the N wall which replaces an original mock window. A stone stair, entered by a door on the N side of the entrance-hall, gives access to the basement, where there is an axial passage flanked by small rooms on the E, and on the W by larger rooms, including a laundry and the original kitchen.

A U-shaped wooden staircase with a moulded wooden hand-rail rises against the N wall of the entrance-hall to give access to the first-floor landing. The stair-well and landing occupy an unusually large proportion of the central division, the remainder of which forms a single round-ended room. There are two bedrooms in each of the flanking divisions. These rooms have no individual features of particular interest.

879252   NM 82 NE   June 1970

327. Kinlochlaich. This house (Pl. 97A, B) comprises a small plain oblong building of the 18th century to which an extensive addition in the Gothic style was made in about 1820. The original house, which now forms a SE kitchen-wing, measures about 12·2 m by 7·0 m over all and comprises two main storeys; the roof is gable-ended. The plan was probably conventional, comprising two main rooms on each floor flanking a central entrance-lobby and staircase. The three-window SW front remains fairly intact but the entrance itself has been converted into a window.

The late Georgian addition, which now constitutes the principal residence, comprises two main storeys and a part basement. The masonry, like that of the original house, is of harled rubble, but the 19th-century work incorporates sandstone dressings. The plan comprises an entrance-vestibule and principal staircase, abutting the NW gable-wall of the old house, together with short projecting wings to the NW and NE, of which the former accommodates the dining-room and the latter the drawing-room. The exterior displays a considerable assortment of simple Gothic detail, including crenellated angle-turrets and diagonal stepped buttresses surmounted by pyramidal finials. Most of the windows comprise twin pointed lights in timber frames set within square-headed surrounds, but the surrounds of the principal windows have pointed arch-heads enriched with hood-moulds. The principal entrance, however, is semicircular-headed, the surround being wrought with a continuous triple roll-moulding beneath a corbelled hood-mould of similar character. The timber staircase,

---

[1] *NSA*, vii (Argyll), 79.
[2] Ibid., 529; Lorn Presbytery Minutes, vi (1829–39), pp. 11–13.

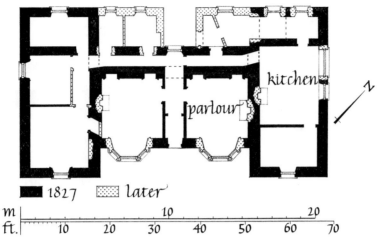

Fig. 219. Kulmani, Duror (No. 328); ground-floor plan

which may replace an earlier one of stone, is of scale-and-platt type with cast-iron balusters and a mahogany hand-rail. The principal rooms have a Gothic flavour, best illustrated by the panelled doors and shutters, and the mock rib-vault of the vestibule (Pl. 97C, D). The drawing-room ceiling has a radial centre-piece (Pl. 97E), and both this room and the dining-room have enriched cornices of simple repetitive patterns.

The house appears to have been erected shortly before 1820 by John Campbell of Lochend, whose father had purchased Kinlochlaich and re-named it Lochend after the Perthshire property from which the family took their designation.[1]

939466   NM 94 NW   June 1971

328. Kulmani, Duror. This building, now occupied as a private residence, was one of a group of Highland manses built at government expense to standard designs. It was completed in 1827,[2] and stands 60 m SE of the church (No. 244) that was built at the same time.

The existing structure (Pl. 97G) is H-shaped on plan (Fig. 219) and conforms closely to Telford's published design for 'a manse of one story',[3] the principal variation being that the NW portion of the SW wing, shown by Telford as a byre, projects no further than the corresponding part of the NE wing. Numerous minor alterations have taken place, including the remodelling of all fireplaces and the insertion of two bay-windows in the central division of the principal, or SE, façade. The re-entrant angles between the rear parts of the wings and the central block have been infilled to provide additional accommodation, that to the NE forming part of a kitchen which replaces the original one, now the sitting-room, in the NE wing. Despite these alterations, the building, which has harled and whitewashed walls and slated roofs neatly trimmed with lead ridging, retains much of its original character.

994552   NM 95 NE   July 1971

329. Lerags House. This small late-Georgian mansion-house (Pl. 97F) is situated 1·8 km SW of Kilbride, overlooking an inlet of Loch Feochan. The original building, which appears to date from the first quarter of the 19th century, was probably built by Alexander Campbell of Lerags, who succeeded his father, Archibald Campbell, and was in possession of the estate in 1821.[4] It comprises a rectangular two-storeyed block measuring 13·4 m from N to S by 8·2 m transversely over all, which has received two successive extensions towards the E during the 19th century. A further Victorian addition at the S end of the W front was demolished in 1960, thus restoring the original appearance of the principal façade, which is of three bays with a centrally-placed doorway. The slated roof with sprocketed eaves is of late 19th-century date, being similar to that of the E extension.

Although the interior has undergone considerable alteration, it retains the original arrangement at ground-floor level of one principal room on each side of a central wooden stair. The first floor was divided into three rooms.

843245   NM 82 SW   April 1970

330. Lochnell House. Lochnell House (Pls. 98A, B, 99A) stands in wooded policies near the head of Ardmucknish Bay, some 10 km NE of Oban. The existing building incorporates work of four main periods ranging in date

[1] Campbell, M O, *A Memorial History of the Campbells of Melfort* (1882), 57–9; S.R.O., Abbreviated Register of Sasines (Argyll), 1781–1820, nos. 1474–5, 2905, 3175. In 1822 it was reported that the house had been erected 'within these few years' (*Edinburgh Evening Courant*, 14 September 1822).
[2] '6th Report of Commissioners for Building Churches in the Highlands of Scotland', 24, in *Parliamentary Papers, 1831*, ix.
[3] Telford, *Atlas*, pl. 59.
[4] S.R.O., Abbreviated Register of Sasines (Argyll), 1821–30, no. 81.

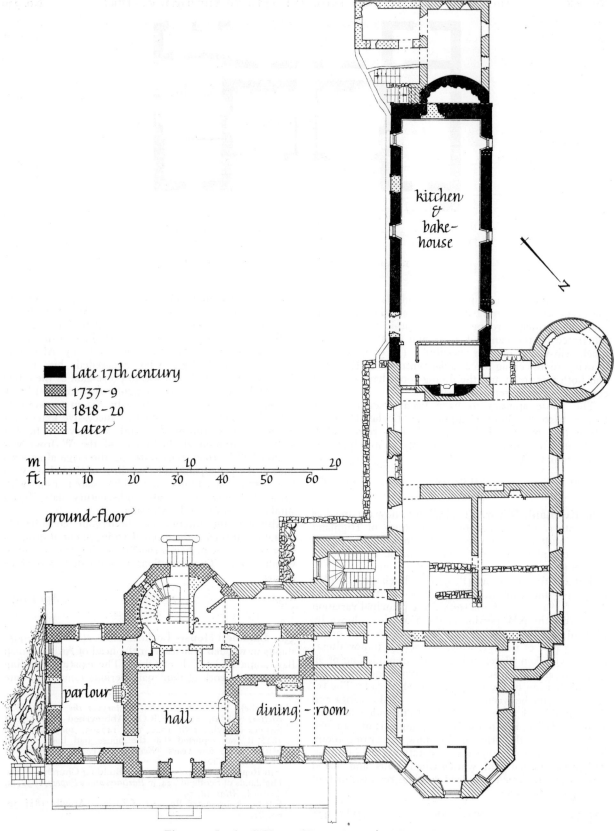

late 17th century
1737-9
1818-20
later

m
ft.   10   20   30   40   50   60

10   20

ground-floor

kitchen
&
bake-
house

N

parlour

hall

dining-room

Fig. 220. Lochnell House (No. 330); ground-floor plan

from about the end of the 17th century to about the end of the 19th century. The late 17th-century house is now represented only by a service-wing, which forms the SW range of the present building (Fig. 220), but a main block of contemporary, or of earlier, date must formerly have occupied the NE portion of the site. In about 1737–9 the house was altered and enlarged by the erection of a new dwelling-house to the SE of this earlier main block. Between about 1818 and 1820 the house was again remodelled, the early NE main block being swept away and its site utilized for the erection of a substantial mansion in the castellated style, to which the SW service-wing and the early Georgian dwelling-house formed flanking appendages. At the same time a court of offices, also in the castellated style, was constructed on the NW side of the house, and the SW service-wing was extended in length. In 1853 the greater part of the house was gutted by fire, and the building appears to have remained unoccupied until towards the end of the century, when the early Georgian dwelling-house and the SW service-wing were restored. Of the late Georgian mansion, however, only the NE portion was reoccupied, the remainder being patched up and allowed to remain as a roofless shell.

THE SOUTH-WEST SERVICE-WING. This comprises two main storeys and a basement (Pl. 99A). The masonry is of random rubble with offset margins of dressed sandstone having slightly rounded arrises, and the wall-surfaces appear to have been harled. The SE wall rises to an ovolo-moulded eaves-cornice, and the gables are crow-stepped and have moulded skewputs. The chimney-stack, which is panelled, is surmounted by a moulded coping. The S corner of the building incorporates a bi-faceted sundial situated a little below the cornice (Pl. 99C). At the junction of the NW wall of the wing with the SW wall of the late Georgian mansion there is a stone bearing the inscription: THIS / STONE / MOV[ED] / & / REPLACED / AUG(US)T 21 / 1818. The stone in question probably formed one of the N quoins of the wing.

The lowest storey of the range incorporates a series of four intercommunicating barrel-vaulted cellars entered from doorways in the NE and SW gable-walls. Each cellar is lit by means of a single window in the NW wall. The upper two storeys now comprise a single lofty apartment having a gallery at the NE end, but this arrangement was probably not introduced before the end of the 19th century. The ground-floor seems originally to have served as a kitchen and bake-house, as evidenced by the survival of two sink-outlets in the NW wall, and by the existence of what appears to be the remains of a large bake-oven projecting beyond the lower portion of the SW gable-wall. This last is now inaccessible, but must formerly have opened off the fireplace of which some traces can be seen in the gable-wall. The original entrance-doorway to the kitchen in the SE wall is now blocked, access being obtained through a former window-opening. The original arrangement of the first-floor rooms is uncertain. The roofless outbuilding that extends south-westwards from the SW

gable-wall of the service-wing appears to be largely of late Georgian date, but it incorporates re-used stone dressings of 17th-century character, probably quarried from buildings demolished during the alterations of 1818–20.

THE EARLY GEORGIAN DWELLING-HOUSE. This building was probably erected for the purpose of providing a more conveniently disposed series of living-rooms than was available within the earlier NE main block. Although evidently designed to be incorporated within an existing complex of buildings, however, the house appears to have been largely self-contained, and the plan conforms closely to that found in many small mansion-houses of the period. As first constructed (Fig. 221), the building comprised an oblong hip-roofed block of three main storeys measuring about 18·3 m from NW to SE by 9·1 m transversely over walls some 1·0 m in thickness, and having a semi-octagonal staircase-bay projecting from the centre of the rear elevation. The masonry is of rubble, now cement-rendered but no doubt originally harled, with rusticated quoins and dressings of light grey sandstone. Most of the doorway- and window-surrounds of the NE front seem to have been removed during the late 19th-century restoration, but care has been taken to copy the original mouldings.

The central portion of the principal, or NE, façade is advanced and rises to a triangular pediment surmounted by elaborately carved urn-finials. The tympanum contains a much-weathered relief-carving evidently representing the full heraldic achievement of the Campbells of Lochnell. The shield bears quarterly: 1st and 4th, gyronny of eight, for Campbell; 2nd, a boar's head [erased] for Gordon; 3rd, a galley sail furled, for Lorn. The dexter supporter is a lion rampant [guardant] and the sinister a swan, while for crest there is a dexter hand holding a lance. The ground- and second-floor windows in this portion of the façade have lug-moulded surrounds, those on the first floor being semicircular-headed with pronounced keystones. These latter windows are traversed at springing-level by a continuous moulded string-course, and above the level of the string the rusticated quoins give way to panelled pilasters. The main entrance-doorway, which is centrally placed at ground-floor level, is surmounted by a segmental pediment containing an inscribed marble tympanum. This incorporates a central monogram evidently comprising the initials D C and M C, flanked by the date 1737 in Roman numerals, and commemorating the erection of the house in that year by Sir Duncan Campbell, 7th of Lochnell, and his second wife, Margaret, daughter of Daniel Campbell of Shawfield. On each side of the central panel there is carved a crest and motto, the dexter one, for Campbell of Lochnell, comprising a dexter hand holding a lance and surmounted by a label bearing the inscription ARMA PARATA FERO ('I carry my arms at the ready'), and the sinister one, for Campbell of Shawfield, a griffin erect, holding the sun between his forepaws, and surmounted by a label bearing the inscription FIDUS AMICIS ('Loyal to my friends'). It is uncertain whether this tympanum is original, or whether it was

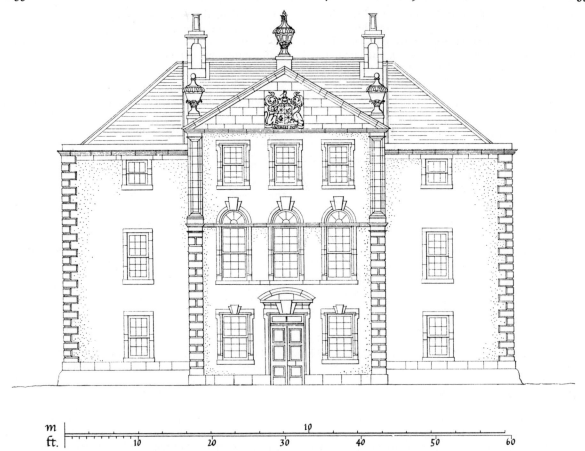

Fig. 221. Lochnell House (No. 330); principal elevation of early Georgian house (partially reconstructed)

inserted during the late Victorian restoration in order to preserve information in danger of being lost through the weathering of carving in the main pediment. The flanking portions of the façade, of which only the SE bay now survives, were treated very simply, the windows having plain round-arrised surrounds, and the walls rising directly to a moulded eaves-cornice.

The main feature of the rear elevation (Pl. 99A) is the semi-octagonal staircase-bay, which incorporates two main ranges of plain rectangular windows together with a pair of small segmental-headed keystoned windows at ground-floor level. The doorway that now occupies a central position at this level is clearly an insertion and the original arrangement is uncertain. Between first- and second-floor levels there is a series of sunk circular panels probably designed to house busts. Certain minor alterations to the fenestration of the bay seem to have been made during the late 19th-century restoration.

The interior of the early Georgian house has been remodelled on at least two occasions and few original features remain. The plan appears to have been of simple tripartite form, with the chimney-flues housed in the two internal partition-walls (Fig. 220). Each of the three divisions of the main block probably contained a single large room at each level, those on the ground-floor

comprising a central hall, a parlour and a dining-room. The dining-room was remodelled and enlarged in 1818–20, while the existing marble chimney-piece of mid-18th-century date is said to have been brought from Gwrych Castle, Denbighshire, in more recent times.[1] To the rear of the dining-room there is a small barrel-vaulted apartment, which may have served as a strongroom. The arrangement at first-floor level is similar, even to the provision of a barrel-vaulted chamber situated directly above the one on the ground-floor. The room occupying the central division of the house at this level has an elaborate Victorian ceiling. The existing geometric staircase with pine balustrade is probably of Victorian date, but may incorporate some of the stone treads of an earlier stair. Pococke's description of the house indicates that the bay originally contained both the principal staircase and a service-stair.[2]

THE LATE GEORGIAN MANSION. This is a substantial four-storeyed block having its principal façade facing NW. Here the main components are asymmetrically grouped, and comprise circular and octagonal angle-

[1] Information from the present proprietor, The Rt Hon. the Earl of Dundonald.
[2] Pococke, *Tours*, 72.

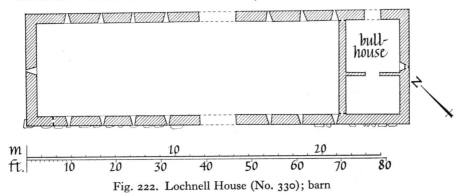

Fig. 222. Lochnell House (No. 330); barn

towers flanking a central bay which contains three main ranges of window-openings of diverse size and form. The principal window (Pl. 99B) has a balcony and is segmental-arched beneath a square-headed hood-mould; the date 1820 is inserted within the spandrels. The walls rise to corbelled and crenellated parapets and the W angle-tower incorporates a number of boldly proportioned crosslet arrow-loops (Pl. 99D). Apart from these features, however, the mouldings are for the most part classical in character, those on the NE front, in particular, evidently being designed to harmonize with the adjacent early Georgian house. The masonry is of exposed random rubble with light brown sandstone dressings, except in the basement-storey, where the dressings are mostly of granite. The basement is sunk on the SE side, while to the NW it is masked by the court of offices. The front elevation of the court of offices, which thus constitutes a forescreen to the principal façade of the mansion, comprises an entrance-gateway and battlemented screen-wall flanked by low octagonal corner-towers.

Only the NE portion of the mansion is now roofed, and of the series of spacious apartments that formerly occupied the first floor only the N drawing-room (Pl. 99E) remains in occupation. This incorporates a handsome marble chimney-piece in the Adam manner decorated with medallion figurines.[1]

STABLE-COURT AND BARN. The stable-court to the E of the house, now somewhat remodelled, appears to belong to about the second quarter of the 19th century, but the adjacent barn (Pl. 98c) may be a little older. This is a substantially-built structure measuring 25·9 m by 7·5 m over all, and having its walls pierced by a regularly disposed series of ventilation-slits (Fig. 222); the existing roof is modern. One end of the building is partitioned off to form a bull-house.

ICE-HOUSE. About 50 m to the S of the house there is a subterranean ice-house of 18th- or early 19th-century date. This comprises a vaulted egg-shaped chamber having a maximum diameter of about 3·2 m and a height of at least 5·3 m; the lower part of the chamber is filled with debris. The approach is by means of an L-shaped passage formerly provided with three separate doorways.

LADY MARGARET'S TOWER. This outlook-tower is prominently situated upon the summit of a rock ridge about 800 m SW of the house, from which position it commands a magnificent prospect of Loch Linnhe, Loch Etive and the island of Mull. The structure is executed in the castellated style and comprises a small square tower having angle-turrets which oversail on semicircular-headed arches to carry a corbelled and crenellated parapet (Fig. 223). Within there is a turnpike-stair of stone, lit by lunettes situated beneath the oversailing arches, and rising to a square cap-house having a domed roof and corbelled parapet. The building, which is constructed of random rubble without dressings, measures about 4·9 m square at base and rises to a height of about 12 m. The entrance-doorway on the NW side is surmounted by a corbelled drip-course, above which there is a stone panel framed within classical half-columns and an entablature, and inscribed: ERECTED / BY LADY CAMPBELL / ANNO 1754. Lady (Margaret) Campbell was the second wife of Sir Duncan Campbell, 7th of Lochnell (cf. p. 280). The tower was visited by Bishop Pococke during his tour of Scotland in 1760.[2]

The family most closely associated with the history of this house is that of Campbell of Lochnell, whose founder John, second son of Colin, 3rd Earl of Argyll, is on record as laird of Lochnell in 1536. This branch of the family took their title from that portion of their estates situated around Loch Nell, in the parish of Kilmore and Kilbride, but subsequently transferred the name to their Benderloch property of Ardmucknish, which became their principal residence. Pont's map[3] indicates the existence of a residence in this locality at about the beginning of the 17th century, but the oldest portion of the present structure can probably be ascribed to Alexander Campbell, 6th of Lochnell, who succeeded to the property in about 1671 and who died in 1713. His son Sir Duncan Campbell, 7th of Lochnell, built the early Georgian house. Little is known about the circumstances of its erection, but it would appear that in October 1738 building-operations at Lochnell were

---

[1] This chimney-piece, like the one in the dining-room, was formerly at Gwrych Castle, Denbighshire.
[2] Pococke, *Tours*, 71.
[3] Blaeu's *Atlas* (Lorn).

U

N W *elevation*

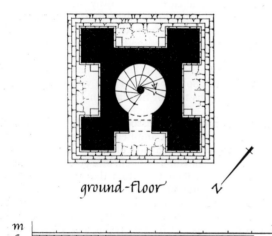

ground-floor

Fig. 223. Lochnell House (No. 330); Lady Margaret's Tower

being supervised by John Johnstone, a close associate of the architect John Baxter, elder.[1] It seems possible, therefore, that Baxter played some part in the design of Lochnell. The late Georgian mansion was erected by Lt. Gen. Duncan Campbell, 8th of Lochnell, at a cost of more than £15,000,[2] the architect on this occasion probably having been Archibald Elliot.[3] The late 19th-century restoration of the house, following the fire of 1853,[4] was probably carried out by Archibald Campbell,

13th of Lochnell, whose successor Archibald, 14th of Lochnell, sold the property to the 12th Earl of Dundonald in 1918.[5]

886389 (House)   NM 83 NE   June 1968
882383 (Tower)

331. Muckairn Manse, Taynuilt. This is a good example of the two-storeyed type of manse designed by Thomas Telford for the Parliamentary Commission set up in 1824 to provide a number of new churches and manses in the Highlands (cf. also No. 244). The manse seems to have been built at the same time as the adjacent church (No. 269), that is to say in 1829, the total cost being £724 5s 6d.[6] It comprises a gable-ended main block of T-plan having a porch on each side and lean-to offices at the rear (Pl. 100E). The masonry is of well-coursed rubble blocks of dressed granite and the roof is slated. The S front contains two rows of regularly-spaced windows, the principal entrance-doorway being contained within the E porch. The interior has been somewhat altered, but in the original arrangement the ground-floor probably contained a kitchen, parlour and small study, while three bedrooms occupied the first floor. The entrance-vestibule opens into a corridor at the rear of the main block from which access is obtained to the principal apartments and to the staircase-projection. There was originally no direct access from the main body of the house to the offices at the rear, which then included a stable, byre, coal-house and larder.

005309   NN 03 SW   August 1970

332. Old Schoolhouse, North Ledaig. This is a plain two-storeyed structure with a hipped roof and gable-chimneys. Although the building is basically oblong on plan, the main front projects as a semi-hexagonal bay (Pl. 100D). The masonry is of harled rubble without free-stone dressings. Single-storeyed outshots adjoin each gable-wall, while at the rear of the building there is a central staircase-wing, evidently an addition. The interior has been remodelled for domestic use, but in the original arrangement the whole of the ground-floor area is said to have been occupied as a schoolroom, while the first floor, which was approached by means of a stone forestair at the rear, served as the schoolmaster's residence.

[1] S.R.O., Clerk of Penicuik Collection, GD 18/5009. Johnstone, a wright by trade, lived on Sir John Clerk's estate at Penicuik, and is known to have worked with Baxter at Mavisbank, Midlothian; Haddo, Aberdeenshire; and Galloway House, Wigtownshire. Cf. Simpson, Ann M, 'The Architectural Work of the Baxter family in Scotland 1722–98', p. 22 (unpublished Edinburgh University thesis, 1971, copy in N.M.R.S.).
[2] *NSA*, vii (Argyll), 501.
[3] Elliot's will (S.R.O., Commissariot of Edinburgh, 28 June 1825) indicates a debt of £113 by 'General Campbell'.
[4] Name Book, No. 1, p. 11.
[5] *Burke's Landed Gentry* (1939 ed.), 337–8.
[6] Telford, *Life*, 490–1; Telford, *Atlas*, pl. 59; *NSA*, vii (Argyll), 521.

The building is probably of early 19th-century date, being one of the three public schools that served the parish of Ardchattan at this period (cf. also No. 319).[1]

905373   NM 93 NW   June 1967

333. Rarey. This is a tacksman's house of the second quarter of the 18th century which has subsequently been extended and remodelled (Pl. 100A). The original house appears to have been single-storeyed, comprising a simple oblong block with a central entrance-doorway behind which a staircase rose to give access to a low attic. The masonry is of harled rubble and the roof is of slate. The interior now presents no features of interest. Above the original entrance-doorway, which is now blocked, there is a slate panel bearing the initials I C dividing the date 1743. Above the inscription there is a wreath, a boar's head couped for crest, and the motto FOLLOW ME. The date evidently commemorates the erection of the oldest portion of the house.

Prior to the middle of the 17th century Rarey was in the possession of the MacDougalls, who had a residence in the immediate vicinity of the present house (cf. No. 297). Following the acquisition of the Nether Lorn estate by the Campbell Earls of Breadalbane at the end of the 17th century, however, Rarey seems to have been farmed by tacksmen. The initials on the carved panel described above are probably those of John Campbell, younger, of Barcaldine, whose name appears in a rental of the property dated 1730,[2] and who may be the same person as the John Campbell, tacksman of Rarey in Lorn, who is on record in 1777.[3]

830206   NM 82 SW   April 1970

334. Taynuilt Hotel. This is a plain two-storeyed building of harled rubble fronting the main Dalmally–Oban road (A85), and incorporating outbuildings and offices at the rear. The oldest part of the structure appears to be the central portion of the main block which, with its small widely-spaced windows and projecting chimney-stack at the back, may be ascribed to about the middle of the 18th century. Some of the offices may also be of 18th-century date, while the Tuscan entrance-porch was probably erected following the extension of the main block eastwards sometime during the early 19th century. Further additions have been made in more recent years. The interior has been remodelled on several occasions and now presents no features of special interest.

003310   NN 03 SW   May 1968

335. Tigh Mór, Stronmilchan (Site). The only visible remains are the footings of two sub-rectangular buildings, one of which measures about 15·0 m in length and 7·5 m in width over all, and the other about 8·0 m in length and 5·5 m in width over all. There is little exposed stonework and it is possible that both buildings were constructed mainly of turf.

This is said to have been a residence of the MacGregors of Glen Strae (cf. Nos. 283 and 314).[4]

154288   NN 12 NW   September 1967

336. Upper Sonachan House. This is a small laird's or tacksman's house of about the middle of the 18th century which has subsequently been remodelled and enlarged. The original house appears to have been a plain two-storeyed block having a central staircase with a single main room on each side on both floors. The masonry is of harled rubble and the roof is gabled and slated. The front elevation (Pl. 100B) remains largely intact, although the ground-floor windows have been enlarged and a porch added; the interior has been extensively remodelled. The flanking wings of the house are probably of early 19th-century date, but have recently been partially reconstructed. The E wing incorporates a panel with an heraldic crest figuring a swan (Pl. 100C), which formed part of the armorial achievement of the Campbells of Sonachan (cf. No. 274).

Upper Sonachan appears to have belonged to the Sonachan estate until 1877, when the trustees of Robert Campbell of Sonachan disponed it to the 8th Duke of Argyll.[5]

061210   NN 02 SE   May 1968

FARMS, TOWNSHIPS AND SHIELINGS

337. Shielings, Airidh nan Sileag. This site (Fig. 224) lies in the upper reaches of Glen Strae at a height of about 150 m OD. The huts stand on rising ground above the right bank of the River Strae, the site being traversed by a small burn, known as Allt Airidh nan Sileag, which today comprises two separate but adjacent water-courses. This burn is evidently subject to severe flooding, and it is clear that a number of huts have been washed away or buried beneath debris during the spates of the past century or so.

All the buildings are of dry-stone construction. They vary a good deal in size and shape, and likewise in their degree of preservation, but the most complete examples stand to a height of rather more than 1·0 m. The huts can be classified into two main groups, of which the first comprises structures of sub-rectangular plan having an average overall size of 5·8 m by 3·8 m, while the second comprises structures of sub-circular plan having an average overall diameter of 4·5 m. The thickness of the

---

[1] *NSA*, vii (Argyll), 507.
[2] S.R.O., Breadalbane Collection, GD 112/9/1, fol. 2.
[3] *Clan Campbell*, iii, 141.
[4] *NSA*, vii (Argyll), 97.
[5] Documents in the possession of the present proprietor, Sir Charles M'Grigor, Bt.

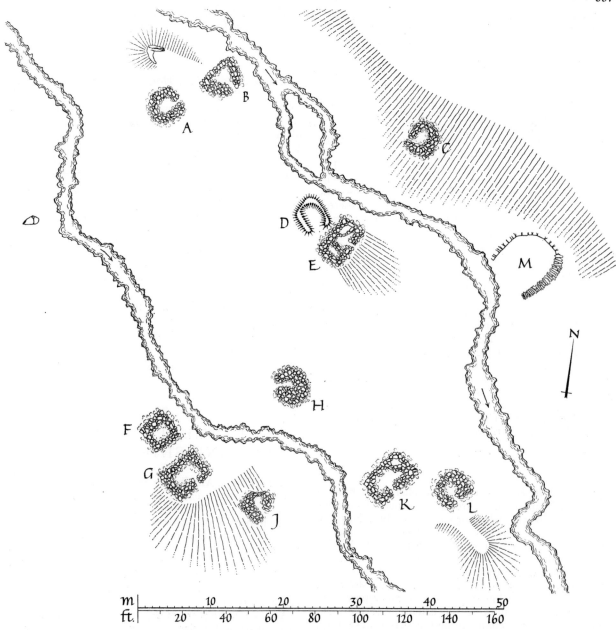

Fig. 224. Shielings, Airidh nan Sileag (No. 337); plan

walls varies from 1·5 m to 0·6 m. Most of the huts have their doorways on the downhill, or SE, side, where they are sheltered to some extent from the prevailing wind, and some are partly built into the slope of the hill. One of the larger huts (E) appears to have contained two apartments, while two (E and K) incorporate modern ewe-pens. In addition to the eleven huts identified within the area covered by the site-plan (Fig. 224), a number of outlying examples of similar character were also observed. Towards the E extremity of the site there are the remains of an enclosure (M), part of which has been

washed away by the adjacent burn. The enclosure appears to have been approximately circular on plan, with an internal diameter of about 6·7 m.

This is probably the 'small shealing at the head of the glen' (Glen Strae), pertaining to the tenants of Edendonich, that is on record in 1790.[1]

191353   NN 13 NE   July 1971

[1] S.R.O., Breadalbane Collection, GD 112/48, bundle labelled 'other bridges', letter from John Campbell to 4th Earl of Breadalbane, 18 April 1790.

338. Cruck-framed Byre, Bonawe. This building stands directly behind the E end of the row of workers' dwellings described on p. 291, and was formerly utilized as a byre and storehouse. It is constructed of local rubble masonry laid in mud mortar and is roughly oblong on plan, measuring about 7·3 m from N to S by 4·6 m transversely over walls some 0·6 m in thickness (Fig. 225). The building contains two pairs of crucks,

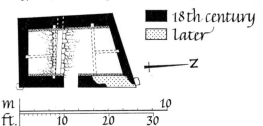

■ 18th century

░ later

⊢ Z

Fig. 225. Cruck-framed byre, Bonawe (No. 338); plan

with additional blades at the centre of each end-wall to receive a hipped roof. The crucks are scarf-jointed and pegged at wall-head level, but the upper portions of the blades were evidently sawn off when the existing covering of corrugated iron was substituted for the original thatch.

The building is probably of 18th- or early 19th-century date.

010317   NN 03 SW   April 1972

339. Cruck-framed Building, Cadderlie. This is the best preserved of a small group of buildings situated on level ground about 220 m from the W shore of Loch Etive and 5 km NE of Bonawe Quarries. It comprises a dwelling-house and byre, each originally of five bays divided by cruck-trusses, and is probably of late 18th- or early 19th-century date. The byre, which is now roofless, remains substantially unaltered, although the wall-head has been raised by 0·53 m at a recent period. The dwelling-house was remodelled in about the middle of the 19th century, and further blocking of windows took place when it subsequently passed out of domestic use.

The building measures 22·5 m by 5·3 m over walls

0·7 m in thickness; the byre and dwelling are of equal size (Fig. 226). The long axis runs from ESE to WNW but will be described as if from E to W. A massive boulder-plinth supports walls of lime-mortared granite rubble which have been harled and whitewashed. In both parts of the building the cruck-couples have been sawn off below wall-head level; the surviving stumps are scarf-jointed with wooden pegs. The byre, which occupies the W portion of the structure, is entered by a door in the N wall; there are no other openings. A stone-built drain passes below the wall to the E of the door and can be traced for about 6 m, leading into lower ground to the N of the dwelling.

In the original arrangement, the dwelling-house had opposed doorways in the N and S walls about 7·6 m from the E wall. There is no evidence of window-openings; if these existed, they must have been in the central bay where there are later openings. The substantial wall separating byre from dwelling, although not bonded into the side-walls, is probably an original feature; the consistent spacing of the cruck-couples suggests this, and the wall certainly antedates the comprehensive remodelling that turned this simple dwelling into an improved cottage of normal 19th-century type. In its altered form the house had a central doorway in the S wall, flanked by windows; in the N wall there is an additional opening which preserves its small sash-window. Although no evidence of internal partitions survives, there were evidently two principal rooms, each having an inserted fireplace in the end-wall. The new plan required a different system of bays, and the cruck-couples were removed before alterations began.

046369   NN 03 NW   July 1970

340. Cruck-framed Building, Clachadow. One of the ruinous outbuildings of this farm formerly contained two pairs of crucks, which recently collapsed into the interior. The crucks (Fig. 227, Pl. 101E) were scarf-jointed and pegged at wall-head level, and were strengthened by collars; the ridge-pole appears to have been carried upon a yoke. The building in which the crucks were incorporated is partly of dry-stone and partly of

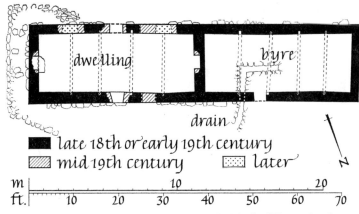

dwelling   byre

drain

↗ N

■ late 18th or early 19th century

░ mid 19th century

░ later

Fig. 226. Cruck-framed building, Cadderlie (No. 339); plan

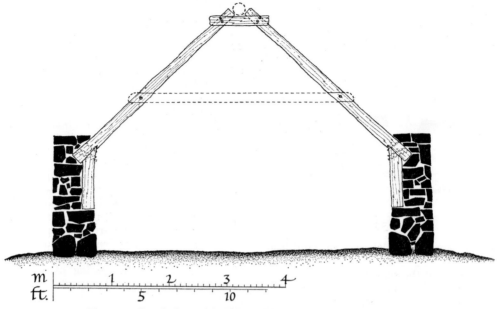

Fig. 227. Cruck-framed building, Clachadow (No. 340); section

stone-and-lime construction; it has evidently been remodelled on more than one occasion, but in its present form is probably of 19th-century date.

947274   NM 92 NW   July 1968

341. Dunstaffnage Mains Farm. This farmhouse, which is of late 18th- or early 19th-century date, is a substantial two-storeyed building of whitewashed rubble masonry with slated roof (Pl. 101F). It differs from other improved farmhouses of the same period in Lorn, however, in that the central block, of three bays, is flanked by single-storeyed hip-roofed pavilions, one of which contains the kitchen and the other a bedroom. The two-storeyed block comprises two rooms at each level, flanking a central staircase.

877337   NM 83 SE   June 1970

342. Cottages, Glencoe Village. This pair of cottages (Pl. 101A) stands 45 m E of the school, on the N side of the main street of Glencoe Village. In 1972 the buildings were converted for use as a folk museum; a large opening was formed in the dividing-wall, and the roof-structure was completely renewed to take a covering of heather thatch. The following description relates to the structure as it appeared prior to these alterations.

The W building, which is cruck-framed, is the earlier, and measures 10·8 m by 5·1 m over walls 0·8 m in thickness. The walls are built of granite with frequent courses of slate, bound with lime mortar; there is a chimney in each gable. The side-walls have subsequently been heightened with two courses of bricks to carry a corrugated-iron roof above the thatch. The building comprises four bays, defined by three pairs of cruck-couples, one pair of which has been removed. Thin partition-walls of mortared slate, which appear to be original, divide the interior into three apartments of approximately equal size (Fig. 228, Pl. 101B).

The easternmost pair of crucks is shown in the section (Fig. 229). The cruck-feet (Pl. 101C) rest on slabs of slate 0·5 m above floor-level. Each cruck-blade is in two sections, scarf-jointed and pegged below wall-head level, and the blades are joined by a cambered yoke (Pl. 101D).

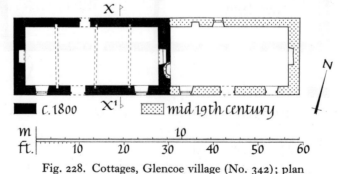

Fig. 228. Cottages, Glencoe village (No. 342); plan

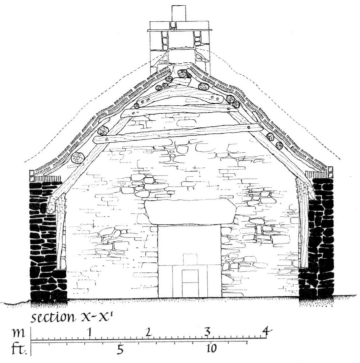

section X-X¹

Fig. 229. Cottages, Glencoe village (No. 342); section

The upper blades taper from 0·15 m by 0·20 m at wall-head level to 0·13 m by 0·11 m at the top. There are two collar-beams. The purlins are formed by several poles which show no systematic arrangement, each being only a single bay in length. The three thin poles that form the ridge rest on a block of wood above the yoke. The central pair of crucks is similar, but has only one collar-beam. The W pair has been removed but the mural slots remain. Short poles, laid close together, rest on the purlins and support a continuous layer of turf, above which are the remains of a straw thatch. A layer of peats rests on the wall-head to provide packing at the feet of these poles.

At a later period another cottage, measuring 8·8 m by 5·0 m over all, was added to the E gable, into which a fireplace and chimney were cut. The masonry is similar in character to that of the earlier building. The roof consists of six pairs of coupled rafters resting on the wall-head, each with a single collar-beam and a straight yoke.

An outhouse, whose N end has been destroyed, stands 2·1 m W of the earlier cottage. Its walls consist of alternate courses of slate and round boulders, and the corners are rounded. Slots survive for one pair of crucks and for an end-cruck.

A small township is shown at Carnach on Roy's Map of c. 1750 but the present village is said to date from about the end of the 18th century, when the upper part of the Glen was cleared for sheep farming.[1] The original cottage was probably built in the early years of the 19th

century, and the addition made before the middle of the century.

102589   NN 15 NW   October 1968

343. Shielings, Glen Risdale. This area of former upland pasture, situated on the NW slope of Glen Risdale at a height of about 150 m OD, is named 'Drimnatoull' in an estate-survey of 1809 by Alexander Langlands.[2] This map shows two separate 'shieling' symbols, which probably correspond to the existing groups, of two and three huts respectively, situated NE and SW of a marshy hollow which Langlands represents as a stream. Shortly before the date of visit the area was ploughed by the Forestry Commission in preparation for tree-planting, and several small hut-foundations of turf which had been observed on a previous visit in June 1970 cannot now be identified.

The three surviving huts in the SW cluster are single-chambered structures of sub-rectangular plan, each having a single entrance in the NW wall. Two of the huts (A, C on Fig. 230) measure about 6·7 m from NE to SW by 3·4 m transversely over walls having an average thickness of 0·9 m, while the third (B) measures some 6·3 m by 4·0 m. The dry-stone walls, which consist of a single course of substantial rubble blocks with smaller stones above, stand to a height of about 0·6 m and have

---

[1] National Trust for Scotland, *Glencoe and Dalness* (1968), 40.
[2] S.R.O., RHP 720.

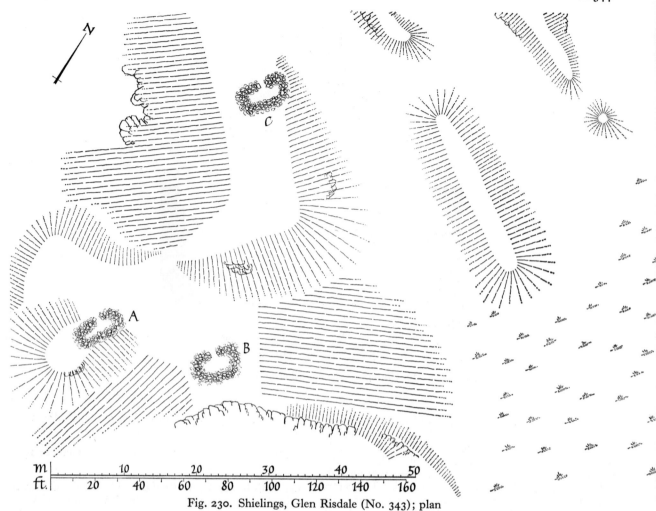

Fig. 230. Shielings, Glen Risdale (No. 343); plan

probably never been much higher; the roofs were probably formed by turf and branches.[1]

The two huts that lie 75 m to the NE are somewhat different in type. One (D) measures about 5·5 m by 3·7 m and has opposed entrance-doorways, while the other (E), which is very poorly preserved, appears to have been two-chambered, with the only identifiable doorway opening into the smaller E chamber.

The summer grazing of black cattle formed an important part of the economy of Nether Lorn until the end of the 18th century, and the area of high ground between Loch Seil and Glen Risdale was used for that purpose by the tenants of the coastal townships of Ardnahua (No. 345) and Duachy. The practice came to an end c. 1790, when the area was included in a sheep-walk based on the farm of Barrnayarry, managed by John Campbell, son of the factor for the Breadalbane estate in Nether Lorn.[2] The huts described above were probably used by the tenants of Ardnahua and Duachy, and may be ascribed to the last quarter of the 18th century.

810188   NM 81 NW   July 1971

344. Cruck-framed Building, Narrachan. This is a small house of dry-stone construction which has subsequently been patched and repaired with lime mortar. It now measures about 10·1 m in length by 5·3 m transversely over walls some 0·84 m in thickness, but may originally have been somewhat longer. The corners are rounded externally, and the only openings are an entrance-doorway and a window. The building was evidently cruck-framed, with a hipped roof supported on end-crucks, one of which survives; the existing roof is of modern construction. The crucks appear to have been of two-piece construction with scarfed and pegged joints at wall-head level.

110365   NN 13 NW   July 1968

[1] For the use of turf in shieling-huts at the nearby township of Barrachrail in the late 18th century, cf. *SHR*, xvi (1919), 150–1.

[2] S.R.O., RHP 972/5, 'Report on Nether Lorn by R Robertson, 1796', *passim*.

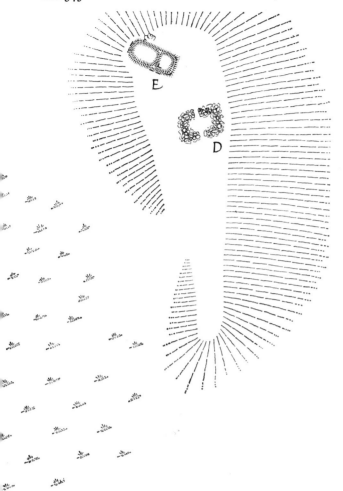

345. Tigh-cuil Township. The remains of this small township (Fig. 231, Pl. 102) are situated about 530 m W of Barrnacarry farmhouse, and are now included in that property. During the 18th and 19th centuries, however, the area formed part of the farm of Ardnahua, whose extent is shown in an estate-map of 1809 (Pl. 103A).[1] Until the last decade of the 18th century the only buildings on Ardnahua, a joint-farm of eight tenants comprising about 165 ha (407 acres), were situated in an irregular group 750 m SSE of Tigh-cuil; in 1788 it was reported that the tenants had 'their houses all in one corner at a distance from some of their best land'. The factor's recommendation that the farm be divided into smaller lots was implemented two years later, when the SE portion was split into three farms, each leased by two tenants who were allocated part of the original township for their dwellings. The remainder of the property, an area of 77 ha (190 acres) of which 11·7 ha (29 acres) was arable, became North Ardnahua, and in 1796 it was 'possessed by Archibald Clark and Alexander McCowan, both in the town upwards of twenty years, who have removed to this division six years ago when the town was divided, and have built a new toft at their own expences'.[2]

Several of the existing structures are identifiable on the estate-map of 1809, and it is evident that these are the original buildings of the new settlement, erected in or shortly after 1790. Two buildings are shown as still roofed on the O.S. map of 1897, but the township was probably abandoned by that date, or shortly thereafter.

The settlement, which is situated at an altitude of about 70 m OD, on the SE side of a long ridge which slopes to the NE, comprises two byre-dwellings (A, B, on Fig. 231) and a number of smaller buildings and enclosures. The even nature of the terrain is interrupted by two low parallel rocky ridges on a SW–NE axis, forming a small hollow in which one of the byre-dwellings (B) is situated. Most of the buildings are preserved, at least partially, to their original height and are gable-ended, the masonry in all cases being of slate- and whinstone-rubble, bonded for the most part with clay mortar. Three of the larger buildings (A, B, D), display wall-sockets which formerly held crucks, and through-stones project from their gables to fasten the ropes formerly used to hold the roofing-thatch in position.

One of the byre-dwellings (A) is situated close to a dry-stone head-dyke which separates the area of settlement and arable from higher rough pasture to the SW. The building is of five cruck-bays, measuring 16·0 m from NW to SE by 6·1 m transversely over walls some 0·8 m in thickness. Access was by opposed doorways set centrally in the side-walls, and by additional doorways, one in each side-wall, which may be later insertions. The NW portion of the building, lit by two windows in the end-bay, was probably the dwelling, but the other part also has two windows of moderate size, in addition to a small window in the SE gable-wall. Against the NE wall there is built a later annexe which is itself of two periods, a single enclosure having subsequently been divided into three small compartments. The NE end of this annexe extends on to a stone-revetted raised platform rising about 1·2 m above an area of marsh that separates Building A from the remainder of the township.

Associated with this building, and situated 24 m to the S of it, is a rectangular outhouse (A1) having two doorways in the N wall and a small annexe against the E gable-wall. Although constructed of dry-stone masonry, this structure is of later date than the byre-dwelling; it may, however, replace a small building situated W of the latter, which is shown on the estate-map of 1809 but has now disappeared completely.

The second byre-dwelling (B) is of six cruck-bays and measures 18·6 m from SW to NE by 6·0 m transversely over walls 0·9 m in thickness. The two divisions of the building were entered by separate doorways in the SE wall, and in the original arrangement were probably of equal length, being divided by a partition on the line of the central cruck-couple. Subsequently a stone partition-wall incorporating a fireplace and cupboard was built, and this encroached on the original area of the byre.

[1] S.R.O., RHP 720, Plan of Nether Lorn estate by Alexander Langlands.
[2] S.R.O., Breadalbane Collection, GD 112/9/3, Nether Lorn Rental, Crop 1788, p. 13; S.R.O., RHP 972/5, 'Report on Nether Lorn by R Robertson, 1796'.

The SW gable-wall was rebuilt, probably in the second quarter of the 19th century, together with the adjacent portion of the SE wall in which there is a window of some size; the gable-wall contains a fireplace and a cupboard-alcove, above which there is a small horizontal recess, perhaps designed to hold the family bible. This portion of the dwelling evidently constituted the 'room', while the NW portion, with its large inserted fireplace and a door communicating with the byre, was the kitchen. This apartment was lit by small windows in the NW and SE walls; another window in the NW wall, in the central bay of the dwelling, probably served a bed-closet, which was provided with a small aumbry near the window. The byre was lit by a small opening near the NE end of the SE wall. At a later date the byre-dwelling was extended to the NE by the construction of a narrower annexe, communicating with the byre by a doorway formed in the NE gable-wall of the original building, and also having an entrance-doorway in the SE wall. This annexe was of dry-stone masonry, but apart from the NE wall, which is preserved as the SW gable-wall of a second annexe, comprising two bays divided by a single cruck-couple, it is now reduced to foundation-level.

Immediately to the SE of the byre-dwelling there is a small rectangular structure (B1) whose SE wall is formed by a natural rock-face. This building, which is window-less, has a small fireplace in its SW gable-wall and may have been a workshop or smithy. To the NE of Building B there is a rectangular enclosure (C), and outside the SW wall of this there are the scanty remains of a small shed formed by two dry-stone walls set at right angles to a natural rock-face. The enclosure was evidently a kail-yard created after 1809, when it appears on the estate-map as part of a larger area of unenclosed arable-ground.

To the E of Enclosure C there is a building (D), probably a barn, which stands within a small walled enclosure, built up artificially on the NW to a height of 1·2 m above an area of marsh. The building, which is represented, with the enclosure, on the estate-map of 1809, was of four cruck-bays, although the slots of the central cruck-couple have been obscured. It was entered by a doorway in the NW wall, the only other opening being a small triangular window in the NE gable-wall.

Even after the division of Ardnahua in 1790, the tenants of each portion continued to cultivate their land in run-rig, and the arable fields of North Ardnahua were never enclosed. They lie scattered in small parcels over a wide area, where traces of rig-cultivation are still visible, but one of the main areas of cultivation was on sloping ground immediately SE of Tigh-cuil, between the settlement and a small unnamed burn which formed the boundary with Mid Ardnahua. A roadway, embanked on the E, runs S from Building A1, along the W edge of the area of arable, as far as the burn, and is represented in the same position on the estate-map of 1809. The farm is bounded on the NW by 1·3 km of rocky coastline; the only suitable boat-landing, however, is on the SW shore of Barrnacarry Bay, and when Ardnahua was divided in 1790, this area was separated as a croft.

806222   NM 82 SW   June 1971

346. Cruck-framed Byre, Torr-an-tuirc. This building is of some interest inasmuch as it combines an orthodox cruck-framework with a hipped roof supported on end-crucks. It measures 12·8 m by 5·9 m over walls some 0·6 m in thickness (Fig. 232), and is constructed of

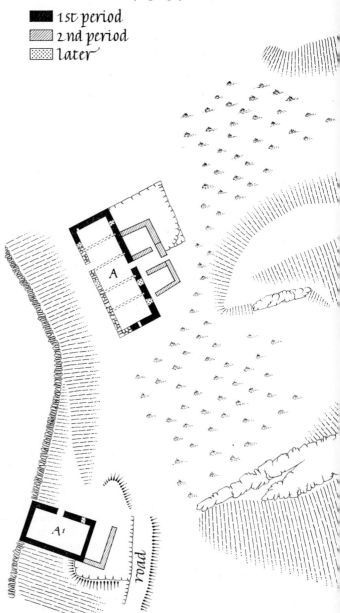

Fig. 231. Tigh-cuil township (No. 345); plan

random rubble laid in coarse lime-mortar. There are five cruck-bays, including the two end-bays, in which the crucks are centrally placed in the end-walls. All the crucks have been sawn off at wall-head level to accommodate a secondary roof, but they were originally scarf-jointed and pegged at about wall-head level. The lower portions of the crucks are slotted into the walls, the bases

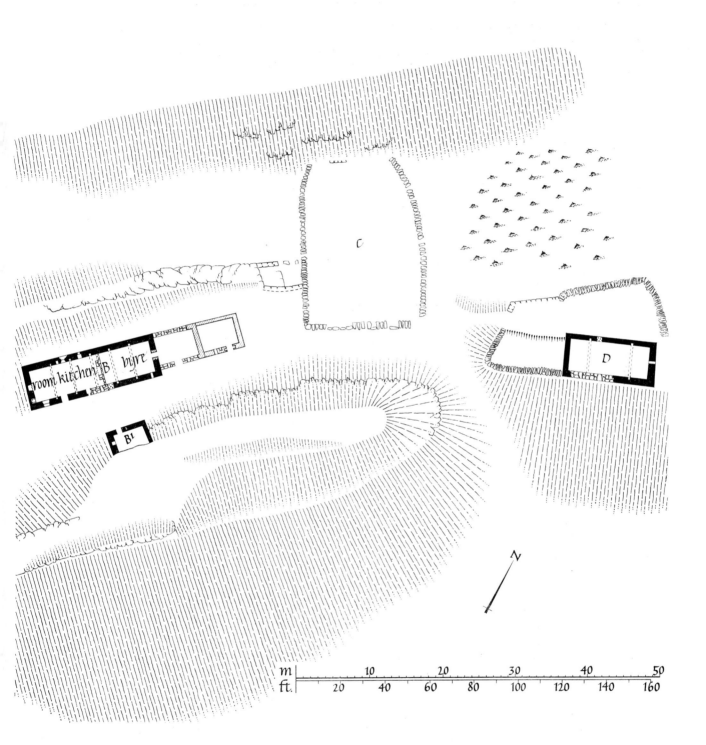

room kitchen B byre

B¹

C

D

N

m		10		20		30		40		50
ft.	20	40	60	80	100	120	140	160

being about 0·6 m above floor-level. The crucks appear to be of pine or larch, and measure about 0·20 m square at base. The roof was probably originally of thatch. The byre has two doorways in the E wall, but these appear to have been reconstructed, since the adjacent stretch of wall now contains no cruck-sockets corresponding with those in the opposite wall. There is a drain-outlet at the base of the N wall.

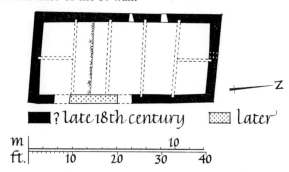

Fig. 232. Cruck-framed brye, Torr-an-tuirc (No. 346); plan

The byre, which is probably of late 18th- or early 19th-century date, seems originally to have been associated with a house of which the remains are situated immediately to the S. Other ruined buildings can be seen in the same area, together with a solitary occupied house, and these evidently comprised the former township of Torr-an-tuirc, which is indicated ('Turnturk') on Roy's Map of about 1750.

903277   NM 92 NW   July 1970

INDUSTRIAL AND ENGINEERING WORKS, INCLUDING QUARRIES

347. Charcoal-burning Stances, Achanlochan. A number of charcoal-burning stances are known to exist in the mixed oak and birch woodland to the S of Achanlochan Farm. A representative example, situated beside a track some 180 m SW of the farmhouse, is approximately circular on plan within a slight earthen bank and

has a diameter of about 6 m. The charcoal was presumably used at Lorn Furnace (No. 362). The process of manufacture is described by Lord Teignmouth, who visited the locality shortly before 1836. 'The wood used is both oak and birch; the former is first stripped of its bark, which forms an inconsiderable part of the profit. The birch, which is about half the value of the oak, is charred together with the bark, which facilitates the process, and is of itself of no value. The charring-mills are rudely constructed in the copse, being made of circular enclosures of turf, covered with a basket-work, formed of the poles of trees; and the air is admitted but partially, in order that the ignition may not be too rapid. The charcoal is bagged and conveyed to the smelting-houses in carts. The bark is stacked in a creel barn, made of wicker of any sort of copse-wood, and pervious to air'.[1]

9831   NM 93 SE   July 1968

348. Limestone-quarries and Workers' Dwellings, An Sàilean, Lismore. The remains of this small industrial complex (Pl. 104A) lie on the NW coast of the island, about 2 km W of Achnacroish, where a limestone cliff some 50 m in height overlooks a well-sheltered bay. At the foot of the cliff there are two pairs of lime-kilns (Pl. 104B), situated about 150 m apart. The larger and better-preserved pair lies to the N, the loading-mouths of the kilns having been approached by means of a bridge which spanned the access-road to the quarry-face. The structure measures about 13·5 m by 10·7 m over all at base and rises to a height of 8·5 m. The kiln-chambers are approximately ovoid in shape, having a mouth-diameter of about 2·4 m and a maximum diameter of about 3·7 m.

The quarry-workers appear to have been accommodated mainly in small detached cottages of which three more or less intact examples survive in different parts of the site. In addition to these, and of greater interest, is a row of ruinous buildings which stands near the N extremity of the site (Fig. 233). Like the cottages already mentioned, these were single-storeyed structures of stone and lime, but in the original arrangement, at least, they were evidently cruck-framed, the crucks being housed in wall-slots, some of which still survive. Latterly,

[1] Teignmouth, Lord, *Sketches of the Coasts and Islands of Scotland and of the Isle of Man* (1836), ii, 362–3.

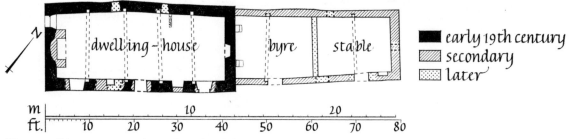

early 19th century
secondary
later

Fig. 233. Limestone-quarries and workers' dwellings, An Sàilean, Lismore (No. 348); plan of dwelling-house

this row of buildings appears to have comprised a two-roomed dwelling-house with an adjacent byre and stable, but originally the SW portion of the structure seems to have been a freestanding pair of single-roomed workers' dwellings. Lime was shipped from a nearby quay, which is built of stone with the facing-blocks set on end; it incorporates a single-storeyed building which served latterly as a coal-store.

The lime-burning industry on Lismore seems to have been initiated shortly before the end of the 18th century, and was continued until the opening years of the present century.[1] The existing buildings at An Sàilean probably date mainly from the first half of the 19th century.

8341   NM 84 SW   June 1970

349. Old Quarries, Ardentallan. A quarry extends for about 100 m along the SE shore of Ardentallan Point, the working-face being visible at high-water level, lying beneath a substantial lava-flow (Pl. 104C). The stone is a grey medium-grained sandstone of Lower Old Red Sandstone age. Further quarries and refuse-tips extend for about 400 m immediately to the NW of the road that runs along the NW shore of Loch Feochan, some 800 m NE of Ardentallan Point. Drill-holes may be seen in various parts of the quarries. The material was probably transported from the site by water, and some remains of a roughly-formed jetty may be seen directly opposite the main working-face.

This quarry was described as a suitable source of freestone for the repair of the Old Parish Church, Kilmore (No. 264) in 1859,[2] and may be the 'slate and freestone quarry' on the property of Mr MacDougall of Gallanach that the author of the *New Statistical Account* mentions as a source of freestone of superior quality in 1843.[3] Stone was also supplied from Ardentallan for use in the construction of the Caledonian Canal.[4] The stone resembles that found at Barrnacarry (No. 351), on the opposite side of Loch Feochan, and closely matches samples of building-stone from Dunollie Castle (No. 286), Gylen Castle (No. 291), Lismore Cathedral (No. 267), Ardanaiseig House (No. 307) and the Free High Church, Oban (No. 270).

8222, 8223,   NM 82 SW   April 1970
8323

350. Slate-quarries and Workers' Dwellings, Ballachulish. Extensive remains of former slate-quarries (Pl. 105A, B) are to be seen at West Laroch and East Laroch, about 3 km SE of South Ballachulish. The largest and most recently worked quarry is situated at East Laroch, where there is also a harbour formed out of banks of quarry waste. Two other quarries and a harbour exist at West Laroch, and many smaller workings can be seen above the village in the valley of the River Laroch.

Writing in 1841 the author of the *New Statistical Account* stated that the quarry-workers were accommodated in houses of stone and lime with slated roofs.

'The accommodation in each is three apartments, all plastered, with chimnies and grates in the principal one, and an open garret above. To most of them a cow-house is attached'.[5] Numerous rows of cottages of this description were formerly to be seen at Laroch, and beside the road leading from Laroch to Glencoe, but few examples (Pl. 105C) remain today. A typical cottage measured 7·6 m by 6·1 m over all and incorporated a room on each side of a central entrance-doorway, together with a small closet centrally placed at the rear.

The Ballachulish slate-quarries were first opened by the proprietor, Mr Stewart of Ballachulish, about the year 1693, and a century later the industry employed 74 families numbering 322 persons, and slate was being exported to many different parts of Scotland, as well as to England, Ireland and America. Maximum production was reached during the last quarter of the 19th century, when the total labour-force rose to just under 600 men with an annual production of 26 million slates. The industry declined rapidly during the present century and the last quarry was closed in 1955.[6]

0758, 0858   NN 05 NE   July 1970

351. Old Quarry, Barrnacarry. This quarry extends some 400 m northwards along the E shore of Barrnacarry Bay, commencing at a point about 500 m NNE of Barrnacarry House. The stone is a grey, medium- to coarse-grained sandstone of Lower Old Red Sandstone age containing pebbles up to 0·15 m in diameter. The quarry was evidently utilized mainly for the supply of building-stone, but the seaward inclination of the beds also facilitated the production of millstones. The latter were detached by means of wedges inserted at intervals around the perimeter. A number of partially detached stones remain *in situ* (Pl. 104D), and these vary in diameter from 1·0 m to 1·2 m. Drill-holes may also be seen in various parts of the quarry. The material was presumably transported directly from the site by water.

The stone is similar in character to that found at Ardentallan Point (No. 349), and closely matches samples of building-stone from Dunollie Castle (No. 286), Gylen Castle (No. 291) and the W wall of Lismore Cathedral (No. 267). Accounts survive for the transport of stone from Barrnacarry for use in the coach-house at Ardmaddy Castle (No. 310) in 1838, and the entire court of offices is constructed of the same stone.[7]

8122   NM 82 SW   April 1970

[1] *Stat. Acct.*, i (1791), 500; *Third Stat. Acct.* (Argyll), 164.
[2] S.R.O., HR 526/5, Kilmore and Kilbride Heritors' Records, specification for repairs, 1859.
[3] *NSA*, vii (Argyll), 528.
[4] Lee, G W and Bailey, E B, *The Pre-Tertiary Geology of Mull, Loch Aline, and Oban* (Memoirs of the Geological Survey, Scotland, 1925), 125.
[5] *NSA*, vii (Argyll), 250.
[6] *Stat. Acct.*, i (1791), 499–500; *NSA*, vii (Argyll), 247–251; Bremner, D, *The Industries of Scotland* (1869), 429–432; Fairweather, B, *A Short History of Ballachulish Slate Quarry* (1968), *passim*.
[7] S.R.O., Breadalbane Collection, GD 112/20/5, Ardmaddy Building-Papers.

352. Millstone-quarry, Barran. About half a kilometre NE of Barran farmhouse there is a boulder-outcrop which has been quarried in an unsuccessful attempt to detach a millstone. The stone was intended to have a diameter of about 1·3 m and thickness of about 0·20 m, and quarrying was probably abandoned because of the appearance of fractures in the exposed face. The diameter of the millstone suggests that this quarry is of 18th- or 19th-century date.

168252   NN 12 NE   September 1967

353. Whisky-still, Brackley (Site). About 275 m SE of Brackley a small platform, enclosed on its lower side by a dry-stone wall, stands at the intersection of two unnamed tributary streams of Allt a' Chruaidh-ghrainne. The platform is roughly rectangular on plan and measures about 7·6 m by 4·6 m over all. At one of the inner corners a small slab-roofed shelter, measuring about 1·07 m square and 0·76 m in height, has been formed beneath the outcropping rock. This is said to have been the site of an illicit still.[1]

181262   NN 12 NE   September 1967

354. Old Quarry (possible), Bridge of Awe. Variegated pink and white sandstone of a very coarse texture can be seen outcropping on both banks of the River Awe in the vicinity of the old Bridge of Awe (No. 368). Although no traces of quarrying-operations are now visible, the stone matches closely with samples of freestone dressings from Fraoch Eilean Castle (No. 290) and the church of Baile Mhaodain, Ardchattan (No. 220), and was in all probability utilized in the construction of these buildings.

0329   NN 02 NW   July 1970

355. Marble-quarry, Caddleton. This quarry is situated in the valley of an unnamed burn, about 150 m from the E shore of Ardmaddy Bay and about 660 m S of Ardmaddy Castle (No. 310). Beds of marble, red and white or grey and white in colour, are exposed in the floor of the valley; the sides of the valley are formed by igneous rocks which overlie the marble. A ridge of marble on the SW bank of the burn, which appears to have been originally about 6 m in length and 2·9 m in height, has been completely quarried away, leaving a vertical face which displays evidence of the removal of slabs about 0·9 m in length. The worked surface bears drill-holes 0·04 m in diameter, spaced at intervals of from 0·11 m to 0·20 m. Another worked face is visible at the base of the cliff about 12·2 m W of this, and others are concealed by dense vegetation. A well-built track leads from the quarry to the jetties that are situated about 320 m to the SW (p. 251). At the side of this track, about 120 m NW of the quarry, there lies a roughly-squared block of red and white marble measuring 0·7 m by 1·4 m by 0·9 m, which bears drill-marks similar to those already described.

This quarry was worked from 1745 to 1751 by the 'Marble and Slate Company of Netherlorn', which also operated the slate-quarries at Easdale (No. 356) and elsewhere. The leading partners were Colin Campbell of Carwhin (cf. p. 252), who acted as manager, and John Campbell, cashier of the Royal Bank of Scotland. By February 1748 several large blocks of marble had been raised, and in May of that year the company 'being strangers, in many respects, to the nature of marble', prepared a list of questions concerning the quarrying and sale of marble, which were answered by Andrews Jelfe, the London architect and stone-carver. In the same year a pier was completed, and the road leading to it was begun. Chimney-pieces were supplied to several Scottish landowners; but when Charles Erskine, Lord Tinwald, supplied designs for elaborate chimney-pieces, he was asked to accept a simpler design with few mouldings, which could be supplied at £8 or £9 apiece. The fire-place-surrounds at Ardmaddy Castle (p. 250) are probably typical of those produced by the company, which found difficulty in obtaining reliable skilled workmen. The method of working, as described in 1749, was for one workman to hold a drill or 'jumper' in place vertically, while another struck it with a heavy hammer, and this operation was repeated at intervals of about 0·03 m. Similar drill-holes were made on all sides of the block, which was finally removed with iron wedges, and trimmed by sawing. An improvement which had been introduced involved single workmen using a jumper fitted with a 16-pound weight, but the operation continued to be 'expensive and tedious'. In 1750 it was reported that thirteen men were employed, but that the marble being worked was mixed with whinstone, and blasting was necessary; at the end of the following season the quarry was abandoned.[2]

786157   NM 71 NE   May 1970

356. Slate-quarries and Workers' Dwellings, Easdale, Seil. Slate has been quarried at several sites on the islands of Nether Lorn, and remains of old workings with accompanying dwellings may be seen at Cullipool, Black Mill Bay and Toberonochy, Luing, and at Balvicar and Ardencaple, Seil. The most important quarries, however, were on the island of Easdale and the smaller island of Ellanbeich (Pl. 106A) which, during the first half of the 19th century, became united to Seil by a causeway formed by a vast accumulation of quarry-waste.[3]

In contrast to the quarries at Ballachulish (No. 350), most of the beds of good slate at Easdale lay near or below ground-level, and as more efficient pumps were introduced during the 19th century the workings were carried down to considerable depths. In 1869 the principal quarry at Ellanbeich had a surface area of about 140 m

---

[1] Information from Mrs J Crerar, Brackley.
[2] S.R.O., Breadalbane Collection, GD 112/18/22, Marble Company Minute-book, 1745–57, *passim*.
[3] The sound separating Ellanbeich from Seil is represented on a map of 1787 by G Langlands (S.R.O., RHP 975/1). Cf. Leyden, *Tour*, 56.

by 75 m, and a depth of some 50 m. This quarry, which contained an elaborate system of railway-tracks, was protected from the sea by a narrow wall of unquarried rock strengthened by a masonry wall, and when this was breached by a storm in November 1881 the entire quarry was flooded,[1] so that it now presents the appearance of a tidal basin. Most of the disused workings on Easdale, the oldest of which are two situated near the SE shore of the island, are also flooded. The only industrial building of importance is the ruinous engine-house, probably of mid-19th-century date, situated immediately E of Ellanbeich quarry. This provided motive power for the railway-system and also for the pumps in the quarry.

The harbours at Ellanbeich and Easdale (Pl. 106c, D) were built c. 1826[2] and both have jetties constructed with vertically-set masonry. The NW quay at Easdale, incorporating a flight of steps, is particularly well preserved; the area to the NW is divided by rows of slate slabs, resembling headstones, into a series of compartments, originally ten in all, for stacking graded loads of slates ready for shipping.

Most of the quarriers' dwellings, both at Ellanbeich and Easdale, are single-storeyed cottages of rubble masonry, harled and whitewashed, having slate paving-slabs at the street-front and neatly slated roofs (Pl. 106B). The existing buildings probably date from the first quarter of the 19th century, and their internal layout corresponds closely with that represented on a survey plan of 1856 which forms the basis of the accompanying plan (Fig. 234).[3] Each cottage has two main rooms

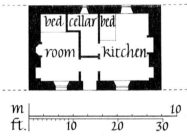

Fig. 234. Slate-quarries and workers' dwellings, Easdale, Seil (No. 356); plan of cottage

separated by a lobby and closet, the latter normally entered from the kitchen, and the internal partitions are timber-framed with slate infilling. The main group of cottages at Ellanbeich is arranged as two back-to-back rows, each in blocks of five, four and four, separated by streets from a third row of dwellings on the WSW and a series of walled gardens on the ENE. The arrangement of the cottages on Easdale is less systematic; some are grouped round three sides of a square, while others extend W and NW of the harbour. A considerable part of the island of Easdale is covered by an intricate network of dry-stone walls forming small closely-grouped enclosures. Similar enclosures formerly existed at Ellanbeich, and may be the remains of allotments used for the intensive potato-cultivation that was observed there in 1800.[4]

Quarrying operations at Easdale were at first con-

ducted on an *ad hoc* basis, the necessary materials being gathered from the slate debris on the shore, or quarried above water-level by the workmen engaged on particular building-works (cf. p. 34). During the first half of the 18th century the quarries were greatly developed, with permanent crews of quarriers preparing slates for shipment on vessels engaged in trade between the Clyde and the East Coast.[5] When the management was taken over by the 'Marble and Slate Company of Netherlorn' in 1745 (cf. p. 278), eight crews of four men were employed, with an annual production of about 500,000 slates. By 1771 the work-force had increased to thirteen crews at Easdale, five at Ellanbeich, and nineteen elsewhere on Seil and Luing, and production in 1795 was about five million slates.[6] At this period quarrying was restricted to the seams above low-water level, although a system of outflow-channels and sluices allowed these levels to be worked at all states of the tide.

In 1800 the quarries at Ellanbeich, which had apparently been worked down to low-water level, were described as exhausted,[7] but the introduction soon after this of improved sources of power for pumping and transport, including a windmill and steam engines, permitted work at Easdale and Ellanbeich to be carried down to the great depths described above. Peak production was estimated in 1869 as about nine million slates, but this output was greatly reduced by the flooding of Ellanbeich quarry in 1881; production at Easdale continued intermittently until c. 1914.[8]

7316, 7317,   NM 71 NW   July 1971
7416, 7417

357. Lighthouse, Eilean Musdile, Lismore. This lighthouse (Pls. 107–9) was erected in 1833 at a cost of £11,230 by the Inverness contractor, James Smith, under the supervision of Robert Stevenson, engineer to the Commissioners of Northern Lights.[9] It comprises a lighthouse-tower and a pair of dwelling-houses symmetrically disposed about a small oblong courtyard. The tower has a diameter of 5·8 m at base over walls 1·4 m in thickness, and rises to a height of 19·6 m at the corbelled parapet-walk, the lantern (Pl. 110A) being 31·4 m above the high-water level of spring tides.[10] The masonry is of coursed lime-washed rubble, with painted

[1] Gillies, *Netherlorn*, 16.
[2] Bremner, D, *The Industries of Scotland* (1869), 427.
[3] 'Ground Plan of present Quarriers Houses' inset in unexecuted plan for rebuilding of houses at Ellanbeich, 1856 (S.R.O., RHP 970/13).
[4] Leyden, *Tour*, 56.
[5] Mackay, W, *The Letter-Book of Bailie John Steuart of Inverness 1715–1752*, SHS (1915), Index, s.v. 'Slate'.
[6] S.R.O., Breadalbane Collection, GD 112/18/nos. 21–4, 54–5, Marble Company Ledgers, Minute-books, Journals, *passim*; *Stat. Acct.*, xiv (1795), 161–2.
[7] Leyden, *Tour*, 56.
[8] *NSA*, vii (Argyll), 77–8; Gillies, *Netherlorn*, 10–16; Bremner, D, *The Industries of Scotland* (1869), 425–8.
[9] 'Report of the Commissioners appointed to inquire into the condition and management of Lights, Buoys and Beacons . . .', *Parliamentary Papers*, 1861, xxv, vol. ii, 177.
[10] Ibid.

dressings of freestone; stone for the construction of the lighthouse is said to have been quarried at Loch Aline.[1] The parapet-walk (Pl. 110B) has a lozenge-patterned hand-rail of cast iron, within which there rises the cast-iron superstructure of the light-room, pierced by two rows of square glass panes. The glazing-bars incorporate cast-iron hand-grips, fashioned in the form of dolphins, while the base and cornice of the superstructure are decorated with panels of the same material which display various nautical and heraldic insignia (Pl. 110C, D). All these details seem to belong to the original period of construction, but the reflector-mechanism has been renewed.

The keeper's houses (Pl. 110E) are plain single-storeyed buildings with flat roofs surmounted by prominent chimney-stacks; the central bays are advanced. The coursed sandstone-rubble masonry is exposed externally, but lime-washed on the courtyard side. The courtyard entrance (Pl. 110G), which is centrally placed, comprises a lintelled doorway set within a flat-arched recess whose blocking-course echoes that of the flanking houses. In front of the entrance there is a walled garden traversed by a sinuous path leading to an outer gateway, beyond which there are two slipways, one on each side of the island.[2]

It was originally proposed to improve communication by the construction of a roadway and bridges linking Eilean Musdile with the island of Lismore, but the scheme was abandoned following the completion of a segmental-arched bridge (Pl. 110F) spanning the gorge that bisects Eilean Musdile itself.

778351   NM 73 NE   July 1971

358. Glen Kinglass Ironworks. The remains of this ironworks occupy a grassy haugh on the NE bank of the River Kinglass about 800 m above its debouchment into Loch Etive at Ardmaddy. The buildings are ruinous and incomplete, and the entire site is rapidly being eroded by the action of the river. The best-preserved building is the furnace itself (Fig. 235), which occupies a bankside position towards the SE corner of the site. This is a substantially-built structure of local granite boulders laid in lime mortar measuring about 7·9 m square over all at base, and now rising to a maximum height of about 4·0 m. The internal dimensions of the building cannot be determined because of the accumulated debris

that now chokes the interior, but traces of splayed apertures communicating with the furnace-hearth can be seen on the NW and SW sides. The furnace was presumably charged by means of a bridge spanning the cavity formed between the SE wall and the bank at the rear, and some fragmentary remains, together with deposits of charcoal, can be seen upon the summit of the bank in this quarter.

Immediately to the SW of the furnace there are the remains of a rectangular building measuring about 6·4 m from N to S by 5·0 m transversely over all, while the flat low-lying ground to the W and NW appears to have been enclosed by a wall some 0·68 m in thickness. Within this latter area there may be seen considerable deposits of iron slag, together with fragments of two rectangular buildings lying adjacent and parallel to one another. One of these measures about 11·6 m by 5·2 m and the other about 10·0 m by 6·4 m over all.

The buildings whose remains are visible on the opposite bank of the river probably belonged mainly to Inverkinglass Farm, but one of them, a substantially built structure of granite boulders laid in lime mortar, of which a fragment now stands directly upon the edge of the river bank, may have been associated with the ironworks.

This ironworks was established by an Irish company which had negotiated contracts for timber rights with a number of local landowners, including Sir Duncan Campbell, 7th of Lochnell, and the 2nd Earl of Breadalbane, in 1721–3.[3] The initial partners in the company appear to have been Roger Murphy, tanner, of Enniskillen and Dublin, and Captain Arthur Galbraith, of Dublin, but other Irish and Scottish co-partners subsequently joined the enterprise, including Sir Duncan Campbell, who leased the ground upon which the furnace was built.[4] The company seems to have traded mainly in sawn timber and bark, but iron-smelting must have been begun before February 1725, when mention is made of 'an Iron forge or worke now erected and built at Glankileness'.[5] In May 1727 Manus MacDonald, an Irish founder, travelled from 'Glenkenlish' to Fort William to give advice in connection with the establishment of the Invergarry Furnace, while later in the same year Thomas Rawlinson, manager at Invergarry, visited Glen Kinglass to consult Captain Galbraith.[6] It is known that a bull's hide was supplied for the furnace bellows at Glen Kinglass in August

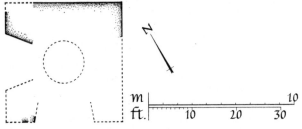

Fig. 235. Glen Kinglass Ironworks (No. 358); plan of furnace

[1] Gaskell, P, *Morvern Transformed* (1968), 171.
[2] As first planned the keepers' houses were semi-detached and there was no direct access from the garden to the courtyard (Contract-drawings, dated 1829, in the possession of the Northern Lighthouse Board).
[3] Campbell of Ardchattan Papers, Ardchattan Priory, disposition and assignation between Roger Murphy and Arthur Galbraith dated 9 July 1722, registered 29 January 1726; S.R.O., Breadalbane Collection, GD 112/16/11.
[4] Campbell of Ardchattan Papers, draft tack of lands of Ardmaddy etc. by Sir Duncan Campbell to Captain Galbraith and Roger Murphy, n.d.
[5] Ibid., deed of conveyance, Roger Murphy to Edward Nixon and Robert Maine, dated 5 February 1724/5.
[6] S.R.O., Invergarry Ironworks Papers, GD 1/168/1, pp. 16–17.

1730,[1] while there is evidence to show that the ironworks was still in operation two years later.[2] The enterprise probably collapsed before 1738, however, in which year the Irish company's rights in Glenorchy Woods were sold to another contractor.[3]

082371   NN 03 NE   July 1968

359. Whisky-stills (Sites), Lismore. Despite a serious shortage of natural fuel, the island of Lismore was notorious in the early 19th century as a centre of illicit distilling; barley was grown in abundance, and the limestone cliffs of the coast provided many sheltered valleys where small pot-stills could be established with little risk of detection.[4] Two sites that appear to be associated with this illicit industry have been identified near Tirefour farm.

One site occupies a small wooded valley, about 12 m in width and running N–S, into which a stream flows by a waterfall on the W side. This stream runs S for about 40 m to enter the sea at Port Maluag, and immediately S of the waterfall the valley has been blocked by a dam of dry-stone masonry measuring 0·7 m in thickness and originally forming a pool 5 m in length. Above the pool there are two artificial terraces, the lower one measuring 2·0 m from N to S and the higher one about 3·0 m; the latter, which is about 1·5 m above the lower terrace and is supported by a roughly-built retaining-wall, is bounded on the N by steeply-rising ground.

The second site is situated 550 m NNE of that just described, immediately E of a nameless group of ruined buildings. A rocky cleft which runs NW into the limestone cliff narrows to a width of 2·6 m, and at this point the floor of the cleft is 2·7 m below the level of the field to the W. The extremity of the cleft has been blocked by a dry-stone wall, 0·6 m in thickness and incorporating an opening 0·6 m in width and 0·9 m in height, to form an irregular chamber measuring 1·4 m in width and 2·2 m in length, and having a height of 1·1 m. The walls of the chamber are formed partly by the rock face and partly by dry-stone masonry lining, and the roof is constructed of massive slab-lintels of limestone, covered with soil and turf to form part of the field above. Dense vegetation renders the entrance to the chamber completely invisible from below, while the adjacent cliff-top is an excellent look-out point covering the Lynn of Lorn in all directions. Local tradition associates this site, and a nearby spring called Tobar an Fhìon ('the well of the wine'), with illicit distilling, and it is admirably suited to be a hiding-place for distillers, as well as for their equipment and product.[5]

871433 (Illicit Still)   NM 84 SE   July 1970
875437 (Hiding-place)

360. Charcoal-burning Stances, Loch Creran. This group of about a dozen stances lies in scrub birch on the lower slopes of Coire Circe about 60 m above the S shore of Loch Creran. The platforms are similar in size and shape to those described under No. 361, but because

of the comparatively gentle incline of the ground little cutting and banking was necessary for their construction, and dry-stone revetments are seldom employed. The charcoal was probably transported by sea for use at the neighbouring ironworks of Glen Kinglass (No. 358) and Bonawe (No. 362).

988437   NM 94 SE   May 1972

361. Charcoal-burning Stances, Loch Etive. About twenty stances lie scattered along a steep hillside, immediately above the pier at the head of Loch Etive at an altitude of between 75 m and 150 m. The platforms are D-shaped or oval on plan, measuring about 9 m in width and 7 m in depth, and most of them have been formed by cutting and banking, their forward lips being supported by massive revetments of dry-stone masonry up to 1·7 m in height. In some instances traces of a drainage-channel can be seen leading out of one side of the platform. The platforms are now turf-covered, and many are overgrown with scrub birch, but where the surface has recently been disturbed fragments of charcoal[6] are visible immediately beneath the turf. Similar stances occur on the opposite, or SE, shore of Loch Etive at various points between Kinlochetive and Inverliever Bay, a particularly well-preserved group, numbering upwards of thirty platforms, lying about 2 km SW of Kinlochetive.

The timber-rights of the lands of Kinlochetive were included in a contract[7] drawn up in 1723 between the 2nd Earl of Breadalbane and the Irish company that was then seeking to establish an ironworks in Glen Kinglass (cf. No. 358). No doubt many of the stances were constructed at this time, falling out of use when the Glen Kinglass furnace was closed down some time during the 1730s. There was probably a second and more protracted period of activity, however, following the establishment of the Bonawe ironworks (No. 362) in 1753, and the acquisition of many of the local timber-rights by the operating company.[8]

1044   NN 14 SW   May 1972
1045   NN 14 NW

362. Lorn Furnace, Bonawe. The buildings associated with the former ironworks occupy an extensive tract of gently sloping ground lying close to the south shore of

---

[1] Campbell of Ardchattan Papers, account of money disbursed by Sir Duncan Campbell on the Ironworks of Glen Kinglass and Firwoods of Glen Orchy, May 1729—October 1730.
[2] Ibid., obligation by Colin Campbell of Inveresragan to Donald Campbell of Achendoun endorsed by Alexander McMillan, 18 November 1732. Cf. also No. 303.
[3] S.R.O., Breadalbane Collection, GD 112/16/11.
[4] MacCulloch, J, The Highlands and Western Isles of Scotland (1824), iv, 367–72.
[5] The Commissioners are indebted to Mr R Miller, Tirefour, for information about this site.
[6] Fragments collected at the date of visit were identified as birch and hazel by the Royal Botanic Garden, Edinburgh.
[7] S.R.O., Breadalbane Collection, GD 112/16/11, contract dated 14 September 1723.
[8] Fell, Iron Industry, 391–2, 441–8.

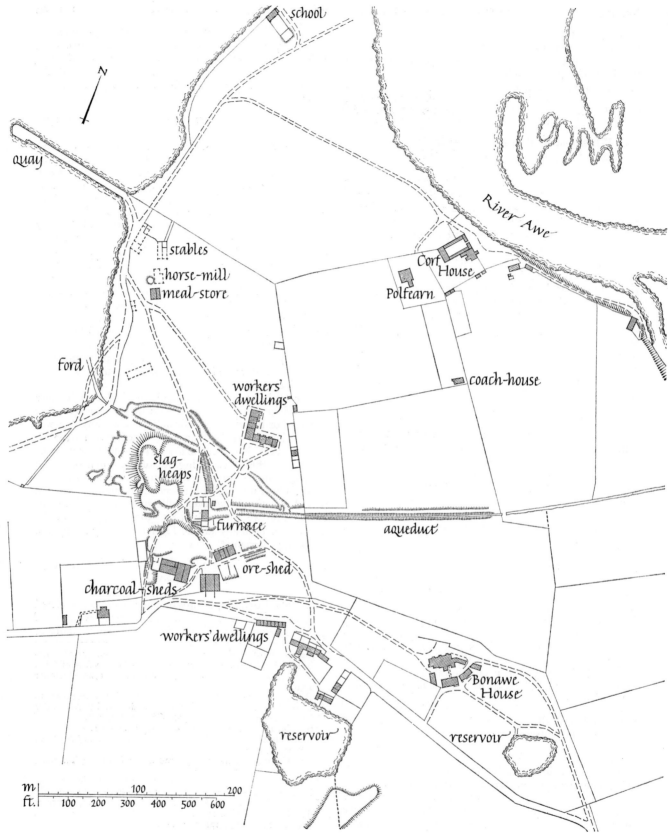

school

quay

N

stables

horse-mill

meal-store

ford

workers'
dwellings

slag-
heaps

Corf
House

Polfearn

coach-house

furnace

aqueduct

ore-shed

charcoal-sheds

workers' dwellings

Bonawe
House

reservoir

reservoir

River Awe

m
ft.

100   200
100   200   300   400   500   600

Fig. 236. Lorn Furnace, Bonawe (No. 362); site-plan

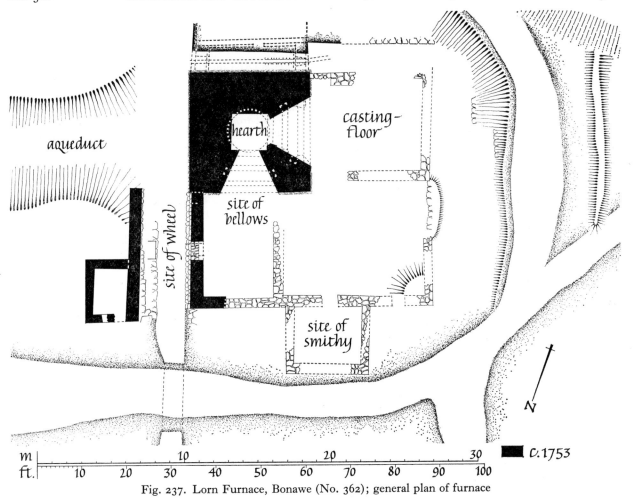

Fig. 237. Lorn Furnace, Bonawe (No. 362); general plan of furnace

Loch Etive between Airds Bay and the mouth of the River Awe. The furnace was established in 1753 by a group of Lakeland ironmasters led by Richard Ford (generally known as the Newland Company), with the object of utilizing locally produced charcoal to smelt haematite ore brought in by sea from Lancashire and Cumberland. Agreements for the supply of wood were negotiated with a number of local landowners, including the 3rd Earl of Breadalbane and Sir Duncan Campbell of Lochnell, who had been closely associated with the similar but ill-fated project at Glen Kinglass (No. 358), and the company embarked upon a period of considerable prosperity, iron of good quality being produced at a cost which compared favourably with that in the Lake District. Local labour was extensively employed to cut wood and to manufacture and transport charcoal (cf. Nos. 360 and 361), while subsidiary industries included tanning and spinning. As well as constructing a furnace and workers' dwellings, the company erected numerous ancillary buildings, including a school, a church and a quay, thus creating a small industrial community which soon became an object of some curiosity to travellers in the Highlands.[1]

After the expiry of the original lease of wood rights in 1863, a new lease was obtained by Alexander Kelly, who sub-let the furnace to the Company (by now known as the Lorn Furnace Company) whilst himself supplying charcoal. After a short period of further activity, however, the furnace was finally closed down in 1874, and the buildings were thereafter abandoned or put to other uses. An extensive programme of repair and consolidation is currently being undertaken by the Department of the Environment.[2]

The more important of the surviving buildings are described below, and their locations are illustrated on the accompanying site-plan (Fig. 236). Most of these structures exhibit building-techniques of English Lakeland origin, and there can be little doubt that imported craftsmen and materials were used in their construction.

THE FURNACE. The furnace buildings occupy a focal position on the site, standing a little to the N of the coal-

[1] St Fond, *Journey*, ii, 149–50; Garnett, *Tour*, i, 130.
[2] Fell, *Iron Industry*, 390–414; Cadell, H M, *The Story of the Forth* (1913), 148–50; (MacDonald, Mrs T H L), *Taynuilt: Our History* (n.d.), 21–6.

houses and ore-shed (Pl. 111), and immediately beside the principal access-road from the quay. They comprise the blast-furnace itself, which survives more or less intact, together with the ruins of a number of ancillary structures. All these buildings probably originated about the year 1753, but the furnace was subsequently raised in height, and minor alterations and additions were made to some of the outbuildings from time to time.

The buildings (Figs. 237, 238, 239, 241; Pl. 112) are for the most part constructed of local rubble masonry, chiefly granite, strongly bound in lime mortar, the lintels being either of cast iron or of timber. The furnace-tunnel is lined with firebrick, while the chimney is also of brick, the upper courses being constructed of bricks somewhat larger in size than those in the lower courses. The existing tunnel-lining and chimney are clearly of secondary construction, however, having probably been inserted when the furnace was raised in height. Some of the facing-bricks of the tunnel-lining bear the incised stamp CWM BRAN FIRE CLAY CO., a firm which is known to have operated at Cwmbran, Monmouthshire, prior to about 1850.[1] It seems probable, therefore, that the

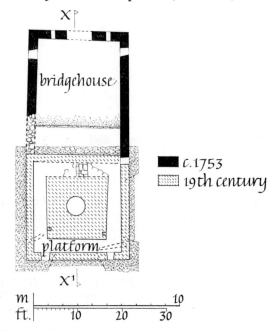

Fig. 238. Lorn Furnace, Bonawe (No. 362); upper plan of furnace

furnace was raised in height and relined about the second quarter of the 19th century.

The furnace measures about 7·9 m square at base, but the walls batter sharply inwards as they ascend, so that at a height of about 6·4 m the structure measures only about 7·0 m square. Above this level the masonry appears to be of secondary construction, and the walls are vertical. The existing wall-head rises to a height of 8·9 m, the total height of the structure to the top of the

chimney being 11·7 m; in the original arrangement, however, the wall-head and chimney were evidently somewhat lower.

Access to the furnace-hearth is obtained by means of deeply-splayed apertures on the N and W sides (Pl. 113C), of which the former gave entry for the blast, while the latter was utilized for the tapping process and for the clearance of slag. Each of these openings is spanned by three cast-iron lintels, some of the upper ones being supported on massive stone corbels. The spaces between the lintels are for the most part ceiled with slabs of red sandstone laid corbelways, but the upper portion of the N ceiling is corbelled with granite. The two upper lintels of the W opening, and the uppermost one of the N opening, bear the cast inscription BUNAW. F. (Bonawe Furnace) 1753 (Pl. 113B), while the central lintel of the N opening appears to bear the ligatured initials NE (?Newland) and the date 175[?3]. These lintels were probably cast by Richard Ford & Company at Newland, Lancashire, preparatory to the construction of the furnace, and subsequently transported northwards by sea; the red-sandstone slabs may also be of Lake-District origin. A similar procedure for the supply of materials had been adopted at the establishment of the Invergarry Furnace in 1727.[2]

The furnace-hearth measures about 2·4 m square at the present floor-level, but at a height of about 1·5 m the internal corners are spanned by curved cast-iron lintels, and the chamber becomes circular on plan, having a diameter of 2·7 m. Above the boshes the tunnel is of inverted conical form: the loading-mouth (Pl. 113A), which is situated at a height of 8·7 m above the present floor-level, has a diameter of 1·0 m. The mouth itself splays outwards to meet the base of the square brick chimney, which rises to a height of 2·1 m. Access to the mouth was obtained by means of steps leading up from a bridgehouse situated on the S side of the furnace, where the ground-level is considerably higher than on the remaining sides. The existing steps, which are of firebrick, were evidently installed during the reconstruction of the upper portion of the furnace, but the original loading-arrangements were probably similar, although conducted at a slightly lower level. One of the steps bears the maker's stamp: LUCOOK.

At this upper level a cavity formed between the outer walls of the furnace and the casing of the tunnel allows a continuous walk or platform, about 1·0 m in width, to pass round all four sides of the building. This platform was evidently roofed on three sides with lean-to roofs butted on to the chimney, the double-pitched roof on the S side being continuous with that of the adjacent bridgehouse. The platform is lit by two windows in the N wall, by another in the W wall, and perhaps formerly by a fourth in the E wall. The present roof is modern, but two timber posts associated with an earlier roof can

---

[1] Information from Mr G Seabridge, Director and Works Manager, South Wales Refractories Limited.
[2] Fell, *Iron Industry*, 351. Many of the red-sandstone slabs have recently been renewed by the Department of the Environment.

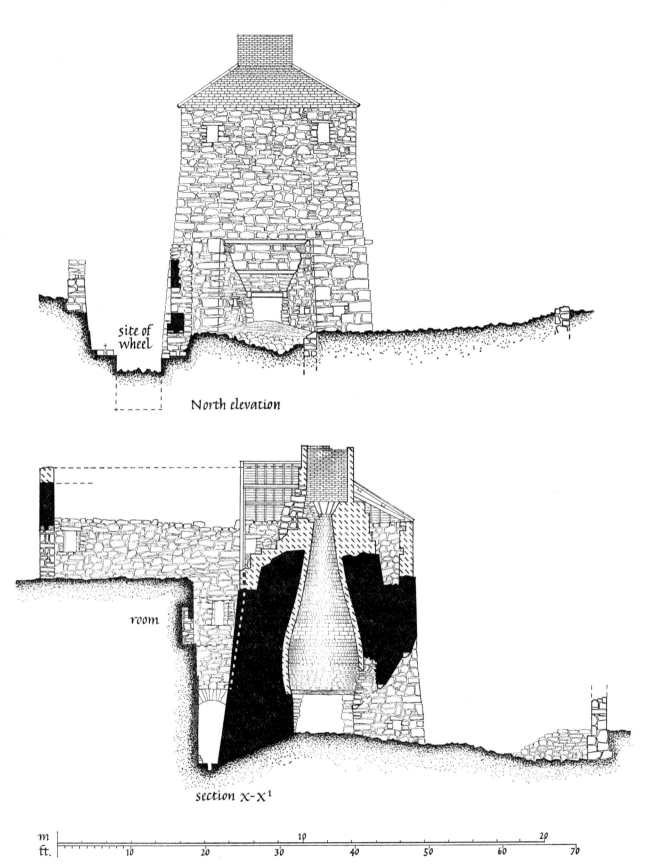

site of wheel

North elevation

room

section X-X¹

m

ft.

| 10 | 20 | 30 | 40 | 50 | 60 | 70 |

10   20

Fig. 239. Lorn Furnace, Bonawe (No. 362); elevation and section of furnace

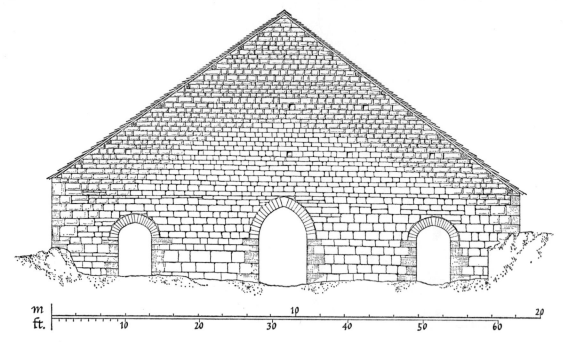

Fig. 240. Lorn Furnace, Bonawe (No. 362); elevation of E charcoal-shed

be seen encased in the masonry of the tunnel-lining close to the NW and NE corners of the platform. About 1·0 m beneath the level of the platform a number of small square openings, some of them provided with drip-stone lintels, may be seen in the external faces of the W and E walls of the furnace. These appear to be the mouths of vents designed to permit the escape of steam and other exhaust-gases during the blowing-in of the furnace.[1]

The bridgehouse was entered by a wide timber-lintelled doorway in the S wall. Because of the bankside position of the building, this doorway is situated at approximately the same level as the unloading-doors of the adjacent charcoal and ore storage-sheds, an arrangement which must have greatly facilitated the charging of the furnace. The doorway appears to have been protected by a gabled porch. In the original arrangement the floor-level of the bridgehouse was evidently some 0·7 m lower than it is today, the floor having been raised and the wall-heads correspondingly heightened at the time of the reconstruction of the upper part of the furnace. The S portion of the floor of the bridgehouse rests upon made-up ground supported by a retaining-wall, but the N portion was supported on joists bridging a cavity formed between the retaining-wall and the S wall of the furnace. Some of these joists still remain *in situ*, being located at the original floor-level of the bridgehouse, which approximately corresponds to that of the platform surrounding the furnace.

Beneath this joisted floor the cavity contained a long narrow apartment evidently entered by means of a forestair leading to a doorway in the E wall. This chamber was lit by a window in the W wall, while the retaining-wall to the S incorporates a timber-lintelled fireplace having a curiously-constructed horizontal flue with outlets in the W and E walls. This room may have been provided for the accommodation of the founder, whose constant attendance at the furnace was necessary during smelting-operations. Beneath the joisted floor of the apartment the lower part of the cavity appears to have contained a drain, which was carried under the side-walls of the building by means of flat voussoired arches.

The other ancillary buildings are all in a ruinous condition, and some are represented only by wall-foundations. The aqueduct approached from the E, making a right-angled turn before flowing past the E side of the furnace to drive a water-wheel situated in a forebuilding. This wheel, which was probably of breast-shot construction, provided power to operate a large bellows situated immediately in front of the N face of the furnace. Other buildings on this side are known to have included a smithy and a pay-office.[2] The casting-floor lay immediately outside the W aperture of the furnace, being covered with a pitched roof whose outline may still be traced on the furnace-wall. The aqueduct was fed from the River Awe at a point about 1 km from the furnace, while reservoirs situated in the neighbourhood of the manager's house and adjacent workers' dwellings provided an emergency supply.

[1] Cf. Schubert, H R, *History of the British Iron and Steel Industry from c. 450 B.C. to A.D. 1775* (1957), 197, 203.
[2] Cadell, op. cit., 149.

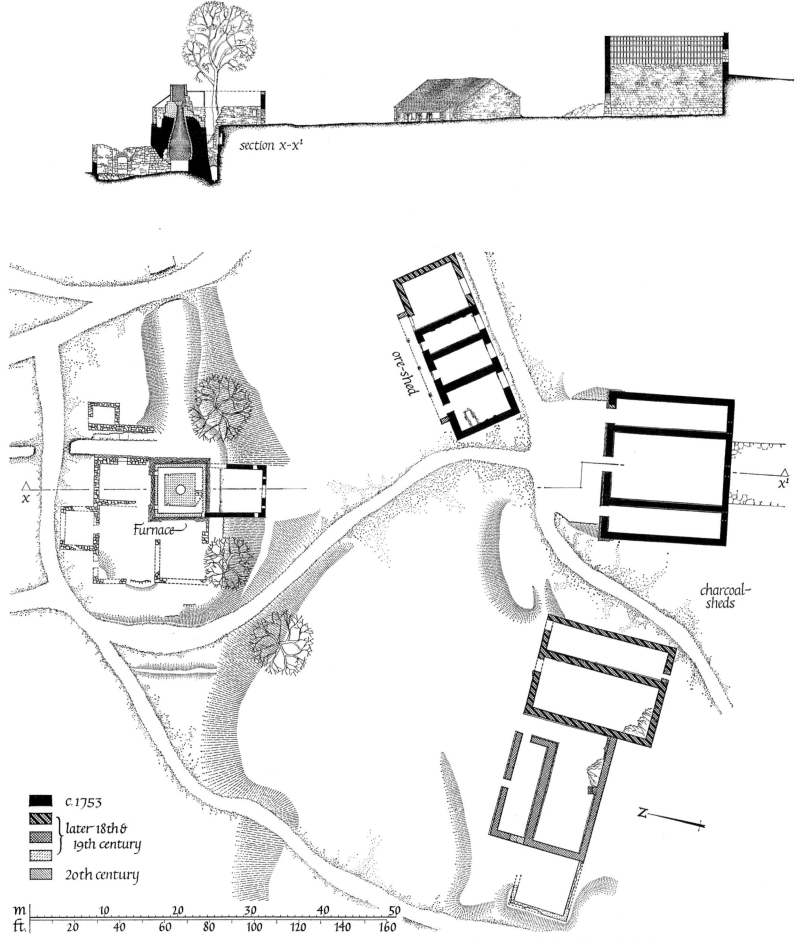

section x-x¹

ore-shed

Furnace

charcoal-sheds

x

x¹

Z

c. 1753

} later 18th & 19th century

20th century

m | 10 20 30 40 50
ft. | 20 40 60 80 100 120 140 160

Fig. 241. Lorn Furnace, Bonawe (No. 362); plan and section of furnace, ore-shed and charcoal-sheds

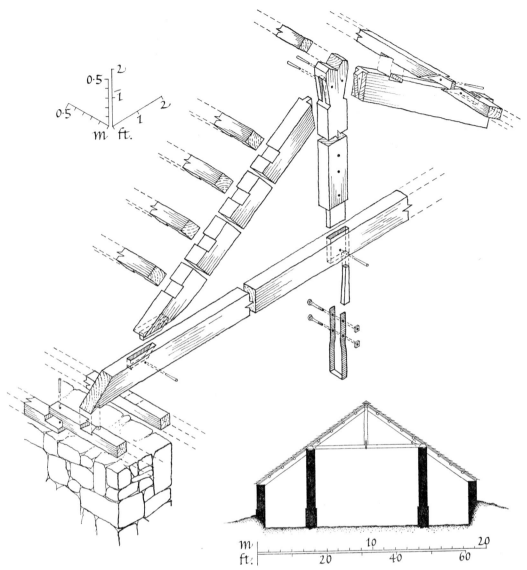

Fig. 242. Lorn Furnace, Bonawe (No. 362); roof-details and section of E charcoal-shed

ORE-SHED. This building (Fig. 241, Pl. 114A) measures 22·7 m from NE to SW by 9·1 m transversely over walls about 1·0 m in thickness. As first built, in or about 1753, however, it had a length of only 15·4 m, the NE portion having been added to the original structure at some later date. The masonry of the original building is of light-grey granite, and free use is made of through-stones: the lower portions of the walls incorporate offset-courses. The masonry of the NE addition, on the other hand, is composed primarily of reddish-brown porphyrite, although a number of light-grey granite quoins have been employed. The roof is of collar-and-tie-beam truss construction, the slates being nailed to battens; the ridge-piece is of stone.

In the original arrangement the building contained three storage-bays of unequal size, each provided with a high-level loading-door in the SE wall and a low-level unloading-door in the opposite wall, which faces the furnace. Similar access-arrangements are found in the NE addition, which incorporates a single large storage-bay. Some time after the erection of the NE addition an open gallery, supported on timber posts, was constructed along the greater part of the NW wall to permit unloading to take place under cover. At the same time the wall-head was raised to accommodate the gallery. The floors of the storage-bays appear to have been cobbled. Most of the internal wall-surfaces are deeply stained with haematite. The structure was repaired, partly re-roofed

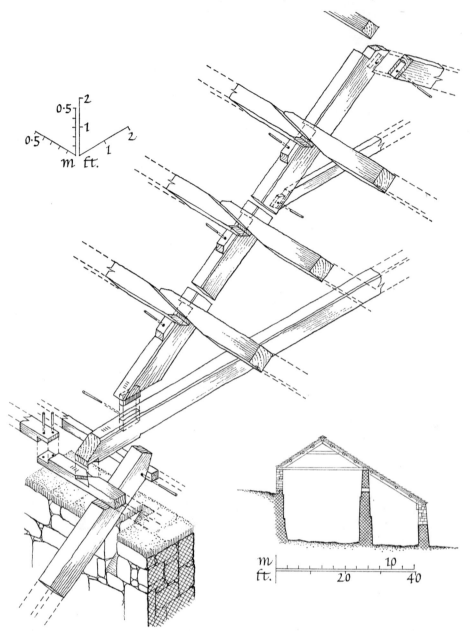

Fig. 243. Lorn Furnace, Bonawe (No. 362); roof-details and section of W charcoal-sheds

and re-slated by the (then) Ministry of Public Building and Works in 1967–8, the timber posts of the gallery being renewed at that time.

CHARCOAL-SHEDS. These extend westwards from the ore-shed and comprise a large detached shed, together with a group of three smaller attached sheds, beyond which there may be seen what appears to be the site of another detached shed, now completely ruinous. All the sheds occupy bankside positions that allow high-level loading-doors to be incorporated at the back and low-level unloading-doors at the front, where there is direct access to the bridgehouse of the furnace. The E detached shed is evidently the oldest, and probably dates from the establishment of the foundry, while the three sheds forming the adjacent group appear to have been erected successively during the course of the late 18th and early 19th centuries, progressing from E to W.

The oldest shed (Figs. 240, 241, Pl. 114B) is constructed of coursed rubble masonry composed partly of grey Bonawe granite and partly of dark-red porphyrite. The upper portions of the walls are successively diminished

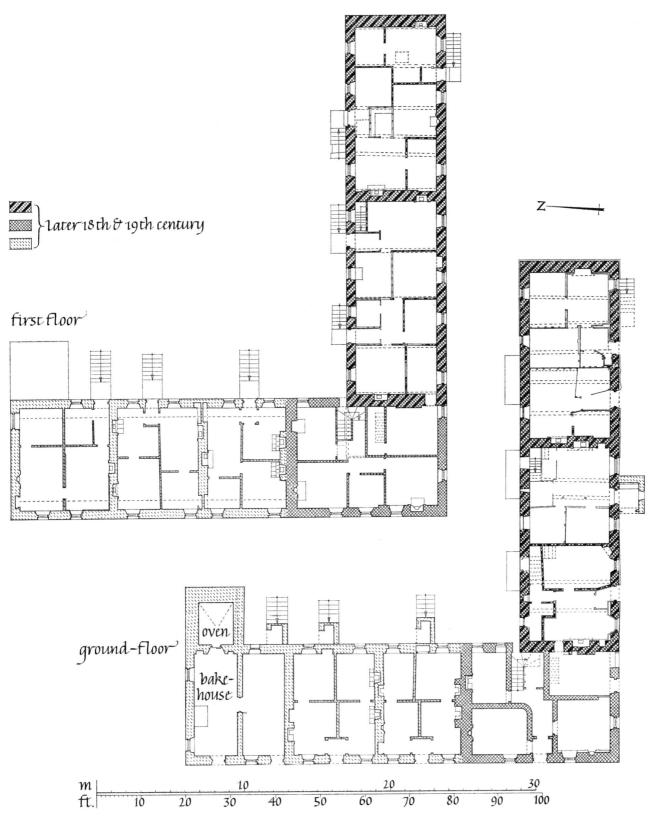

later 18th & 19th century

first floor

ground-floor

oven

bake-house

z

m

ft.

10   20   30   40   50   60   70   80   90   100

10   20   30

Fig. 244. Lorn Furnace, Bonawe (No. 362); ground- and first-floor plans of NE workers' dwellings

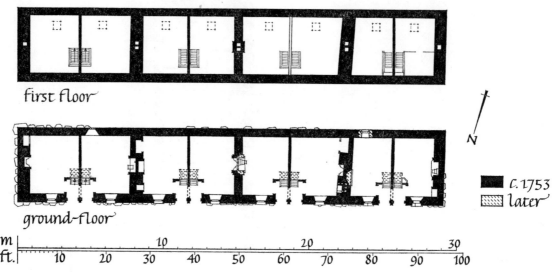

first floor

ground-floor

■ c.1753
▨ later

Fig. 245. Lorn Furnace, Bonawe (No. 362); ground- and first-floor plans of SE workers' dwellings

in thickness by means of offset-courses, and the masonry incorporates occasional through-stones and numerous put-log holes, the latter presumably being designed to support scaffolding during building- and maintenance-operations. The unloading-doors have arched heads formed with dark-grey greywacke dressings probably imported from the Lake District, the central arch being obtuse in form, and the flanking arches four-centred. One of the latter has at some period been superseded by a timber lintel. The interior is divided into three parts and has a total floor-area of about 246 sq. m and a capacity of 1296 cu. m; there is no provision for upper floors. The roof is of king-post tie-beam truss construction (Fig. 242, Pl. 115A) with graded Lake-District slates nailed to battens,[1] and stone ridge-pieces. The S gable-wall is surmounted by a brick belfry.

The three attached sheds (Fig. 241, Pl. 114C) are generally similar in character to the one just described, but the doorways are spanned with massive timber lintels. One of the loading-doors of the E shed appears to have been protected by an external canopy. The E and central sheds contain two storage compartments of unequal size, the former having a total floor-area of about 170 sq. m and a capacity of 782 cu. m, and its neighbour a floor-area of about 166 sq. m and a capacity of 585 cu. m. The roofs (Pl. 115B–D) are of tie-beam truss construction, the trusses of the central shed being also collared (Fig. 243). The roof of the E shed is pitched from W to E, and that of the central one from N to S, the roof of the larger storage-compartment in each case being extended downwards at the same pitch to cover the smaller one. The W shed, now very ruinous, appears to have contained a single storage-compartment having a floor-area of about 52 sq. m.

WORKERS' DWELLINGS. There are two main groups of workers' dwellings, of which the larger comprises a two-storeyed block of L-plan standing about 100 m NE of the furnace (Fig. 244, Pl. 116A). This appears to have been erected in three successive stages, the E range possibly dating from about the second half of the 18th century, the southern portion of the N range from the early 19th century, and the remainder of the N range from a somewhat later period in the same century. All the buildings are constructed of local rubble laid in lime mortar, and the roofs are slated. Timber lintels are used throughout, and those in the E range appear to have been protected externally by stone drip-courses, a characteristic which suggests that this portion of the structure was erected by Lakeland workmen.

The building has been altered to a considerable extent during occupation, and part of the interior has recently been gutted by fire, so that it is now difficult to determine the precise nature of the original layout. Thus, the E range may originally have been divided into flats, as it is today, having a series of three- or four-roomed dwellings at each level, of which those on the first floor were approached from forestairs on the N side. On the other hand, it is clear that some, at least, of the present forestairs are of secondary construction, while the existence of blocked-up internal staircases at the W end of the range indicates that at some period provision was made for a pair of two-storeyed dwellings, each containing about half a dozen rooms. The southern portion of the N range, which local tradition holds to have been an overseer's house, appears to have been designed as a substantial two-storeyed dwelling, but the remainder of

---

[1] Although many of the foundry buildings are today covered with Lakeland slate, there is evidence to suggest that local slate was much used at first: 'That Mr Ford's people at the Furnace of Bunaw preferr'd the Easedale slate to those of Westmorland, and made use of lathing instead of sarking, . . . only they plaster'd the lath on the inside and thereby answer'd every way as well as the sarking' (S.R.O., Breadalbane Collection, GD 112/18/22, letter from Colin Campbell of Carwhin, dated 18 March 1754).

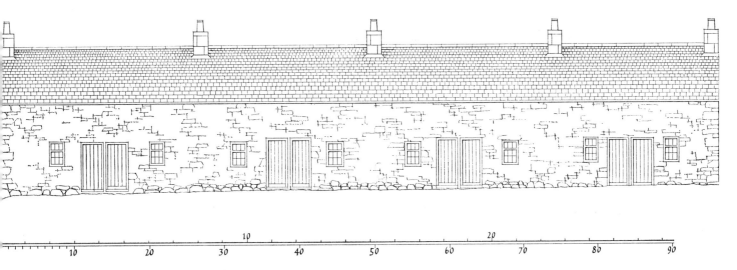

Fig. 246. Lorn Furnace, Bonawe (No. 362); elevation of SE workers' dwellings

the N range was probably always divided into flats. This latter portion of the building comprises a series of four-room dwellings of which those on the first floor are reached by means of forestairs on the E side. The northernmost section of the ground-floor area was a bake-house, and incorporates a brick-vaulted bake-oven housed in an adjacent outshot.

The second group of dwellings (Figs. 245, 246, Pl. 116B) stands about 100 m SE of the ore- and charcoal-sheds, and comprises a row of single-storeyed cottages. Each cottage formerly contained a single living-room with a loft above, reached by means of a steep timber staircase opening off a small entrance-lobby (Pl. 116C). The general character of the building is similar to that of the first group of dwellings, but the cottages are probably somewhat older, and may have been erected at the establishment of the foundry.

BONAWE HOUSE. This mid-18th-century house was built as the residence of the manager of the Lorn Furnace Company, and is situated in wooded grounds about 300 m ESE of the main group of furnace-buildings. The original house comprises three principal storeys with basement and garret, and is oblong on plan, measuring 13·9 m from E to W by 11·7 m transversely over walls varying from 0·8 m to 1·0 m in thickness (Fig. 247). The walls are of rubble masonry, harled and whitewashed, and the roof is covered with Westmorland slates. A prominent feature of the S elevation is the use of long thin slabs set horizontally with their edges projecting a short distance from the wall-face to form

rough drip-stones above the window-openings. A two-storeyed wing was built against the W gable-wall in the early years of the present century, and smaller additions were made against the S wall at the same period.

The principal (N) façade (Pl. 116D) is of five bays, having the entrance-doorway placed centrally at ground-floor level. The ground-floor windows, however, have been replaced by large modern bay-windows. The windows of the second floor are not so tall as those of the first floor. The doorway (Pl. 116E), which is reached by a short flight of steps, is framed within an imposing timber surround incorporating fluted pilasters and a triglyph-frieze which supports a Doric pediment. The S elevation, now much obscured by recent additions, has been of four bays, having a doorway in the second bay from the W at ground-floor level. At first-floor level the opening above this doorway is a Venetian window whose principal light contains wooden mullions which intersect in the window-head, while the W side-light is a mock opening, probably originally painted to imitate glazing-bars. The E and W gable-walls terminate in long chimney-stacks which have been rebuilt during the present century.

The original internal arrangement remains substantially unaltered; there are, however, few original furnishings, all of the fireplaces having been replaced. Several of the doorways retain their original moulded architraves and six-panelled doors, and the openings leading into the principal rooms at ground- and first-floor level are ornamented with panelling in the jambs

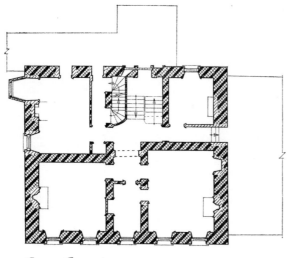

first floor

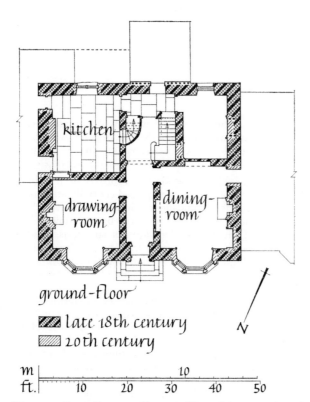

ground-floor

▨ late 18th century
▨ 20th century

N

m | 10
ft. | 10   20   30   40   50

Fig. 247. Lorn Furnace, Bonawe (No. 362); ground- and
first-floor plans of Bonawe House

and soffits. The entrance-doorway gives access to a hall flanked on the E by the drawing-room and on the W by the dining-room; the latter apartment has two elliptical-headed recesses in the S and E walls. An elliptical-headed timber arch springing from fluted pilasters divides the entrance-hall from the staircase-hall, where

the rebuilt stair rises on the W, while a rounded projection on the E conceals a service-stair. A stone-flagged corridor containing the S door gives access to a large stone-flagged kitchen in the SE angle, from which the service-stair rises in the W wall, and to a smaller room, perhaps a study or office, in the SW angle. This room originally communicated directly with the staircase-hall, but the doorway is now obstructed by the lower part of the rebuilt stair, and has been blocked. A stone stair situated below the principal staircase leads down to the basement, which underlies the W part of the house; it comprises a wine-cellar and an apartment said to have been a dairy.

The disposition of rooms on the first floor is generally similar to that below. To the N of the stair-head there is a small lobby which gives access to both of the principal bedrooms, and between these rooms there is a closet; this was originally attached to the NE room, but is now entered by modern doorways from the NW room and also from the lobby. The apartment in the SW angle has been reduced in area by the insertion of a partition-wall to form a corridor giving access to the early 20th-century W wing. An original partition-wall forms a corridor in the W part of the SE division of the house; the service-stair from the kitchen, which is lit by the splayed E side-light of the Venetian window, enters at the S end of the W wall of this corridor, and a similar stair, which provides the only means of access to the second floor, rises from a door in the same wall. The corridor and the SE room were originally lit by windows in the S wall, both of which have now been enlarged to form doors communicating with a modern extension.

The second floor has been extensively remodelled and contains no features of interest. The greater part of one original roof-truss is, however, visible in the garret. This is of a type commonly found in 18th-century pattern-books,[1] incorporating a shouldered king-post and two queen-posts with four diagonal struts. There are four purlins on each side, rebated into the principal rafters, and an obliquely-set ridge-piece. The slates are now carried on sarking-boards in the Scottish manner, but this is probably the result of re-roofing.

This is probably the house, 'built by a Mr. Knott of Coniston Water-head, a partner in the iron-foundry at Bunawe', the appearance of which failed to please Dorothy Wordsworth, when she visited the place in 1803.[2]

0031, 0032,   NN 03 SW   September 1971
0131, 0132

363. Gunpowder-works, Melfort. This enterprise was established by Harrison, Ainslie and Co., proprietors of the Lorn Furnace (No. 362), who purchased the estate of Melfort, with extensive woodlands, from Colonel John Campbell in 1838. It is said that produc-

---

[1] E.g., Hoppus, E, *The Gentleman's and Builder's Repository* (4th ed., 1760), pl. 76, no. 2; Pain, W and J, *Pain's British Palladio* (1786), pl. 13.
[2] Wordsworth, *Tour*, 145; Fell, *Iron Industry*, 273, 406.

tion was discontinued after a serious explosion in 1867, and the estate was sold to a private owner in 1874.[1] The mill-lade and some of the buildings remained in use after this date as part of a saw-mill. Normal practice required that buildings where the manufacturing processes took place should be of light construction; most of those at Melfort were built of brick, and have completely disappeared, although their sites are identifiable. The large-scale map prepared by the Ordnance Survey in 1871, however, shows the full extent of the works shortly before they closed.[2]

The works were situated in the valley of the River Oude, E and NE of Melfort House, the buildings being spaced out over a distance of about 700 m. Parts of the complex were linked by a tram-way which continued WSW for 800 m to a pier at Fearnach Bay. To the N, the Eas Tarsuinn stream was dammed just above its junction with the River Oude, at a height of 75 m OD, forming a pool which served a mill-lade. The lade, which is still well preserved, was constructed by quarrying the steep hillside to form a sheer rock-face on the W, and building a wall of rubble masonry, having an average thickness of 0·8 m, on the E. It ran S for 550 m into a rock-cut reservoir with a sluice-gate, beyond which it continued SW to operate in succession four mills, each placed at a lower level, before flowing E into the River Oude. Three of these mills probably ground the individual constituents of the powder, while the fourth was an incorporating-mill where the ingredients were mixed; each had a charge-house, for temporary storage, attached or nearby. The two lower mills, which survive in a fragmentary state, each comprised two chambers, 4·6 m square within 0·8 m rubble walls, separated by a narrow compartment containing a water-wheel, probably of over-shot construction.

The remaining processing-buildings, situated NNE of the mills, but not disposed altogether in accordance with the sequence of operations, were the corning-house, press-house, glazing-house, packing-house, dusting-house and two stove-houses served by a single boiler-house. A short distance N of the reservoir is the 'suspense magazine', roofless but otherwise intact, measuring 5·5 m by 6·1 m over walls of rubble masonry 0·6 m thick.

Large storage-sheds were required for sulphur and saltpetre, both imported by sea from abroad, and for charcoal which was produced locally in charcoal cylinders formerly situated on the SE bank of the River Oude, and which was used in large quantities. These sheds remain intact although the 'saltpetre and refinery house' which adjoined them on the NE has completely disappeared. The largest shed, measuring 26·2 m from E to W by 10·4 m transversely over 0·6 m walls, is built against the hill-side and, like the similar sheds at Bonawe, had loading-doors, now blocked, high up in the N wall. It is divided into two compartments by a stone partition-wall, and these contain respectively three and two king-post roof-trusses (Pl. 117A), carrying a roof of local slate. This building was subsequently extended for 10·4 m to the W, the addition being lofted. Adjoining the large shed on the SE, and probably contemporary

with it, is another measuring 13·6 m from N to S by 8·5 m transversely, having roof-trusses of similar form.

To the W of the storage-sheds there is a group of buildings (Pl. 117B) which, although used as a cooperage in connection with the powder-works, is probably of early 19th-century date and may have been the original court of offices for Melfort House. The buildings surround three sides of a square, and that on the N side is a two-storeyed structure of five bays, with hipped roof, having round-headed louvred openings at first-floor level.

Some 600 m W of the main group of buildings, and 60 m N of the road from Melfort to Degnish, there stands the principal magazine, consisting originally of two simple stone-built sheds, each measuring 8·8 m by 6·7 m, one of which was subsequently doubled in length. These structures are now roofed with asbestos sheeting.

8314, 8414   NM 81 SW   July 1971

364. Old Ferryhouse, Port Appin. This name applies to a pair of early 19th-century cottages situated immediately behind Port Appin pier. The cottages are constructed of lime-washed rubble with slate roofs, and are built parallel to each other with bowed gable-ends overlooking the shore (Pl. 117D); both have been remodelled internally within recent years. According to local information, the space between the two cottages was formerly roofed over to serve as a boat-house. The Lismore–Appin ferry is on record as early as c. 1630, and is also mentioned by the authors of the first and second *Statistical Accounts*.[3]

902453   NM 94 NW   July 1968

365. Lime-kilns, Port Kilcheran, Lismore. Port Kilcheran is a small bay situated on the SE coast of Lismore, about 200 m SE of Kilcheran House (No. 257). Bishop John Chisholm established a lime-burning industry there soon after the Roman Catholic Highland Seminary occupied Kilcheran House in 1803, and bricks for lining the kiln were being shipped from Glasgow in 1804.[4] When Walter Scott visited the area in 1814, he recorded in his journal 'Chisholm has established a seminary . . . and what is a better thing, a valuable lime-work. Reports speak well of the lime. . . .'.[5] Despite this good reputation, the lime-works were never profitable, and there is no evidence that they remained in operation after the departure of the seminary in 1828.[6]

[1] S.R.O., Abbreviated Register of Sasines (Argyll), 1831–40, no. 1310; ibid., 1869–75, no. 2157; Shedden, *Lorn*, 80–1.
[2] O.S., 1 : 2500 map, Argyllshire, sheet cxxii, 13. For descriptions of the manufacture of gunpowder, cf. 'Report of the Select Committee on Explosive Substances', *Parliamentary Papers, 1874*, ix; Hodgetts, E B, *The Rise and Progress of the British Explosives Industry* (1909); *Industrial Archaeology*, v (1968), 128.
[3] *Geog. Coll.*, ii, 155; *Stat. Acct.*, i (1791), 499; *NSA*, vii (Argyll), 255.
[4] *The Innes Review*, viii (1957), 31–2.
[5] Lockhart, J G, *Memoirs of Sir Walter Scott* (1882), iv, 343.
[6] *The Innes Review*, viii (1957), 32.

The earliest structure on the site (Pl. 118A) is a free-standing single kiln constructed of harled rubble masonry, which measures 6·7 m from N to S by 6·1 m transversely over all and stands to a height of about 6 m. In the N and E sides there are openings with arch-pointed heads roughly formed by corbelled stones; that on the N has an aumbry above the lintel of the draw-hole. There is no surviving means of access to the top of the kiln, and a cottage of mid-19th-century date abuts it on the W. About 14 m to the N there is another building, 7·6 m in height, which measures 12·2 m from N to S by 10·7 m transversely over all; the NE and SE angles are bevelled. The W part of this structure contains two barrel-vaulted store-rooms, each measuring 4·9 m by 3·8 m, while the E portion forms a double kiln, each kiln having two draw-holes. The draw-holes set in the bevelled angles have segmental outer arches of stone, and inner arches of brick, while those in the E side have straight-sided arched heads. The top of this structure, which is enclosed by a low parapet, is reached by a ramp from higher ground on the N. Against the E wall there is built a long rectangular shed, the E gable-wall of which contains a door from which a small boat could be loaded at high tide. The face of the limestone cliff about 80 m W of this site shows traces of extensive quarrying.

825386   NM 83 NW   June 1970

366. Limestone-quarries and Workers' Dwellings, Port Ramsay, Lismore. This village (Pl. 118B, D) stands close to the NE tip of Lismore, overlooking the best anchorage in the island.[1] Port Ramsay was thus well situated for the prosecution of the two enterprises to which it owed its development in the 19th century, namely the local fishing-industry and the export of lime.[2] The village comprises a single row of cottages standing close to the water's edge. These cottages are plain single-storeyed dwellings of rubble masonry with lime-washed walls and slate roofs, and each contains two main rooms. The principal limestone-quarries lie immediately to the NE of the village, where there is also a quay and a pair of lime-kilns (Pl. 118C). Another group of quarries with an associated kiln may be seen on the opposite side of the bay, beyond Fennacrochan.

8845   NM 84 NE   May 1968

367. Old Ferryhouse, South Shian. This is a plain two-storeyed building of oblong plan with a gable-ended roof; the masonry is of harled rubble (Pl. 117C). The interior, now somewhat remodelled, seems originally to have comprised two main rooms on each floor flanking a central staircase of timber. A single-storeyed wing extends southwards from the rear of the house towards a detached group of outbuildings, whose walls contain cruck-stumps associated with an earlier roof.

Although there was a ferryhouse here at least as early as 1777, the existing buildings probably date from the second quarter of the 19th century. The wing of the ferryhouse and the outbuildings appear to form part of a group of buildings erected by Sir Duncan Campbell of Barcaldine in 1831–2, while the ferryhouse itself, which also served as an inn, is probably of slightly later date.[3]

908421   NM 94 SW   July 1970

ROADS AND BRIDGES

368. Bridge of Awe. This fine three-arched bridge (Pl. 119A) spans the River Awe about 100 m upstream from the present road-bridge that replaced it in 1938. Construction was completed in 1779, and the original structure remains substantially intact although much of the rubble stonework has been refaced during the present century.

The 18th-century road from Dalmally to Bonawe crosses the bridge from E to W. The overall length of the bridge and approaches is 72 m, the length spanned by the three segmental arches is 50 m, and the spans of the individual arches, from E to W, measure 13·6 m, 15·2 m and 14·2 m respectively. At its highest point, above the central arch, the top of the parapet is 8·2 m above water-level; the height to the arch-soffit is 6·5 m. The roadway has a width of 4·2 m between parapets 0·38 m in thickness. There are refaced triangular cut-waters on both sides of the central piers.

In 1776 the Commissioners of Supply for Argyll applied to the Commissioners of Forfeited Estates for financial assistance to bridge the River Awe. They claimed that, since the river could seldom be forded, Lorn, Morvern and the Islands were cut off from the road via Dalmally to Stirling, which was the best route to Crieff cattle-fair. Local landowners had contributed £400 of the £600 required, and the Forfeited Estates Board agreed to supply the balance. Work was well advanced in 1778, when the central part of the bridge was swept away by a flood while the centering was in place for forming the arches. Despite this mishap, the bridge was completed in the following year.[4]

030297   NN 02 NW   July 1970

369. Clachan Bridge, Seil. This bridge, which joins the island of Seil to the mainland, spans Clachan Sound at a point about 4·5 km SW of Kilninver. The bridge (Pl. 119B) crosses the narrow tidal channel by a single bold segmental arch having a span of 22 m and a height above high-water level of about 8·5 m. The overall length of the bridge with approaches is about 95 m, and the road-

[1] *NSA*, vii (Argyll), 229.
[2] *Stat. Acct.*, i (1791), 500; *NSA*, vii (Argyll), 251; *Third Stat. Acct.* (Argyll), 164.
[3] S.R.O., Campbell of Barcaldine Collection, GD 170/381/12; ibid., GD 170/514/17; RHP 12330 and 12336.
[4] S.R.O., Forfeited Estates Papers, E 728/29/ nos. 16 and 20; ibid., E 727/34/14; Smith, *General View*, 276–7.

way measures 4·7 m in width between parapets 0·4 m in thickness. The masonry is of roughly-coursed boulder-rubble with copious pinnings, and the form of the arch is emphasised by long thin voussoir-slabs. Within the haunches of the arch there are circular recesses, 2·1 m in diameter; the central portion of the parapet is defined by small pyramidal blocks set above these recesses.

This site had been selected for a bridge as early as 1787, when it was identified as 'Intended Bridge' on an estate-plan by George Langlands.[1] In 1790 John Campbell of Lochend, Chamberlain of the Breadalbane estate in Argyll, rejected a suggestion that the channel should be filled in, and obtained a plan from John Stevenson, an Oban contractor, for a bridge having a main arch of 21·3 m span, high enough to allow the passage of small vessels, together with a smaller arch of 6·1 m span. The greater part of the estimated cost of £450 was to be divided between Lord Breadalbane, the Easdale Slate Company, and MacDougall of Ardencaple. Lord Breadalbane suggested that a professional architect should be consulted, and it is probable that the design was amended by Robert Mylne.[2] The bridge was constructed in 1791 by John Stevenson, who made a considerable financial loss for which he received partial compensation from Lord Breadalbane in 1795.[3]

785196   NM 71 NE   June 1970

370. Bridge and Embankment, Dalmally.
A three-arched bridge (Pl. 119C) carries the old road from Bonawe via Stronmilchan to Dalmally across the River Orchy at a point about 150 m NNW of Glenorchy Church (No. 246). The bridge was constructed by the contractor who had built Bridge of Awe (No. 368), using machinery and centering from the latter, and was completed in 1780.

The S bank of the river is somewhat higher than the N bank; the bridge therefore reaches its highest point above the S arch. Although the rubble masonry has been refaced in the upper parts, the triangular cut-waters remain intact and preserve their stepped tops. The overall length of the bridge and approaches is 55 m and the distance spanned by the three segmental arches is 43 m. The spans of the individual arches, from N to S, measure 9·2 m, 12·9 m and 14·8 m respectively, and the heights of the arches above water-level measure 4·6 m, 5·6 m and 6·7 m respectively. The width of the roadway is 4·1 m between parapets 0·38 m in thickness.

South-east of the church, an embankment incorporating three arches carries the road across a backwater of the River Orchy and an area of marshy ground for an overall distance of 63 m. This structure has been extensively rebuilt during the present century; the central arch, which has a span of 8·6 m and a height above water-level of 3·2 m, is now the only part that appears to be of the same date as the larger bridge.

In July 1778, when the construction of Bridge of Awe was under way, the Commissioners of Supply for Argyll petitioned the Forfeited Estates Commissioners for financial assistance to build an additional bridge across the Orchy. The need for this was explained in terms

similar to those of the previous petition (cf. No. 368), with the added benefit of facilitating troop-movements during winter. It was stated that the lowest estimate obtained was £650, if the bridge were to be built immediately using wood and machinery from Bridge of Awe; of this sum £300 had been subscribed locally. Construction was completed in August 1780, when the masons received a gift from Glenorchy parish poor-fund, 'upon finishing Bridge of Urchay'.[4]

166276 (Dalmally Bridge)
168274 (Embankment)   NN 12 NE   July 1970

371. Military Road, Inveraray–Tyndrum.
This road was begun in 1757 under the direction of Major Caulfield in order to carry the line of the recently completed Dumbarton–Inveraray road into Lorn and establish a link with the main Stirling–Fort William road (No. 372). Prior to 1757 communication between Inveraray and Dalmally had been obtained by means of a road maintained by the local Commissioners of Supply. The initial work of construction was probably completed in the early 1760s, but considerable sums of money were expended on repairs and maintenance before the responsibility for upkeep passed to the Parliamentary Commissioners in 1814, and this process of improvement has continued up to the present day, with the result that few stretches of the road now remain in anything like their original condition.[5]

The road enters Lorn on the line of the present highway at Taynafead (NN 093182), but almost immediately diverges westwards on to higher ground, running adjacent and approximately parallel to the highway for a distance of about 2 km. This section of the road, which has evidently been disused for a considerable time, takes the form of a rough track, some 4·5 m in width, heavily overgrown with reeds and grasses. The road rejoins the present highway at NN 099206, and between this point and Achlian there are no identifiable

---

[1] S.R.O., RHP 975/1, Survey of Seil and Luing.
[2] During the period when the design of Clachan Bridge was being discussed, Mylne was preparing plans for extensive works at Taymouth. In his diary for 13 April 1790 there appears the entry 'Gave Earl of Bread Albane . . . a small drawing for the side of a Road Bridge' (Richardson, A E, *Robert Mylne, Architect and Engineer, 1733 to 1811* (1955), 137). The Earl's intention of consulting an architect is acknowledged by John Campbell in a letter of 18 April 1790, before news of the meeting with Mylne could have reached him from London. It seems probable that Mylne suggested the omission of the smaller arch in Stevenson's original design, and included the decorative recesses which may be compared with those used at Hexham (ibid., pl. 42). There is no evidence to support the attribution of the bridge to Thomas Telford (made by, e.g., Gillies, *Netherlorn*, 35).
[3] S.R.O., Breadalbane Collection, GD 112/48, Bridges Correspondence, 18 February, 18 April 1790; ibid., GD 112/9/3, Nether Lorn Rental, 1794-5.
[4] S.R.O., Forfeited Estates Papers, E 728/29/20; New Register House, Glenorchy Parish Register, OPR/512/2, fol. 31.
[5] Mackenzie, Sir K S, 'Military Roads', *TISS*, v (1895-9), 369, 371, 374n; Mactavish, D S, 'Argyllshire Roads prior to 1800', *TGSI*, xxxviii (1937-41), 329, 350.

features of interest apart from the bridges at Cladich (NN 096220) and Inistrynich (NN 111234). These are both plain single-arched structures with 3·5 m carriageways, and probably date from the 18th century, but the one at Cladich has subsequently been widened. Between Achlian and Dalmally the military road remains in use as a minor vehicle-road, the average width of the carriageway being 4·0 m. The single-arched bridge that spans the Teatle Water (NN 127250) has a span of 9·7 m and, like the smaller bridge at Ardteatle itself (NN 135257), a carriageway of 3·5 m; both bridges are probably of 18th-century date. The bridge at Croft-in-tuime (NN 157271), on the other hand, which has a 4·8 m carriageway, bears the date 1812, and evidently replaces an earlier bridge.[1]

Between Dalmally and Inverlochy the road again forms part of a modern highway and there are no features of interest with the exception of the disused bridge at Inverlochy (NN 196275). This is a two-arched structure with a cut-water pier; the main arch has a span of 10·4 m and the carriageway has a width of 3·4 m. A stone bridge across the River Lochy was constructed in this vicinity by James Duff, mason, about the year 1734,[2] but the existing structure probably dates from the second half of the 18th century.

The old road can be seen crossing and re-crossing the modern highway on the ascent between Inverlochy and Strone, beyond which the two roads run more or less parallel to each other for about 3 km, the earlier one taking the higher ground to the N. Here the old road takes the form of a metalled track some 3·6 m in width, the burns being spanned by culverts. Another section of the early road, again running a little to the N of the modern highway, can be identified between Arrivain and Arinabea, but here the road has evidently remained in use until the present century. The carriageway has a width of about 4·6 m and the larger burns are spanned by well-constructed bridges of 19th-century date. The road enters Perthshire on the line of the present highway about 1 km NW of Tyndrum (NN 320309), where it joins the Stirling–Fort William road (cf. No. 372).

093182–320309   May 1972
NN 01 NE, NN 02 SE, NN 12 SW,
NN 12 NW, NN 12 NE, NN 22 NW,
NN 22 NE, NN 23 SE, NN 33 SW

372. Military Road, Tyndrum–Kinlochleven.

The construction of the military road from Stirling to Fort William was begun in 1748, under the direction of Major Edward Caulfield.[3] The section between Fort William and Kinlochleven was completed in 1750,[4] while a substantial portion of the road through Argyll was made in the following year by five companies each of the Buffs and of Colonel Rich's Regiment. A plan by H Gordon[5] shows that this work comprised the sections from Loch Dochart, Perthshire, to Auch Bridge, and from Bridge of Orchy to Forest Lodge. The road, when completed, was maintained at considerable expense. A new road from Altnafeadh through Glencoe to Ballachulish was constructed by the local Commissioners of Supply

between 1776 and 1782, and responsibility for it was assumed by the military authorities in 1786, when the difficult section from Altnafeadh over the Devil's Staircase to Kinlochleven was abandoned.[6] Improved lines of road were constructed c. 1800 on several sections between Bridge of Orchy and Kingshouse.

Responsibility for the upkeep of the military roads was transferred to the Commissioners for Highland Roads and Bridges in 1814.[7] In 1829 it was stated that steamboats on the West Coast had much diminished the traffic and that only drovers now used the road; it remained an important droving route throughout the 19th century.[8] The improved line of the military road was retained, with minor alterations, until 1932, when the present A82 was constructed on an entirely different route. Portions of the older road remain in use for estate purposes, although only one section, from Bridge of Orchy to Victoria Bridge, is classified as a public highway.

Where it has been least altered, in those sections that were abandoned by c. 1800, the road appears as a level track about 4·6 m in width flanked by upcast mounds and drainage ditches, with small roadside quarries at frequent intervals. A kerb of earth-fast boulders is found at the S approach of the Devil's Staircase, and on the abandoned section N of Forest Lodge. The technique of terracing known as 'cut-and-bank' is employed on hillsides, particularly NW of Bridge of Orchy, and the embankments in this section have been revetted with dry-stone masonry; elsewhere the marks of quarrying are still visible. The surface is normally overgrown with heather, but a metalled surface with gravel infilling survives at Màm Carraigh, NW of Bridge of Orchy.

In addition to the large bridges that are described individually below, there are many small segmental-arched bridges and straight-lintelled 'culvert-bridges', the oldest of which are of dry-stone masonry. A typical example, which crosses the Easan Dubh at NN 275442, has a span of 1·7 m and a height to the arch-soffit of 0·6 m, the width of the roadway being some 4·6 m. These small bridges, and two others whose span is 3·8 m, carry a roadway of the normal width; the larger bridges that may be ascribed to 1751–2, however, are somewhat narrower, the roadway varying in width from 3·5 m (bridge at Bà Cottage) to 4·0 m (Inveroran Bridge).

The military road enters Argyll some 2·8 km N of Tyndrum (NN 329332), at a height of 320 m OD. Gordon's plan shows that at this point the road is following an older local track which General Roy's survey

---

[1] This is probably the bridge near Dalmally that was rebuilt in 1812 at a cost of £113 7s 8d (*Parliamentary Papers, 1813–14*, iii, 59).

[2] Mactavish, op. cit., 344; S.R.O., Campbell of Barcaldine Collection, GD 170/834/2.

[3] *TISS*, v (1895–9), 370.

[4] Nat. Lib. of Scot. MS 1649.Z.3/40a.

[5] P.R.O., MR 479, no. 5.

[6] S.R.O., Forfeited Estates Papers, E 728/30/1, petitions dated 9 December 1776, 15 June 1782; *TISS*, v (1895–9), 378–9.

[7] Haldane, A R B, *New Ways Through The Glens* (1962), 160.

[8] S.R.O., Breadalbane Collection, GD 112/47/4, letter from D Campbell, 30 July 1829; Haldane, A R B, *The Drove Roads of Scotland* (1952), 80–2, 211–13.

indicates leading from Tyndrum through Achallader and Glencoe to Ballachulish. A short section of the military road can be traced on the hillside above the improved Parliamentary road, from the county boundary to a point about 100 m N of the modern railway-bridge. Thereafter the road merges with the Parliamentary road, which has itself suffered greatly from erosion. The road along the 'Braes of Auch' was repaired at great expense in 1802–4,[1] and has undergone constant improvement since that date; only the lower, dry-stone courses of some of the many culvert-bridges and embankments can be ascribed to the military period.

The section constructed in 1751 terminates NE of Auch at NN 327357, where the Allt Chonoghlais is crossed by an early bridge having a span of 11·7 m and a height to the arch-soffit of 3·4 m. The next section, on the SE slope of Beinn Dorain, adheres to the line of the older track referred to above, diverging from it near Bridge of Orchy Station. No early work can be identified on this part of the road, which is maintained in good order for vehicular use.

Bridge of Orchy (NN 296396) is a single-arched structure of local rubble-masonry (Pl. 119D), much of which has been refaced during the present century. The overall length of the bridge with approaches is 49 m, and the roadway at the approaches has a width of 5·8 m, diminishing at the abutments to 3·7 m, all within parapets 0·36 m in thickness. The segmental arch has a span of 18·9 m, and the height to the arch-soffit is 6·7 m. The bridge appears on Gordon's plan, and was built in or shortly before 1751.

The road over the NE shoulder of Beinn Inverveigh, some 3·5 km in length from Bridge of Orchy to Inveroran, was abandoned before 1803[2] and preserves its original appearance better than any other section of the military road in Lorn. The track rises steadily through a Forestry Commission plantation, where it is interrupted in places by modern trenches, to a large zigzag in open moorland 1·2 km NW of Bridge of Orchy. The stream NNW of this bend crosses the road at a ford (NN 288405) bottomed with flat slabs and having a cobbled approach from the S. From that point, over the summit at 320 m OD and on the descent to Inveroran by a series of four zigzags, the road corresponds closely with Gordon's plan in the arrangement of quarry-pits and drainage-trenches, which are confined to the upper side of the track and led away at regular intervals through culvert-bridges into streams.

The military road rejoins the present highway at Inveroran (NN 274414), formerly an important drove-stance, the point of junction being 50 m E of an early bridge, which has a low-set segmental arch with a span of 6·3 m and a height of 2·3 m. The next bridge to the E, crossing the Allt Tolaghan, has a roadway some 4·7 m in width and was probably rebuilt by the Parliamentary Commissioners. Some 420 m to the N of this bridge the military road diverges to the W of the present road, then crosses it and, as shown on Gordon's plan, originally continued to a bridge spanning the Linne nam Beathach downstream of the late 19th-century Victoria Bridge.

From Forest Lodge (NN 271424) to its junction with the Parliamentary road at NN 283468, the military road runs along the hillside some 500 m W of the later route, rising to a height of about 360 m OD. The first 700 m of this section was completed in 1751, as recorded on Gordon's plan, while the remainder was probably constructed in the following year. This part of the route is characterized by several well-preserved culvert-bridges and arches, although the condition of the road-way is inferior to that SE of Inveroran. Some 900 m S of Bà Bridge (NN 279474), and 330 m N of it (NN 277486), there are two early bridges of similar scale, each having a flat segmental arch with a span of 3·8 m and a height of 1·2 m and carrying a roadway 4·6 m in width. Bà Bridge (NN 277483) is of mid-19th-century date, but the abutment of an earlier bridge is visible immediately to the E. The bridge that crosses the Allt Creagan nam Meann near Bà Cottage (NN 278494) has a span of 6·2 m and a height to the arch-soffit of 2·1 m; it is approached from the N by a causeway of dry-stone masonry incorporating a small culvert-bridge.

The next improved line of road begins at NN 280498, about 400 m N of the bridge last described. The original road, some 3 km in length and rising to a height of almost 520 m OD, is considerably eroded and presents no features of particular interest. This section was abandoned shortly before 1803, when Dorothy Wordsworth, travelling S from Kingshouse, 'came upon a new road, one of the finest that was ever trod'; 'a new road in the Black Mount', evidently the improved line either in this area or else immediately N of Forest Lodge, was built by local contractors in 1796 at a cost of £290.[3] The original and improved lines of the road join at NN 270526, and immediately N of the junction there is an early bridge having a span of 2·8 m and an arch-height of 1·3 m. The condition of the Parliamentary road in this area is deteriorating rapidly; at the date of visit it was negotiated in a vehicle with some difficulty.

From Blackrock Cottage to Kingshouse the military road has been rebuilt and is in regular use. At NN 252549, about 900 m WNW of Kingshouse, it traverses the hillside above the modern road and can be traced for a distance of 2·3 km to NN 231558, where it merges with the A 82 trunk road. The only feature of interest in this section is a well-bottomed ford at NN 246555. At Altnafeadh the trunk road continues W through Glencoe, replacing the improved route that was constructed in 1776–82, while the original line of the military road follows the direct route NW to Kinlochleven, a distance of some 8·7 km. This portion of the road, which replaced an earlier track shown on Roy's map, was never suitable for wheeled vehicles.[4] After its abandonment by the military, however, it remained in use as a drove-road,

---

[1] 'Statement of the Origin and Extent of the Several Roads in Scotland', *Parliamentary Papers, 1813–14*, iii, 48–9.
[2] Dorothy Wordsworth (*Tour*, 183) records that her route from Inveroran to Tyndrum led close to Loch Tulla, apparently on the line of the present A 8005.
[3] Wordsworth, *Tour*, 181; *Parliamentary Papers, 1813–14*, iii, 23.
[4] *TISS*, v (1895–9), 378.

Fig. 248. Graffito, Creagan (No. 373; scale 1:5)

and during the present century it has become a popular pedestrian route. The effect of this continuous use, and of the erosive action of streams, has been to destroy the surface of the road, particularly in the area N of Altnafeadh where it runs beside the Allt a' Mhaim. At the Devil's Staircase (NN 216573), an impressive series of zigzags which carries the road over the E shoulder of Stob Mhic Mhartuin, the original track has been further affected by short cuts at the bends. The summit (NN 215576) is reached at a height of 552 m OD, and thereafter the roadway is better preserved. Immediately W of the road, on the S bank of the Allt a' Choire Odhair-bhig (NN 213583), there are the fragmentary remains of a sub-rectangular building of dry-stone masonry, measuring some 6·1 m by 2·7 m within walls 0·9 m in thickness. About 1 km N of this building, at NN 214593, the rock face W of the road has been cut back to form a roadway some 4·3 m in width, and thereafter the route descends in a series of zigzags through an area of exposed rock and small precipices. The identifiable track of the military road terminates at the electricity sub-station at NN 202605; from this point to the county boundary at Kinlochleven the road has been improved for vehicular use and presents no features of interest.

329330–192618   August 1971
        NN 16 SE, NN 23 NE, NN 24 SE,
    NN 24 NE, NN 25 SE, NN 25 NW,
    NN 26 SW, NN 33 SW, NN 33 NW

ARCHITECTURAL FRAGMENTS, CARVED STONES ETC.

373. Graffito, Creagan. About 1·6 km E of Creagan, the road that runs along the N side of Loch Creran crosses the twin tributaries of a small unnamed burn. If the easternmost branch is followed northwards for some 200 m up the steep face of Beinn Churalain, and beyond the point where it is first marked on the O.S. map, a natural terrace is reached upon which there is a rock outcrop bearing an incised representation of a galley of the kind used in the Western Isles throughout the medieval period. The outcrop lies close to the E side of the burn, and 15 m SE of a small cairn composed largely of white stones.

The galley (Fig. 248, Pl. 120B) is merely sketched and measures only 0·43 m in length by 0·42 m in height, but it is strikingly similar in essentials to the elaborately carved galley on the tomb built in 1528 for Alexander MacLeod in St Clement's Church at Rodel.[1] The high stem and stern, the stern rudder, the centrally-stepped mast supported by shrouds and stays, and the yard controlled by braces are all features of the Rodel boat, but in the present instance no sail is shown. Below the sketch the initials DS and the date 1729 have been incised, apparently with the same instrument as that

---

[1] Steer and Bannerman, *Monumental Sculpture*, fig. 25.

employed to delineate the greater part of the vessel. This type of galley can hardly have survived, however, until the 18th century, and there are in fact indications that the graffito is of greater antiquity. As the photograph shows, the forestay running from the top of the mast to the stem-post is less distinct than the rest of the rigging, while on the hull there are faint traces of a group of letters beginning AST, the letter A being of the form with a V-shaped cross-bar which is commonly found in monumental inscriptions of the late-16th and 17th centuries. It seems probable, therefore, that the original sketch was made at a time when such galleys were still plying on Loch Creran, perhaps in the latter half of the 16th century, but that it was substantially re-cut in 1729.

The small cairn referred to above does not appear to be sepulchral, but may rather have been intended to mark a basin-shaped hollow, 0·30 m in diameter at the mouth and 0·25 m in depth, which has been excavated out of the rock at this point and which is covered by a stone lid worked into a circular shape. The purpose of this feature is not known.

990450   NM 94 NE   June 1970

374. Architectural Fragments, Druimneil House. Although the house itself does not fall within the scope of this *Inventory*, some of the fittings call for mention. The most interesting item is an open-well staircase (Pl. 120A) of pine having turned balusters and a heavy moulded hand-rail. This staircase is evidently of mid-18th-century date, and although its provenance is not known it may possibly be of Scottish origin. In addition, a number of the principal rooms are decorated with oak panelling of Jacobean date, said to have been brought from Ickworth, Suffolk.[1]

910446   NM 94 SW   March 1968

375. Armorial Panel, Dunstaffnage House. Incorporated within the N gable-wall of Dunstaffnage House there is a marble panel carved with the full armorial achievement of the Campbells of Dunstaffnage (Pl. 120C). The shield is charged: quarterly, 1st, a castle of three towers, on the top of the middle tower a cock, and on each of the others an eagle; 2nd, gyronny of eight; 3rd, a fess checky; 4th, a boar's head cabossed between a crescent and a mullet. For supporters there are two foot-soldiers armed with swords and muskets, while the crest is an anchor in pale; the motto is VIGILANDO ('Watchful'). This panel, which appears to be of 18th-century date, is said to have been brought from Dunstaffnage Castle (No. 287),[2] and is evidently the one found in the garden there in 1826.[3]

899334   NM 83 SE   July 1968

376. Armorial Panel, Old Smithy, Port Appin. Built into the SW gable-wall of the old smithy at Port Appin there is a sandstone panel (Pl. 120D) of unknown provenance bearing a shield parted per fess and charged: in dexter chief a lion rampant; in sinister chief gyronny of eight; in base a galley, sail furled, oars in action, a beacon on the topmast. The identification of this coat of arms is uncertain. The panel appears to be of 17th- or 18th-century date.

907454   NM 94 NW   July 1968

377. Architectural Fragments, St Conan's Church, Lochawe. St Conan's Church, a large building of eclectic style erected between 1881 and 1930 at the expense of, and largely to the designs of, Walter D Campbell of Blythswood, incorporates a number of imported architectural fragments and other fittings. These include the following:

(1) The 15th-century W window of St Mary's Parish Church, South Leith, removed from that building at the restoration of 1848 and re-erected here, with the original outer face turned inwards, in the S wall of the Bruce chapel.[4] The arch-head of the six-light window (Pl. 120E) is filled with flamboyant tracery, and the jambs are wrought with alternating ovolo and hollow-chamfer mouldings. The stops of the filleted hood-mould are carved with human heads, now greatly worn. The original outer faces of the mullions are wrought with hollow chamfers and filleted rolls, while internally the mullions and jambs are chamfered.

(2) Portions of the original tracery of the E window of the S choir-aisle of Iona Abbey (Pl. 120F), now built into a recess in the N wall of the S nave-aisle. The original window was restored in 1904, at the expense of Miss Campbell of Blythswood,[5] and the fragments preserved are greatly weathered. They comprise the cusped heads of the two lower lights, a wheel composed of six trefoil lights, and a small quatrefoil opening at the apex of the arch-head.

(3) The head of a lancet-window of 13th-century type, rebated externally but not chamfered, which lies at the W end of the nave. This is of doubtful authenticity, and may have been carved for use in the present building, like many fragments preserved in the gardens near the church.

(4) A bell (Pl. 120G), 0·76 m in diameter, now kept in the Bruce chapel, bearing the inscription: THOMAS MEARS FOUNDER LONDON 1843 / NORTH LIGHTHOUSES / IN SALUTEM OMNIUM. This is said[6] to have come from Skerryvore Lighthouse, and was evidently one of the three bells purchased, at a total cost of £107 6s 3d, for use in foggy weather.[7]

---

[1] Information from the proprietor, Mr B M Yeaman.
[2] Information from the Captain of Dunstaffnage.
[3] *Dunstaffnage Case*, 62, 253.
[4] A measured drawing by T Ross was published in *TSES*, vii (1921–4), part ii, opp. p. 79.
[5] *TGAS*, new series, v (1905–8), 86–7.
[6] Martin, J C, *Saint Conan's Kirk, Loch Awe* (1950), 11.
[7] Stevenson, A, *Account of the Skerryvore Lighthouse, with Notes on the Illumination of Lighthouses* (1848), 381.

Also preserved in the Bruce Chapel are two wooden screens, each of four bays. These are said to be from Eton College Chapel,[1] but are of modern workmanship.

115267   NN 12 NW   June 1971

INDETERMINATE REMAINS

378. Indeterminate Remains, Saulmore. About 135 m NW of Saulmore farmhouse a prominent rocky knoll named Tom a' Chrochaidh rises to a height of about 15 m OD on the S side of the public road from Connel to Oban. By tradition a place of execution, it is marked on the second edition of the O.S. 6-inch map as a 'Tumulus',[2] and it is recorded[3] that in 1870 traces of 'a small circular mound' were distinctly visible on the summit. At the present time the E and NE faces of the knoll are scarred by several small quarry-scoops, and the summit itself, which measures about 14·6 m by 7·6 m, carries a very light scatter of stones, now almost completely hidden under the turf. The central area is slightly hollowed and is surrounded by a ragged peripheral stony fringe about 1 m thick and not more than 0·2 m high; this latter feature may be the residue of the small mound already mentioned. No burials are known from the site, and although the remains may represent the debris resulting from the severe robbing of a cairn, this can only be determined by excavation.

891338   NM 83 SE   April 1967

[1] Martin, loc. cit.
[2] Sheet lxxxvii SW.
[3] Name Book, No. 19, p. 23.

ARMORIAL

Breadalbane, Earl of, see *Campbell of Glenorchy.*

Cameron of Corrychiracha. Three bars (p. 131).

Cameron of Culchennan. Three bars (p. 131).

Campbell of Airds. Quarterly, 1st, a hart's head cabossed; 2nd, gyronny of eight; 3rd, a galley, sail furled, oars in action and pennons flying; 4th, on a fess three buckles (p. 244).

Campbell of Airds. Quarterly, 1st, gyronny of eight; 2nd, ? a galley, sail furled; 3rd, illegible; 4th, ? a hart's head cabossed; on a chief a ? buckle between two mullets (p. 191).

Campbell of Balligown. Quarterly, 1st and 4th, gyronny of eight; 2nd, a boar's head erased; 3rd, a galley, sail furled (p. 115).

Campbell of Barcaldine, see *Campbell of Inneryeldies.*

Campbell of Clathic. Gyronny of eight, within a bordure ? vair (p. 114).

Campbell of Dunstaffnage. Quarterly, 1st and 4th, gyronny of eight; 2nd and 3rd, a galley, sail furled (pp. 128, 204).

Campbell of Dunstaffnage. Quarterly, 1st, a castle of three towers, on the top of the middle tower a cock, and on each of the others an eagle; 2nd, gyronny of eight; 3rd, a fess checky; 4th, a boar's head cabossed between a crescent and a mullet (p. 299).

Campbell of Glenorchy. Quarterly, 1st and 4th, gyronny of eight; 2nd, a galley, sail furled, pennons flying; 3rd, checky (in error for a fess checky) (p. 177).

Campbell of Glenorchy impaling Stewart of Atholl. Dexter, quarterly, 1st and 4th, gyronny of eight; 2nd, a galley, sail furled, pennons flying; 3rd, checky (in error for a fess checky); sinister, quarterly, 1st and 4th, paly of six; 2nd, illegible; 3rd, checky (in error for a fess checky) (p. 177).

Campbell of Glenorchy, Earl of Breadalbane. Quarterly, 1st and 4th, gyronny of eight; 2nd, a galley, sail furled, oars in action and pennon flying; 3rd, a fess checky (pp. 234, 249).

Campbell of Inneryeldies. Quarterly, 1st and 4th, gyronny of eight; 2nd and 3rd, a galley, sail furled, oars in action (p. 114).

Campbell of Inneryeldies. Quarterly, 1st and 4th, gyronny of eight; 2nd, a galley, sail furled, oars in action; 3rd, a fess checky between three ? crescents (p. 114).

Campbell of ? Inverawe. Quarterly, in each quarter, gyronny of eight (p. 113).

Campbell of ? Inverawe. Quarterly, 1st and 4th, gyronny of eight; 2nd, a galley, sail furled; 3rd, a ? salmon naiant (p. 114).

? Campbell of Inverawe. Quarterly, 1st, 2nd and 4th, gyronny of eight; 3rd, gyronny of eight, in base a ? salmon naiant (pp. 113–14).

Campbell of Lerags. Quarterly, on a field bearing gyronny of eight; 1st and 4th, a galley, sail furled; 2nd and 3rd, a ? boar's head erased (p. 143).

Campbell of Lochnell. Quarterly, 1st and 4th, gyronny of eight; 2nd, a boar's head erased; 3rd, a galley, sail furled (pp. 114–15, 263).

Campbell of Lossit. Quarterly, 1st, a hart's head cabossed; 2nd, gyronny of eight; 3rd, a galley, sail furled; 4th, on a chief, ? an unidentified charge (p. 165).

Campbell of Scammadale. Quarterly, 1st, a castle of three towers; 2nd, gyronny of eight; 3rd, a fess checky; 4th, a ? boar's head cabossed (p. 128).

Campbell. Quarterly, 1st and 4th, gyronny of eight; 2nd, a boar's head couped; 3rd, a galley, sail furled (p. 165).

Campbell. Quarterly, 1st and 4th, gyronny of eight; 2nd, a galley, sail furled; 3rd, a ? salmon naiant (p. 165).

? Campbell. Quarterly, 1st and 4th, gyronny of eight; 2nd and 3rd, a galley, sail furled (p. 113).

Downie of Appin. A fess between three boars' heads couped (p. 246).

Fletcher. A Greek cross, a ? flagon in the centre, between four pellets, each charged with a pheon (p. 97).

MacDougall of Lunga. Quarterly, 1st and 4th, a lion rampant; 2nd and 3rd, a galley, sail furled, pennons flying (pp. 145–6).

MacDougall of MacDougall and Dunollie. Quarterly, 1st, a lion rampant; 2nd, a castle of three towers; 3rd, a galley; 4th, a dexter hand couped fessways holding a cross-crosslet (p. 143).

McDougall. Quarterly, 1st, a lion rampant; 2nd, a castle of three towers; 3rd, a galley; 4th, a dexter hand couped fessways holding a cross-crosslet (p. 140).

MacDougall. Quarterly, 1st and 4th, a lion rampant; 2nd and 3rd, a galley, sail furled (p. 142).

MacGregor of Correctled. A fir-tree surmounted by a sword in bend, on the point an imperial crown in the dexter chief canton (p. 162).

McIntyre of Gleno. A stag tripping having its chest pierced by an arrow; a galley, sail furled, pennon flying; a mullet; a salmon naiant (p. 113).

McIntyre. Quarterly, 1st and 4th, an ? eagle displayed; 2nd, a galley, sail furled; 3rd, a dexter hand couped fessways holding a cross-crosslet (p. 149).

McLauchlane. Quarterly, 1st, a lion rampant; 2nd, an open book; 3rd, a galley, pennon flying; 4th, a salmon naiant (p. 140).

McLachlan. Quarterly, 1st, a ? lion passant; 2nd, a sinister hand couped fessways holding a cross-pattée; 3rd, a galley; 4th, a salmon naiant (p. 140).

Macnab of Barran. On a chevron three crescents; in dexter chief a dexter arm couped holding a sword; in sinister chief a sinister arm couped holding a sword; in base a galley, oars in action (p. 134).

Stewart of Appin. Quarterly, 1st and 4th, a fess checky; 2nd and 3rd, a galley, sail furled (p. 114).

Stewart of Atholl, see *Campbell of Glenorchy.*

Stewart. On a field or, a fess checky surmounted by a bend, a cinquefoil in chief (p. 131).

Unidentified. In dexter chief a lion rampant; in sinister chief gyronny of eight; in base a galley, sail furled, oars in action, a beacon on the topmast (p. 299).

GLOSSARY

Abacus. The uppermost member of a capital.

Achievement. In heraldry, the coat of arms (helmet, crest, mantling, motto) fully emblazoned according to the rules of heraldry.

Acroterion. A pedestal for a statue, or other ornament, placed at the angles of a pediment. Also, more loosely, the ornament itself.

Aisle. (1) An internal subdivision of a church, formed by an arcade separating it from the main body of the nave or chancel. (2) A projecting wing or chapel, often for purposes of family burial (Scots).

Aketon. A quilted coat worn under armour or as an independent defence.

Annulet. (1) In architecture, a small raised moulding encircling a shaft or column. (2) In heraldry, a ring.

Architrave. (1) A moulded frame round a door, window or similar opening. (2) The lowest member of an entablature, resting directly upon the column or pier.

Arris. The external angle at the meeting of two surfaces.

Ashlar. Masonry wrought to an even or rusticated face and square edges, and bedded with a fine joint.

Aumbry. A small cupboard or closed recess in a wall.

Bailey. An open space or court within a castle enclosure.

Bailie. (1) A municipal officer or magistrate. (2) The principal administrative officer of a barony (Scots).

Bar. In heraldry, a diminutive of the fess (*q.v.*) occupying one-fifth of the shield.

Barmkin. A defensive enclosure, usually attached to a tower-house.

Barrel-vault. A continuous vault, semicircular, segmental or pointed in section.

Bascinet. A light helmet, generally egg-shaped with a pointed apex.

Base. In heraldry, the lowest part of the shield.

Batter. An inward-sloping face of a wall, terrace or bank.

Beaker. In archaeology, a type of pottery vessel used in the early 2nd millennium B.C.

Bell-cast. In architecture, of a roof, or similar feature, having a bell-shaped profile.

Bend. In heraldry, a charge formed by two lines drawn diagonally from the dexter chief to the sinister base of the shield.

Billet-ornament. An ornament, used mainly in Romanesque architecture, comprising small oblong or cylindrical blocks placed at regular intervals.

Black letter. A type of lettering used by the early printers and for inscriptions; also termed 'Gothic' or 'Old English'.

Bloomery. A site used for primitive iron-smelting.

Bordure. In heraldry, a border round the edge of the shield.

Boshes. In a blast-furnace, the lower part(s) of the tunnel.

Breast-shot. Of a water-wheel in which the water is admitted to the buckets approximately at the level of the axle.

Bretasche. A defensive gallery of timber.

Cabossed. In heraldry, of an animal's head cut off above the neck and shown full-faced.

Cap-house. The small roofed superstructure of a stair leading to the parapet-walk or garret of a building.

Cavetto. A concave moulding of one-quarter of a circle.

Chamfer. The bevelled surface left by cutting away an angle or arris (*q.v.*).

Chancel. That part of a church east of the nave or crossing in which the altar is placed.

Chape. The protective metal plate at the tip of a scabbard.

Charge. In heraldry, the figures or bearings contained in an escutcheon.

Checked, see *Rebated.*

Checky. In heraldry, divided alternately into equal squares of two different tinctures.

Chevron. (1) In architecture, a Romanesque moulding of zigzag form. (2) In heraldry, a charge of pointed-gable form.

Chief. In heraldry, the upper third of a shield.

Cinerary Urn. In archaeology, a type of pottery vessel used for containing a cremated burial in the 2nd millennium B.C.

Cinquefoil. In heraldry, five leaves conjoined in the centre. See also *Foil.*

Corbel. A block of stone or timber projecting from a wall to support a superincumbent weight.

Corinthian, see *Orders of Architecture.*

Cornice. (1) In Classical architecture, the uppermost member of an entablature. (2) A moulded projection which crowns or finishes the part to which it is attached.

Corning-house. In gunpowder-manufacture, a building where the blended gunpowder is separated into individual grains.

Cote-hardie. A long tunic worn by ladies during the medieval period.

Couped, see *Erased.*

Coving. The concave profile sometimes formed between a ceiling and the walls of a room.

Crenelle. An opening in an embattled parapet, between two merlons (*q.v.*).

Crescent. In heraldry, the crescent moon with its horns turned upwards.

Crest. In heraldry, the ornament on the upper part of the helmet placed over coats of arms.

Cross, Greek. A plain cross in which all four limbs are of equal length.

Cross, Latin. A cross of which the stem is longer than the other limbs.

Cross, Maltese. In heraldry, a cross similar to the cross-pattée (*q.v.*) but having the extremities of the limbs slightly indented.

Cross-crosslet. In heraldry, originally a cross with limbs ending as trefoils, but later one with limbs ending in squarely-cut plain crosses.

Cross-pattée. In heraldry, a cross with expanding limbs cut square at the ends.

Cross-potent. In heraldry, a cross having a small transverse arm at the extremity of each limb.

Crow-stepped. Of a gable having a stepped profile (Scots).

Cruck. A principal roof-member springing from a point below wall-plate level.

Cusp. In architecture, each of the projecting points between the small arcs or 'foils' (*q.v.*) in Gothic tracery, arches, etc. A surface so treated is said to be *cusped.*

Dexter. In heraldry, the right-hand side, opposite to the spectator's left.

Diaper. A floral or geometric pattern, often repeated over a considerable surface.

Displayed. In heraldry, of a bird whose wings are expanded and legs spread.

Dog-tooth. In Gothic architecture, an ornament consisting of a series of pyramidal flowers.

Doric, see *Orders of Architecture.*

Dorter. A monastic dormitory.

Edge-roll. A moulding of circular section, quirked and set on an external angle.

Enceinte. An enclosure.

Entablature. In Classical architecture, the whole of the horizontal members above the column (architrave, frieze, cornice).

Erased. In heraldry, ragged as if torn off, as distinct from *couped,* or cut evenly.

False Portal. In archaeology, a setting of stones designed to represent the entrance to a burial-chamber in a pre-historic cairn or barrow.

Fess. In heraldry, a horizontal band across the centre of a shield.

Fillet. In architecture, a narrow flat band running down a shaft or along a moulding, or separating two mouldings.

Flabellum. A long-handled fan used for liturgical purposes in the Early Christian Church.

Foil (trefoil, quatrefoil, cinquefoil). In architecture, the lobe, often leaf-shaped, of three, four, five or more arcs formed by the cusps (*q.v.*) of an arch or other opening, or in panelling.

Food Vessel. In archaeology, a type of pottery vessel used in the 2nd millennium B.C.

Frieze. In Classical architecture, the member in the entablature of an order that occurs between the architrave and the cornice. Also applied to a band below a ceiling-cornice.

Gablet. A small gable.

Garderobe. A medieval latrine; known as a close-garderobe when it has no soil-shaft.

Gibbs-surround. The surround of a door or window composed of either alternating larger and smaller blocks of stone set quoinwise, or of intermittent large blocks, often connected by a narrow raised band.

Groin-vault. A type of vault formed without ribs, the groin being the sharp edge formed at the intersection of two barrel-vaults at right angles.

Guardant. In heraldry, looking out from the field.

Gyron. In heraldry, a triangular figure formed by two lines drawn respectively from one of the angles and one of the adjacent sides of the shield to the centre.

Gyronny. In heraldry, when the field is covered with gyrons of a stated number.

Harled. Rough-cast (Scots).

Hipped roof. A roof pitched back at the end instead of being formed with a gable.

Hood-mould. A projecting moulding above an arch or lintel, also called a drip-stone or label.

Impost. In architecture, the member from which an arch springs.

Ingo, ingoing. In architecture, the return face of a wall, usually where it forms the inner side of a doorway or window-opening.

Jamb. (1) The side of a door or window. (2) A wing of a building (Scots). (3) In heraldry, the leg of an animal.

Keeled. In architecture, of a column slightly pointed in section.

King-post. In roof-construction, an upright post connecting the ridge-piece with the centre of a tie-beam or collar-beam.

Label. In heraldry, a piece of silk, or linen, usually depicted as a narrow horizontal band with three pendants, generally used as a mark of cadency.

Label-mould, see *Hood-mould.*

Laich. Low (Scots).

Lancet. In architecture, a slender window with an arch-pointed head.

Langet. A strip of metal projecting from the centre of the quillons (*q.v.*) of a sword over the base of the blade, as a protection for the hand.

Lugged, lug-moulded. Having an 'ear' or projecting piece.

Machicolation. A slot or shaft, particularly an opening between corbels, through which missiles could be directed downwards.

Mensal. Of a church whose revenues are appropriated to the maintenance of the domestic economy of a monastery or cathedral (from Latin *mensa*, 'table').

Merlon. The part of an embattled parapet that stands between two openings (*see Crenelle.*)

Mid-annulet, see *Annulet.*

Mortsafe. An iron frame placed over a coffin as a protection against body-snatchers (Scots).

Mullet. In heraldry, a five-pointed spur-rowel, like a star, but with a hole in the centre.

Naiant. In heraldry, of an animal swimming in a horizontal position.

Newel. (1) The central column of a spiral staircase, from which the steps radiate. (2) The principal posts of a staircase, into which the string and hand-rail of the stair are framed.

Nook-shaft. A shaft set in an angle or nook.

Ogee. A continuous double curve, one concave and the other convex.

Oppidum. An Iron Age hill-fort whose exceptional size and particularly commanding position suggests that it was a tribal centre (Latin).

Or. In heraldry, gold or yellow, conventionally represented in monochrome by small dots.

Orders of Architecture. In Classical or Renaissance architecture, the five systems of columnar architecture, known as Tuscan, Doric, Ionic, Corinthian and Composite.

Over-shot. Of a water-wheel in which the water is admitted to the buckets over the top of the wheel.

Ovolo moulding. A convex moulding.

Pale. In heraldry, a wide vertical band down the middle of a shield.

Palmette. A fan-shaped ornament somewhat resembling a palm-leaf.

Paly. In heraldry, of a field divided by vertical lines into several parts of a stated even number.

Passant. In heraldry, of an animal walking.

Patera. In architecture, a small, flat, circular or oval ornament.

Pediment. A gable used in Classical architecture above a portico, doorway or window; it may be triangular or segmental.

Pend. A covered passage (Scots).

Perpendicular. In architecture, the last of the three phases into which the Gothic style in Britain is conventionally divided. It begins about the middle of the 14th century.

Pheon. In heraldry, the barbed head of a dart or arrow.

Piano nobile. In Renaissance architecture, the principal storey of a building, raised above ground-level and containing the reception rooms.

Pilaster. A rectangular column, of shallow projection, attached to a wall.

Piscina. A basin in which Eucharistic vessels are washed, usually set in a niche or recess to the south of the altar, and provided with a drain discharging into the thickness of the wall.

Pit-prison. A castle prison, usually in the form of a sunk chamber entered from above through a hatch.

Plinth. The projecting base of a wall or column.

Pommel. The knob terminal of a sword-hilt.

Presbytery. The part of the church reserved for the officiating clergy, east of the choir.

Pulpitum. A screen, usually of stone, separating the nave and choir in a major church.

Putto. A small figure of a naked boy.

Quatrefoil, see *Foil.*

Queen-post. In roof-construction, one of two upright posts placed symmetrically on a tie-beam and connecting it with a collar-beam or the rafters above.

Quillons. The arms forming the cross-guard of a sword.

Quirk. In architecture, a sharp-edged groove separating other members of a moulding.

Quoin. An external corner-stone of a building.

Raggle. A groove cut in masonry to receive the material forming a joint, especially on the face of a wall to receive the edge of a roof.

Rampant. In heraldry, of an animal standing erect on the hind legs, with both forelegs and tail elevated and the head in profile.

Rear-arch. A constructional arch to carry the inner side of a wall over the back of a door or window.

Rebated. Recessed to receive a door-frame, etc., or to act as a stop.

Redented. Of a gun-loop whose outer embrasure is stepped back with a series of rebates designed to deflect missiles.

Relieving-arch. An arch built over a lintel, to relieve it of superincumbent weight.

Roll-and-hollow moulding. A roll-moulding combined with one or more concave ones.

Rood. Christ's Cross.

Rubble. Masonry of rough unsquared stones.

Rusticated. In architecture, of masonry in which only the margins of the stones are worked, the faces being left rough, e.g. 'rock-faced'; also of ashlar having the joints emphasised by channelling.

Rybat. A dressed stone forming the reveal of a window- or door-opening (Scots).

Sarking. Boarding laid on the rafters as a base for the roofing-material (Scots).

Scale-and-platt. Of a stair having straight flights of steps with landings.

Scarcement. A narrow ledge formed where a wall is set back.

Scarf-joint. A longitudinal joint between two timbers, bevelled or notched at their ends and pinned through the bevelled portion.

Scollop-thatching. A method of thatching in which the straw is secured by thin rods called scollops (Gaelic, *sgolban*).

Segmental arch. An arch whose arc is less than a semicircle.

Sinister. In heraldry, the left-hand side, opposite to the spectator's right.

Skew. The slope of a gable head.

Skewput. The lowest stone in the coping of a gable (Scots).

Soffit. The underside of a stair, lintel, cornice, arch, canopy, etc.

Solar. An upper chamber in a medieval house, usually approached from the dais end of the hall.

Sole-piece.   A short horizontal roof-member supporting the foot of a rafter.

Spandrel.   The triangular-shaped space above the haunch of an arch.

Sprocket.   A short member nailed to the foot of a rafter to form tilted eaves or a bell-shaped roof.

Stanchours, Stenchers.   Stanchions (Scots).

String-course.   A projecting horizontal band or moulding carried along the face of a wall.

Stugged.   Of masonry dressed with a punch so as to produce close pock-markings.

Tack.   A lease, usually of landed property, the lessee being known as a tacksman (Scots).

Tau-headed.   Of a cross or crozier, in the form of a T (Greek).

Teind.   Tithe (Scots).

Tirl-pin.   A form of door-knocker, having a metal ring which rasps against a serrated edge (Scots).

Tòiseach.   In medieval Celtic society, the head of a clan or family group, sometimes identified with the office of thane.

Trefoil, see *Foil.*

Trumbel.   A spiral stair (Scots).

Turnpike stair.   A spiral stair (Scots).

Tusking.   In architecture, of stones left projecting from the surface of a wall to allow the bonding in of another wall. Also used of the ragged end of a ruinous wall.

Tympanum.   An enclosed space in the head of an arch, doorway, etc., or in the triangle of a pediment.

Undercroft.   An underbuilding, often vaulted, beneath a principal room such as a church or hall.

Univallate.   In fortification, having a single line of defence.

Vair.   In heraldry, a kind of fur, often represented by bell-like figures ranged in rows.

Vitrifaction.   In archaeology, the fused condition to which the rubble core of a timber-laced fort-wall is reduced by the action of fire.

Volute.   A spiral scroll used especially in Ionic capitals (see *Orders of Architecture*).

Voussoirs.   The wedge-like stones that form an arch.

Wadset.   A type of mortgage, in which the lender becomes possessor of the property mortgaged (Scots).

Wreath.   In heraldry, the circular fillet or twisted band by which the crest is joined to the helmet.

INDEX

Where necessary for ease of identification, page references to main entries are given in bold type.

Abbeys: Inchaffray (Perthshire), p. 135; Iona, pp. 23, 36, 142, 144, 149, 299, pl. 120F; Movilla (Co. Down), p. 102n; Saddell (Kintyre), p. 161; *see also* **Religious houses.**
Abbreviations, pp. xli-xliii.
Abernethy (Inverness-shire), ironworks, p. 34.
Achacha, cairn *and* standing stone, pp. 10, **45,** fig. 15.
Achadun Castle, Lismore: pp. 26-7, **168-71,** 186, figs. 159-61, pls. 37-8B; farm, p. 171.
Achaleven, cairn, p. 45.
Achallader, burial-ground, pp. **97,** 173.
Achallader, Treaty of, p. 174.
Achallader Castle, pp. 29, 97, **171-5,** 238, figs. 162-4, pls. 38C-9C.
Achalladoure, *see* Achallader Castle.
Achanamoine, cairn, pp. 11, **45.**
Achanancarn, cairn, pp. 11, **45.**
Achanlochan, charcoal-burning stances, p. 276.
Achanrear, Barcaldine, bronze axe, p. 13, pl. 5A.
Acharra, standing stone, p. 62, pl. 9C.
Achchalder, *see* Achallader Castle.
Achlian, pp. 31, 94, **243,** pl. 78A-D.
Achlian, crannog, p. 94.
Achnaba, pp. 31, 45, 57, **243-4,** pl. 78E.
Achnaba: cairns, pp. 11, **45;** church, *see* **Ardchattan,** parish church; cist, pp. 45, **57.**
Achnacarron, *see* Càrn Bàn, Achnacarron.
Achnacree, chambered cairn, pp. 7-8, **37,** 50, fig. 7, pl. 3A.
Achnacreebeag, chambered cairn, pp. 7-9, **37,** 40, fig. 8, pl. 6.
Achychendone, *see* Achadun Castle.
Agriculture, pp. 3, 32-3.
Airds House, pp. 30-1, 194, **244-5,** fig. 212, pls. 79-82.
Airidh nan Sileag, shielings, pp. 33, **267-8,** fig. 224.
Alan, p. 113.
Albany Street, Oban, p. 242.
Alexander, p. 112.
Alexander, p. 113.
Alexander II, King of Scotland, p. 141.
Alexander III, King of Scotland, pp. 27, 217.
Allan, p. 113.
Allt an Dùnain, cairn, p. 45.
Allt Chonoghlais, bridge, p. 297.
Allt na h-Annait, p. 115.
Allt Tolaghan, bridge, p. 297.
Altars, pp. 26, 103, 136, 167, fig. 125.
Amisfield Tower (Dumfriesshire), p. 219n.
Anaid, p. 22.
An Caisteal, dun, *see* **Leccamore, Luing.**
An Doirlinn, Eriska, crannog, pp. 20, **93.**
Andrew, bishop of Argyll, p. 171.
An Dùn, Clenamacrie, dun, pp. 77-8, fig. 46.
An Dùn, Loch Fiart, Lismore, broch, pp. 20, **75,** fig. 43.
An Dùn, Sloc a' Bhrighide, Lismore, dun, pp. 19, **78,** fig. 47.
An Dùnan, Dalintart, dun, p. 77.
An Dùnan, Minard Point, dun, p. 77, fig. 45.
Angus, p. 149.
Angus, George, architect, p. 211.
Annaid, pp. 22n, 98.
Annat, pp. 22n, 98.
An Sàilean, Lismore, limestone-quarries *and* workers' dwellings, pp. 3, 35, **276-7,** fig. 233, pl. 104A-B.
An Sithean, mesolithic flints, p. 5.
Aon Garbh, Lismore: cairns, pp. 45-6; cist, p. 57.
Appin, Tynribbie, old parish church, pp. 22n, **98-9,** 161, fig. 86, pl. 12A-C.

Appin House, pp. 30-1, **245-7,** figs. 213-14, pls. 83-4C.
Appin-murder cairn, Ballachulish, pp. 97-8, 256.
Appin Post-office, Tynribbie, p. 247, pl. 84D.
Archer-slits, *see* Arrow-slits.
Architects: Angus, George, p. 211; Baxter, John (the elder), pp. 31, 266; Bryce, David, pp. 248, 252; Burn, Robert, p. 255; Burn, William, pp. 31, 247, 255; Burnet, Sir John James, p. 255; Campbell, John, of Lochend, pp. 33, 155, 249n, 252, 256, 261, 268n, 272, 295; Cousin, David, pp. 25, 165-6; Dalzel, Mr, p. 153; Douglas, John, p. 31n; Edgar, J, p. 147n; Elliot, Archibald, pp. 31, 266; Elliot, James, pp. 25, 132; Graham, James Gillespie, pp. 31, 248-9, 251-3, 255; Jelfe, Andrews, p. 278; Lindsay, Ian G, p. 161; Lorimer, Sir Robert, p. 259; MacDougald, Donald, p. 147; McNab, Mr, p. 166; Morris, Roger, p. 30n; Mylne, Robert, pp. 36, 295; Norton, L C, p. 259; Pugin, Augustus Welby Northmore, pp. 25, 165; Smith, James, pp. 25n, 129; Stevenson, John, pp. 132, 242, 254, 295; Telford, Thomas, pp. 25n, 129, 164, 261, 266, 295n; Thom, John, pp. 99, 260; Wilson, Charles, pp. 30, 110.
Architectural fragments, *see* Carved stones.
Ardachy, burial, pp. 57-8.
Ardanaiseig, pp. 31, 61, 94, **247,** 277, pls. 85-6B.
Ardanaiseig, crannogs, p. 94.
Ardanstur, duns (1) *and* (2), pp. 78-9, figs. 48-9; forts (1) *and* (2), p. 64, fig. 28.
Ardantrive, Kerrera, cave, p. 12.
Ardchattan: Baile Mhaodain, burial-ground and church, pp. 25, 99, 110, **115-16,** 278, figs. 6, 102, pl. 21C; old parish church, pp. 99, 110, 116, 211n, 247n; parish church, pp. 25, **99,** fig. 87, pl. 12D-F; well, p. 116; *see also* **Ardchattan Priory.**
Ardchattan Priory: pp. 22-3, 26, **99-115,** 116, 125, 157n, 179n, 210, figs. 88-101, pls. 13-20.
  ARCHITECTURAL DESCRIPTION:
    Building material, p. 101.
    Burial-aisles, pp. 101-3, **104-5,** pls. 13B, 14A, 16D-F.
    Choir: pp. 23, **101-3,** 105, 110, figs. 90-1, pls. 13B, 14-15C, E; sacristy, pp. 101-2.
    Conventual buildings: pp. 23, 101, 103, **105-10,** figs. 88, 94-8, pls. 17-18; chimney-pieces, pp. 109-10, pl. 18G; fish-pond, p. 109; panelling, p. 109, pl. 18G; Prior's Room, pp. 106, 109, pl. 18G; pulpit, pp. 23, 105, 108, figs. 94A, D-E, 95-7, pls. 17A, 18A-E; refectory, pp. 23, 101, 105-8, figs. 94-8, pls. 17-18F; timber roof, pp. 23, 106, 108, fig. 98, undercroft, pp. 105-6.
    Crossings and transepts: pp. 101, **103-4,** 105, 125, figs. 88, 89D, F-G, 92-3, pls. 15D, F, 16A-C; chapels, pp. 101, 103, 105; pulpitum, p. 103, fig. 90E.
    Masons' marks, p. 101, fig. 89.
    Nave: pp. 101, **105,** pl. 16G; consecration crosses, p. 105.
  FUNERARY MONUMENTS AND OTHER CARVED STONES:
    Early Christian, pp. 22, 110-11, fig. 99; medieval, pp. 26, 102, **111-13,** figs. 100-1, pl. 19; post-Reformation, pp. 26, 103-5, **113-15,** 179n, pl. 20.
  HISTORICAL NOTE, p. 110.
  MANSION, pp. 101, 105-6, 108-10, figs. 88, 98, pls. 13A, 18G.
Ardchonnell: chambered cairn, pp. 7, **40,** fig. 9; crannog, p. 94; house, p. 231.
Ardencaple, Seil, quarry *and* workers' dwellings, p. 278.
Ardencaple House, Seil, pp. 31, **247-8,** pl. 86C-D.
Ardentallan, old quarries, pp. 35, 141, 153, 157, 166, 195, 217, 222, **277,** pl. 104C.

Ardfad Castle, Seil, p. 175, fig. 165, pl. 39D.
Ardlarach, Luing, pp. 31, 33, 96, **248**, pl. 86E.
Ard Luing, Luing, earthwork, pp. 21, **95**, fig. 80.
Ardmaddy, quarry, *see* **Caddleton.**
Ardmaddy Castle, pp. 28, 30-1, 242, **248-52**, 277-8, figs. 215-16, pls. 87-9.
Ardnacloich, *see* **Cladh Churiollan, Creagan.**
Ardnahua, pp. 33, 272-4, pl. 103A.
Ardteatle: bridge, p. 296; cup-markings, p. 61.
Ardtornish (Morvern), quarry, pp. 115, 151, 156, 159, 163, 184, 199, 216, 225, 247.
Arduaine, dun, p. 79.
Argyll, Archibald Campbell, 8th Earl of, aft. 1st Marquess of, pp. 179, 194, 198, 211, 239, 249, 252.
——Archibald Campbell, 9th Earl of, pp. 171, 194, 198, 210-11, 239, 252.
——Archibald Campbell, 10th Earl of, aft. 1st Duke of, p. 211.
——Campbell family, Dukes of, pp. 211n, 242, 254.
——Campbell family, Earls of: pp. 30, 186, 198, 210, 217, 231; *see also* **Argyll,** Campbell family, Dukes of, *and* **Campbell family,** of Lochawe.
——Colin Campbell, 1st Earl of, pp. 179, 186, 231, 238.
——Colin Campbell, 3rd Earl of, p. 265.
——George Douglas Campbell, 8th Duke of, pp. 138n, 267.
——George William Campbell, 6th Duke of, pp. 242-3.
——John Campbell, 2nd Duke of, p. 30n.
——John Campbell, 5th Duke of, p. 231.
——John Douglas Sutherland Campbell, 9th Duke of, p. 211.
Argyllshire Gathering Halls, Breadalbane Street, Oban, burial, p. 60.
Argyll Square, Oban, p. 242.
Ariogan, cairns (1) *and* (2), p. 46.
Armlets, bronze, pp. 12-13, 59, pl. 4C.
Armorial, pp. 26, **301-2.**
Armorial insignia: p. 26; Achallader, burial-ground, p. 97; Airds House, p. 244, pls. 80, 81A, C; Appin House, p. 246; Ardchattan Priory, pp. 26, 113-15, pl. 20; Ardmaddy Castle, p. 249, pl. 88C; Barcaldine Castle, pp. 177, 179, pls. 41A-B, 43C; Castle Stalker, pp. 191, 194, pl. 50A; Degnish, p. 254; Dunstaffnage Castle, p. 204; Dunstaffnage Chapel, pp. 128-9; Dunstaffnage House, p. 299, pl. 120C; Eilean Munde, old parish church, p. 131, pl. 25A, C; Eilean Musdile, lighthouse, p. 280; Glenorchy, parish church, p. 134; Inishail, old parish church, p. 136, fig. 125; Kilbrandon, Seil, old parish church, p. 140, pl. 29D; Kilbride, old parish church, pp. 142-3, pl. 29B; Kilchattan, Luing, old parish church, pp. 145-6, pl. 30D; Kilchrenan, parish church, p. 149, pl. 31E; Kilchurn Castle, p. 234, pl. 72F; Lismore, St Moluag Cathedral and parish church, p. 162, pl. 34F; Lochnell House, p. 263; Muckairn, parish church, p. 165, pl. 35A; Port Appin, old smithy, p. 299, pl. 120D; Sonachan, burial-enclosure, p. 167, pl. 36D; Upper Sonachan House, p. 267, pl. 100C.
Arrow-slits, pp. 27, 175, 208-9, 225-6, 265, figs. 186, 204, pl. 99D.
Artists: Pierie, John, p. 254n; Sandby, Paul, p. 246n; Stanley, A, pl. 77A; Watts, W H, p. 216n.
Ath Dearg: burial-ground, p. 115; shielings, p. 115.
Atholl, John Murray, 1st Marquess of, pp. 210-11, 239.
——John Stewart, 4th Earl of, p. 177.
——Stewart family, Earls of, p. 177.
'Atlantic Bridge', *see* **Clachan Bridge, Seil.**
Auchachenna, chambered cairn, pp. 7, **40-1**, fig. 10.
Auchalladour, *see* **Achallader Castle.**
Auch Gleann, burial-ground *and* chapel, pp. 22n, **115.**
Auchindoun, *see* **Achadun Castle.**
Auchindrain (Mid Argyll), cruck-framed buildings, p. 32.
Auchnacloich, Cladh na h-Anaid, burial-ground, pp. 22, **120-1.**
Augustinian Order, p. 135.
Axes: bronze, p. 13, pl. 5A, C; jadeite, p. 9; stone, p. 9.

Bà Bridge, p. 297.
Bachull mór (crozier), p. 21.
Back Combie Street, Oban, pp. 30, **243.**

Bà Cottage, bridge, pp. 296-7.
Baile Mhaodain, Ardchattan, burial-ground, church and well, pp. 25, 99, 110, **115-16**, 278, figs. 6, 102, pl. 21C.
Baileys, pp. 181, 184, 186, 194, 213, 216-17, 222-3, 225, 229-31, figs. 168, 170, 188, 191, 197-204.
Ballachuan, Seil, burial-ground *and* chapel, pp. 25, **116-17**, fig. 103.
Ballachulish: Appin-murder cairn, pp. **97-8**, 256; slate-quarries, pp. 3, 32, 34-5, 178, **277**, 278, pl. 105A-B; workers' dwellings, pp. 35, **277**, pl. 105C.
Ballachulish House: pp. 31, 46, **252-3**, pl. 90A-B; cairn, pp. 10, **46**, fig. 16; carved stone, p. 253.
Ballevoadan, *see* **Baile Mhaodain.**
Ballimeanoch: cairns, p. 46; *see also* **Creag a' Chaibeil.**
Balliveolan, pp. 117, **253**, pl. 91A.
Balliveolan, burial-ground, p. 117.
Balliveolan, Lismore, enclosure, p. 95, fig. 81.
Balloch, *see* **Taymouth Castle.**
Ballycastle, Luing, dun, pp. 18, **79-80**, fig. 50.
Baltersan Castle (Ayrshire), p. 219n.
Balure: cairns, pp. 11, **46-7**; cists, pp. 12, **58.**
Balvicar, Seil: fort, pp. 16-18, **64-5**, fig. 29; quarry *and* workers' dwellings, p. 278.
Balygrundle, Lismore: cairns (north) *and* (south), p. 47; *see also* **Dùn Mór.**
Bar-a-goan, Kilvarie, burial-ground *and* chapel, p. 117.
Barbreck, cairn, p. 47.
Barcaldine: standing stones, p. 62; *see also* **Achanrear** and **Castle Farm.**
Barcaldine Castle: pp. 29, 114, **176-81**, 238, 253, figs. 166-7, pls. 1, 40-3; architectural description, pp. 176-9; historical note, pp. 179-80; inventory of furnishings, pp. 180-1.
Barcaldine House: pp. 180, 211n, **253**, 258, pl. 90C-E.
Barcaltin, Barchaltan, Barchaltane, *see* **Barcaldine Castle.**
Barguillean, dun, p. 80, fig. 51.
Barmkins, pp. 28, 188-9, 232, 238, fig. 173.
Barns, pp. 32-3, 161, 244, 258, 265, 274, fig. 222, pl. 98C.
Barochreal, cairn, p. 47.
'Baron's Cairn', *see* **Lochan nan Ràth.**
Barr a' Chaistealain, dun, pp. 18, **80**, fig. 52.
Barrachrail, township, pp. 142, 272n.
Barran, millstone-quarry, pp. 35, **278.**
Barr Beag, cairn, p. 47.
Barr Mór, dun, p. 80, fig. 53.
Barr Mór, Lismore: bronze axe, p. 13, pl. 5C; cairns (1) *and* (2), p. 47, fig. 17; cist, p. 58.
Barrnacarry: farm, p. 272; old quarry, pp. 35, 141, 153, 157, 166, 195, 251, **277**, pl. 104D.
Barrow, Lochnell Arms Hotel, pp. 10, **54.**
Barr Phort, crannog, p. 94.
Baxter, John (elder), architect *and* mason, pp. 31, 266.
Beacharra ware, p. 8.
Beakers, pp. 9, 12, 40, 43, 59-61, pl. 3B.
Bealwothar, *see* **Castle Coeffin.**
Beauly Priory (Inverness-shire), p. 23.
Belfries, *see* **Bell-cots.**
Bell, Henry, engineer, p. 243.
Bell-cots, pp. 99, 121, 129, 132-3, 139, 146, 148, 154, 159, 163, 167, 290, figs. 136, 155, pls. 12D, 24A, 26A, C, 30A, 31D, 32A-B, 35B.
Bell-founders: Maxwell, Robert, p. 164; Mears, Thomas, p. 299.
Bells, pp. 21n, 121, 132-3, 164, 299, pls. 35F, 120G.
Benderloch: Cill Choluim-chille, burial-ground, pp. 118-19; standing-stones (1) *and* (2), p. 62.
Beothail, p. 187.
Bernera, burial-ground *and* chapel, p. 117.
Beuge, John, engraver, p. 254n.
Bishop's Well, *see* **Tobar an Easbuig.**
Black Crofts, North Connel, field-bank, pp. 13, 21, **95-6**, pl. 11E.
Black Lynn, Oban, p. 242.
Black Mill Bay, Luing, quarry *and* workers' dwellings, p. 278.
Blairquhan Castle (Ayrshire), p. 220.
Bloomeries: p. 33; *see also* **Ironworks.**
Boat-houses, pp. 216, 251, 254, 293, pl. 89A.

Boat-landings: pp. 4, 138, 166, 182, 184, 189, 216, 220, 222, 230-1, 241, 274, figs. 173, 188, 197, 210; *see also* **Harbours** *and* **Jetties.**

Bonawe: church, p. 283; cruck-framed byre, pp. 32, **269,** fig. 225; Dùn Mór, earthwork, p. 96, fig. 83; Lorn Furnace, ironworks, pp. 3, 33-4, 63, 128, 276, **281-92,** 293, figs. 236-47, pls. 111-16; quarry, pp. 3, 163, 288; workers' dwellings, pp. 34, 269, 283, **290-1,** figs. 236, 244-6, pl. 116A-C.

Bonawe House, pp. 34, **291-2,** figs. 236, 247, pl. 116D-E.

Bothan na Dige, Stronmilchan, pp. 187, **254,** 267.

Brackley, whisky still, p. 278.

Breachacha Castle (Coll), pp. 34n, 188.

Breadalbane, Campbell family, Earls of, pp. 182, 234, 249, 252, 267.

——John Campbell, of Glenorchy, 1st Earl of, pp. 28, 174, 179, 180n, 232, 234, 239, 252.

——John Campbell, 2nd Earl of, pp. 30, 139n, 239, 252n, 258, 280-1.

——John Campbell, 3rd Earl of, pp. 240, 283.

——John Campbell, 4th Earl of, aft. 1st Marquess of, pp. 25, 33, 132, 252, 254, 268n, 295.

——John Campbell, 2nd Marquess of, pp. 25, 139, 166, 242, 252.

——Mary Campbell, Countess of, p. 234.

Breadalbane Place, Oban, cists, p. 59.

Breadalbane Street, Oban, burial and cists, pp. 59-60.

Bridge of Awe: bridge, pp. 4, 36, 278, **294,** 295, pl. 119A; old quarry, pp. 35, 115, 182, 213, 216, **278.**

Bridge of Jure, *see* **Glenure.**

Bridge of Orchy, pp. 36, 296-7, pl. 119D.

Bridges: pp. 4, 36; Allt Chonoghlais, p. 297; Allt Tolaghan, p. 297; Ardmaddy Castle, pp. 248, 251, pl. 89B; Ardteatle, p. 296; Bà Bridge, p. 297; Bà Cottage, pp. 296-7; Bridge of Awe, pp. 4, 36, 278, **294,** 295, pl. 119A; Bridge of Orchy, pp. 36, 296-7, pl. 119D; Clachan Bridge, Seil, pp. 36, 49, **294-5,** pl. 119B; Cladich, p. 296; Croft-in-tuime, p. 296; Dalmally, pp. 36, **295,** pl. 119C; Easan Dubh, p. 296; Eilean Musdile, p. 280, pl. 110F; Glenure, p. 258; Hexham (Northumberland), p. 295n; Inistrynich, p. 296; Inverlochy, p. 296; Inveroran, pp. 296-7; Linne nam Beathach, p. 297; River Lochy, p. 296; Teatle Water, p. 296; Victoria Bridge, pp. 296-7.

Bridget, p. 184.

Bridge of Urchay, *see* **Dalmally,** bridge.

Brochs: pp. 16, 20, fig. 5; An Dùn, Loch Fiart, Lismore, pp. 20, **75,** fig. 43, pl. 10; Tirefour Castle, Lismore, pp. 16, 20, **75-7,** fig. 44, pl. 10.

Bronze Age: pp. 9-15; distribution maps, figs. 2-4; monuments (descriptions), pp. 45-64, 95-6, figs. 15-27, pls. 8-9, 11E; relics, pp. 9-10, 12-15, 43, 46, 49, 51-5, 57-61, pls. 3B-5C.

Brooches, pp. 58, 60, 223.

Brooch of Lorn, p. 223.

Bruce family, p. 299.

Bryce, David, architect, pp. 248, 252.

Building-contractors: Dalziel, William, p. 166; Drummond, John, pp. 110, 253; Johnstone, Allan, p. 132; Simpson, John, p. 254n; Smith, James, p. 279; Spottiswoode, Mr, p. 255; Stevenson, John, pp. 132, 242, 254, 295; Thom, John, pp. 99, 260; Watherston and Son, John, p. 255.

Building materials: firebrick, p. 284; iron, p. 284, pl. 113B; slate, pp. 34n, 132, 178, 225, 239, 290-1; stone, pp. 101, 115, 141, 151, 153, 156-7, 159, 163, 166, 168, 177, 182, 184, 189, 195, 199, 211n, 213, 216-17, 222, 225, 247, 251, 277-8, 280, 288, 290; timber, p. 132, pl. 27A; *see also* **Chimney-pieces, Quarries** *and* **Timber roof-structures.**

Bunaw, Bunawe, *see* **Bonawe.**

Burghs: p. 30; *see also* **Oban.**

Burial-enclosures: Airds House, p. 245; Shuna, Nether Lorn, p. 167; Sonachan, pp. **167,** 267, pl. 36D; *see also* **Burial-grounds.**

Burial-grounds: pp. 21-2, 25; Achallader, pp. **97,** 173; Ath Dearg, p. 115; Auch Gleann, pp. 22n, **115;** Baile Mhaodain, Ardchattan, pp. 115-16; Ballachuan, Seil, pp. 25, **116-17,** fig. 103; Balliveolan, p. 117; Bar-a-goan, Kilvarie, p. 117;

Bernera, p. 117; Caibeal, Lochavich, pp. 117-18, fig. 104; Cill an Inbhire, p. 118; Cill-an-Suidhe, Lismore, pp. 21, **118,** 119, 121, fig. 105; Cill Choluim-chille, Benderloch, pp. 118-19; Clachan, Lismore, pp. 21, 118, **119,** 121, fig. 106; Cladh Churiollan, Creagan, pp. 25, **122,** fig. 110; Cladh na h-Anaid, Auchnacloich, pp. 22, **120-1;** Cladh na h-Anaid, Taynuilt, pp. 22, 118-19, **121,** fig. 108; Cladh Uaine, pp. 25, **121,** fig. 109; Creag a' Chaibeil, Ballimeanoch, pp. 25, **123,** fig. 112; Creag Mhór, p. 124; Eilean Munde, pp. 25-6, **129-31,** 139, fig. 120, pls. 24C-25; Kilbride, Glen Feochan, p. 143; Kilcheran, Lismore, p. 146; Kilchoan House, p. 146; Kilmaha, pp. 21, **149-50,** figs. 139-41; Kilmaronag, pp. **150-3,** 163, fig. 142; Kilmarow (Killarow, Killocraw) (Kintyre), p. 110; Kilmun, pp. 25, **155,** fig. 147; Kilninver, pp. 155-6; *see also* **Burial-enclosures, Chapels, Churches** *and* **Monasteries.**

Burials: p. 12; Ardachy, pp. 57-8; Cnoc Aingil, Lismore, p. 58; Dùn an Fheurain, p. 58; Dunollie, pp. 58-9; Kames, p. 59; Kilcheran, Lismore, p. 59; Mount Pleasant House, Kerrera, p. 22; Oban, pp. 12, 22, **59-60,** pl. 4A; *see also* **Cists.**

Burn, Robert, architect *and* marble-carver, p. 255.

——William, architect, pp. 31, 247, 255.

Burnet, Sir John James, architect, p. 255.

Byres: pp. 32, 188, 243-4, 247, **258,** 261, 266, 269, 273-4, 276-7, figs. 225-6, 231-3, pls. 84D, 102B.

Cadderlie, cruck-framed building, pp. 32-3, **269,** fig. 226.

Caddleton, marble-quarry, pp. 35, 250-1, **278.**

Caibeal, Lochavich, burial-ground, pp. 117-18, fig. 104.

Caibeal Chiarain, chapel, p. 117.

Caifean, p. 187.

Cailean Mór, *see* **Campbell,** Sir Colin (Cailean Mór), of Lochawe.

Cairnbane, *see* **Portnacroish.**

Cairns: pp. 9-13, fig. 2; Achacha, pp. 10, **45,** fig. 15; Achaleven, p. **45;** Achanamoine, pp. 11, **45;** Achanancarn, pp. 11, **45;** Achnaba, pp. 11, **45;** Allt an Dùnain, p. 45; Aon Garbh, Lismore, pp. 45-6; Appin-murder cairn, Ballachulish, pp. **97-8,** 256; Ariogan (1) *and* (2), p. 46; Ballachulish House, pp. 10, **46,** fig. 16; Ballimeanoch, p. 46; Balure, pp. 11, **46-7;** Balygrundle (north) *and* (south), Lismore, p. 47; Barbreck, p. 47; Barochreal, p. 47; Barr Beag, p. 47; Barr Mór (1) *and* (2), Lismore, p. 47, fig. 17; Càrn Bàn, Achnacarron, p. 47; Càrn Breugach, Kerrera, p. 48; Carn Chailein, pp. 115, **118;** Càrn Mór, Lismore, p. 48; Castle Farm, Barcaldine, pp. 10-11, **48-9,** fig. 18; Clachadow (1) *and* (2), pp. 10, **49,** 50, fig. 19, pl. 8B; Clachan Bridge, Seil, p. 49; Clenamacrie (east) *and* (west), p. 49; Cnoc Aingil, Lismore, pp. **49,** 58; Connel, p. 49; Corrielorne, p. 50; Creagan, p. 299; Creag an Fhithich, Lismore, p. 50; Cruach Achadh na Craoibhe, p. 50; Culcharron, pp. 10, 12, 49, **50,** 51, 54, fig. 20; Dalnacabeg, p. 50; Dalranach, pp. 50, 55; Dalvuie (1) *and* (2), pp. 11, **50-1;** Druim an Uinnsinn (1) *and* (2), Lismore, p. 51, fig. 21; Dùnan Buiaig, p. 51; Dunstaffnage House, p. 51; Duntanachan, pp. 51-2; Fasnacloich, p. 52; Glen Etive, p. 52; Gualachulann, p. 52; Kilmartin (Mid Argyll), p. 10; Kilmelford, p. 52; Kilmore, pp. 10-11, 13, 43, **52-3,** 96, figs. 22-3, pl. 4B; Kintraw (Mid Argyll), p. 10; Lagganbeg, p. 53; Làrach Bàn, pp. 10, **53-4,** fig. 24; Ledaig, p. 54; Lerags, pp. 10, **54,** fig. 25; Lochan a' Chuirn, pp. 11, **54;** Lochan na Beithe, pp. 11, **54;** Lochan nan Ràth, pp. 11, 37, **54,** pl. 8A; Moss of Achnacree, pp. 11, **55;** Musdale, p. 55; Pennyfuir, p. 55; Rockhill, p. 55; Salachail, p. 55; Sgeir Carnaich, p. 55; Shelachan, p. 55; Shuna Cottage (1) *and* (2), Shuna, Nether Lorn, pp. **55,** 57; Shuna Point, Shuna, Nether Lorn, p. 57; Slatrach Bay, Kerrera, p. 57; Stronmilchan, p. 57; Strontoiller, pp. 10, 51, **57,** 63, fig. 26, pl. 9A; West Laroch, p. 57; *see also* **Barrow, Burials, Chambered cairns** *and* **Cists.**

Caisteal Ach-a-luachrach, *see* **Camuslaich.**

Caisteal na Gruagaich (Morvern), p. 182.

Caisteal nan Con, Torsa, pp. 28, **181-2,** fig. 168, pl. 44.

Caisteal na Nighinn Ruaidhe, Loch Avich, pp. 28-9, **182-4,** fig. 169.

Caisteal Suidhe Cheannaidh, dun, pp. 19, **81,** fig. 54.
Caithness: John Campbell of Glenorchy, 6th Earl of, p. 179; *see also* **Breadalbane,** 1st Earl of.
Caledonian Canal (Inverness-shire), p. 277.
Caledonii, p. 16.
Calton Jail (Edinburgh), p. 31.
Cameron, Alan, 16th of Lochiel, p. 131n.
——Allan, of Corrychiracha, p. 131.
——Anne, p. 131.
——Donald, of Corrychiracha, p. 131.
——Sir Ewen, 17th of Lochiel, p. 131.
——John, of Culchennan, p. 131.
——John, younger of Lochiel, p. 131.
Cameron family, of Corrychiracha, p. 131.
——of Culchennan, p. 131.
Campbell (Cambel), Alexander, p. 134.
——Alexander (d. 1829), p. 146.
——Alexander, bailie of Ardnamurchan, p. 165.
——Alexander, tacksman, p. 243.
——Alexander, 4th of Airds, p. 162.
——Alexander, 1st of Ardchattan, pp. 101, 104, 110.
——Alexander, of Arrivean, p. 114.
——Alexander, of Barcaldine, pp. 174n, 179-80, 239.
——Alexander, of Barcaldine and Glenure, p. 258.
——Alexander, 10th of Dunstaffnage, pp. 128, 211.
——Alexander, 19th of Dunstaffnage, p. 259.
——Alexander, of Lerags, p. 261.
——Alexander, 3rd of Lochnell, pp. 105, 114.
——Alexander, 6th of Lochnell, pp. 105, 114-15, 265.
——Alexander, of Sonachan, p. 148.
——Allane (d. 1671), p. 114.
——Angus, of Ardlarach, p. 167.
——Angus (Aeneas), 11th of Dunstaffnage, pp. 204, 207, 211.
——Angus, 20th of Dunstaffnage, p. 211.
——Anna, p. 165.
——Annabella, p. 114.
——Archibald (*flor. c.* 1567), p. 174.
——Archibald (d. 1788), p. 145.
——Archibald, innkeeper, p. 165.
——Archibald, tacksman (*flor. c.* 1741), p. 128.
——Archibald, of Inverawe, p. 223.
——Archibald, of Lerags (*flor. c.* 1516), pp. 26, 143, 168, 242.
——Archibald, of Lerags (*flor. c.* 1800), p. 261.
——Archibald, 13th of Lochnell, p. 266.
——Archibald, 14th of Lochnell, p. 266.
——Lord Archibald, pp. 142, 149.
——Archibald, of Melfort, p. 254.
——Arthur, constable of Dunstaffnage Castle, pp. 197, 210.
——Beatrix, p. 128.
——Charles, p. 252.
——Charles, of Combie, p. 242.
——Colin, p. 134.
——Colin (d. 1671), p. 114.
——Captain Colin, p. 258.
——Colin, of Achnaba, minister of Ardchattan and Muckairn, p. 244.
——Colin, of Balligown, p. 115.
——Colin, of Carwhin, pp. 248, 252, 278, 290n.
——Sir Colin, 1st of Glenorchy, pp. 28, 174, 179, 186, 211, 232, 238.
——Sir Colin, 3rd of Glenorchy, p. 238.
——Colin, 6th of Glenorchy, pp. 174n, 179, 232, 238.
——Colin, of Glenure, pp. 98, 256, 258.
——Colin, of Inveresragan, p. 281n.
——Sir Colin (Cailean Mór), of Lochawe, pp. 118, 149, 231.
——Sir Colin, of Lochawe (d. *c.* 1343), pp. 197, 231.
——Colin, 5th of Lochnell, p. 171.
——Captain Colin, of Skipness, p. 240.
——Daniel, of Shawfield, p. 263.
——David, of Combie, p. 256.
——Donald, of Achendoun, p. 281n.
——Donald, 5th of Airds, pp. 30n, 245.
——Donald, of Ardentallan, p. 115.
——Sir Donald, of Ardnamurchan and Airds, pp. 29, 194, 245.
——Donald, of Lossit, p. 165.
——Donald, of Scammadale, p. 128.
——Donald, of Sonachan, pp. 147-8.
——Captain Dougall, p. 114.
——Dougall, of Inverawe, p. 114.
——Dugald, tacksman, p. 243.
——Dugald (*flor. c.* 1728), p. 252n.
——Dugald, of Craignish, p. 184.
——Col. Dugald, of Inverawe, p. 113.
——Dugall, of Lochawe, p. 242.
——Duncan (*flor.* 1831), p. 247n.
——Duncan, mason, pp. 256, 258.
——Duncan, tacksman (*flor.* 1634), p. 174.
——Sir Duncan, 1st Bt of Barcaldine and Glenure, pp. 180, 253n, 258, 294.
——Sir Duncan, 3rd Bt of Barcaldine, p. 180.
——Duncan, of Blarochorin, p. 134.
——Sir Duncan, 2nd of Glenorchy, pp. 232, 238, 251n.
——Sir Duncan, 4th of Glenorchy, pp. 238, 252.
——Sir Duncan, 1st Bt and 7th of Glenorchy, pp. 29, 114, 132, 171, 174, 176-7, 179, 187, 238.
——Duncan, of Glenure, p. 258.
——Duncan, of Inverawe, p. 243.
——Duncan, of Jura, p. 252.
——Sir Duncan, of Lochawe, pp. 184, 211, 231, 238.
——Sir Duncan, 7th of Lochnell, pp. 30, 164, 244, 263, 265, 280, 281n, 283.
——Lt. Gen. Duncan, 8th of Lochnell, pp. 152n, 164, 266.
——Duncan, of Sonachan, p. 148.
——George, 2nd of Airds, p. 245.
——Helen, of Blythswood, p. 299.
——Isabella, of Glenfeochan, p. 154.
——Isobel, p. 145.
——James, minister of Kilmore and Kilbride, p. 155.
——Sir James, of Lawers, p. 204.
——James Archibald, of New Inverawe, p. 247.
——Jane, p. 259.
——John, commendator of Ardchattan, aft. bishop of the Isles, p. 110.
——John, cashier of Royal Bank of Scotland, p. 278.
——John, factor of Breadalbane estate in Argyll, p. 32.
——John, 3rd of Airds, p. 194.
——John, 2nd of Ardchattan, p. 110.
——John, of Ardentallan, p. 115.
——John, of Auchinryre, p. 179.
——John, of Balliveolan, pp. 117, 253.
——John, younger of Barcaldine, p. 267.
——Sir John, 9th of Calder (Cawdor), p. 110.
——John, 11th of Calder (Cawdor), pp. 245, 251.
——John, of Clathic, p. 114.
——John, 9th of Dunstaffnage, p. 128.
——Sir John, 2nd Bt and 8th of Glenorchy, p. 239.
——Sir John, 5th of Glenorchy, p. 238.
——John, of Invergeldie (Inneryeldies, Inverzaldies), pp. 114, 179.
——John, of Lochend, chamberlain of Breadalbane estate in Argyll, pp. 33, 155, 249n, 252, 256, 261, 268n, 272, 295.
——John, younger of Lochend, pp. 256, 261, 272.
——John, 1st of Lochnell, p. 265.
——John, 4th of Lochnell, p. 115.
——John, of Lossit, p. 165.
——John, of Melfort, p. 254.
——Col. John, of Melfort, p. 292.
——Lachlan, p. 145.
——Dame Lillias, pp. 204, 207.
——Margaret (d. 1657), p. 114.
——Margaret (d. 1681), p. 140.
——Margaret (*flor. c.* 1803), p. 256.
——Lady Margaret, pp. 263, 265.
——Margaret, p. 131.
——Marjory, p. 162.
——Mary, p. 113.
——Mary, p. 134.
——Mary, p. 167.
——Captain Neil, of Degnish, p. 254.
——Sir Neil, of Lochawe, p. 231.
——Lord Neil, pp. 140, 145, 249, 252.
——Niall, 15th of Dunstaffnage, p. 146.

Campbell, Patrick, of Barcaldine, pp. 211n, 253, 258.
——Patrick, of Invergeldie (Inneryeldies, Inverzaldies), pp. 114, 134, 179-80.
——Robert, merchant, p. 258.
——Robert, of Finab and Monzie, pp. 217, 243, 259.
——Sir Robert, of Glenfalloch, aft. 3rd Bt and 9th of Glenorchy, pp. 131n, 179-80.
——Robert, of Monzie, pp. 217, 243, 259.
——Robert, of Sonachan, pp. 242, 267.
——Ronald, of Craignish, p. 184.
——Walter Douglas, of Blythswood, p. 299.
Campbell family: pp. 113, 124, 140, 149, 155, 165, 180, 210; *see also* **Argyll**, Campbell family, Earls of.
——of Achalader, p. 174n.
——of Achnaba, p. 244.
——of Airds, pp. 30, 191, 194, 244-5.
——of Ardchattan, pp. 101, 104, 110.
——of Ardnamurchan and Airds, p. 194.
——of Balligown, p. 115.
——of Balliveolan, pp. 117, 253.
——of Barcaldine: pp. 114, 179-80, 244, 253; *see also* **Campbell family,** of Invergeldie.
——of Calder (Cawdor), pp. 140, 153.
——of Combie, pp. 242, 256.
——of Craignish, pp. 182, 184.
——of Dunstaffnage, pp. 114, 124, 128-9, 198, 204-5, 210, 217, 242, 299.
——of Glenlyon, p. 175.
——of Glenorchy: pp. 28, 174, 177, 179, 187, 238; *see also* **Breadalbane** *and* **Caithness**.
——of Inverawe, pp. 102-3, 113-14, 217, 223, 247, 259.
——of Invergeldie (Inneryeldies, Inverzaldies), pp. 114, 179.
——of Lerags, pp. 26, 143, 168.
——of Lochawe: pp. 115, 118, 149, 155, 182, 184, 210, 231; *see also* **Argyll**, Campbell family, Earls of.
——of Lochnell, pp. 26, 30, 103-4, 110, 114-15, 242, 263, 265.
——of Lorn, *see* **Lorn**, lordship of.
——of Lossit, p. 165.
——of Melfort, p. 153.
——of Scammadale, pp. 128-9.
——of Shawfield, p. 263.
——of Sonachan, pp. 167, 267.
Campbell of Lerags Cross, pp. 26, **143**, 168, pl. 29B-C.
Campbeltown (Kintyre), p. 30.
Camserney (Perthshire), p. 32n.
Camuslaich, Seil, dun, p. 81, fig. 55.
Canna (Inverness-shire), cashel, p. 120n.
Cannon (Canon), Colonel Alexander, p. 174n.
Carlingford Mint (Co. Louth), p. 111n.
Carnach, township, p. 271.
Càrn an Ròin, crannog, p. 94.
Càrn Bàn, cairn, *see* **Balure**.
Càrn Bàn, Achnacarron, cairn, p. 47.
Càrn Bàn, Achnacree, cairn, *see* **Achnacree**.
Càrn Breugach, Kerrera, cairn, p. 48.
Carn Chailein, cairn, pp. 115, **118**.
Càrn Dubh, crannog, p. 94.
Càrn Mhic Chealair, crannog, p. 94.
Càrn Mór, Lismore, cairn, p. 48.
Carsaig (Mull), quarry, pp. 35, 101, 168, 199.
Carved stones, architectural fragments etc.:[1] p. 36; Ballachulish House, p. 253; Castle Coeffin, p. 186, fig. 171; Druimneil House, p. 299, pl. 120A; Dunollie Castle, p. 197, fig. 179, pl. 54F; Eilean Munde, p. 131, pl. 25D; Fort William, p. 259; Fraoch Eilean, pp. 216-17, fig. 190, pl. 62F; Gylen Castle, Kerrera, pp. 217, 219, 222-3, 254, pl. 65D-E, G; Ickworth (Suffolk), p. 299; Inverawe House, p. 259; Kilchurn Castle, p. 238, pl. 75C; Lochawe, St Conan's Church, pp. 36, 299, pl. 120E-F; *see also* **Armorial insignia, Funerary monuments, Graffiti, Masons' marks** *and* **Rock-carving**.
Carvers: Burn, Robert, p. 255; Jelfe, Andrews, p. 278; O Brolchan, John, p. 112; Smith, D, p. 155; *see also* **Carving** *and* **Masons**.

Carving, schools of (medieval): p. 26.
    IONA, pp. 26, 102, 111-12 (nos. 9-10, 11(i), pl. 19C), 130-1 (no. 1), 142 (nos. 8-9), 149 (no. 5), 161 (nos. 1-5, pl. 34D).
    LOCH AWE, pp. 26, 111 (nos. 7-8), 133-4 (nos. 2-10, pl. 26B, D), 135-6 (nos. 2-5), 140 (no. 4), 142 (nos. 1-7), 148-9 (nos. 2-4, 9), 153 (no. 2), 154-5 (nos. 2-5), 161-2 (nos. 6-7).
Cashels: p. 21; Cladh a' Bhearnaig, Kerrera, pp. 21, **119-20**, fig. 107; Sgor nam Ban-naomha, Canna (Inverness-shire), p. 120n; Strathcashel Point (Stirlingshire), p. 120n; *see also* **Religious houses**.
Castel Kaven, *see* **Castle Coeffin**.
Castill, *see* **Castles Farm**.
Castle Carra (Co. Mayo), p. 28n.
Castle Coeffin, Lismore, pp. 28, 171, **184-7**, figs. 170-1, pls. 45-6C.
Castle Coeffin, Lismore, fort, pp. 16, **65**.
Castle Farm, Barcaldine, cairns and standing stone, pp. 10-11, **48-9**, fig. 18.
Castle Hill, *see* **Rarey**, castle.
Castles, dun, pp. 19, **81-2**, 187, fig. 56.
Castles of enclosure, pp. 26-7.
Castles Farm, castle, pp. 82, **187**, 254, 267.
Castle Shuna, Shuna, Appin, pp. 187-8, fig. 172, pl. 46D-E.
Castle Stalker, pp. 29, 43, 187, **188-94**, figs. 173-6, pls. 47-51.
Castles and Tower-houses: pp. 25-9, 31; Achadun Castle, Lismore, pp. 26-7, **168-71**, 186, figs. 159-61, pls. 37-8B; Achallader Castle, pp. 29, 97, **171-5**, 238, figs. 162-4, pls. 38C-9C; Amisfield Tower (Dumfriesshire), p. 219n; Ardfad Castle, Seil, p. 175, fig. 165, pl. 39D; Ardmaddy Castle, pp. 28, 30-1, 242, **248-52**, 277-8, figs. 215-16, pls. 87-9; Baltersan (Ayrshire), p. 219n; Barcaldine Castle, pp. 29, 114, **176-81**, 238, 253, figs. 166-7, pls. 1, 40-3; Blairquhan Castle (Ayrshire), p. 220; Breachacha Castle (Coll), pp. 34n, 188; Caisteal na Gruagaich (Morvern), p. 182; Caisteal nan Con, Torsa, pp. 28, **181-2**, fig. 168, pl. 44; Caisteal na Nighinn Ruaidhe, Loch Avich, pp. 28-9, **182-4**, fig. 169; Castle Carra (Co. Mayo), p. 28n; Castle Coeffin, pp. 28, 171, **184-7**, figs. 170-1, pls. 45-6C; Castles Farm, pp. 82, **187**, 254, 267; Castle Shuna, Appin, pp. 187-8, fig. 172, pl. 46D-E; Castle Stalker, pp. 29, 43, 187, **188-94**, figs. 173-6, pls. 47-51; Castle Sween (Mid Argyll), p. 27; Castle Tioram (Inverness-shire), pp. 29n, 195n; Coull Castle (Aberdeenshire), p. 27; Craignish Castle (Mid Argyll), p. 184; Dirleton Castle (East Lothian), p. 27; Duart Castle (Mull), p. 27; Duffus Castle (Morayshire), p. 28n; Dunans Castle (Cowal), pp. 172n, 175; Dundarave Castle (Mid Argyll), pp. 29, 217, 220; Dunollie Castle, pp. 22, 28-9, 58-9, **194-8**, 202, 277, figs. 177-9, pls. 52-4; Dunstaffnage Castle, pp. 27, 89, 121, 124, 127n, 128, 147, 197, **198-211**, 226, 299, figs. 180-6, pls. 55-9; Fincharn (Mid Argyll), p. 184; Finlarig Castle (Perthshire), pp. 238-9; Fraoch Eilean, pp. 27-9, 35, 134-5, **212-17**, 225, 232, 259, 278, figs. 188-90, pls. 60-2; Greencastle (Co. Down), pp. 28, 217; Gwrych Castle (Denbighshire), pp. 264, 265n; Gylen Castle, Kerrera, pp. 29, 175, **217-23**, 254, 277, figs. 191-6, pls. 63-5; Haggs Castle (Renfrewshire), p. 220; Innis Chonnell Castle, pp. 25-7, 29, 94, 138, 155, 210, **223-31**, figs. 197-204, pls. 66-8; Inverlochy Castle (Inverness-shire), p. 27; Kenmure Castle (Kirkcudbrightshire), p. 220; Kilchurn Castle, pp. 28-9, 177, 179, **231-40**, figs. 205-9, pls. 69-75; Knock Castle (Skye, Inverness-shire), p. 28; Loch Dochart Castle (Perthshire), pp. 228, 238; Loch na Sreinge, pp. 29-30, **241**; Lochranza Castle (Arran, Buteshire), p. 28; Moy Castle (Mull), p. 34n; New Murthly Castle (Perthshire), p. 252; Rarey, pp. 96, **242**, 251, 267, fig. 211; Rothesay Castle (Buteshire), p. 202n; Saddell Castle (Kintyre), p. 171; Tarbert Castle (Kintyre), pp. 26n, 27; Taymouth Castle (Perthshire), pp. 132, 238, 252, 295n; *see also* **Fortified dwellings**.
Castle Sween (Mid Argyll), p. 27.
Castle Tioram (Inverness-shire), pp. 29n, 195n.
Cathedrals: pp. 21-3, 26; Dunblane (Perthshire), p. 159n; Fortrose (Ross and Cromarty), p. 23n; Kirkwall (Orkney), p. 165n; Lismore, St Moluag, pp. 21-3, 26, 48-9, 142, **156-63**, 166, 171, 186, 277, figs. 148-52, pls. 32-4.

[1] Excluding those which form part of other monuments.

Caulfield, Major Edward, engineer, pp. 36, 295-6.
Cave of the Crags, rock shelter, p. 5.
Caves: pp. 5-6, 12, 58-9, 60; An Sithean, p. 5; Ardantrive, Kerrera, p. 12; Cave of the Crags, p. 5; Creag an Èig, p. 12, pl. 3C; Dunollie, pp. 58-9; Oban, pp. 5-6, 12, 60, pl. 2; *see also* **Rock-shelters.**
Cave of the Skulls, Oban, burials, p. 60.
Cawdor Place, Oban, pp. 30, **243.**
Cerones, p. 16.
Chaben, *see* **Castle Coeffin.**
Chambered cairns: pp. 6-9, 11, fig. 2; Achnacree, pp. 7-8, **37, 50,** fig. 7, pl. 3A; Achnacreebeag, pp. 7-9, **37, 40,** fig. 8, pl. 6; Ardchonnell, pp. 7, **40,** fig. 9; Auchachenna, pp. 7, **40-1,** fig. 10; Cladich, pp. 7, **41, 43,** fig. 11; Dalineun, pp. 7-9, 11, **43,** fig. 12, pl. 7; Portnacroish, pp. 6, **43;** Port Sonachan, pp. 7-8, **43-4,** fig. 13; Shuna Cottage, Shuna, Nether Lorn, pp. 7, **44, 57,** fig. 14.
Chapels: pp. 23, 25-6; Annaid, p. 98; Auch Gleann, pp. 22n, **115;** Ballachuan, Seil, pp. 25, **116-17,** fig. 103; Bar-a-goan, Kilvarie, p. 117; Bernera, p. 117; Caibeal Chiarain, p. 117; Cill-an-Suidhe, Lismore, pp. 21, **118,** 119, 121, fig. 105; Cill Choluim-chille, Benderloch, pp. 118-19; Cladh Churiollan, Creagan, pp. 25, **122,** fig. 110; Cladh Uaine, pp. 25, **121,** fig. 109; Creag a' Chaibeil, Ballimeanoch, pp. 25, **123,** fig. 112; Dunstaffnage, pp. 23, 26, 105, **124-9,** 198-9, 205, figs. 6, 114-17, pls. 22-3; Innis Sèa-Ràmhach, pp. 25, **138,** figs. 6, 126; Iona, p. 142; Keil, pp. 23, 26, **139,** 161, figs. 6, 128, pl. 28B-E; Kilbride, Seil, p. 144; Kilcheran, Lismore, p. 146, pl. 30A; Kilchoan House, p. 146; Kilchurn Castle, pp. 232, 235, 239; Killandrist, Lismore, pp. 119, **149;** Kilmaha, pp. 21-2, **149-50,** figs. 139-41; Kilmun, pp. 25, **155,** fig. 147; Lismore, p. 162; Port Maluag, Lismore, p. 166; *see also* **Burial-enclosures, Burial-grounds, Churches** *and* **Monasteries.**
Charcoal-burning stances: p. 34; Achanlochan, p. 276; Loch Creran, pp. 34, **281,** 283; Loch Etive, pp. 34, **281,** 283.
Charles II, King of Great Britain, pp. 110, 252.
Chimney-pieces: pp. 109-10, 204, 245-8, 250-1, 253, 255, 264-5, 278, fig. 214B, pls. 18G, 82C-D, 84A-C, 86D, 89C-D, 90D-E, 93B, 99E; *see also* **Firebacks** *and* **Fireplaces.**
Chisholm, Bishop Aeneas, p. 146.
——Bishop John, pp. 146, 293.
Christie, Andrew, master-mason, pp. 179, 239.
Churches: pp. 23, 25-6; Appin, Tynribbie, old parish church, pp. 22n, **98-9,** 161, fig. 86, pl. 12A-C; Ardchattan, old parish church, pp. **99,** 101, 110, 116, 211n, 247n; Ardchattan, parish church, pp. 25, **99,** fig. 87, pl. 12D-F; Baile Mhaodain, Ardchattan, pp. 25, 99, 110, **115-16,** 278, figs. 6, 102, pl. 21C; Bonawe, p. 283; Cladich, parish church, pp. **121,** 135; Cleigh, pp. 141, 153; Dalavich, parish church, pp. **124,** 146, 165, fig. 113, pl. 21A-B; Duror, pp. 130, 139, 161; Duror, parish church, pp. 25, **129,** 164, 261, 266, figs. 118-19, pl. 24A-B; Edinburgh, Leith, St Mary's parish church, pp. 36, 299, pl. 120E; Eilean Munde, parish church, pp. 25-6, **129-31,** 139, figs. 6, 120, pls. 24C-25; Glenorchy, Dalmally, parish church, pp. 25-6, **132-4,** 295, figs. 121-2, pls. 26-7; Inchcailleach (Stirlingshire), parish church, p. 125n; Inishail, old parish church, pp. 22, 25-6, 121, 129, **134-6, 138,** 149, figs. 6, 123-5, pl. 28A; Inverghiusachan, pp. 138-9, fig. 127, pl. 28F; Kilbrandon and Kilchattan, Seil, old parish church, pp. **139,** 144; Kilbrandon, Seil, old parish church, pp. 139-40, pl. 29D; Kilbride, old parish church, pp. 25-6, **140-3,** 153, figs. 129-30, pl. 29A-C; Kilchattan, Luing, old parish church, pp. 23, 25, 36, **144-6,** 167, figs. 6, 131-4, pl. 30B-E; Kilchousland (Kintyre), parish church, p. 25; Kilchrenan, parish church, pp. 25-6, **146-9,** figs. 135-8, pl. 31C-F; Kilespickerill, p. 163; Killean (Kintyre), old parish church, pp. 23, 124-5, 144; Kilmaronag, pp. **150-3,** 163, fig. 142; Kilmarow (Killarow, Killocraw) (Kintyre), p. 110; Kilmelford, parish church, p. 153; Kilmore, old parish church, pp. 25-6, 116, 141, **153-5,** 260, 277, figs. 6, 143-6, pl. 31A-B; Kilmun (Cowal), collegiate church, p. 231; Kilninver, parish church, pp. 110, **155-6;** Lismore, parish church, pp. 21-3, 26, 48-9, 142, **156-63,** 171, 186, 277, figs.
148-52, pls. 32-4; London, St George's Fields, p. 165n; Manchester, St Wilfrid's, p. 165n; Muckairn, Taynuilt, old parish church, pp. **163,** 164-5, figs. 6, 153; Muckairn, Taynuilt, parish church, pp. 25, 124, 149, **163-5,** 168, 266, figs. 154-6, pl. 35; Oban, Free High Church, pp. 25, 30, **165-6,** 243, 277, pl. 36A-C; Portnacroish, Episcopal church, pp. 25, **166-7,** figs. 157-8, pl. 36E; Rodel, St Clement's Church, Harris (Inverness-shire), pp. 135n, 165n, 298; Soroby (Tiree), p. 110; Southport (Lancashire), St Mary's, p. 165n; *see also* **Burial-enclosures, Burial-grounds, Chapels** *and* **Monasteries.**
Cill an Inbhire, burial-ground, p. 118.
Cill-an-Suidhe, Lismore, burial-ground *and* chapel, pp. 21, **118,** 119, 121, fig. 105.
Cill Choluim-chille, Benderloch, burial-ground *and* chapel, pp. 118-19.
Cill Easpuig Chaorrail, p. 163n.
Cill Mo-Thatha, *see* **Kilmaha.**
Cinerary Urns: pp. 12, 57-8, 60, pl. 4A; *see also* **'Urns'.**
Cistercian Order, pp. 23, 161.
Cists: pp. 9-12, fig. 3; Achnaba, pp. 45, **57;** Aon Garbh, Lismore, p. 57; Balure, pp. 12, **58;** Barr Mór, Lismore, p. 58; Cleigh, p. 58; Dengish, p. 58; Dunollie, pp. 58-9; Gallanachbeg, pp. 9, 12, **59,** 60; Keil, pp. 12, **59;** Kintaline, p. 59; Ledaig, p. 59; Melfort House, pp. 12-13, **59,** pl. 4C; Oban, pp. 12, **59-60,** pls. 3D, 4A; Saulmore, pp. 60-1; Slaterich, Kerrera, pp. 12, **61,** pl. 3B; *see also* **Burials, Cairns** *and* **Chambered cairns.**
Clachadow: cairns (1) *and* (2), pp. 10, **49,** 50, fig. 19, pl. 8B; cruck-framed buildings, pp. 269-70, fig. 227, pl. 101E; cup-markings, p. 61; dun, p. 82.
Clachan, Lismore, burial-ground, pp. 21, 118, **119,** 121, fig. 106.
Clachan Bridge, Seil: bridge, pp. 36, 49, **294-5,** pl. 119B; cairn, p. 49.
Clachan Dysart, *see* **Glenorchy, Dalmally.**
Clach na h-eala, Lismore, standing stone, p. 162.
Cladh a' Bhearnaig, Kerrera, cashel, pp. 21, **119-20,** fig. 107.
Cladh Churiollan, Creagan, burial-ground, chapel, well *and* well-house, pp. 25, **122,** fig. 110.
Cladhmorrie, *see* **Cladh Uaine.**
Cladh na h-Anaid, Auchnacloich, burial-ground, pp. 22, **120-1.**
Cladh na h-Anaid, Taynuilt, burial-ground, pp. 22, 118-19, **121,** fig. 108.
Cladh Uaine: burial-ground *and* chapel, pp. 25, **121,** fig. 109; shielings, p. 121.
Cladich: bridge, p. 296; chambered cairn, pp. 7, **41, 43,** fig. 11; parish church, pp. **121,** 135.
Clark, Archibald, p. 273.
Clazemorrie, *see* **Cladh Uaine.**
Cleidh-na-h-Annait, p. 22n.
Cleigh: p. 13; cairns, *see under* **Kilmore,** cairns; church, pp. 141, 153; cist, p. 58; earthwork, p. 96.
Clenamacrie: cairns (east) *and* (west), p. 49; cross-decorated stone, pp. 22, **122-3,** fig. 111; cup-markings, p. 61; dun, pp. 77-8, fig. 46; standing stone, pp. 49, **62.**
Clerk, John, mason, p. 155.
——Sir John, of Penicuik, pp. 31, 266n.
Climate, p. 3.
Clyde-type chambered cairns, pp. 6-7, 11, 40-4.
Clyvernock, *see* **Cladh a' Bhearnaig.**
Cnoc Aingil, Lismore: burial, p. 58; cairn, pp. **49,** 58.
Cnocan Dubha, fort, pp. 65-6, fig. 30.
Cnoc an Tighe Mhóir, Seil, fort, pp. 17, **66,** fig. 31.
Cnoc Buidhe, cairn, *see under* **Kilmore,** cairns.
Cnoc Sligeach (Oronsay), mesolithic occupation, pp. 5-6.
Cochrane, *see* **Dundonald.**
Coire na h'Anaid, p. 98n.
Coire na h-Annait, p. 115.
Colagin, fort, pp. 66-7, fig. 32.
Colin, son of Patrick, p. 140.
Colin's cairn, *see* **Carn Chailein.**
Colinus, son of Angus, p. 149.
Combie Street, Oban, pp. 242-3.
Communications, pp. 3-4.

Connel: cairn, p. 49; ferry, p. 110; standing stone, pp. 13, **62, 64.**

Consecration crosses, p. 105.

Corran Esplanade, Oban, p. 30.

Corran Park, Oban, cist, pp. 12, **60,** pl. 3D.

Corrielorne, cairn, p. 50.

Coull Castle (Aberdeenshire), p. 27.

Courts of offices, pp. 195, 220, 246, 248, 251-3, 263, 265, 277, 293, pls. 89F, 117B.

Cousin, David, architect, pp. 25, 165-6.

Craignish Castle (Mid Argyll), p. 184.

Craikwherreellan, *see* **Cladh Churiollan,**

Crannogs: pp. 16, 20; An Doirlinn, Eriska, pp. 20, **93;** Loch a' Mhuillin, p. 93; Lochan Dughaill (Kintyre), p. 20; Lochan na Gealaich, p. 93; Loch Awe, pp. 20, **94,** fig. 79; Loch Seil, p. 94; Milton Loch (Kirkcudbrightshire), pp. 20, 94; Moss of Achnacree, pp. 20, **94-5;** *see also* **Fortified dwellings.**

Creag a' Chaibeil, Ballimeanoch, burial-ground *and* chapel, pp. 25, **123,** fig. 112.

Creagan: cairn, p. 299; Cladh Churiollan, burial-ground *and* chapel, pp. 25, **122,** fig. 110; graffito, pp. 36, **298-9,** fig. 248, pl. 120B.

Creag an Eig Cave, Food Vessel, p. 12, pl. 3C.

Creag an Fhithich, Lismore, cairn, p. 50.

Creag Aoil, fort, p. 67.

Creag Mhór, burial-ground *and* well, p. 124.

Creones, p. 16.

Creran, *see* **Cladh Churiollan.**

Croft-in-tuime, bridge, p. 296.

Cross-decorated stones, *see under* **Funerary monuments.**

Crosses, *see under* **Funerary monuments.**

Cruach Achadh na Craoibhe, cairn, p. 50.

Cruck-framed buildings: pp. 32-3; Auchindrain (Mid Argyll), p. 32; Bonawe, pp. 32, **269,** fig. 225; Cadderlie, pp. 32-3, **269,** fig. 226; Clachadow, pp. 269-70, fig. 227, pl. 101E; Glencoe village, pp. 32, **270-1,** figs. 228-9, pl. 101A-D; Narrachan, pp. 32, **272;** Torr-an-tuirc, pp. 32, **274, 276,** fig. 232; Upper Gylen Farm, Kerrera, p. 32n; *see also* **Townships** *and* **Workers' dwellings.**

Crucks, pp. 32-3, 269-74, 276, 294, figs. 227, 229, pl. 101C-E.

Culcharron: cairn, pp. 10, 12, 49, **50,** 51, 54, fig. 20; cup-markings, pp. 12, **50.**

Cullipool, Luing, quarry *and* workers' dwellings, p. 278.

Cup-and-ring markings and Cup-markings: p. 12, fig. 3; Ardteatle, p. 61; Clachadow, p. 61; Clenamacrie, p. 61; Culcharron, pp. 12, **50;** Keppochan, p. 61; Kilchrenan, p. 61; Killiechonich, p. 61; Kilmaronag, p. 62; Leccamore, Luing, pp. 12, **91;** Loch Gleann a' Bhearraidh, p. 62; Oban Esplanade, p. 62.

Currie, James, p. 259.

Custom-house, Oban, pp. 3, 242.

Cwm Bran Fire Clay Co., p. 284.

Dagger, bronze, pp. 10, 13, 53, pl. 4B.

Dalavich, parish church, pp. **124,** 146, 165, fig. 113, pl. 21A-B.

Dalfuir, *see* **Barcaldine House.**

Dalineun: cairns, *see under* **Kilmore,** cairns; chambered cairn, pp. 7-9, 11, **43,** fig. 12, pl. 7.

Dalintart, An Dùnan, dun, p. 77.

Dalmally: bridge and embankment, pp. 36, **295,** pl. 119C; Glenorchy, parish church, pp. 25-6, **132-4,** 295, figs. 121-2, pls. 26-7; manse, pp. 31, **254,** pl. 91B; St Conan's Well, p. 124.

Dalnacabeg, cairn, p. 50.

Dalranach, cairn, pp. **50,** 55.

Dalriada, p. 1.

Dalrigh, burial, p. 60.

Dalvuie, cairns (1) *and* (2), pp. 11, **50-1.**

Dalzel, Mr, architect, p. 153.

Dalziel, J and W, wrights, p. 99.

——William, builder, p. 166.

David II, King of Scotland, pp. 186, 197, 210.

Dedications: Holy Cross, p. 167n; St Andrew, p. 149; St Baedan, p. 116; St Bean, pp. 153, 155; St Brendan of Clonfert, p. 139; St Bridget, pp. 141, 144; St Cairrell, pp. 122, 163n; St Cathan, p. 144; St Columba, pp. 119, 139; St Comghan, p. 146; St Congan, p. 146; St Conuall, p. 138n; St Cronoc, p. 152; St Cyril of Alexandria, p. 122; St John, pp. 118, 167n; St John the Baptist, p. 110; St Kentigern, p. 150; St Lugaidh, p. 156; St Maelrubha, pp. 121, 153; St Mary, p. 110; St Mary the Virgin, p. 117; St Mochoe, *see* St Kentigern; St Mochoe of Nendrum, p. 150; St Modan, p. 116; St Moluag, p. 156; St Munn, pp. 130, 155; St Peter the Deacon, p. 146; St Ronan, p. 152; St Tua, p. 150.

Degnish, pp. 31, 33, 58, **254,** pl. 91F.

Degnish, cist, p. 58.

Dirleton Castle (East Lothian), p. 27.

Distillery, Oban, pp. 242-3.

Distillery Cave, Oban, mesolithic implements, p. 5, pl. 2.

Distilling (illicit), pp. 35, **278, 281.**

Dogs' Castle, *see* **Caisteal nan Con, Torsa.**

Domestic architecture, 17th-19th c.: pp. 28, 30-1; Achlian, pp. 31, 94, **243,** pl. 78A-D; Achnaba, pp. 31, 45, 57, **243-4,** pl. 78E; Airds House, pp. 30-1, 194, **244-5,** fig. 212, pls. 79-82; Appin House, pp. 30-1, **245-7,** figs. 213-14, pls. 83-4C; Appin Post-office, Tynribbie, p. 247, pl. 84D; Ardanaiseig, pp. 31, 61, 94, **247,** 277, pls. 85-6B; Ardchattan Priory, *see under* **Ardchattan Priory;** Ardchonnell House, p. 231; Ardencaple House, Seil, pp. 31, **247-8,** pl. 86C-D; Ardlarach, Luing, pp. 31, 33, 96, **248,** pl. 86E; Ardmaddy Castle, pp. 28, 30-1, 242, **248-52,** 277-8, figs. 215-16, pls. 87-9; Ballachulish House, pp. 31, 46, **252-3,** pl. 90A-B; Balliveolan, pp. 117, **253,** pl. 91A; Barcaldine House, pp. 180, 211n, **253,** 258, pl. 90C-E; Blairquhan Castle (Ayrshire), p. 220; Bonawe House, pp. 34, **291-2,** figs. 236, 247, pl. 116D-E; Bothan na Dige, Stronmilchan, pp. 187, **254,** fig. 233; Castle Shuna, Appin, p. 188; Dalmally Manse, pp. 31, **254,** pl. 91B; Degnish, pp. 31, 33, 58, **254,** pl. 91F; Dunans Castle (Cowal), pp. 172n, 175; Dungallon, Manor House, p. 254, pl. 91C; Dunollie House, pp. 195, 197-8, 217, 219, 221n, **222-3,** 254, figs. 179, pls. 54F, 65D-E, G, 91E; Dunstaffnage Castle, *see under* **Dunstaffnage Castle;** Eilean Musdile, p. 280, pls. 108-9, 110E; Ferlochan, old schoolhouse, pp. **254-5,** 267, pl. 91D; Fraoch Eilean Castle, *see under* **Fraoch Eilean;** Gallanach, pp. 31, 90, **255,** pls. 92-4; Galloway House (Wigtownshire), p. 31n, 266n; Glenstockdale, pp. 255-6, pl. 96B; Glenure, pp. 31, **256-8,** fig. 217, pl. 95; Gwrych Castle (Denbighshire), pp. 264, 265n; Haddo House (Aberdeenshire), p. 266n; Hayfield, pp. 31, 33, **258-9,** pl. 96E; Inverawe House, p. 259; Kilbrandon House, Seil, pp. 31, 116, **259-60,** pl. 96A; Kilcheran, Lismore, p. 146, pl. 30A; Kilchoan House, p. 146; Kilmore House, pp. 31, **260,** fig. 218, pl. 96C-D; Kinlochlaich, pp. 31, 256, **260-1,** pl. 97A-E; Kulmani, Duror, pp. 31, 129, **261,** fig. 219, pl. 97G; Lerags House, pp. 31, 54, **261,** pl. 97F; Lochnell House, pp. 30-1, 33, 59, 164, 242, **261-6,** figs. 220-3, pls. 98-9; Mains of Glins (Stirlingshire), p. 256n; Manor House, Dungallon, p. 254, pl. 91C; Marble Hill House, Twickenham (Middlesex), p. 30; Mavisbank House (Midlothian), p. 266n; Melfort House, p. 293; Muckairn manse, Taynuilt, pp. 31, **266,** pl. 100E; New Murthly Castle (Perthshire), p. 252; North Ledaig, old schoolhouse, pp. 54, **266-7,** pl. 100D; Oban, pp. 30, **242-3,** pls. 76-7; Rarey, pp. 31, 242, **267,** pl. 100A; Smeaton (East Lothian), p. 245; Taymouth Castle (Perthshire), pp. 132, 238, 252, 295n; Taynuilt Hotel, p. 267; Tigh Mór, Stronmilchan, pp. 187, 254, **267;** Upper Sonachan House, pp. 31, **267,** pl. 100B-C; Valleyfield House (Fife), p. 109; *see also* **Cruck-framed buildings, Farms, Old ferryhouses, Shielings, Townships** *and* **Workers' dwellings.**

Door furniture, pp. 178, 244-6, 250, pls. 42C-D, 82F, 89E.

Dorrett, James, surveyor, p. 120.

Douglas, John, architect, p. 31n.

Doun Donacky, *see* **Gylen Castle.**

Downie, Robert, of Appin, pp. 246-7.

——Sara, p. 124.

Downie family, of Appin, p. 246.

Drawbridge (and **drawbridge-pit**), pp. 27, 189, 191, 202.

Drimnatoull, *see* **Glen Risdale.**

Droving, p. 4.

Druim an Duin (Mid Argyll), dun, p. 19n.

Druim an Uinnsinn, Lismore, cairns (1) *and* (2), p. 51, fig. 21.

Druimavuic, *see* **Balliveolan.**

Druimneil House, architectural fragments, p. 299, pl. 120A.

Druimvargie Rock-shelter, Oban, p. 5, pl. 2.

Drummond, John, builder *and* mason, pp. 110, 253.

Duachy: standing stones, pp. 12–13, **62-3,** pl. 9B; township, p. 272.

Duart Castle (Mull), p. 27.

Duff, James, mason, pp. 99, 211, 247, 253, 296.

Duffus Castle (Morayshire), p. 28n.

Dugall, p. 113.

Dùn Ablaich, Luing, earthwork, pp. 21, **96,** fig. 82.

Dunach, dun, p. 82, fig. 57.

Dùnan Buiaig, cairn, p. 51.

Dùnan Corr, fort, p. 67.

Dùn an Fheurain: burials, p. 58; dun, pp. 18, 20, 58, **82-3.**

Dùnan Molach, dun, p. 83, fig. 58.

Dùnans, Glen Cruitten, fort *and* well, p. 67.

Dunans Castle (Cowal), pp. 172n, 175.

Dùn Aorain, Seil, dun, pp. 19, **83-4,** 88, fig. 59.

Dùn Athaich, dun, p. 84.

Dùn Bachlach, dun, p. 84, fig. 60.

Dunbeg, fort, p. 67.

Dùn Bhlaran, dun, pp. 18, **84,** fig. 61.

Dunblane Cathedral (Perthshire), p. 159n.

Duncan's Castle, *see* **Gylen Castle.**

Dùn Chathach, dun, pp. 18, **84-5,** fig. 62.

Dùn Chrùban, Lismore, dun, pp. 19, **85,** fig. 63, pl. 11A.

Dùn Creagach: dun, p. 85; fort, pp. 17, **67-8,** fig. 33.

Dùn Cuilein, Lismore, dun, p. 86, fig. 64.

Dùn Daraich (Cowal), dun, p. 18.

Dundarave Castle (Mid Argyll), pp. 29, 217, 220.

Dundonald, Sir Douglas Mackinnon Baillie Hamilton Cochrane, 12th Earl of, p. 266.

Dundouchie, *see* **Gylen Castle.**

Dùn Fadaidh, dun, pp. 19, **86,** fig. 65.

Dungallon, The Manor House, p. 254, pl. 91C.

Dùn Iadain, fort, pp. 17-18, **68,** fig. 34.

Dùn Leigh, dun, pp. 18, **86,** fig. 66.

Dùn Mac Sniachan, dun, forts *and* well, pp. 16-18, **68-70,** fig. 35.

Dùn Mhic Raonuill, dun, pp. 86-7, fig. 67.

Dùn Mhuirageul, dun, pp. 18-19, **87,** fig. 68.

Dùn Mór, Balygrundle, Lismore, dun, pp. 47, **88,** fig. 69.

Dùn Mór, Bonawe, earthwork, p. 96, fig. 83.

Dùn Mucaig, Seil, dun, p. 88, fig. 70.

Dùn na Cuaiche, dun, pp. 47, **88.**

Dùn Neil, dun, pp. 19, **88-9.**

Dunollie: bronze axe, p. 13; burials *and* cist, pp. 58-9.

Dunollie Castle, pp. 22, 28-9, 58-9, **194-8,** 202, 277, figs. 177-9, pls. 52-4.

Dunollie House, pp. 195, 197-8, 217, 219, 221n, 222-3, **254,** fig. 179, pls. 54F, 65D-E, G, 91E.

Dùn Ormidale, fort, pp. 16, **70,** fig. 36.

Duns: pp. 16-20, fig. 5; An Dùn, Clenamacrie, pp. 77-8, fig. 46; An Dùn, Sloc a' Bhrighide, Lismore, pp. 19, **78,** fig. 47; An Dùnan, Dalintart, p. 77; An Dùnan, Minard Point, p. 77, fig. 45; Ardanstur (1) *and* (2), pp. 78-9, figs. 48-9; Arduaine, p. 79; Ballycastle, Luing, pp. 19, **79-80,** fig. 55; Castles, pp. 19, **81-2,** 187, fig. 56; Clachadow, p. 18; Druim an Duin (Mid Argyll), p. 19n; Dunach, p. 82, fig. 57; Dùn an Fheurain, pp. 18, 20, 58, **82-3;** Dùnan Molach, p. 83, fig. 58; Dùn Aorain, Seil, pp. 19, **83-4,** 88, fig. 59; Dùn Athaich, p. 84; Dùn Bachlach, p. 84, fig. 60; Dùn Bhlaran, pp. 18, **84,** fig. 61; Dùn Chathach, pp. 18, **84-5,** fig. 62; Dùn Chrùban, Lismore, pp. 19, **85,** fig. 63, pl. 11A; Dùn Creagach, p. 85; Dùn Cuilein, Lismore, p. 86, fig. 64; Dùn Daraich (Cowal), p. 18; Dùn Fadaidh, pp. 19, **86,** fig. 65; Dùn Leigh, pp. 18, **86,** fig. 66; Dùn Mac Sniachan, pp. 16-18, **68-70,** fig. 35; Dùn Mhic Raonuill,
pp. 86-7, fig. 67; Dùn Mhuirageul, pp. 18-19, **87,** fig. 68; Dùn Mór, Balygrundle, Lismore, pp. 47, **88,** fig. 69; Dùn Mucaig, Seil, p. 88, fig. 70; Dùn na Cuaiche, pp. 47, **88;** Dùn Neil, pp. 19, **88-9;** Dùn Skeig (Kintyre), pp. 18, 70n; Dunstaffnage, pp. **89,** 198; Duntanachan, p. 89; Eilean an Atha, Luing, pp. 19, **89,** fig. 71; Fiart, Lismore, pp. 89-90, fig. 72; Gallanach, pp. 19, 78, **90,** fig. 73; Kilcheran, Lismore, p. 90, fig. 74; Kilchoan Loch, p. 90; Kildalloig (Kintyre), p. 19n; Leccamore, Luing, pp. 12, 18-19, **91-2,** fig. 75, pl. 11B-D; Loch a' Phearsain, p. 92, fig. 76; Park, Lismore, p. 92; Rahoy (Morvern), p. 18; Rubh' an Tighe Loisgte, p. 92; Sean Dùn, Lismore, pp. 21, **92-3,** fig. 77; Sunadale (Kintyre), p. 18; Tom a' Chaisteil, p. 93, fig. 78.

Dùn Skeig (Kintyre), dun *and* forts, pp. 18, 70n.

Dunstaffnage, dun, pp. **89,** 198.

Dunstaffnage Castle: pp. 27, 89, 121, 124, 127n, 128, 147, 197, **198-211,** 226, 299, figs. 180-6, pls. 55-9.

ARCHITECTURAL DESCRIPTION:

Building material, pp. 199, 211n.

East range and east curtain-wall, pp. 27, 198-9, **204-5,** 211, figs. 180-1, 183-5.

Gatehouse, pp. 27, 198, **199, 202, 204,** 207, 211, figs. 180-1, 183, pls. 57B, 58C-E, 59A.

North tower, pp. 27, 198-9, 204, **205-6,** 211, figs. 180-1, pl. 55A.

North-west range and north-west curtain-wall: pp. 27, 198-9, 204-5, **206-8,** 211, figs. 180-1; dwelling-house, pp. 198, 204, 206-7, 211, fig. 181, pl. 58A-B.

South-west and south-east curtain-walls, pp. 27, 198-9, 205, **209-10,** pl. 59B-D.

Well, p. 208, fig. 180.

West tower, pp. 27, 198-9, 205, **208-9,** 211, figs. 180-1, 186, pls. 56B, 57A.

HISTORICAL NOTE, pp. 210-11.

SUMMARY, p. 198.

Dunstaffnage Chapel, pp. 23, 26, 105, **124-9,** 198-9, 205, figs. 6, 114-17, pls. 22-3.

Dunstaffnage House: armorial panel, p. 299, pl. 120C; cairn, p. 51.

Dunstaffnage Mains Farm, pp. 33, **270,** pl. 101F.

Duntanachan: cairn, pp. 51-2; dun, p. 89.

Dùn Uabairtich, fort, pp. 18, **70, 72,** fig. 37.

Dùn Uamha Chradh, *see* **Balygrundle.**

Durobwar, *see* **Keil Chapel.**

Duror: church, pp. 130, 139, 161; houses, pp. 32n, 33n; manse, *see* **Kulmani;** parish church, pp. 25, **129,** 164, 261, 266, figs. 118-19, pl. 24A-B.

Early Christian period: pp. 21-2, 117-21, 149-50, 156, 160, 197, figs. 104-8, 139-41; relics, pp. 21-2; *see also under* **Funerary monuments.**

'Earth house', Kerrera, p. 22, pl. 5D.

Earthworks: pp. 16, 21-2; Ard Luing, Luing, pp. 21, **95,** fig. 80; Cleigh, p. 96; Dùn Ablaich, Luing, pp. 21, **96,** fig. 82; Dùn Mór, Bonawe, p. 96, fig. 83; Dunollie Castle, pp. 22, 197; Lochan nan Ràth, p. 97; Rarey, pp. 96, **242, 251,** 267, fig. 211; South Ledaig, p. 97.

Easan Dubh, bridge, p. 296.

Easdale, Seil, slate-quarries *and* workers' dwellings, pp. 3, 33-5, 132, 225, 239, **278-9,** fig. 234, pl. 106.

Easdale Slate Co., p. 295.

East Laroch, *see* **Ballachulish,** slate-quarries.

Edendonich, *see* **Airidh nan Sileag.**

Edgar, J, architect, p. 147n.

Editorial Notes, pp. xlv-xlvi.

Edward II, King of England, p. 231.

Effigies, *see under* **Funerary monuments.**

Eilean an Atha, Luing, dun, pp. 19, **89,** fig. 71.

Eilean an Stalcaire, *see* **Castle Stalker.**

Eilean Balnagowan, enclosure, p. 96.

Eilean Mór, fort, p. 72.

Eilean Munde, burial-ground *and* old parish church, pp. 25-6, **129-31,** 139, figs. 6, 120, pls. 24C-25.

Eilean Musdile, Lismore: bridge, p. 280, pl. 110F; lighthouse, pp. 35, 63, **279-80,** pls. 107-10; standing stone, p. 63.

Eilean Stalcair, Loch Tulla, fortified dwelling, pp. 29-30, 174, **211.**

Eilean Tighe Bhàin, Loch Tromlee, fortified dwelling, pp. 29-30, **212,** fig. 187.

Elanelochtollyff, *see* **Eilean Stalcair.**

Elankylquhurne, *see* **Kilchurn Castle.**

Elanmunde, *see* **Eilean Munde.**

Ellanbeich, quarry *and* workers' dwellings, pp. 278-9, fig. 234, pl. 106B.

Elliot, Archibald, architect, pp. 31, 266.

——James, architect, pp. 25, 132.

Embankment, Dalmally, p. 295.

Enclosures: pp. 16, 21; Balliveolan, Lismore, p. 95, fig. 81; Eilean Balnagowan, p. 96; Kilmun, p. 97, fig. 84; Làrach na h-Iobairte, p. 97, fig. 85; Sean Dùn, Lismore, pp. 21, **92-3,** fig. 77.

Engineering works and buildings, *see* **Industrial works and buildings.**

Engineers: Bell, Henry, p. 243; Caulfield, Major Edward, pp. 36, 295-6; Mitchell, Joseph, pp. 25, 129; Stevenson, Robert, pp. 35, 279; Telford, Thomas, pp. 25n, 129, 164, 261, 266, 295n; Watson, David, p. 194.

Engraver, Beuge, John, p. 254n.

Epidii, p. 16.

Episcopal Church, Portnacroish, pp. 25, **166-7,** figs. 157-8, pl. 36E.

Erc, p. 1.

Eredine, crannog, p. 94.

Erskine, *see* **Tinwald,** Lord.

Esplanade, Oban, cup-markings, p. 62.

Farms: pp. 31-3; Achadun, p. 171; Achnaba, pp. 45, 57, **243-4;** Airds House, Home Farm, p. 245, pl. 82E; Ardlarach, Luing, pp. 31, 33, 96, **248,** pl. 86E; Ardnahua, pp. 33, 272-4, pl. 103A; Auch Gleann, farmhouse, p. 115; Barrnacarry, p. 272; Dunstaffnage Mains Farm, pp. 33, **270,** pl. 101F; Hayfield, steading, pp. 33, 259, pl. 96E; Mid Ardnahua, p. 274; North Ardnahua, pp. 273-4; *see also* **Barns, Byres, Cruck-framed buildings, Shielings, Townships** *and* **Workers' dwellings.**

Fasnacloich, cairn, p. 52.

Fennacrochan, lime-kilns *and* quarries, p. 294.

Ferlochan, old schoolhouse, pp. **254-5,** 267, pl. 91D.

Ferryhouses, *see* **Old ferryhouses.**

Fiart, Lismore, dun, pp. 89-90, fig. 72.

Field-bank, Black Crofts, North Connel, pp. 13, 21, **95-6,** pl. 11E.

Fincharn Castle (Mid Argyll), p. 184.

Finlarig Castle (Perthshire), pp. 238-9.

Firearm defence, pp. 28-9, 97, 172-3, 178-9, 193, 198, 202, 205, 209-10, 219-23, 225, 229, 235-8, figs. 163-4, 195, 203, 209, pls. 39A-B, 50E, 51D, 67E, 72G.

Firebacks (cast-iron), pp. 109, 244, pl. 78E.

Fireplaces: pp. 28-9, 178, 184, 186-8, 191, 193, 204, 207-8, 221, 228, 236-7, 258, 286, figs. 176, 183A, 202B, pls. 43B, 51F, 58A, 65B, 67C, 68B, 75B, 95B; *see also* **Chimney-pieces** *and* **Firebacks.**

Fletcher, John, p. 97.

Fletcher family, pp. 97, 174-5.

Fonts, pp. 128, 162.

Food Vessels, pp. 9-10, 12, 43, 46, 60-1, pl. 3C-D.

Forbes, Bishop Robert, p. 130.

Ford, Richard, ironmaster, pp. 283-4, 290n.

Forfeited Estates, Commissioners for, pp. 294-5.

Fortified dwellings: pp. 29-30; Eilean Stalcair, Loch Tulla, pp. 29-30, 174, 211; Eilean Tighe Bhàin, Loch Tromlee, pp. 29-30, **212,** fig. 187; Loch a' Phearsain, Kilmelford, pp. 29-30, **240-1,** fig. 210; Loch Nell, pp. 29-30, **242;** *see also* **Crannogs.**

Fortrose Cathedral (Ross and Cromarty), p. 23n.

Forts: pp. 16-18, fig. 5; Ardanstur (1) *and* (2), p. 64, fig. 28; Balvicar, Seil, pp. 16-18, **64-5,** fig. 29; Castle Coeffin, Lismore, pp. 16, **65;** Cnocan Dubha, pp. 65-6, fig. 30; Cnoc an Tighe Mhóir, Seil, pp. 17, **66,** fig. 31; Colagin, pp. 66-7, fig. 32; Creag Aoil, p. 67; Dùnan Corr, p. 67; Dùnans, Glen Cruitten, p. 67; Dunbeg, p. 67, Dùn

Creagach, pp. 17, **67-8,** fig. 33; Dùn Iadain, pp. 17-18, **68,** fig. 34; Dùn Mac Sniachan, pp. 16-18, **68-70,** fig. 35; Dunollie, pp. 22, 197; Dùn Ormidale, pp. 16, **70,** fig. 36; Dùn Skeig (Kintyre), pp. 18, 70n; Dùn Uabairtich, pp. 18, **70, 72,** fig. 37; Eilean Mór, p. 72; Kilcheran, Lismore, pp. 16, **72-3,** fig. 38; Kilmore, p. 73; Little Horse Shoe, Kerrera, p. 73, fig. 39; Losgann Larnach, pp. 18, **73-4,** fig. 40; Tom an Iasgaire, pp. 18, **74,** fig. 41; Torr a' Chlaonaidh, pp. 74-5, fig. 42.

Fort William (Inverness-shire), carved stone, p. 259.

Fraoch Eilean, castle: pp. 27-9, 35, 134-5, **212-17,** 225, 232, 259, 278, figs. 60-2, pls. 62A; bailey, pp. 213, **216,** fig. 188, pl. 62A; boat-landing, p. 216, fig. 188; building material, pp. 213, 216; carved stone, pp. 216-17, fig. 190, pl. 62F; dwelling-house, pp. 28, 213, **215-16,** figs. 188-9, pl. 62C, E; hall-house, pp. 27, **213,** 215, 216, figs. 188-9, pl. 62B, D; historical note, p. 217.

Frechelan, *see* **Fraoch Eilean.**

Free High Church, Oban, pp. 25, 30, **165-6,** 243, 277, pl. 36A-C.

Friary: Ross Errilly (Co. Galway), p. 157n; *see also* **Religious houses.**

Funerary monuments and other carved stones:

EARLY CHRISTIAN: p. 22.

Cross-decorated stones: Ardchattan Priory, pp. 110-11 (no. 1, fig. 99); Clenamacrie, pp. 22, **122-3,** fig. 111; Inishail, pp. 134, 135 (no. 1, pl. 28A); Kilmaha, p. 150 (nos. 1-2, figs. 140-1).

Rock-carving, Kilmaha, p. 150, fig. 139.

MEDIEVAL: pp. 25-6; *see also* **Graffiti.**

Altar-frontal, Inishail, p. 136 (no. 13, fig. 125).

Carved fragments: Ardchattan Priory, p. 111 (nos. 2-6, figs. 100-1, 19A-B); Dunstaffnage Chapel, p. 128 (nos. 1-3); Muckairn, Taynuilt, p. 165 (no. 2, pl. 35D).

Cross-base, Lismore, p. 162 (no. 15).

Crosses: p. 26; Ardchattan Priory, pp. 111-12 (no. 10); Kilbride, p. 143 (no. 15); Kilbride (Lerags Cross), pp. 143, 168, pl. 29B-C; Taynuilt, pp. 167-8.

Effigies: p. 26; Ardchattan Priory, p. 111 (no. 7); Inishail, p. 138 (no. 17).

Sheela-na-gig, Taynuilt, p. 165 (no. 1, pl. 35E).

Slabs: p. 26; Ardchattan Priory, pp. 111-13 (nos. 8-9, 11(i), 12-17, pl. 19C); Eilean Munde, pp. 130-1 (nos. 1-3); Glenorchy, Dalmally, pp. 133-4 (nos. 1-11, fig. 122, pl. 26B, D); Inishail, pp. 135-6, 138, 149 (nos. 2-10, 14-19); Iona, p. 144, 149; Kilbrandon, Seil, p. 140 (nos. 1-4); Kilbride, pp. 142-3 (nos. 1-14, 16); Kilchrenan, pp. 148-9 (nos. 1-6, 8-9, fig. 138, pl. 31C); Kilmelford, p. 153 (no. 2); Kilmore, pp. 154-5 (nos. 1-5, fig. 146); Lismore, pp. 161-2 (nos. 1-7, 10-12, pl. 34D); Muckairn, Taynuilt, p. 149, 165 (nos. 3-5, fig. 156), 168.

Tomb-chests: p. 26; Ardchattan Priory, pp. 102, 112 (no. 11(ii)); Glenorchy, p. 134 (no. 12); Inishail, p. 136 (nos. 11-12); Kilchrenan, p. 149 (no. 7); Kilmichael Glassary (Mid Argyll), p. 162; Lismore, p. 162 (nos. 8-9, pl. 34E).

POST-REFORMATION: p. 26.

Cairn, Appin-murder cairn, pp. **97-8,** 256.

Carved fragments, Eilean Munde, p. 131, pl. 25D.

Headstones: Achallader, p. 97; Appin, p. 99 (no. 2); Cladh Churiollan, p. 122; Glenorchy, Dalmally, p. 134 (nos. 18-19); Kilbrandon, Seil, p. 140 (no. 10); Kilchattan, Luing, p. 146 (nos. 4-5, pl. 30E).

Mural: Ardchattan Priory, pp. 104-5, 113-14 (no. 22, pl. 20D); Balliveolan, p. 117; Dunstaffnage Chapel, p. 129 (no. 6, pl. 23D); Kilchattan, Luing, p. 146 (no. 5); Kilchrenan, p. 148, 149 (no. 12, pl. 31F); Kilmore, pp. 154, 155 (no. 6); Lismore, p. 162 (no. 17, pl. 34F); Sonachan, p. 167, pl. 36D.

Obelisk, Kilchrenan, p. 149 (no. 13, pl. 31E).

Recumbent slabs: p. 26; Airds House, p. 245; Ardchattan Priory, pp. 103, 113-14 (nos. 18-21, 23-5, pl. 20A-B); Cladh Churiollan, p. 122; Dalavich, p. 124 (pl. 21B); Dunstaffnage Chapel, pp. 128-9 (nos. 4-5, pl. 23E); Eilean Munde, p. 131 (nos. 4-5, 8-9, pls. 24D-E, 25B-C);

Glenorchy, Dalmally, p. 134 (nos. 13-17); Keil, p. 139 (nos. 1-2, pl. 28B-C); Kilbrandon, Seil, p. 140 (nos. 5, 7-8, pl. 29D); Kilbride, p. 143 (no. 18); Kilchattan, Luing, p. 145 (nos. 1-2); Kilcheran, p. 146; Kilchrenan, p. 149 (nos. 10-11); Kilninver, p. 156; Lismore, p. 162 (no. 16); Shuna, Nether Lorn, p. 167.
Table-tombs: p. 26; Ardchattan Priory, pp. 114-15 (nos. 26-30, pl. 20C); Eilean Munde, p. 131 (nos. 6-7, pl. 25A); Innis Sèa-Ràmhach, p. 138; Kilbrandon, Seil, p. 140 (nos. 6, 9); Kilbride, p. 143 (no. 17); Kilchattan, Luing, pp. 145-6 (nos. 3, 5, pl. 30D); Kilmore, p. 155 (no. 7); Muckairn, Taynuilt, pp. 124, 165 (nos. 6-9, pl. 35A).
Tomb-chest, Kilmore, p. 154.
UNCLASSIFIED:
Cairn, Carn Chailein, pp. 115, **118**.
Carved fragment, Dunstaffnage Chapel, p. 129 (no. 7).
Cross, Kilmelford, p. 153 (no. 1).
Slab, Appin, p. 98 (no. 1).
Tomb-chests, Lismore, p. 162 (nos. 13-14).

Galbraith, Captain Arthur, p. 280.
Gallanach, pp. 31, 90, **255**, pls. 92-4.
Gallanach, dun, pp. 19, 78, **90**, fig. 73.
Gallanachbeg, cist, pp. 9, 12, **59**, 60.
Galloway House (Wigtownshire), pp. 31n, 266n.
Gasworks, Oban, burial, pp. 12, **60**.
Geology, p. 2.
George Street, Oban, p. 242.
Gillespie, James, see **Graham**, James Gillespie.
Gillinge, see **Gylen Castle**.
Glankileness, see **Glen Kinglass**.
Glencairn, William Cunningham, 8th Earl of, p. 110.
Glencoe: pp. 32-3, **270-1**, figs. 228-9, pl. 101A-D; see also **Keil Chapel**.
Glencown, see **Keil Chapel**.
Glen Cruitten, see **Dùnans**.
Glen Etive, cairn, p. 52.
Glen Feochan, Kilbride, burial-ground, p. 143.
Glengarry, see **Invergarry**.
Glenkenlish, see **Glen Kinglass**,
Glen Kinglass, Loch Etive, ironworks, pp. 3, 34, 244, **280-1**, 283, fig. 235.
Glenlyon brooch, p. 223n.
Glenorchy, Lord, see **Breadalbane**, John Campbell, 3rd Earl of.
Glenorchy, Dalmally, parish church, pp. 25-6, **132-4**, 295, figs. 121-2, pls. 26-7.
Glen Risdale, shielings, pp. 33, **271-2**, fig. 230.
Glenstockdale, pp. 255-6, pl. 96B.
Glen Strae, see **Airidh nan Sileag**.
Glen Strae Castle, see **Castles Farm**.
Glenure: pp. 31, **256-8**, fig. 217, pl. 95; barn, pp. 33, 258; bridge, p. 258.
Glenurquhay, see **Kilchurn Castle**.
Goatfield (Mid Argyll), ironworks, p. 34.
Gordon, H, surveyor, pp. 296-7.
Gordon family, p. 263.
Graffiti: p. 36; Creagan, pp. 36, **298-9**, fig. 248, pl. 120B; Kilchattan, Luing, pp. 36, **144-5**, figs. 132-4, pl. 30C.
Graham, James Gillespie, architect, pp. 31, 248-9, 251-3, 255.
Grant, Mrs Elizabeth, of Laggan, p. 246n.
——**Robert**, of Branchell, p. 140.
Grave-monuments, see **Funerary monuments**.
Graveyards, see **Burial-enclosures** and **Burial-grounds**.
Great Western Hotel, Oban, p. 30.
Greencastle (Co. Down), pp. 28, 217.
Grierson, Sir Richard, 7th Bt of Lag, p. 259.
Grieve, A Mackenzie, p. 258.
Gualachulain, cairn, p. 52.
Gun-loops, see **Firearm defence**.
Gunpowder-works, Melfort, pp. 34, **292-3**, pl. 117A-B.
Guthrie, James, Dingwall Pursuivant, p. 194.
Gwrych Castle (Denbighshire), pp. 264, 265n.
Gylen Castle, Kerrera: pp. 29, 175, **217-23**, 254, 277, figs. 191-6, pls. 63-5; boat-landings, pp. 220, 222; building

material, pp. 217, 222; carved stones, pp. 217, 219, 222-3, 254, fig. 196, pls. 64C, 65D-E, G; forework, pp. 217, 222; gun-loops, pp. 220-2, fig. 195; historical note, p. 223; oriel-window and box-machicolation, pp. 219-20, 222, figs. 194C, 196, pl. 64C; outer bailey, pp. 217, 222, fig. 191.

Haddo House (Aberdeenshire), p. 266n.
Haggs Castle (Renfrewshire), p. 220.
Hall-houses, pp. 27-8.
Hamilton, David, bishop of Argyll, p. 171.
Hammerman, Smith, James, p. 239.
Harbours: pp. 30, 35, 277, 279, pl. 106C-D; see also **Boat-landings** and **Jetties**.
Harrison, Ainslie and Co., p. 292.
Hayfield: pp. 31, 33, **258-9**, pl. 96E; steading, pp. 33, 259, pl. 96E.
Henry VIII, King of England, p. 113.
Heraldic insignia, see **Armorial insignia**.
Hexham (Northumberland), bridge, p. 295n.
Highland Roads and Bridges, Commissioners for, pp. 295-7.
Holy Stone, see **Kilchrenan**, cup-and-ring markings.
Home Farm, Airds House, p. 245, pl. 82E.
Hunter's Island, see **Castle Stalker**.

Ice-houses, pp. 58, 265.
Ickworth (Suffolk), architectural fragments, p. 299.
Inchaffray Abbey (Perthshire), p. 135.
Inchcailleach (Stirlingshire), parish church, p. 125n.
Indeterminate remains, Saulmore, p. 300.
Industrial Works and Buildings: pp. 3-4, 33-5; bloomeries, p. 33; boat-landings, pp. 4, 138, 166, 182, 184, 189, 216, 220, 222, 230-1, 241, 274, figs. 173, 188, 197, 210; charcoal-burning stances, pp. 34, **276, 281**, 283; custom-house, pp. 3, 242; distillery, pp. 242-3; distilling (illicit), pp. 35, **278, 281**; gunpowder-works, pp. 34, **292-3**, pl. 117A-B; harbours, pp. 30, 35, 277, 279, pl. 106C-D; ironworks, pp. 3, 33-4, 128, 244, 276, **280-92**, 293, figs. 235-47, pls. 111-16; jetties, pp. 216, 231, 251, 277-9, 284, pl. 106C-D; kilns, pp. 32, 35, 51, 276, 293-4, pls. 104B, 118A, C; lighthouses, pp. 35-6, 63, **279-80**, 299, pls. 107-10, 120G; Lorn Furnace, Bonawe, pp. 3, 33-4, 63, 128, 276, **281-92**, 293, figs. 236-47, pls. 111-16; mills, pp. 32, 34, 279, 293; millstones, pp. 35, 182, 212, 277, pl. 104D; old ferryhouses, pp. 176, **293-4**, pl. 117C-D; old schoolhouses, pp. 54, **254-5**, **266-7**, pls. 91D, 100D; quarries, see **Quarries**; workers' dwellings, pp. 33-5, 269, **276-9**, 283, **290-1**, 294, figs. 233-4, 236, 244-6, pls. 104A, 105C, 106, 116A-C, 118B, D.
Inishail: crannog, p. 94; old parish church, pp. 22, 25-6, 121, 129, **134-6, 138**, 149, figs. 6, 123-5, pl. 28A.
Inistrynich: bridge, p. 296; crannog, p. 94.
Inistrynich House, see **Hayfield**.
Inninmore Bay (Morvern), quarry, pp. 101, 189.
Innis Chonnell Castle: pp. 25-7, 29, 94, 138, 155, 210, **223-31**, figs. 197-204, pls. 66-8.
ARCHITECTURAL DESCRIPTION: entrance-gateway, p. 225, fig. 202A, pl. 66D, F; gatehouse, pp. 223, **230**; inner bailey, pp. 223, **225**, 231, figs. 198-204, pls. 66-8; middle bailey, pp. 223, 225, 229, **230-1**; north and east curtain-walls, pp. 223, **228-9**, pl. 68C; outer bailey, pp. 223, 230, **231**; parapet-walks, pp. 223, 226, 228, **229-30**, fig. 199, pl. 68D-E; south range and south-east tower, pp. 27, **225-7**, figs. 201, 203, pls. 66B, 67A-B, E; west range and south-west tower, pp. 27, 223, **227-8**, fig. 202B, pls. 67C-D, F, 68A-B.
HISTORICAL NOTE, p. 231.
SYNOPSIS, p. 223.
Innis Sèa-Ràmhach, chapel, pp. 25, **138**, figs. 6, 126.
Inveraray (Mid Argyll), pp. 30, 32n, 231, 252.
Inveraray-Tyndrum, military road, pp. 36, **295-6**.
Inverawe, carved stone ball, p. 259.
Inverawe House: p. 259; carved stone, p. 259.
Inverfolla, standing stone, p. 63.
Invergarry Furnace (Inverness-shire), pp. 34, 280, 284.
Inverghiusachan, church, pp. 138-9, fig. 127, pl. 28F.
Inverinan, crannog, p. 94.

Inverkinglass, *see* **Glen Kinglass.**
Inverlochy, bridge, p. 296.
Inverlochy Castle (Inverness-shire), p. 27.
Inveroran, bridge, pp. 296-7.
Iona: abbey, pp. 23, 36, 142, 144, 149, 299, pl. 120F; medieval school of carving, *see under* **Carving;** monastery (Early Christian), p. 21; nunnery, pp. 124, 165n.
Iron Age: pp. 16-21, fig. 5; distribution map, fig. 5; monuments (descriptions), pp. 64-97, figs. 28-85, pls. 10-11D; relics, pp. 20, 70, 78, 83, 92.
Iron-founder, MacDonald, Manus, p. 280.
Ironmasters: p. 34; Ford, Richard, pp. 283-4, 290n; Knott, George, p. 292; Rawlinson, Thomas, p. 280.
Ironwork (noteworthy), pp. 35, 106, 109, 134, 177-9, 205, 244, 280, 284, pls. 27B, 42, 78E, 110A-D, 113B.
Ironworks: pp. 3, 33-4; Abernethy (Inverness-shire), p. 34; Glen Kinglass, pp. 3, 34, 244, **280-1,** 283, fig. 235; Goatfield (Mid Argyll), p. 34; Invergarry (Inverness-shire), pp. 34, 280, 284; Lake District, pp. 34, 283-4; Lorn Furnace, pp. 3, 33-4, 63, 128, 276, **281-92,** 293, figs. 236-47, pls. 111-16.

Jack, Alexander, slater, p. 179.
James IV, King of Scotland, pp. 110, 161, 194.
James V, King of Scotland, pp. 110, 193-4.
James VII and II, King of Great Britain, p. 239.
Jedburgh Prison (Roxburghshire), p. 31.
Jelfe, Andrews, architect *and* marble-carver, p. 278.
Jet, pp. 9, 12, 40, 59.
Jetties: pp. 216, 231, 251, 277-9, 284, pl. 106C-D; *see also* **Boat-landings** *and* **Harbours.**
John, p. 113.
John, p. 136.
John of Islay, Lord of the Isles, p. 139.
Johnstone, Allan, mason *and* contractor, p. 132.
——John, mason *and* wright, pp. 31, 266.
Joiners: MacNab, Peter, p. 141; Thompson, William, p. 258.
Julius II, Pope, p. 161.

Kames, burial, p. 59.
Keil, cist, pp. 12, **59.**
Keil Chapel, pp. 23, 26, **139,** 161, figs. 6, 128, pl. 28B-E.
Kelly, Alexander, p. 283.
——John, plasterer, p. 239.
Kenmure Castle (Kirkcudbrightshire), p. 220.
Kentallen, quarry, p. 3.
Keppochan: crannog, p. 94; cup-markings, p. 61.
Kerr (Ker): Vere, p. 249; *see also* **Lothian,** William Kerr, 3rd Earl of.
Kerrera: Ardantrive, cave deposit, p. 12; Càrn Breugach, cairn, p. 48; Cladh a' Bhearnaig, cashel, pp. 21, **119-20,** fig. 107; 'earth house', p. 22, pl. 5D; Gylen Castle, pp. 29, 175, **217-23,** 254, 277, figs. 191-6, pls. 63-5; Little Horse Shoe, fort, p. 73, fig. 39; Mount Pleasant House, 'Viking burial', p. 22; quarries, pp. 35, 195, 217; Slaterich, cists, pp. 12, **61,** pl. 3B; Slatrach Bay, cairn, p. 57; Upper Gylen Farm, cruck-framed building, p. 32n.
Kilbrandon, Seil, old parish church, pp. 139-40, pl. 29D.
Kilbrandon House, Seil, pp. 31, 116, **259-60,** pl. 96A.
Kilbrandon and Kilchattan, Seil, old parish church, pp. **139,** 144.
Kilbride, old parish church, pp. 25-6, **140-3,** 153, figs. 129-30, pl. 29A-C.
Kilbride, Glen Feochan, burial-ground, p. 143.
Kilbride, Seil, chapel, p. 144.
Kilchallumchill, *see* **Keil Chapel.**
Kilchattan, Luing, old parish church, pp. 23, 25, 36, **144-6,** 167, figs. 6, 131-4, pl. 30B-E.
Kilcheran, Lismore: burial, p. 59; burial-ground, p. 146; chapel and house, p. 146, pl. 30A; dun, p. 90, fig. 74; fort, pp. 16, **72-3,** fig. 38; seminary, pp. **146,** 293.
Kilchoan House, burial-ground *and* chapel, p. 146.
Kilchoan Loch, dun, p. 90.

Kilchousland (Kintyre), parish church, p. 25.
Kilchrenan: cup-and-ring markings, p. 61; parish church, pp. 25-6, **146-9,** figs. 135-8, pl. 31C-F; thatching, pp. 32n, 33n, pl. 103B.
Kilchurn Castle: pp. 28-9, 177, 179, **231-40,** figs. 205-9, pls. 69-75.
ARCHITECTURAL DESCRIPTION: barrack-blocks, pp. 28, 232, 234, 236-9, figs. 205-6; chapel, pp. 232, 235, 239; courtyard buildings, pp. 232, **235-8,** 239, figs. 205-6, pls. 73-5; laich hall, pp. 232, **238-9;** tower-house, pp. 232, **234-5,** 238-9, figs. 206-9A, pl. 72.
BOAT-LANDING, p. 231.
CARVED STONES, p. 238, pl. 75C.
HISTORICAL NOTE, pp. 238-40.
SYNOPSIS, p. 232.
Kilcongen, *see* **Kilchoan House.**
Kildalloig (Kintyre), dun, p. 19n.
Kilespickerill, *see* **Muckairn, old parish church.**
Killandrist, Lismore, chapel, pp. 119, **149.**
Killchallumchill, *see* **Cill Choluim-chille, Benderloch.**
Killean, chapel, *see* **Cill-an-Suidhe, Lismore.**
Killean (Kintyre), old parish church, pp. 23, 124-5, 144.
Killiechonich, cup-markings, p. 61.
Kilmaha: burial-ground *and* chapel, pp. 21-2, **149-50,** figs. 139-41; monastery (Early Christian), p. 21.
Kilmaluag, *see* **St Moluag Cathedral.**
Kilmaronag: burial-ground *and* church, pp. **150-3,** 163, fig. 142; cup-markings, p. 62.
Kilmarow (Killarow, Killocraw) (Kintyre), burial-ground *and* church, p. 110.
Kilmartin (Mid Argyll), cairns, p. 10.
Kilmelford: cairn, p. 52; parish church, p. 153; *see also* **Loch a' Phearsain.**
Kilmichael Glassary (Mid Argyll): bell-shrine, p. 21n; medieval funerary monuments, p. 162.
Kilmore: cairns, pp. 10-11, 13, 43, **52-3,** 96, figs. 22-3, pl. 4B; dagger, bronze, pp. 10, 13, 53, pl. 4B; fort, p. 73; neolithic relics, p. 9; old parish church, pp. 25-6, 116, 141, **153-5,** 260, 277, figs. 6, 143-6, pl. 31A-B.
Kilmore House, pp. 31, **260,** fig. 218, pl. 96C-D.
Kilmorrie, *see* **Cladh Uaine.**
Kilmun: burial-ground *and* chapel, pp. 25, **155,** fig. 147; enclosure, p. 97, fig. 84; *see also* **Caibeal, Lochavich.**
Kilmun (Cowal), collegiate church, p. 231.
Kilninver: burial-ground *and* parish church, pp. 110, **155-6;** standing stone, p. 63.
Kilns: pp. 32, 51; *see also* **Lime-kilns.**
Kilvarie, *see* **Bar-a-goan.**
Kinlochlaich, pp. 31, 256, **260-1,** pl. 97A-E.
Kinlochleven-Tyndrum, military road, pp. 36, 295, **296-8,** pl. 119D.
Kintaline, cist, p. 59.
Kintraw (Mid Argyll), cairn, p. 10.
Kirkwall Cathedral (Orkney), sheela-na-gig, p. 165n.
Knock Castle, Skye (Inverness-shire), p. 28.
Knott, George, ironmaster, p. 292.
Kulmani, Duror, pp. 31, 129, **261,** fig. 219, pl. 97G.

Lady Margaret's Tower, Lochnell House, p. 265, fig. 223.
Lagganbeg, cairn, p. 53.
Lake District: ironworks, pp. 34, 283-4; quarries, pp. 290-1.
Landing-places, *see* **Boat-landings.**
Langlands, Alexander, surveyor, pp. 242n, 248n, 271, 273n, pl. 103A.
——George, surveyor, pp. 98n, 156n, 242, 251n, 278n, 295.
Làrach Bàn: cairn, pp. 10, **53-4,** fig. 24; crannog, p. 94.
Làrach na h-Iobairte, enclosure, p. 97, fig. 85.
Laroch, workers' dwellings, p. 277.
Lauder, George, bishop of Argyll, pp. 161, 171.
Leccamore, Luing: cup-markings, pp. 12, **91;** dun, pp. 12, 18-19, **91-2,** fig. 75, pl. 11B-D.
Ledaig: cairn, p. 54; cist, p. 59; Food Vessel, p. 12, pl. 3C.
Lerags: cairn, pp. 10, **54,** fig. 25; *see also* **Campbell of Lerags Cross.**
Lerags House, pp. 31, 54, **261,** pl. 97F.
Leslie, General David, p. 223.

Lighthouses: Eilean Musdile, Lismore, pp. 35, 63, **279-80**, pls. 107-10.

Lime-kilns, pp. 35, 276, **293-4**, pls. 104B, 118A, C.

Limestone-quarries, pp. 3, 35, **276-7, 294**, pls. 104A-B, 118B.

Lindsay, Dougall, minister of Glenorchy and Inishail, p. 134.

——Ian G, architect, p. 161.

Linne nam Beathach, bridge, p. 297.

Lismore: Achadun Castle, pp. 26-7, **168-71**, 186, figs. 159-61, pls. 37-8B; An Dùn, Loch Fiart, broch, pp. 20, **75**, fig. 43; An Dùn, Sloc a' Bhrighide, dun, pp. 19, **78**, fig. 47; An Sàilean, cruck-framed buildings, harbour, kilns, limestone-quarries and workers' dwellings, pp. 3, 35, **276-7**, fig. 233, pl. 104A-B; Aon Garbh, cairns and cist, pp. **45-6, 57**; Balliveolan, enclosure, p. 95, fig. 81; Balygrundle, cairns (north) and (south), p. 47; Barr Mór, axe, cairns (1) and (2), and cist, pp. 13, **47, 58**, fig. 17, pl. 5C; Càrn Mór, cairn, p. 48; Castle Coeffin, pp. 28, 171, **184-7**, figs. 170-1, pls. 45-6C; Castle Coeffin, fort, pp. 16, **65**; Cill-an-Suidhe, burial ground and chapel, pp. 21, **118**, 119, 121, fig. 105; Clachan, burial-ground, pp. 21, 118, **119**, 121, fig. 106; Cnoc Aingil, burial and cairn, pp. **49, 58**; Creag an Fhithich, cairn, p. 50; distilling (illicit), pp. 35, **281**; Druim an Uinnsinn, cairns (1) and (2), p. 51, fig. 21; Dùn Chrùban, dun, pp. 19, **85**, fig. 63, pl. 11A; Dùn Cuilein, dun, p. 86, fig. 64; Dùn Mór, Balygrundle, dun, pp. 47, **88**, fig. 69; Eilean Musdile, bridge, lighthouse and standing stone, pp. 35, **63, 279-80**, pls. 107-10; Fiart, dun, pp. 89-90, fig. 72; Kilcheran, burial, burial-ground, dun, fort and house, pp. 16, **59, 72-3, 90, 146**, 293, figs. 38, 74, pl. 30A; Killandrist, chapel, pp. 119, **149**; Park, dun, p. 92; Port Kilcheran, lime-kilns, pp. 35, **293-4**, pl. 118A; Port Maluag, chapel and well, p. 166; Port Ramsay, limestone-quarries and workers' dwellings, pp. 3, 35, **294**, pl. 118B-D; St Moluag Cathedral and parish church, pp. 21-3, 26, 48-9, 142, **156-63**, 171, 186, 277, figs. 148-52, pls. 32-4; Sean Dùn, dun and enclosure, pp. 21, **92-3**, fig. 77; Tirefour Castle, broch, pp. 16, 20, **75-7**, fig. 44, pl. 10; Tobar na Slainte, p. 166.

Little Horse Shoe, Kerrera, fort, p. 73, fig. 39.

Livingstone, Sir James, p. 171.

Livingstone family, of Bachuil, p. 21.

Loarn Mór, son of Erc, p. 1.

Loch Aline (Morvern), quarry, pp. 35, 280.

Loch a' Mhuillin, crannog, p. 93.

Lochan a' Chuirn, cairn, pp. 11, 54.

Lochan Dughaill (Kintyre), crannog, p. 20.

Lochan na Beithe, cairns, pp. 11, 54.

Lochan na Gealaich, crannog, p. 93.

Lochan nan Ràth: cairn, pp. 11, 37, **54**, pl. 8A; earthwork, p. 97.

Loch a' Phearsain: dun, p. 92, fig. 76; fortified dwelling, pp. 29-30, **240-1**, fig. 210.

Loch Avich (Lochavich), see **Caibeal** and **Caisteal na Nighinn Ruaidhe.**

Lochaw, see **Kilchrenan,** parish church.

Loch Awe: crannogs, pp. 20, **94**, fig. 79; medieval school of carving, see under **Carving;** monasteries (Early Christian), p. 21; quarry, p. 177; St Conan's Church, carved fragments, pp. 36, **299-300**, pl. 120E-F.

Loch Creran, charcoal-burning stances, pp. 34, **281**, 283.

Loch Dochart Castle (Perthshire), pp. 228, 238.

Loch Etive: charcoal-burning stances, pp. 34, **281**, 283; see also **Glen Kinglass.**

Loch Fiart, An Dùn, Lismore, broch, pp. 20, **75**, fig. 43.

Loch Gleann a' Bhearraidh, cup-markings, p. 62.

Loch Greverin, see **Cladh Churiollan.**

Loch na Sreinge, castle, pp. 29-30, **241.**

Loch Nell: fortified dwelling, pp. 29-30, **242;** see also **Kilmore,** cairns.

Lochnell Arms Hotel, barrow, pp. 10, **54.**

Lochnell House: pp. 30-1, 33, 59, 164, 242, **261-6**, figs. 220-3, pls. 98-9; early Georgian dwelling-house, pp. 30, **263-4**, 265, fig. 221, pl. 99A; Lady Margaret's Tower, p. 265, fig. 223; late Georgian mansion, pp. 31, 263, **264-5**, 266, pl. 99B, D-E; south-west service-wing, p. 263, pl. 99A.

Lochranza Castle, Arran (Buteshire), p. 28.

Loch Seil, crannog, p. 94.

Loch Tromlee, see **Eilean Tighe Bhàin.**

Loch Tulla: p. 174; see also **Eilean Stalcair.**

Loerni, Genus, p. 1.

Lorimer, Sir Robert, architect, p. 259.

Lorn, Archibald Campbell, Lord, see **Argyll,** Archibald Campbell, 8th Earl of.

Lorn, lords of: MacDougall, pp. 23, 110, 139, 171, 186, 197-8, 210, 231; Stewart, pp. 186, 193, 197-8, 210, 238; see also **Argyll,** Campbell family, Earls of.

Lorn, lordship of, pp. 186, 197-8, 210, 263.

Lorn Furnace, Bonawe: pp. 3, 33-4, 63, 128, 276, **281-92**, 293, figs. 236-47, pls. 111-16; ancillary buildings, pp. 34, 283-4, 286, fig. 236; Bonawe House, pp. 34, **291-2**, figs. 236, 247, pl. 116D-E; charcoal-sheds, pp. 34, **288**, 290, figs. 236, 240-3, pls. 114-15; furnace, pp. 34, **283-6**, 288, figs. 236-9, pls. 111-13; ore-shed, pp. 34, 284, 286, **287-8**, fig. 241, pl. 114A; workers' dwellings, pp. 34, 269, 283, **290-1**, figs. 236, 244-6, pl. 116A-C.

Lorn Furnace Company, pp. 283, 291.

Losgann Larnach, fort, pp. 18, **73-4**, fig. 40.

Lothian, William Kerr, 3rd Earl of, p. 249.

Luing: Ardlarach, pp. 31, 33, 96, **248**, pl. 86E; Ard Luing, earthwork, pp. 21, **95**, fig. 80; Ballycastle, dun, pp. 18, **79-80**, fig. 50; Black Mill Bay, quarry and workers' dwellings, p. 278; Cullipool, quarry and workers' dwellings, p. 278; Dùn Ablaich, earthwork, pp. 21, **96**, fig. 82; Eilean an Atha, dun, pp. 19, **89**, fig. 71; Kilchattan, old parish church, pp. 23, 25, 36, **144-6**, 167, figs. 6, 131-4, pl. 30B-E; graffiti, pp. 36, **144-5**, figs. 132-4, pl. 30C; Leccamore, cup-markings and dun, pp. 12, 18-19, **91-2**, fig. 75, pl. 11B-D; Toberonochy, quarry and workers' dwellings, p. 278.

Lussa Bay (Jura), mesolithic occupation, p. 6.

McAllum, William, p. 138.

MacArthur (McArthur), Archibald, p. 146.

——Duncan, Captain of Innis Chonnell, p. 231.

——Duncan, prior of Ardchattan, p. 110.

——John, surveyor, p. 33.

MacArthur family, Captains of Innis Chonnell, p. 231.

——of Inistrynich, p. 259.

MacArthur Cave, Oban: burials, p. 60; mesolithic implements, p. 5, pl. 2.

MacCauis, Duncan, vicar of Inishail, p. 136.

MacColl (McColl), Duncan (d. 1772), p. 122.

——Duncan (d. 1822), p. 139.

——Hugh, p. 122.

——Rachel, p. 139.

MacColl family, p. 122.

MacCorquodale family, of Phantilands, p. 212.

McCowan, Alexander, p. 273.

MacDonald (Macdonald), Alasdair 'Colkitto', younger of Colonsay, pp. 110, 212.

——Alasdair, 12th of Glencoe, p. 131.

——Coll, of Keppoch, p. 174n.

——John, 13th of Glencoe, p. 131.

——John, of Islay, Lord of the Isles, p. 139.

——Katherine, p. 104.

——Manus, iron-founder, p. 280.

——Mary, p. 143.

MacDonald family, of Glencoe, pp. 130-1, 174n.

——of Sleat, p. 143.

MacDougald, Donald, architect, p. 147.

McD[ougall], A, piper, p. 143.

MacDougall (McDougall, McDowgall, McDugall), Alan, p. 112.

——Alan, p. 112.

——Alexander, tacksman, p. 140.

——Alexander, lord of Lorn, p. 210.

——Alexander, 12th of MacDougall and Dunollie, p. 113.

——Alexander, 23rd of MacDougall and Dunollie, p. 198.

——Allan, p. 140.

——Allan, of Balichun, p. 140.

——Allan, of Gallanach and Hayfield, p. 259.

MacDougall (McDougall, McDowgall, McDugall),
——Allan, of Rarey, pp. 223, 251.
——Allan, of Torsa, p. 182.
——Coll, of Ardencaple, pp. 248, 295.
——Dougall, 15th of MacDougall and Dunollie, p. 223.
——Dougall, of Rarey, p. 223.
——Dugald, of Gallanach, pp. 255, 277.
——Dugall, prior of Ardchattan, p. 112.
——Duncan, prior of Ardchattan, p. 112.
——Duncan, lord of Lorn, pp. 23, 110, 171, 210.
——Duncan, 16th of MacDougall and Dunollie, pp. 217, 222-3.
——Eugenius, prior of Ardchattan, p. 112.
——Ewen, lord of Lorn, pp. 171, 186, 210.
——Hugh, p. 145.
——Lady Isobell, p. 114.
——Janet, p. 186.
——Jean, p. 131.
——John, p. 113.
——John, p. 139.
——John, of Ardencaple, pp. 175, 248.
——John, of Gallanach, p. 255.
——John (Bacach), lord of Lorn, pp. 197, 210, 231.
——John, lord of Lorn, pp. 139, 186, 197, 210.
——John, of Lunga, p. 145.
——John, of MacDougall and Dunollie (*flor. c.* 1451), p. 197.
——John, 19th of MacDougall and Dunollie, p. 198.
——John (Iain Ciar), 22nd of MacDougall and Dunollie, pp. 143, 198.
——John, of Rarey (*flor. c.* 1479), p. 251.
——John, of Rarey (d. *c.* 1660), p. 252.
——Katrin, p. 140.
——Patrick, p. 248.
——Somerled, pp. 26, 112.
MacDougall family, pp. 26, 112-13, 115, 118, 139, 142-3.
——of Ardencaple, pp. 175, 248.
——of Balichun, p. 140.
——of Gallanach, pp. 182, 259.
——of Kilmun, pp. 117-18.
——lords of Lorn, pp. 23, 186, 197-8, 210, 231.
——of Lunga, pp. 145-6.
——of MacDougall and Dunollie, pp. 26, 29, 102, 112-13, 142-3, 197-8, 223.
——of Rarey, pp. 114, 118, 175, 182, 242, 248, 251-2, 267.
——of Torsa, p. 255.
McDowgall, *see* **MacDougall.**
McDugall, *see* **MacDougall.**
MacFie, Robert, of Airds and Langhouse, p. 245.
MacFie family, of Airds, p. 245.
MacGregor (V'Gregour), Alastair, of Glenstrae, p. 174.
——Gregor, 8th of Glenstrae, p. 187.
——James, of Correctled, p. 162.
——John M'Conoquhy, p. 238.
MacGregor Clan (Clan Gregor), pp. 132, 174, 238.
MacGregor family, p. 174.
——of Correctled, p. 162.
——of Glen Strae, pp. 174, 187, 238, 254, 267.
MacInnes (McInnes), Angus, piper, p. 122.
——Mary, p. 131.
MacIntyre (McIntyre), Duncan, of Gleno, p. 113.
——Duncan Ban, p. 84.
——Robert, surgeon, p. 149.
MacIntyre family, p. 149.
——of Gleno, p. 113.
MacKay Cave, Oban, mesolithic implements, p. 5.
MacKay (Mackay), Janet, p. 258.
MacKellar, Dugall, p. 149.
McKelvie Hospital, Oban, burials, p. 60, pl. 4A.
MacKenzie (McKenzie), Duncan, p. 131.
——Duncan, smith, p. 131.
MacLachlan (McLachlan, McLauchlane),
Colin, of Craiginterve, p. 231.
——Donald, of Innis Chonnell, p. 231.
——Duncan, minister of Strachur and Strathlachlan, p. 140.
——John, minister of Kilbrandon and Kilchattan, p. 140.
——John, minister of Kilninver and Kilmelford, pp. 139-40.
——Patrick, p. 231.

MacLachlan family, p. 140.
——Captains of Innis Chonnell, p. 231.
Maclaine, Hector, bishop of Argyll, p. 171.
MacLauchlane (McLauchlane), *see* **MacLachlan.**
MacLean (Maclean, McLean), Alexander, of Shuna, p. 167.
——Allan, of Shuna, p. 145.
——John, of Shuna, p. 167.
——Margaret, p. 222n.
MacLean family, of Duart, pp. 140, 182, 198, 222n.
——of Shuna, p. 167.
McLerran, Dugald, p. 124.
——John, p. 124.
McMillan, Alexander, p. 281n.
MacNab (Macnab, McNab), Mr, architect, p. 166.
——Alexander, of Barran, p. 134.
——John, of Barran, p. 134.
——Peter, joiner, p. 141.
MacNab family, of Barran, p. 134.
MacNaughton (MacNachdan, MacNachtan, Macnaughton), Ath, pp. 134-5.
——Gillechrist, p. 217.
——Malcolm, pp. 134-5.
MacNaughton family, p. 217.
MacNeil, William, p. 259.
MacNicol family, p. 174.
MacPherson (McPherson), Alexander, p. 134.
——Malcolm, shepherd, p. 155.
MacPherson family, p. 134.
McVean, John, minister of Glenorchy and Inishail, p. 134.
Maine, Robert, p. 280n.
Mains of Glins (Stirlingshire), p. 256n.
Makcaw, John, archdeacon of Argyll, p. 161.
Malcolm, Neil, of Poltalloch, p. 99.
Manor House, Dungallon, p. 254, pl. 91C.
Marble carvers, *see* **Carvers.**
Marble Hill House, Twickenham (Middlesex), p. 30.
Marble-quarry, Caddleton, pp. 35, 250-1, **278.**
Marble and Slate Company of Netherlorn, pp. 278-9.
Masons and master-mason: Baxter, John (elder), pp. 31, 266; Campbell, Duncan, pp. 256, 258; Christie, Andrew, pp. 179, 239; Clerk, John, p. 155; Drummond, John, pp. 110, 253; Duff, James, pp. 99, 211, 247, 253, 296; Johnstone, Allan, p. 132; Johnstone, John, pp. 31, 266; Menelaws, John, p. 253; Smeeton, Robert, p. 258; Tainsh, John, p. 258; *see also* **Carvers.**
Masons' marks, pp. 101, 124, 159, 168, 171, 225, 232, 235, figs. 89, 115, 151, 161, 201, 207.
Mavisbank House (Midlothian), p. 266n.
Maxwell, Robert, bell-founder, p. 164.
Mckichan, p. 111.
Mears, Thomas, bell-founder, p. 299.
Melfort: gunpowder-works, pp. 34, **292-3,** pl. 117A-B; mesolithic implements, p. 5.
Melfort Cottage, *see* **Kilchoan House.**
Melfort House: p. 293; bronze armlets, pp. 12, 59, pl. 4C; cists, pp. 12-13, 59, pl. 4C; jet necklace, pp. 12, 59.
Melville, David Melville, 2nd Earl of, p. 174.
Menelaws, John, mason, p. 253.
Mesolithic period: pp. 5-6; relics, pp. 5-6, pl. 2.
Mid Ardnahua, farm, p. 274.
Middleton, General John, p. 239.
Military roads: p. 36; Inveraray-Tyndrum, pp. 36, **295-6;** Tyndrum-Kinlochleven, pp. 36, 295, **296-8,** pl. 119D.
Mills, pp. 32, 34, 279, 293.
Millstone-quarries and millstones: pp. 35, 182, 212; Barran, pp. 35, **278;** Barrnacarry, pp. 35, **277,** pl. 104D.
Milton Loch Crannog (Kirkcudbrightshire), pp. 20, 94.
Minard Point, An Dùnan, dun, p. 77, fig. 45.
M'Inleister, *see* **Fletcher.**
Mitchell, Joseph, engineer, pp. 25, 129.
Mochoe, *see* **St Kentigern.**
Moleigh, *see* **Kilmore,** cairns.
Monasteries (Early Christian): Cladh a' Bhearnaig, pp. 21, **119-20,** fig. 107; Iona, p. 21; Kilmaha, p. 21; Lismore, pp. 21, 156, 160; Loch Awe, p. 21; *see also* **Religious houses.**
Monck, General, p. 239.

Montrose, James Graham, 1st Marquess of, pp. 32, 179.
Monzie, Patrick Campbell, Lord, p. 139n.
Morris, Roger, architect, p. 30n.
Morrison, James, wright, p. 258.
Mortsafe, p. 134, pl. 27B.
Moss of Achnacree: bronze axe, p. 13; cairn, pp. 11, **55**; crannog, pp. 20, **94-5.**
Mount Pleasant House, Kerrera, 'Viking burial', p. 22.
Movilla Abbey (Co. Down), p. 102n.
Moy Castle (Mull), p. 34n.
Muckairn, Taynuilt: manse, pp. 31, **266**, pl. 100E; old parish church, pp. **163**, 164-5, figs. 6, 153; parish church, pp. 25, 124, 149, **163-5**, 168, 266, figs. 154-6, pl. 35; *see also* **Kilmaronag.**
Murphy, Roger, tanner, p. 280.
Musdale, cairn, p. 55.
Musketry embrasures, *see* **Firearm defence.**
Mutloe, Captain, Governor of Dunstaffnage, p. 110.
Mylne, Robert, architect, pp. 36, 295.

Narrachan, cruck-framed buildings, pp. 32, **272.**
Neolithic period: pp. 6-9, 11; distribution map, fig. 2; monuments (descriptions), pp. 37-44, figs. 7-14, pls. 6-7; relics, pp. 8-9, 37, 40, 43, pl. 3A.
New Inverawe, *see* **Ardanaiseig.**
Newland Company, pp. 34, 283.
Newland (Lancashire), ironworks, pp. 283-4.
New Murthly Castle (Perthshire), p. 252.
Nixon, Edward, p. 280n.
North Ardnahua, farm, pp. 273-4.
North Connel, Black Crofts, field-bank, pp. 13, 21, **95-6**, pl. 11E.
Northern Lighthouses, Commissioners for, pp. 35, 279, 280n, 299.
'North Fort', *see* **Ballycastle, Luing.**
North Ledaig, old schoolhouse, pp. 54, **266-7**, pl. 100D.
Norton, L C, architect, p. 259.
Nunneries: Iona, pp. 124, 165n; Lismore, pp. 162-3; *see also* **Religious houses.**

Oban: pp. 3, 5-6, 9-10, 12-13, 25, 30, 33n, 35; Albany Street, p. 242; anchorage, p. 242; Argyll Square, p. 242; Back Combie Street, pp. 30, **243**; Black Lynn, p. 242; Breadalbane Place *and* Street, burial *and* cists, pp. 59-60; burials *and* cists, pp. 12, 22, **59-60**, pls. 3D, 4A; Cave of the Skulls, burials, p. 60; Cawdor Place, pp. 30, **243**; Combie Street, pp. 242-3; Corran Esplanade, p. 30; Corran Park, cist, pp. 12, **60**, pl. 3D; custom-house, pp. 3, 242; Dalrigh, burial, p. 60; distillery, pp. 242-3; Distillery Cave, p. 5, pl. 2; Druimvargie, rock-shelter, p. 5, pl. 2; Esplanade, cup-markings, p. 62; Free High Church, pp. 25, 30, **165-6**, 243, 277, pl. 36A-C; Gasworks, burial, pp. 12, **60**; George Street, p. 242; Great Western Hotel, p. 30; harbour, p. 242; MacArthur Cave, burials *and* mesolithic implements, pp. 5, **60**, pl. 2; MacKay Cave, p. 5; McKelvie Hospital, burials, p. 60, pl. 4A; piermaster's house, pp. 30, **243**, pl. 77B; quarries, p. 35; ship-building, p. 3; Shore Street, pp. 242-3; South Pier, pp. 30, 243; Star Brae, p. 243; topography, pp. 30, **242**, pls. 76, 77A.
O Brolchan, John, stone-carver, p. 112.
Old ferryhouses: Port Appin, p. 293, pl. 117D; South Shian, pp. 176, **294**, pl. 117C.
Old schoolhouses: Ferlochan, pp. **254-5**, 267, pl. 91D; North Ledaig, pp. 54, **266-7**, pl. 100D.
Old smithy, Port Appin, armorial panel, p. 299, pl. 120D.
Oronsay, mesolithic occupation, pp. 5-6.

Pacifying the Highlands, Commissioners for, p. 174.
Parish list of monuments, pp. xxxv-xxxix.
Park, Lismore, dun, p. 92.
Passage-grave chambered cairns, pp. 6-7, 37, 40.
Paterson, George, wright, pp. 256, 258.
Patrick, p. 140.
Pennyfuir, cairn, p. 55.
Perth, Treaty of, p. 217.

Pierie, John, artist, p. 254n.
Piermaster's House, Oban, pp. 30, **243**, pl. 77B.
Piscinae, pp. 23n, 102, 159, fig. 150, pl. 33E.
Pistol-holes, *see* **Firearm defence.**
Pit-prisons, *see* **Prisons.**
Place-names, pp. 1, 16, 21-2, 98, 115, 117, 150, 152, 182, 187.
Plasterer, Kelly, John, p. 239.
Plasterwork (ornamental), pp. 245, 248, 253-4, 261, pl. 97D-E.
Pluscarden Priory (Moray), p. 23.
Port Appin: old ferryhouse, p. 293, pl. 117D; old smithy, armorial panel, p. 299, pl. 120D.
Port Dubh, Kerrera, quarry, pp. 35, 195, 217.
Port Kilcheran, Lismore, lime-kilns, pp. 35, **293-4**, pl. 118A.
Port Maluag, Lismore, chapel *and* well, p. 166.
Portnacroish: chambered cairn, pp. 6, **43**; Episcopal church, pp. 25, **166-7**, figs. 157-8, pl. 36E.
Port Ramsay, Lismore: lime-kilns, limestone-quarries *and* workers' dwellings, pp. 3, 35, **294**, pl. 118B-D.
Port Sonachan: chambered cairn, pp. 7-8, **43-4**, fig. 13; crannog, p. 94.
Post-office, Tynribbie, Appin, p. 247, pl. 84D.
Priories: Ardchattan, pp. 22-3, 26, **99-115**, 116, 125, 157n, 179n, 210, figs. 88-101, pls. 13-20; Beauly (Inverness-shire), p. 23; Pluscarden (Moray), p. 23; *see also* **Religious houses.**
Prisons: pp. 31, 178, 189, 208, 213, 216, 227-8, 234, fig. 180, pls. 50F, 51G; Calton Jail (Edinburgh), p. 31; Jedburgh (Roxburghshire), p. 31.
Pugin, Augustus Welby Northmore, pp. 25, 165.
Pulpita, pp. 23, 103, 156-7, 160-1, fig. 90E, pl. 33F.
Pulpits, pp. 23, 25, 98-9, 105, 108, 129, 132, 139, 141, 148, 154, 156, 159, 163, 166-7, figs. 94A, D-E, 95-7, pls. 17A, 18A-E, 36B.

Quarries: pp. 3, 26, 34-5; An Sàilean, Lismore, pp. 3, 35, **276-7**, pl. 104A-B; Ardencaple, Seil, p. 278; Ardentallan, pp. 35, 141, 153, 157, 166, 195, 217, 222, **277**, pl. 104C; Ardtornish (Morvern), pp. 115, 151, 156, 159, 163, 184, 199, 216, 225, 247; Ballachulish, pp. 3, 32, 34-5, 178, **277**, 278, pl. 105A-B; Balvicar, Seil, p. 278; Barran, pp. 35, **278**; Barrnacarry, pp. 35, 141, 153, 157, 166, 195, 251, **277**, pl. 104D; Black Mill Bay, Luing, p. 278; Bonawe, pp. 3, 163, 288; Bridge of Awe, pp. 35, 115, 182, 213, 216, **278**; Caddleton, pp. 35, 250-1, **278**; Carsaig (Mull), pp. 35, 101, 168, 199; Cullipool, Luing, p. 278; Easdale, Seil, pp. 3, 34-5, 132, 225, 239, **278-9**, pl. 106A; Ellanbeich, pp. 278-9, fig. 234, pl. 106B; Fennacrochan, p. 294; Inninmore Bay (Morvern), pp. 101, 189; Kentallen, p. 3; Kerrera, pp. 35, 195, 217; Lake District, pp. 290-1; Loch Aline (Morvern), pp. 35, 280; Loch Awe, p. 177; Oban, p. 35; Port Kilcheran, Lismore, p. 294; Port Ramsay, Lismore, pp. 3, 35, **294**, pl. 118B; Toberonochy, Luing, p. 278.
Quays, *see* **Jetties.**

Rahoy (Morvern), dun, p. 18.
Rankin, William, p. 131.
Rarey, pp. 31, 242, **267**, pl. 100A.
Rarey, castle, pp. 96, 242, 251, 267, fig. 211.
Rawlinson, Thomas, ironmaster, p. 280.
Religious houses, *see* **Abbeys, Friary, Monasteries (Early Christian), Nunneries** *and* **Priories.**
Risga (North Argyll), mesolithic occupation, p. 6.
River Lochy, bridge, p. 296.
Roads: pp. 3-4, 36; drove-roads, pp. 4, 296; Inveraray-Tyndrum, pp. 36, **295-6**; Parliamentary roads, pp. 295, 297; Tyndrum-Kinlochleven, pp. 36, 295, **296-8**, pl. 119D.
Robert I, King of Scotland, pp. 186, 197, 210, 231, 242.
Rock-carving, Kilmaha, pp. 21-2, **150**, fig. 139.
Rockhill: cairn, p. 55; crannog, p. 94.
Rock-shelters: Cave of the Crags, p. 5; Druimvargie, p. 5, pl. 2; Shuna, Appin, p. 5.
Rodel, St Clement's Church (Inverness-shire), pp. 135n, 165n, 298.
Roderick, parson of Eilean Fhianain, bishop elect of the Isles, p. 112.
Roman relics, pp. 20, 83.

Ross Errilly (Co. Galway), friary, p. 157n.
Rothesay Castle, Bute (Buteshire), p. 202n.
Rubh' an Tighe Loisgte, dun, p. 92.

Saddell Abbey (Kintyre), p. 161.
Saddell Castle (Kintyre), p. 171.
St Andrew, p. 149.
St Andrew's Well, p. 149.
St Baedan, p. 116.
St Bean, pp. 153, 155.
St Brendan of Clonfert, p. 139.
St Bridget, pp. 141, 144.
St Cairrell, pp. 122, 163n.
St Cathan, p. 144.
St Clement's Church, Rodel (Inverness-shire), pp. 135n, 165n, 298.
St Columba, pp. 119, 139.
St Comghan, p. 146.
St Conan, p. 124.
St Conan's Church, architectural fragments, pp. 36, **299-300**, pl. 120E-G.
St Conan's Well, Dalmally, p. 124.
St Congan, p. 146.
St Conuall, p. 138n.
St Cronoc, p. 152.
St Cyril of Alexandria, p. 122.
St Findoca of Inchealt, *see* **Inishail**, old parish church.
St George's Fields (London), p. 165n.
St Gregory the Great, p. 122.
St Gwenfaen's Well, Rhoscolyn (Anglesey), p. 25n.
St John, pp. 118, 167n.
St John the Baptist, p. 110.
St John's Episcopal Church, Portnacroish, pp. 25, **166-7**, figs. 157-8, pl. 36E.
St Kentigern, p. 150.
St Lugaidh, p. 156.
St Maelrubha, pp. 121, 153.
St Mary, p. 110.
St Mary the Virgin, pp. 112, 117.
St Mary's Church, Southport (Lancashire), p. 165n.
St Mary's Parish Church, Leith (Edinburgh), architectural fragment, pp. 36, 299, pl. 120E.
St Mochoe, *see* **St Kentigern**.
St Mochoe of Nendrum, p. 150.
St Modan, p. 116.
St Moluag, pp. 156, 166.
St Moluag Cathedral and parish church, Lismore: pp. 21-3, 26, 48-9, 142, **156-63**, 171, 186, 277, figs. 148-52, pls. 32-4.
ARCHITECTURAL DESCRIPTION: choir, pp. **156-60**, 161, figs. 148-52, pls. 33-4C; nave, pp. 156, **160**, 161, figs. 148-9, pls. 32-3A; west tower, pp. 156, 160, fig. 148, pl. 32.
CHAPEL, p. 162.
FONT, p. 162.
FUNERARY MONUMENTS AND OTHER CARVED STONES, pp. 26, 142, **161-2**, pl. 34D-F.
HISTORICAL NOTE, pp. 160-1.
NUNNERY, pp. 162-3.
SANCTUARY, p. 162.
STANDING STONE, p. 162.
St Munn, pp. 130, 155.
St Oran's Chapel (Iona), p. 142.
St Patrick, p. 122.
St Peter the Deacon, p. 146.
St Ronan, p. 152.
St Tua, p. 150.
St Wilfrid's, Manchester (Lancashire), p. 165n.
Salachail, cairn, p. 55.
Salt-boxes *and* **recesses**, pp. 187, 207, 221.
Sandby, Paul, artist, p. 246n.
Saulmore: cist, pp. 60-1; indeterminate remains, p. 300.
Schoolhouses, *see* **Old schoolhouses**.
Scott, Andrew, wright, p. 239.
——Sir Walter, p. 293.
Sculptors, *see* **Carvers**.
Sean Dùn, Lismore, dun and enclosure, pp. 21, **92-3**, fig. 77.

Seil: Ardencaple, quarry *and* workers' dwellings, p. 278; Ardencaple House, pp. 31, **247-8**, pl. 86C-D; Ardfad Castle, p. 175, fig. 165, pl. 39D; Ballachuan, burial-ground *and* chapel, pp. 25, **116-17**, fig. 103; Balvicar, quarry *and* workers' dwellings, pp. 16-18, **64-5**, **278**, fig. 29; Camuslaich, dun, p. 81, fig. 55; Clachan Bridge, pp. 36, 49, **294-5**, pl. 119B; Clachan Bridge, cairn, p. 49; Cnoc an Tighe Mhóir, fort, pp. 17, **66**, fig. 31; Dùn Aorain, dun, pp. 19, **83-4**, 88, fig. 59; Dùn Mucaig, dun, p. 88, fig. 70; Easdale, slate-quarries *and* workers' dwellings, pp. 3, 33-5, 132, 225, 239, **278-9**, fig. 234, pl. 106A, C-D; Kilbrandon, old parish church, pp. 139-40, pl. 29D; Kilbrandon House, pp. 31, 116, **259-60**, pl. 96A; Kilbrandon and Kilchattan, old parish church, pp. **139**, 144; Kilbride, chapel, p. 144.
Selbach, p. 197.
Seminary, Kilcheran, Lismore, pp. **146**, 293.
Seton, Hugh, of Touch, pp. 246n, 247.
Sgeir Carnaich, cairn, p. 55.
Sgor nam Ban-naomha, Canna (Inverness-shire), cashel, p. 120n.
Sheela-na-gig, p. 165, pl. 35E.
Shelachan, cairns, p. 55.
Shielings: p. 33; Airidh nan Sileag, pp. 33, **267-8**, fig. 224; Ath Dearg, p. 115; Cladh Uaine, p. 121; Glen Risdale, pp. 33, **271-2**, fig. 230.
Shore Street, Oban, pp. 242-3.
Shuna, Appin: Castle Shuna, pp. 187-8, fig. 172, pl. 46D-E; rock-shelter, p. 5.
Shuna, Nether Lorn: bronze swords, p. 13, pl. 5B; burial-enclosure, p. 167; *see also* **Shuna Cottage** *and* **Shuna Point**.
Shuna Cottage, Shuna, Nether Lorn: cairns (1) *and* (2), pp. **55**, **57**; chambered cairn, pp. 7, **44**, 57, fig. 14.
Shuna Point, Shuna, Nether Lorn, cairn, p. 57.
Simpson, John, builder, p. 254n.
Sinclair, Elizabeth, p. 177.
Skerryvore lighthouse, bell, pp. 36, 299, pl. 120G.
Slate-quarries, pp. 3, 32, 34-5, 132, 178, 225, 239, **277-9**, pls. 105A-B, 106A.
Slaterich, Kerrera, cists, pp. 12, **61**, pl. 3B.
Slaters: Jack, Alexander, p. 179; Williamson, Thomas, p. 239.
Slatrach Bay, Kerrera, cairn, p. 57.
Slaughter Stone, *see* **Kilchrenan**, cup-and-ring markings.
Sloc a' Bhrighide, An Dùn, Lismore, dun, pp. 19, **78**, fig. 47.
Smeaton (East Lothian), p. 245.
Smeeton, Robert, mason, p. 258.
Smith, D, sculptor, p. 155.
——James, architect, pp. 25n, 129.
——James, building contractor, p. 279.
——James, hammerman, p. 239.
Smith, McKenzie, Duncan, p. 131.
Smith's insignia, p. 134.
Solomon, p. 143.
Sonachan, burial-enclosure, pp. **167**, 267, pl. 36D.
Soroby (Tiree), church, p. 110.
Southey, Robert, pp. 132, 134.
'South Fort', *see* **Leccamore, Luing**.
South Ledaig, earthwork, p. 97.
South Pier, Oban, pp. 30, 243.
South Shian, old ferryhouse, pp. 176, **294**, pl. 117C.
Spottiswoode, Mr, building contractor, p. 255.
Standing stones: pp. 10, 12-13, fig. 3; Achacha, pp. 10, **45**; Acharra, p. 62, pl. 9C; Barcaldine, p. 62; Benderloch (1) *and* (2), p. 62; Castle Farm, Barcaldine, pp. 10, **48-9**; Clenamacrie, pp. 49, **62**; Connel, pp. 13, **62**, 64; Duachy, pp. 12-13, **62-3**, pl. 9B; Eilean Musdile, Lismore, p. 63; Inverfolla, p. 63; Kilninver, p. 63; Lismore, p. 162; Strontoiller, pp. 10, **57**, 63, pl. 9A; Taynuilt (1) *and* (2), pp. 13, **63-4**.
Stanley, A, artist, pl. 77A.
Star Brae, Oban, p. 243.
Stevenson, Hugh, p. 242.
——John, building-contractor, pp. 132, 242, 254, 295.
——Robert, engineer, pp. 35, 279.
——Robert, surveyor, p. 242n.

Stewart (Stuart), *see also* **Atholl.**
——Alan, 3rd of Appin, pp. 29, 193-4.
——Ann, p. 131.
——Mr, of Ballachulish, p. 277.
——Prince Charles Edward, p. 131.
——Dugald, 9th of Appin, p. 247.
——Duncan, 2nd of Appin, pp. 193-4.
——Duncan, 5th of Appin, p. 187.
——Duncan, 6th of Appin, pp. 193-4.
——Duncan, younger of Appin, p. 194n.
——James, of Fasnacloich, p. 122.
——Lady Janet, p. 186.
——Lady Jean, p. 177.
——John, p. 131.
——John (d. 1817), p. 131.
——John, 4th of Appin, p. 187.
——John, 3rd of Ardsheal, p. 194.
——John, of Ballachulish, p. 174.
——John, 5th of Ballachulish, p. 253.
——John, of Innermeath, lord of Lorn, pp. 186, 197, 210.
——John, lord of Lorn, pp. 197, 238.
——Margaret, p. 114.
——Robert, 8th of Appin, pp. 194, 247.
——Sir Robert, lord of Lorn, p. 186.
Stewart family: pp. 131, 166, 174; *see also* **Atholl,** Earls of.
——of Appin, pp. 99, 114, 193-4, 246, 256.
——of Innermeath, pp. 186, 197.
——lords of Lorn, pp. 186, 193, 197-8, 210.
Stone-carvers, *see* **Carvers.**
Stone circle, Strontoiller, pp. 13, 57, **63,** fig. 27.
Strathcashel Point (Stirlingshire), cashel, p. 120n.
Stronmilchan: Bothan na Dige, pp. 187, **254,** 267; cairn, p. 57; Tigh Mór, pp. 187, 254, **267;** township, p. 33.
Strontoiller: cairns *and* standing stone, pp. 10, 51, **57,** 63, fig. 26, pl. 9A; Cleidh-na-h-Annait, p. 22n; stone circle, pp. 13, 57, **63,** fig. 27.
Stuart, *see* **Stewart.**
Sunadale (Kintyre), dun, p. 18.
Sundials, pp. 179, 263, pls. 43C, 99C.
Supply for Argyll, Commissioners for, pp. 36, 294-6.
Surveyors: Dorrett, James, p. 120; Gordon, H, pp. 296-7; Langlands, Alexander, pp. 242n, 248n, 271, 273n; Langlands, George, pp. 98n, 156n, 242, 251n, 278n, 295; MacArthur, John, p. 33; Stevenson, Robert, p. 242n.
Sutherland, Mr, p. 140.
——Elizabeth, p. 140.
Swords, pp. 13, 58, 70, 81, pl. 5B.

Tainsh, John, mason, p. 258.
Tanner, Murphy, Roger, p. 280.
Tarbert Castle (Kintyre), pp. 26n, 27.
Taymouth Castle (Perthshire), pp. 132, 238, 252, 295n.
Taynuilt: Cladh na h-Anaid, burial-ground, pp. 22, 118-19, **121,** fig. 108; cross, pp. 167-8; neolithic relics, p. 9; standing stones (1) *and* (2), pp. 13, **63-4;** *see also* **Muckairn.**
Taynuilt Hotel, p. 267.
Teatle Water, bridge, p. 296.
Telford, Thomas, architect *and* engineer, pp. 25n, 129, 164, 261, 266, 295n.
Thatching, pp. 32-3, pl. 103B.
Thom, John, architect *and* builder, pp. 99, 260.
Thomas, p. 113.
Thompson, William, joiner, p. 258.
Tigh-cuil township, pp. 32-3, 272, **273-4,** fig. 231, pls. 102-3A.
Tigh Mór, Stronmilchan, pp. 187, 254, **267.**
Timber resources, pp. 3, 34, 276, 280-1, 283.
Timber roof-structures: pp. 23, 28, 106, 108, 132-3, 166-7, 257, 287, 290, 292-3, figs. 98, 242-3, pls. 27A, 36C, 115A, 117A; *see also* **Crucks.**
Tinwald, Charles Erskine, Lord, p. 278.
Tirefour Castle, Lismore, broch, pp. 16, 20, **75-7,** fig. 44, pl. 10.
Tirevadich, *see* **Hayfield.**

Toad of Lorn, *see* **Losgann Larnach.**
Tobar an Easbuig, p. 143.
Tobar an Fhion, p. 281.
Tobar Bial na Buaidh, p. 124.
Tobar Mhaodain, p. 116.
Tobar na Slainte, p. 166.
Toberonochy, Luing, quarry *and* workers' dwellings, p. 278.
Tom a' Chaisteil: dun, p. 93, fig. 78; *see also* **Rarey,** castle.
Tom an Iasgaire, fort, pp. 18, **74,** fig. 41.
Tombstones, *see* **Funerary monuments.**
Tom na Croise, *see* **Clenamacrie,** cross-decorated stone.
Torr a' Chlaonaidh, fort, pp. 74-5, fig. 42.
Torr-an-tuirc: cruck-framed byre, pp. 32, **274, 276,** fig. 232; township, p. 276.
Torsa, Caisteal nan Con, pp. 28, **181-2,** fig. 168, pl. 44.
Tower-houses: pp. 26-30; *see also* **Castles and Tower-houses.**
Townships: pp. 32-3; Ardnahua, pp. 33, 272-4, pl. 103A; Barrachrail, pp. 142, 272n; Carnach, p. 271; Duachy, p. 272; Stronmilchan, p. 33; Tigh-cuil, pp. 32-3, 272, **273-4,** fig. 231, pls. 102-3A; Torr-an-tuirc, p. 276.
Turnturk, *see* **Torr-an-tuirc.**
Tweeddale, George Hay, 7th Marquess of, p. 247.
Tyndrum-Inveraray, military road, pp. 36, **295-6.**
Tyndrum-Kinlochleven, military road, pp. 36, 295, **296-8,** pl. 119D.
Tynribbie: old parish church, Appin, pp. 22n, **98-9,** 161, fig. 86, pl. 12A-C; post-office, Appin, p. 247, pl. 84D.

Uamh nan Claigionn, *see* **Cave of the Skulls.**
Upper Gylen Farm, Kerrera, cruck-framed building, p. 32n.
Upper Sonachan House, pp. 31, **267,** pl. 100B-C.
Urns: pp. 12, 49, 51, 53-5, 57-60; *see also* **Cinerary Urns.**

Valleyfield House (Fife), cast-iron grate, p. 109.
Valliscaulian Order, pp. 23, 101, 110.
V'Gregour, *see* **MacGregor.**
Victoria Bridge, pp. 296-7.
'Viking burial', p. 22.
Vitrifaction, pp. 17-18, 64-5, 70.

Wade, General George, p. 247n.
Watherston, John & Son, building-contractors, p. 255.
Watson, David, engineer, p. 194.
Watts, W H, artist, p. 216n.
Well-houses, pp. 25, 122, fig. 110.
Wells: p. 25; Auch Gleann, p. 115; Cladh Churiollan, Creagan, pp. 25, **122,** fig. 110; Dalmally, St Conan's Well, p. 124; Dùnans, Glen Cruitten, p. 67; Dùn Mac Sniachan, p. 70; Dunstaffnage Castle, p. 208; Rhoscolyn, St Gwenfaen's (Anglesey), p. 25n; St Andrew's Well, p. 149; Tobar an Easbuig, p. 143; Tobar an Fhion, p. 281; Tobar Bial na Buaidh, p. 124; Tobar Mhaodain, p. 116; Tobar na Slainte, p. 166.
West Laroch: cairns, p. 57; *see also* **Ballachulish,** slate-quarries.
Whisky-stills (illicit): p. 35; Brackley, p. 278; Lismore, pp. 35, **281.**
Wicker-centering, pp. 29, 195, pl. 54B.
William, bishop of Argyll, pp. 171, 186.
Williamson, Thomas, slater, p. 239.
Wilson, Charles, architect, pp. 30, 110.
——Margaret, p. 253.
——William, of Murrayshall, p. 253.

Woodwork (decorative), pp. 109, 244-6, 260-1, 291, 299, pls. 18G, 82D, 83B, 116E, 120A.

Workers' dwellings: pp. 33-5; An Sàilean, Lismore, pp. 35, **276-7,** fig. 233, pl. 104A; Ardencaple, Seil, p. 278; Balla-chulish, pp. 35, **277,** pl. 105C; Balvicar, Seil, p. 278; Black Mill Bay, Luing, p. 278; Cullipool, Luing, p. 278; Easdale, Seil, pp. 33, 35, **278-9,** fig. 234, pl. 106; Ellanbeich, p. 279, pl. 106B; Lorn Furnace, Bonawe, pp. 34, 269, 283, **290-1,** figs. 236, 244-6, pl. 116A-C; Port Ramsay, Lismore, p. 294, pl. 118B, D; Toberonochy, Luing, p. 278.

Wrights: Dalziel, J and W, p. 99; Johnstone, John, pp. 31, 266; Morrison, James, p. 258; Paterson, George, pp. 256, 258; Scott, Andrew, p. 239.

Yetts, pp. 172, 178, 189, 234, 239, pl. 42A-B.

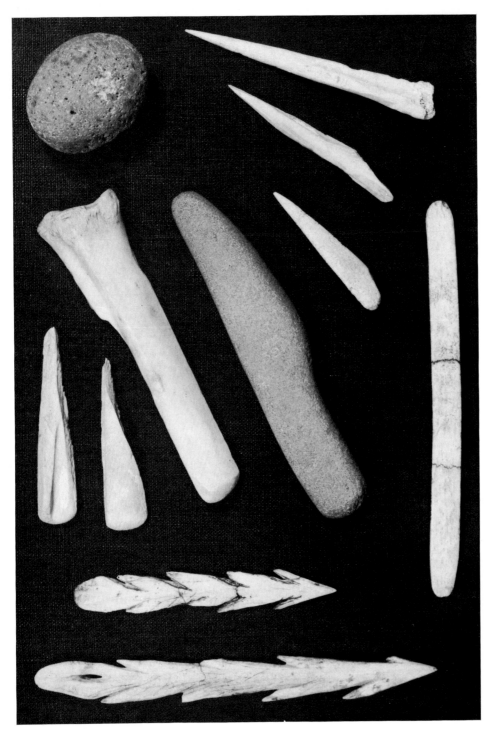

MESOLITHIC IMPLEMENTS (*scale* 2 : 3), OBAN (p. 5)

PLATE 2

A

C

B

D

A. POTTERY VESSEL (*scale* 1 : 2),
   ACHNACREE (1)

B. BEAKER (*scale* 1 : 2),
   SLATERICH, KERRERA (100, 1)

C. FOOD VESSEL (*scale* 1 : 2),
   LEDAIG (p. 12)

D. FOOD VESSEL (*scale* 1 : 2),
   CORRAN PARK, OBAN (98, 8)

PLATE 3

A

B

C

A. CINERARY URN (*scale* 1 : 4), MCKELVIE HOSPITAL, OBAN (98, 7)

B. BRONZE DAGGER (*scale* 1 : 1), KILMORE (57, 4)

C. BRONZE ARMLET (*scale* 1 : 1), MELFORT HOUSE (97)

PLATE 4

A

C

B

D

A. BRONZE AXE (*scale* 1 : 1), ACHANREAR (p. 13)

B. BRONZE SWORDS (*scale* 1 : 4),
   SHUNA, NETHER LORN (p. 13)

C. BRONZE AXE (*scale* 1 : 1),
   BARR MÓR, LISMORE (p. 13)

D. BONE PIN (*scale* 1 : 1), KERRERA (p. 22)

PLATE 5

CHAMBERED CAIRN, ACHNACREEBEAG (2);
   A. SE chamber from E
   B. SE chamber from N (*scale in feet*)
   C. NW chamber from N (*scale in feet*)

PLATE 6

CHAMBERED CAIRN, DALINEUN (6);
    A. chamber from N
    B. secondary cist from SE

PLATE 7

A

B

CAIRNS;
    A. LOCHAN NAN RÀTH (64), from S
    B. CLACHADOW 2 (34), from NW

PLATE 8

A

B

C

A. CAIRN AND STANDING STONE, STRONTOILLER (78), from E
B. STANDING STONES, DUACHY (116), from W
C. STANDING STONE, ACHARRA (110), from N

PLATE 9

A

B

C

D

BROCH, TIREFOUR CASTLE, LISMORE (147);
    A. view from s
    B. view from sw
    C. detail of walling from NE
    D. mural gallery from s

PLATE 10

A

B

C   D

DUN, DÙN CHRÙBAN,
    LISMORE (171);

  A. view from sw

DUN, LECCAMORE, LUING (189);

  B. sw entrance, from outside

  C. sw entrance,
     detail of jamb and
     bar-hole

  D. staircase

FIELD-BANK, BLACK CROFTS,
NORTH CONNEL (203);

  E. view from above

E

PLATE II

OLD PARISH CHURCH, APPIN (214);
    A. view from SE
    B. S doorway
    C. detail of S doorway
PARISH CHURCH, ARDCHATTAN (216);
    D. view from N
    E. communion-table
    F. interior

PLATE 12

A

B

ARDCHATTAN PRIORY (217); A. mansion from SE B. choir and Ardchattan burial-aisle from SE

PLATE 13

ARDCHATTAN PRIORY (217);
    A. choir and Lochnell burial-aisle from N
    B. interior of choir from SE

PLATE 14

A

B

C

D

ARDCHATTAN PRIORY (217):
   A. detail of recesses in s choir wall
   B. recesses in s choir wall
   C. detail of recess in N choir wall
   D. interior of s transept from SE
   E. NE angle-shaft and plinth of choir
   F. archways of crossing from W

E

F

PLATE 15

ARDCHATTAN PRIORY (217);

A. N transept window

B, C. details of N transept window

D. doorway of Ardchattan burial-aisle

E. W doorway of Lochnell burial-aisle

F. N doorway of Lochnell burial-aisle

G. window in N nave-aisle

PLATE 16

ARDCHATTAN PRIORY (217);
    A. refectory pulpit
    B. heads of refectory windows

PLATE 17

A

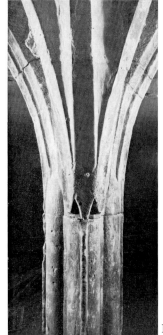
B

C

D

E

F

G

ARDCHATTAN PRIORY (217);
A–E. details of refectory pulpit
F. detail of refectory doorway
G. Prior's Room

PLATE 18

A

B

C

ARDCHATTAN PRIORY (217);
 A, B. carved stones
 C. grave-slab

PLATE 19

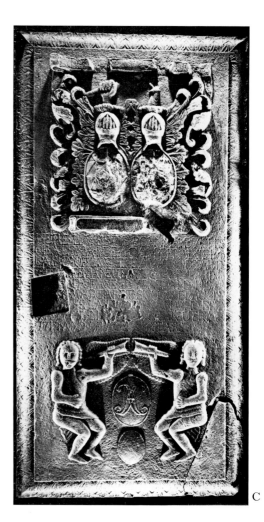

ARDCHATTAN PRIORY (217);
A, B. recumbent slabs
C. table-tomb
D. armorial panel

PLATE 20

A

C

B

PARISH CHURCH, DALAVICH (241);
   A. view from sw
   B. recumbent slab
CHURCH, BAILE MHAODAIN, ARDCHATTAN (220);
   C. interior of E wall

PLATE 21

A

B

C

D

DUNSTAFFNAGE CHAPEL (243);
 A. view from sw
 B. exterior of s wall
 C. s chancel windows
 D. interior of n wall

PLATE 22

A

B

C

D

E

DUNSTAFFNAGE CHAPEL (243);

    A. detail of E window

    B. base of N doorway

    C. Dunstaffnage burial-aisle

    D. pediment

    E. detail of recumbent slab

PLATE 23

A

B

C

E

D

PARISH CHURCH, DUROR (244); A. view from N

B. interior

OLD PARISH CHURCH, EILEAN MUNDE (245); C. view from S

D. recumbent slab

E. detail of recumbent slab

PLATE 24

A

B

C

OLD PARISH CHURCH,
EILEAN MUNDE (245);
  A. table-tomb
  B, C. recumbent slabs
  D. pediment

D

PLATE 25

A

B

C

D

PARISH CHURCH, GLENORCHY, DALMALLY (246);
   A. view from SW
   B. grave-slab
   C. view from SE
   D. grave-slab of a child

PLATE 26

A

B

C

PARISH CHURCH, GLENORCHY,
DALMALLY (246);
   A. interior of roof
   B. mortsafe
   C. interior

PLATE 27

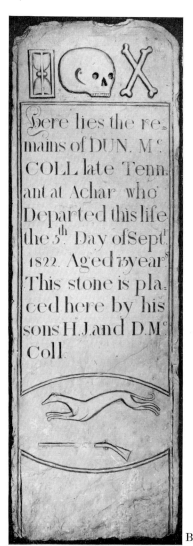

Here lies the remains of DUN. McCOLL late Tennant at Achar who Departed this life the 5th Day of Sept. 1822. Aged 75 year. This stone is placed here by his sons H.J. and D.Mc Coll.

Anno Domini 1825

This Stone is Placed here by John McDougall at Ballachelish and Rachel McColl his spouse In Memory of their Children Alexr who Died 30th Jan. 1822 Aged 28 year. Donn who Died 18th Dec. 1822 Aged 24 years and Ann who Died 21st March 1825 Aged 20 years And of Five Infants.

OLD PARISH CHURCH, INISHAIL (247);
   A. cross-decorated slab
CHAPEL, KEIL (250);
   B, C. recumbent slabs

CHAPEL, KEIL (250);
   D. view from sw   E. s window
CHURCH, INVERGHIUSACHAN (249);
   F. view from s

PLATE 28

A

B

D

C

OLD PARISH CHURCH, KILBRIDE (253);
    A. view from sw
    B. detail of Campbell of Lerags Cross
    C. Campbell of Lerags Cross, front
OLD PARISH CHURCH, KILBRANDON, SEIL (252);
    D. recumbent slab

PLATE 29

KILCHERAN, LISMORE (257);
  A. view from SE
OLD PARISH CHURCH, KILCHATTAN, LUING (256);
  B. view from SW
  C. graffiti
  D. table-tomb
  E. detail of headstone

PLATE 30

A

B

C

D

E

F

OLD PARISH CHURCH, KILMORE (264);

    A. tomb-recess

    B. view from sw

PARISH CHURCH, KILCHRENAN (259);

    C. grave-slab

    D. view from sw

    E. McIntyre monument

    F. McIntyre tablet

PLATE 31

A

B

CATHEDRAL OF ST MOLUAG AND PARISH CHURCH, LISMORE (267);
    A. view from NW
    B. view from SW by Erskine Beveridge, 1882

PLATE 32

CATHEDRAL OF
ST MOLUAG AND PARISH
CHURCH, LISMORE (267);

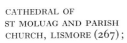

A. exterior of
s choir doorway

B. interior of choir

C. interior of
s choir doorway

D. sedilia

E. piscina

F. archway of
pulpitum

PLATE 33

A

B

C

D

E

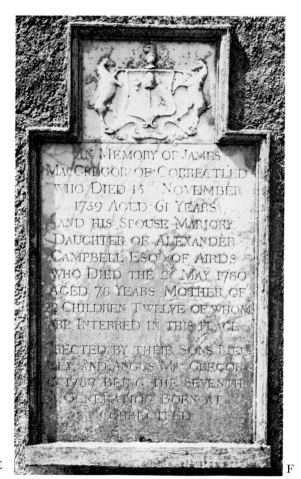

F

CATHEDRAL OF ST MOLUAG AND
PARISH CHURCH, LISMORE (267);

A. corbel-stop of N choir doorway

B. interior of N choir doorway

C. corbel-stop of N choir doorway

D, E. grave-slabs

F. MacGregor monument

PLATE 34

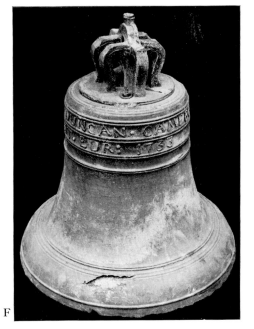

A

B

C

D

E

F

PARISH CHURCH, MUCKAIRN,
TAYNUILT (269);

    A. table-tomb   D, E. carved stones

    B. view from sw   F. bell

    C. interior

PLATE 35

A

B

C

D

E

FREE HIGH CHURCH, OBAN (270);
    A. view from SW
    B. pulpit
    C. interior
BURIAL-ENCLOSURE, SONACHAN (274);
    D. armorial panel
EPISCOPAL CHURCH, PORTNACROISH (272);
    E. view from SE

PLATE 36

A

B

C

D

ACHADUN CASTLE, LISMORE (276);
   A. general view from NE
   B. mural stair
   C. general view from S
   D. exterior of NE curtain-wall

PLATE 37

A

B

C

D

E

F

ACHADUN CASTLE, LISMORE (276);
   A. interior of courtyard from sw
   B. interior of NW curtain-wall
ACHALLADER CASTLE (277);
   C. view from N
   D. view from E
   E. detail of entrance-doorway
   F. window in N wall

PLATE 38

ACHALLADER CASTLE (277);
   A, B. pistol-holes in N wall
   C. interior of E wall
ARDFAD CASTLE, SEIL (278);
   D. view from W

PLATE 39

BARCALDINE CASTLE (279) from S

PLATE 40

A

B

C

D

BARCALDINE CASTLE (279);
  A, B. armorial panels
  C. sw angle-turret
  D. view from NW

PLATE 41

A

C

D

B

BARCALDINE CASTLE (279);
    A. entrance-door and yett
    B. detail of yett
    C, D. door-furniture

PLATE 42

A

B

BARCALDINE CASTLE (279):
  A. hall
  B. kitchen-fireplace
  C. sundial

C

PLATE 43

A

B

C

CAISTEAL NAN CON, TORSA (280);
   A. view from N
   B. view from E
   C. detail of masonry

PLATE 44

A

B

CASTLE COEFFIN, LISMORE (282);
  A. general view from E
  B. view from NE

PLATE 45

A

B

C

D

E

CASTLE COEFFIN, LISMORE (282);
    A. interior from E
    B. mural staircase
    C. fish-trap
CASTLE SHUNA, APPIN (284);
    D. view from S
    E. view from N

PLATE 46

CASTLE STALKER (285) from E

PLATE 47

A

B

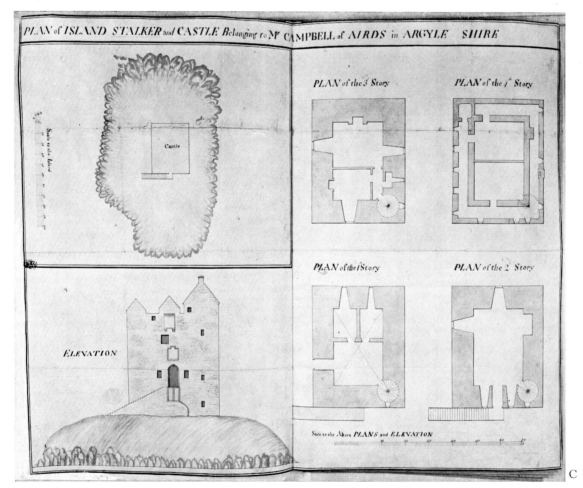

C

CASTLE STALKER (285);   A. view from NW

                               B. view from SW

                               C. Board of Ordnance drawing, *c.* 1748

PLATE 48

Castle of Tene Stalcar.

A

CASTLE STALKER (285);

  A. view from E
    by Richard Pococke,
    1760

  B. view from E
    by John Clerk of
    Eldin, c. 1750–70

B

PLATE 49

CASTLE STALKER (285);
    A. principal entrance
    B. window in NE wall
    C. ground-floor entrance
    D. detail of postern-doorway
    E. gun-loop
    F. vault of pit-prison
    G. carved stone

PLATE 50

CASTLE STALKER (285);

A. garderobe vent-shaft
B. detail of window
   in s angle-round
C. s angle-round
D. pistol-hole
E. detail of stair-newel
F. fireplace-jamb
G. stair-doorways and
   prison hatch

PLATE 51

A

B

DUNOLLIE CASTLE (286);
   A. view from SE
   B. tower-house and courtyard from SE

PLATE 52

DUNOLLIE CASTLE (286);
  A. view from W
  B. tower-house
     from SW
  C. tower-house
     and courtyard
     from NW

PLATE 53

DUNOLLIE CASTLE (286):

A. interior of tower-house
B. imprint of wicker-centering
C. exterior of w curtain-wall
D. interior of w curtain-wall
E. slab-corbelled ceiling
F. carved fragment

PLATE 54

PLATE 55

A

B

DUNSTAFFNAGE CASTLE (287);
  A. view from NE
  B. view from E

A

B

DUNSTAFFNAGE CASTLE (287);
  A. view from SE
  B. view from SW

PLATE 56

A

DUNSTAFFNAGE CASTLE (287);
   A. view from NW
   B. gatehouse from E

B

PLATE 57

DUNSTAFFNAGE CASTLE (287);
A. interior of dwelling-house
B. interior of courtyard from s
C. first-floor apartment of gatehouse
D. window-embrasure in gatehouse
E. dormer-windows of gatehouse
F. window in dwelling-house

PLATE 58

DUNSTAFFNAGE CASTLE (287);
   A. interior of courtyard from W
   B. interior of courtyard from N
   C. detail of SW parapet-walk
   D. SE parapet-walk

PLATE 59

A

B

CASTLE, FRAOCH EILEAN (290);
   A. aerial view from NE
   B. view from SE

PLATE 60

A

CASTLE,
FRAOCH EILEAN (290);
  A. aerial view from E
  B. view from E

B

PLATE 61

CASTLE, FRAOCH EILEAN (290);

  A. view from s

  B. pilaster-buttress

  C. dwelling-house from NW

  D. mural staircase

  E. interior of
     dwelling-house from NE

  F. carved fragment

PLATE 62

A

B

GYLEN CASTLE, KERRERA (291);
  A. general view from NW
  B. general view from SE
  C. view from SW

C

PLATE 63

A

B

C

D

GYLEN CASTLE, KERRERA (291);

    A. view from NE

    B. view from N

    C. detail of NE façade

    D. N angle-turret

PLATE 64

A

B

C

D

E

F

G

GYLEN CASTLE, KERRERA (291):
  A. detail of window
  B. fireplace
  C. interior from E
  D, E. carved fragments
  F. archway of pend
  G. carved fragment

PLATE 65

A

B

C

D

E

F

INNIS CHONNELL CASTLE (292); inner bailey

    A. view from s   B. se angle-tower

    C. view from w

    D. exterior of entrance-gateway

    E. view from NE

    F. interior of entrance-gateway

PLATE 66

INNIS CHONNELL CASTLE (292); inner bailey

A. S courtyard-range
B. interior of SE tower
C. hall and kitchen
D. hall forestair
E. window and gun-loop
F. cellar doorway

PLATE 67

INNIS CHONNELL CASTLE (292); inner bailey
    A. hall lobby
    B. canopied fireplace

C. forestair of N curtain-wall
D. S parapet-walk
E. W parapet-walk

PLATE 68

KILCHURN CASTLE (293);
  A. view from s
  B. view from NE

PLATE 69

A

B

KILCHURN CASTLE (293);
   A. view from NW
   B. view from W

PLATE 70

A

B

KILCHURN CASTLE (293);
    A. view from E, 1808
    B. view from SW by P Sandby, *c.* 1779

PLATE 71

A

B

C

D

F

E

G

KILCHURN CASTLE (293);
tower-house

    A. view from W

    B. N angle-turret

    C. E angle-turret

    D. interior from N

    E. interior from SE

    F. lintel of
       entrance-doorway

    G. interior of pistol-hole

PLATE 72

KILCHURN CASTLE (293);
   A. s angle-tower from NE
   B. courtyard from E
   C. SE curtain-wall

PLATE 73

A

B

C

KILCHURN CASTLE (293);
    A. courtyard from SE
    B. interior of NE range
    C. NE range from E

PLATE 74

A

B

KILCHURN CASTLE (293);
   A. interior of NE range from S
   B. interior of NW range
   C. dormer-window pediment
   D. water-inlet in NE range

C

D

PLATE 75

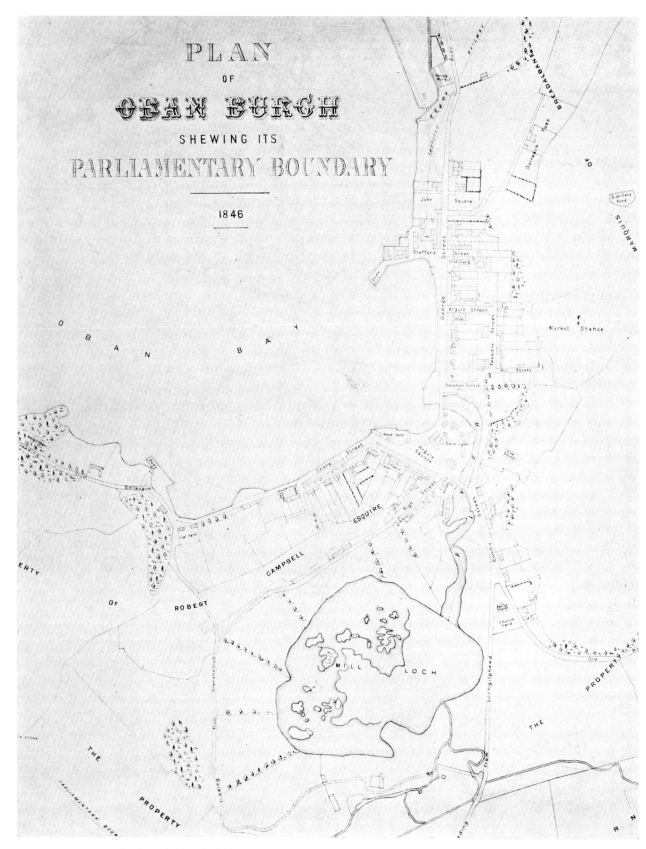

THE BURGH OF OBAN (298–301); detail of plan by R Stevenson, 1846

PLATE 76

THE BURGH OF OBAN (298–301);
    A. view from s by A Stanley, *c.* 1857
PIERMASTER'S HOUSE, SOUTH PIER, OBAN, (301);
    B. view from E

PLATE 77

A

B

C

D

E

ACHLIAN (302);
    A. view from N
    B. entrance-doorway
    C. drawing-room
    D. staircase
ACHNABA (303);
    E. cast-iron fireback

PLATE 78

AIRDS HOUSE (304);
    A. view from sw
    B. view from ne

PLATE 79

AIRDS HOUSE (304); principal façade

PLATE 80

A

B

AIRDS HOUSE (304):
   A. detail of principal façade
   B. pavilions
   C. entrance-doorway
   D. doorway in quadrant-wall

C   D

PLATE 81

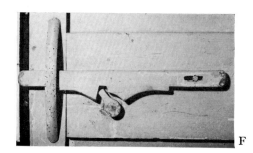

AIRDS HOUSE (304):
   A. principal staircase
   B. entrance-hall
   C. drawing-room chimney-piece
   D. second-floor room
   E. home farm
   F. timber door-lock
   G. gatelodge

PLATE 82

A

B

C

APPIN HOUSE (305);
   A. view from s
   B. cupboard
   C. staircase

PLATE 83

A

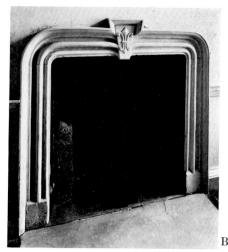

B

C

D

APPIN HOUSE (305);
   A, B, C fireplaces
APPIN POST-OFFICE, TYNRIBBIE (306);
   D. view from W

PLATE 84

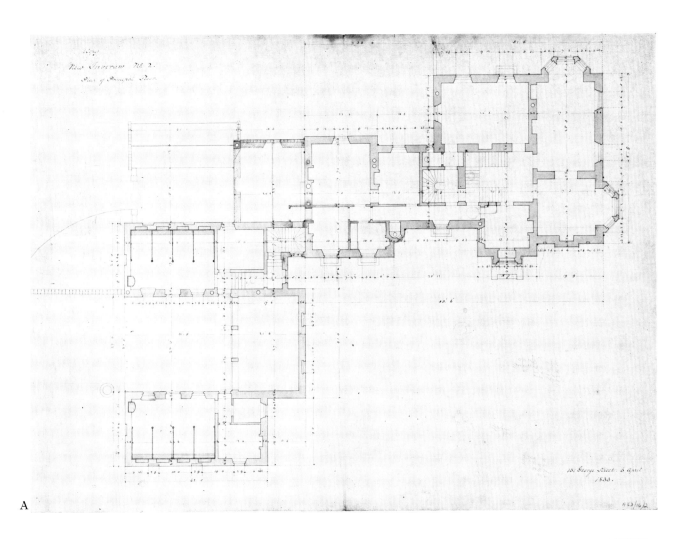

A

B

ARDANAISEIG (307); A. ground-floor plan by William Burn, 1833
B. view from E

PLATE 85

A

B

C

D

E

ARDANAISEIG (307);
   A. entrance-doorway
   B. main block from sw
ARDENCAPLE HOUSE, SEIL (308);
   C. view from N
   D. chimney-piece
ARDLARACH, LUING (309);
   E. view from s

PLATE 86

ARDMADDY CASTLE (310);
   A. view from N
   B. window
   C. SW range from S

PLATE 87

A

C

B

D

ARDMADDY CASTLE (310);
    A. view from N, *c.* 1772
    B. forestair and portico
    C. detail of pediment
    D. carved panel

PLATE 88

A

B

C

D

E

ARDMADDY CASTLE (310);
  A. boat-house
  B. bridge
  C. dining-room fireplace
  D. first-floor room
  E. brass rim-lock
  F. court of offices from sw

F

PLATE 89

A

B

C

D

E

BALLACHULISH HOUSE (311);
    A. view from NW
    B. staircase

BARCALDINE HOUSE (313);
    C. view from NW
    D. dining-room chimney-piece
    E. library chimney-piece

PLATE 90

A

B

C

E

D

A. BALLIVEOLAN (DRUIMAVUIC) (312) from W
B. DALMALLY MANSE (315) from SE
C. THE MANOR HOUSE, DUNGALLON (317), from SE
D. OLD SCHOOLHOUSE, FERLOCHAN (319), from NE
E. DUNOLLIE HOUSE (318) from S
F. DEGNISH (316) from SE

F

PLATE 91

A

B

C

GALLANACH (320);
 A. early view from N
 B. detail of view, 1800
 C. view from NE

PLATE 92

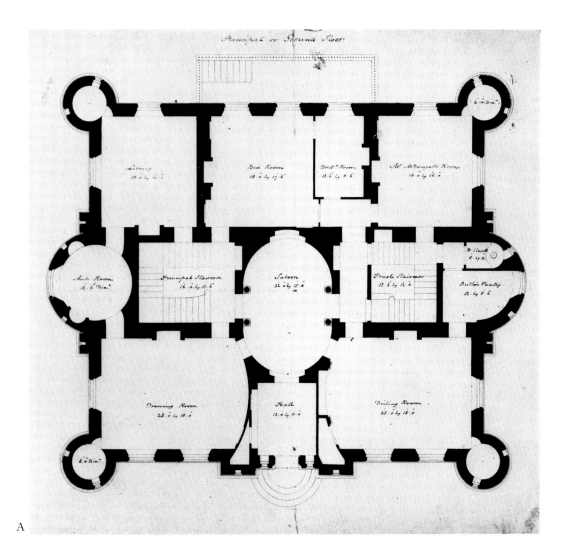

A

B

C

GALLANACH (320);
   A. ground-floor plan by William Burn, 1814
   B. drawing-room
   C. staircase

PLATE 93

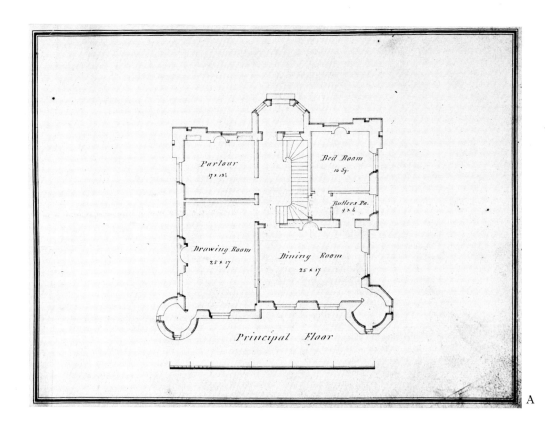

A

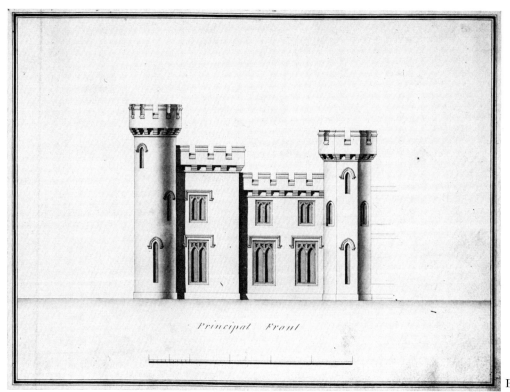

B

GALLANACH (320); designs, probably by Gillespie Graham, 1812
    A. ground-floor plan
    B. principal elevation

PLATE 94

GLENURE (322);
    A. view from NW
    B. kitchen-fireplace
    C. staircase
    D. first-floor room

PLATE 95

A. KILBRANDON HOUSE, SEIL (325), from S

B. GLENSTOCKDALE (321) from N

C. KILMORE HOUSE (326) from E

D. KILMORE HOUSE (326) from W

E. HAYFIELD (323); steading from SE

PLATE 96

A

B

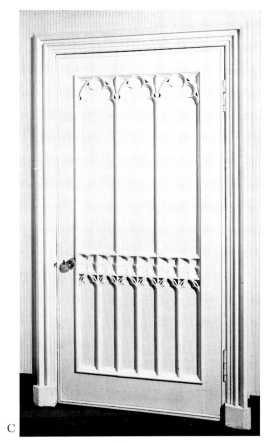

C

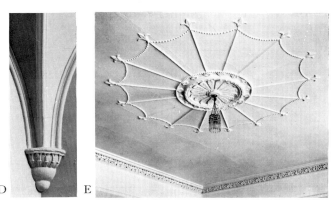

D   E

F

KINLOCHLAICH (327);

    A. view from NW

    B. view from W

    C. door-case

    D. detail of plaster vault

    E. detail of drawing-room ceiling

F. LERAGS HOUSE (329) from W

G. KULMANI, DUROR (328), from SE

G

PLATE 97

A

B

C

LOCHNELL HOUSE (330);
  A. view from NE
  B. view from NW
  C. barn

PLATE 98

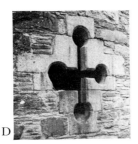

LOCHNELL HOUSE (330);

    A. view from s

    B. oriel-window

    C. sundial

    D. mock arrow-loop

    E. drawing-room chimney-piece

PLATE 99

A. RAREY (333) from N
B. UPPER SONACHAN HOUSE (336) from N
C. UPPER SONACHAN HOUSE (336); carved panel
D. OLD SCHOOLHOUSE, NORTH LEDAIG (332), from W
E. MUCKAIRN MANSE, TAYNUILT (331), from SE

PLATE 100

A

C

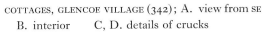

B

D

E

F

COTTAGES, GLENCOE VILLAGE (342); A. view from SE
    B. interior   C, D. details of crucks
E. CRUCK-FRAMED BUILDING, CLACHADOW (340);
   cruck-truss
F. DUNSTAFFNAGE MAINS FARM (341) from NE

PLATE 101

TIGH-CUIL TOWNSHIP (345);

    A. general view from N

    B. byre-dwelling A

    C. general view from SW

PLATE 102

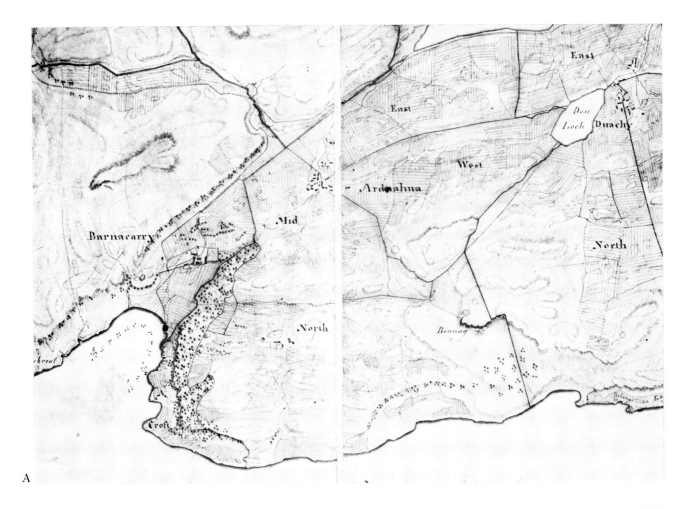

A

B

A. TIGH-CUIL TOWNSHIP
(345);
detail of estate-plan
by Alexander Langlands,
1809

B. THATCHED HOUSES,
KILCHRENAN (p. 32);
view by the Rev
J B MacKenzie,
c. 1870–80

PLATE 103

A

B

C

D

LIMESTONE-QUARRIES AND WORKERS' DWELLINGS,
AN SÀILEAN, LISMORE (348);

    A. general view from SE

    B. lime-kilns

OLD QUARRIES, ARDENTALLAN (349);

    C. working-face

OLD QUARRY, BARRNACARRY (351);

    D. millstone-quarry

PLATE 104

SLATE-QUARRIES AND WORKERS'
DWELLINGS,
BALLACHULISH (350);

    A. general view of East
       Laroch quarry from SE

    B. view of East Laroch
       quarry from NW

    C. cottages, West Laroch

PLATE 105

A

B

C

D

SLATE-QUARRIES AND
WORKERS' DWELLINGS,
EASDALE, SEIL (356);

    A. general view
        from NE

    B. cottages,
        Ellanbeich

    C, D. harbour,
         Easdale Island

PLATE 106

LIGHTHOUSE, EILEAN MUSDILE,
LISMORE (357);
   A. view from SW
   B. view from NE

PLATE 107

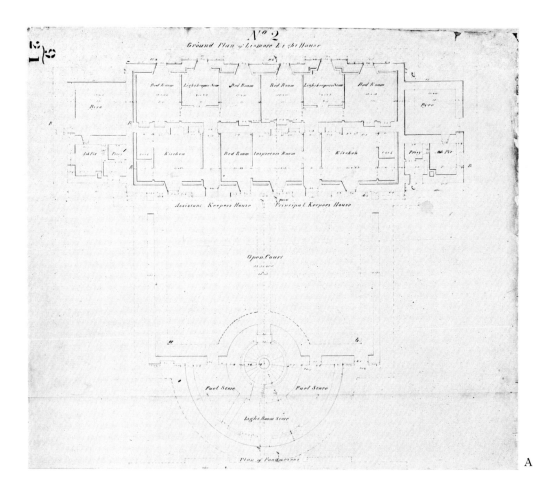

A

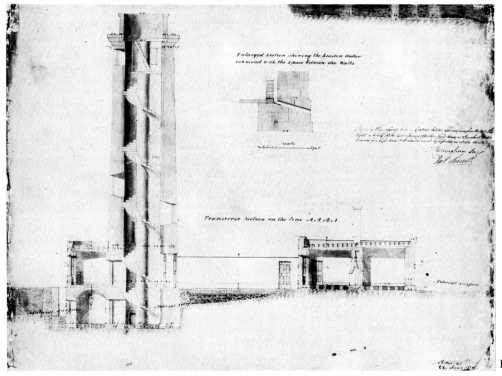

B

LIGHTHOUSE,
EILEAN MUSDILE,
LISMORE (357);

A. ground-floor
plan, 1829

B. section, 1829

PLATE 108

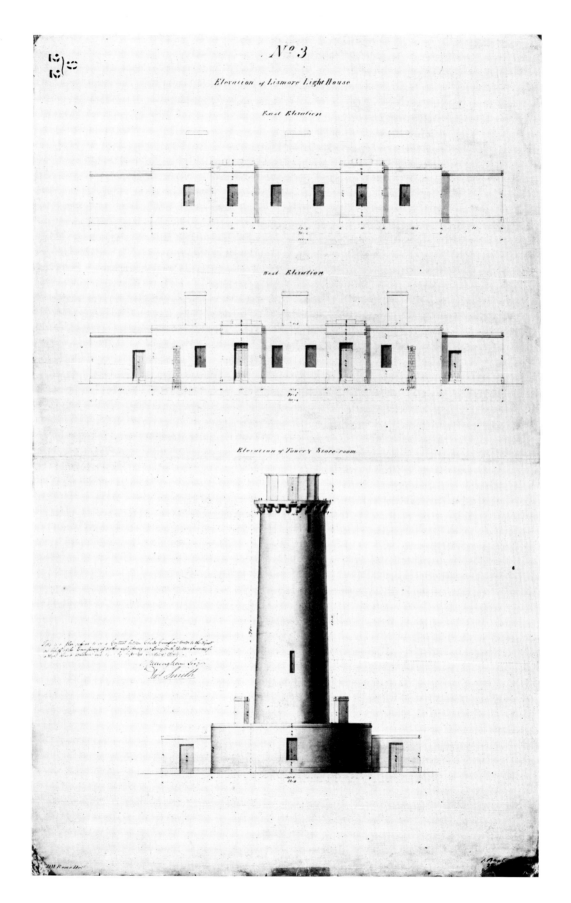

No 3

Elevation of Lismore Light House

East Elevation

West Elevation

Elevation of Tower & Store-room

LIGHTHOUSE,
EILEAN MUSDILE,
LISMORE (357);
elevations, 1829

PLATE 109

A

B

C

D

E

F

G

LIGHTHOUSE, EILEAN MUSDILE, LISMORE (357);
  A. lantern
  B, C, D. details of superstructure
  E. keeper's house   F. bridge
  G. courtyard entrance

PLATE 110

A

B

LORN FURNACE, BONAWE (362);
  A. general view from S
  B. general view from E

PLATE III

LORN FURNACE, BONAWE (362);
  A. early view of furnace from N
  B. furnace from NW

PLATE 112

A

B

C

LORN FURNACE, BONAWE (362);
   A. loading-mouth
   B. cast-iron lintel
   C. furnace-hearth

PLATE 113

A

B

C

LORN FURNACE,
BONAWE (362);

   A. ore-shed and
      E charcoal-shed
      from NE

   B. E charcoal-shed
      from N

   C. W charcoal-sheds
      from SE

PLATE 114

LORN FURNACE,
BONAWE (362);

    A. E charcoal-shed roof

    B, C, D. details of W
       charcoal-shed roofs

PLATE 115

A

C

B

E

D

LORN FURNACE, BONAWE (362);
- A. NE workers' dwellings from N
- B. SE workers' dwellings from NE
- C. staircase in SE workers' dwellings
- D. Bonawe House from N
- E. entrance-doorway of Bonawe House

PLATE 116

A

B

C

D

GUNPOWDER-WORKS, MELFORT (363);
    A. storage-shed roof
    B. court of offices

C. OLD FERRYHOUSE, SOUTH SHIAN (367), from NE
D. OLD FERRYHOUSE, PORT APPIN (364), from N

PLATE 117

LIME-KILNS,
PORT KILCHERAN,
LISMORE (365);

  A. view from W

LIMESTONE-
QUARRIES AND
WORKERS'
DWELLINGS,
PORT RAMSAY,
LISMORE (366);

  B. general view
    from W

  C. lime-kilns

  D. cottages
    from E

PLATE 118

A

B

C

D

A. BRIDGE OF AWE (368) from NW

B. CLACHAN BRIDGE, SEIL (369), from SW

C. BRIDGE AND EMBANKMENT, DALMALLY
   (370); bridge from E

D. MILITARY ROAD, TYNDRUM–
   KINLOCHLEVEN (372);
   Bridge of Orchy from SW

PLATE 119

A

B

C

D

E

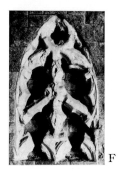

F

G

A. ARCHITECTURAL FRAGMENTS, DRUIMNEIL HOUSE (374); staircase
B. GRAFFITO, CREAGAN (373)
C. ARMORIAL PANEL, DUNSTAFFNAGE HOUSE (375)
D. ARMORIAL PANEL, OLD SMITHY, PORT APPIN (376)
ARCHITECTURAL FRAGMENTS, ST CONAN'S CHURCH, LOCHAWE (377);
    E. window from St Mary's Parish Church, South Leith
    F. window-tracery from Iona Abbey
    G. bell from Skerryvore Lighthouse

PLATE 120